New Testament I and II

Augustinian Heritage Institute

THE WORKS OF SAINT AUGUSTINE
A Translation for the 21st Century

Part 1 - Books
Volumes 15 and 16:
The New Testament

THE WORKS OF SAINT AUGUSTINE

A Translation for the 21st Century

New Testament I and II

I/15 and I/16

The Lord's Sermon on the Mount
(De sermone Domini in monte)
translated by Michael G. Campbell, O.S.A.,
introduced and annotated by Boniface Ramsey

Agreement among the Evangelists
(De consensu evangelistarum)
translated, introduced and annotated by Kim Paffenroth

Questions on the Gospels
(Quaestiones evangeliorum)
translated, introduced and annotated by Roland Teske, S.J.

Seventeen Questions on Matthew
(Quaestiones XVII in Matthaeum)
translated, introduced and annotated by Roland Teske, S.J.

editor
Boniface Ramsey

New City Press
Hyde Park, New York

Published in the United States by New City Press
202 Comforter Blvd., Hyde Park, New York 12538
©2014 Augustinian Heritage Institute

Cover artwork by Leandro DeLeon

Library of Congress Cataloging-in-Publication Data:
Augustine, Saint, Bishop of Hippo.
The works of Saint Augustine.

"Augustinian Heritage Institute"
Includes bibliographical references and indexes.
Contents: — pt. 1, Books. v. 5. The Trinity /
introduction, translation, and notes / Edmund Hill. —
pt. 3. Sermons. v. 1. 1–19. Introduction /
Michele Pellegrino.
1. Theology — Early Church, ca. 30–600. I. Hill,
Edmund. II. Rotelle, John E.   III. Augustinian
Heritage Institute. IV. Title.
BR65.A5E53   1990   270.2   89–28878
ISBN 1–56548–055–4 (series)
ISBN 978–1–56548–529–7 (pt. 1, v. 15 & 16)
ISBN 978–1–56548–531–0 (pt. 1, v. 15 & 16: pbk.)

Printed in the United States of America

Contents

General Introduction

The present volume contains the translations of four works of Saint Augustine, all of which are exegetical treatises of one sort or another. Aside from the fact that all of them are based on the Gospels, they have little else in common.

The Lord's Sermon on the Mount is of course an exegesis of chapters five through seven of Matthew's Gospel, but Augustine's explanation of the Sermon is more a charter of Christian morality and spirituality than mere exegesis of the text and brings a unity to the lengthy discourse that goes far beyond an account of what the text says.

Agreement among the Evangelists is basically an attempt to defend the veracity of the four evangelists in the face of seeming incompatibilities in their record of the gospel events, especially against some pagan philosophers who raised objections to the gospel narratives based on alleged inconsistencies.

Questions on the Gospels is a record of questions that arose when Augustine was reading the Gospels of Matthew and Luke with a disciple. The answers to the questions are not intended to be commentaries on the Gospels in their entirety but merely represent the answers to the questions that arose for the student at the time.

Seventeen Questions on Matthew is similarly in the question-and-answer genre and is mostly likely by Augustine, but it includes some paragraphs at the end that are certainly not his. The work has traditionally been called *Seventeen Questions*, although it would be more correctly called *Sixteen Questions*, since, as the critical edition has shown, question eleven had been mistakenly split into two questions.

THE LORD'S SERMON ON THE MOUNT

(De sermone Domini in monte)

Introduction

The Lord's Sermon on the Mount is reliably dated to the period 393–394, early in Augustine's career. At that point Augustine had been a priest at Hippo for two or three years, having probably been ordained in early 391. Soon after his ordination he had begged Valerius, his ordaining bishop, for time to study the Scriptures in preparation for his priestly ministry,[1] and he had most likely devoted about a year to that task. The first exegetical work that he produced after this period of study was his unfinished *Literal Commentary on Genesis* (he had already written *On Genesis: A Refutation of the Manicheans* in 389). *The Lord's Sermon on the Mount* was his initial foray into the New Testament, and it represented the first time that anyone had separated the Sermon on the Mount from the rest of the Gospel of Matthew and treated it independently. That Augustine chose these three chapters (5–7) from Matthew as his first New Testament project suggests that, at least at the time, it held the same attraction, or fascination, for him as it has for many other commentators and countless readers. But it was not merely the attractiveness of such passages from the Sermon on the Mount as the Beatitudes and the oft-commented-on Lord's Prayer that led Augustine to delve into Christ's great Matthean discourse: he clearly viewed it at the time as perhaps the primary exposition of the New Law as seen from a moral perspective. Yet, although he dealt with passages from Matthew again in his sermons and in such works as his *Questions on the Gospels*, he never treated it again in such detail and at such length as he did in the present work; his theological concerns caused him to concentrate instead on John and even more so on Paul.

Augustine divided *The Lord's Sermon on the Mount* into two books of nearly equal length, the first of which covers the fifth chapter of Matthew, arguably the most important part of the Sermon, and the second its sixth and seventh chapters. Inasmuch as the sixth chapter contains the Lord's Prayer, a commentary on it, one of several produced by him,[2] can be found in the second book (II,4,15–11,39). Whether or not or to what degree Augustine may have intentionally borrowed from his great predecessors — and in particular from the three seminal treatises by Tertullian, Origen and Cyprian — when he interpreted this prayer, his own commentary is certainly well within the tradition established by them. Of particular interest is his understanding that the *daily bread* of the fourth petition of the Lord's Prayer implies three realities rather than just the one or two that are typical of other writers — namely, the bread that supports physical life, the eucharist, and "the divine precepts, which we should daily reflect on and put into practice" (II,7,25–27).

When Augustine composed *The Lord's Sermon on the Mount* he was very sensitive to both Manicheanism and Donatism, each of which was active in North Africa at the end of the fourth century, although he never mentions either of these

---

1. See Letter 21.
2. See Sermons 56–59; Letter 130,11,21–12,22.

two unorthodox movements by name in his work. Unmistakable allusions to Manicheanism occur, however, in I,20,65, II,9,31–33, and II,24,79, while Donatism is referred to more obliquely in I,5,13. Pelagianism and the great controversy over grace, on the other hand, was still in the future, and the closest thing that Augustine does to raising the issue of the role of grace, which would preoccupy him during his final two decades, is a brief and uncontroversial statement in II,4,16, which could have been made at any time during the period of his theological maturity: "And because it is not through any merits of our own but by the grace of God that we are called to an eternal inheritance, to be coheirs with Christ and attain adoption as sons, we place that same grace at the beginning of the prayer when we say *Our Father.*"

The modern and in some respects unfortunate distinction among theology, morality and spirituality would have been unknown to Augustine. Nonetheless, acknowledging a certain usefulness in that distinction, we can say that *The Lord's Sermon on the Mount* emphasizes morality much more than it does theology or spirituality, and it is from that perspective that Augustine begins his commentary: "If anyone were to ponder with piety and seriousness the sermon which our Lord Jesus Christ gave on the mount, I believe that he would discover there, as far as norms for high moral living are concerned (*quantum ad mores optimos pertinet*), the perfect way to lead the Christian life" (I,1,1). As proof that "all the precepts necessary for regulating a person's life are contained in it," he quotes from the Sermon's conclusion the gospel analogy of the wise man and the foolish man who built their houses on rock and sand respectively (Mt 7:24–27) (I,1,1). Since Augustine deals with the sections of the Sermon on the Mount in the order in which they appear, the interpretation of this analogy serves as the conclusion of the whole work, and for him it represents a call to put into action the precepts with which the entire Sermon is charged (II,25,87). The treatise is thus sandwiched between an initial citation of Mt 7:24–27 and a final one, which are together intended to emphasize the moral thrust of Christ's long discourse.

Of course Matthew's text cries out for the sort of moral commentary that Augustine provides as he goes through it word by word, and several moral questions engage his interest more than others. Chief among them is the issue of marriage and separation that is raised in Mt 5:31–32 and that he discusses extensively in I,14,39–16,50. The exact meaning of the term "fornication" (the Latin text that Augustine used translated the Greek *porneia* by *fornicatio* rather than by a word with a more specific connotation), which constituted the exception whereby a wife could be dismissed from an otherwise inviolable union, exercised Augustine a great deal. In *Revisions* I,19 (18),6 he notes that there is still room for debate on the matter, and he recommends reading later works of his own and even those of other authors. Other passages in the Sermon on the Mount also elicit similar if not quite such extended attention — for example, the section that advises the Christian not only to yield to his antagonists but even to exceed their demands (Mt 5:38–42), which is treated in I,19,56–20,68; the precept to pray for one's enemies (Mt 5:44), the discussion of which in I,21,69–22,77 includes a digression on the sin that leads to death, mentioned in 1 Jn 5:16–17; and the relationship between catering to the needs of this life on the one hand and living for the kingdom of God on the other, occasioned by Mt 6:33 and discussed in II,16,53–17,58.

Augustine's approach to the moral teaching of the Sermon on the Mount is relatively straightforward and non-allegorical when the text, at least from his standpoint, lends itself to this kind of exegesis. A good example of such is I,9,21–25, where he interprets Mt 5:20–22, in which Jesus first distinguishes between the righteousness of the scribes and Pharisees and that of his own disciples. Augustine gives a fairly unvarnished explanation of the passage and does not have recourse to allegory. Some of what he says, in fact, has enduring exegetical validity — for instance, his insight that there is an ascending order of punishment in the series of judgment, the council, and the fire of Gehenna in Mt 5:22. In his interpretation of Mt 6:26–30 (*Consider the birds of the air...*) in II,15,51–52 Augustine even warns against over-allegorizing: the birds of the air and the lilies of the field stand for nothing but themselves, just as, in his view, the unjust judge in Lk 18:2–8 is a mere illustration and cannot be a symbol of God. With respect to other passages, though, Augustine burnishes his allegorical credentials. Thus, in explicating Mt 5:39 in I,19,58 he identifies a person's right cheek with divine qualities and his left with human qualities. For the right and left hands, referred to by Jesus in the context of almsgiving in Mt 6:3 and discussed in II,2,6–7, Augustine discusses three interpretations, one of which (that the left hand represents a man's wife) he rejects as absurd. And, finally, there are the allegorical possibilities that certain numbers suggest — three (I,19,61), seven (I,4,11–12), eight (I,4,12) and fifty (I,4,12).

None of Augustine's emphasis on the moral means that he neglects the spiritual opportunities that a reading of the Sermon on the Mount would bring to mind. A more spiritual approach is especially evident in his treatment of the Beatitudes in I,1,3–5,15, which for him constitute a kind of ladder of perfection, as outlined in I,3,10. In terms of the theological, however, in the most narrow sense of an investigation of the nature of God or Christ, there is very little, if anything, that qualifies, apart from the commentary on the opening lines of the Lord's Prayer in II,5,17–18, and this is no more than a standard reflection on the immateriality of God. But had Augustine seen in the Sermon on the Mount an occasion to confront Arianism, which was active in North Africa during his time, he would certainly have had something to say in the area of christology.

The most original aspect of *The Lord's Sermon on the Mount*, the result both of Augustine's synthesizing genius and of his conviction that the number seven had deep mystical meaning, is his pairing of the Beatitudes with other teachings from the Sermon on the Mount, with the gifts of the Holy Spirit as set out in Is 11:2, and with the petitions of the Lord's Prayer.[3] He begins by explaining each Beatitude in I,3,10, sometimes mentioning a related virtue (humility, for example, in the case of

---

3. Augustine almost certainly knew Ambrose's *Exposition of the Gospel according to Luke* V,49–68, in which Ambrose pairs both Matthew's eight and Luke's four Beatitudes (Lk 6:20–23) not

Blessed are the poor in spirit), and in I,4,11 he joins the Beatitudes with the gifts. In order to draw a connection between the two, though, inasmuch as there are eight Beatitudes and seven gifts, he has to claim that the eighth Beatitude is basically an elaboration of the first, which he finds hinted at by the fact that each makes explicit mention of the kingdom of heaven (I,3,10; 4,12). In addition, so as to be able to link the ones with the others in a way that is satisfactory to him, he has to reverse Isaiah's sequence of the gifts, since, at least as he sees it, the Beatitudes are listed in ascending order[4] and the gifts in descending order. Using the sequence of the Beatitudes as his pattern, he justifies reversing the gifts, which begin with wisdom, the loftiest of them, and conclude with the fear of the Lord, the lowliest of them, by recalling that *the beginning of wisdom is the fear of God* (Sir 1:16; Ps 111:10); this allows him to start with the fear of the Lord and conclude with wisdom.[5] In II,11,38, Augustine adds the seven petitions of the Lord's Prayer, in the order of their appearance, to the different sets of Beatitudes and gifts. Meanwhile, as he proceeds along in his treatise, he also links the Beatitudes, in the sequence in which they appear, with the segments of the Sermon that he is discussing; this is a connection that he does not stress to the same extent as he does the others, and it has been mostly overlooked by the expositors of *The Lord's Sermon on the Mount*. The result is a tour de force of systematization, for the most part arbitrary, with important spiritual implications. The following table shows the relationship, as delineated by Augustine, among the Beatitudes (with the corresponding sections of the Sermon that Augustine connects with the Beatitudes, and where they are discussed in the work), the gifts of the Holy Spirit, and the petitions of the Lord's Prayer respectively:

1. *Blessed are the poor in spirit, for theirs is the kingdom of heaven.*
     Mt 5:13–24 (I,6,16–10,28).
        The fear of the Lord.
           Hallowed by thy name.

2. *Blessed are the meek, for they shall inherit the earth.*
     Mt 5:25–26 (I,11,29–32).
        Piety.
           Thy kingdom come.

3. *Blessed are the sorrowful, for they shall be comforted.*
     Mt 5:27–28 (I,12,33–36).
        Knowledge.
           Thy will be done on earth as it is in heaven.

---

with the gifts of the Holy Spirit or with the petitions of the Lord's Prayer but with the cardinal virtues of temperance, justice, prudence and fortitude (in that order).

4.   Thus also Gregory of Nyssa's sermons on the Beatitudes, with which Augustine may or may not have been familiar. See especially the beginning of Sermon 2.

5.   The connection of the Beatitudes with the reversed gifts of the Holy Spirit, as well as the justification for reversing them, is also found in Sermon 347 and *Teaching Christianity* II,7,9–11.

4. *Blessed are those who hunger and thirst for righteousness, for they shall be satisfied.*

> Mt 5:29–37 (I,13,37–18,54).
>> Fortitude.
>>> *Give us this day our daily bread.*

5. *Blessed are the merciful, for they shall obtain mercy.*

> Mt 5:38–48 (I,19,58–23,80).
>> Counsel.
>>> *Forgive us our trespasses as we forgive those who trespass against us.*

6. *Blessed are the pure of heart, for they shall see God.*

> Mt 6:1–7:12 (II,1,1–22,76).
>> Understanding.
>>> *Lead us not into temptation.*

7. *Blessed are the peacemakers, for they shall be called sons of God.*

> Mt 7:13–23 (II,23,77–25,86).
>> Wisdom.
>>> *Deliver us from evil.*

* * *

Although Jerome's translation of the Gospels into Latin was available when Augustine wrote *The Lord's Sermon on the Mount*, he used the Latin translation with which he was familiar, which was a version of the so-called Old Latin. He seems not to have adopted Jerome's translation of the Bible, known as the Vulgate, until around the year 400.

The entry on *The Lord's Sermon on the Mount* in *The Revisions* (I,19 [18]) is one of the longest in that work, and in it Augustine qualifies fourteen statements or phrases that appear in his commentary; only the entry on *A Miscellany of Eighty-three Questions* contains more such qualifications. Yet Augustine gives no indication that he in any way regretted or rejected this early treatise of his. Its extensive manuscript tradition[6] and the frequency with which it has been both published in the original Latin and translated into modern languages[7] suggests that it has been seen through the centuries as a worthy production of a great theologian, even if it may not be on a par with the other groundbreaking works that are more readily associated with his name.

* * *

The present translation of *The Lord's Sermon on the Mount* was made from the Latin text published in *Nuova Biblioteca Agostiniana* X/2, 82–285; it is pre-

---

6. See Almut Mutzenbecher, "Handschriftenverzeichnis zu Augustinus De sermone domini in monte," in *Sacris Erudiri* 16 (1965) 184–197.

7. The edition used for this translation (pp. 71–72) lists fifteen Latin editions since the late fifteenth century and as many translations into major languages since the late eighteenth century.

ceded by a detailed introduction by Salvino Caruana (in Italian) on pp. 7–69.
Almut Mutzenbecher's critical text of the treatise in *Corpus Christianorum, Series
Latina* 35 was consulted in establishing the text for the Italian series. Mutzen-
becher's introduction (in German), although earlier, is a valuable complement to
Caruana's. There are several extant English translations, most notably William
Findlay, *Our Lord's Sermon on the Mount,* revised and edited by Philip Schaff in
A Select Library of the Nicene and Post-Nicene Fathers of the Christian Church,
First Series 6 (New York 1903; repr. 1979) 1–63; John J. Jepson, *St. Augustine, The
Lord's Sermon on the Mount* (Westminster, Md. 1948) = *Ancient Christian Writ-
ers* 5; Denis J. Kavanagh, *Commentary on the Lord's Sermon on the Mount, with
Seventeen Related Sermons* (New York 1951) = *Fathers of the Church* 11, 17–199.

Revisions I,19 (18)

1. At that time I wrote two volumes on the Lord's Sermon on the Mount according to Matthew. In the first of them, in regard to what is written, *Blessed are the peacemakers, for they shall be called sons of God* (Mt 5:9), I said, "Wisdom accords with the peacemakers. In them everything is ordered, and no affection vies with reason, but all things are subject to the spirit of man, because he himself in turn obeys God."[1] The way in which I spoke is truly problematic. For no one can make such progress in this life that the law fighting against the law of our mind[2] is utterly absent from our members, since, even if a person's spirit resisted it in such a way that it never slipped into giving assent to it, it[3] would still continue to fight against it. What I said, then, that there would be no vying with reason, can be correctly understood with regard to those who are now acting on behalf of peace by overcoming the desires of the flesh, so that at some time that fullness of peace may be attained.

2. Then, in another passage, when I had repeated the same words of the Gospel, *Blessed are the peacemakers, for they shall be called sons of God*, I added, "All of these can certainly be accomplished in this present life, just as we believe that they were accomplished in the life of the apostles."[4] This should not be understood in such a way that we would think that in the apostles, while they were living here, there was no movement of the flesh fighting against the spirit; rather, these things can be accomplished here to the same extent that we believe they were accomplished in the apostles, namely, in accordance with that measure of human perfection which is as much perfection as can exist in this life. For it was not said that these things could be accomplished in this life because we believe that they were accomplished in the life of the apostles, but what was said was "as we believe that they were accomplished in the life of the apostles," so that they would be accomplished as they were accomplished in them, that is, to the degree of perfection that this life is capable of, and not as they are going to be accomplished, thanks to that utter peace for which we hope, when it will be said, *Where, O death, is your strife?* (1 Cor 15:55)

3. In another passage I used the testimony, *For God gives the Spirit without measure* (Jn 3:34),[5] without having understood at the time that this is more accurately taken to refer to Christ himself. For, indeed, unless the Spirit were given to other men according to measure, Elisha would not have asked for the double of what Elijah had.[6]

---

1. *The Lord's Sermon on the Mount* I,4,11.
2. See Rom 7:23.
3. I.e., the law of our mind.
4. *The Lord's Sermon on the Mount* I,4,12.
5. *The Lord's Sermon on the Mount* I,6,17.
6. See 2 K 2:9.

Again, when I was explaining what was written, *Not one jot or one stroke shall pass from the law until everything is complete* (Mt 5:18), I said, "This can only be understood as a vigorous expression of completion."[7] Here the question is appropriately raised as to whether this completion can be understood in such a way that it is still true that no one who is now making use of the choice of the will lives here in sin. For by whom can the law be completely carried out, even to a stroke, except by one who accomplishes all the divine commandments? But among these same commandments there is also what we are commanded to say, *Forgive us our trespasses, as we forgive those who trespass against us* (Mt 6:12), which is the prayer that the entire Church says until the end of the world. All the commandments are therefore considered to have been accomplished when whatever is not accomplished is pardoned.

4. What the Lord said, *Whoever abolishes one of the least of these commandments and so teaches* (Mt 5:19), and so forth, up to the passage where it says, *Unless your righteousness surpasses that of the scribes and Pharisees, you shall not enter the kingdom of heaven* (Mt 5:20),[8] I certainly explained much better and more suitably in other later sermons of mine,[9] which would take too long to repeat here. The thrust [of these words] leads to the conclusion that the righteousness of those who speak and do is greater than that of the Pharisees. The Lord himself says of the scribes and the Pharisees in another passage, *For they speak and do not do* (Mt 23:3).

We also understood better afterwards[10] what is written, *Anyone who is angry with his brother for no reason* (Mt 5:22).[11] For the Greek codexes do not have *for no reason*, as appears here, although the sense is the same. For we said that one must see what it means to be angry with one's brother, because one who is not angry with his brother is not angry at his brother's sin. One who is not angry at his brother's sin, then, is angry for no reason.

5. Again, I said, "This is how we must understand what is said about father and mother and the other blood ties, that we hate in them what is the lot of the human race by being born and dying."[12] This sounds as though these relationships would not have existed if, without some antecedent sin of human nature, no one were going to die. This understanding I have already condemned previously.[13] For there would certainly have been families and blood ties even if there had been no original sin; the human race would have increased and multiplied without death. And so the problem as to why the Lord commanded that enemies be loved[14] must be solved in another way, given that in another passage he commands that parents and

---

7.   *The Lord's Sermon on the Mount* I,8,20.
8.   See ibid. I,8,20–9,21.
9.   These sermons seem not to have survived.
10. See *The City of God* XXI,27.
11. See *The Lord's Sermon on the Mount* I,9,22.25.
12. Ibid. I,15,41. See Lk 14:26.
13. See *Revisions* I,10,2; 13,8.
14. See Mt 5:44; Lk 6:27.

children be hated. It is not solved as it is here but as we often solved it later,[15] that is, that we should love our enemies in order to gain them for the kingdom of God and hate in those nearest to us whatever obstacle there is to the kingdom of God.

6. Again, I certainly discussed here very carefully the precept forbidding the dismissal of one's wife except by reason of fornication.[16] But what the Lord wanted to be understood by the fornication by reason of which he would permit a wife to be dismissed must repeatedly be thought through and investigated — whether what is condemned is lewd behavior or that of which it is said, *You have destroyed everyone who fornicates away from you* (Ps 73:27), which certainly includes the previous one (for he who *takes the members of Christ and makes them members of a prostitute* [1 Cor 6:15] is also fornicating away from the Lord). I do not want the reader to think that, in regard to this matter, which is so important and so difficult to make a determination about, this discussion of ours should suffice. He should read other works as well, whether works of ours that were written later[17] or those of others that offer a more careful treatment. Otherwise, if he can, he himself should pursue with an especially vigilant and probing mind those things that could rightfully cause confusion here. Because not every sin is fornication and because God, who hears his holy ones when each day they say, *Forgive us our trespasses*, does not destroy every sinner (although *he destroys everyone who fornicates away from him*), the most obscure question is how this fornication should be understood and defined, and whether even by reason of it one is permitted to dismiss one's wife. On the other hand, there is no question that it is permitted by reason of what is perpetrated in lewd behaviour. And when I said that this was permitted and not commanded, I did not heed another passage that says, *He who takes an adulteress is foolish and wicked* (Prv 18:22). I certainly would not have said that that woman should be considered an adulteress, even after she heard from the Lord, *Nor do I condemn you; go, and from now on do not sin anymore* (Jn 8:11), if she listened obediently to this.

7. In another passage touching on what John says, *I do not say that one should pray for this* (1 Jn 5:16), I defined a sin of a brother which leads to death in this way: "I believe that there is a sin of a brother which leads to death when, after having come to the knowledge of God through the grace of our Lord Jesus Christ, someone attacks the brotherhood and is on fire with envy against that same grace by which he has been reconciled to God."[18] I did not actually affirm this, because I said that this was what I thought, but this should nonetheless have been added — "if he were to finish his life in this wicked perversity of mind"[19] — because a very bad

15. See *The City of God* XXI,26.
16. See *The Lord's Sermon on the Mount* I,16,43. See Mt 5:32.
17. See *Observations on the Heptateuch* II,71; Sermon 162.
18. *The Lord's Sermon on the Mount* I,22,73.
19. Augustine's original sentence would then be modified as follows: "I believe that there is a sin of a brother which leads to death when, after having come to the knowledge of God through the grace of our Lord Jesus Christ, someone attacks the brotherhood and is on fire with envy

person living in this life should certainly not be despaired of, nor is it imprudent to pray for a person who is not despaired of.

8. Again, in the second book I said, "No one will be permitted to ignore the kingdom of God when his only-begotten Son comes from heaven in a way that is not only intellectually comprehensible but also visible, as the Lordly Man, to judge the living and the dead."[20] But I do not see whether he who is *the mediator of God and men, the man Jesus Christ* (1 Tm 2:5), is appropriately referred to as a Lordly Man, although he is certainly the Lord. Who in his holy household cannot be called a lordly man?[21] And indeed, as for my saying this—I read it in some Catholic commentators on the Divine Scriptures. But wherever I said this, I wish that I had not said it.[22]

Again, what I said, "Practically no one in conscience can hate God,"[23] I see should not have been said, for there are many of whom it is written, *The pride of those who hate you* (Ps 74:23).

9. There is another passage in which I said, "The Lord said, *Its own trouble is sufficient for the day* (Mt 6:34), because necessity itself will compel the taking of food, which in my judgment is called *trouble* because it is a punishment as far as we are concerned, for it belongs to the infirmity that we have merited by sinning."[24] Here I failed to recall the foods for the body that were also given to the first human beings in paradise before they merited the punishment of death by sinning.[25] For, in a body that was not yet spiritual but animal, they were immortal in such a way that, in this kind of immortality, they still made use of bodily foods.

Again, I said, "The glorious Church which God chose for himself, having neither spot nor wrinkle."[26] I did not say this because now and in every regard it is already such, although there should be no doubt that it has been chosen for this, so that it may be like that when Christ, its life, appears,[27] for then it will also appear with him in the glory on account of which the Church has been called glorious.

Again, apropos of what the Lord said, *Ask and you shall receive; seek and you shall find; knock and it shall be opened to you* (Mt 7:7), I thought that how these three things differ from one another should be painstakingly examined,[28] but all of them are much better reduced to a very urgent petition. This is clear, in

---

against that same grace by which he had been reconciled to God, and if he were to finish his life in this wicked perversity of mind."

20. *The Lord's Sermon on the Mount* II,6,20. See 2 Tm 4:1.
21. "Lordly Man": *homo dominicus*. The expression can also be rendered as "man of the Lord" or "the Lord's man," which are probably better translations for members of the "holy household"—namely, the Church. They do not make sense, however, in reference to Christ himself.
22. On this controversial term and its use in patristic literature see Alois Grillmeier, "Jesus Christ, the Kyriakos Anthropos," in *Theological Studies* 38 (1977) 275–293; idem, "*O kyriakos anthropos*: Eine Studie zu einer christologischen Bezeichnung der Väterzeit," in *Traditio* 33 (1977) 1–63.
23. *The Lord's Sermon on the Mount* II,14,48.
24. Ibid. II,17,56.
25. See Gn 1:29; 2:9.16.
26. *The Lord's Sermon on the Mount* II,19,66. See Eph 5:27.
27. See Col 3:4.
28. See *The Lord's Sermon on the Mount* II,21,71–73.

fact, from when he concluded everything with the same word and said, *How much more will your Father who is in heaven give good things to those who ask him* (Mt 7:11), for he did not say "to those who ask and seek and knock."

This work begins in this way: "[If anyone were to ponder with piety and seriousness] the sermon which our Lord [Jesus Christ] gave."

Book One

1,1. If anyone were to ponder with piety and seriousness the sermon which our Lord Jesus Christ gave on the mount, I believe that he would discover there, as far as norms for high moral living are concerned, the perfect way to lead the Christian life. We would not be rash enough to make this promise of ourselves, but we deduce it from the very words of that same Lord. Indeed, from the conclusion of the sermon it is evident that all the precepts necessary for regulating a person's life are contained in it. His words are as follows: *Anyone who hears my words and does them I shall compare to a wise man who built his house upon rock. The rain fell, floods came, the winds blew and battered that house, and it did not fall, for it was built on rock. But anyone who hears my words and fails to act on them I shall compare to a foolish man who built his house on sand. The rains fell, floods came, the winds blew and battered that house, and it fell, and its ruin was great.* (Mt 7:24–27) The fact that the Lord did not merely say, *Anyone who hears my words,* but said instead, *Anyone who hears these words of mine,* is proof enough, then, in my judgment, that the words he spoke on the mount serve as such a perfect template of instruction for those people who wish to model their lives on them that they can rightly be compared to the man who built his house on rock. What I have said is intended to show that this sermon embodies the perfect summary of all those precepts necessary for leading the Christian life. We shall discuss this assertion in more detail in its appropriate place.

1,2. The sermon, then, begins as follows: *Seeing the large crowd, he went up the mount, and when he had sat down his disciples came to him. And opening his mouth he taught them, saying.* (Mt 5:1–2) If we look for the meaning of *mount* it could justifiably be understood as signifying the greater precepts of righteousness,[1] because those of less importance had been given to the Jews. Yet it was the one God who gave the lesser precepts, through his holy prophets and servants, to a people for whom it was still opportune to be bound by fear, in accordance with a most just ordering of times. And through his Son he gave the greater ones to a people for whom it was now fitting to be set free by charity. Since the lesser ones were given to those not yet fully mature and the greater ones to those who had come of age, they were given by him who alone is competent to dispense the appropriate medicine to the human race, suitable for its time. Nor should we wonder that the greater precepts have been given for the sake of the kingdom of heaven and the lesser ones for the sake of the earthly kingdom by one and the same God who made heaven and earth.[2] The prophet remarks of that greater righteousness, *Your*

---

1. "Righteousness": *justitiae.* This is the usual translation of *justitia* throughout.
2. "Who made heaven and earth": a phrase possibly inspired by the creed, although it does not seem to have formed part of the creed that was used in Hippo. See J. N. D. Kelly, *Early Christian Creeds,* 3rd ed. (New York 1972) 176.

righteousness is like the mountains of God (Ps 36:6), and this expresses well how such sublime truths are to be taught on the mount by one single competent teacher.[3]

He taught them sitting down, which pertains to the dignity of a teacher. His disciples came closer to him in body in order to hear his words, for they were already close in mind as far as the fulfilling of his precepts was concerned. *He opened his mouth and taught them, saying.* The expression that says, *And opening his mouth*, could be a device which suggests that the sermon to follow will be an extended one, or perhaps it means that he who was once accustomed to opening the mouths of the prophets in the Old Testament was now opening his own mouth.[4]

1,3. What then does he say? *Blessed are the poor in spirit, for theirs is the kingdom of heaven* (Mt 5:3). In a text about the desire for earthly possessions we read, *All is vanity and presumption of spirit* (Qo 1:14). Presumption of spirit means arrogance and pride. Generally speaking, proud people are said to have inflated spirits, and rightly so, since spirit is also called wind. Scripture says, *Fire, hail, snow, ice, stormy wind* (Ps 148:8). Who does not know that the proud are described as inflated, blown up as though with wind? Hence we have the words of the Apostle, *Knowledge inflates, love builds up* (1 Cor 8:2). With good reason, therefore, can the poor in spirit be understood as those who are humble and fear God — who do not, in other words, possess an inflated spirit. Indeed, blessedness can have no other beginning if we wish to arrive at perfect wisdom. *The beginning of wisdom is the fear of the Lord* (Sir 1:14; Ps 111:10), because in contrast it is written, *Pride is the beginning of all sin* (Sir 10:13).[5] Let the proud, therefore, desire and love the kingdoms of this world, but *blessed are the poor in spirit, for theirs is the kingdom of heaven.*

2,4. *Blessed are the meek, for they shall inherit the earth* (Mt 5:4). I believe that the earth referred to here is the one spoken of in the Psalms: *You are my hope, my heritage in the land of the living* (Ps 142:5). It indicates that the eternal inheritance has a kind of solidity and stability where the soul, possessed of true affection, rests in its own place as a body does on the earth, and is nourished there on its own food just as a body is from the earth. Such is the repose and life of the saints. The meek are those who yield to insults and do not resist evil but conquer evil with good.[6] Let the violent dispute and fight over what is earthly and temporal, but *blessed are the meek, for they shall inherit the earth,* from which they cannot be driven out.

---

3. See Mt 23:8.
4. The expression (*circumlocutio*) is in fact a standard Hebraicism to which Augustine, in his second suggested interpretation, gives a rich allegorical meaning.
5. The text that Augustine had before him cited Sir 10:13 here (and also below at I,11,32) in this version. But the best Hebrew and Greek manuscripts cite the verse otherwise: *The beginning of all pride is sin.* Augustine often referred to his version (as in *The City of God* XIV,13 and elsewhere) to demonstrate the primacy of pride among the vices. See William M. Green, "Initium omnis peccati superbia: Augustine on Pride as the First Sin," in *University of California Publications in Classical Philology* 13 (1949) 407–431.
6. See Rom 12:21.

2,5. *Blessed are the sorrowful, for they shall be comforted* (Mt 5:5). Sorrow is sadness at the loss of what we hold dear. But those who have turned to God let go of the things which they held dear in this world. They no longer find pleasure in them as they once did, and until they experience the love of what is eternal they are in some way grief-stricken. The Holy Spirit will therefore comfort them, because he is first and foremost named the Paraclete, or Consoler, so that in letting go of what is temporal they may rejoice in what is eternal.

2,6. *Blessed are those who hunger and thirst for righteousness, for they shall be satisfied* (Mt 5:6). Such people he declares to be lovers of that good which is true and steadfast. They will find satisfaction in that food of which the Lord himself says, *My food is to do the will of my Father* (Jn 4:34), which is righteousness, and with that water of which he says that, whoever drinks of it, *it shall become in him a spring of water, welling up to eternal life* (Jn 4:14).

2,7. *Blessed are the merciful, for they shall obtain mercy* (Mt 5:7). He declares blessed those who come to the help of the unfortunate, for they will be repaid by being delivered themselves from misfortune.

2,8. *Blessed are the pure of heart, for they shall see God* (Mt 5:8). How foolish then are those people who search for God with the outer eyes, since it is by the heart that he is seen, as we find written elsewhere, *Seek him with an undivided heart* (Wis 1:1). In fact, a pure heart is an undivided heart.[7] And just as we cannot see the light except with eyes that are pure, neither can God be seen unless that through which we see him is pure.

2,9. *Blessed are the peacemakers, for they shall be called sons of God* (Mt 5:9). Perfection is to be found in peace, where nothing is at odds, and therefore the peacemakers are sons of God, because nothing is opposed to God, and sons indeed ought to bear the likeness of their Father. But those who order all the affections of the soul and subject them to reason — that is, to the mind and to the spirit — and have subdued the desires of the flesh are peacemakers within themselves and become the kingdom of God. In that kingdom everything is ordered in such a way that what distinguishes and is surpassing in man rules over those other things which do not resist and which we have in common with the animals. And so that very thing which is outstanding in man, his mind and reason, becomes subject to one who is more powerful, Truth itself,[8] the only-begotten Son of God. For man could not rule over what is inferior to himself were he not subject to one higher than himself. This is the peace that is given on earth to people of goodwill;[9] this is the life of the wise person who has attained the summit of perfection. The prince of this world has been expelled from this most peaceful and ordered kingdom,[10] for he exercises his dominion over those who lead obdurately wayward and dis-

---

7. "*Undivided heart*...undivided heart": *simplicitate cordis...simplex cor.* "Undivided" is the usual translation of *simplex* throughout.
8. See Jn 14:6.
9. See Lk 2:14.
10. See Jn 12:21.

ordered lives. Firmly established and ordered from within, and notwithstanding the persecutions stirred up from without by the one who has been expelled, this peace only serves to enhance that glory which is according to God. Nor does he cause anything to collapse within this edifice, but through his abortive scheming he only succeeds in making clear just how solid its internal construction is. And so it follows, *Blessed are those who suffer persecution for the sake of righteousness, for theirs is the kingdom of heaven* (Mt 5:10).

3,10. The total number of these maxims amounts to eight. Referring to others, he goes on to address those present with the words, *Blessed are you whenever they curse you and persecute you* (Mt 5:11). He expressed the previous maxims in general terms, for he did not say, "*Blessed are the poor in spirit,* for yours is the kingdom of heaven," but rather, *for theirs is the kingdom of heaven.* Nor did he say, "*Blessed are the meek,* for you shall inherit the earth," but rather, *for they shall inherit the earth,* and so on as far as the eighth maxim, which states, *Blessed are those who suffer persecution for the sake of righteousness, for theirs is the kingdom of heaven.*[11]

He now turns his attention to those who are present and addresses them, since what he said just previously also concerned those who were present and heard these things. What was to follow, which also appeared to refer in a particular way to those who were present, was intended to apply as well to those who were not present or who would come afterwards. For this reason the number of those maxims merits careful consideration.

Blessedness begins from humility.[12] *Blessed are the poor in spirit,* meaning those who are not puffed up, because their soul is subject to divine authority, lest after this life it suffer punishment, even if by chance it believed itself to be blessed in this life. From here the soul proceeds to an acquaintance with Sacred Scripture, where it must show itself to be meek in piety, lest it dare disparage what appears absurd to the unlearned and, through engaging in obstinate disputes, no longer be docile. From here it begins to discover the nature of the ties of this world because of carnal habit and sin. And so at this third stage where there is knowledge, because of its involvement in things which are inferior, it mourns the loss of the supreme good. The fourth stage involves toil, where the soul labors strenuously to extricate itself from the attachments which have entrapped it with their deadly sweetness. Here there is hunger and thirst for righteousness, and fortitude is absolutely necessary, because what is adhered to out of pleasure is not relinquished without pain. The fifth stage counsels a means of exit to those who persevere in their struggle, because unless they are aided by a higher power they are in no way capable of extricating themselves from such powerful snares of misery. The counsel is indeed a just one, that whoever wishes to receive help from someone more powerful must

---

11.   Had Christ spoken in the second person rather than in the third, he would have been addressing only those who were present. In the following section Augustine points out that Christ now addresses those present in particular.

12.   The role of humility as the basis of the spiritual life is especially evident in Letter 118,3,22.

himself assist someone weaker in a situation where he finds himself the stronger. Therefore, *Blessed are the merciful, for they shall obtain mercy.* The sixth stage concerns purity of heart, which is the result of a sound conscience and good works that enable the soul to contemplate the supreme good, which is only perceptible through an intellect that is pure and serene. Finally, the seventh stage is wisdom itself, the contemplation of truth, bringing peace to the whole person and establishing a likeness to God, which reaches its apogee in this way: *Blessed are the peacemakers, for they shall be called sons of God.*[13] The eighth stage returns, as it were, to the beginning, because it shows and demonstrates what is in fact complete and perfect.

In the first and eighth stages mention is made of the kingdom of heaven: *Blessed are the poor in spirit, for theirs is the kingdom of heaven*, and: *Blessed are those who suffer persecution for the sake of righteousness, for theirs is the kingdom of heaven.* We read in Scripture, *Who will separate us from the love of Christ: tribulation, distress, persecution, hunger, nakedness, peril, or the sword?* (Rom 8:35) There are seven beatitudes, therefore, which lead to perfection, for the eighth, starting again from the outset as it were, adds clarity and shows what has been accomplished, so that through these gradations the others may reach completion.

4,11. And in my opinion the sevenfold working of the Holy Spirit, of which Isaiah speaks,[14] corresponds to these stages and maxims. But the order is different. For in Isaiah the list begins with what is more excellent, whereas here we start with what is less so. The prophet begins with wisdom and concludes with the fear of God, but *the beginning of wisdom is the fear of God* (Sir 1:16; Ps 111:10).[15] Therefore, if we ascend by stages and in numerical order, as it were, the first stage is the fear of God, the second piety, the third knowledge, the fourth fortitude, the fifth counsel, the sixth understanding, and the seventh wisdom. The fear of God accords with the humble, of whom it says here, *Blessed are the poor in spirit*, those who are not puffed up or proud, whom the Apostle exhorts, *Do not aspire to what is beyond you, but be fearful* (Rom 11:20), in other words, do not exalt yourself. Piety accords with the meek. The pious seeker honors Sacred Scripture and finds no fault with what he does not yet understand, nor does he set his mind against it, which is what it means to be meek. So it is said here, *Blessed are the meek.* Knowledge accords with the sorrowful, who have discovered from the Scriptures what evils have held them bound, which the uninstructed pursue as good and beneficial. So it is said here, *Blessed are the sorrowful.* Fortitude accords with those who hunger and thirst, for they struggle in their desire for the joy which comes from truly good things and are eager to divert their love from what is material and pertains to the body. So it is said here, *Blessed are those who hunger and thirst for righteousness.* Counsel

---

13. The supremacy of wisdom is often stressed in Augustine's writings, especially since it is sometimes identified with God. See, e.g., *Confessions* IX,10,24; *Teaching Christianity* I,8,8.
14. See Is 11:2–3.
15. The Latin editor variously reads "God" (*Dei*), as here, and the more familiar and scripturally correct "Lord" (*Domini*), as in I,4,12.

accords with the merciful. This is the one remedy for escaping great evils: that we forgive just as we wish to be forgiven,[16] and help others as far as we are able in the same way that we desire assistance when we are unable to help ourselves. So it is said here, *Blessed are the merciful.* Understanding accords with the pure of heart, like an eye that has been cleansed. Through it can be discerned *what the eye of the body has not seen, nor ear heard, nor has it entered into the human heart* (Is 64:4; 1 Cor 2:9). Of such people it is said here, *Blessed are the merciful.* Wisdom accords with the peacemakers. In them everything is ordered, and no affection vies with reason, but all things are subject to the spirit of man, because he himself in turn obeys God.[17] Of them it is said here, *Blessed are the peacemakers.*

4,12. The one single reward for all these differently named stages, however, is the kingdom of heaven. In the first place comes, as is proper, the kingdom of heaven, which constitutes the perfect and supreme wisdom of the rational soul. And so it is stated, *Blessed are the poor in spirit, for theirs is the kingdom of heaven,* which is the equivalent of saying, *The beginning of wisdom is the fear of the Lord.* Their inheritance is given to the meek, as to those who devoutly seek the Father's will: *Blessed are the meek, for they shall inherit the earth.* Consolation is given to the sorrowful, as to those who are aware of what they have lost and are immersed in the troubles in which they find themselves: *Blessed are the sorrowful, for they shall be consoled.* Satiety is given to those who hunger and thirst, as refreshment to those who struggle and fight with fortitude for salvation: *Blessed are those who hunger and thirst for righteousness, for they shall be satisfied.* Those who have been merciful will receive mercy, as those who have followed the truest and best counsel, and so they will receive from someone more powerful what they have shown to others weaker than themselves: *Blessed are the merciful, for they shall obtain mercy.* Those who are pure in heart will be empowered to see God, as those who have the clarity of vision to understand things that are eternal: *Blessed are the pure of heart, for they shall see God.* The likeness of God will be conferred on the peacemakers, as on those who possess the fullness of wisdom and have been formed in the image of God through the regeneration of the new man: *Blessed are the peacemakers, for they shall be called sons of God.* All of these can certainly be accomplished in this present life, just as we believe that they were accomplished in the life of the apostles,[18] although the transformation into angelic form promised us after this life[19] can in no way be expressed in words. *Blessed are those who suffer persecution for the sake of righteousness, for theirs is the kingdom of heaven.*

This eighth maxim, which returns to the beginning and evokes the image of the perfect man, is perhaps signified by the Old Testament practice of circumci-

---

16. See Mt 6:12.14–15.
17. See *Revisions* I,19 (18),1, where Augustine observes that such a state cannot in fact be attained in this life.
18. See *Revisions* I,19 (18),2, where Augustine denies that the apostles were no more capable than anyone else of achieving anything more than could be achieved in this life.
19. See Mt 22:30 par.

sion on the eighth day[20] and by the Lord's resurrection after the sabbath day,[21] which is both the eighth and the first day, and by the celebration of eight days of rest which we mark in the rebirth of the new man, and by the very number of Pentecost. For when we multiply seven by seven we have forty-nine, and, if an eighth [day] is added, the number fifty is complete, and in a manner of speaking we arrive back at the beginning.[22] On this day the Holy Spirit was sent, by whom we are led into the kingdom of heaven and by whose doing, thanks to whom we receive our inheritance, we are consoled and fed, obtain mercy, are purified and restored to peace. And so, having attained perfection, we endure for the sake of truth and righteousness all those external trials which come our way.

5,13. *Blessed are you,* he says, *when people curse and persecute you and, lying, speak all kinds of evil against you because of me. Rejoice and be glad, for your reward is great in heaven.* (Mt 5:11–12) Whoever in the name of a Christian seeks the pleasures of this world and an abundance of temporal things should be aware that our blessedness is to be found within, as the prophetic word says of the soul of the Church, *All the beauty of the king's daughter is within* (Ps 45:13). For curses, persecutions and slander are promised externally to those whose great reward is in heaven, which is perceived in the hearts of those who suffer, who can now declare, *We glory in our afflictions, knowing that affliction brings patience, patience brings endurance, and endurance hope. And hope is not deceived, because the love of God has been poured into our hearts through the Holy Spirit who has been given to us.* (Rom 5:3–5) Suffering such things brings no benefit, but rather bearing them for the name of Christ not only with an outlook that is serene but also with joy. In fact many heretics, using the Christian name to lead others astray, undergo many such sufferings, but they are excluded from the reward that has been spoken of, for it says not only *Blessed are those who suffer persecution* but also *for the sake of righteousness.* Where sound faith is not found, then there can be no righteousness, for *the righteous man lives by faith* (Hab 2:4; Rom 1:27). Nor should schismatics promise themselves any part of this reward, for, likewise, where there is no charity there can be no righteousness, because *love does no wrong to the neighbor* (Rom 13:10). If they possessed it, they would not tear asunder the body of Christ, which is the Church.[23]

---

20. See Gn 17:12 and frequently thereafter.
21. See Mt 28:1.
22. In Augustine's numerology, the numbers seven, eight and fifty signify completion or perfection; see, e.g., *The City of God* II,31 (seven); ibid. XXII,30 (eight); *Teaching Christianity* II,16,25 (fifty). Seven, however, is made even more perfect by the addition of one; see, e.g., *The City of God* XXII,30.
23. See Col 1:24. In this section Augustine has referred to both heretics and schismatics and seems to make a distinction between them, which was not always made in Christian antiquity. Although it is not evident who the heretics might be, the schismatics are almost certainly the Donatists, who were frequently accused by Augustine of being without charity and of divisiveness, as they are here. See in particular the *Homilies on the First Epistle of John* passim. Augustine's next two writings after *The Lord's Sermon on the Mount* were the first that he directed against the Donatists—*A Psalm against the Party of Donatus* and *One Book in Answer to a Letter of the*

5,14. We may ask what difference there is between the words *when they curse you* and *speak all manner of evil against you,* inasmuch as "to curse" means "to speak evil." But it is one thing to add insult to a curse in the presence of the one who is being cursed, as was said to our Lord, *Are we not speaking the truth, that you are a Samaritan and are possessed by a devil?* (Jn 8:48) It is quite another when in his absence a person's good name is sullied, just as the Scriptures also record of him, *Some say that he is a prophet; others say no, but that he leads the people astray* (Jn 7:12). To persecute someone is to use violence or to resort to plotting. This is exactly what the one who betrayed him and those who crucified him did. But it is not just said, *And speak all kinds of evil against you,* but *lying* is added, and further, *because of me.* I think that this has been added because of those people who want to boast of their persecutions and the aspersions cast on their good name, and who therefore claim that Christ belongs to them in view of the many evil things said about them, although the truth is being spoken when it refers to their errors. And if by chance some false accusations are leveled against them, which usually occurs through the rashness of others, they do not, however, suffer these for the sake of Christ. For, if he fails to bear the Christian name in accordance with the true faith and Catholic teaching, he is not a follower of Christ.

5,15. *Rejoice and be glad,* he continues, *for your reward is great in heaven.* I do not think that in this instance *heaven* means the higher parts of our visible world, for our reward, which ought to be stable and eternal, must not be located in elements which are changeable and subject to time. I believe that reference is being made to the spiritual firmaments where eternal righteousness is to be found.[24] In comparison, the sinful soul is described as earth, and because it is sinful it is told, *You are earth, and to earth you shall return* (Gn 3:19).[25] Speaking of these heavens the Apostle says, *For our homeland is in heaven* (Phil 3:20). Those who rejoice in spiritual things experience even now that reward, but afterwards it will reach perfection in every respect, when this mortal as well puts on immortality.[26] *For in the same way,* he adds, *they persecuted the prophets before you* (Mt 5:12). Here, broadly speaking, he applies persecution both to those who are cursed and to the defamation of a person's good name, and he rightly exhorts by way of an example, because those who speak the truth usually suffer persecution. However, the ancient prophets were not found wanting in proclaiming the truth through fear of persecution.

Heretic Donatus. The idea which Augustine expresses here and in the following section — that heretics and schismatics could suffer for their beliefs and not be martyrs (and hence receive the martyrs' reward) because their beliefs and practices were erroneous — is a commonplace in early Christian thought. See, e.g., Irenaeus, *Against Heresies* IV,33,9; Cyprian, *On the Unity of the Catholic Church* 14; Eusebius, *Ecclesiastical History* V,16,20–22; Augustine, Sermon 53A,13.

24. See 2 Pt 3:13.
25. For the symbolism of heaven and earth see also below at II,6.21–24.
26. See 1 Cor 15:53–54.

6,16. He therefore most fittingly continues, *You are the salt of the earth* (Mt 5:13), showing how the foolish are going to be judged—those who, either pursuing an abundance of temporal goods or fearing their lack, have suffered the loss of eternal goods, which can neither be conferred nor removed by human agency. Therefore, *if salt loses its savor, how will it become salt again?* (Mt 5:13) In other words, if you, being the ones through whom the nations are somehow to become salt, forfeit the kingdom of heaven for fear of persecution, whence are those to come through whom your error will be taken away, since God has chosen you as his means to take away the error of others? And so *the salt that has lost its savor is fit for nothing except to be thrown out and trampled underfoot by men* (Mt 5:13). It is certainly not trampled underfoot by those who suffer persecution; rather, it becomes useless through those who fear persecution. Only what lies on the earth can be trampled upon, but that person is not earthbound who, although he may endure much physical suffering on earth, in his heart remains steadfastly rooted in heaven.

6,17. *You are the light of the world* (Mt 5:14). As he said previously *salt of the earth,* so now he says *light of the world. Earth* must not be understood here as it was previously, as what we tread with our feet, but as the people who live on the earth, or even sinners, for it was to dispel their foul odor and give them flavor that the Lord sent the salt of his apostles. Likewise, *world* must be taken to refer not to heaven and earth but to the inhabitants of the world or to those who love the world. It was to enlighten them that the Lord sent his apostles. *A city set upon a hilltop cannot be hidden* (Mt 5:14), that is, one which is founded upon a righteousness which is distinguished and outstanding, symbolized by the very mount itself on which the Lord speaks. *Nor do they light a lamp and place it under a bushel but on a lampstand* (Mt 5:15). What are we to think? Is *under a bushel* just taken to refer to hiding a lamp, as if he were to say, "No one lights a lamp and then hides it"? Or does *a bushel* mean something else, so that placing a lamp under a bushel is to prefer the wellbeing of the body to preaching the truth, with the result that a person does not proclaim the truth lest he suffer some difficulty in matters pertaining to his body and to temporal affairs?

A bushel is spoken of with good reason, perhaps because of the relationship existing between punishment and measure,[27] since everyone receives recompense according to measure for what he has done in the body. Thus, *in this regard,* as the Apostle says, *everyone receives for what he has done in the body* (2 Cor 5:10), and, somewhat analogous to this bushel of the body, it is said elsewhere, *The measure you give shall be the measure you receive* (Mt 7:2). Or it may be because temporal goods which originate in the body begin and pass within a certain measure of days, which is perhaps what *a bushel* symbolizes. But those things which are

---

27. The Latin for "bushel" (*modius*) can also be used for "measure," which allows Augustine to treat the one word as referring to both an individual unit of measure (a bushel) and measure in general. But *mensura,* the more common word for "measure," is also used in the scriptural citations and elsewhere in this section.

by nature eternal and spiritual are subject to no such limitation, *for God gives the Spirit without measure* (Jn 3:34).[28] The person who places a lamp under a bushel for the sake of temporal benefits, therefore, is obscuring and concealing the light of sound teaching, whereas the person who masters his body in the service of God puts it on a lampstand to show how the proclamation of the truth pertains to a higher order, while mastery of the body belongs to a lower order. Through this very mastery of the body, however, the light of instruction should shine ever more brightly, and by good works through the various offices of the body — voice, tongue, and other movements of the body — it should be imparted to those who aspire to learn. And so a person places his light on a lampstand in accordance with the Apostle's words, *I do not box like someone beating the air, but I chastise my body and bring it into subjection, lest by chance while preaching to others I become a castaway myself* (1 Cor 9:26–27). I think that when the Lord says, *So that it might give light to everyone in the house* (Mt 5:15), by *house* he means the dwelling place of men, the world itself, because of what he said earlier, *You are the light of the world* . Or, if someone wanted to understand *house* as Church, that is by no means farfetched.

7,18. He continues, *So let your light shine before men that they may see your good works and glorify your Father who is in heaven* (Mt 5:16). If he were only to say, *So let your light shine before men that they may see your good works,* he would appear to be declaring that their purpose was human praise, which is something that the hypocrites seek, and those who solicit honors and go in pursuit of the most futile forms of renown.[29] Against such people it is written, *If I were still striving to please men, I would no longer be a servant of Christ* (Gal 1:10); and in the words of the prophet, *Those who set out to please men have been put to shame, for God has reduced them to nothing* (Ps 53:5); and again, *God has shattered the bones of those who please men* (Ps 53:5); and once more the Apostle, *Let us not become avid for vain glory* (Gal 5:26); and he again, *Let a person examine himself, and then he will glory in himself and not in another* (Gal 6:4). Not only, then, did the Lord say, *That they may see your good works,* but he added, *and glorify your Father who is in heaven,* meaning that the fact that a person pleases men through his good works should not establish the pleasing of men as its end but that he should refer this to the praise of God, and that they should be pleasing to men so that in him God may be glorified. It befits those who give praise to honor God and not man, as the Lord pointed out in the case of that man brought before him when the crowd praised his power in healing the paralytic, as it is written in the Gospel, *They feared God and gave glory to him who gave such power to men* (Mt 9:8). Paul, his imitator, says, *They had only heard that he who once persecuted*

---

28. See *Revisions* I,19 (18),3, where Augustine qualifies his use of this verse by saying that it applies only to Christ, while the Spirit is given in a measurable quantity to others.

29. The issue raised here, of a person's motivations for performing good works, is treated at much greater length below at II,1,1–3,12.

us now proclaims the faith which he formerly tried to destroy, and they glorified God in me (Gal 1:23–24).

7,19. After he has urged his hearers to endure everything for the sake of truth and righteousness and not to conceal the good they were going to receive but to learn with generosity so as to teach others, not performing good works so as to win praise for themselves but for the glory of God instead, he then sets himself to instruct and teach them what they are to teach, as if they had put the question to him, "We are indeed willing to put up with everything for your name's sake and not conceal your teaching. But what exactly is it that you forbid to be hidden? And for what exactly do you command us to endure everything? Surely you are not going to contradict what is written in the law?" No, he says. *Do not think that I have come to abolish the law or the prophets; I have come not to abolish them but to fulfill them* (Mt 5:17).

8,20. This statement has two meanings, each of which must be carefully examined. For whoever says, *I have come not to abolish the law but to fulfill it,* speaks either of adding something which the law lacks or of carrying out what it contains. Let us then examine first my first suggestion. Whoever adds what is lacking does not therefore annul what he finds but instead affirms it by completing it. Consequently he goes on to say, *Amen, I say to you, until heaven and earth pass away not one jot or one stroke shall pass from the law until everything is complete* (Mt 5:18). For while those things come to be which, through their addition, bring completion, even more so do those things come to be which are initial premises. So the words, *Not one jot or one stroke shall pass,* can only be understood as a vigorous expression of completion[30] demonstrated through individual letters, among which an iota is smaller than all the others because it is made with a single dash, and the stroke is a small mark above it. By these words he shows that the law is to be fulfilled down to its smallest details. He then adds, *Whoever abolishes one of the least of these commandments and so teaches others shall be called least in the kingdom of heaven* (Mt 5:19).[31] One jot or one stroke therefore refers to the least commandments. *Whoever abolishes and so teaches*—that is, according to what he has abolished, not according to what he has found and read—*shall be called least in the kingdom of heaven*, and perhaps he may not even be found in the kingdom of heaven, where only those who are great may be found. *Whoever observes and so teaches, he shall be called great in the kingdom of heaven* (Mt 5:19). *Whoever observes* refers to the one *who does not abolish and so teach*, meaning that he does not abolish on this basis. But that *he shall be called great in the kingdom of heaven* entails that he will also be in the kingdom of heaven, where the great are given entrance. What follows relates to this.

---

30. In *Revisions* I,19 (18),3 Augustine questions whether this completion, or perfection, can be acquired in this life, given that it would mean an observance of every commandment.

31. In *Revisions* I,19 (18),4 Augustine says that he explained Mt 5:19–20 better in some later sermons of his, which seem not to have survived.

9,21. For I tell you, unless your righteousness surpasses that of the scribes and Pharisees, you shall not enter the kingdom of heaven (Mt 5:20). This means that you must observe not only the smallest precepts of the law, from which a person starts out, but also those which are added by me, who *have come not to abolish the law but to fulfill it*; otherwise *you shall not enter the kingdom of heaven*. But you say to me in reply, "When speaking just now of the least commandments he declared that whoever abolished one of them and taught that it was abolished would be called least in the kingdom of heaven. Yet that person would be called great who observed them and so taught, and consequently he will be in the kingdom of heaven because he is great. If this is the case, what need is there to add the least precepts of the law if it is possible for someone to be already in the kingdom of heaven, inasmuch as whoever observes them and so teaches is great?" For this reason the sentence—*Anyone who observes them and so teaches them shall be called great in the kingdom of heaven*—should be understood as applying not to the least commandments but to those that I am going to speak of. What are they? That your righteousness, he states, should surpass that of the scribes and Pharisees, *for, unless it surpasses it, you shall not enter the kingdom of heaven*. Hence whoever abolishes those least commandments and so teaches shall be called least. But anyone who keeps the least of the commandments and so teaches shall not be regarded as great and fit for the kingdom of heaven but as not as small as the person who abolishes them. In order to be great and fit for that kingdom he must observe and teach just as Christ now teaches, which means that his righteousness must surpass that of the scribes and Pharisees.

The righteousness of the Pharisees consists in refraining from killing, whereas the righteousness of those who will enter the kingdom of God consists in not being angry for no reason. Not to kill is the least of the commandments, and whoever annuls that will be called least in the kingdom of heaven. Yet whoever observes it and refrains from killing does not immediately become great and fit for the kingdom of heaven, but he has made some progress. If he is not angry for no reason he will advance in perfection; should he attain this perfection, so much the more distant will he be from murder. Therefore, he who teaches that we should not be angry is not abolishing the law against killing but rather completing it, so that, when we refrain externally from killing and do not bear anger in our heart, we preserve our integrity.

9,22. You have heard, he continues, *that it was said to the people of old, You shall not kill, and anyone who does kill shall be liable to judgment. But I say to you that anyone who is angry with his brother for no reason*[32] *shall be liable to judgment; and anyone who says raca to his brother shall be liable to the council; and whoever says fool shall be liable to the fire of Gehenna.* (Mt 5:21–22) What difference is there among being liable to judgment, liable to the council, and liable

---

32. The commonly accepted text omits *for no reason*, although it was found in the version that Augustine had before him, and elsewhere as well. In *Revisions* I,19 (18),4 Augustine notes that he later came to reject this reading because it was not in the original Greek.

to the fire of Gehenna? For this last punishment sounds most serious, and there is the indication of a certain gradation from what is lighter to what is more serious, until it reaches the fire of Gehenna. Therefore, if being liable to judgment is of less consequence than being liable to the council, and likewise if being liable to the council is less serious than being liable to the fire of Gehenna, it inevitably follows that we must understand that being angry with one's brother is less serious than saying "raca," and, further, that saying "raca" is not as serious as saying "fool." For there would be no gradations of guilt had not the offences been enumerated in gradated fashion.

9,23. An obscure word occurs here, for *raca* is neither Greek nor Latin, whereas the other terms are familiar from our own language. There are some who wish to derive the meaning of this word from the Greek, being of the opinion that *raca* means "ragged," for the Greek for "rag" is said to be *hrachos*. Yet, when people are asked what the Greek word for "ragged" is, they do not reply *raca*. If that were the case, a Latin translator could put down "ragged" instead of *raca* and so refrain from using a term which does not exist in Latin and is not used in Greek. A more likely explanation is the one which I heard from a certain Hebrew when I inquired of him. He said that the word had no meaning but expressed rather the emotion of an agitated mind. These are what grammarians call interjections, small parts of a discourse, suggesting the emotion of an agitated mind, as when a suffering person says "Alas!" or an irritated person says "Hmm!" Such words are unique to each language and do not translate easily into another language. This undoubtedly compelled both the Greek and Latin translators to transcribe the word itself since they were unable to translate it in any way.

9,24. These sins consequently admit of varying grades. The first is when a person gets angry and contains the emotion he has conceived in his heart. However, if such an upset provokes a meaningless utterance from someone who is angry, the very fact of the outburst, which is a proof of a mental upset and hurts the person with whom he is angry, is certainly more serious than if his rising anger were suppressed in silence. But if not only the angry person's voice is heard but also the word against whom it is directed designates and implies a kind of outrage, who can doubt that this represents a further stage than if the mere sound of anger were expressed? Consequently, in the first case there is one element, that is, anger alone; in the second there are two elements, both anger and the tone of voice which denotes anger; in the third there are three, anger, the voice which denotes anger, and the tone of the voice which carries with it a certain outrage. Now you see the three stages of accusation, that of judgment, that of the council, and that of the fire of Gehenna. Where judgment is concerned, there is still room to defend oneself. In the council, however, although there is usually judgment as well, the distinction here compels us to keep them separate. It seems that it belongs to the council to pass sentence, when it is no longer a question of deciding whether or not the guilty person is to be condemned; rather, those who pass sentence confer among themselves as to what punishment should be imposed on the person they have agreed should be condemned. The fire of Gehenna, however, admits of no doubt as far as condemnation is concerned, as in the case of judgment, nor as far as the imposition of punishment is concerned, as in the case of the council. In Gehenna both the condemnation and the punishment of the condemned person are certain.

Different levels, therefore, appear to exist in the matter of sins and guilt. But who can say in what unseen ways these are apportioned according to the merits of souls? Hence we must pay attention to the great distance that exists between the righteousness of the Pharisees and that greater righteousness which leads to the kingdom of heaven. For, since killing is more serious than accusing by word and thereby renders one liable to judgment, in this instance anger causes one to be liable to judgment, which is the least of the three sins. In the first case people are debating the question of murder among themselves, whereas in this instance all is left to divine judgment, where the fate of the condemned is the fire of Gehenna. Yet, if an insult is to be punished by the fire of Gehenna, and if someone says that, in accordance with a higher righteousness, murder will be subject to a more severe punishment, then he is obliged to acknowledge that there are different states in Gehenna.

9,25. In these three statements, though, we must certainly discern a further meaning implied in the words. The first proposition has all the words required so that nothing more is to be understood: *Anyone who is angry,* he says, *with his brother for no reason shall be liable to judgment.* But in the second statement, when he says, *Anyone who says raca to his brother,* the words "for no reason" are implied, and so he adds, *shall be liable to the council.* In the third, when he declares, *Anyone who says fool,* two things are to be understood, both "to his brother" and "for no reason." We can therefore defend the fact that the Apostle calls the Galatians stupid, whom he also calls brothers. Nor does he do this *for no reason.* Therefore "brother" is to be understood in this text, because in the discourse on one's enemy which follows it is said that even he should be treated with a greater righteousness.

10,26. He then continues, *If therefore you are offering your gift at the altar and there remember that your brother has something against you, leave your gift there before the altar and go first to be reconciled with your brother, and then come and offer your gift* (Mt 5:23–24). So it is evident that he was referring to one's brother earlier, for the sentence which follows is connected by the conjunction which witnesses to what has preceded. For he does not say, "If you are offering your gift at the altar," but, *If therefore you are offering your gift at the altar.* So, if it is not lawful to be angry with a brother without reason, or to say "raca" or to say "fool," much less is it lawful to suppress something within oneself, with the result that anger turns into hatred. What is said elsewhere has application here: *Do not let the sun go down on your anger* (Eph 4:26). And so we are commanded that, when offering a gift at the altar, if we remember that a brother has something against us, we are to leave the gift before the altar and go and be reconciled with that brother and then come and offer the gift. Were this to be taken literally, perhaps someone would think that it had to be carried out in the brother's presence; it could not be postponed for a time, since you are commanded to leave your gift before the altar. But should such a thought come to mind in the brother's absence and even, as can happen, while he is living overseas, it is absurd to believe that you should leave your gift before the altar and then offer it to God after land and sea have been traversed. Hence we have no option but to resort to a spiritual interpretation, so that what is said may be understood without absurdity.

10,27. And so we can interpret the altar in God's inner temple in a spiritual sense as signifying faith itself, whose sign is the visible altar. For whatever the gift we are offering to God, be it prophecy, teaching, prayer, hymn or psalm, or any other kind of spiritual gift which comes to mind, it cannot be acceptable to God unless it is supported by a sincere faith and is, as it were, firmly and unshakeably founded on it, so that what we are saying can be perfect and blameless. There are many heretics who do not have an altar, that is, the true faith, and who utter blasphemies in place of praise. They are burdened by the opinions of this world and, as it were, cast their act of devotion down upon the ground. But the intention of the person who is making the offering must also be beyond reproach.

Suppose, then, that we are on the point of offering something in our heart, that is, in God's inner temple (*for God's temple, which is what you are, is holy* [1 Cor 3:17], the Apostle says, and, *Christ dwells in the inner man through faith in your hearts* [Eph 3:16–17]), and that it should come to mind that a brother has something against us, meaning that, if we have offended him in some way, then he has something against us. (For, should he offend us, we have something against him, and then there is no need to go and be reconciled, for you will not be seeking pardon from the person who has offended you but only forgiving in the same way that you wish to be forgiven by the Lord for what you yourself have committed.) We must therefore go and be reconciled when we remember that we have perhaps offended a brother in some way. We must go not with the feet of the body, though, but with the affections of the mind, so that with a humble demeanor you prostrate yourself before the brother to whom you hasten with a warm disposition, in whose presence you will make your offering. For in this way, should he even be present, you will be able to soothe him with genuine warmth and recall him to grace by asking pardon, so long as you do this first before God, making your way to him not with a sluggish movement of the body but with the disposition of an urgent love. And returning from there, by recalling the intention with which you initially started out, you will offer your gift.

10,28. Yet who behaves in such a way that he is never angry with his brother for no reason, or does not say "raca" for no reason, or does not call him "fool" for no reason, all of which is evidence of great pride? If by chance a person has fallen into any one of these faults there is one remedy—that he should beg for pardon in humility of soul, provided that he is not puffed up with a spirit of vain arrogance. *Blessed,* therefore, *are the poor in spirit, for theirs is the kingdom of heaven.* Let us now see what follows.

11,29. *Come to terms with your adversary quickly,* the Lord says, *while you are on the way with him, lest your adversary hand you over to the judge, and the judge hand you over to the attendant, and you be thrown into prison. Amen, I say to you, you shall not go out from there until you pay back the last penny.* (Mt 5:25–26) By the term *judge* I understand this: *For the Father does not judge anyone but has handed over all judgment to the Son* (Jn 5:22). By *attendant* I understand this: *And angels attended on him* (Mt 4:11); and we believe that he will come with his angels to judge the living and the dead.[33] By *prison* I understand the punishments of darkness, which he calls *external* in another text.[34] I do in fact believe that the joy of the divine reward lies inwardly, within the mind itself, or somewhere even more secluded if such can be conceived. Of this it is said to the faithful servant, *Enter into the joy of your Lord* (Mt 25:23), just as in the ordering of public life the person who is thrown into prison is sent out of the courtroom or out of the judge's chamber.

11,30. The payment of the last penny can reasonably be interpreted as meaning that nothing will go unpunished, just as we are accustomed to say "down to the dregs" when we wish to express the fact that something is so exhaustive that nothing remains. Or the term *last penny* may refer to earthly sins. For the fourth member of the different constituents of this world, and the last, is earth, so that if you start from heaven, then number air as second and water third, earth comes fourth.[35] The statement, *until you pay the last penny,* can be conveniently taken to mean "until you atone for your earthly sins," for this is what the sinner heard: *You are earth, and to earth you shall return* (Gn 3:19). I wonder if the words *until you pay* do not refer to that punishment which is called everlasting. For how can the debt be paid where no place is allowed for repentance and for leading a more upright life? Perhaps then the words found here, *until you pay,* are to taken in the same sense as the text where it is said, *Sit on my right until I put all your enemies under your feet* (Ps 110:1), for once his enemies have been put under his feet he will not cease to sit on the right; or as when the Apostle says, *He must reign until he puts all his enemies under his feet* (1 Cor 15:25), for once they have been put there he will not cease to reign. In the same way, therefore, when it is said of him, *He must reign until he puts his enemies under his feet,* it means that he will always reign because his enemies will always be under his feet, so likewise what is said here — *You shall not go out from there until you pay the last penny* — can be understood in a similar way, meaning that he will never go out but will always be paying the last penny inasmuch as he is paying an eternal penalty for earthly sins. I have not asserted this so that I might appear to be evading a more searching

---

33. Christ's coming to judge the living and the dead is mentioned in every major ancient creed. See Mt 13:41; 24:31.
34. See Mt 8:12; 22:13; 25:30.
35. Augustine is not speaking here of the four elements of classic philosophical thought, inasmuch as he leaves out fire, which was one of them. His four *distincta membra* are simply the observable parts of the universe as he knew it, arranged in descending order of materiality. See also, e.g., *Confessions* XI,5,7.

examination of the punishments for sins, in the sense that Sacred Scripture calls them eternal, although whatever may be the manner of their presentation they are to be avoided rather than experienced.

11,31. But let us see who exactly the adversary is, whom we are enjoined to come to terms with quickly, while we are still on the way with him. He is either the devil or a human being or the flesh or God or his precept. Yet I cannot see how we are enjoined to come to terms with the devil, in other words to be of the same mind and in agreement with him. Some have translated the word in the Greek text, *eunoon,* as "being of one mind," others as "being in agreement." But we are not enjoined to show goodwill to the devil, for where there is goodwill there is also friendship, nor has anyone ever said that we must offer friendship to the devil; nor is it appropriate to be of one mind with him on whom we declared war when we first renounced him[36] and at whose conquest we shall receive the crown of victory; nor is it right to be in agreement with him, for had we never consented to him we would never have fallen into such misery.

As for a human being, although we are enjoined to be at peace with everyone insofar as it lies in our power,[37] where indeed goodwill, harmony and agreement are to be understood, yet I cannot see how I can accept that we should be handed over by a human being to the judge, when I understand Christ to be the judge, *before whose judgment seat we must all appear* (2 Cor 5:10), as the Apostle says. How then can a person hand someone over to the judge when he himself must likewise stand before the judge? Or, if someone is handed over to the judge because he has offended someone else, and although the person he has offended has not handed him over, it is perfectly acceptable that he should be handed over to the judge by the law itself, which he contravened when he offended someone. For, if the offence results in a person's death, there is no longer any time to reach agreement with him, for he is no longer with him on the way, that is, in this life.[38] Yet he will be healed by doing penance and by taking refuge with a contrite heart in the mercy of him who forgives the sins of those who turn to him and who rejoices more over one repentant sinner than over ninety-nine who are righteous.[39]

Even less do I see how we are enjoined to be benevolent, to be of one mind and in agreement with the flesh. It is rather sinners who love their own flesh and are of one mind with it and are in agreement with it, whereas those who keep it in servitude are not in agreement with it but compel it to be in agreement with them.

11,32. Perhaps then we are being enjoined to be in accord with God and to come to terms with him, so that we may be reconciled to him from whom we have turned away through sinning, and for that reason he can be said to be our adversary. For he can justifiably be called the adversary of those whom he resists,

---

36. The baptismal renunciation of Satan is being referenced.
37. See Rom 12:18.
38. The way or the path as a metaphor for life (repeated below at I,11,32) is extremely ancient, accentuated in Latin, where "way" is *via* and "life" is *vita.*
39. See Lk 15:7.

for *God resists the proud but gives grace to the humble* (Jas 4:6), and, *Pride is the beginning of all sin, while the beginning of man's pride is to fall away from God* (Sir 10:13.12), and the Apostle says, *If, when we were enemies, we were reconciled to God through the death of his Son, all the more shall we saved by his life now that we have been reconciled* (Rom 5:10). From this it can be inferred that there is no evil nature that is hostile to God, since those who were enemies have now in fact been reconciled. Anyone, therefore, on this way, that is, in this life, who has not been reconciled to God through the death of his Son will be handed over to the judge by him, because *the Father does not judge anyone but has handed over all judgment to the Son.* The remainder of what is written in this chapter follows logically on what we have been explaining.

There is only one thing which could pose a difficulty to this explanation: I mean in what sense we can be said to be on the way with God, if from this text he has to be understood as the adversary of the wicked, with whom we are enjoined to be quickly reconciled, unless perhaps, because he is everywhere, we ourselves are indeed with him when we are on this way. For, it says, *if I climb to the heavens, you are there; if I go down to the lower regions, you are there; if I take wings towards the horizon and dwell in the furthest parts of the sea, even there your hand would bring me, and your right hand would lead me* (Ps 139:8–10).

Or, if it is not acceptable that the wicked should be with God, although there is no place where God is not present (just as we do not say of the blind that they are in the light even if the light shines on their eyes), only one option remains, that in this context we take the adversary to mean God's precept. For what is adversarial to those wishing to sin other than God's precept, that is, his law and the Sacred Scripture which are given to us in this life, so that they may accompany us on the way, and which we must not oppose, lest he hand us over to the judge, but which it behoves us to come to terms with quickly? For no one knows when he must leave this life. But who is the one who comes to terms with Sacred Scripture except the one who reads it or listens to it with devotion and acknowledges its supreme authority, so that what he understands he does not hate because he is aware that it is adversarial to his sins but rather loves its correction and rejoices that it does not spare his diseases until they are healed? But whenever something appears obscure or absurd to him, he refrains from stirring up arguments and disputes but prays for understanding and remembers that goodwill and respect must be shown to such eminent authority. Yet who accomplishes this except the one who approaches the discovery and knowledge of the Father's testament not with litigious threats but with meekness and piety? *Blessed,* therefore, *are the meek, for they shall inherit the earth.* Let us examine what follows.

12,33. *You have heard that it was said, You shall not commit adultery. But I say to you that anyone who looks upon a woman with lustful desire has already committed adultery with her in his heart.* (Mt 5:27–28) The lesser righteousness, therefore, consists in not committing adultery through the joining of bodies, but the greater righteousness of the kingdom of God is not to commit adultery in one's heart. Whoever refrains from committing adultery in his heart all the more easily safeguards himself from committing adultery in his body. The one who commanded this, therefore, confirmed it; for he did not come to abolish the law but to fulfill it. Particular attention must be paid to the fact that he did not say, Anyone "who desires a woman" but *who looks upon a woman with lustful desire*, meaning that, for this purpose and with this intention, he aims at lustfully desiring her. This is no longer a matter of being teased by the pleasure of the flesh but clearly a surrender to lust, with the result that the unlawful appetite is not restrained but would be sated if the opportunity arose.

12,34. There are three stages by which sin comes about—suggestion, pleasure, and consent. Suggestion occurs either through memory or through the bodily senses, as when we see, hear, smell, taste or touch something. But if there is pleasure in enjoyment, illicit pleasure must be curbed. When we are fasting, for example, the sight of food activates the gustatory appetite, which occurs only through pleasure; yet we do not succumb to this but restrain it instead by the higher law of reason. If, however, consent is given, sin takes place in the full sense of the word, known to God in our heart, even if the deed does not become apparent to others. That is how these stages unfold, analogous to the suggestion of the serpent, deceitful and slippery, that is, by the movement of bodies that takes place in time, and should such fantasies be played out within the soul they are abstracted externally from the body. And if a hidden motion of the body touches the soul, apart from those five senses, it also belongs to time and is deceitful. Therefore, the more it insinuates itself in hidden fashion and impinges upon the faculty of thought, so much the more aptly can it be compared to the serpent. These three stages, as I began to say, are similar to what took place as recorded in Genesis, when on the part of the serpent there was a suggestion, even persuasion, and on the part of Eve there was pleasure in the desire of the flesh, whereas on the part of the man there was consent in the act of reason.[40] Man, having passed through these three stages, was driven out of paradise, that is, from the most blessed light of righteousness to death. And that most righteously! For anyone who persuades does not compel. All natural beings in their own order and according to their own kind are beautiful, but from the higher grades, within which the rational mind is ranked, there should be no descent to lower grades. Nor is anyone compelled thus. If it happens, the person is subject to the punishment of the righteous law of God, for it does not happen unwillingly. However, the pleasure which precedes the habit is either of no account or so insignificant as not to matter; but to yield to it is a great sin, for it is forbidden. As soon as a person yields he has committed sin in his heart. If he proceeds to the deed itself, the desire appears to be satisfied and quenched. But afterwards, when the suggestion returns, a still greater desire is kindled, but much less than the desire which turns into habit through constant acts. It is extremely

---

40. See Gn 3:1–7; 2 Cor 11:3. The woman, in other words, symbolizes the flesh and the man symbolizes reason or intellect. Augustine later rejected this opinion in *The Trinity* XII,13,20, where he also discussed the temptation of Adam and Eve.

difficult to conquer this; yet, if a person does not neglect himself or flinch from Christian warfare, with the guidance and help of God he will conquer even this habit. And so there will be a return to the original peace and order, and the man is subjected to Christ and the woman to the man. [41]

12,35. Just as we arrive at sin through these three stages, suggestion, pleasure, consent, so sin itself may be differentiated in three ways, in the heart, by deed, and by habit; they are like three deaths. One takes place as though at home, when a person gives way to pleasure in his heart; the second is brought out, as though outside the door, when consent eventuates in deed; the third occurs when, through force of bad habit, the soul is crushed as if by a mound of earth and now lies putrefying as though in the grave. Anyone who reads the Gospel knows that the Lord raised three types of dead people to life, and perhaps he reflects on what differences are implied in the very words that he uses in raising them up. In one place he says, *Little girl, get up!* (Mk 5:41) Elsewhere, *Young man, I say to you, Get up!* (Lk 7:14) And still elsewhere, *He groaned in spirit, wept, and again groaned*; then afterwards *he cried out in a loud voice, Lazarus, come forth!* (Jn 11:33.35.43)

12,36. We should therefore take the term "adulterers," mentioned in this chapter, to refer to every lustful desire of the flesh. For, since Scripture repeatedly calls idolatry fornication,[42] while Paul the apostle names greed as idolatry,[43] who can doubt that all wicked desire is justifiably called fornication when the soul becomes corrupt by disregarding the rule of its higher law and by prostituting itself for reward through the base pleasure derived from animal impulses? Consequently, anyone who is conscious of the rebellion of carnal pleasure against an upright will, because of sinful habits, and is dragged into captivity by its untamed violence should recall as far as he is able the kind of peace he has lost through sinning, and he should exclaim, *Wretched man that I am! Who will free me from the body of this death? The grace of God through our Lord Jesus Christ.* (Rom 7:24–25) For when he bewails how wretched he is, in his grief he is imploring the help of the consoler. And the awareness of one's wretched state represents no small opening to happiness, and therefore, *Blessed* also *are the sorrowful, for they shall be comforted.*

13,37. He then continues as follows, *If your right eye scandalizes you, pull it out and cast it away from you. For it is better for you that one of your members perish than that your whole body go to Gehenna.* (Mt 5:29) To cut out one's members is a task requiring great fortitude. For whatever it is that the eye signifies, it is without doubt something greatly loved. Those who wish to express the intensity of their love are accustomed to say, "I love him like my eyes" or even "more than my eyes." The addition of *right* perhaps serves to increase the force of love. For, although the eyes of the body are jointly directed to seeing, and both are equally capable if focused, people fear more the loss of the right eye. So the meaning is this:

41.   See 1 Cor 11:3. Following Augustine's symbolism, reason will be subjected to Christ and the flesh to reason.
42.   See Ez 16:15–22; Hos 4:11–12.
43.   See Col 3:5.

whatever it is that you love so much that you cherish it as though it were your right eye, *if it scandalizes you,* if it is an impediment to true happiness, *pull it out and cast it away from you. For it is better for you that one of these perish,* which you love like one of your bodily members, *than that your whole body go to Gehenna.*

13,38. But because he continues by speaking in a similar way about the right hand, *If your right hand scandalizes you, cut it off and cast it away from you. For it is better for you that one of your members perish than that your whole body go to Gehenna* (Mt 5:30), we are compelled to examine more closely what he means by *eye.* In this regard nothing strikes me as being more appropriate than a very dear friend. For this is what we can correctly call a member that we dearly love, and a counselor as well, particularly where the things of God are concerned (because it is the right one), since the eye as it were points out the way to us, whereas the left is loved as a counselor (although in matters of this world which pertain to the body), and it would have been superfluous to speak of it as causing scandal, since not even the right would be spared. As regards the things of God, a counselor causes scandal if he attempts to mislead anyone into some dangerous heresy in the name of religion and doctrine. The right hand, therefore, is to be taken as a cherished helper and a minister in matters pertaining to God; for, just as contemplation is understood as belonging to the eye, so action is correctly associated with the hand, such that the left hand is understood to pertain to the works necessary for this life and for the body.

14,39. *It was said, Whoever dismisses his wife should give her a bill of repudiation* (Mt 5:31). This is the lesser righteousness of the Pharisees, and what the Lord says does not contradict it: *But I say to you, Whoever dismisses his wife, except by reason of fornication, makes her an adulterer, and whoever marries a woman dismissed by her husband commits adultery* (Mt 5:32).[44] Whoever commands that a bill of repudiation be given is not the one who commands that the wife be sent away, but *whoever dismisses her,* he says, *should give her a bill of repudiation,* so that the thought of a bill might temper the precipitate anger of the man who is dismissing his wife. The one who sought a pause before dismissal, then, gave notice as far as he could to hardhearted men that he was not in favor of separation. And so, when the Lord was questioned elsewhere on this point, he replied, *Moses conceded this because of your hardness of heart* (Mt 19:8). For, however hardhearted the man might be who wanted to dismiss his wife, when he reflected that once the bill of repudiation had been given she could safely marry someone else, he might easily be placated. In order, therefore, to emphasize that a wife might not be dismissed lightly, the Lord made fornication the only exception. All the other difficulties, should such exist, he commands to be courageously

---

44. The literature on these two verses, like that on Mt 19:3–9, is immense, and Augustine himself devotes substantial effort to understanding them. His position, briefly summarized, is the traditionally Catholic one, which allows for separation of the spouses under certain circumstances (characterized as fornication) but not for remarriage. Notably, he allows wives to dismiss their husbands as well as husbands to dismiss their wives.

endured for the sake of marital fidelity and chastity. He even declares a man to be an adulterer who marries a woman who has been released by her husband. The apostle Paul shows the limit of such an obligation which, he says, must be observed as long as the husband lives; by his dying, though, he gives his consent to marry.[45] He himself maintained this ruling and pointed out that it was not his own counsel, as was the case in much of his teaching, but a precept given by the Lord when he stated, *I command those who are married, not I but the Lord, that a woman should not leave her husband. But if she does leave she is to remain unmarried or else be reconciled to her husband. Nor is a man to send his wife away.* (1 Cor 7:10–11).

I believe that a similar criterion applies, that if a man sends his wife away he should not marry another, or else he should be reconciled to his wife. It can happen that he may dismiss his wife by reason of fornication, which the Lord allowed as an exception. Now, if the wife is not permitted to marry another while her husband is still alive, nor can he marry while the wife whom he dismissed is still alive, much less is it right for him to engage in despicable sexual relationships with others. Those marriages are to be considered more blessed where — once they have generated offspring, or even if they have refused to have earthly progeny — the couple is able to observe chastity by mutual consent, since that precept in which the Lord forbade the dismissal of the wife is not contravened. For he who lives with her not carnally but spiritually is not dismissing her, and what the Apostle said is safeguarded, *For the rest, let those who have wives live as if they did not have them* (1 Cor 7:29).

15,40. The words which the Lord spoke on another occasion as a rule perturb the outlook of those who are less advanced but who are nonetheless already striving to model their lives on the precepts of Christ: *Anyone who comes to me and does not hate his father and mother and wife and children and brothers and sisters, and even his own soul, cannot be my disciple* (Lk 14:26). To those with less insight it can appear contradictory that here he forbids a wife to be dismissed, except by reason of fornication, whereas elsewhere he denies the possibility of discipleship to someone who does not hate his wife. But if he were referring to cohabitation, he would not be putting mother and father and brothers in the same category. Yet how true it is that *the kingdom of heaven suffers force, and those who use force seize it* (Mt 11:12)! What great force does a man not require to love his enemies and to hate father and mother and wife and sons and brothers! For the one who invites to the kingdom of heaven commands both. And with the help of his guidance it is easy to show how these do not contradict one another; but it is difficult to put into practice even when it has been understood, although in this instance it becomes very easy with his help. For the eternal kingdom, to which he condescends to call his disciples, whom he also names brothers,[46] does not have temporal necessities of this kind. In fact, *There is not Jew or Gentile, male or female, slave or free,*

---

45.   See Rom 7:2.
46.   See Mt 12:49.

but Christ is all and in all (Gal 3:28; Col 3:11). And the Lord himself says, *In the resurrection of the dead they will take neither husband nor wife but will be like the angels in heaven* (Mt 22:30). It is essential, therefore, for anyone who here wants to reflect on the life of that kingdom to hate not those particular persons but rather the necessities which by nature are temporal and which prop up this transitory life that undergoes the process of being born and dying. And if anyone does not hate it, then he does not yet love that other life which is not subject to the condition of being born and dying, which binds together earthly marriages.

15,41. If I were to ask a good Christian, who still has a wife and continues to beget children with her, whether he would want her as a wife in that kingdom, and, being mindful of the promises of God and of that life where this corruptibility will put on incorruptibility and this mortality will put on immortality,[47] being possessed by a great or at least some love, he will reply forcefully and with an exclamation that he would not want it. Or again, if I were to ask him whether after the resurrection, when he has been transformed like the angels, as promised to the saints, he would want her to live with him, he will answer that he would wish for that just as forcefully as he answered the first question negatively. So here we find a good Christian who loves a woman as a creature of God, whom he desires to be restored and made new, but who hates the bonding and copulation which is corruptible and mortal. In other words, he loves her insofar as she is a human being but hates the fact that she is a wife. In the same way he loves an enemy not because he is an enemy but because he is a human being he wishes for him what he wishes for himself, which is to be reformed and renewed so that he may reach the kingdom of heaven. This is how we must understand what is said about father and mother and the other blood ties, that we hate in them what is the lot of the human race by being born and dying,[48] but that we love what can be brought with us to that kingdom where no one says "my father" but all address the one God as *our Father,*[49] and no one says "my mother" but all refer to that Jerusalem as our mother,[50] and no one says "my brother" because everyone will be each person's brother.[51] Brought together into unity, our marriage bond will be as with a single husband[52] who freed us from the prostitution of this world through the shedding of his blood. The disciple of Christ must therefore hate the things which are transitory in those whom he wishes to come with him to the things which remain forever. And the more he hates in them what is transitory, so much the more does he love them.

15,42. A Christian can therefore live in harmony with his wife, whether satisfying the needs of the flesh with her, which the Apostle says is by way of concession

---

47. See 1 Cor 15:53.
48. In *Revisions* I,19 (18),5 Augustine regrets the impression which he gave here that such blood ties would not have existed had there been no original sin and no death.
49. See Mt 23:9; 6:9.
50. See Gal 4:26.
51. See Mt 23:8.
52. See 2 Cor 11:2.

rather than command,[53] or for the purpose of begetting children, which in some sense can be praiseworthy, or for fraternal companionship without any sexual intercourse, as though having a wife without having one,[54] which in a marriage between Christians is to be regarded as most excellent and sublime, so that he hates in her what goes under the name of temporal necessity and loves the hope of eternal blessedness. For we undoubtedly hate what we certainly desire one day should no longer exist, just as, if we were not to hate the life of this present time which is transitory, we would not desire the life to come which is not subject to time. It is for this life that the soul has been created, of which it is said, *Whoever does not, moreover, hate even his own soul cannot be my disciple* (Lk 14:26). For corruptible food is essential for this life, of which the Lord says, *Is not the soul of more value than food?* (Mt 6:25) that is, this life, for which food is necessary. When he says that he lays down his life for his sheep[55] he is certainly referring to this life, signifying that he is going to die for us.

16,43. Another question arises at this point. Since the Lord permits a wife to be dismissed by reason of fornication, in what sense is fornication to be understood here?[56] Is it to be taken as everyone has hitherto understood fornication, as that which occurs through libidinous acts, or rather as what Scripture usually means by fornication, as said above, as all corrupt and illicit behavior such as idolatry or greed and every violation of the law resulting from unlawful desire? But let us consult the Apostle lest we say something rashly. He states, *I command those who are married, not I but the Lord, that a wife should not leave her husband. But if she does leave she is to remain unmarried or else be reconciled to her husband.* It is possible, then, that she can leave for the reason which the Lord permits. But if it is lawful for a woman to send her husband away even not by reason of fornication and not lawful for a man, what answer shall we give to what he appended, *Nor is a man to send his wife away?* Why did he not add *except by reason of fornication,* which the Lord permits, unless he wants a similar formula to be understood, that, if he does send her away, which is permitted by reason of fornication, he should remain without a wife or else be reconciled to his wife? It would not be wrong for her husband to be reconciled to that woman who was addressed by the Lord when no one dared stone her, *Go, and take care that you do not sin again* (Jn 8:3–11). For the one who said that it was not lawful to dismiss a wife, except by reason of fornication, obliges a man to keep his wife except by reason of fornication; but, if there is such a reason, he does not oblige but permits it. In the same way it is said that it is not lawful for a woman to marry someone else unless her husband is dead; should she marry prior to her husband's death she is culpable. If she does not

---

53. See 1 Cor 7:3–6.
54. See 1 Cor 7:29.
55. See Jn 10:15.
56. In *Revisions* I,19 (18),6 Augustine observes that his discussion of the meaning of fornication here is not the last word on the matter, and he recommends that other writings, either by him or by other authors, be consulted.

marry after the death of her husband, she is not culpable, for she is not commanded to marry but is permitted to do so.[57] If, therefore, the formula applies equally, in terms of the law of marriage, to a man and a woman, to the extent that the Apostle not only has the same thing to say with regard to the woman, *A woman does not have power over her own body, but the husband,* but also does not pass over in silence its application to the husband, *Likewise, a man does not have power over his own body, but the woman* (1 Cor 7:4) — if, then, the formula is identical, we may not infer that it is lawful for a woman to send her husband away, except by reason of fornication, any more than it is for a man to do so.

16,44. We must examine what we understand by fornication, therefore, and consult the Apostle, as we did at the outset. He goes on to say, *To the rest I say, not the Lord* (1 Cor 7:12). We must first look here at the identity of *the rest*; he spoke earlier in the Lord's name to those who are married, but now he does so in his own name *to the rest.* Perhaps he is even addressing those who are not married. But this does not follow, for he adds, *If a brother has an unbelieving wife and she consents to live with him, he should not dismiss her* (1 Cor 7:12). Consequently, he is now speaking to those who are married. What can his reference *to the rest* mean, then, except that previously he spoke to those who were united in such a way as to share in the faith of Christ, whereas now he says *to the rest* to those who are united in such a way as not to share the faith? What has he to say to them? *If a brother has an unbelieving wife and she consents to live with him, he should not dismiss her, and if a wife has an unbelieving husband and he consents to live with her, she should not dismiss her husband* (1 Cor 7:12–13). If he is not giving a command in the Lord's name, then, but admonishing in his own name, the advice he gives is such that, if someone were to act differently, then he would not be contravening a command. It is the same as when, in the matter of virgins, he says a little later that he has no command from the Lord but offers his own advice and praises virginity to such a degree as to attract her who desires it, although she is not to be judged as violating the command if she chooses otherwise.[58] What is commanded is one thing, what is advised is another, and what is forgiven is something else. A woman is forbidden to *leave her husband. But if she does leave, she is to remain unmarried or else be reconciled to her husband.* She is not permitted, therefore, to act otherwise. The believing husband who has an unbelieving wife who agrees to live with him is advised not to dismiss her. It is therefore permissible to dismiss her, for it is not the Lord's command that forbids dismissing her but the Apostle's counsel. In the same way a virgin is advised not to marry, but, should she marry, she will indeed not be heeding but will not be acting against the precept. Yet she is excused, since he says, *I say this by way of concession, not by way of command* (1 Cor 7:6). Consequently, if it is permissible to dismiss an unbelieving wife (although it would be better not to dismiss her, and yet, according to the Lord's command,

---

57. See 1 Cor 7:9.
58. See 1 Cor 7:25–28.

it is not permissible to dismiss a wife except by reason of fornication), unbelief itself is the equivalent of fornication.

16,45. What are you saying, Apostle? Apparently, that a believing husband with an unbelieving wife who consents to live with him should not dismiss her. That is what he says. Since the Lord, then, also commands that a husband is not to dismiss his wife, except by reason of fornication, why do you say, *I say, not the Lord*? Because the idolatry practised by unbelievers, and any other kind of harmful superstition, is fornication. The Lord allowed a wife to be dismissed by reason of fornication, but, since he permitted but did not command it, he gave scope to the Apostle to advise that he who wanted to do so should not dismiss an unbelieving wife, because there was the possibility that she would become a believer. He says, *For an unbelieving husband is made holy in his wife, and an unbelieving wife is made holy in the brother* (1 Cor 7:14). I think it transpired that some women had already come to the faith on account of their believing husbands, and some men on account of their believing wives; and, although he did not mention names, he offered encouragement by way of these examples to lend weight to his advice. He then continues, *Otherwise your children would be unclean, whereas now they are holy* (1 Cor 7:14). For there were already children who were Christians, who had been made holy thanks to the authoritative consent of either one or both parents. This would not have happened if the marriage had been dissolved by the believing party and the unbelief of the other partner had not been tolerated until a favorable moment for believing had arisen. This is the advice of the one to whom I think it was said, *If you incur any added expense, I shall repay you on my return* (Lk 10:35).

16,46. If unbelief, therefore, is fornication, and idolatry is unbelief, and avarice is idolatry, there can be no doubt that avarice is fornication as well. Who then can justifiably distinguish any form of unlawful desire from fornication in general, if avarice is fornication? Hence we are to infer that, because of unlawful desires (and not only those which accompany libidinous acts committed with others' husbands or wives, but all those that cause the soul to deviate from the law of God through its misuse of the body, causing injury to it in a destructive and dishonorable manner), a husband can dismiss his wife without guilt, and a wife her husband, because the Lord made an exception by reason of fornication. We must of necessity understand the nature of fornication, as discussed above, in a generic and universal sense.

16,47. When he said, *except by reason of fornication,* he did not specify on the part of whom, whether the man or the woman. For not only is it permissible to dismiss a wife who is guilty of fornication, but the man who dismisses his wife by whom he is compelled to commit fornication assuredly does so by reason of fornication. Take for example someone whose wife compels him to sacrifice to idols, who dismisses her by reason not only of her fornication but of his as well—of hers because she has committed fornication, of his lest he commit fornication. Nothing could be more unjust than to dismiss a wife by reason of fornication if the husband is also shown to have committed fornication. The text comes to mind: *Inasmuch as you judge another, you condemn yourself, for you do those very things which you judge* (Rom 2:1). Therefore, whoever intends to dismiss his wife by reason of fornication ought first to purify himself of fornication, and I would say the same about the woman.

16,48. When he says, *Whoever marries a woman dismissed by her husband commits adultery* (Mt 5:32), the question can be asked whether the woman is also guilty of adultery in the same way as the man who marries her. For she is commanded to remain unmarried or else be reconciled with her husband — if, it says, she has left her husband.[59] There is no small difference between dismissing and being dismissed. If she dismisses her husband and marries another, she is considered to have left her husband with the desire of exchanging him for another, which without question is the attitude of an adulteress. But were she to be dismissed by the husband with whom she wanted to stay, the person who married her would be committing adultery, according to the Lord's teaching, but whether she herself would be guilty of the same misdeed is uncertain. What is even less easy to determine is, in the case when a man and woman engage in sexual relationships with mutual consent, whether one is an adulterer and the other is not. Moreover, there is the additional fact that, if the man is guilty of adultery by marrying a woman who is separated from her husband, although she did not dismiss her husband but was herself dismissed, she causes him to commit adultery, which the Lord also forbids. From this we deduce, whether she has been dismissed or has dismissed her husband, that she is obliged to remain unmarried or else be reconciled with her husband.

16,49. Again, the question may be raised as to whether a husband, with the consent of his wife, either because she is sterile or does not wish to have marital relations, may take another woman, who is neither someone else's nor separated from her husband, without being guilty of fornication. An example of this can in fact be found in an account in the Old Testament.[60] But in this present age, at the stage at which the human race has now arrived, the precepts are of a superior order. They must be viewed in a context which distinguishes the ages disposed by divine providence, which assists the human race in a most orderly fashion, yet does not arrogate to itself norms for the conduct of life.[61] But can the words of the Apostle, *A woman does not have power over her own body, but the husband; and likewise a husband does not have power over his own body, but the woman,* have such validity that, with the permission of the wife, who has power over her husband's body, a man can have sexual relations with a woman who is neither someone else's wife nor separated from her husband? But we must not conclude

---

59. See 1 Cor 7:11.
60. See Gn 16:1–3. The example is of Abraham, Sarah and Hagar. Augustine seeks to justify their behavior in his *Answer to Faustus, a Manichean* XXII,30–32; Sermon 51,28.
61. Augustine is alluding briefly to his oft-repeated view that the history of the world is divided into ages, usually numbered six — five in the Old Testament and the sixth beginning with the coming of Christ and ending with his second coming. See, e.g., *Miscellany of Eighty-three Questions* 58,2; *The City of God* XXII,30.

thus, lest it seem possible for a woman to do the same with the permission of the man, a practice which common sense forbids.[62]

16,50. Some instances can arise, however, where even the wife may be able to do this with the husband's consent on behalf of the husband himself, as is said to have taken place at Antioch about fifty years ago around the time of Constantius. Acyndinus was prefect then, and he was also consul, when he demanded from a certain public debtor a pound of gold.[63] Inspired by what motive I do not know (and this is something that tempts those who hold positions of authority like that, to whom anything is lawful or is rather what they suppose to be lawful), he made threats with an oath, affirming strongly that, if on a certain day fixed by him the debtor did not pay the aforementioned gold, he would be put to death. And so, while he was being detained in cruel confinement and was unable to free himself of the debt, the dreaded day began to approach and draw near. He had by chance a most beautiful wife, but she had no money to come to the aid of her husband. A certain wealthy man, infatuated with the woman's beauty and aware that her husband was in such a predicament, sent to her and promised that, if she consented to spend one night with him and have intercourse, he would provide the pound of gold. Thereupon the woman, knowing that not she but her husband had power over her own body, sent word to him that she would agree to do this for her husband, provided that he, the lord of her body in marriage, to whom she owed absolute chastity, was willing to allow this to happen, disposing as it were of his own property for the sake of his life. He thanked her and ordered that it be done, in no way judging that the sexual union was adulterous, because there was an absence of lust and because a great love for her husband required it, he himself having willed and commanded it. The woman came into the house of that wealthy man, and he unchastely carried out what he desired. But she gave her body in sexual union to no one except her husband, who desired not his marital rights, as he was accustomed to, but life. She received the gold, but the one who gave it fraudulently withdrew what he had given and substituted a similar bag full of earth. But when the woman arrived home and discovered it, she rushed out into the street to declare what she had done, inspired by the same tender love for her husband which had compelled her to do it. She has recourse to the prefect, tells everything that happened, and shows how she was

---

62. Whereas the question of whether a husband can, in very specific circumstances, be given permission by his wife to have sexual relations with another woman is briefly but seriously discussed from a biblical perspective, that of whether a woman can be given permission by her husband to have sexual relations with another man is dismissed out of hand as being contrary to common sense (*quod omnium sensus excludit*). Yet the account that immediately follows, regarding which Augustine sympathetically withholds judgment, shows a remarkable openness to the moral complexity of the issue at the time that he wrote *The Lord's Sermon on the Mount*, and in concluding the account he suggests that a real-life moral struggle has an authority that the mere citation of a moral precept does not have. It is worth noting that Augustine did not qualify the views presented here in his *Revisions*.

63. Constantius II was emperor, sometimes with co-emperors, from 337 until 361. Acyndinus was governor of the Orient from 338 until 340 and, with Valerius Proculus, was consul in 340. Hence the incident that is described, which Augustine accurately says had happened about fifty years previously, must have occurred around 340.

deceived. The prefect then first pronounces himself guilty, since his threats were the cause of what happened, and, as though passing sentence on someone else, orders that a pound of gold be brought into the treasury from the possessions of Acyndinus and that the woman be given ownership of the land from which she received earth instead of gold.

I offer no opinion on any part of this story. Let each person judge as he pleases, for the story is not drawn from divinely inspired sources. However, when the story is told, human instinct does not disapprove of what the woman did at her husband's bidding, as we were horrified previously when the subject itself was discussed and no example was given. But in this chapter of the Gospel nothing is to be more carefully pondered than the great evil which is fornication, so that, although a couple may be united in marriage with the tightest of bonds, for this reason alone it may be dissolved. What fornication means has been sufficiently discussed.

17,51. Jesus continues, *Again, you have heard it said to the people of old, You shall not swear, but you shall fulfill your oath to the Lord. But I say to you not to swear at all, not by heaven, for it is the throne of God, nor by the earth, for it is his footstool, nor by Jerusalem, for it is the Great King's city. Nor are you to swear by your head, for you cannot make one hair white or black. But let your discourse be yes, yes, no, no. Anything more comes of evil.* (Mt 5:33–37) The righteousness of the Pharisees consists in not committing perjury. He confirms this who prohibits swearing, which belongs to the righteousness of the kingdom of heaven. Just as one who does not speak is unable to speak falsely, so one who refrains from swearing cannot commit perjury. Yet, since a person who calls upon God as his witness is swearing, this passage deserves careful consideration lest the Apostle, who often swore in this manner, appears to have contradicted the precept of the Lord when he says, *What I am writing to you, behold before God I am not lying* (Gal 1:20), and again, *The God and Father of our Lord Jesus Christ, who is blessed for ever, knows that I am not lying* (1 Cor 11:31). The same holds for what follows, *God is my witness, whom in my spirit I serve in the gospel of his Son, how I always remember you without ceasing in my prayers* (Rom 1:9–10), unless perhaps one maintains that what constitutes an oath is what is sworn through something else which is true, which would mean that Paul did not swear, for he did not say "by God" but *God is my witness.* To think this way is absurd. However, because of those who are fractious or quite backward in understanding, lest anyone think that there is a difference, he should know that the Apostle swore in this way when he said, *By your glory I die each day* (1 Cor 15:31). One should not interpret the phrase as saying, "Your glory causes me to die each day," as in the words, "By his teaching he was instructed," that is, by his teaching it came about that he was perfectly instructed. The Greek manuscripts make a distinction; in them the phrase is *Ne ten humeteran kauchesin,*[64] which is only uttered by someone taking an oath.

---

64. The reference is to 1 Cor 15:31, which may mean literally either " by your glory" or "by your boasting" (as in "glorying").

Hence we must understand that the Lord commands that a person should not swear so that no one may have recourse to an oath as to something good and, by frequent swearing, lapse into perjury out of habit. For this reason, whoever feels that an oath is necessary, not in good actions but in situations of necessity, should exercise restraint as much as possible and not resort to one apart from necessity, when he sees how slow people are to believe what is to their advantage unless it is confirmed by an oath. In this instance the words are applicable, *Let your discourse be yes, yes, no, no.* This is the ideal to aspire to. *Anything more comes from evil,* meaning that, if you are compelled to swear, you should know that it has become necessary through the weakness of those whom you are trying to persuade. And this weakness is certainly an evil, from which we daily pray to be delivered when we say, *Deliver us from evil* (Mt 6:13). And so he did not say, "Anything more is evil," for you are not behaving wrongly when you swear to good effect, which although not commendable is necessary, so as to convince someone that what you are advocating is advantageous, but it arises from the evil of the person because of whose weakness you were compelled to swear. Yet no one knows, unless he experiences it personally, just how difficult it is to overcome the habit of swearing and never to do rashly what necessity sometimes compels.

17,52. The question may be asked as to why, after he said, *But I say to you not to swear at all,* there follows, *not by heaven, for it is the throne of God,* and all the rest as far as *nor by your head.* I believe the reason is that the Jews, if they swore for these reasons, did not consider themselves bound by an oath. And because they had heard, *You shall fulfill your oath to the Lord,* they did not think that they owed the Lord what they had sworn if they swore by heaven or earth or by Jerusalem or by their head. This happened not because of an omission on the part of the one who commanded it but because they interpreted it wrongly. And so the Lord teaches that that there is nothing so base in what God has created that anyone should consider committing perjury by it, since created things from the highest to the lowest are ruled by divine providence, beginning from the throne of God and extending to white or black hair. He says, *Not by heaven, for it is the throne of God, nor by the earth, for it is his footstool,* meaning that when you swear by heaven or by earth you should not consider yourself absolved from your oath to the Lord, because through him you are truly bound by your oath, inasmuch as heaven is his throne and earth his footstool. *Nor by Jerusalem, for it is the Great King's* city; this is better than if he had said "my," although it is evident that he meant this.[65] And because he himself is indeed the Lord, whoever swears by Jerusalem is bound by oath to the Lord. *Nor are you to swear by your head.* What can a man claim is closer to him than his head? But how does it belong to us, when we do not possess the power to turn one hair white or black? Anyone, therefore, who wishes to swear by his head is bound by oath to God, who sustains everything in a manner beyond our understanding and is everywhere present. And in this regard the

---

65. I.e., "for it is *my* city."

other forms are included, all of which cannot be stated, as in the example we have quoted from the Apostle, *By your glory I die each day.* To show that he was bound by such an oath to the Lord, he added, *which I have in Christ Jesus* (1 Cor 15:31).[66]

17,53. But, for the sake of those whose outlook is fleshly, I say that, when heaven is referred to as God's throne and the earth as his footstool, it must not be taken to mean that God has members located in heaven and earth just as we have when we sit down; rather, the seat in question signifies judgment.[67] And, since in the physical structure of the universe heaven presents the greatest spectacle and the earth the least, as though the divine power were more present to what is surpassingly beautiful while ordering what is least attractive in its remotest and most inferior parts, he is said to be seated in heaven while his feet are on the earth. Taken spiritually, however, the word *heaven* refers to holy souls and *earth* to sinners.[68] And, because a spiritual person judges everything while he is judged by no one,[69] he is appropriately named *the throne of God.* On the other hand, the sinner, to whom it was said, *You are earth, and to earth you shall return* (Gn 3:19), through that justice which rewards according to merit, is placed in the most inferior parts and, being unwilling to abide by the law, is punished by the law and may be fittingly described as God's footstool.

18,54. But, so as now to conclude this section, which is also of the greatest importance, what can be said or conceived of to be more laborious or demanding than when the faithful soul stretches every sinew in an effort to overcome the habits of vice? Let him cut off those members which are an impediment to the kingdom of heaven lest he be crushed by pain. Let him endure in married fidelity all those things which, although irksome in the extreme, do not involve corrupt and illicit acts, by which I mean fornication. For instance, if a person has a wife who is infertile, or physically deformed, or weak in body, or blind, or deaf, or lame, or whatever else, or afflicted with sickness or general debility, or anything most horrific that can possibly be imagined, apart from fornication, let him tolerate it for the sake of faith and companionship. He should not only not cast off such a wife, nor, if he does not have one, marry a woman who is separated from her husband and is beautiful, healthy, rich and fertile. And, if behavior of this kind is not permissible, much less should it be considered lawful for him to engage in any other kind of illicit sexual relationship. Let him flee from fornication so as to extricate himself from every kind of decadent behavior. Let him speak the truth and commend it not with frequent oaths but with upright morals. Taking refuge within the citadel of Christian warfare, as from a superior vantage point, let him lay low the rebellious throng of all evil habits (only a few of which have been mentioned, but in such a way that all are implied) that are arrayed against him. But who would be so bold as to undertake such labors except someone who is on fire with the love of

---

66. The verse thus becomes: *By your glory, which I have in Christ Jesus, I die each day.*
67. Somewhat the same concern is expressed below at II,5,17–18.
68. Augustine returns to this interpretation below at II,6,22.
69. See 1 Cor 2:15.

righteousness, completely ablaze, as it were, with hunger and thirst and considering his life to be of no value until it achieves satisfaction, and who assails the kingdom of heaven with force?[70] For in no other way will he be able to have the strength to bear all the things that, as far as severing habits goes, the lovers of this world consider altogether toilsome, arduous and difficult. *Blessed, therefore, are those who hunger and thirst for righteousness, for they shall be satisfied.*

18,55. Throughout these struggles, however, when a person experiences hardship as he makes his way through circumstances which are difficult and unforgiving, and he is surrounded by trials of every kind, and on all sides he views the weight of his past life, and he is fearful that he may not be able to complete what he has undertaken, then let him take counsel so as to merit help. And what else is counsel if not tolerating the weakness of others and supporting it as far as one can, as one who himself desires to receive divine help? And so it follows that we should look at the precepts pertaining to divine mercy. Being meek and being merciful appear to be one and the same thing. But the difference is that the meek person, of whom we spoke previously, does not in his piety contradict the divine teachings which address his sins nor those words of God which he does not yet grasp, but he affords no advantage to the one whom he does not contradict or resist. The merciful person, however, does not resist in such a manner that by his correction he would worsen the person whom he is resisting.

19,56. The Lord therefore goes on to say, *You have heard that it was said, An eye for an eye and a tooth for a tooth. But I say to you not to resist evil, but, if anyone strikes you on the right cheek, offer him the other as well; and whoever wishes to contend in judgment with you and to take your coat, give him your cloak as well; and whoever forces you to go one mile, go with him another two.*[71] *Give to everyone who asks of you, and do not turn away from one who would borrow from you.* (Mt 5:38–42) The lesser righteousness of the Pharisees consists in not being excessive in revenge, so that no one would retaliate more than he received, and this marks an important stage.

It is no simple matter to find someone who, on receiving a single blow, would want to retaliate by a single blow, or who, on hearing a single word from an accuser, would be content to retaliate to precisely the same extent rather than exact an excessive degree of revenge, whether because his anger has been aroused or because he thinks it right that he who first caused the hurt should be more grievously hurt than he who had not caused the hurt was hurt. The law for the most part restrains such an attitude, where it is written, *An eye for an eye and a tooth for a tooth* (Ex 21:24), indicating by these words the manner whereby revenge would not exceed the offense. And this is the beginning of peace, but perfect peace consists in not desiring vengeance at all.

---

70. See Mt 11:12.
71. Augustine's text of Mt 5:41 had this version of the Lord's saying, which added the word *another*, rather than the more familiar and better attested *go with him two*. Below at I,19,61 he uses *another two* to arrive at the allegorically satisfying number three.

19,57. Therefore, between that which comes first, which is beyond the law, that a greater evil should be repaid for a lesser evil, and that which the Lord tells his disciples for their perfection, that evil should not be repaid with evil, to pay back in the measure one has received holds something like an intermediary position. In this way, in accordance with the variation of eras, there is a transition from extreme discord to supreme concord. Consider the difference between someone who with the premeditated intention of offending and injuring does wrong and the person who on being offended does not retaliate. Yet the person who initially has done wrong to no one, but when offended retaliates excessively either in will or in deed, has moved away from the height of wrongdoing and made progress towards the height of righteousness but has yet to observe what the law, which was given through Moses, lays down.

Therefore, whoever retaliates only to the extent that he has been offended has already forgiven something, for he does not merit the same punishment by offending as that person suffers who, though innocent, was offended by him. Consequently, he who came not to abolish but to fulfill the law brings to perfection this righteousness, which is initially not severe but merciful. He left the two remaining intervening stages to be understood and preferred to speak from the very summit of mercy. The person who fails to meet the magnitude of this precept, which is proper to the kingdom of heaven, still has something to do: he must not repay in equal measure, but less so, for example with one blow for two, or by severing an ear for having his eye torn out. Moving in ascending order from here, the person who does not retaliate at all is approximating the Lord's command, but he has not yet arrived. For it still appears a small matter to the Lord if you do not pay back the evil that you have received with no evil in return, unless you are prepared to receive more. For this reason he does not say, "But I say to you not to repay evil for evil," even though this is a great command. Instead he says, "Do not resist evil in such a way that you not only do not repay the injury done to you but even so that you do not resist for fear that something else may be inflicted on you." This is what he goes on to explain: *But if anyone strikes you on the right cheek, offer him the other as well.* He does not say, "If anyone strikes you, do not strike back," but, "Present yourself again to the one who strikes you."

That this pertains to mercy will be perceived especially by those people who greatly love and care for children or others very dear to them who are sick or infants or weaklings, and from whom they often have to endure much, and, if their wellbeing requires it, must resign themselves to suffer considerably until the weakness of age or illness passes. What else, therefore, could the Lord, the physician of souls,[72] possibly teach those whom he was instructing to care for the wellbeing of their neighbor except to endure with equanimity the weaknesses of those whose welfare they wished to promote? In fact, every kind of dishonesty

---

72. The theme of the Lord as physician, usually expressed as "Christ the physician," is a frequent one in Augustine and recurs below at II,17,58. See Rudolph Arbesmann, "The Concept of 'Christus Medicus" in St. Augustine," in *Traditio* 10 (1954) 1–28.

derives from a weakness of mind, because there is no one more innocent than the person who has attained perfection in virtue.

19,58. The question may be asked as to the significance of the right cheek, which is what in fact is found in the Greek manuscripts that are to be considered more reliable. Many Latin texts mention only a cheek, and not the right one.[73] Now, a person is recognized by his face. And we read in the Apostle, *You put up with it if anyone reduces you to slavery, if anyone preys upon you, if anyone exploits you, if anyone acts arrogantly towards you, if anyone strikes you in the face,* and then he immediately adds, *I speak out of shame* (2 Cor 11:20–21), in order to clarify what is meant by being struck in the face, which means to be disdained and despised. The Apostle does not say this to stop them from tolerating such people but rather to point out that he himself, who loves them as much as he loves himself, would willingly spend himself for them.[74] But because the face cannot be spoken of in terms of right and left, while there can be a nobility both according to God and according to this world, it is symbolized by the right cheek and the left,[75] so that in whatever way a disciple of Christ is despised because he is a Christian, it makes him even better prepared to be despised if he possesses any of the honors of this world.

Thus the same Apostle, when he was being persecuted because of the Christian name, would not have presented the other cheek to those who struck the right one had he remained silent about the dignity that was his in the world. For, by declaring, *I am a Roman citizen* (Acts 22:25), he was by no means implying that he was not prepared to have despised in himself something he held to be of little account on the part of those who had displayed contempt for such a surpassing and salutary name in him. Was he then less tolerant later of the chains that were forbidden to be placed on Roman citizens, or did he wish to accuse anyone of this insult? And if on the grounds of Roman citizenship he did not refrain from offering to those who spared him what they could strike, it was because he wanted through his patience to correct those of such great perversity who he perceived were honoring in him those parts that were of the left rather than the right. We must pay the greatest attention to the state of mind with which he carried out everything, how kindly and mercifully he acted towards those at whose hands he endured these things. For when he was given a slap by the command of the high priest he appeared to react bitterly with the words, *God shall strike you, whitewashed wall!* (Acts 23:2–3), which to those of slower understanding sounds like a reproach but to those with understanding is a prophecy. A whitewashed wall means hypocrisy, that is, a simulation of the priestly dignity through pretence, concealing under this name, as under a white covering, an interior which is foul and base. As far as humility was concerned, he guarded it in a remarkable way when it was said to him, *Are you slandering the chief priest?* and he replied, *Brothers, I did not know he was the chief priest, for*

---

73. See Lk 6:29.
74. See 2 Cor 12:15.
75. Augustine has recourse here to the ancient symbolism of right and left. Since the right is superior to the left, it has divine and Christian resonances, whereas the left has a this-worldly symbolism. Further right-left symbolism occurs below at II,2,6–9.

it is written, You shall not slander the leader of your people (Acts 23:4–5). He here demonstrates with what calmness he had uttered the words that he appeared to have spoken in anger, because such a quick and gentle response would not be possible on the part of persons who were irate and disturbed. And by that very fact he spoke the truth to those who grasped what he was saying, *I did not know he was the chief priest,* as if to say, "I have known another chief priest, for whose name I am enduring these things, and whom it is not right to insult but you are insulting, since what you hate in me is nothing other than his name."

Hence a person must not boast pretentiously of such things but be ready in his heart for anything, so as to be able to sing the words of the prophet, *My heart is ready, O God, my heart is ready* (Ps 57:7). Many indeed know how to present the other cheek but do not know how to love the person who strikes them. The Lord himself, however, who was assuredly the first to practice the precepts that he himself taught, did not present the other cheek to the servant of the priest who struck him but said, *If I have spoken wrongly, show me the wrong. If I have spoken correctly, why do you strike me?* (Jn 18:23) Nonetheless, he was not unprepared in his heart not only to be struck on his other cheek for the salvation of all but for his whole body to be crucified as well.

19,59. In the case of what follows, *And whoever wishes to contend in judgment with you and to take your coat, give him your cloak as well,* the precept's proper meaning pertains to the disposition of the heart and not to ostentatious display. But what is stated about the coat and cloak must not be referred to these things alone but to everything else which we may claim by some right to belong to us on a temporal basis. For if this is what is enjoined where necessities are concerned, how much more fittingly should there be contempt for what is superfluous! However, those things of ours of which I spoke must be included within that range prescribed by the Lord when he said, *If anyone wishes to contend in judgment with you and to take your coat.* All those things about which we can contend in judgment, such as might pass from our possession to that of the person contending with us or to the one on whose behalf he contends, should be understood here, like clothes, house, land, livestock, or wealth in general. Whether this should apply as well in the case of slaves is a question of considerable importance. For it is inappropriate for a Christian to possess a slave in the same way as he would a horse or an article of silver, although it could happen that a horse might be worth more than a slave, and an article of gold or silver a great deal more. But if the slave is taught by you, his master, to worship God more appropriately, and is trained in a manner more fitting and virtuous than he would be by another who wishes to have him, I do not know whether anyone would be so bold as to say that he should be treated with the same contempt as an item of clothing. A human being in fact ought to love another human being like himself, since he is commanded by the Lord of all to love even his enemies, as what follows demonstrates.[76]

---

76. This passage demonstrates that Augustine accepted slavery as part of the world in which he lived, although he acknowledged the special quality of the relationship between a Christian

19,60. It must certainly be noted that every coat is an item of clothing, but not every item of clothing is a coat. The term "clothing" therefore has a wider significance than the term "coat." And so I understand the words, *If anyone wishes to contend in judgment with you and to take your coat, give him your cloak as well,* to mean that, if anyone wishes to take your coat, give him also any other garment that you have. Consequently, many have rendered this as "mantle," which is *himation* in Greek.

19,61. *And whoever forces you to go one mile,* says the Lord, *go with him another two,* and indeed you should be prepared to do this not so much with your feet as with a willing attitude. For in Christian history itself, where authority resides, you will find nothing of this kind undertaken by the saints or by the Lord himself, when he bequeathed us a pattern for living in the humanity that he deigned to assume.[77] Yet in practically every place you will find such people ready to bear with equanimity whatever has been unjustly inflicted upon them. But could we possibly surmise from what was said, *Go with him another two,* that he wanted to arrive at three? The number three signifies perfection,[78] so that when anyone accomplishes this action he may realize that he is fulfilling perfect righteousness by compassionately tolerating the infirmities of those whom he wishes to become healthy. Moreover, it is possible to discern from the three examples a hint of these precepts, the first being, if anyone strikes you on the cheek; the second, if anyone wishes to take your coat; the third, if anyone forces you to go a mile, and in this third example two is added to one, which makes three. If this number in the present passage does not signify perfection, as has been said, let it be acknowledged that, when he lays down these precepts, the Lord begins with what is more tolerable and gradually ascends until he arrives at the point of enduring the other two. At first he wished you to turn the other cheek when the right one was struck, so that you would be prepared to endure less than you already endured (for whatever the meaning ascribed to the right may be, and it is certainly of greater value than that ascribed to the left, a person who has suffered hurt in something more precious can also endure it when it is of little value). He then commands that the person who wants to take your coat be given your cloak as well, which amounts to about

---

master and his Christian slave. Augustine's most important statement on slavery is found in *The City of God* XIX,15, where he says that it is the result of general human sinfulness and not a natural condition.

77. "In the humanity that he deigned to assume": *in homine quem suscipere dignatus est.* Augustine's wording reflects a so-called *homo assumptus* (or *susceptus*) Christology, which until the early fifth century tended to be an acceptable way of understanding the relationship between the divine person and the human nature of Christ. But it came to be associated with Nestorianism, which held that Christ was composed of two distinct persons. It was in any event an imperfect expression that Augustine later rejected. See Alois Grillmeier, *Christ in Christian Tradition I: From the Apostolic Age to Chalcedon (451),* trans. by John Bowden (2nd rev. ed., Atlanta: John Knox Press 1975) 407.

78. In Augustinian numerology, three plays a minor role apart from its obvious connection to the Trinity, and other numbers (e.g., 6, 7, 8, 10, 40, 50) are far better suited to symbolize perfection. Augustine himself suggests in the next few lines that not everyone may agree with the role that he assigns to the number three here.

the same value or not much more, but by no means double. The third begins with a mile, to which he said two miles must be added, commanding you to endure twice that amount. By this he indicates that you must bear it with equanimity if a person acts basely towards you in a manner less so than previously, or to the same degree, or more so.

20,62. I note that in these three kinds of examples no category of offence has been overlooked. For all the circumstances in which we suffer some abuse can be divided into two types: one in which it is not possible to retaliate, the other in which it is possible. But in the case where it is not possible to retaliate, relief is usually sought in revenge. When you are struck, what good does it do to strike back? Is the part of the body that has been hurt thereby restored to its full integrity? But an enraged mind desires such alleviations, although they are of no help to a sane and balanced mind, which judges that another's weakness should be endured with compassion rather than that one's own, which is of no account, should be eased by another's punishment.

20,63. What is not forbidden here is the punishment which leads to correction. For this too pertains to mercy, nor does it hinder that disposition with which a person is prepared to endure much from the one whom he wishes to be corrected. But the only person in a position to requite such punishment is the one who has overcome hatred, a vice that usually inflames those who are keen to vindicate themselves, with an intense love. Nor is it to be feared that parents appear to hate their small son when they beat him for wrongdoing, lest he continue to do wrong.[79] In truth, the perfect love of God the Father himself is proposed to us for imitation,[80] for it is said in what follows, *Love your enemies, do good to those who hate you, and pray for those who persecute you* (Mt 5:44). And through the prophet it is said of the Lord, *The Lord corrects the one whom he loves and chastises every son whom he receives* (Prv 3:12). The Lord also declares, *The slave who does not know his master's will and behaves in a manner worthy of punishment will receive few lashes, but the slave who does know his master's will and behaves in a manner worthy of punishment will receive many lashes* (Lk 12:47–48). All that is asked is that the only person to punish be he who has the authority for the correct ordering of affairs and possesses the same will to punish as a father does in the case of his small son, whom he cannot yet hate because of his age. From this most appropriate example it should be sufficiently clear that sin can be punished by love rather than left unpunished, in such a way that whoever administers the punishment would not leave the person downcast because of it but happy because of the correction. Yet he should be prepared, if necessary, to endure with equanimity all that is leveled against him by the person he desires to correct, whether he has the authority to correct him or not.

---

79. See *Homily on the First Epistle of John* 7,8 for the identical example and an exposition of the thought underlying it.
80. See Mt 5:48.

20,64. There were some great and holy men who were well aware that death, which separates the soul from the body,[81] was not something to be feared but who, in accordance with the outlook of those who had a fear of death, punished certain sins by death, so that in the living a salutary fear would be instilled while, in the case of those who were punished by death, it was not death itself that would inflict harm but sin, which could increase were they to remain alive. Those to whom God had given such a judgment did not judge rashly. Hence it was that Elijah dealt out death with his own hand and through the lightning that he beseeched from heaven,[82] and many other great and godly men, imbued with a like spirit and considering the human circumstances, acted in the same way in a manner that was not intemperate. When the disciples gave the example of Elijah to the Lord, recalling what had been done by him, so that he would give them the power to demand fire from heaven in order to consume those who had refused them hospitality, the Lord rebuked them not because of the example of the holy prophet but for their ignorance where revenge was concerned, which was a mark of their still untutored state, observing that they were animated not by a love of correction but by the hateful desire of revenge.[83] Therefore, after he had taught them what it meant to love one's neighbor as oneself,[84] and, even after the outpouring of the Holy Spirit, whom he sent down from on high ten days after his ascension,[85] as he promised,[86] such acts of punishment were not wanting, although they were much rarer than in the Old Testament. (There, for the most part, they were constrained through fear, like slaves, whereas here they were nurtured as sons principally through love.) For, as we read in the Acts of the Apostles, Ananias and his wife fell down dead at the words of the apostle Peter and were not raised to life but buried.[87]

20,65. But if those heretics opposed to the Old Testament are unwilling to believe this book, let them cast a glance at Paul the apostle, whom they read as well as we do,[88] when he speaks of a certain sinner whom he handed over to Satan for the destruction of the flesh, so that his soul might be saved.[89] And if they are reluctant to understand this as meaning death, for a degree of doubt surrounds it, let them acknowledge some sort of punishment from Satan orchestrated by the

---

81. Augustine cites the classic definition of death, accepted by pagans and Christians alike, here as he does elsewhere (see, e.g., *The City of God* XIII,6). Christian authors who also used this definition include Athenagoras, *On the Resurrection* 16; Tertullian, *On the Soul* 51; Gregory of Nyssa, *The Great Catechism* 8.
82. See 1 K 18:36–40.
83. See Lk 9:53–55.
84. See Mt 19:19 par.
85. See Acts 2:1–4.
86. See Jn 14:16–17.
87. See Acts 5:1–10.
88. These unnamed heretics are the Manicheans, who rejected the Hebrew Scriptures but accepted Paul and other parts of the New Testament in a qualified way. For their rejection of the Old Testament see, e.g., *Answer to Faustus, a Manichean*, passim; for their rejection of the Acts of the Apostles see, e.g., ibid. XIX,31; and for their acceptance of Paul see, e.g., ibid. XI,1–8. The Manicheans are referred to again, although not by name, below at II,9,31 and II,24,79.
89. See 1 Cor 5:1–5.

Apostle. That he acted not out of hatred but out of love is clear from what was added, *that his soul might be saved* (1 Cor 5:5). Or let them heed what we are referring to in those books to which they ascribe great authority, where it is written that the apostle Thomas invoked the curse of a most cruel death on someone who slapped him but commended his soul, so that it would be spared in the world to come. A dog brought the man's hand, which was severed from the rest of his body, to the table where the apostle was dining; he had been killed by a lion.[90] We are not permitted to believe this book, for it is not found in the Catholic canon, whereas they read it and revere it as being completely incorrupt and truthful,[91] and they rage fiercely against the physical punishments contained in the Old Testament with what blindness I know not, being altogether unaware of the mentality and the particular times that marked these deeds.

20,66. Therefore, in the type of offense that is requited by punishment, the standard to be observed by Christians is not to allow hatred to arise when an offense has been committed. Rather, out of compassion for weakness, one's soul should be ready to undergo a great deal; yet it should not neglect correction and should be able to resort to advice or authority or power. There is yet another type of offense which can be repaid in full and of which there are two kinds: one relates to money, the other to action. The first is exemplified by the coat and cloak, the other by the constraint of the one mile and two miles. For a cloak can be given back, and the person whom you help by an action can help you if the need arises. Perhaps a distinction should be made here. The first example, which refers to being struck on the cheek, represents everything brought upon us by base people that could not be requited except by punishment. The second example of the cloak represents everything that can be paid back without punishment, and hence perhaps this addition was made, *If anyone wishes to contend in judgment with you,* because whatever is taken away judicially is not considered to be removed by the sort of force that punishment demands. The third example, however, represents a combination of both in such a way that restitution could be made either without punishment or with punishment. For whoever violently insists on an unowed action without judgment, like someone who unjustly compels another's help unlawfully even though he is unwilling, can pay the penalty for his injustice and atone for the act if the person who suffered the injustice should request it. By means of this whole range of offenses, then, the Lord teaches how the Christian soul must be patient and compassionate to the highest degree and be very prepared to put up with a great deal.

20,67. But since it is a small thing not to do harm, unless you also do a good turn insofar as you are able, he is consistent in adding, *Give to everyone who asks of you, and do not turn away from whoever wishes to borrow from you* (Mt 5:41).

---

90. See *Acts of Thomas* 6.8.
91. The Manicheans claimed that some passages of the New Testament with which they disagreed had been interpolated. See, e.g., *Answer to Faustus, a Manichean* XXII,15; XXXIII,6. They accepted the apocryphal *Acts of Thomas*, on the other hand, in its entirety.

To everyone who asks, he says, not "to the one who asks for everything," so that you give honestly and justly what you can afford. What if he looks for money so as to try to oppress an innocent person with it? What if, most wickedly, he solicits an unchaste act? Yet, lest I broach too many possibilities, which are countless, that assuredly should be given which harms neither you nor another person, insofar as it can be humanly known or believed. And when you rightly refuse to give what he asks, that should be considered an act of righteousness in itself, inasmuch as you do not send him away with nothing. In this way you will give to everyone who asks of you, even though you will not always give what he asks. And on occasion you will be giving something better, when you correct someone who is asking for what is unrighteous.

20,68. The words, *Do not turn away from whoever wishes to borrow from you,* must be addressed to one's conscience, *for God loves a cheerful giver* (2 Cor 9:7). Everyone who receives is a borrower, even should he be unable to repay. Since God abundantly repays the merciful, everyone who does a favor receives interest. Or, if there is no satisfaction in accommodating a borrower unless the recipient is going to pay back, we must understand that the Lord included both ways of giving a loan. For we either give what we give with generosity, or we lend to someone who will repay us. And most people who are prepared to give at the prospect of a divine reward become hesitant when a loan is asked for, as though they are going to receive nothing from God if the person who receives what is given repays it. Hence divine authority rightly encourages this kind of generosity in us with the words, *And do not turn away from whoever wishes to borrow from you,* that is, do not withdraw your concern from the person who seeks something because your money will lie idle and God will not repay you if man does so. But when you do this because of God's precept, it is impossible for it to remain unproductive in the sight of him who commands these things.

20,69. He then continues and says, *You have heard that it was said, You shall love your neighbor and hate your enemy. But I say to you, Love your enemies, do good to those who hate you, and pray for those who persecute you, so that you may be sons of your Father who is in heaven, who commands his sun to rise upon the good and the bad and rains upon the righteous and the unrighteous. For if you love those who love you, what reward will you have? Do not the publicans do this? And if you greet your brothers only, what are you doing that is exceptional? Do not the heathens do this very thing? Be perfect, therefore, just as your Father who is in heaven is perfect.* (Mt 5:43–48) Without this kind of love, by which we are commanded to love even our enemies and persecutors, who can fulfill what was previously spoken of? The perfection of mercy, through which the struggling soul is greatly assisted, cannot be extended beyond love of one's enemy. And so the passage concludes thus, *Be perfect, therefore, just as your Father who is in heaven is perfect,* in such a way, however, that God is understood to be perfect as God, and the soul to be perfect as the soul.

21,70. Yet, that there is some progress in the righteousness of the Pharisees, which pertains to the old law, can be deduced from the fact that many people hate even those who love them, just as dissolute children hate parents who curb their excesses. Whoever loves his neighbor, therefore, has made some progress, although he still hates his enemy. But by the rule of the one who came to fulfil the law, not to abolish it, he will make benevolence and goodness perfect when he has brought it as far as loving his enemy. For that former amount of progress, although not insignificant, is nonetheless so small that it can even be had in common with the publicans. And what is said in the law, *You shall hate your enemy,*[92] must not be taken as the word of one who commands the righteous but of one who yields to the weak.

21,71. A question arises at this juncture which must not in any way be brushed aside. Many other texts of Scripture can be found which, to those who reflect on them in a less careful and prudent manner, appear to contradict this precept of the Lord, whereby he exhorts us to love our enemies, to do good to those who hate us, and to pray for those who persecute us. For in the prophetic writings there are to be found numerous imprecations against enemies that can be considered curses, such as this one, *Let their table become a snare* (Ps 69:22), and other things that are said there; and this, *Let his children become orphans and his wife a widow* (Ps 109:9); and everything else which is spoken before or after in the same Psalm through the prophet with reference to Judas.[93] Numerous other passages exist throughout Scripture which seem opposed both to this precept of the Lord and to that of the Apostle when he says, *Bless, and do not curse* (Rom 12:14), while it is even written of the Lord that he cursed those cities which did not accept his word.[94] And the aforementioned Apostle also said of someone, *The Lord will repay him according to his works* (2 Tm 4:14).

21,72. But these problems are easily solved, because the prophet uttered in terms of an imprecation what was to take place in the future not with the longing of one who wished it but in the spirit of one who foresaw it; so also in the case of the Lord and in that of the Apostle, for neither are their words the expression of what they wished but of what they predicted. For when the Lord said, *Woe to you, Capernaum* (Mt 11:21 par.),[95] no other meaning is intended except that something bad would befall it because of its infidelity, which the Lord did not wish to happen out of malevolence but discerned through his divinity. And the Apostle did not say, "May he repay," but, *The Lord will repay him according to his works,* which are the words of someone predicting, not cursing. The same applies to the hypocrisy of the Jews that has already been spoken of, whose downfall he saw was imminent, when

---

92. These are the words not of the old law, which does not have them, but of Jesus.
93. In his *Exposition of Psalm* 108,1, Augustine says that much of Psalm 109 has to do with Judas, but that not everything that pertains to a bad man in the Psalm applies to him. Ps 109:8 is already cited in reference to Judas in Acts 1:20.
94. See Mt 11:20–24 par.
95. The words are actually *Woe to you, Chorazin.*

he said, *The Lord shall strike you, whitewashed wall!* The prophets were very much accustomed to predict future events using the language of imprecation, just as they often resorted to the past tense to declare what would take place in the future, as in the text, *Why have the nations raged and the peoples planned vain things?* (Ps 2:1) For the prophet did not say, "Why will the nations rage and the peoples plan vain things?" since he was aware that it was not as though the events had already taken place, but he foresaw that they would take place. This text is similar: *They divided my garments among them and cast lots for my clothes* (Ps 22:18). He did not say here either, "They will divide my garments among them and will cast lots for my clothes." No one should be scandalized at these words unless he fails to perceive that the range of these figures used in speaking in no way detracts from the truth of the events but rather reinforces the sentiments of the mind.

22,73. But the words of the apostle John raise this pressing question: *If someone knows that his brother commits a sin which does not lead to death, he will pray and God will give life to him whose sin does not lead to death. But there is a sin which leads to death, and I do not say that you should pray for it.* (1 Jn 5:16) He is clearly pointing out that there are certain brothers for whom we are not obliged to pray, although the Lord commands us to pray even for our enemies. This question cannot be resolved unless we acknowledge that there are some sins among the brothers which are more serious than the persecution of enemies.

Now it can be demonstrated from many texts of Sacred Scripture that Christians are called brothers. This is what the Apostle sets down as something very obvious: *For an unbelieving husband is made holy in his wife, and an unbelieving wife is made holy in the brother* (1 Cor 7:14). He did not say "our"[96] but considered it obvious, since by the name *brother* he intended to understand the Christian who had an unbelieving wife. And so he says shortly afterwards, *But if the unbeliever wishes to depart, let him depart; a brother or a sister is not subject to bondage of this sort* (1 Cor 7:15).

I believe, then, that there is a sin of a brother which leads to death when, after having come to the knowledge of God through the grace of our Lord Jesus Christ, someone attacks the brotherhood and is on fire with envy against that same grace by which he has been reconciled to God.[97] But there is a sin which does not lead to death if someone does not become estranged from the love of his brother but through some weakness of character fails to meet the necessary obligations of brotherhood. For this reason even the Lord on the cross said, *Father, forgive them, for they do not know what they are doing* (Lk 23:34). For, since they had not yet become sharers in the grace of the Holy Spirit, they were not joined to the fellowship of the holy brotherhood. And in the Acts of the Apostles blessed

---

96. I.e., "our brother."
97. In *Revisions* I,19 (18),7 Augustine says that this sentence gives the impression that there is no hope for such a person and that, since no one should be despaired of in this life, the sentence should be completed with the words "if he were to finish his life in this wicked perversity of mind."

Stephen prays for those who are stoning him,[98] for they had not yet come to believe in Christ nor were they struggling against the grace which was held in common. The apostle Paul, I believe, does not pray for Alexander because he was already a brother and was guilty of the sin which leads to death, that is, he had attacked the brotherhood out of envy. However, in the case of those who did not break the bond of love but succumbed through fear, he prays that they be forgiven. His words are as follows: *Alexander the coppersmith has done me considerable harm; the Lord will repay him according to his works. You also must avoid him, for he has vigorously resisted our preaching.* He then goes on to speak about those for whom he prays: *There was no one with me at my first defense, but everyone abandoned me; may they not be held accountable.* (2 Tm 4:14–16)

22,74. This difference between sins separates Judas the betrayer[99] from Peter the denier[100] not because there should be no forgiveness for someone who repents (lest we find ourselves contravening those words of the Lord whereby he commanded that a brother who asked his brother to forgive him should always be forgiven[101]) but because the depravity of such a sin is so great that a person is unable to humble himself and beg for forgiveness, even if he is compelled through a bad conscience to acknowledge and own up to his sin. For when Judas said, *I have sinned because I have betrayed innocent blood* (Mt 27:4), he more easily rushed to the noose in desperation[102] than begged pardon in humility. Consequently God's forgiveness is greatly dependent on the quality of the repentance. Many indeed are quick to confess that they have sinned and are so annoyed with themselves that they wish vehemently that they had never sinned, but they do not commit themselves to humbling their soul and to bruising their heart and to imploring pardon. It must be believed that, because of this attitude, these people have a sense of being already condemned on account of the magnitude of their sin.

22,75. And this is perhaps what the sin against the Holy Spirit means, namely, the undermining of brotherly charity out of spite and envy after the grace of the Holy Spirit has been received. This sin, the Lord says, will be forgiven neither here nor in the world to come.[103] The question may therefore be asked whether the Jews sinned against the Holy Spirit when they claimed that the Lord drove out devils by the power of Beelzebul, the prince of devils.[104] Are we to say that this was spoken directly against the Lord, for he says of himself in another passage, *If they called the father of the house Beelzebul, how much more his servants* (Mt 10:25)? Or could it be that, thankless as they were for such present blessings, they spoke out of great envy and that, although they were not as yet Christians, they are to be regarded as having sinned against the Holy Spirit because of the very greatness of

98. See Acts 7:59–60.
99. See Mt 26:47–50.
100. See Mt 26:69–75.
101. See Lk 17:3–4.
102. See Mt 27:5.
103. See Mt 12:31–32.
104. See Mt 12:24.

their envy? Such a conclusion does not follow from what the Lord said. For, although in the same passage he says, *Whoever speaks evil against the Son of Man will be forgiven, but whoever speaks against the Holy Spirit will be forgiven neither in this world nor in the world to come* (Mt 12:32), this can nonetheless be construed as a warning to them to draw near to grace and, once having received grace, not to sin in the way that they were then sinning. For then they spoke evil against the Son of Man, and they could be forgiven if they were converted and believed in him and received the Holy Spirit. Once they had received it, if they set themselves to envying the brotherhood and to attacking the grace that they had received, they would be forgiven neither in this world nor in the world to come. For, if he had considered them to be so condemned as to be bereft of hope, he would not have judged them as still worthy of correction when he went on to say, *Either make the tree good and its fruit good, or make the tree bad and its fruit bad* (Mt 12:33).

22,76. Let it be accepted, therefore, that we must love our enemies and do good to those who hate us and pray for those who persecute us, as long as it is understood that we are not commanded to pray on behalf of certain sins even of our brothers, lest because of our ignorance Sacred Scripture seem to contradict itself, which is not possible. But it is not altogether clear whether there are some people for whom we should not pray or still others against whom we should pray. The general principle has been enunciated, *Bless, and do not curse* (Rom 12:14), and again, *Return no one evil for evil* (Rom 12:17). Yet, if you are not praying for a person, you are not praying against him. You can see that his punishment is assured and that his salvation is utterly hopeless, and it is not through hatred that you fail to pray for him but because you feel that it is of no avail, and you do not wish your prayer to be spurned by the most just judge.

But what are we to make of those against whom we understand that the saints prayed, not that they would be corrected (for in that regard they had already been prayed for) but for their final condemnation? What is at issue here is not what the prophet said about the Lord's betrayer, for, as has been noted, that was a prediction of future events and not a wish for punishment, nor what was said by the Apostle against Alexander, about which enough has been said, but rather what we read in the Apocalypse of John, that the martyrs prayed to be vindicated,[105] although the protomartyr himself prayed for the forgiveness of those who stoned him.[106]

22,77. Yet we should not allow ourselves to be persuaded by this. For who would dare to say for certain, when those white-clad saints[107] prayed to be vindicated, whether they were praying against human beings themselves or against the reign of sin? In fact the heartfelt and most righteous and merciful vindication of the martyrs consists in the overthrow of the reign of sin, a reign that caused them such great suffering. The Apostle encourages the overthrow of this reign when he says, *Do not therefore let sin reign in your mortal body* (Rom 6:12). The reign of sin is

---

105. See Rv 6:10.
106. The protomartyr is Stephen. See Acts 7:60.
107. See Rv 6:11.

destroyed and overthrown partly by people's conversion, when the flesh becomes subject to the spirit, and partly by the condemnation of those who persist in sin, when they are constrained in such a way as to be unable to harm the righteous who are reigning with Christ. Look at the apostle Paul: do you not think that he was vindicating Stephen the martyr in his own person when he declared, *I do not fight as one beating the air, but I chastise my body and bring it into subjection* (1 Cor 9:26–27)? For what he was subduing and weakening and bringing to order in himself was that urge which he had conquered and which had driven him to persecute Stephen and other Christians.[108] Who, then, can show that the holy martyrs did not pray to the Lord for such vindication, since they were able to wish freely for the end of a world in which they had suffered so greatly? And those who do pray even for their enemies pray for those who can be reformed, and they do not pray against those who wish to remain beyond reform, for the God who punishes them is not an evil torturer but a most just regulator. Without any shadow of doubt therefore, let us love our enemies, do good to those who hate us, and pray for those who persecute us.

23,78. What comes next, *So that you may be sons of your Father who is in heaven,* is to be understood on the basis of that norm of which John also speaks, *He gave them power to become sons of God* (Jn 1:12). There is one who is Son by nature and is altogether incapable of sinning, whereas we are made sons once we have received the power and insofar as we carry out the precepts that he lays down. For this reason the apostolic teaching refers to the adoption by which we are called to an eternal inheritance, so that we can become coheirs with Christ.[109] We become sons, therefore, through spiritual rebirth, and we are adopted into the kingdom of God not as strangers but as those made and created — that is, fashioned — by him. Thus there is one blessing whereby he has made us by his almighty power, when previously we did not exist, and a second whereby he has adopted us, so that as sons we may enjoy eternal life in return for sharing in adoption. Accordingly he does not say, "Do these things because you are sons," but, "Do these things *so that you may be sons.*"

23,79. Since he calls us to this through the Only-Begotten himself, he calls us to his own likeness. For, as he goes on to say, he *makes his sun rise upon the good and the bad and rains upon the righteous and the unrighteous* (Mt 5:45). You may understand *his sun* to refer not to the one which is visible to the eyes of the body but to that wisdom of which it is said, *She is the brightness of eternal light* (Wis 7:26), of which it is also said, "The sun of righteousness has risen for me,"[110] and again, *But for you who fear the Lord's name the sun of righteousness shall rise* (Mal 4:2), in which case you will interpret the rain as the outpouring of the teaching of truth, because it has appeared to the good and the bad, and Christ has been preached to the good and the bad. Or you may prefer to understand the

---

108. See Acts 7:58; 8:1–3; 9:1–2.
109. See Rom 8:17.
110. These words do not occur in the Bible.

sun as that which is visible not only to the bodily eyes of human beings but also to those of beasts, and the rain as that by which fruit is brought forth that is given for bodily nourishment. I consider this to be the most likely interpretation, that that spiritual sun rises only for the good and the holy, for this is what the wicked lament in the book entitled The Wisdom of Solomon, *And the sun has not risen for us* (Wis 5:6), and that that spiritual rain moistens the good alone, because the vine of which it is said, *I shall command my clouds not to rain upon it* (Is 5:6), symbolizes the wicked. But whether you understand the one or the other, they result from God's great goodness, which we are commanded to imitate if we wish to be sons of God. For who could be so ungrateful as not to notice the comfort afforded by that visible light and earthly rainfall? We see that this comfort is extended in this life to righteous and sinners alike. For he does not say, *He makes* the *sun rise upon the good and the bad*, but he specifies *his*, namely, that which he himself created and established, when he produced something from nothing in order to make it, as is recorded in Genesis about all the heavenly lights[111]—he who with justice can claim everything to be his which he created from nothing. And so we are reminded by his command with what great liberality (which we ourselves have not created but have received with his gifts) we should treat our enemies.

23,80. Who, then, is able or prepared to suffer wrongdoings from the weak, insofar as it assists their wellbeing, and prefers to suffer more evil from another than to pay back what he has suffered; or to give something to everyone who asks, or whatever he asks, if he possesses it and it is right to give it, or to give good advice or to show a kindly disposition, and not to turn away from whoever wants to borrow; to love one's enemies, to do good to those who hate him, to pray for those who persecute him? Who, then, discharges all these obligations unless he is fully and completely merciful? By this single counsel misery is avoided with the help of him who says, *I desire mercy rather than sacrifice* (Hos 6:6). *Blessed are the merciful,* then, *for they shall obtain mercy.*[112] But I feel that it is appropriate now for the reader, tired from such an extended volume, to pause for a while and renew his energies in anticipation of what remains to be considered in another book.

---

111. See Gn 1:16.
112. "Misery...*mercy...merciful...mercy*": *miseria...misericordiam...misericordes...miserebitur.*

Book Two

1,1. Purity of heart, with which this book commences, follows a discussion of mercy, with which the first book concludes. Purity of the heart may be compared to that of the eye, through which God is seen, and the greatest care must be devoted to keeping it unclouded, as the dignity of the object that can be seen with this sort of eye demands. But it is difficult for this eye, which has been mostly purified, to avoid the incursion of certain impurities that derive from those things which usually accompany our good actions, such as the praise of others. If indeed it is ruinous not to live uprightly, what is it to live uprightly and to be unwilling to receive praise from others except to be hostile to human affairs, which in truth become all the more wretched the less people's upright way of life is given approval? Therefore, if those among whom you live do not extol you for leading an upright life, they are in the wrong. Yet you are in danger if they do extol you, unless you possess a heart that is so undivided and pure that what you do from the right motives does not depend on people's praise, and you should take all the more delight in that they give praise for the right reason and are approving not you but what is good. For, if you do lead an upright life, and even if no one praises you, then you will understand that the praise they confer on you is beneficial to those who praise you, if they honor not you but God because of your good life. For anyone who leads an upright life becomes his temple, so as to fulfill what David says, *In the Lord shall my soul find praise; let the meek hear and be glad* (Ps 34:2).

It pertains to a pure eye, then, to disregard people's praises in doing what is right and not to draw their attention to the good that you do, in other words, to do something so as to win people's approval. For even the pretence of doing good will be appealing when all that is sought is the praise of a person who, because he is unable to look into the heart, can even praise things that are false. Those who behave in this manner, by feigning goodness, have a divided heart. And so no one possesses an undivided heart, that is, a pure heart, unless he transcends human praise, fixes his gaze on him alone when he leads an upright life, and endeavors to please him who alone scrutinizes the conscience. And whatever emerges from such a clear conscience is all the more praiseworthy the less desirous it is of human praise.

1,2. *Beware then,* he says, *of parading your righteousness before people, to be seen by them* (Mt 6:1). He means by this that you should beware of living righteously with this in mind and of placing your good in being seen by people. *Otherwise you will have no reward from your Father who is in heaven* (Mt 6:1) — not if you are seen by people, but if being seen by people is the reason why you lead a righteous life. For what, then, would the words found at the beginning of this Sermon mean, *You are the light of the world. A city set on a hilltop cannot be hidden. Nor do they light a lamp and place it under a bushel but on a lampstand, so that it may give light to all who are in the house. So let your light shine before men that they may see your good works*? But he did not stop here, for he added, *and glorify your Father who is in heaven.* (Mt 5:14–16) Yet, since he reproves such behavior here if the reason for our upright works is to act uprightly with the sole intention of being seen by people, he said afterwards, *Beware of parading your righteousness before people, to be seen by them,* but he added nothing further. From this it is clear that he did not forbid upright behavior before people but rather that upright behavior take place before people in order to be seen by them, that is, that such an outlook be the determining factor of our activity.

1,3. For the Apostle also says, *If I still sought to please people, I would not be a servant of Christ* (Gal 1:10), although he says elsewhere, *Aim to please everyone in all things, just as I please everyone in all things* (1 Cor 10:32–33). Those who fail to understand this conclude that it is contradictory, because he asserted that he did not aim to please people, for he would not be acting rightly by pleasing people rather than God. But insofar as he did please people, it was his intention to turn their hearts to the love of God. And so he was speaking correctly about not pleasing people, because he saw that by that very fact he would please God, and he rightly commanded that people must be pleased, not that this should be sought as the reward of upright behavior, but because a person could not please God if he failed to present himself as a model to imitate to those whom he wished to be saved, for under no circumstances can a person imitate someone who is not pleasing to him. Just as a person would not be speaking irrationally were he to say, "In this work for which I am looking for a ship, it is not a ship that I am looking for but my homeland," likewise the Apostle could appropriately say, "In this work whereby I am pleasing people, it is not people that I am pleasing but God, for that is not what I seek, but my intention is that those whom I wish to be saved should imitate me." He says the same about the collection that is taken up for the saints, *Not that I am looking for a gift, but I am seeking its fruit* (Phil 4:17), which means, "Even though I am looking for your gift, that is not what I am looking for, but your fruit." This could be seen as a clear sign of just how far they had progressed in God, since they freely did what was asked of them not because of the joy accruing from their gifts but from their communion in charity.

1,4. And when he also goes on to add the phrase, *Otherwise you will have no reward from your Father who is in heaven,* he is stating nothing other than that we must beware of seeking human approval as a reward for what we do, in the belief that this will make us happy.

2,5. *When you give alms,* therefore, says the Lord, *do not have it trumpeted before you, as the hypocrites do in the synagogues and in the streets, so that they may be praised by people* (Mt 6:2). Do not, he says, wish to become known as hypocrites. For it is evident that what hypocrites pretend to do in the presence of people differs from what lies in their hearts. Hypocrites are impersonators, mouthpieces for other characters, as in stories from the theatre. For example, the one who plays the part of Agamemnon in a tragedy,[1] or of anyone else who fea-

---

1. Agamemnon, according to Greek legend, was king of Mycenae and leader of the Greek forces against the Trojans. Murdered by his wife Clytemnestra and her lover Aegisthus, his death

tures in history or fable, is not really that person but is impersonating him and is called a hypocrite.[2] Similarly, in the Church or in human life of any kind, whoever wishes to appear what he is not is a hypocrite. For he impersonates a righteous man but does not exhibit his qualities, because he derives all his satisfaction from the praise of people, which impersonators can also do, as long as they deceive those to whom they seem to be good and are praised by them. But people of this kind receive no reward from God, who scrutinizes the heart, except punishment for their deceit. *They have received their reward*, however, *from men* (Mt 6:2), he says. Most justly will it be told them, *Depart from me, you workers of iniquity* (Mt 7:23), for you had my name but did not perform my works. Those have received their reward, therefore, who give alms for no other reason than to win people's praise — not if they should happen to be praised by people, but if they behave in such a way as to win praise, as has been previously discussed. For people's praise must not be the aim of someone who behaves uprightly but ought to accompany someone who behaves uprightly, so that those who can imitate what they praise may advance, not so that anyone would think that through their praise they are conferring some benefit on him.

2,6. *But when you give alms, do not let your left hand know what your right hand is doing* (Mt 6:3). If you take the left hand to mean unbelievers, it will be clear that there is no fault in wanting to please believers, although we are nonetheless absolutely forbidden to make the praise of any people whatsoever the fruit and purpose of our good actions. Where the situation arises, however, that they imitate you because your good actions please them, it must be manifest not only to believers but to unbelievers as well, so that in praising our good actions they may honor God and attain to salvation. Yet, should you understand the left hand to mean an enemy, so that your enemy is unaware that you are giving alms, why did the Lord himself heal people out of compassion when he was surrounded by the Jews who were his enemies? Why did the apostle Peter, having healed the cripple on whom he had taken compassion at the Beautiful Gate, endure the anger of his enemies towards him and the other disciples of Christ?[3] And if the enemy is not to know when we give alms, how are we to deal with that very same enemy so as to fulfill the precept, *If your enemy is hungry, feed him; if he is thirsty, give him a drink* (Rom 12:20).

2,7. Those of a materialistic outlook usually hold a third opinion, which is so absurd and laughable that I would not mention it unless I had experienced that not a few people have been erroneously led into thinking that the term *left hand* refers to a wife. Thus, since in household matters women tend to be more spar-

---

was avenged by his son Orestes. Augustine's choice of him as an example of a tragic figure is perfectly understandable, as he appears frequently in Greek literature, beginning with Homer.

2. *Hypocrita* was a Latin word, derived from the Greek, whose original and innocuous meaning was related to the theater. It was first used in a derogatory sense in the Greek of the Gospels, as here. See also below at II,19,64.

3. See Acts 3:1–8.

ing with money, it should be concealed from them, in order to avoid domestic quarrels, when out of compassion their husbands give some of it to the needy. As though men alone were Christians, and this command were not enjoined on women too! From which left hand is a woman commanded to conceal her work of mercy? Or shall a husband also be the left hand to a woman? An assertion of this kind is utterly ridiculous. Or perhaps someone thinks that there are two left hands in mutual opposition and that, if something is distributed from the family purse by one person in a way that was contrary to the wishes of the other, such a marriage is not Christian. But it follows of necessity that, if one of them wishes to give alms in accordance with God's precept, whichever one of them opposes it is an enemy of God's precept and is therefore to be counted among unbelievers. The precept governing such cases is that by his good manner of life and behavior a believing husband can win over his wife or a believing wife her husband.[4] Consequently, they must not conceal from one another the good actions by which they should challenge one another, so that one may be able to spur the other on to share the Christian faith. Nor must such actions be done in secret so as to win God's favor. But if something must be kept hidden so long as the weakness of the other is unable to bear it with equanimity, then this is neither wrong nor unlawful. However, from an examination of the whole chapter it is now quite clear that she[5] is not signified by the left hand, and from this it will likewise be discovered what the Lord means by the left hand.

2,8. *Beware*, says the Lord, *of parading your righteousness before people, to be seen by them; otherwise, you will have no reward from your Father who is in heaven.* He mentioned righteousness in a general sense here, and then he goes on to speak of its parts. For the work of almsgiving forms part of righteousness, and by way of connection he says, *When you give alms, therefore, do not have it trumpeted before you, as the hypocrites do in the synagogues and in the streets, so that they may be praised by people.* He referred to this when he said earlier, *Beware of parading your righteousness before people, to be seen by them.* But what follows, *Amen, I tell you, they have received their reward,* refers to what was said above, *Otherwise you will have no reward from your Father who is in heaven.*

Then it follows, *But when you give alms.* When he says, *But when you,* what else does he mean than "not like them"? What, then, is he commanding me to do? He says, *When you give alms, do not let your left hand know what your right hand is doing.* People like that, then, act in such a way that their left hand knows what their right hand is doing. Hence you are forbidden to do what is reproachable in them. What is reproachable in them, though, is that they behave so as to seek people's praise. It follows logically that the left hand seems to mean nothing other than the love of praise, while the right hand denotes the intention to fulfill the divine precepts. As a result, when the desire for human approval impinges on

---

4.   See 1 Cor 7:14.
5.   I.e., the wife.

the consciousness of the person giving alms, then the left hand becomes conscious of what the right hand is doing. *Do not,* therefore, *let your left hand know what your right hand is doing*; in other words, do not let the desire for human praise encroach on your consciousness when you endeavor to fulfill the divine precept of giving alms.

2,9. *So that your almsgiving may be in secret* (Mt 6:4). What does *in secret* mean if not within a good conscience that cannot be shown to the human eye nor disclosed in words? For many people tell many lies. If the right hand, therefore, acts interiorly in secret, everything external that is visible and temporal pertains to the left hand. Let your almsgiving then be in your conscience itself, where many people practice almsgiving with goodwill, even if they lack money or whatever else should be given to the needy. But there are many who give outwardly but do not do so inwardly, who through ambition or for the sake of some temporal benefit wish to appear merciful, and in the case of such people only the left hand is to be considered at work. Likewise, others hold as it were a middle position between the two, so that they give alms with their intention directed towards God, and yet into this excellent choice there also insinuates itself a certain longing for praise or some such fragile and ephemeral thing. But our Lord much more vehemently forbids the working of the left hand alone within us when he also prohibits its infiltration into the actions of the right hand, so that we should both beware of giving alms out of a desire for temporal benefits and, when we have God in mind in this work, not allow a longing for advantages either to infiltrate or to attach itself. It is a matter of purifying the heart, for unless it is undivided it cannot be pure. For how can it be undivided if it serves two masters[6] and does not purify its vision by concentrating solely on eternal realities but instead obscures it with the love of those that are mortal and fragile? *Let your almsgiving be in secret,* then, *and your Father, who sees in secret, will repay you* (Mt 6:4). Absolutely just and right! For, if you are looking for a reward from the one who alone scrutinizes the conscience, let conscience itself suffice to merit your reward. Many Latin codices read as follows, *And your Father, who sees in secret, will repay you openly.* Yet since we do not find "openly" in the Greek codices, which are earlier, we did not feel that it should be discussed here.[7]

3,10. *And when you pray,* he says, *you are not to be like the hypocrites, who love to stand in synagogues and pray in street corners, so that they may be seen by people* (Mt 6:5). It is not wrong in this case to be seen by people but rather to do these things so that you may be seen by them. The same thing is said repeatedly and superfluously, although there is only one rule to be observed, by which it is made known that these things are not to be feared and avoided if people know them but if they are done with the intention that the benefit sought from them is to please people. The Lord himself uses the same words when he adds, as he did

6. See Mt 6:24.
7. Some important Greek versions, as well as some Latin ones (notably of the so-called Old Latin), do in fact have the word or words for "openly."

previously, *Amen, I tell you, they have received their reward* (Mt 6:5), demonstrating here that he forbids the desire for a reward which is a source of joy to the foolish, inasmuch as they are praised by others.

3,11. *But when you pray,* he says, *go into your bedrooms* (Mt 6:6). What are those bedrooms if not our very hearts, which are also signified by the words of the Psalm, *What you say in your hearts, repent also upon your beds* (Ps 4:4)? *And closing the doors,* the Lord continues, *pray to your Father in secret.* It is of little consequence to go into bedrooms if the door is left open for intruders, for the things on the outside burst through the door with abandon and seek out our innermost recesses. We have said that the term "outside" refers to all the temporal and visible things that enter our thoughts by the door of the fleshly senses and disturb them through a multitude of futile images.[8] The door must therefore be kept closed — that is, we must resist the fleshly senses so that a spiritual prayer which comes into being in the inner recesses of the heart, where we pray to the Father in secret, may be directed to the Father. *And,* he says, *your Father who sees in secret will reward you* (Mt 6:6). And this ought to be brought to an end with a similar conclusion, for we are not being told now *that* we should pray but rather *how* we should pray. Nor did he do so previously, when it was not a matter of giving alms but rather of the attitude with which we should give them, because he enjoined purification of the heart, and simply being single-mindedly intent on eternal life can accomplish that purification through a love of wisdom that is sole and pure.

3,12. *When you pray,* he says, *do not use many words, as the heathens do, for they think that by speaking much they will be heard* (Mt 6:7). Just as the hypocrites present themselves to the public gaze when they pray, the effect of which is to please people, so do the heathens, that is, the gentiles, who believe that by speaking much their prayers will be heard. And in truth all excessive speech comes from the gentiles, for they devote their energies to the training of the tongue rather than the purification of the mind.[9] They attempt as well to apply to God this kind of trivial pursuit to appease him by prayer, believing that he can be prevailed upon to give a decision, like a human judge, by the power of words. *Do not be like these, therefore,* says the only true teacher, *for your Father knows what you need even before you ask him* (Mt 6:8). For, if many words are spoken so as to instruct and teach someone who is unlearned, what need is there of them for him who knows everything, to whom all things that exist, by the very fact that they exist, speak and declare that they have come into being?[10] And those things that are yet to be do not escape his skill and wisdom, in which both things that have passed away and things that will pass away are all present and do not pass away.

---

8. Origen expresses the same thought in *On Prayer* 20,2.
9. Augustine is criticizing the emphasis on rhetorical training that was central to the education of young men in Greek and Roman culture, as he does in *Confessions* (e.g., I,17,27–29; IV,2,2), the *Sermon on Christian Discipline,* and elsewhere.
10. See *Confessions* X,6,8–9.

3,13. But since the Lord himself is going to teach us how to pray, albeit in a few words, the question may be asked as to why these brief words have to be addressed to the one who knows all things before they exist and is aware, as has already been said, what our needs are before we ask him?[11] We should reply first of all that it is not with words that we must ask God for what we want but with the things that we carry in our minds and with the orientation of our thinking, coupled with a love that is pure and an affection that is sincere. But our Lord has taught us these very things in words, and, having committed them to memory, we shall recall them at the time of prayer.

3,14. But again, whether we are to pray by things or by words, the question can be asked as to why there has to be prayer if God already knows what we need, unless the very intention to pray soothes and purifies our heart and makes it better disposed to receive the divine gifts, which are showered on us spiritually.[12] For God does not hear us through the earnestness of our prayers, because he is always ready to give his light to us, which is not visible but intelligible and spiritual; yet we are not always ready to receive it because we are inclined toward other things and are under the shadow of our desire for what belongs to the temporal order. A movement of the heart, therefore, takes place in prayer towards the one who is always prepared to give, provided that we are disposed to receive what he gives, and within that very movement there occurs a purification of the inner eye, once those things we desire in the temporal order are excluded. Thus the vision of an undivided heart can receive the pure light, which shines divinely without decline or alteration,[13] and not simply receive it but even abide in it not only without hindrance but even with unspeakable delight, whereby the blessed life truly and genuinely attains perfection.

4,15. We must now look attentively at what he — from whom we both learn what we should pray for and obtain what we pray for — has commanded us to pray for. *Pray,* he says, *as follows: Our Father, who art in heaven, hallowed be thy name; thy kingdom come, thy will be done on earth as it is heaven. Give us this day our daily bread, and forgive us our trespasses as we forgive those who trespass against us, and bring us not into temptation, but deliver us from evil* (Mt 6:9–13).

Since in every prayer it is necessary to obtain the good will of the one whom we are invoking, and then what we are asking for must be stated, the good will of the one to whom prayer is directed is usually invoked by praising him, and this is customarily placed at the beginning of the prayer.[14] It is there that our Lord commands us to say nothing else than *Our Father, who art in heaven* (Mt 6:9). There are many things spoken in praise of God which are scattered variously and

---

11. The same classic question is raised in Origen, *On Prayer* 5,2, although Origen's answer, ibid. 6,3–5, is very different than Augustine's.
12. There is a similar thought ibid. 8,2.
13. See Jas 1:17.
14. Augustine is applying the ancient rhetorical device of *captatio benevolentiae*, alluded to in Cicero, *The Orator* II,27,115 and elsewhere, to the practice of prayer.

widely throughout Sacred Scripture and which can be pondered by anyone who reads them; nowhere, however, is there a precept given to the people of Israel to say *our Father* or to pray to God as Father, but the Lord made himself known to them as to servants, that is, as to those still living according to the flesh. I say this for the time they received the commandments of the law, which they were ordered to observe. For the prophets often point out that the Lord God could also have been their Father if they had not strayed from his commandments, as in this text, *I have begotten sons and raised them up; but they have spurned me* (Is 1:2); and in this, *I said, You are gods and sons of the Most High, but you shall die like men and fall like one of the princes* (Ps 82:6–7); and in this, *If I am the Lord, where is the fear due to me? And if I am a Father, where is the honor due to me?* (Mal 1:6); and in many other passages in which the Jews stand rebuked because by sinning they were unwilling to become sons of God, except for those words spoken in prophecy about the future Christian people, that they would have God as their Father, in accordance with the gospel passage, *He gave them power to become sons of God* (Jn 1:12). The apostle Paul states, *As long as the heir is a child, he is no different than a slave* (Gal 4:1), and he recalls that we have received the spirit of adoption, *in which we cry out, Abba, Father* (Rom 8:15).

4,16. And because it is not through any merits of our own but by the grace of God that we are called to an eternal inheritance, to be coheirs with Christ and attain adoption as sons,[15] we place that same grace at the beginning of the prayer when we say *Our Father.* By this title charity is aroused, for what ought to be more precious to sons than a father? An attitude of affection is stirred up as well when people call God *our Father,* and also a kind of presumption that we shall receive what we are asking for, since, prior to any petition, we are in possession of the great gift of being permitted to say *our Father.* For what would he not now give his sons who petition him when he has already given them the status of sons? Finally, what great sensibility strikes one's conscience, that the person who says *our Father* should not be unworthy of such a Father! For, if some ordinary person should be permitted by a senator of distinguished lineage to address him as father, he will undoubtedly be cautious and not act impetuously, reflecting on his humble origins, his lack of wealth, and the lowly state of his civic position. With what greater trepidation, therefore, must God be addressed as Father, if there are stains so great and behavior so disgraceful that God would shun them much more justifiably than would that senator the poverty of some beggar, since in fact the condition that he despises in the beggar could become his own as well, given the instability of human affairs, whereas God never lapses into disgraceful behavior. And, thanks to the mercy of him who demands this from us in order to be our Father, what can be purchased at no price can be purchased by good will alone. The rich and those who are wellborn according to the world are warned here, once they have become Christians, not to behave arrogantly to the poor and those of

---

15. See Rom 8:17.23.

lowly birth, because they all say *our Father* together, which they cannot honestly and piously say if they do not recognize one another as brothers.

5,17. Let the new people, then, called to an eternal inheritance, take up the voice of the New Testament[16] and say, *Our Father, who art in heaven,* which means in the saints and in the righteous, for God is not restricted to the dimensions of space.[17] The heavens are indeed noble bodies of the universe, but still bodies, and they cannot exist anywhere other than in space. But if God's place is thought of as being in the heavens, in the higher parts of the universe, then birds, which live closer to God, are of greater merit. Yet it is not written in Scripture that the Lord is close to tall people or to those who live in the mountains, but it is written, *The Lord is close to the brokenhearted* (Ps 34:18), which pertains more to what is lowly. But just as the sinner is called "earth," when it is said to him, *You are of the earth, and to earth you shall return* (Gn 3:9), so by way of contrast the righteous person can be called "heaven."[18] For it is said to the righteous, *The temple of God is holy, which is what you are* (1 Cor 3:17). Therefore, if God dwells in his temple, and the saints are his temple, it is correctly said, *who art in heaven,* you who are in the saints. And this comparison is most apt, since it shows that the vast spiritual difference between the righteous and sinners is just as great as the bodily one that exists between heaven and earth.

5,18. As an indication of this, when we stand to pray we turn to the east, from where the heavens rise.[19] It is not as though God dwells there and has abandoned the other parts of the world, for he is present everywhere not in physical space but by the power of his majesty, but we do this in order that the mind may be encouraged to turn to a more excellent nature, that is, to God, when its body, which is earthly, turns to a more excellent body, that is, to the heavenly body. It is in keeping with the various stages of religion and most beneficial that, through the awareness of all things both great and small, God can indeed be perceived. And therefore, as for those who have applied themselves to what is visible and beautiful and are unable to conceive of anything immaterial, because they necessarily prefer heaven to earth, their opinion is more acceptable if they believe that God, whom they still conceive of in bodily terms, is in heaven rather than on earth. When they eventually come to realize that the dignity of the soul surpasses even that of the heavenly body,

---

16. See *Homily on the Gospel of John* 65,1: "new men, heirs of the New Testament, singers of a new song."

17. These thoughts also appear in Origen, *On Prayer* 23.

18. The notion that heaven symbolizes the righteous and earth sinners also appears below at II,6,22.

19. Praying while standing and facing east was the normal practice in Christian antiquity, attested by numerous patristic texts. See, e.g., Origen, *On Prayer* 31,2–3 (where standing is implied rather than stated).32; Basil, *On the Holy Spirit* 27,66. But kneeling was also an acceptable posture. See Paul F. Bradshaw, *Daily Prayer in the Early Church* (London 1981) 18. It is interesting to note that, in *A Miscellany of Questions in Response to Simplician* II,4, written a few years after the present work, Augustine flouts the longstanding tradition and says that the posture for prayer is a matter of indifference. On the rich symbolism of the east, which was the reason for praying in that direction, see Jean Daniélou, *The Bible and the Liturgy* (Notre Dame 1956) 30–33.

they search for him more in the soul than in the heavenly body. And, when they realize how great the difference is between the souls of sinners and those of the righteous, just as when their outlook was still that of the flesh[20] they did not dare to locate God on earth but in heaven, so afterwards they will seek him with greater faith and understanding in the souls of the righteous more than in those of sinners.

The correct understanding, therefore, of the words *Our Father, who art in heaven* is that he is said to dwell in the hearts of the righteous as in his holy temple. Let the person who prays also be desirous that the one whom he invokes dwell within him, and, as he aspires to this, let him hold fast to righteousness, for by this kind of service God is invited to dwell within his soul.

5,19. Let us now see what we should ask for. Who it is that is invoked and where he dwells has been explained. The first petition, which ranks before all, is this: *Hallowed be thy name* (Mt 6:9). This petition is not made as if God's name were not hallowed but so that people may hallow it,[21] that is, so that God may be so well known to them that they would not consider anything else more hallowed which they would more dare to offend. The passage which reads, *God is made known in Judea, in Israel his name is great* (Ps 76:1), should not be taken to mean that in one place God is smaller, in another greater; but his name is great wherever he is named because of the greatness of his majesty. And so his name is said to be holy whenever it is spoken of with reverence and with fear of giving offence. This is what is now happening when, by making it known throughout the different nations, the Gospel proclaims the name of the one God through the mediation of his Son.

6,20. He then continues, *Thy kingdom come* (Mt 6:10). As the Lord himself teaches in the Gospel, there will be a day of judgment once the Gospel has been preached to every nation; this pertains to the holiness of God's name. What is said here, *Thy kingdom come,* should not be understood as if God does not already reign. But perhaps someone would maintain that the word *come* is spoken with regard to the earth, as if he does not now reign on earth and as if he has not in fact reigned on earth from the beginning of the universe. *Thy kingdom come* therefore means that it is to be revealed to mankind. For just as the visible light is invisible to those who are blind and to those who close their eyes, so it is with the kingdom of God, which has never been absent from the earth, although it is invisible to those who do not know it. But no one will be permitted to ignore the kingdom of God when his only-begotten Son comes from heaven in a way that is not only intellectually comprehensible but also visible, as the Lordly Man,[22] to judge the living and the dead. After this judgment, when the sifting and separation of the righteous from the unrighteous has taken place, God will dwell within the righteous in such a way that there will be no need for anyone to be taught by man but, as it is writ-

---

20. See Rom 8:5.
21. This notion is a commonplace. See Tertullian, *On Prayer* 3; Origen, *On Prayer* 24,1; Cyprian, *On the Lord's Prayer* 7.
22. In *Revisions* I,19 (18),8 Augustine regrets his use of the term "Lordly Man" (*homo dominicus* in Latin, *kyriakos anthropos* in Greek) as being imprecise.

ten, *Everyone will be taught by God* (Jn 6:45). Then the blessed life will reach full perfection among the saints eternally, in a manner similar to that of the most holy and blessed angels of heaven, who are now wise and blessed through their enlightenment by God himself, because the Lord has promised this also to those who are his own: *In the resurrection,* he declares, *they will be like the angels in heaven* (Mt 22:30).

6,21. And so, after the petition in which we say, *Thy kingdom come,* he continues, *Thy will be done on earth as it is in heaven* (Mt 6:10), that is, in the same way that your will prevails among the angels in heaven, who are completely united to you and rejoice in you, with no shadow of error obscuring their wisdom or distress hindering their blessedness, so let it be among your saints who are on earth and who are of the earth as far as their bodies are concerned, but who are to be taken up from the earth into the unchanging abode of heaven. In the same vein is the angelic proclamation, *Glory to God in the highest, and peace on earth to men of good will* (Lk 2:14), so that when our good will precedes, following the one who calls, the will of God comes to completion within us, as is the case among the angels in heaven, and no obstacle stands in the way of our happiness, which is peace.

Thy will be done is also properly understood as meaning that your precepts should be obeyed *on earth as in heaven,* in other words, by human beings just as by the angels. For the Lord himself speaks of fulfilling God's will when his precepts are obeyed when he says, *My food is to do the will of him who sent me* (Jn 4:34), and frequently, *I have not come to do my own will, but the will of him who sent me* (Jn 5:30; 6:38), and when he says, *Behold, my mother and your brothers. And whoever does the will of God is my brother and mother and sister* (Mt 12:49–50). The will of God is indeed accomplished in those who do the will of God, not that they themselves do it so that God may will it but that they do what he wills; in other words, they act according to his will.

6,22. The words, *Thy will be done on earth as it is in heaven,* can also mean that, as it is with the righteous and the saints, so also with sinners.[23] This can be taken in two ways: either that we pray for our enemies (for what else should they be considered who willfully oppose the spread of the Christian and Catholic name?[24]), with the result that the phrase, *Thy will be done on earth as it is in heaven,* could mean that, just as the righteous do your will, so also may sinners, so that they may return to you; or, alternatively, *Thy will be done on earth as it is in heaven* could mean that each be given what is his own, which will happen at the last judgment, when the righteous will receive their reward and sinners condemnation, and the sheep will be separated from the goats.[25]

---

23. The same symbolism occurs in Cyprian, *On the Lord's Prayer* 12.
24. Since, by the time Augustine wrote this work, Catholic Christianity had been declared the official religion of the Roman Empire (in an imperial edict issued in 380), it is hard to know whom he has in mind.
25. See Mt 25:32–33.

6,23. It is also not absurd, and indeed it fits in perfectly with our faith and hope, to understand heaven and earth to mean spirit and flesh.[26] And because the Apostle says, *With my mind I serve the law of God, but in my flesh the law of sin* (Rom 7:25), we see that the will of God is accomplished in the mind, that is, in the spirit. But when death is swallowed up in victory and this mortal puts on immortality, which will occur at the resurrection of the flesh and through that transformation promised to the righteous in accordance with the preaching of the same Apostle,[27] then the will of God will be done on earth as it is in heaven; that is, just as the spirit does not resist God but follows and fulfills his will, neither will the body offer resistance to the spirit or the soul, which is presently burdened by the weakness of the body and prone to the habits of the flesh. In eternal life the plenitude of peace will consist not only in the closeness at hand of willing the good but also in the accomplishing of it. *Now, the Apostle says, the will to do good is close at hand to me, but its accomplishment is not* (Rom 7:18), for it is not yet done on earth as it is in heaven, in other words, the will of God is not yet accomplished in the flesh as it is in the spirit. For it is in our wretched state that the will of God is accomplished, when we suffer through the flesh what is due to us through the law of mortality, which our nature incurred through sinning. But the object of our prayer must be that, just as the will of God may be done on earth as it is in heaven, and just as we may delight in the law of God in our inner selves, in the same way, once our bodies have been transformed, nothing of ours may stand in the way of this delight of ours as a result of earthly sufferings or pleasures.

6,24. It by no means deviates from the truth if we accept *Thy will be done on earth as it is in heaven* as applying to the Lord Jesus Christ himself and similarly to the Church:[28] as in the man who accomplished the Father's will, so in the woman to whom he was betrothed. In fact heaven and earth may be appropriately understood as a man and woman, since by the fecundating heavens the earth becomes fruitful.[29]

7,25. The fourth petition is *Give us this day our daily bread* (Mt 6:11). *Daily bread* represents all that is necessary to sustain us in this life, and when he was issuing his precepts he said about this, *Do not be concerned about tomorrow* (Mt 6:34), which is why he adds *Give us this day*. It may also refer to the sacrament of the body of Christ, which we receive daily,[30] or to the spiritual food of which the same Lord says, *Work for the food which does not perish* (Jn 6:27), and again, *I*

---

26. For this symbolism see also Tertullian, *On Prayer* 4; Cyprian, *On the Lord's Prayer* 11.
27. See 1 Cor 15:53–54.
28. For this symbolism see also Origen, *On Prayer* 26,3.
29. The idea that heaven is masculine and earth feminine is an ancient one and is reflected in the genders of the words themselves: "heaven" is masculine in Greek and early Latin (by Augustine's time it was neuter), while "earth" is feminine in both languages. In Greek and Roman mythology Ouranos/Uranus/Coelus, the god of heaven, is married to Titaea/Thea/Rhea/Terra, the goddess of earth.
30. Augustine occasionally speaks of the daily reception of the eucharist as a practice both of the church of Hippo (see, e.g., Sermon 227) and of other churches as well (see, e.g., Letter 54,2). That daily reception was more a Western custom, or at least a custom in the local churches with which Augustine was familiar, than an Eastern one is suggested by what is said below at II,7,26, although see p. 81, note 32.

am the bread of life which has come down from heaven (Jn 6:41). We can reflect as to which of these three options is the most probable.[31] For perhaps someone may be troubled because we pray to receive what is necessary for this life, such as food and clothing, whereas the Lord himself says, *Do not be anxious about what you are to eat or what you are to wear* (Lk 12:22). Or is it possible for someone not to be anxious about the object of his prayer, since that prayer is directed with such intensity of purpose that what was said about closing the bedroom doors is entirely applicable to it, as well as what the Lord said, *Seek first the kingdom of God, and all these things will be given to you* (Mt 6:33)? He does not say, "*Seek first the kingdom of God,* and afterwards seek those things." Instead he says, *All these things will be given to you,* in other words, even if you do not ask for them. I cannot in any way see how someone could be correctly said not to seek something for which he prays to God in the most intense fashion.

7,26. But let us turn our attention to the sacrament of the Lord's body, so that many of those who live in the East and do not partake daily of the table of the Lord may not object, since this bread is spoken of as *daily*.[32] Let them remain silent and not defend their stance on this question on the grounds of Church authority, because they do this without giving offence, nor are they forbidden from doing so by those in charge of the Churches or condemned if they do not obey.[33] From this it is evident that *daily bread* is not understood in this sense in those places, for those who do not partake of it every day would stand accused of a grave sin.[34] But, as has been remarked, let us refrain from discussing them in any way; yet what must surely occur to those who reflect on it is that we have received a rule of prayer from the Lord which must not be infringed by either addition or omission. This being the case, who would be so bold as to claim that we should say the Lord's Prayer only once, or even, if a second or a third time, only until the hour when we partake of the body of the Lord, but should not pray it again afterwards for the rest of the day? For then we could not say *give us this day* what we have already received. Or could someone compel us to celebrate that sacrament at the very last part of the day?[35]

---

31. All three options are also mentioned in Tertullian, *On Prayer* 6; Cyprian, *On the Lord's Prayer* 13–14.
32. Daily reception of the eucharist was certainly not unknown in the East. See, e.g., Basil, Letter 93 (which is devoted entirely to eucharistic practices).
33. In Letter 54,2 Augustine recognizes the legitimacy of different practices in regard to the eucharist — whether of reception every day, or on certain days during the week, or only on Sunday.
34. I.e., in the places where the eucharist was not received daily, the words *daily bread* were not given a eucharistic interpretation; were it otherwise, those who were not daily recipients would be committing a serious sin.
35. Augustine's argument here is that, if one were to require a eucharistic interpretation of the words *Give us this day our daily bread*, then one would not be able to say the Lord's Prayer after having received the eucharist. The fact that this is absurd, particularly inasmuch as the eucharist was almost invariably celebrated in the morning in Augustine's time (see Letter 54,5–9), serves to buttress his contention that a non-eucharistic understanding of this phrase was completely acceptable, although his insistence that all three understandings — material,

7,27. What remains, then, is to interpret *daily bread* in a spiritual sense, as meaning the divine precepts, which we should daily reflect on and put into practice. For it is with these in mind that the Lord says, *Work for the food which does not perish* (Jn 6:27). This daily food signifies what endures as long as this temporal life, through the days that pass and give way to one another. And indeed, as long as the soul's yearning alternates between what is higher and what is lower, between things which are spiritual at one time and things which are fleshly at another, it may be compared to a person who at one time feeds on food and at another suffers the pangs of hunger, to whom bread is necessary on a daily basis, by which he is restored when hungry and raised up when faint. Hence, just as our body is restored by food in this life — that is, before that transformation[36] — because it experiences a diminution, so also our soul is restored by the food of the precepts because, as a result of its temporal yearnings, it suffers as it were from a diminution of attentiveness to God. *Give us this day* is said *as long as it is called today* (Heb 3:13), that is, in this temporal life. For, when this life is ended, we shall be replenished for ever with spiritual food, so that it will no longer be called *daily bread*, because then the passing of time, which causes the days to succeed one another and which gives rise to the term "daily," will no longer obtain. What was said, *Today if you hear his voice* (Ps 95:7), was rephrased by the Apostle in the Epistle to the Hebrews,[37] *As long as it is called today,* and that is how we must understand *Give us this day.* But if anyone wishes to understand the phrase as referring to the food that is necessary for the body or to the sacrament of the Lord's body, it is imperative to group all three together, so that, as we ask for the daily bread that is necessary for the body, we should also do so for that which is consecrated and visible and for that which is the invisible word of God.

8,28. The fifth petition follows: *And forgive us our trespasses as we forgive those who trespass against us* (Mt 6:12).[38] It is apparent that by *trespasses* sins are to be understood, either from what the same Lord says, *You shall not go out from there until you have paid back the last penny* (Mt 5:26), or from what he called those trespassers when he was told of the persons who were killed by the collapse of the tower and also of those whose blood Pilate mingled with the sacrifice.[39] For he said that people thought that they were sinners in the extreme, and he added, *Amen, I say to you, unless you do penance you also will die* (Lk 13:5). It is not that someone is being urged here to forgive people their monetary debts,

---

spiritual and sacramental — should be maintained together (see the end of II,7,27) seems to undercut this.

36. I.e., the transformation effected by the resurrection of the body.

37. There were different opinions on the Pauline authorship of the Epistle to the Hebrews in Christian antiquity. Augustine observes in *The City of God* XVI,22 that the majority held that Paul (whom he, like others, regularly calls "the Apostle") was the author, and he himself was evidently of that persuasion.

38. *Trespasses*: *debita. Trespasses* has been maintained in order to conform to the traditional translation of the Lord's Prayer, but "debts" and "debtors" generally fit better in the context and are used in what follows when it would make no sense to do otherwise.

39. See Lk 13:1.4.

therefore, but rather whatever sin another person has committed against him. For we are enjoined to forgive a monetary debt by the precept that was previously stated, *If anyone wants to take your coat and to contend in judgment with you, give him your cloak as well* (Mt 5:40).[40] Nor does it necessarily follow from this that every debtor should be forgiven the money he owes but rather the one who is so unwilling to repay it that he would even be ready to engage in litigation. *It is not fitting,* as the Apostle says, *for a servant of the Lord to engage in litigation* (2 Tm 2:24). Anyone, therefore, who either spontaneously or when summoned to do so refuses to pay his monetary debt should be forgiven it. There are two reasons why he would be unwilling to repay — either because he does not have it or because he is greedy and desirous of another's goods. Both belong within the context of neediness: the former is poverty of material goods, the latter of soul. Whoever, therefore, forgives such a person's debt is forgiving a poor person and performing a Christian act, in adherence to the teaching that he should be willingly disposed to lose what is owed him. But if he behaves in an altogether restrained and gentle manner in order to be repaid, seeking not so much interest from his money[41] as to correct the one who is certainly acting wickedly by possessing what he should repay and not repaying it, he will not only not be sinning but will even be acting greatly to his advantage, so that he will not suffer the loss of his faith while looking for profit from another's money. It follows then from this fifth petition, in which we say, *Forgive us our trespasses as we forgive those who trespass against us,* that it is referring not to money but to all the ways a person can sin against us, and consequently also by means of money. For the person who owes you money sins against you when he has the means to repay and refuses to repay. If you do not forgive such a sin, you will be unable to say, *Forgive us as we forgive,* but, if you do forgive, you will see that whoever is commanded to say such a prayer is admonished even to forgive what is monetary.

8,29. It can certainly be discussed that, when we say, *Forgive us as we forgive,* we are proven guilty of having contravened this rule if we do not forgive those who seek pardon, because we ourselves wish to be forgiven when we ask pardon from a most gracious Father. On the other hand, the precept which bids us pray for our enemies[42] does not command us to pray for those who seek pardon. For such people cannot be enemies. Yet in no way can someone claim to pray for a person whom he does not forgive. Consequently, it must be acknowledged that all sins committed against us have to be forgiven if we wish our Father to forgive

40. Both the word order and some of the words themselves differ significantly from how this verse is cited above at I,19,56.60, thus suggesting that Augustine was quoting Scripture here (as elsewhere in this work) from memory.

41. "Interest from his money": *fructum pecuniae.* Augustine merely hints here at his strong opposition to the taking of interest on borrowed money. See, e.g., Sermon 38,8. In his condemnation of usury he is consonant with both the Old Testament and the teaching of the ancient Church. See R. P. Maloney, "The Teaching of the Fathers on Usury: An Historical Study on the Development of Christian Thinking," in *Vigiliae Christianae* 27 (1973) 241–263.

42. See Mt 5:44.

those which we have committed. As for revenge, I consider that enough has been said about it previously.[43]

9,30. The sixth petition is *And bring us not into temptation* (Mt 6:13).[44] Some manuscripts have *lead*, which in my view is just as valid, for both are translations of the one Greek word *eisenegkes*.[45] Many people, when they pray, do so as follows, *Do not permit us to be led into temptation,* showing in what sense *lead* is used.[46] For of himself God does not lead, but he permits that person to be led whom in a most secret dispensation in accordance with his merit he deprives of his help. Often, also, for manifest reasons he judges worthy the one he deserts and permits to be led into temptation. It is one thing to be led into temptation and another to be tempted. For no one can be proven without temptation, whether in his own regard, as it is written, *What sorts of things does that person know who has never been tempted?* (Sir 34:9) or in someone else's, as the Apostle says, *And you did not despise your trial in my flesh* (Gal 4:14). That is how he knew that they[47] were steadfast, because out of charity they did not turn away from those trials which befell the Apostle in the flesh. For even prior to all temptations we are known to God, who knows all things before they happen.

9,31. The text that is found in Scripture, *The Lord your God is testing you, to know if you love him* (Dt 13:3), expresses a manner of speaking, inasmuch as *to know* is tantamount to saying "to make you know," just as we say that a day is joyful when it makes us joyful, and that cold weather is sluggish because it makes us sluggish, and countless other examples which are found either in common language or in the discourse of the educated or in Sacred Scripture. The heretics who are opposed to the Old Testament fail to understand this, and they think that that person should be branded with the vice of ignorance of whom it is said, *The Lord your God is testing you,* [48] as if it were not written of the Lord in the Gospel, *He said this to test him, for he himself knew what he was going to do* (Jn 6:6). For if he knew the heart of the one whom he was testing, what did he wish to see by testing him? But undoubtedly the reason for that was that he who was being tested would grow in self-knowledge and be critical of his lack of faith, once the Lord had fed the multitude on bread, since he had believed that they would not have anything to eat.[49]

---

43. The reference is probably to I,19,56–20,66 above.
44. "Temptation," "trial" and "test," in what follows, are all translations of *tentatio*, as their verb forms are of *tentare*.
45. *Bring: inferas; lead: inducas. Inducas* was used by Jerome in his Vulgate translation; Augustine consistently used *inferas*.
46. See Cyprian, *On the Lord's Prayer* 3.17. Ambrose, *On the Sacraments* 5,29, has a version differing only slightly from Cyprian's.
47. I.e., the Galatians.
48. The unnamed heretics in question (as also below at II,9,32) are the Manicheans, who looked askance at the entire Old Testament and in particular at God as he was portrayed there. In this instance they evidently understood that God was trying to find out something that he did not already know.
49. See Jn 6:7–13.

9,32. The purpose of our prayer here is not that we should not be tempted but that we should not be brought into temptation, as in the case of someone who has to be tested by fire and who does not pray that the fire not touch him but rather that he not be burned. For *the furnace tests the work of the potter, and trial by suffering those who are righteous* (Sir 27:5). And so Joseph was tested by seductive enticements but was not brought into temptation.[50] Susanna was tested but was not led or brought into temptation.[51] And there were many others of both sexes, but, above all, Job.

The heretics, enemies of the Old Testament, are fond of scoffing sacrilegiously at his remarkable steadfastness in the Lord his God, brandishing most of all the fact that Satan sought to test him.[52] They inquire of ignorant people, who are unable to understand such things, how it could be possible for Satan to speak with God. They do not grasp (and are unable to, being blinded by superstition and disputation) that God does not physically occupy space in bodily form and so is in one place and not another, or that one part of him is here and another there, but that through his greatness he is everywhere, not divided into parts but complete in every place.[53] Yet, if with their fleshly outlook they interpret the passage, *Heaven is my throne and earth my footstool* (Is 66:1), as a place to which the Lord himself refers when he says, *You shall not swear by heaven, for it is the throne of God, nor by the earth, for it is his footstool* (Mt 5:34–35), how strange is it if the devil, while on earth, stood at the feet of God and spoke in his presence?[54] For when will they succeed in understanding that there exists no soul, however perverse, although still capable of any degree of rational thought, in whose conscience God does not speak? For who has inscribed the natural law in the hearts of human beings if not God? The Apostle says of this law, *For when the gentiles who do not have the law perform by nature what the law prescribes, although they do not have the law, they are a law unto themselves; they show that the law is written in their hearts, with their conscience bearing witness and their thoughts either accusing them or excusing them among themselves, on the day when God will judge the hidden secrets of men* (Rom 2:14–16).

Consequently, whenever a soul endowed with reason, even if blinded by lustful passion, reflects and exercises its reason, whatever is true in that act of reasoning should not be attributed to it but rather to the light of truth itself by which it is enlightened, albeit tenuously and in accordance with its capacity, with the result that it perceives some vestige of truth in its act of reasoning. What is so remarkable, then, if the soul of the devil, perverted by a passionate depravity, nonetheless thought something true of the righteous man when he wished to test him, thanks to

---

50. See Gn 39:7–12.
51. See Dn 13:19–23.
52. See Jb 1:9–12.
53. The Manicheans believed that God was material, albeit brilliant and massive, and hence confined to a place. See, e.g., *Confessions* III,7,12; V,10,19–20.
54. See Jb 1:7.

the voice of God himself—that is, that he should be presented as having listened to the voice of Truth itself[55]—whereas whatever is false is attributed to that passion from which the devil's name is derived?[56] As the Lord and ruler of all, however, and as the disposer of all things in accordance with the merits of each, God has often spoken, whether to the good or to the wicked, even by way of the bodily and visible creation, as in the case of angels who have appeared in human guise,[57] and in that of the prophets who declared, "The Lord says these things." What is so remarkable, then, if, although not in thought itself but certainly by means of some creature fitted for such a purpose, God is said to have spoken with the devil?

9,33. Nor should they suppose that it was due to the merit of his dignity or of his righteousness, as it were, that God spoke to him, because he spoke to an angelic soul, although stupid and grasping, as if he were speaking to a stupid and grasping human soul. Or let them explain how God spoke to that rich man, whose utterly grasping foolishness he wished to censure with the words, *Fool, this night your soul is demanded of you. And the things that you have prepared, whose will they be?* (Lk 12:20) The Lord does indeed say this in the Gospel, to which the heretics, willingly or unwillingly, submit their necks.[58] If, then, they are so concerned about Satan's request to God to put a righteous man to the test, I am not going to explain why this took place, but I am going to demand that they explain what was said by the Lord himself to his disciples in the Gospel, *Behold, Satan is seeking to sift you like wheat* (Lk 22:31), and what he said to Peter, *But I have prayed that your faith may not fail* (Lk 22:32). Once they explain this to me, they will be explaining to themselves at the same time what they are asking of me. But if they cannot explain this, they should not be so bold as to find fault rashly with what they read in another book and what they do not censure when they read it in the Gospel.

9,34. Tests occur through Satan, then, not by his power but by the Lord's permission, either to punish people for their sins or to prove and test them through God's mercy. And there is a vast difference in the kind of test a person falls into. For Judas, who sold the Lord,[59] fell into one that was different than that of Peter, when in panic he denied the Lord.[60] There are tests of a human kind, I believe, when a person of good intentions nonetheless fails in carrying out some plan through human frailty or is provoked against a brother in his zeal to correct him, a little more than Christian serenity demands. Speaking of these things, the Apostle says, *Let not temptation take hold of you if it is not human*, although the same Apostle says, *God is faithful and will not allow you to be tempted beyond what you can bear, but with the temptation he will also provide a way out, so that you can endure*

---

55. See Jb 1:8; 2:3.
56. It is uncertain what Augustine might have meant here, unless perhaps he is referring to Jn 8:44, where the devil is characterized as the father of lies.
57. Or, less likely, "who have appeared before the eyes of men."
58. "The heretics" are, once again, Manicheans, who were more accepting of the New Testament than of the Old.
59. See Mt 26:14–16,50.
60. See Mt 26:69–75.

it (1 Cor 10:13). In these words he clearly shows that we should not pray so as not to be tempted but so as not to be led into temptation. We are being led, however, if we are unable to bear whatever befalls us. But when dangerous temptations arise from temporal things, whether prosperous or adverse, and ruin could result if we are brought or led into them, the person who is not seduced by the attraction of prosperity will not be broken by the burden of adversity.

9,35. The last and seventh petition is *But deliver us from evil* (Mt 6:13). For we must pray not only that we may not be led into the evil that we have avoided, which is the prayer of the sixth petition, but that we may also be delivered from that which we have been led into. Once this has happened, nothing fearful will remain, and no temptation at all will frighten us. Yet we must not hope that this can happen in this life, as long as we bear about this mortal condition into which we have been led through the serpent's wiles,[61] but our hope must be that it can happen in the future, and this is the hope which is not seen. Speaking of this, the Apostle says, *Hope which is seen is not hope* (Rom 8:24). But we must not despair of the wisdom which is granted the servants of God in this life. For such is its nature that with the utmost vigilance we should flee from what, thanks to the Lord's revelation, we understand must be fled from, and with the most ardent charity we should desire what, thanks to the Lord's revelation, we understand must be desired. For, when the last vestige of this mortal condition is laid aside through death itself, at the appropriate time there will be perfected in every part of man the blessedness that was begun in this life, for the seizing and procuring of which every effort is now expended.

10,36. But there is a distinction among these seven petitions that should be examined and discussed. For, since our life is now lived in the present and eternal life is an object of hope, and since those things which are eternal rank first in dignity, although it is by means of temporal actions that we begin to arrive at them, the carrying out of the first three petitions, therefore, starts in this life, which unfolds in this world. For the hallowing of God's name has its beginnings in the very coming of the Lord of humility; and the coming of his kingdom, in which he will come in glory, will be revealed not when time is finished but at the end of time; and the perfect accomplishment of his will on earth as in heaven—whether you understand heaven and earth as the righteous and the sinners, or the spirit and the flesh, or the Lord and the Church, or all together—will be complete when our blessed state attains perfection, which will be at the end of time; yet all three will remain forever. For the hallowing of God's name is eternal, and his reign will have no end, and eternal life is promised as the perfection of our blessedness. Those three will therefore remain perfect and complete in that life which is promised to us.

10,37. But the remaining four petitions, in my view, pertain to this temporal life. The first of them is *Give us this day our daily bread*. By the very fact that it is called *daily bread*—whether it is to be understood as spiritual or as sacramental

---

61. See Gn 3:4–5,13.

or as visible nourishment—it pertains to this world, which the Lord called *this day*, not because spiritual food is not eternal but because the bread which Scripture calls *daily* is presented to the soul either by the spoken word or by certain temporal signs. None of these will exist then, when everyone will be taught by God[62] and will not hint at the ineffable light of truth through bodily movements but will drink deeply from it in purity of mind. And it is very likely referred to as bread and not as drink because bread becomes nourishment through being broken and consumed, just as the Scriptures feed the soul when they are opened and examined, whereas drink, taken as it is found, passes into the body, with the result that in this present time bread is truth, since it is called *daily bread*, while then it will be drink, because no effort will be required in examining and discoursing, breaking and digesting as it were, but it will only be necessary to drink deeply of the pure and translucent truth. And now sins are forgiven us, and now we forgive them, which is the second of these four petitions, but then there will be no forgiveness of sins, because there will be no sins. And trials trouble this temporal life, but they will not exist when what has been said is complete, *You shall hide them in the shelter of your face* (Ps 31:20). And the evil from which we desire to be delivered, as well as the very deliverance from evil, belongs indeed to this life, a mortality which we have merited through the justice of God and from which, through his mercy, we shall be delivered.

11,38. It seems to me as well that these petitions, which number seven, correspond to the number seven from which this whole sermon proceeds. For if through the fear of God the poor in spirit are blessed, because theirs is the kingdom of heaven, let us pray that the name of God may be hallowed among men with a chaste and enduring fear for all time. If it is through piety that the meek are blessed, because they will inherit the earth, let us pray that his kingdom may come, whether in ourselves, so that we may become meek and offer him no resistance, or from heaven to earth in the glorious splendor of the Lord's coming, when we shall rejoice and be found worthy of praise, as the Lord says, *Come, blessed of my Father, receive the kingdom which has been prepared for you since the foundation of the world* (Mt 25:34). For *in the Lord,* says the prophet, *shall my soul find praise; let the meek hear and be glad* (Ps 34:2). If it is through knowledge that those who are sorrowful are blessed, because they shall be comforted, let us pray that his *will may be done on earth as it is in heaven*, because when the body, insofar as it is earth, is at one with the spirit, insofar as it is heaven, in total and perfect peace, we shall not be sorrowful. For the struggle of this present age consists in nothing else than when they conflict with one another and compel us to say, *I see another law in my members, opposed to the law of my mind* (Rom 7:13), and to acknowledge our struggle with a tearful cry, *Miserable man that I am! Who will free me from the body of this death?* (Rom 7:24) If it is through fortitude that those who hunger and thirst for righteousness are blessed, because they shall be satisfied, let us pray

---

62. See Jn 6:45.

that our daily bread may be given to us today, and that, supported and sustained by it, we may be able to arrive at that complete satiety. If it is through counsel that the merciful are blessed, because they shall obtain mercy, let us forgive the trespasses of those who trespass against us, and let us pray that ours may be forgiven us. If it is through understanding that the pure of heart are blessed, because they shall see God, let us pray not to be led into temptation, so that we may not have a divided heart, inasmuch as we do not yearn for the one good to which we may refer everything that we do, but simultaneously pursue temporal and eternal things. For temptations which arise from things that, humanly speaking, appear to be oppressive and ruinous exert no power over us, provided that those things resulting from the allurements of what people consider to be good and praiseworthy do not exert such power. If it is through wisdom that the peacemakers are blessed, because they shall be called sons of God, let us pray that we may be freed from evil, for this very freedom will make us free,[63] that is, sons of God, so that we may cry out in the spirit of adoption, *Abba, Father!* (Gal 4:6)

11,39. But we must not be negligent and overlook the fact that, in all of these phrases in which the Lord commanded us to pray, he judged to be particularly worthy of emphasis the one which pertains to the forgiveness of sins, by means of which he wanted us to be merciful and which is the sole counsel for avoiding misery. For in none of the other phrases do we pray as if we were bargaining with God, for we say, *Forgive us, as we forgive.* If we are not faithful to this bargain, our whole prayer is fruitless. This is what he says: *For if you forgive people their sins, your Father who is in heaven will also forgive you yours. But if you do not forgive people, neither will your Father forgive you your sins.* (Mt 6:14–15)

12,40. There follows a precept on fasting which pertains to the same purity of heart that is now under discussion. For in this practice great care must be taken lest any ostentation and desire for human praise should creep in, which would result in a divided heart and would prevent it from being pure and undivided, so as to be able to focus on God. *But when you fast,* he says, *do not be sad like the hypocrites; for they distort their face in order that people may see that they are fasting. Amen, I say to you, they have received their reward. But when you fast, anoint your heads and wash your faces, so that people may not see that you are fasting, but your Father who is in secret; and your Father who sees what is in secret will repay you.* (Mt 6:16–18) It is clear from these precepts that our attention must be focused completely on joys of an interior kind, so that we may not search for an external reward and be conformed to this world and so forfeit the promise of interior blessedness, which is so much more stable and solid, by which God has chosen us *to be conformed to the image of his Son* (Rom 8:29).

12,41. It should be very carefully noted in this passage that there can be pridefulness not only in the splendor and glamour of bodily things but also in those

---

63. "For this very freedom will make us free": *ipsa enim liberatio liberos nos faciet.* Augustine surely intended the pun which arises from the fact that *liberos* means both "free" and "children," and especially "sons."

which are dirty and mournful and all the more insidious when they deceive under the pretext of the service of God. Someone, therefore, who shines out because of an exaggerated cult of the body or of clothing or of other things is easily exposed by the very existence of such ostentation as a follower of the world, and he deceives no one by his false display of holiness. But if, in his profession of the Christian faith, someone attracts the attention of others through conspicuous squalor and filthiness, and when he does so freely and does not allow it to happen through necessity, it can be deduced from the rest of his behavior whether he is acting out of contempt for excessive refinement or because of some kind of ambition, because the Lord instructed us to beware of wolves in sheep's clothing.[64] *By their fruits,* he said, *you will know them* (Mt 7:15–16). For when, as a result of some trials, these very things are taken from them, or what they have acquired or hope to acquire by this apparel is denied them, then it inevitably becomes clear whether the person is a wolf in sheep's clothing or a sheep in its own. Consequently, a Christian ought not to attract people's attention through excessive adornment because impostors also often assume modest and basic attire so as to mislead the unwary, for the sheep must not discard their own skins, even if at times wolves clothe themselves in them.

12,42. People frequently inquire as to the meaning of the words, *But when you fast, anoint your heads and wash your faces, so that people may not see that you are fasting.* Although, as is customary, we wash our face daily, no one with good reason has ever taught that we should also anoint our heads when we fast. But if everyone acknowledges that this is very unseemly, the command regarding the anointing of the head and the washing of the face must be understood as referring to the inner person. Anointing the head, therefore, pertains to joy,[65] and washing the face to purity; and so whoever anoints his head is rejoicing inwardly in his mind and with his reason. For this reason we correctly understand the head to represent what predominates in the soul, by which it is clear that the other aspects of a person are governed and directed. And this is accomplished by the person who does not seek delight in what is external, deriving joy from the praises of human beings according to the outlook of the flesh. For the flesh, which ought to be subordinate, can in no sense be the head of human nature in its totality. *No one*, indeed, *ever hates his own flesh* (Eph 5:29), as the Apostle says when he gives instructions on how one's wife must be loved, but the head of the woman is the man, and the head of the man is Christ.[66] Therefore, whoever desires his head to be anointed in accordance with this teaching should by his fasting rejoice inwardly, since by his very fasting he is turning away from the pleasures of the world in order to be subject to Christ. In like manner he will also wash his face, meaning that he will purify the heart by which he will see God, without the imposition of a veil polluted

---

64. Similar concern is expressed in Jerome, Letter 22,27.
65. Augustine elsewhere associates joy with oil (see, e.g., *Confessions* V,13,23; *Exposition of Psalm* 22,5), but it is somewhat surprising that he does not cite obvious scriptural support for this interpretation here — e.g., Pss 23:5; 45:7; 133:2.
66. See 1 Cor 11:3.

by the filth of weakness; he will be firm and stable because he is pure and single-minded. *Wash yourselves,* it says, *make yourselves clean; remove the wrongdoing from your souls and from my sight* (Is 1:16). We must wash our face of those filthy deeds which offend the gaze of God. *For we, with unveiled face, reflect the glory of the Lord and shall be transformed into the same likeness* (2 Cor 3:18).

12,43. The thought of the necessities pertaining to this life also often wounds and sullies our inner eye and for the most part divides our heart, so that, in the case of those matters where we seem to engage righteously with people, we are not behaving with the kind of heart demanded by God, that is, not because we love them but because we want to derive some benefit from them for the sake of the needs of this present life. We ought, then, to act well towards them for the sake of their eternal salvation and not for the sake of our own temporal benefit. May the Lord, then, turn our heart to his testimonies and not to gain.[67] *For the aim of the precept is charity coming from a pure heart and a good conscience and a faith that is genuine* (1 Tm 1:5). For the person who takes thought for a brother because of some necessity pertaining to this life is not doing so in charity, since he is putting his own interests first and not those of his brother, whom he must love as himself. In fact he is not even pursuing his own interests, since his behavior results in a divided heart which prevents him from seeing God, in whose vision alone is true and enduring blessedness found.

13,44. With good reason, then, he who insists on the purification of our heart goes on to say and commands, *Do not store up treasure for yourselves on earth, where moth and rust destroy, and where thieves break in and steal, but lay up treasure for yourselves in heaven, where neither moth nor rust destroy, and where thieves do not break in and steal. For where your treasure is, there also will your heart be.* (Mt 6:19–21) So, if one's heart is on the earth, meaning that if someone does something from that heart in order to gain an earthly advantage, how can what is wallowing about on the earth be pure? But if it is in heaven it will be pure, because all that is heavenly is pure. For a thing becomes debased when it is mixed with something of an inferior nature, although in its own kind it is not debased, because even gold mixed with pure silver is debased. Consequently our soul becomes debased by the desire for earthly attractions, although the earth is itself beautiful in its own kind and according to its own arrangement. In this context I would take heaven to mean what is not corporeal, for everything corporeal is to be understood as the earth. Whoever lays up treasure for himself in heaven—in that heaven, then, of which it is said, *The heaven of heavens is the Lord's* (Ps 115:16), that is, in the spiritual firmament—ought to despise the world in its totality. For we must not locate and set our treasure and our heart in what is transitory but in what remains forever, because *heaven and earth will pass away* (Mt 24:35).

13,45. And he clearly demonstrates here that everything he commands relates to the purification of the heart when he states, *Your eye is the lamp of your body.*

---

67. See Ps 119:36.

If, then, your eye is undivided, your whole body will be full of light, but if your eye is evil, your whole body will be darkness. If, then, the light which is in you is darkness, how great is the darkness? (Mt 6:22–23) This passage is to be seen in such a way that we may understand that all our actions are pure and pleasing in the sight of God if they are done from an undivided heart, that is, with our intention fixed on the sublime goal of charity, because *the fullness of the Law* is also *charity* (Rom 13:10). We must interpret the eye, therefore, as the intention underlying everything that we do. And if it is pure and upright and looks at what should be looked at, all our actions that are done in accordance with it will necessarily be good. All these actions he referred to as the whole body, because the Apostle also describes our members as the kinds of works that he disapproves of and commands to be put to death, when he says, *Therefore, put to death your members which are on the earth: fornication, impurity, greed,* and other things of this kind (Col 3:5).

13,46. It is not what a person does that must be examined, therefore, but the intention informing his action. For this is the light dwelling within us, because by this it is manifest to us that what we are doing is being done with a good intention, *for everything that is made manifest is light* (Eph 5:13). In fact, those actions pertaining to human society which proceed from us have an uncertain outcome, and hence he called them *darkness.* For I cannot tell when I offer money to a needy person who requests it what he is going to do or undergo as a result, and it can happen that he may either do something bad with it or undergo something bad because of it which I, when I gave it, did not wish to happen, nor did I give it with this intention. And so, if I did something with a good intention that was known to me when I did it and is therefore called light, the thing that I did, irrespective of its outcome, is light. But the outcome, since it is uncertain and unknown, is called darkness. But if I acted with an evil intention, even that light itself is darkness. For it is called light because each person knows the intention with which he acts, including when it is with an evil intention. But that very light is darkness because the intention is not undivided and directed to what is above, but instead it descends to what is inferior and casts a shadow, as it were, because of a divided heart. *If then the light which is in you is darkness, how great is the darkness?* This means that, if the very intention of the heart by which you do what you do and which is known to you is befouled and blinded by the desire for earthly and temporal things, how much more is the deed itself—whose outcome is uncertain—foul and dark. In fact, even if what you do, based on an intention that is not upright and pure, turns out to someone's advantage, the way you acted and not how it benefited the other person will be imputed to you.

14,47. The words that follow, *No one can serve two masters,* are to be referred to that same intention, which he goes on to explain when he says, *for he will either hate one and love the other, or endure one and despise the other.* These words need to be carefully examined. He proceeds to show who these two masters are when he says, *You cannot serve God and mammon* (Mt 6:24). *Mammon* is said to be the Hebrew word for "riches."[68] The Punic word agrees with this, for in Punic "gain" is referred to as *mammon*.[69] But whoever serves mammon in fact serves him who, because of his wickedness, has been placed over all earthly goods and is named by the Lord as the ruler of this world.[70] *A person, therefore, will either hate one and love the other,* who is God, *or he will endure one and despise the other.* For whoever serves mammon endures a hard and cruel taskmaster; caught up in his own evil desires, he becomes subject to the devil yet does not love him – for who would love the devil? – but endures him. It is like being in a large household, where someone becomes involved with another person's maidservant and endures servitude because of his passion, even if he has no affection for the one whose maidservant she is.

14,48. *But he will despise the other,* says the Lord, not hate him. Practically no one in conscience can hate God,[71] but he can despise him—that is, not fear him—when, so to speak, he rests secure in his own uprightness. The Holy Spirit counsels against such negligence and reckless security when he says through the prophet, *My son, do not add sin upon sin, and say, The mercy of God is great, being unaware that God's patience calls you to repentance* (Sir 5:5–6). For what greater mercy can be called to mind than that of him who forgives all the sins of those who have turned to him and makes the wild olive share in the fruitfulness of the olive? And whose severity is as great as that of him who did not spare the natural branches but cut them off because of their infidelity?[72] Yet anyone who wishes to love God and to be careful not to offend him should not think that he can serve two masters, and he should rid the upright intention of his heart of all duplicity. In this way he will *think of the Lord in goodness and seek him with an undivided heart* (Wis 1:1).

15,49. *Therefore,* he says, *do not be anxious in your soul about what you should eat, nor how you should clothe your body* (Mt 6:25), lest perhaps, although superfluities may not be sought after, the heart may be divided because of necessities, and in seeking them our intention may be perverted. The reason is that, when we perform a deed on the grounds of mercy, that is, when we wish to appear to be acting on another person's behalf, we may have our own advantage in mind rather than the other person's benefit, and we may not seem to ourselves to be sinning inasmuch as we are seeking to obtain not what is superfluous but what is necessary. The Lord, however, is instructing us to bear in mind that, when God created us and endowed us with a body and soul, he gave us much more than food and clothing, and he does not want anxiety for these things to result in a divided heart. He says,

---

68. See Origen, *Fragment* 129 *on Matthew.*
69. Punic was the language native to North Africa in Augustine's time, although it disappeared a few centuries later. He defends the Punic language and Punic literature against a detractor in Letter 17,2.
70. See Jn 12:31; 14:30.
71. In *Revisions* I,19 (18),8 Augustine cites Ps 74:23 (*the pride of those who hate you*) to show that he was mistaken in saying that no one could in conscience hate God.
72. See Rom 11:17–20.

Is not the soul worth more than food? so that you may understand that he who gave the soul will much more easily give food, *and the body more than clothing?* (Mt 6:25)—that is, of much greater worth, so that you may likewise understand that he who gave the body will much more unhesitatingly give clothing.

15,50. In this regard the question is usually asked whether that food pertains to the soul, since the soul is incorporeal but food is material. But we know that in this passage the soul stands for that life whose support is bodily nourishment. In accordance with this meaning there is also the saying, *Whoever loves his soul will lose it* (Mt 16:25). Unless we understand that this applies to this life, which we must lose for the sake of the kingdom of God (which it is clear that the martyrs were able to do), this precept will contradict the words that state, *What does it profit a man were he to gain the whole world but suffer the loss of his own soul?* (Mt 16:26)

15,51. *Consider,* he says, *the birds of the air, that they neither sow nor reap nor gather into barns, and your heavenly Father feeds them. Are you not of more value than these?* (Mt 6:26) That is, you are more precious. For in truth a rational animal, such as man is, has been given a more elevated status in the natural order than irrational animals, such as birds are. *Which of you,* he says, *for all your efforts is able to add a single cubit to his stature? And why are you anxious about clothing?* (Mt 6:27–28) In other words, your body can be clothed by the providence of him through whose power and sovereignty it has transpired that it has been brought to its present stature. The fact that your body has attained its present stature and is not due to your own solicitude can be deduced from the fact that, if you are solicitous and wish to add a single cubit to your stature, you cannot do so. Therefore leave concern for clothing the body to him through whose solicitude you see that you possess a body of such stature.

15,52. It was also necessary that a teaching be given for clothing, just as it was for food. And so he goes on to say, *Consider how the lilies of the field grow; they neither labor nor spin. Yet I tell you that not even Solomon in all his glory was clothed like one of these. Now, if God so clothes the grass of the field which is here today and tomorrow is cast into the furnace, how much more you of little faith?* (Mt 6:28–30) But these teachings are not to be treated as allegories, so that we would ask what the birds of the air or the lilies of the field mean, for they have been presented in order that greater realities may become apparent from lesser ones. It is the same with the judge who neither feared God nor respected man and yet acceded to the widow's incessant pleading that he take note of her case, not out of pity or kindness but lest he be exhausted,[73] for in no way is that unjust judge an allegory of the person of God.[74] However, insofar as God, who is good and just,

---

73. See Lk 18:2–5.

74. Augustine, one of the greatest allegorists of the ancient Church, here set limits to what could be allegorized. The allegory that he so strongly rejected, however, seems not to have been unheard of. Cardinal Angelo Mai, a nineteenth-century philologist, mistakenly attributed to Cyril of Alexandria, via the eleventh-century Byzantine bishop Theophylact, the opinion that the unjust judge was an allegory of God. See *A Commentary on the Gospel of Saint Luke by Saint Cyril of Alexandria*, trans. by R. Payne Smith (Oxford 1859; reprinted 1983) 479, note 1. But admitting

cares for those who pray to him, the Lord in this instance wanted it to be inferred that even an unjust person cannot disdain those who assail him with their incessant requests, even if for the sake of avoiding exhaustion.

16,53. *Therefore,* he says, *do not be anxious, and say, What shall we eat or what shall we drink or how shall we be clothed? For the gentiles seek all these things. Your Father knows that you need all these things. Seek first the kingdom and the righteousness of God and all these things will be given to you as well* (Mt 6:31–33). He points out here in the clearest possible manner that these things, although necessary, are not to be desired as though they were goods for us of the sort that for their sake we would do well whatever we do. He explained the difference between the good, which is to be pursued, and the necessary, which is to be used, when he said, *Seek first the kingdom and the righteousness of God, and all these things will be given to you as well* (Mt 6:33). Therefore, the kingdom and the righteousness of God is our good, which must be aspired to and set as our goal, for whose sake we do whatever we do. Yet, since we do battle in this life in order to arrive at that kingdom, we cannot live this life without these necessities. *These things will be given to you as well,* he says, but *seek first the kingdom and the righteousness of God.* Since he said that this was *first,* he indicated that the other is to be sought afterwards, in terms not of time but of dignity: the one as our good, the other as necessary for us, but necessary in view of that good.

16,54. For example, we should not proclaim the Gospel so that we may eat but rather eat so that we may proclaim the Gospel. For, if we proclaim the Gospel so that we may eat, we are valuing the Gospel more cheaply than food, and our good will now consist in eating but our necessity in proclaiming the Gospel. The Apostle himself forbids this when he states that it is lawful for him, and indeed permitted by the Lord, for those who proclaim the Gospel to earn their livelihood from the Gospel; in other words, they should derive from the Gospel what is necessary for this life but not misuse this authority.[75] For there were many who sought an occasion to acquire and sell the Gospel. The Apostle, in his desire to deprive them of this occasion, supported himself by the work of his own hands.[76] Referring to these people elsewhere, he says, *That I may deprive of an occasion those who seek an occasion* (2 Cor 11:12). Even if, as in the case of those other and good apostles, he could gain his livelihood from the Gospel with the Lord's permission, he did not postulate food to be the purpose of proclaiming the Gospel but instead located the purpose of that very food itself within the Gospel; in other words, as I have observed above, he did not proclaim the Gospel to gain food and whatever else was necessary but availed himself of the latter so as to carry out the former, lest he proclaim the Gospel not willingly but from necessity. For he disapproves of this when he says, *Do you not know that those who minister in the temple eat*

that an attribution is mistaken does not account for the existence of the mistakenly attributed opinion.

75. See 1 Cor 9:12–14.
76. See Acts 20:34.

what comes from the temple, and those who serve at the altar have a share in what comes from the altar? In the same way, the Lord ordained that those who proclaim the Gospel are to live from the Gospel. But I did not avail myself of any of these things. (1 Cor 9:13–15) He points out here that this was permitted and not commanded; otherwise he could stand accused of contravening a precept of the Lord.

He goes on to say, *I have not written these things so that they may be thus in my regard. It is better for me to die than to have anyone deprive me of my boast.* (1 Cor 9:15) He said this because he had now decided, on account of those who were seeking an occasion, to earn his livelihood by his own hands. *For, if I proclaim the Gospel,* he adds, *it is not a boast on my part* (1 Cor 9:16); in other words, if I proclaim the Gospel *so that they may be thus in my regard,* that is, if I proclaim the Gospel to acquire those things, I am locating the purpose of the Gospel in food and drink and clothing. But why is this not a boast on his part? *For,* he declares, *necessity is laid upon me* (1 Cor 9:16), that is, that I should proclaim the Gospel, because I do not have the means to live or to gain temporal advantage from preaching eternal truths. So the proclamation of the Gospel entails necessity, not free choice. *Alas for me,* he declares, *if I do not proclaim the Gospel* (1 Cor 9:16). But how should he proclaim the Gospel? By positing his reward in the Gospel itself and in the kingdom of God, for in this way he can willingly and without constraint proclaim the Gospel. *For, if I do it willingly,* he says, *I have my reward; if I do it unwillingly, a charge has been entrusted to me* (1 Cor 9:17). By this he means, if I am compelled to preach the Gospel through the lack of those things necessary for temporal life, others, who love the Gospel because of my preaching, will have the reward of the Gospel through me, but I shall not gain any reward, because I love not the Gospel but rather its recompense as found in those temporal things. But it would be outrageous if someone were to act as a minister of the Gospel not as a son but as a slave to whom a charge has been entrusted and who dispenses what belongs to another, while he himself obtains nothing apart from his means to live, which is something that is granted externally, not as a share in the kingdom but to support a wretched slavery. However, he describes himself elsewhere as a steward.[77] For, once a slave has been numbered among the sons through adoption, he can faithfully dispense to his fellow participants the same patrimony in which he as a coheir has merited a share. But when he now states, *If I do it unwillingly, a charge has been entrusted to me,* he wants such a steward to be understood as one who dispenses what belongs to another, from which he himself gains nothing.

16,55. Therefore, anything that is sought for the sake of something else is undoubtedly inferior to the object for which it is sought. And so the object for whose sake you are seeking something else comes first, not the thing for whose sake you are seeking it. Consequently, if we are seeking the Gospel and the kingdom of God for the sake of food, we are giving food priority and then afterwards the kingdom of God; the upshot is that, if there were no lack of food, we would

---

77.　See 1 Cor 4:1.

not seek the kingdom of God. Therefore, to seek food first and then the kingdom of God is tantamount to giving the former first place and the latter second. If, however, we seek food in order to possess the kingdom of God, we are doing what has been said: *Seek first the kingdom and the righteousness of God, and all these things will be given to you as well.*

17,56. If we seek first the kingdom and the righteousness of God, that is, if we have laid aside all other considerations so that we seek those other things for the sake of this, we should not be anxious that we would lack the necessities of this life for the sake of the kingdom of God. For the Lord said earlier, *Your Father knows that you need all these things* (Mt 6:32). And so when he had said, *Seek first the kingdom and the righteousness of God,* he did not add, "Then seek these other things, even though they may be necessary," but he said, *These things will be given to you as well,* meaning that they will follow if you seek them without imposing any obstacle of yours, lest in seeking them you be torn in different directions or establish dual goals, desiring both the kingdom of God for its own sake and also those things which are necessary. Seek rather the latter for the sake of the former, and as a result you will not lack them, because you cannot serve two masters. The person who seeks both the kingdom of God as a surpassing good and these temporal things is trying to serve two masters. For he cannot have an undivided eye and serve the one Lord God unless he accepts all the other things, if they are necessary, for the sake of this one thing, that is, for the sake of the kingdom of God.

Just as all those in military service receive provisions and pay, so also all those who proclaim the Gospel receive food and clothing. But not all who serve in the military do so for the sake of the wellbeing of the state but for the sake of what they receive; likewise, not all who serve God do so for the sake of the wellbeing of the Church but for the sake of these temporal things, which they acquire as provisions and pay, or for the sake of both one and the other. But it has been already said, *You cannot serve two masters.* Therefore only with an undivided heart, for the sake of the kingdom of God, should we do good to all, but in so doing we should not think of the reward of temporal things either by itself or in conjunction with the kingdom of God. The Lord included all these temporal things under the term *tomorrow* when he said, *Do not be anxious, then, about tomorrow* (Mt 6:34). For the morrow can be spoken of only within time, where the future follows the past. When we perform a good deed, therefore, let us think not of what is temporal but of what is eternal. That deed will then be good and perfect. *For tomorrow,* he says, *will be anxious for itself* (Mt 6:34); that is, take food or drink or clothing when it is appropriate, when necessity itself compels you to do so. These things will be at your disposal, because our Father knows that we need them all. For, he says, *Its own trouble is sufficient for the day* (Mt 6:34); that is, what necessity compels us to use of such things is sufficient, which in my judgment is called *trouble* because it is a punishment as far as we are concerned, for it belongs to the infirmity and

mortality which we have merited by sinning.[78] Do not, then, increase the gravity
of the punishment pertaining to this temporal necessity so that you not only suffer
the lack of these things but even enlist in God's service in order to meet this need.

17,57. At this point we need to be very careful lest perhaps, whenever we notice
a particular servant of God acting with foresight so that he does not lack these
necessities either for himself or for those entrusted to his care, we judge him as
acting contrary to the Lord's precept and as being anxious about the morrow. For
even the Lord himself, to whom the angels ministered,[79] when he deputed one of
his servants to procure these necessities, deigned to have purses with money that
would be available to meet whatever needs arose, although he did this by way of
example lest anyone be scandalized afterwards. The keeper and robber of these
purses, as Scripture records, was Judas, who also betrayed him.[80] The apostle Paul
might also appear to have been preoccupied about the morrow when he wrote,
*Now, concerning the collections for the saints: as I directed the churches in
Galatia, so you also are to do. On the first day of the week, each of you is to put
something aside and store it up, depending on his prosperity, so that collections
need not be taken up when I come. But when I arrive, I shall send those whom you
approve by letter to carry your gift to Jerusalem. But if it seems advisable that I
should go as well, they will go with me. I shall come to you when I pass through
Macedonia, for I am going through Macedonia. Perhaps I shall stay with you and
even remain for the winter, so that you can speed me on my way whenever I do go.
For I do not want to see you now just in passing, for I hope to spend some time
with you, if the Lord permits it. But I shall stay in Ephesus until Pentecost.* (1 Cor
16:1–8) It is likewise recorded in the Acts of the Apostles how things necessary
for sustenance were procured for the future in view of the impending famine. For
this is what we read: *Now in those days prophets came down from Jerusalem to
Antioch, and there was great rejoicing. When we had assembled, one of them
called Agabus stood up and foretold through the Holy Spirit that a great famine
would take place throughout the world, and this happened under Claudius. On
learning this, the disciples decided, everyone according to his ability, to send
relief to the brethren who were living in Judea, and they did so, sending it to the
elders by the hand of Barnabas and Saul.* (Acts 11:27–30) And when the apostle
Paul was about to embark, the necessities which they gave to him by way of gifts
seemed more than provisions for a single day.[81] He also wrote, *Let him who used
to steal no longer steal, but instead let him work honestly with his own hands, so
that he may have something to give to the person in need* (Eph 4:28). It may appear
to those who misunderstand him that Paul is not following the precept of the Lord,
who said, *Consider the birds of the air, that they neither sow nor reap nor gather*

---

78. In *Revisions* I,19 (18),9 Augustine qualifies this thought by noting that he had forgotten that the
    first parents were created to make use of food even in paradise itself.
79. See Mt 4:11 par.
80. See Jn 12:6.
81. See Acts 28:10.

into barns, and, *Consider how the lilies of the field grow; they neither labor nor spin* (Mt 6:28), when he instructs such people to work with their own hands, so that they may be in a position to give to others. And when he often remarks of himself that he worked with his own hands, lest he become a burden to anyone,[82] and it is recorded of him that he associated with Aquila, who had a trade similar to his own, so that they could work together to earn a living,[83] he does not appear to have imitated the birds of the air and the lilies of the field.

It is sufficiently clear from these and other passages of Scripture that our Lord does not disapprove if someone acquires these things in human fashion but rather if someone enrolls in God's service because of them, so that in his doings he is focused not on the kingdom of God but on the acquisition of such things.

17,58. This entire precept, then, is reducible to this rule, that even in providing for these things we must be thinking of the kingdom of God, but in the service of the kingdom of God we should give no thought to them. And consequently, even if on occasion they are not available because God often permits it thus as part of our training, they not only do not weaken our resolve but even confirm it as tested and tried. For in fact, as the Apostle says, *We glory in our trials in the knowledge that trials produce patience, patience endurance, and endurance hope; but hope does not deceive, because the charity of God has been poured into our hearts through the Holy Spirit, who has been given to us* (Rom 5:3–5). When he reflects on his trials and ordeals, the same Apostle recalls that he suffered not only in prisons and shipwrecks and in many afflictions of this sort but also in hunger and thirst, in cold and nakedness.[84] When we read this, we must not think that the Lord was wavering in his promises, so that the Apostle suffered hunger and thirst and nakedness while seeking the kingdom and the righteousness of God, since we have been told, *Seek first the kingdom and the righteousness of God, and all these things will be given to you as well.* That physician, to whom we have entrusted ourselves totally and once and for all and from whom we have the guarantee of the present and the future life, knows well that these things are like remedies, and sometimes he bestows them and sometimes he removes them, according to what he judges is beneficial for us. And indeed he guides and directs us when we should be consoled and when we should be tried in this life, and when we should be established and confirmed after this life in perpetual rest. For a man who on occasion takes provender away from his beast of burden is not relinquishing his care for it but is doing this, instead, in order to care for it.

18,59. And, whenever such things are either procured for the future or, if there is no reason for you to use them, laid up in reserve, because it is unclear what the intention might be, since it could arise from an undivided heart or from a divided heart, he fittingly added in this place, *Do not judge, lest you be judged; for by the judgment with which you judge you yourselves will be judged; and by*

---

82. See 1 Thes 2:9.
83. See Acts 18:2–3.
84. See 2 Cor 11:23–27.

the measure with which you have measured it will be measured out to you (Mt 7:1–2). I believe that nothing else is being imposed upon us in this passage save to place a favorable interpretation on those actions where the intention behind them is doubtful. The phrase, *By their fruits you shall know them* (Mt 7:16), refers to what is manifest and cannot have been engaged in with a good intention, such as debauchery or blasphemy or robbery or drunkenness and the like, and we are permitted to pass judgment on these things because the Apostle says, *For what concern of mine is it to judge outsiders? Is it not those who are within that you should judge?* (1 Cor 5:12)

With regard to types of food, since any kind of foods adapted for human use can be eaten indifferently without greed and with a good intention and an undivided heart, the same Apostle forbids those who ate meat and drank wine to be judged by people who abstained from food of this kind. *The person who eats*, he says, *should not despise the one who does not eat; and the person who does not eat should not pass judgment on the one who eats.* He also adds, *Who are you who pass judgment on someone else's slave? It is before his own master that he stands or falls.* (Rom 14:3–4) In the case of such actions which can arise from an intention that is good and undivided and honorable (although they can also arise from one that is not good), those people, although they were human, wished to pass judgment on the hidden matters of the heart, which God alone judges.

18,60. What the Apostle says elsewhere also pertains to this, *Do not judge anything before the time, until the Lord comes and reveals what is now hidden in the dark and makes known the purposes of the heart. And then there will be praise to each person from God.* (1 Cor 4:5) Certain actions, then, are indifferent, and we do not know the intention behind them, because it can be either good or bad, and it would be rash to pass judgment on them and especially to condemn them.[85] The time for judging these matters will come when the Lord reveals what is hidden in darkness and makes known the intentions of the heart. The same Apostle likewise says elsewhere, *The sins of some people are manifest, leading to judgment, but those of others appear later* (1 Tm 5:24). He is saying that it is clear what the intention is behind those things that are manifest; they lead to judgment; that is, if judgment follows those things it is not rash. Those which are hidden follow afterwards, for not even they will be hidden when their time comes. And this we must also understand of good deeds. For he adds, *Similarly, good deeds are also manifest, and those which are otherwise cannot be hidden* (1 Tm 5:25). Let us therefore pass judgment on things that are manifest, but let us leave the judgment to God concerning things that are hidden, because even they cannot remain hidden, be they bad or good, when the time comes for them to be made manifest.

18,61. There are two instances in which we must avoid rash judgment: when the intention behind an action is uncertain, or when it is uncertain how someone

---

85. The categories of good, bad and indifferent (*medium*) are Stoic in origin. See Johannes von Arnim, ed., *Stoicorum veterum fragmenta* I (Leipzig-Berlin 1921) 47–48; III (1923) 17–39.

who is now either bad or good will turn out to be in the future. If, for example, someone with a stomach ailment did not want to fast, and you did not believe him and attributed the vice of gluttony to him, you would be judging him rashly. Likewise, if you became aware of someone's obvious gluttony and drunkenness and censured him as though he were beyond correction and change, you would nonetheless be passing a rash judgment. Let us, then, not censure those things whose motivations we do not know, nor censure those that are manifest as if despairing of improvement, and we shall escape the judgment of which it is said, *Do not judge, lest you be judged.*

18,62. What he says next might sound strange: *For by the judgment with which you judge you yourselves will be judged; and by the measure with which you have measured it will be measured out to you.* If we make a rash judgment, will God judge us rashly as well? Or if we measure with a false measure, does God have a false measure with which to measure us in return? For I take the term *measure* to mean judgment. In no way does God either judge rashly or repay anyone by a false measure. But this has been said because it necessarily follows that the very same rashness with which you punish another person will punish you as well, unless perhaps it must be surmised that wrongdoing does some harm to the person against whom it is directed but nothing to the person from whom it comes. Rather it is often the case that nothing harms the person who suffers the wrong, whereas the one who perpetrates the wrong is inevitably hurt. What harm did the malice of the persecutors do to the martyrs? It did a great deal to the persecutors themselves. Even if some of them emended their ways, they were blinded by malice at the time they were persecuting. Similarly, a rash judgment for the most part does no harm to the person who is judged rashly, but the rashness itself inevitably harms the one who judges rashly. I think that this is also formulated in the rule, *Everyone who strikes with the sword will die by the sword* (Mt 26:52). How many in fact strike with the sword yet do not die from the sword, like Peter himself! But someone might think that he escaped such a punishment through the forgiveness of his sins, although nothing could be more ridiculous than to think that there could be a punishment greater than the sword, which did not befall Peter, apart from the cross, which did befall him.[86] What is to be said about the thieves who were crucified with the Lord, because the one who merited pardon merited it after he had been crucified, while the other did not merit it at all?[87] Or did it happen that all those whom they killed they had first crucified, and that consequently they too deserved to suffer the same penalty? It is ridiculous to think like this. What else, then, could the saying mean, *Everyone who strikes with the sword will die by the sword,* if not that the soul dies from whatever sin it has committed?

19,63. The Lord warns us in this passage, therefore, against making rash and false judgments, for he desires that anything we do should come from a heart that

---

86. Augustine is aware of the tradition, first alluded to by Tertullian in *On the Prescription of Heretics* 36, that Peter was crucified.
87. See Lk 23:2–43.

is undivided and intent on God alone, and there are many actions whose intentions are uncertain and on which it is rash to pass judgment. Those people are particularly guilty of rash judgment regarding matters which are uncertain, and who prefer to censure and condemn rather than improve and correct, which is a fault attaching either to pride or to envy. So he goes on to say, *Why do you notice the splinter in your brother's eye but do not see the beam in your own eye?* (Mt 7:3) If he sinned out of anger, for example, you censure out of hatred. The difference between a splinter and a beam is as great as that between anger and hatred, for hatred is inveterate anger which becomes so strong over the course of time that it is rightly called a beam. It can happen that, if you are angry with someone, you wish him to mend his ways, whereas if you hate him you cannot want to correct him.

19,64. *For how can you say to your brother, Allow me to take the splinter from your eye, and see, there is a beam in your own eye? Hypocrite, first take the beam from your own eye, and then you will see to take out the splinter from your brother's eye.* (Mt 7:4–5) That is, first get rid of hatred from yourself and then you can correct the person you love. With good reason he says *hypocrite*, for to censure fault is the prerogative of upright and well-disposed persons, but when the wicked do it they are acting the part of others like hypocrites, who disguise behind a mask what they are and display with a mask what they are not. By the term "hypocrites," therefore, you should understand impostors. And this troublesome kind of impostors must truly be avoided at all costs, who out of hatred and spite bring accusations against every kind of vice and wish to be perceived as counselors at the same time. And therefore we must act vigilantly, with care and kindness, so that, when necessity compels us to rebuke or censure someone, we ourselves would first reflect whether such a fault was one that we never had or are lacking now. And if we never had it, we should bear in mind that we are human and could have had it; but if we did have it and no longer have it, let our common frailty come to mind, so that compassion and not hatred may precede the rebuke or censure, so that whether what we do results in another's improvement or makes him worse (for the outcome is uncertain), we may nonetheless rest secure because our eye is undivided. But if on reflection we discover that we are guilty of the same fault as the person whom we were prepared to blame, let us neither blame nor censure but rather groan together, and let us invite him not to pay heed to us but to strive together with us.

19,65. As the Apostle says, *To the Jews I became like a Jew so as to win over the Jews; to those who are subject to the law like one subject to the law, although I myself am not subject to the law, so as to win over those who were subject to the law; to those who are outside the law like one outside the law, although I am not without the law of God but am under the law of Christ, so as to gain those who are outside the law; to the weak I became weak so as to win over the weak. I have become all things to all people, so as to win them all.* (1 Cor 9:20–22) He was certainly not acting from pretence, as some would understand it, in order to safeguard their own despicable pretence by such an eminent authority, but he did this out of charity, by which he felt that the weakness of the person whom he wished to assist was his own. For he also prefaced this by saying, *For, although I am free from all, I have made myself the slave of all so as to gain the greater number* (1 Cor 9:19). And so, in order that you may understand that this comes not from pretence but from charity, whereby we exercise compassion towards people who are weak like us, he gives this warning in another passage: *Brothers, you have been called to freedom; only do not let freedom give the flesh its opportunity, but serve one another in charity* (Gal 5:13). And this is not possible unless each one takes on the other's weakness as his own, to bear it with patience, until the one for whose wellbeing he is concerned is freed from it.

19,66. Rebukes, therefore, are to be administered rarely and in cases of great necessity, so that even in these instances our concern may be the service of God and not ourselves. For the aim is to do nothing with a divided heart, so that, by removing the beam of envy or spite or pretence from our own eye, we may see to remove the splinter from our brother's eye. We shall then see it with the eyes of a dove,[88] like those that are praised in the bride of Christ, the glorious Church which God chose for himself, having neither spot nor wrinkle, that is, pure and undivided.[89]

20,67. But, since the notion of undividedness can mislead some people who wish to obey God's precepts, so that they consider it wrong at times to conceal what is true, just as it is wrong at times to say what is false, with the result that matters are disclosed to persons who are unable to cope with them, which causes greater damage than if they were to conceal them completely and forever, the Lord most correctly adds, *Do not give what is holy to dogs nor cast your pearls before swine, lest they trample them underfoot and turn and tear you to pieces* (Mt 7:6). The Lord himself, although he never lied, showed that he kept some truths hidden when he said, *I still have many things to say to you, but you cannot bear them now* (Jn 16:12). And the apostle Paul said, *I have not been able to speak to you as to spiritual persons but as to fleshly persons. Like little ones in Christ, I gave you milk to drink, not solid food, for you were not capable, but neither are you now, for you are still fleshly.* (1 Cor 3:1–2)[90]

20,68. In this precept, though, which forbids us to give what is holy to dogs and to cast our pearls before swine, we must examine carefully what is meant by *holy*, by *pearls*, by *dogs*, by *swine*. What is holy is that which it is wrong to violate and corrupt. Attempt and will pertain to the guilt of this crime, although what is

---

88. See Sgs 4:1.
89. See Eph 5:27. In *Revisions* I,19 (18),9 Augustine distinguishes between the Church as it presently is, which is imperfect, and the Church as it will be, when it will appear with Christ in glory. See also *Revisions* II,18(45) for the identical concern.
90. This and the following sections seem to refer to the so-called discipline of the secret, or rule of secrecy, which was especially in vogue during the fourth and fifth centuries and whose purpose was to hinder Christians from disclosing certain aspects of their religion, particularly with regard to the sacraments, to non-Christians.
   Augustine is careful to distinguish between concealing the truth and telling a lie. His teaching on lying is very strict: see, e.g., *Lying*; *Against Lying*.

holy by its nature remains inviolable and incorruptible. Certain spiritual things of great importance are to be considered pearls; because they lie hidden, it is as though they have to be hauled out of the deep, and, like shells that have been prised open, they are found in allegorical clothing. Hence the following interpretation is permissible: what is holy and what is a pearl may be said to be one and the same thing, but what is holy derives from the fact that it must not be corrupted, and a pearl from the fact that it must not be despised. A person attempts to corrupt what he does not want to remain whole, but he despises what he considers worthless and thinks is, as it were, beneath him, and therefore whatever is despised is said to be trampled upon. Dogs are so called because they lunge to tear apart, and what they tear apart they do not allow to remain whole. *Do not give,* he says, *what is holy to dogs,* because, even if it cannot be torn apart and corrupted but remains whole and inviolable, we must reflect on the purpose of those who keenly and most ferociously resist and, insofar as lies within their power, attempt to suppress the truth. As for swine, although they do not attack with their teeth like dogs, they filthy everything by trampling on it. *Do not,* then, he says, *cast your pearls before swine, lest they trample them underfoot and turn and tear you to pieces.* I understand dogs not inappropriately as assailants of truth, and swine as its despisers.

20,69. He says, *They will turn and tear you to pieces.* He does not say, "They will tear the pearls themselves to pieces." For while trampling upon them, when they turn in order to hear something else, they also still tear apart the person who cast the pearls which they trampled upon. You will not find it simple to discover what could be pleasing to someone who tramples upon pearls, that is, who despises divine truths which have been discovered by dint of great effort. I do not see how someone who teaches such people is not torn to pieces through anger and indignation. Each animal, both the dog and the swine, is impure.[91] Care must therefore be taken lest something be revealed to a person who is unable to understand it; it is better that he seek what is hidden rather than attack or neglect what is clear. Nor in fact can any other reason be found as to why things that are clear and important are not accepted apart from hatred or contempt, which is why the first is signified by dogs and the second by swine. All such impurity is conceived through the love of what is temporal, that is, through the love of this world, which we are commanded to renounce, so that we can be pure. Anyone who longs to have a heart that is undivided and pure must not feel guilty if he conceals something that the person from whom he conceals it cannot grasp. But it must not be deduced from this that it is permissible to tell a lie, for it does not follow that, when the truth is concealed, falsehood is spoken. The first thing that must be done, then, is to remove the obstacles which prevent the person from understanding, because if he fails to understand by reason of some uncleanness, he must be purified either in word or deed, insofar as this is in our power.

---

91. "Impure": *immundum*. The usual designation for such animals is "unclean," but *immundum* translates not only as "unclean" but also as "impure," and the latter both maintains the sense and is in keeping with the use of the word in what follows.

20,70. Although our Lord is found to have said things that many of those present did not accept either through opposition or disdain, it must not be thought that he gave to dogs what was holy or that he cast his pearls before swine, for he did not give to those who were unable to understand but to those who were capable and present at the same time, whom it would not have been right to neglect because of others' impurity.[92] And when those who were testing him questioned him, he replied to them in such a way that they could not contradict him, although they were consumed by their own poison rather than fed on his food. But the ones who were able to understand because of those others heard much to their advantage.

I have said this lest perhaps someone, unable to respond to a questioner, might feel himself excused by this text if he should say that he was unwilling to give to dogs what was holy or to cast his pearls before swine. The person who knows what to reply should give an answer, especially for the sake of others who might despair were they to believe that the question proposed admitted of no answer, if this pertained to matters that were useful and instructive for salvation.

For there are many questions that can be asked by those with time on their hands, redundant and inane and for the most part harmful, about which nonetheless something has to be said, yet it is precisely why such things should not be inquired about that should be opened up and explained. But when it is a case of beneficial things we must sometimes give an answer to what we are asked, just as the Lord did when the Sadducees questioned him about the woman who had seven husbands and which one would be hers in the resurrection.[93] For he replied that *in the resurrection they will neither marry nor be given in marriage but will be like the angels in heaven* (Mt 22:30).

Sometimes the one who asks the question must himself be questioned about something else, and if he responded he would be answering for himself the question he originally asked, but if he declined to speak it would not appear wrong to those who were present if he did not receive an answer to the question he asked. For those who put him to the test by asking whether tribute should be paid were themselves questioned about something else, namely, whose image was on the coin that they brought to him; and because they replied to what they had been asked, that the coin bore Caesar's image, they answered for themselves the question that they had put to the Lord.[94] And so he concluded on the basis of their response, *Give to Caesar, therefore, what belongs to Caesar, and to God what belongs to God* (Mt 22:21). When the chief priests and elders of the people asked by what authority he performed his works, he questioned them about the baptism of John, and, since they were unwilling to say something which they saw could be used

---

92. Augustine seems to be saying that Christ only intentionally taught those who could understand and accept what he was saying, but that there were others among his listeners — allegorically dogs and swine — who happened to hear his words at the same time and whom he could not prevent from doing so.

93. See Mt 22:23–28 par.

94. See Mt 22:15–21 par.

against them (for they did not dare say anything derogatory about John because of the bystanders),[95] he said, *Nor will I tell you by what authority I do these things* (Mt 21:27), and this appeared perfectly acceptable to the bystanders. They said that they did not know what they were ignorant of, but they did not want to acknowledge it. And indeed it was right that those who wanted an answer to the question they asked should first do what they asked be done for them; if they had done this they would in fact have answered for themselves. For they had themselves sent to John, inquiring who he was, or rather priests and Levites were sent who thought that he was the Christ, although he denied that he was and gave witness to Christ.[96] Had they been willing to acknowledge such testimony, they would have taught themselves by what authority Christ did these things, but as if feigning ignorance they put the question in order to find a pretext to level false accusations.

21,71. When, therefore, it was stipulated that what was holy should not be given to dogs or pearls be cast before swine, a listener could have responded and said, being aware of his ignorance and frailty, and being commanded not to give what he believed that he had not yet received—he could have responded, then, and said, "What holy thing do you forbid me to give to dogs and what pearls do you forbid me to cast before swine, since I do not see that I yet possess such things?" Most fittingly, therefore, the Lord added and said, *Ask and it shall be given to you; seek and you shall find; knock and it shall be opened to you. For everyone who asks receives, and whoever seeks finds, and to whoever knocks it shall be opened.* (Mt 7:7–8)[97] To ask pertains to acquiring a healthy and undistracted mind, so that we may be able to fulfill what is commanded, whereas to seek pertains to discovering the truth. For, since the blessed life reaches completion through action and knowledge, action requires a supply of strength, and contemplation the manifestation of realities. The first of these is to be asked for, the second is to be sought, so that the former may be given and the latter found. But in this life knowledge belongs to the way rather than to possession itself. But when anyone finds the true way, he will arrive at possession itself, which will be opened to the one who knocks.

21,72. In order, then, that these three may stand out clearly, asking, seeking, finding, let us use the example of a person who has lame feet and is unable to walk. He must first be healed and given strength to walk, and this relates to what the Lord said, *Ask*. Yet what does it benefit him to be able to walk now or even to run if he goes astray through misleading paths? The second thing, therefore, is to find the way to the destination where he wishes to arrive. When he has reached and come to it, if he finds the place itself closed where he wishes to dwell, neither having been able to walk nor having walked and arrived will be of any use unless it is open; to this pertains what is said, *Knock*.

---

95. See Mt 21:23–27 par.
96. See Jn 1:19–27.
97. In *Revisions* I,19(18),9 Augustine says that these three things—asking, seeking and knocking—could be reduced to a single urgent petition and did not need to be explained as though they were entirely distinct from each another.

21,73. He who does not deceive in his promises has afforded great hope, for he says, *Everyone who asks receives, and whoever seeks finds, and to whoever knocks it shall be opened* (Mt 7:8). Perseverance is therefore required so that we may obtain what we are asking for, and find what we are seeking, and that it may be opened when we knock. Just as he cited the example of the birds of heaven and the lilies of the field, so that we might not be preoccupied with nourishment and clothing in the future, and so that hope might ascend from matters of less importance to those of greater, he speaks as follows in this passage: *Or which of you, if his son asked for bread, would give him a stone? Or, if he asked for a fish, would give him a snake? If you, therefore, although you are evil, know how to give good gifts to your sons, how much more will your Father who is in heaven give good things to those who ask him!* (Mt 7:9–11) How do the evil give good things? But he called evil those who still love this world, and sinners. The good things which they give must be said to be good in accordance with their outlook, for they are convinced that these are good. And although in the nature of things these may be good, they are nonetheless temporal and belong to this mortal life. Anyone who is evil and gives such things does not give from what is his own, for *the Lord's is the earth and its fullness* (Ps 24:1), *he who made heaven and earth and the sea and all that is in them* (Ps 146:6). What great hope must we have, then, that God will give good things to us who ask him and that we cannot be deceived by receiving one thing instead of another when we ask him, when we ourselves, although we are evil, know to give what we are asked for! For we do not deceive our sons, and, whatever good things we give, we are giving not from what is ours but from what is his.

22,74. A certain endurance and vigor for walking along the path of wisdom have been fixed in good morals, which lead to a pure and undivided heart. He spoke of this at length, and now he concludes, *Whatever good you wish that people should do to you, then, do so to them, for this is the law and the prophets* (Mt 7:12). We read in the Greek manuscripts, *Whatever you wish that people should do to you, do so to them.* I think, however, that *good* was added by Latin speakers to clarify the phrase.[98] For it could happen that someone would shamefully wish some act to be perpetrated against himself and would refer to this phrase. For example, if a person wanted to be provoked to drink to excess and get drunk, and he did this first to the one from whom he wanted to be provoked, it would be absurd to think that such a person had adhered to this teaching. Because, in my view, this was a cause of concern, a single word was added for clarity's sake, and hence in the phrase, *Whatever you wish that people should do to you, do so also to them,* the word *good* was added.[99] If this is not found in the Greek manuscripts, even they should be corrected. But who would dare to do this? We must therefore understand

---

98. *Good* is found only in some Latin texts; see, e.g., Cyprian, *On the Lord's Prayer* 18.
99. The word actually occurs at the end of the phrase in Latin, as Augustine himself says ("so that after the phrase"), but the translation of his words ("so that in the phrase") reflects its placement in the English.

that the phrase is complete and altogether perfect, even though this word is not added. For the expression *whatever you wish* must be taken in its strict sense and not as colloquially and commonly used. For only in good things does the will come into play, whereas, in deeds that are evil and shameful, desire rather than will is properly at issue. It is not that Scripture always speaks this way, but where necessary it employs terms which are strictly appropriate and do not permit of any other interpretation.

22,75. It appears that this precept pertains to the love of neighbor but not to the love of God as well, since he says elsewhere that there are two precepts on which *the whole law depends and all the prophets* (Mt 22:40).[100] For if he had said, "Whatever you wish to be done to you, you also do the same," by reason of this one phrase this precept would have included both, since it would have been said at once that each person wished to be loved by both God and human beings. And so, when he is commanded that he should do what he would wish done to himself, he is indeed commanded to love both God and human beings. But when it is said more specifically of human beings, *Whatever you wish that people should do to you, do so also to them,* nothing other seems to be said than *You shall love your neighbor as yourself.* Yet we must not carelessly overlook what he added here, *For this is the law and the prophets.* (Mt 22:39–40) Of those two precepts not only did he say, *The law depends and the prophets,* but he added, *The whole law and all the prophets,* by which he meant every prophecy. Although he did not include it here, he reserved a place for the other precept, which concerns the love of God. Hence — because this follows the precepts about an undivided heart, and care should be exercised in regard to those (lest anyone have a divided heart) to whom one's heart may be hidden, that is, in regard to human beings — this very precept had to be given. There is practically no one who would wish another person with a divided heart to have dealings with him. But what is not possible is for someone with an undivided heart to give something to someone else, unless he gives it without seeking some temporal advantage from him and does so with the intention that we discussed at length earlier, when we were speaking about an undivided eye.[101]

22,76. Therefore, an eye that has been made pure and undivided will be fit for and capable of perceiving and contemplating its own interior light, for this is the eye of the heart. That person possesses such an eye who has determined that the purpose of his good works is that they should truly be good works, not for winning people's approval. If he happens to please them, though, he thinks rather in terms of their salvation and the glory of God and not of his own vain boastfulness. Nor does he perform a good deed for the salvation of his neighbor in order to acquire things that are necessary for maintaining his livelihood. Nor does he rashly pass judgment on a person's intention and will, inasmuch as it is not apparent with what intention and will a deed may be done. And whatever service he may render to

---

100. *All* is not in the original Greek or in the common Latin translations of Matthew, nor in some manuscripts of *The Lord's Sermon on the Mount*, but it makes sense in the context.

101. See above at II,13,45–46.

another person he performs with the same intention with which he would want it rendered to himself, that is, in such a way that he would not expect some temporal gain from him. This is how the heart with which we seek God will be undivided and pure. *Blessed,* then, *are the pure in heart, for they shall see God* (Mt 5:8).

23,77. But because this applies to a few, the Lord now begins to speak about searching for and acquiring wisdom, which is the tree of life.[102] In searching for and acquiring it, which means contemplating it, an eye of this sort is led through everything that has gone before, so that in this way the hard path and the narrow door can be seen. What he now says — *Enter by the narrow door, because the door is wide and the path broad which leads to perdition, and there are many who enter it. How narrow is the door and how hard the path which leads to life, and there are few who find it!* (Mt 7:13–14) — he does not say, then, because the Lord's yoke is harsh or his burden heavy, but because those who wish to put an end to their labors are few, and they do not believe in the one who cries out, *Come to me, all you who labor, and I shall give you rest. Take up my yoke and learn from me, for I am meek and humble of heart, for my yoke is easy, and my burden light.* (Mt 11:28–30) (It was at this point that the Sermon began — with the humble and meek of heart.[103]) They are numerous who reject this easy yoke and light burden, while few submit to it. Consequently, the path is hard which leads to life, and the door narrow through which it is entered.

24,78. Here, then, those who promise wisdom and the knowledge of truth, which they do not have, must be approached with the greatest caution; they are like the heretics who habitually commend themselves because they are so few. Therefore, when the Lord said that there are few who find the narrow door and the hard path, lest those people insinuate themselves under the guise of their fewness, he immediately added, *Beware of false prophets who come to you in sheep's clothing, while inwardly they are ravenous wolves* (Mt 7:15). But they do not deceive the undivided eye, which knows how to recognize a tree by its fruits, for he says, *By their fruits you shall know them* (Mt 7:16). He then adds some analogies: *Can grapes be gathered from thorns, or figs from thistles? In the same way, every good tree bears good fruit, but a bad tree bears bad fruit. A good true cannot bear bad fruit, nor can a bad tree bear good fruit. Every tree which does not bear good fruit will be cut down and cast into the fire. Therefore by their fruits you shall know them.* (Mt 7:16–20)

24,79. At this point the error should at all costs be avoided on the part of those who believe that two natures can be inferred from these two trees, one of which is of God, but the other neither of God nor from God. This error has already been discussed at length in other books and, if that is still insufficient, will continue to be discussed, but now it must be pointed out that those two trees are of no help to

---

102. See Prv 3:18.
103. See Mt 5:3–4.

them.[104] In the first place it is so abundantly clear that the Lord is referring to human beings that whoever reads what precedes and what follows will be amazed at their blindness. They next focus their attention on the phrase, *A good tree cannot bear bad fruit, nor can a bad tree bear good fruit* (Mt 7:18), and conclude from it that a bad soul cannot be changed for the better nor a good soul for the worse, as though it were said, "A good tree cannot become bad nor a bad tree become good." But what it says is, *A good tree cannot bear bad fruit, nor can a bad tree bear good fruit.* The tree in fact signifies the soul itself, that is, the person himself, and the fruit is the person's deeds. A bad person, therefore, cannot perform good deeds, nor a good person bad deeds. If a bad person, then, wishes to perform good deeds, let him first become good. The Lord himself expresses it more clearly elsewhere: *Either make the tree good, or make the tree bad* (Mt 12:33). But if he were symbolizing the two natures of those people[105] by these two trees, he would not say *make.* For what person can make a nature? And next, even there, having mentioned the two trees, he added, *Hypocrites, how can you speak what is good, since you are bad?* (Mt 12:34) As long as someone is bad, then, he cannot produce good fruit, for, if he produces good fruit, he will no longer be bad. Thus it could be stated most truthfully: snow cannot be hot, for when it begins to get hot we no longer call it snow but water. It can happen that what was snow is no longer snow, but it is not possible for snow to be hot. It is possible, therefore, for someone who was bad to be bad no longer, but it is not possible for a bad person to do what is good. Even if sometimes he behaves in a beneficial manner, it is not he himself who is doing it, but it is the result of providence, which accomplishes it through him, as was said of the Pharisees, *Do what they say, but do not do what they do* (Mt 23:3). The fact that they said what was good, and that what they said was heard to good advantage and put into practice, was not due to them, for the Lord said, *They sit on the chair of Moses* (Mt 23:2). Those who preach the law of God through divine providence, then, can be of benefit to their listeners, although they might not be to themselves. Regarding such people it was said through the prophet in another passage, *You sow wheat and reap thorns* (Jer 12:13), because they command what is good and do what is bad. Those who listened to them and did what was said by them, then, did not gather grapes from thorns but gathered grapes from the vine through the thorns. It is as if someone were to put his hand through a hedge or were to pick grapes from a vine surrounded by a hedge: in that case the fruit would come not from the thorns but from the vine.

---

104. Augustine is referring here to Manicheanism, which postulated an ongoing cosmic struggle between two natures, one good and the other evil; the good nature was represented by God. For Manichean use of the gospel passage about the two trees as symbolizing these two natures see *Answer to Felix, a Manichean* II,2.

    The books that Augustine devoted to a refutation of Manicheanism before he wrote *The Lord's Sermon on the Mount* are *The Catholic Way of Life and the Manichean Way of Life, On Genesis against the Manicheans, True Religion,* and *The Acts of a Debate with Fortunatus, a Manichean.* Several writings came after, including the monumental *Answer to Faustus, a Manichean.*

105. I.e., the Manicheans.

24,80. The question may rightly be raised as to what kind of fruit he wishes us to consider, by which we can distinguish the tree. Many impute certain things to the fruit which pertain to sheep's clothing, and in this way they are deceived by wolves; these are things like fasting and prayer and almsgiving. If all of these things could not be done by hypocrites as well, he would not have said earlier, *Beware of parading your righteousness before people, to be seen by them* (Mt 6:1). Once he has made this statement, these three things follow — almsgiving, prayer, fasting. There are many who give much to the poor not out of mercy but out of self-promotion; and there are many who pray, or rather seem to pray, not with their gaze fixed upon God but from a desire to please people; and there are many who fast and put on a show of astonishing abstinence for the benefit of those to whom these practices appear arduous, and are considered worthy of honor. Through guile of this kind they entrap them, and while they pretend one thing in order to deceive, they employ another to rob or kill those who are unable to see that they are wolves in sheep's clothing. These things, then, are not the fruits by which the Lord admonishes us to recognize the tree. Those which are done with a good intention and in truth are the clothing characteristic of sheep, but when they are done with a bad intention and in error, they do nothing other than clothe wolves. Yet sheep should not hate their own clothing because wolves often conceal themselves in it.

24,81. The Apostle tells us by what kind of fruits, when they are found, we can recognize a bad tree: *But the works of the flesh are manifest. They are fornication, impurity, licentiousness, idolatry, sorcery, enmity, strife, jealousy, anger, dissension, divisions, envy, drunkenness, carousing and the like. I warn you, as I warned you before, that those who do such things shall not possess the kingdom of God.* And he goes on to detail the fruits by which we may recognize a good tree: *But the fruit of the Spirit is love, joy, peace, patience, kindness, goodness, faith, gentleness, self-control.* (Gal 5:19–23) It should be noted that *joy* is used here in its strict sense, for bad people are not said to rejoice but, strictly speaking, to put on an act, just as we observed previously[106] that bad people, strictly speaking, do not have a will, where it was said, *Whatever you wish people to do to you, do these things also to them.* Using the term in its strict sense, according to which joy is only spoken of with regard to good persons, the prophet also says, *There is no joy for the wicked, says the Lord* (Is 48:22). Likewise, when faith is mentioned, it is not any kind of faith but true faith, and other kinds that are mentioned here have certain likenesses of themselves in bad and deceitful people, with the result that they can be completely deceptive, unless a person possesses an eye that is both pure and undivided by which to recognize these things. In the most appropriate sequence, therefore, the purification of the eye was first discussed, and then the things that were to be avoided were spoken of.

25,82. Yet, even if someone should have a pure eye, that is, if he should live by a heart that is sincere and undivided, he is nonetheless unable to gaze into the

---

106. See above at II,22,74.

heart of another person, and there are things that are disclosed through trials which are not manifest in deeds or words.

There are two kinds of trial: in the hope of gaining some temporal benefit and in the fear of losing it. And we must be very much on guard as we move towards wisdom, which can be found in Christ alone, *in whom are hidden all the treasures of wisdom and knowledge* (Col 2:3)—we must be very much on guard, then, lest we be deceived in the name of Christ by heretics or others with a perverted understanding and by the lovers of this world. For he goes on to issue the warning, *Not everyone who says to me, Lord, Lord, will enter the kingdom of heaven; but he who does the will of my Father, he will enter the kingdom of heaven* (Mt 7:21). We must not think that it pertains to that fruit if someone says, *Lord, Lord,* which would make the tree appear good to us. But this is the fruit—to do the will of the Father who is in heaven, for the doing of which Christ condescended to offer himself as an example.

25,83. It can with good reason be puzzling as to how these words accord with what the Apostle says, *No one speaking in the Spirit of God says, Cursed be Jesus, and no one can say, Jesus is Lord, except in the Holy Spirit* (1 Cor 12:3), because we cannot say that some of those who have the Holy Spirit will not enter the kingdom of heaven, if they persevere until the end, nor can we say that those who say, *Lord, Lord,* have the Holy Spirit, and yet do not enter the kingdom of heaven. What can it mean, then, that *no one says, Jesus is Lord, except in the Holy Spirit,* unless the Apostle used the word *says* according to its strict meaning, so that it denotes both the will and the understanding of the person who speaks? The Lord, on the other hand, used the word in a loose sense when he said, *Not everyone who says to me, Lord, Lord, will enter the kingdom of heaven.* For the person who says this seems neither to will nor to understand what he is saying, whereas the person who expresses his will and his thought by the sound of his voice is speaking accurately. In the same way it was said earlier that joy in its strict sense belongs to the fruits of the Spirit, not in the sense in which the Apostle uses it elsewhere, *It does not rejoice over wrongdoing* (1 Cor 13:6), as though anyone could be joyful over wrongdoing, because that is the elation of a soul in wild disarray, not joy, for the good alone possess joy. Therefore, those people seem to speak who do not discern with their understanding and act with their will in accordance with what they utter, but they merely make a sound with their voice; it is in this sense that the Lord says, *Not everyone who says to me, Lord, Lord, will enter the kingdom of heaven.* Those people speak truthfully and in the strict sense, on the other hand, when the utterance of their words is not in disharmony with their will and thought; it is in this sense that the Apostle says, *No one can say, Jesus is Lord, except in the Holy Spirit.*

25,84. And it is particularly relevant to the present discussion that, while striving towards the contemplation of the truth, we not be deceived—either by the name of Christ by those who have the name but not the deeds or by certain works and miracles. When the Lord performed such works for the sake of unbelievers, he nonetheless warned that we should not be led astray by works of this kind, thinking that, where we saw a visible miracle, invisible Wisdom was present as well. He goes on to say, then, *Many will say to me on that day, Lord, Lord, did we not prophesy in your name, and cast out demons in your name, and work many miracles in your name? And then he will say to them, I never knew you; depart from me, you who work iniquity.* (Mt 7:22–23) He does not know anyone, then, except the one who works justice.[107] For he also forbade his disciples to rejoice over things like the fact that demons were subject to them, *but rejoice,* he said, *that your names are written in heaven* (Lk 10:20)—in that city of Jerusalem that is in heaven which, I believe, is where the righteous and the holy alone will reign. *Or do you not know,* says the Apostle, *that evildoers will not possess the kingdom of God?* (1 Cor 6:9)

25,85. But perhaps someone will say that it is impossible for the wicked to perform those visible miracles, and he believes instead that they will be speaking falsely when they say, *In your name we have prophesied and cast out demons and worked many miracles.* Such a person should read how many of them the magicians of the Egyptians worked in their opposition to Moses, the servant of God.[108] Or if he does not want to read this, because they were not performed in the name of Christ, he should read what the Lord himself, speaking of false prophets, said, *Then, if anyone says to you, Behold, here is the Christ, or there he is, do not believe him. For many false Christs and false prophets will arise and work great signs and wonders, so that even the elect may be led into error. Behold, I have foretold this to you.* (Mt 24:22–23)

25,86. How necessary it is, then, to have a pure and undivided eye in order to find the path to wisdom, blocked as it is by the deceits and falsehoods of so many bad and perverse people! To avoid all of them means attaining the most assured peace and the unshakeable stability of wisdom. For it is greatly to be feared that, out of zeal for wrangling and contention, a person may not see what can only be seen by a few: that the uproar of the contradictors is insignificant, unless he also cries out against himself. What the Apostle says is also relevant here: *It is not fitting for a servant of the Lord to engage in disputes, but he should be meek towards all, willing to learn, patient, gently rebuking those who think differently, in case perhaps God grants them repentance to know the truth* (2 Tm 24:25). *Blessed, then, are the peacemakers, for they shall be called sons of God* (Mt 5:9).

25,87. We should pay particular attention to how frighteningly this discourse is drawn to a close. *Anyone who hears my words and does them, then,* says the Lord, *will be like a wise man who built his house on rock* (Mt 7:24). For no one makes what he hears or sees permanent except by doing. And if Christ is a rock, as numerous texts of Scripture testify,[109] that person builds on Christ who does what he hears from him. *The rain fell, floods came, the winds blew and battered*

---

107. "Iniquity...justice": *iniquitatem...aequitatem.*
108. See Ex 7:11–22.
109. See Rom 9:32–33; 1 Cor 10:4; 1 Pt 2:4–8.

that house, and it did not fall, for it was built on rock (Mt 7:24). Such a person does not fear any dark superstitions (for what other meaning does rain have when it is used to signify something evil?), or the gossip of men, which in my opinion can be compared to the winds, or the river of this life which, with its lusts of the flesh, flows upon the earth. Whoever is misled by the good fortune of these three things is broken when they turn to adversity. Whoever has his house built on rock fears none of them, since he not only listens to the Lord's precepts but does them as well. And whoever listens but does not do them is veering dangerously close to all of these, for he lacks a solid foundation, and by listening and not doing them he is building for a fall. For the Lord continues, *And anyone who hears my words and does not do them will be like a foolish man who built his house on sand. The rain fell, floods came, the winds blew and battered that house, and it fell, and its ruin was great. And it happened that, when Jesus had finished speaking, the crowds were in amazement at his teaching, for he taught them as one having authority, not like their scribes.* (Mt 7:26–29) This is what I stated earlier was signified by the prophet in the Psalms, when he said, *I will act with trust in him. The words of the Lord are pure words, silver refined by fire, purged of the earth seven times* (Ps 12:6). On the basis of this number, I am inclined to relate these precepts as well to the seven maxims which the Lord enunciated at the outset of this discourse, when he spoke of the blessed, and to those seven workings of the Holy Spirit which the prophet Isaiah enumerates.[110] But whether that sequence or some other one should be considered alongside these, we must act upon what we have heard from the Lord if we wish to build upon rock.

---

110. See Is 11:2–3.

INDEX

(Prepared by Kathleen Strattan)

The first numeral in the Index is the Book number. The numbers following the colons are the Chapter numbers, then the Section numbers in parentheses. (Additional numbers, preceded by the letter n, indicate footnotes.)

Abraham, I:16(49) and n60
action; actions
    See also intention
    contemplation and, II:21(71)
    and disregarding people's praise, II:1
    and sincere faith, I:10(27)
    and what is in a person's heart, II:25
Acts of the Apostles, I:20(64), 22(73);
    II:17(57)
    Manichean rejection of, I:20(65) and
      n88
Acts of Thomas, I:20(65) and nn90–91
Acyndinus, I:16(50) and n63
adoption, II:16(54)
    into kingdom of God, I:23(78);
      II:11(38)
    as sons, I:23(78); II:4(15–16)
adultery, I:12(36), 14(39), 16(48)
    in the heart, I:12(33, 36)
    and spousal permission, I:16(49–50)
      and n62
adversaries
    See also enemies
    God as called adversary, I:11(32)
adversity, II:9(34), 25(87)
affection, I:2(4, 9), 4(11) and *Revisions*
    I,19(18):1, 10(27); II:3(13), 4(16)
    See also love
Agabus, II:17(56)
Agamemnon, II:2(5)
ages: history of the world, I:16(49) and
    n61
air, I:11(30) and n35
Alexander the coppersmith, I:22(73, 76)
allegory, I:19(58); II:2(6–7)
    limits to, II:15(51–52) and n74
    numbers as suggesting, I:4(11–12),
      19(61)
alms; almsgiving, II:2(5–9), 3(11)
altar, I:10(26–27); II:16(54)
Ambrose, *Introduction* and n3
Ananias, I:20(64)

angels, I:11(29), 15(40–41); II:6(20–21),
    17(57), 20(70)
    in human guise, II:9(32)
    likeness of, I:4(12)
anger, I:9(21)–10(26), 14(39), 19(56, 58);
    II:2(6), 19(63), 20(69), 24(81)
    for no reason, I:4, 9(21–22), 10(26,
      28); *Revisions* I,19(18):4
animals:
    impure/unclean, II:20(69–70) and
      nn91–92
    rational and irrational, II:15(51)
antagonists. *See* enemies
Antioch, I:16(50); II:17(57)
anxiety, II:7(25), 15(49, 51), 16(53),
    17(56–57)
Apocalypse, I:22(76)
Apostle, the (St. Paul). *See* Paul, the
    Apostle
apostles, I:6(17); II:16(54)
    capability of, I:4(12); *Revisions*
      I,19(18):2
appetite, carnal, I:12(33–34)
    See also lust
approval, human, II:1(1), 1(4), 2(8),
    22(76)
    See also praise
Aquila, II:17(57)
arrogance. *See* pride
ascension of the Lord, I:20(64)
asking, seeking, and knocking, II:21(71)
    and *Revisions* I,19(18):9
authority, I:20(65)
    in Christian history, I:19(61)
    Church, II:7(26)
    divine, I:3(10), 11(32), 20(68)
    *he taught them as one having
      authority,* II:27(87)
    people in positions of, I:16(50)
    to punish, I:20(63, 66)
    of real-life moral struggle, I:16(49)
      and n62

AGREEMENT AMONG THE EVANGELISTS

(De consensu evangelistarum)

Introduction

Augustine wrote *Agreement among the Evangelists* in 400, contemporaneously with the composition of his *Confessions* (397–401). But the reception and analysis of the *Agreement* has been exactly the opposite of its contemporary, for the work is almost never mentioned, analyzed or taught, possibly because in it we do not see the personal and unique Augustine but rather a more typical fourth-century exegete and apologist. The treatise is not a "harmony" of the Gospels in the usual sense of a work that combines all the elements of all four Gospels into one continuous narrative, such as the popular and widespread second-century *Diatessaron* of Tatian or those pamphlets that are still produced for one's personal piety. Rather, it is a much more general defense of the truth of the Gospels. In that spirit it starts out with a lengthy attack on paganism that occupies most of Book I and that anticipates much of Augustine's more thorough attack on paganism in his *City of God*. The remaining three books present detailed analyses of each gospel passage with an eye towards showing how each passage agrees with every other, or, at the very least, is not in disagreement with any other. Augustine's goal, therefore, is not to replace or combine the individual gospel accounts or even to interpret them; his only purpose is to convince and reassure the reader that each Gospel can be read individually without any danger of inconsistency or contradiction within its own narrative or vis-à-vis the other Gospels. To this end Augustine utilizes several different hermeneutical principles, which are worth enumerating here.

His most frequently-invoked principle is that omission is not contradiction: "For we have already noted something that did not need to be noted and should have been immediately evident to anyone — that there is no contradiction if one omits what the other includes, or if one expresses it one way and the other another way, as long as they both express the truth regarding the subjects and ideas."[1] Two accounts could have absolutely no overlap in their reporting of the events, but each could be completely true, as long as one did not explicitly deny what was reported in the other. This is an enormously useful principle, as it allows Augustine to skip over many of the differences among the Gospels without comment or further analysis. At one point it even appears that omission in fact gives the account a higher level of certainty, for, when only one evangelist reports something, there can be no disagreement, because there is nothing with which to disagree.[2]

Where there is overlap in terms of content, Augustine's most frequent problem is to explain away the discrepancies in order among the Gospels. He does this in accordance with the principle that the evangelists may include something later in their narratives even though it occurred earlier in Jesus' life, or they may anticipate something that occurred later by placing it earlier in their narratives. Augustine says that this is "the manner in which they were accustomed to record things that they

---

1.   II,19,47.
2.   See II,41,88.

had omitted previously or anticipate things that happened later; they knew these things before, but, as they remembered them later, they were divinely prompted to write them down."[3] Augustine is emphatic that this reordering is not done out of forgetfulness but as part of the process of divine inspiration: "This brings to our attention something of the greatest importance to the overriding question of the agreement of the evangelists, which we have attempted to answer with God's help. It is not from ignorance that they omit some things, nor is it from ignorance of the actual order of events that they have kept to the order in which they recall things."[4] The evangelists ordered their narratives for symbolic and not historical reasons, and therefore narrative order implies nothing about the real historical order. Differences in order can therefore be ignored just as easily as omissions.

A similar principle that guides Augustine is that narrative proximity implies nothing about the real time that elapsed. If the evangelists omit mentioning events and sayings, they can also be assumed to have omitted mentioning time intervals.[5] As with the previous principle, this can skew the interpretation of Jesus' words, as we may have lost their original context: two sayings could mean something totally different if they followed each other immediately than if they were spoken or uttered days apart.[6]

This much would allow Augustine to explain all the places where one Gospel includes something that the others do not and any differences in the order of events. But it still leaves many places where the evangelists are narrating the same event but quote Jesus as using different words. This causes Augustine to assert the principle that, as long as they all convey the same meaning or sense, the exact wording is not important: "For now we are dealing with the agreement of the evangelists, from whose diversity of words we learn this helpful truth: the one thing that is necessary in order to hear the truth is not the words but the meaning the speaker wished to convey."[7] A corollary to this principle is that one Gospel may preserve the words actually spoken by Jesus, while the others may preserve the sense behind them.[8] The converse of this principle of one meaning expressed in different words is also stated, namely, that the Gospels may use the same words, but with a different meaning, if this hypothesis is necessary for their narratives to be in agreement, for "there are many words that do not have one meaning but are understood in different ways in different places."[9]

This in turn leads to much-farther-reaching conclusions for Augustine concerning the limitations of language. For if it is possible for the evangelists, who always speak the truth, to vary their wording, then it is also possible for other people to do the same, but for both to be right in their meaning and intention: "And

---

3.   II,19,44.
4.   II,42,90.
5.   See, e.g., II,17,34; 19,45–46.
6.   See, e.g., III,4,11.
7.   III,4,14; see II,24,55–25,57.
8.   See II,28,66.
9.   II,30,72.

if someone says that the evangelists certainly ought to have been given this ability by the power of the Holy Spirit, so that their words would differ in neither kind nor order nor number, then he does not understand that, just as the evangelists' authority is heightened, so too is the credibility strengthened of other people who speak the truth through them. For, if several people narrate the same thing, in no way can one of them be rightly accused of falsehood if he differs from another, because the evangelists give a precedent example in his defense."[10] Whereas we might think that pluralism makes the variations between the Gospels understandable and therefore substantiates their claims to truth, Augustine reasons the other way: the fact that the evangelists express the truth in different words makes it possible that other people may do the same. Augustine says that this "diversity of agreement" is actually preferable to a belief that the evangelists' words are God's own: "Knowing this is advantageous both to morality, for the purpose of guarding against and judging falsehood, and to faith itself, lest we suppose that God would commend the truth to us by giving us not only the thing itself but even the words in which it is expressed, as though they were a kind of deified sound. It is rather the case that the thing which is to be learned is so far above the words by which it is learned that we would not need to ask about them at all if we were able to know the thing itself without them, as God knows it and his angels know it in him."[11] The fact that the Gospels are all true, yet contain different words, shows that God's truth transcends all human attempts at expression; the Gospels' "diversity of agreement" is another curative to human pride and arrogance, undercutting the human temptation to control God and to limit his message to only one "right" version.

Augustine's other principles present us with a variety and combination of methods familiar from ancient and modern attempts at harmonization. The evangelists may individually present Jesus as speaking different words, when in fact all of these were spoken by him; each evangelist's report is accurate, though incomplete, and therefore should be conflated or combined with the others.[12] When the Gospels present similar accounts that cannot be reconciled with one another, it may be because Jesus said or did similar things on different occasions.[13] And if all else fails, Augustine occasionally has recourse to giving the gospel account an allegorical or figurative interpretation.[14] But, on the other hand, some of Augustine's principles are astonishingly modern. When considering whether Mt 27:9 (*Then was fulfilled what had been spoken by the prophet Jeremiah…*) should read *Zechariah* instead of *Jeremiah*, Augustine states the modern principle of accepting the more difficult reading (*lectio difficilior*) exactly: "There would have been no reason to add this name [i.e., Jeremiah], and thereby make the copy misleading.

---

10. II,12,28.
11. II,66,128.
12. See, e.g., II,24,55.
13. See, e.g., II,29,69; 30,77; 50,104–05.
14. See, e.g., II,77,150–151; III,4,14; 7,30; 25,86.

But there would have been a reason to remove it from so many copies."[15] Augustine even concedes the related point that some of the gospel texts may have been "emended," i.e. "corrupted," by later scribes.[16] As on so many other intellectual points, Augustine presents us with a combination of ancient and modern ways of looking at the world, or, in this case, the text.

In the end, Augustine knows that he can never use reason to convince anyone of the truth of the Gospel, for that would be an idolatrous use of human reason: "For what I value is not my own idea but the truth of the Gospel.... But do not ever suppose that any one of all four evangelists is false or has fallen into error from such a holy and high authority."[17] Yet he also knows that reason is a powerful and integral part of the human constitution, and, if it is overlooked and undervalued, it will remain an enemy to faith and not cooperate with it. As Pascal would paraphrase Augustine twelve centuries later: "Reason would never submit unless it judged that there are occasions when it ought to submit."[18] Faith can neither ignore reason nor be merely equivalent to reason. In this work Augustine attempts to show how one who believes in the truth of the Gospels is not being foolish, irrational, or duped. In that respect it is an insightful look at what Augustine thinks is fundamental and necessary to revelation, for, insofar as revelation communicates God and God's plan, it cannot be contained in any human category of language or thought; yet, insofar as revelation is capable of being understood by human beings, it must be contained and limited in this way. Revelation must finally be both reasonable and mysterious, acceptable and incomprehensible, as again Pascal would state in his own way: "If we submit everything to reason our religion will be left with nothing mysterious or supernatural. If we offend the principles of reason our religion will be absurd and ridiculous."[19]

* * *

The present translation of *Agreement among the Evangelists* was made from the Latin Text published in *Nuova Biblioteca Agostiniana* X/1. I occasionally consulted S.D.F. Salmond's English translation, *The Harmony of the Gospels*, edited by Philip Schaff, in *A Select Library of Nicene and Post-Nicene Fathers of the Christian Church*, First Series 6 (New York 1903, repr. 1979) 77–236.

* * *

The translator would like to dedicate this work to his Core Humanities students at Villanova University, who have frequently inspired him with the wit, insight, and enthusiasm that is only possible with those who are in the second decade of their life. They have brought him great pleasure.

---

15. III,7,29.
16. See III,25,71.
17. III,13,43.
18. Blaise Pascal, *Pensées*, trans. by A. J. Krailsheimer (New York 1966) 174 (270).
19. Ibid. 173 (273).

During these same years, when I was dictating the book on the Trinity in piecemeal fashion, I also continually exerted myself in the writing of others, which I interposed at various times. Among them are the four books *On the Agreement among the Evangelists,* [written] because of those who misrepresent them as though they were in disagreement. The first of these books was composed in answer to those who give the impression that they greatly honor Christ as a wise man, or pretend to do so, and do not want to put their trust in the Gospel because they[1] were not written by him but by his disciples, who they think erroneously ascribed to him a divinity whereby he was believed to be God.

In that book I mentioned "Abraham, from whom the nation of the Hebrews began,"[2] and it is almost certainly believable that the Hebrews are thought to have been called something like Abrahews. But they are more correctly understood to have been called something like Hebrews after a man named Heber. I have discussed this matter enough in the sixteenth book of *The City of God.*[3]

In the second [book], when I was dealing with the two fathers of Joseph, I said that he was begotten by one and adopted by the other.[4] But it should have been said that he was adopted in accordance with the law[5] *on behalf of* the one who had died, which is more believable, because he who begot him had taken his mother, the wife of his deceased brother.

Again, I said, "Luke traces the line up to David through Nathan, the prophet by whom God removed [David's] sin."[6] I ought to have said "through the prophet of this name," lest anyone think that this was the same person when it was someone else, although that was what he too was called.

This work begins in this way: "Among all the divine authorities."

---

1. Augustine has gone from the singular ("Gospel") to the plural ("they").
2. I,14,21.
3. See *The City of God* XVI,3.11.
4. See II,3,5.
5. See Dt 25:5–6.
6. II,4,12.

Book One

1,1. Among all the divine authorities that are included in the sacred writings, the Gospel rightly stands out from the rest. For what the law and the prophets foretold for the future is shown in the Gospel as fulfilled and complete. The first preachers of this Gospel were the apostles, who saw our Lord and savior himself, Jesus Christ, when he was still in the flesh. They not only remembered the words they had heard from his mouth and the deeds he had done before their eyes, but when the duty of preaching the Gospel was placed upon them they also took care to announce to the human race those things that had happened before they were his disciples. They were able to inquire and learn about these divine and important events of his birth, infancy and childhood either from Jesus himself, or from his parents, or from others, with totally reliable information and completely trustworthy evidence. Some of them — Matthew and John — also produced in their respective books written accounts of him, containing those things it was necessary to put into writing.

1,2. But one might suppose that, concerning the understanding and proclamation of the Gospel, it might make a difference whether the ones announcing the Gospel were followers of the Lord when he appeared here in the flesh accompanied by his disciples or were people who came to believe by accurately learning from Jesus' followers. So that no one would suppose such a thing, divine providence, by the Holy Spirit, has made sure that some of those who came after the first apostles were given the authority not only to preach the Gospel but even to put it in writing.[1] Such are Mark and Luke. But all the others who have attempted or dared to put in writing the deeds of the Lord or of the apostles have not merited the trust of the Church in their own times, and their writings have not received the canonical authority of the sacred books.[2] This was so not only because their narratives were unfit to be believed but also because they deceptively put into their writings things which the Catholic and apostolic rule of faith and sound doctrine both condemn.[3]

2,3. Therefore there are those four evangelists who are completely familiar to the entire world. (It may be that there are four of them because there are four parts to the world,[4] so that by their number they show, as by some sort of sign,

---

1. Augustine seems to be implying here that writing is a more important and noteworthy undertaking than speaking. Although this may be unsurprising to us, it does run contrary to much of ancient culture, which still regarded writing as a more or less vulgar mnemonic device. On this, see P. J. Achtemeier, "*Omne Verbum Sonat*: The New Testament and the Oral Environment of Late Western Antiquity," in *Journal of Biblical Literature* 109 (1990) 3–27.
2. Augustine clearly presents a rather idealized view of the inclusion and exclusion of books from the canon.
3. On the criteria for inclusion in the New Testament (apostolic authorship and "correct" teaching), see, e.g. Bart D. Ehrman, *The New Testament: A Historical Introduction to the Early Christian Writings* (5th ed. New York 2012) 11. Works such as the *Gospel of Peter* and the *Gospel of Philip* would thereby be excluded.
4. Augustine may simply have in mind the four cardinal directions or perhaps the "four corners" of the world, as in Rv 7:1.

that the Church of Christ has spread everywhere throughout the world.) They are believed to have written in this order: first Matthew, then Mark, thirdly Luke, and finally John. Hence, as regards their knowledge and preaching there was one order among them, but as regards their writing there was another order. For indeed, with regard to knowledge and preaching, those certainly were first who had followed the Lord when he was here in the flesh; they heard what he said and saw what he did and they were sent out to preach the Gospel by a command from his mouth.[5] But with regard to composing a written Gospel, one which must be believed to be divinely ordained, there were only two of those whom the Lord chose before his passion, and these occupy the first place and the last: Matthew the first, John the last. This was done so that the other two, who were not from that group but were nonetheless followers of the Christ who spoke in these others, would be securely held by both of them and set between them like sons who should be embraced.

2,4. It is true that of these only Matthew is said to have written in the Hebrew language; the others wrote in Greek. And however much it might appear that each of them kept his own particular order of narration, it is not the case that any one of them can be found to have chosen to write in ignorance of his predecessor, or to have omitted as unknown something which another is found to have written. But because each was inspired, they refrained from adding any redundancy to their works. For Matthew is understood to have produced an account of the incarnation of the Lord according to the royal lineage and an account of most of his deeds and words as they relate to the present human life. Mark, following him, seems like his acolyte and summarizer. Mark shares no material with John that the others do not also share; he records little on his own that the others do not share; and he has even less in common with Luke unless the others share it also. But with Matthew he has very many agreements, and many of these use the same number of words or identical words; these agreements are either with Matthew alone or also with the others. On the other hand, Luke appears more concerned with the priestly lineage and character of the Lord. For, although he traces Jesus' genealogy back to David,[6] he does not do so by following the royal line but rather the line of those who were not kings; he traces the line through David's son Nathan,[7] who was not a king. But this is not the case with Matthew, who traces Jesus' genealogy through Solomon the king,[8] following the order of the kings; in this way, as we shall note later, he has preserved their mystical number.

3,5. For the Lord Jesus Christ, the one true king and the one true priest[9] (the former to rule us, the latter to make expiation for us), has shown how his own figure maintained these two characterizations, which were recognized only singly by

---

5.   See Mt 10:1–16; 28:19–20; Lk 10:1–12.
6.   Augustine's use of different verbs (*ascendo/descendo*) shows that Luke traced the lineage backwards (to God) and Matthew traced it forwards (to Jesus).
7.   See Lk 3:31.
8.   See Mt 1:6.
9.   See Heb 4:14–5:10; 8:1–13.

the Fathers. This is shown by that title which was put on his cross, *The King of the Jews* (Mt 27:37 par.), about which Pilate responded with cryptic instinct, *What I have written, I have written* (Jn 19:22). Indeed, it was foretold in the Psalms, *Do not destroy the writing of the title* (Ps 75 title). And, regarding his character as priest, it has been shown by his teaching us how to offer and receive. Thus he sent beforehand a prophecy about himself, saying, *You are a priest forever, according to the order of Melchizedek* (Ps 110:4). And there are many other places in Divine Scripture where Christ appears as both king and priest. Thus even David himself, whose son Christ is said to be more often than he is said to be Abraham's son, and whom Matthew and Luke alike have in Jesus' genealogy (the one tracing the genealogy down from him through Solomon, the other tracing it back to him through Nathan), although he was clearly a king, took on the character of a priest when he ate the bread of the presence, which only the priests are allowed to eat.[10] Moreover, it should be noted that only Luke recounts how Mary was found by the angel, and how she was a relative of Elizabeth,[11] who was the wife of Zechariah the priest. Luke also writes that Zechariah's wife was one of the daughters of Aaron, that is, that she was of the priestly tribe.[12]

3,6. Therefore, while Matthew focused on Christ's character as king, and while Luke focused on his character as priest, they both perfectly put forth Christ's humanity, for Christ was made both king and priest according to his humanity. God gave to him the throne of his father David, so that there might be no end to his kingdom[13] and so that there might be a mediator between God and men, the man Christ Jesus,[14] to intercede for us. But Luke had no one following him and acting as his summarizer, as Matthew had Mark. This is perhaps not without some significance, for kings are seldom without obedient followers. Therefore, the evangelist who had attempted to give an account of Christ's royal character had a follower associated with him, one who in some way followed in his steps. But since the priest would enter the holy of holies alone,[15] it is evident that Luke, who focused on Christ's priesthood, would not have a helper coming after him, one who in some way would summarize his narrative.

4,7. However, these three evangelists were concerned primarily with those things which Christ did in an earthly manner by means of human flesh. John, on the other hand, was concerned primarily with the true divinity of the Lord, in which he is equal to the Father; this he attempted most of all to convey in his Gospel, as much as he believed would be sufficient for humanity. Therefore he goes higher and farther than these three. In them you see those who in some way spoke with Christ the man on earth, but in John you see one who has passed beyond the cloud

10. See Lv 24:5–9; 1 S 21:6–7; Mt 12:3–4; Mk 2:25–26; Lk 6:3–4.
11. See Lk 1:36.
12. See Lk 1:5.
13. See Lk 1:32–33; Dn 7:14.
14. See 1 Tm 2:5.
15. See Lv 16:17.

that covers the entire earth and has arrived at the shining heaven from which he has looked with the clearest and steadiest mental eye upon God the Word, who was in the beginning with God, and by whom all things were made.[16] And he has recognized the one who was made flesh in order to dwell among us[17] — one who took on flesh, not one who was changed into flesh. For, if this assumption of flesh had been done without preserving the immutable divinity, it could not have been said that *I and the Father are one* (Jn 10:30), for the Father and the flesh are not one. And John alone has recorded the testimony of the Lord concerning himself, *The one who has seen me has also seen the Father* (Jn 14:9); and *I am in the Father and the Father is in me* (Jn 14:10); and *That they may be one even as we are one* (Jn 17:22); and *Whatever the Father does, these same things the Son does likewise* (Jn 5:19). Whatever other things reveal to the right-minded the divinity of Christ, in which he is equal to the Father, these things John alone has put into his Gospel. It is almost as if, while reclining on the Lord's breast at dinner, as he often did,[18] he drank in the secret of his divinity more fully and in some way more intimately than the others.

5,8. Furthermore, there are presented to the human mind two virtues, one active, one contemplative. Something moves by means of the former, something is arrived at by means of the latter. One labors by means of the former to cleanse the heart in order to see God;[19] one negates[20] oneself by means of the latter and God is seen. The former is concerned with the laws that govern this earthly life, the latter with the doctrine of that life which is eternal. In this way, also, the former acts while the latter rests; for the former is concerned with purifying us from sins, the latter with the light of the purified. In this way, also, the former is seen in this mortal existence in the work of a virtuous way of life,[21] but the latter is seen rather in faith, and only in a very few, through a glass darkly and only in part,[22] like some kind of vision of the immutable truth. These two virtues are understood to be symbolized by the two wives of Jacob.[23] I treated these two as well as I could and as much as seemed necessary in my work against Faustus the Manichean.[24] "Leah" clearly means "working," while "Rachel" means "the visible first principle."[25] By this one can understand (if one considers it carefully) that the three evangelists who were familiar with that active virtue were the ones who

---

16.   See Jn 1:1–3.
17.   See Jn 1:14.
18.   See Jn 13:23.
19.   See Mt 5:8.
20.   Literally "is emptied" (*vacatur*).
21.   See Jas 3:13; 1 Pt 2:12; 3:16.
22.   See 1 Cor 13:12.
23.   See Gn 29:16–28.
24.   See *Answer to Faustus, a Manichean* XXII,52.
25.   See the different allegorizations of the two sisters in Philo, *On Mating with the Preliminary Studies* 24–33, and in Justin Martyr, *Dialogue with Trypho* 134. Augustine's allegorization became widely known, as shown by Dante's use of it in *Purgatorio* XXVII, 97–108. See also the discussion in M. E. Mason, *Active Life and Contemplative Life* (Milwaukee 1961) 27–45.

most fully investigated the Lord's earthly deeds and those utterances of his that most directly pertain to the teaching of the ways of the present life. John, on the other hand, focused his attention and proclamation on the contemplative virtue; therefore he narrates far fewer of the Lord's deeds, but he records more carefully and fully his utterances, especially those that illustrate the unity of the Trinity and the happiness of eternal life.

6,9. Therefore it seems to me that, if one is to interpret the four living creatures of The Apocalypse as representing the four evangelists, then it is more likely that the lion represents Matthew, the man Mark, the calf Luke, and the eagle John, rather than that the man represents Matthew, the eagle Mark and the lion John.[26] This latter formulation focuses only on the beginnings of the books and not on the overall plan of the evangelists, which is what should have been examined more thoroughly. For it is more appropriate that the one who most clearly presented Christ's royal character should be signified by the lion. Thus also in The Apocalypse the lion is mentioned in connection with the royal tribe itself, where it is said, *The lion of the tribe of Judah has conquered* (Rv 5:5). And according to Matthew the magi are said to have come from the east to seek and worship the king whose birth was announced to them by the star;[27] and King Herod himself fears the royal child, so that, in order to kill him, he puts many children to death.[28] Neither [formulation] calls into question that Luke is signified by the calf, because of the priest's greatest sacrifice.[29] For there the narration begins with Zechariah the priest,[30] and the relationship between Mary and Elizabeth is mentioned.[31] There it is narrated that the rites of the earliest priesthood were performed in relation to the infant Christ;[32] and a careful investigation reveals other such things by which Luke shows his interest in the priestly character [of Christ]. Therefore Mark, who wishes to present neither [Christ's] royal lineage nor his priestly nature, whether by descent or by consecration, but who appears to present the things which Christ the man did, seems to be signified by the figure of the man among those four living creatures. But these three creatures, whether lion or man or calf, walk upon the earth; likewise, these three evangelists are concerned primarily with the things that Christ did in the flesh, and with the teachings of his that he gave to those who [also] bear the flesh concerning the conduct of this mortal life. John, on the other hand, soars above the clouds of human weakness like an eagle and gazes upon the light of unchangeable truth with the keenest and steadiest eyes of the heart.[33]

26. See Rv 4:7; 5:6; 7:11; Ezk 1:5. The four creatures are assigned to the evangelists in Irenaeus, *Against Heresies*, III,11,8; Jerome, *Commentary on Matthew*, preface.
27. See Mt 2:1–12.
28. See Mt 2:16–18.
29. See Heb 4:14–5:10; 8:1–13.
30. See Lk 1:5–25.
31. See Lk 1:36.
32. See Lk 2:22–24.
33. See *Homilies on the Gospel of John* 15,1; 36,5.

7,10. But these holy chariots of the Lord, in which he is carried throughout the world, bringing his easy yoke and light burden to the nations,[34] are attacked with false accusations by some people, motivated by either their impious vanity or their ignorant recklessness. They do this in order to diminish the trust put in this true account that has spread the Christian religion throughout the world so successfully that now unbelievers hardly dare to mutter their false accusations among themselves, restrained by the faith of the gentiles and the devotion of all the nations. Nevertheless, by their slanderous arguments they keep some from believing in the faith, while among believers they try as much as possible to trouble them with disturbances. But there are some brethren who, for the benefit of their own faith, want to know how to respond to such questions, either in order to advance their own knowledge or to refute the others' lies. In light of this, with the inspiration and help of the Lord our God (would that it might help in the salvation of such people!), we have undertaken in this work to show the errors and recklessness of those who have decided to make quite definite charges against the four books of the Gospel that have been written separately by the four evangelists. In order to do this, it must be shown that these four writers are not in opposition to one another. For, among their empty complaints, those [who attack the Gospel] usually hold up as their chief accusation that the evangelists disagree with one another.

7,11. But first we must discuss something that often disturbs some people—namely, why the Lord himself wrote nothing, so that we must believe others who wrote about him. This is what is said by pagans in particular when they do not dare to censure or blaspheme the Lord Jesus Christ himself but grant that he had the highest (though still only human) wisdom. Thus they claim that the disciples attributed more to their teacher than he really was by saying that he is the Son of God and the Word of God, by whom all things were made, and that he and God the Father are one; [they say the same] of similar passages in the epistles of the apostles, where we are told to worship him and the Father as one God.[35] For they believe that he should be honored as a very wise man, but they deny that he should be worshiped as God.

7,12. Therefore, when they ask why he himself wrote nothing, they would seem to be prepared to believe whatever he himself might have written about himself but not what others on their own authority might have proclaimed about him. To this I respond that, regarding some of their noblest philosophers, they have believed what their disciples recorded of them, when [the philosophers] themselves wrote nothing about themselves.[36] For Pythagoras, the most shining example that Greece then had of that contemplative virtue, is said to have written nothing either about himself or about anything else. And [much the same goes] for Socrates, whom they

---

34. See Mt 11:30.
35. See, e.g., 2 Cor 1:3; 11:31; Gal 1:1; Eph 1:3; 2:18; 3:14; Phil 2:11; Col 1:3; 2:2; 1 Thes 1:1; 2 Thes 1:1; Tit 1:4; 1 Pt 1:3; 1 Jn 1:3; 2:1.24; 5:7; 2 Jn 3:9.
36. See *The City of God* VIII,2–4.

esteem higher than all in the active [virtue] that forms morals.[37] They even claim he was declared to be the wisest of all by the testimony of their god Apollo. Only when he treated Aesop's fables in a few meager verses did he use his own words and numbers, applying them to another's subject. But really he wanted to write nothing: he says he did this only when compelled by the power of his own deity, as his noblest disciple Plato reports.[38] And in that work he wanted to report another's thoughts rather than his own. What reason then do they have to believe what those [philosophers'] disciples recorded about them when they refuse to believe what Christ's disciples wrote about him? This is especially relevant, since they admit that his wisdom was superior to that of other people, although they refuse to admit that he was God. Can it really be that those who they believe were greatly inferior to him have been able to make completely truthful disciples, while he himself was unable to do so? But if it is most absurd to say this, then they should believe of him, whose wisdom they admit, not what they themselves wish but what they read that was written by those who learned from that wise man.

8,13. Therefore they should say how they have come to know or to hear that he was the wisest person. If this has been spread by popular reports, then is it the case that popular reports form a more dependable account than that of his disciples, by whose proclamation of him the same report has permeated the whole world like a sweet aroma? In short, they should prefer one report over the other, and they should believe the better report. For certainly this report, which is broadcast with remarkable clarity by the Catholic Church, at whose expansion through the whole world they are amazed, unquestionably triumphs over their empty rumors. Furthermore, this report is so great and so renowned that out of fear of it they fret over their nervous and paltry little objections in their own hearts; they fear to be heard more than they want to be believed. [This report] proclaims Christ as the only begotten Son of God and as God, by whom all things were made.[39] If, then, they choose a report as witness, why not choose this one, which shines with such clarity? If written evidence, why not the Gospels, whose authority surpasses all others? Indeed, we believe what is said of their gods in their older writings and in the more renowned reports. But if they are to be worshiped, why do they mock them in the theaters?[40] If they are to be mocked, on the other hand, what could be greater mockery than to worship them in the temples? It is the case that those who wish to be witnesses to Christ, but who speak about what they do not know, thereby rob themselves of the right to know of what they speak. Or if they say that they have any books which they claim to have been written by him, let them show them to us. Indeed, if the man who they admit was the wisest wrote them, then they would be most advantageous and beneficial. If they are afraid to produce them, then those [books] must be evil; but if they are evil, then the wisest man cannot

---

37. See ibid. VIII,4.
38. See Plato, *Phaedo* 61b.
39. See Jn 1:3.
40. See *The City of God* II,13.

have written them. But they admit that Christ was the wisest man; therefore Christ cannot have written any such thing.

9,14. Indeed, they are so foolish as to claim that those books which they consider to have been written by him contain the methods by which they think he performed those miracles which have become well-known everywhere. By such thinking they show what they love and what they are trying to do, for they think Christ was the wisest man only because he knew some unheard-of forbidden arts, which are justly condemned not only by Christian teaching but even by the administration of earthly government itself. Furthermore, if they claim to have read such books of Christ's, why do they themselves not do the sorts of things that so amaze them when done by him in those books?

10,15. In fact, some are so much in error that it seems like a divine judgment; for some who believe or wish others to believe that Christ wrote such things claim that these books bore an address to Peter or Paul, like the heading of a letter. It is possible that either the enemies of the name of Christ or some who thought to give the weight of authority of so glorious a name to such damnable arts may have written such things under the name of Christ and the apostles. But by such deceitful audacity they have been so blinded that they only deserve to be mocked, even by children who are at the level of readers and know Christian literature only in an immature way.[41]

10,16. For when it occurred to them to represent Christ as writing to his disciples in such a way, they deliberated over who would seem the most believable as the addressees of such writing; these would seem to be those who were his intimate followers, to whom he was especially attached. And so Peter and Paul occurred to them, I believe, because in many places they saw pictures of both of them with him. For Rome, with especially solemn renown, commends the merits of Peter and Paul, because their martyrdoms were on the same day.[42] Therefore they deserved to fall completely into error, for they sought Christ and his apostles not in the holy books but on painted walls. Nor is it surprising that these pretenders were deceived by the painters, for, during the whole time that Christ lived in mortal flesh with his disciples, Paul was not yet his disciple. Only after his passion, after his resurrection, after his ascension, after the sending of the Holy Spirit from heaven,[43] after the conversion and astonishing faith of many Jews, after the stoning of Stephen the deacon and martyr,[44] when Paul was still called Saul and was violently persecuting those who believed in Christ[45] — [only then did Christ] call from heaven and

---

41. See Daniel I. Block, " 'That They May Hear': Biblical Foundations for the Oral Reading of Scripture in Worship," in *Journal of Spiritual Formation & Soul Care* 5.1 (2012) 5–34, esp. 11, on "reading" as the lowest level of instruction in the Scriptures (to be used to advance the learner into hearing, learning, fearing, obeying, and living).

42. See Eusebius, *Ecclesiastical History* II,25. Peter and Paul thus share the same feast day, June 29th.

43. See Acts 2:1–4.

44. See Acts 7:54–8:1.

45. See Acts 8:3; Gal 1:13; Phil 3:6.

make him his disciple and apostle.[46] How then could Christ, before he died, have written those books that they claim he wrote to his most intimate disciples Peter and Paul, when Paul was not yet his disciple?

11,17. [There are some] who madly rave that it was by magical arts that he was able [to do] the things [he did], and that by the same arts he made his name sacred to the peoples converted to him. They must answer this: How could he by magical arts, before he was born on earth, have filled with the divine Spirit those prophets who foretold as future events those things about him that we now read in the Gospel as accomplished facts, and the effect of which we now see in the world?[47] For, even if by magical arts he made himself be worshiped (although he was dead!), was he also a magician before he was born? One nation had been given the mission to prophesy his coming; the entire conduct of that state was a prophecy of this king who was to come and who was to establish a heavenly city out of all the nations.[48]

12,18. Moreover, this Hebrew nation (which, as I have said, was commissioned to prophesy Christ) had no other God but one God, the true God, who made heaven and earth and everything that is in them. Often he handed them over to their enemies because of his displeasure; indeed, now it is for their worst crime of murdering Christ that they have been completely banished from Jerusalem itself, which was the capital of their kingdom, and have been conquered by the Roman Empire. Now, the Romans usually appeased the gods of conquered nations by worshiping them, and they usually maintained their sacred rites, but they were unwilling to do this with the God of the Hebrew nation either when they attacked it or when they defeated it. I believe they saw that, if they accepted the sacred rites of a God who commanded that he alone be worshiped and that idols be destroyed, everything they had formerly worshiped would have to be abandoned, but they believed that the veneration of these had made their empire prosper. In this the fraudulence of their demons greatly deceived them. For certainly they should have understood that it was by the hidden will of the true God, who has power over all things,[49] that their kingdom was established and grew; it was not by the favor of those gods who, if they had had any power at all in the matter, would instead have protected their own peoples from being overrun by the Romans, or would have handed the vanquished Romans themselves over to them.

12,19. They cannot say that their own piety and customs became beloved and preferred by the gods of the nations they conquered. They will never say this as long as they recall their early history, when they were a refuge for criminals and when Romulus committed fratricide.[50] For Remus and Romulus established a refuge to which any criminal who had committed any crime could flee unpunished; they

---

46. See Acts 9:1–30.
47. See *Answer to Faustus, a Manichean* XII,45.
48. See ibid. XIII,4.15; XXII,17.24.
49. See *The City of God* V,21.
50. See ibid. I,34; III,6; XV,5.

gave no rules for penitence to rehabilitate the souls of such wretches. Rather, by rewarding impunity they armed the gathered cowardly gang against their cities, whose laws they feared. And when Romulus killed his brother, who had done him no wrong, he did not intend to defend justice but rather to assert brute force. Did the gods then love such actions, making themselves enemies of their own cities by favoring their enemies? No, they did not harm those who were being attacked, nor did they in any way help those [who were attacking], because they do not have the power to give or remove kingship; only the one true God does that by his hidden judgment. Those to whom he gives an earthly kingdom are not necessarily blessed, nor are those from whom he takes [one] necessarily wretched. Rather, he makes people blessed or wretched for other reasons and in other ways, distributing temporal and earthly kingdoms by either permission or gift to whomever he wishes and for however long he wishes, according to the predestined order of the ages.

13,20. Nor can they ask this: Why did the God of the Hebrews, whom you call the supreme and true God, not only not let them vanquish the Romans but not even help them not to be vanquished by the Romans? For they had committed obvious sins, for which the prophets long before had predicted that this would happen to them. Above all, in an evil rage they murdered Christ, and by this sin they were made blind to the guilt of their other hidden sins. That his passion would benefit the nations was predicted by the same prophetic witness. Nothing shows this more clearly than the following—that nation's kingdom, Temple, priesthood, cult and mystical anointing (which is called *chrisma* in Greek, from which the name of "Christ" is derived, and because of which that nation called its kings "christs," or "anointed ones") were established for no other reason than to foretell Christ; all these things ceased after the resurrection of the murdered Christ began to be preached to the believing gentiles. These things ceased because of the Romans' victory and the Jews' defeat, although neither was aware of it.

14,21. The few pagans who have remained [pagan] do not note this truly remarkable fact: the God of the Hebrews was an offense to the conquered and was also rejected by the conquerors[51] but is now preached and worshiped among all the nations. For this is that God of Israel of whom the prophet spoke long ago to the people of God: *And he who brought you out, the God of Israel, shall be called* [the God] *of the whole earth* (Is 54:5). This has been accomplished by the name of Christ, who came to men from the line of that very Israel who was a grandson of Abraham, from whom the nation of the Hebrews began.[52] For it was also to this Israel that it was said, *In your seed shall all the tribes of the earth be blessed* (Gn 28:14). This shows that the God of Israel, the one God, who made heaven and earth and who manages human affairs justly and mercifully in such a way that his justice does not exclude his mercy and his mercy does not hinder his

---

51. See 1 Cor 1:23.
52. In *Revisions* II,16 Augustine notes that the Hebrews may at one time have been called Abrahews after Abraham but that they most likely took their name from a man named Heber. He refers to a discussion of this in *The City of God* (XVI,3.11).

justice, was not himself conquered along with his Hebrew people by letting their kingdom and priesthood be destroyed and overthrown by the Romans. For, in fact, through the Gospel of Christ, the true king and priest, whose coming was prefigured by that kingdom and priesthood, the God of Israel himself is now everywhere overthrowing the idols of the nations. Indeed, it was to stop their destruction that the Romans refused to accept his rites as they accepted those of the gods of the other nations they conquered. Thus did he remove both kingdom and priesthood from the prophetic nation, because he who had been promised by that [nation] had come. And he has made the Roman Empire, which conquered that nation, subject to his name by Christ the king; and he has converted it by the strength and devotion of the Christian faith, overthrowing those idols whose worship had kept his rites from being accepted.

14,22. I do not think that it was by magical arts that Christ, before he was born among men, caused the events of his life to be foretold by so many prophets and also by the kingdom and priesthood of a certain nation. Indeed, the people of that now destroyed kingdom are scattered everywhere by the wonderful providence of God.[53] They have remained without any royal or priestly anointing, in which anointing the name of Christ is clearly seen.[54] Nonetheless, they do retain traces of some of their observances; even though they have been conquered and vanquished, they do not accept those Roman rites of idol worship. They keep the prophetic books as witness to Christ, and thus the truth of Christ, of whom the prophets spoke, is shown by the records of his enemies. What then do these wretches reveal about themselves when, with evil intent, they praise Christ? If anything about magic has been written under his name, while the doctrine of Christ is vehemently opposed to such practices, they ought rather to take this as indicating how great that name is, because even those who live in opposition to his precepts try to legitimate their abominable practices by using his name. For among the diverse human errors, many people have used his name when establishing their various heresies against the truth. In the same way, even Christ's enemies, although they recommend teachings that are against Christ's doctrine, still think they have no weight of authority unless they use Christ's name.

15,23. But those empty praisers of Christ and devious slanderers of the Christian religion do not dare to blaspheme Christ, because some of their philosophers, as Porphyry of Sicily relates in his books,[55] consulted their gods as to how they should respond to Christ, and they were forced by their oracles to praise Christ. Nor is this remarkable, for we also read in the Gospel that the demons confessed him.[56] As it is written in our prophets, *For the gods of the nations are demons* (Ps 96:5). Therefore they do not attempt to go against the responses of their gods,

---

53. See *The City of God* IV,34; XVIII,46.
54. "Anointing…anointing…Christ": *unctione…chrismate…Christi.* "Christ" and "chrism," in other words, are related terms, the former coming from the latter. See above at I,13,20.
55. See *The City of God* VII,25; X,9; XIX,22–23; Eusebius, *Ecclesiastical History* VI,19.
56. See, e.g., Mk 1:24; Lk 4:41.

and so they turn their blasphemies from Christ and heap them upon his disciples. But it seems to me that if these gods of the nations, whom the pagan philosophers may have consulted, were also asked about the disciples of Christ, they would be compelled to praise them too in the same way.

16,24. Nonetheless, these people still argue that this destruction of temples and condemnation of sacrifices and smashing of images is not brought about by the doctrine of Christ but by that of his disciples, who they contend taught something different from what he taught. In this way they intend to tear apart the Christian faith while honoring and praising Christ. But, at the very least, Christ's disciples proclaimed Christ's deeds and words on which this Christian religion is established; there is still a very small number opposed to this [religion], not with open attacks but with muted grumblings nonetheless. But, if they refuse to believe that Christ taught in this way, they should read the prophets, who not only commanded the destruction of the superstitions of idols[57] but even predicted that this destruction would also occur in Christian times. If they were mistaken, why is there so clear a fulfillment? If, on the other hand, they spoke the truth, why resist such divine prophetic power?

17,25. But this question requires more attention from them: What do they think the God of Israel is? Why do they not accept his worship like that of the gods of the other nations vanquished by the Roman Empire, especially since it is their opinion that all gods should be worshiped by the wise? Why then is this one excluded from the number of others? If he is the mightiest, why is he alone not worshiped by them? If he has little or no power, why are the images of [the other gods] smashed by all the nations, so that he is now almost the only one worshiped by them? They shall never be able to cast this question aside as long as they worship greater and lesser gods, who they suppose are gods, while not worshiping this God, who has overpowered all those whom they worship. If he has great power, why is he held in contempt? If he has little or no power, why has he been able [to do] so much, though he is held in contempt? If he is good, why is he alone separated from the other good [gods]? If he is evil, why is he the only one not to be overcome by so many good [gods]? If he is truthful, why are his commands rejected? If he is false, why are his predictions fulfilled?

18,26. In the end they may think of him however they wish. But do not the Romans recognize even the worship of evil gods?[58] Have they not built shrines to Pallor and Fever? Do they not advise that good demons should be treated well[59] and that bad demons should be placated? But, however they regard him, why have they considered him the only god who is neither called upon nor appeased? What is this God, who is either so unknown that he is the only one not yet found among so many gods or so well known that he is now the only one worshiped by so many people? Therefore there is nothing for them to say as to why they have refused to

---

57. See Is 2:18; Ezk 14:6.
58. See *The City of God* II,14; III,12.25; IV,15.23; VI,10; *Answer to Faustus, a Manichean* XX,9.
59. Reading *invitandos*; other editions read *imitandos* ("to be imitated").

accept the rites of this God except that he wishes to be the only one worshiped; he forbade the worship of those gods of the nations that they worshiped then. But this rather requires [an answer] from them: What, or of what kind, do they consider this God to be, who denies the worship of the other gods to whom they built temples and images? He is of such power that his will has succeeded more in destroying their images than theirs [has succeeded] in keeping his rites from acceptance. Indeed, the opinion of that philosopher of theirs is clear—and, based on their own oracle, they hold him to be the wisest of all people. For the opinion of Socrates is that every god should be worshiped in the way that he commanded himself to be worshiped. Therefore it is a matter of the greatest necessity for them not to worship the God of the Hebrews, for, if they want to worship him in a way other than how he has said he is to be worshiped, then they would not really be worshiping him as he is but as they themselves have invented him to be. But if they want [to worship him] in the way that he has said he [is to be worshiped], then they see that they cannot worship the other gods whose worship he forbade. For this reason they have rejected the religion of the one true God so as not to offend the many false ones, thinking that the anger of those would be more harmful to them than the favor of this one would be beneficial.

19,27. But that must have been a useless necessity and a ridiculous cowardice. We ask now what these people, who find pleasure in the worship of all the gods, think of this God. For if this one is not worshiped, how are all worshiped when this one is not worshiped? But if he is worshiped, then not all can be worshiped, because unless he alone is worshiped, he is not really worshiped. But perhaps they will say that he is not a god, while saying they are gods who, as we believe, have no power except what he grants them by his judgment. Not only can they not benefit anyone but they cannot even harm anyone except those whom the one who has all power judges to deserve harm. But, as they themselves are forced to admit, those [gods] are clearly able to do less than he. But are these gods whose prophets—though I do not say they are false—have nonetheless given answers that are well-suited to their own private interests? How then is he not God whose prophets have given answers that were not only correct concerning the things about which they were consulted at the time but are even so concerning things about which they were not consulted, things concerning the whole human race and all the nations, prophesied so long beforehand, which we now read and witness?[60] If they call a god the one who inspired the Sibyl to sing of the fates of the Romans,[61] how is he not God who, as foretold, has caused the Romans and all the nations, through the Gospel of Christ, to believe in him, the one God, and to destroy all the images of their fathers? Finally, if they call those gods, who have never dared through their prophets to say anything against this God, how is he not God who through his prophets not only commanded the destruction of their images but even

---

60. See *Answer to Faustus, a Manichean* XIII,7–11.
61. Reading *fata*; other editions read *facta* ("deeds").

predicted that among all the nations they would be destroyed by those who, having abandoned them, were commanded to worship him, the one God, and were by his command his servants?

20,28. Or let them claim, if they are able, that one of the Sibyls or any one of their other soothsayers predicted that in the future the God of the Hebrews, the God of Israel, would be worshiped by all the nations; and that the worshipers of other gods would have been right in rejecting him previously; and that the future writings of his prophets would be of so high an authority that even the Roman Empire, in order to obey them, would order the destruction of images, although warned not to obey such commands. Let them claim such things, if they are able, from any of the books of their soothsayers. For I do not hesitate to say that the things which are read in their books give testimony to our Christian religion; they might have learned the same thing from the holy angels and from our prophets themselves, just as even the demons were forced to confess Christ when he was present in the flesh.[62] But I leave aside those things we profess which they claim we made up, although they themselves may be pressed to show any prophecy by the soothsayers of their gods against the God of the Hebrews, just as we [can show] many and formidable ones from the books of our prophets against their gods. In ours we see the command, we read the prediction, and we show the accomplished fact. The few remaining pagans like to lament the fulfillment of these things rather than acknowledge that God who is able to foretell their fulfillment. But from their false gods, who are truly demons, they most eagerly desire to be told by their responses something that will happen to them.

21,29. Since these things are so, why do these wretches not understand that this God is the true God? Although they are forced to admit that he is God, they must think that he is separate from the company of their gods. How else could they not allow his worship with the others, when they claim that all gods should be worshiped? Since they cannot be worshiped together with him, why not choose the one who forbids the worship of the others and abandon those who do not forbid the worship of him? If they do forbid it, let us read where. For what could be more important than to read this to their people in their temples, where no such thing has ever been proclaimed? And, indeed, the prohibition of one by so many should be more notable and persuasive than that of so many by one.[63] For if the worship of this God is impious, then those gods are useless, since they do not keep people from such impiety. But if in fact the worship of this one is pious and precludes the worship of others, then their worship is impious. But if they forbid his worship so timidly that they dare to prohibit less than they fear to be heard,[64] who is so unwise as not to realize that this God should be chosen? He very publicly forbids the worship of others. He predicted, commanded, and himself brought about the destruction of their images. We do not know whether those others forbid his wor-

---

62. See, e.g., Mk 1:24; Lk 4:34.41.
63. Reading *notior et potentior.*
64. Reading *audiri timeant.*

ship, we do not read that they predicted such a prohibition, and we do not see that they have the power to bring it about. Why should anyone choose them? I pose the question; let them respond. Who is this God who torments all the gods of the nations, who overturns all their sacred rites, who thus destroys them?

22,30. Who is he? Why do I ask this question of people whose thought is empty? Some say that he is Saturn.[65] I think this is because of the sanctification of the sabbath, for they assign that day to Saturday.[66] Varro himself, whom they deem the most learned among them, thought that the God of the Jews was Jupiter.[67] He thought it did not matter by what name he was called as long as the same thing was understood; I think he was led astray in this regard by his unique supremacy. For the Romans hold Jupiter as the highest object of worship (their Capitol is a clear enough indication of this), and they consider him the king of all the gods. When he noticed that the Jews worship the supreme God, he could only comprehend it as Jupiter. But whether they think the God of the Hebrews is Saturn or Jupiter, let them tell us when Saturn dared to forbid the worship of another god? He did not do this even with Jupiter, the son who is said to have driven his father from his kingdom. And if the more powerful and victorious [Jupiter] is accepted by his worshipers, then they should not worship Saturn, the conquered and expelled. But Jupiter did not forbid his worship, either. Although he had been able to conquer him, he nonetheless let him remain a god.

23,31. They say that our writings are fables which only the wise can interpret or else laugh at. "But we" [they say] "worship Jupiter, of whom Maro says, 'Everything is full of Jupiter,'[68] that is, the life-giving spirit of all things." Varro therefore had reason to think that Jupiter was worshiped by the Jews, for God says by the prophet, *I fill heaven and earth* (Jer 23:24). But what does the same poet mean when he says "ether"? How do they understand it? For he says, "Then omnipotent father Ether, with fruitful rain, came down into the bosom of his joyful bride."[69] Indeed, they say that the ether is not a spirit but a rarefied body in which heaven is stretched above the atmosphere. Do we just give license to the poet [to sound] sometimes like a Platonist (according to whom God is not a body but a spirit) and sometimes like a Stoic (according to whom God is a body)? What then do they worship in the Capitol? If it is a spirit, or if it is the corporeal heaven itself, then what is the purpose of Jupiter's shield, which they call the aegis? Indeed, this name is explained by the story of a goat that fed Jupiter when he was hidden by his mother.[70] Or is this a lie of the poet? Or are the Roman temples the works of the poets? But what is this variability? It is not poetical, though it is clearly comical,

---

65. See *The City of God* VII,19.
66. See *Answer to Faustus, a Manichean* XVIII,5; XX,13.
67. See *The City of God* IV,10–11; VI,6; VII,5.
68. Virgil, *Eclogues* III,60; see *The City of God* IV,9.
69. Virgil, *Georgics* II,325; see *The City of God* IV,10.
70. Explaining *aegis* as derived from the Greek word for goat (*aix*).

that when you seek your gods in books you agree with the philosophers, but when you revere them in temples you agree with the poets.

23,32. But was that Euhemerus also a poet, who most clearly portrayed as men Jupiter himself, his father Saturn, and his brothers Pluto and Neptune?[71] Indeed, their worshipers should rather thank the poets, because they fashioned them so as to exalt them, not to dishonor them. Cicero relates that this Euhemerus was translated into Latin by Ennius the poet. Or was Cicero himself a poet? In the *Tusculan Disputations* he gives the following advice to his discussion partner, with whom he shares secret knowledge: "If one were to search into antiquity and probe what the Greek writers produced, one would find that even the higher sorts of gods went from us up into heaven. Ask whose tombs are found in Greece; remember, since you have been initiated, what is handed on in the mysteries. Then indeed you will understand how widespread this [belief] is."[72] He certainly admits often enough that their gods were human, although he kindly thinks that they went into heaven. But he did not hesitate to say publicly that their honorable reputation was bestowed on them by human beings. For he says of Romulus, "Because of kindness and fame we elevate to the immortal gods Romulus, who founded [this] city."[73] Therefore it is no surprise that ancient people did with Jupiter and Saturn and others the same thing that the Romans did with Romulus; indeed, more recently they wished to do the same with Caesar. Virgil added the flattery of poetry to these, saying, "Behold, the star of Caesar came from Dione."[74] Therefore, let them beware, for historical truth reveals the tombs of false gods on earth, and poetic vanity fabricates rather than authenticates their stars in heaven.[75] For that is not really the star of Jupiter, nor is that one [the star] of Saturn. Rather, people wished to honor some people after their deaths by imposing their names on the stars, which were fixed from the beginning of the world. And, among these, why should chastity be slighted and pleasure rewarded? For, among the heavenly bodies that revolve with the sun and the moon, Venus has a star and Minerva does not.[76]

23,33. But it may be that Cicero the academician is less trustworthy than the poets. He is daring enough to recall the tombs of the gods and to put it in writing, although he does not offer it as his own opinion but recalls it from the traditions of their own shared rites. Or does even Varro fabricate things like a poet or put things dubiously like an academician? For he says that the worship of such gods is based either on the life or on the death they experienced among human beings. Or was Leon the Egyptian priest a poet or academician?[77] For he explained the origin of

---

71.　See *The City of God* IV,27; VI,7; VII,27. Euhemerus was a late-4th-century B.C. Greek thinker who popularized the idea that the gods were once human beings.

72.　Cicero, *Tusculan Disputations* I,13,29; see *The City of God* VIII,5.

73.　Cicero, *Against Catiline* III,13,29; see *The City of God* II,15; III,15.

74.　Virgil, *Eclogues* IX,47.

75.　Punning on *fingere* ("to fabricate") and *figere* ("to authenticate").

76.　Venus was the goddess of love and Minerva the goddess of wisdom.

77.　See *The City of God* VIII,5.27; XII,11.

their gods to Alexander of Macedon differently than the Greeks' opinion, though still showing that those gods had been human.

23,34. But what is this to us? They say that they worship Jupiter and not some dead man and that they have dedicated their Capitol not to some dead man but to the spirit that enlivens everything and fills the entire world. And they may give any interpretation they wish to his shield, which was made of goatskin in honor of his nurse. But what do they say about Saturn?[78] What do they worship in Saturn? Is he not the first one who came from Olympus? "Fleeing from Jupiter's arms and exiled from his kingdom, he brought together the ignorant people scattered on the mountain tops and gave them laws and wished that the place where he lay be called Latium."[79] Does not his image, which includes a covered head, show him as concealed?[80] Did he not introduce agriculture to the Italians, as shown by his sickle? They answer, "No, for you may see whether there was a man or king of whom such things were said. But we interpret Saturn as universal time, as shown by his Greek name. For he is called Kronos, which with the added aspiration is the word for time.[81] Also in Latin he is called Saturn, as though he were saturated with years."[82] I do not know what is to be done with these people. While trying to give a better interpretation of the names and images of their gods, they admit that their greatest god, who is the father of the others, is "Time." But what else do they show by this than that all their gods are temporal, since the father of them all is composed of time?

23,35. Their more recent Platonic philosophers, who have lived during Christian times, have been embarrassed by this. They try to interpret Saturn in another way, saying that the name Kronos indicates fullness of understanding. For fullness is called *choros* in Greek, and understanding or mind is *nous*. In a way the Latin name favors this [interpretation], if the first part is from Latin and the latter part from Greek: he is called Saturnus, as though he were "Satur-*nous*," "full-mind." For they saw how absurd it was if Jupiter were a son of time, while they considered him, or wished others to consider him, as the eternal god. But if their ancient authorities had this [interpretation], it is remarkable that Cicero and Varro failed to mention it.[83] However, according to this novel interpretation they say that Jupiter is the son of Saturn, as though his is the spirit emanating from that supreme mind; they want this [spirit] to be understood as the soul of this world, which fills all heavenly and earthly bodies. Why does Maro say, "Everything is full of Jupiter," as I mentioned a little earlier?[84] If they are able, should they not change human superstition as well as interpretation, and [get rid of] all images, or at least build temples to Saturn rather than Jupiter? For they claim that no rational soul is wise

---

78.   See ibid. VII,13.
79.   Virgil, *Aeneid* VIII,320–324.
80.   Punning on Latium and *latens* ("concealed").
81.   I.e., Ch instead of C or K.
82.   Punning on Saturnus and *saturetur* ("saturated").
83.   See *The City of God* VI,8; VII,9.13.
84.   See above at I,23,31.

except by participation in his supreme and unchangeable wisdom.[85] [They say] this not only of a human soul but even of that world [soul] which they call Jupiter. Now, we not only concede but we specifically proclaim that any soul that is truly wise is so by participation in the supreme wisdom of God.[86] But it is a large and obscure question whether that universal bodily mass, which is called the world, has a kind of soul, or its own soul.[87] Does it have a rational life, which regulates it like any other animal? This opinion should not be accepted unless it is proved true; nor should it be rejected unless it is proved false. But what difference does it make for people if this remains unresolved forever, since no soul becomes wise or blessed by another soul but only by the supreme and unchangeable wisdom of God?

23,36. But the Romans, who have built the Capitol for Jupiter and not Saturn, or those other nations which believe that Jupiter should have special worship above the other gods, do not feel this way. In accord with their own new opinion they would — if they had the power [to do] such things — dedicate even their greatest monuments to Saturn; they would especially eliminate the astrologers and horoscope-makers who make Saturn into an evil god among the other stars,[88] while they would say that he was the creator of the wise. But this opinion is so widespread in people's minds that they refrain from naming him, calling him "the old one" rather than Saturn. This superstition is so fearful that the Carthaginians have nearly changed the name of their town, calling it "the town of the old one" more often than "the town of Saturn."

24,37. Therefore it is obvious what these idolaters worship and what they try to hide. But even these new interpreters of Saturn must explain what they think of the God of the Hebrews. For it seemed right to them also to worship all gods along with the [other] nations, since their pride kept them from humbling themselves under Christ for the remission of their sins. Then what do they think of the God of Israel? For, if they do not worship him, then they do not worship all gods; but if they do worship him, they do not worship him as he commanded, for they also worship others, whose worship he has prohibited. He prohibited this through the prophets, through whom he also foretold those things now done to their idols by Christians. For either angels were sent to those prophets, who figuratively, by the congruence of sensible things, showed them the one true God, the creator of all things, to whom the universe is subject, and they indicated in what way he ordered his own worship, or else the minds of some of them were elevated by the Holy Spirit, so that they saw with angelic vision. Either way, they served that God who prohibited the worship of other gods, and they preserved their country with the faith of piety in the royal and priestly roles and [preserved] those rites that prefigured the coming Christ, king and priest.

---

85. See ibid. X,2.
86. See Jb 12:13; 28:12–28; Prv 8:1–36; 1 Cor 1:30; 2:7; Eph 1:17; Col 1:9; 2:3; Jas 1:5.
87. See *The City of God* VII,23.
88. On astrology see *Confessions* IV,3,4; VII,6,8.

25,38. But, further, let them say why none of the gods of the nations (whom they wish to worship and therefore wish not to worship him who cannot be worshiped with them) has ever prohibited the worship of another. They give them different offices and functions, and have them govern the things appropriate to each of their stations.[89] For Jupiter does not prohibit the worship of Saturn, although this is not because he is just a man who expelled another man, his father, from his kingdom; he is either the body of the heavens or the spirit that fills heaven and earth, and therefore he cannot prohibit the worship of that higher mind from which he is said to have emanated. In the same way, Saturn does not prohibit the worship of Jupiter, although this is not because he is just somebody conquered by some rebel named Jupiter, from whose arms he came fleeing into Italy, but because the first mind favors the soul that it begat. But surely Vulcan would prohibit the worship of Mars, his wife's lover, and Hercules that of Juno, his persecutor. What sort of foul consensus is there among them, so that Diana, the chaste virgin, does not prohibit the worship, I say, not only of Venus but even of Priapus?[90] If one person wants to be both a hunter and a farmer, he will have to be the servant of both, though it will embarrass him even to build their temples near each other. But they may interpret Diana as whatever virtue they wish, and they may interpret Priapus as a god of fecundity, although Juno would rightly be embarrassed to have such a helper with female fertility. Let them say what they please and interpret as they deem wise. The God of Israel will overturn all their arguments nonetheless. He has prohibited the worship of all of them, while his worship is prohibited by none of them. He has also commanded, foretold, and accomplished the destruction of their images and rites, and he has clearly shown that they are false and lying and that he himself is the true and truthful God.

25,39. Who does not wonder at the following? Those worshipers, now few in number, of the numerous and false gods, when asked what god [our God] is, whatever answer they may give, dare not deny that he is a god, [although] they refuse to submit to him. For, if they deny this, they are easily disproved by his actions, both prophesied and fulfilled. I do not speak of those things which they think they are free to disbelieve, such as the fact that in the beginning he made heaven and earth and all that is in them,[91] nor of things in remotest antiquity, such as when he took up Enoch,[92] destroyed the wicked with the flood, and saved the righteous Noah and his household by way of wood.[93] I begin the story of his acts among human beings with Abraham.[94] For a clear promise was given to him by an angelic oracle that we now see fulfilled. To him was said, *In your seed shall all the nations be blessed* (Gn 22:18). From his seed were the people of Israel,

---

89.   See *The City of God* VI,9.
90.   See ibid. II,14; VII,24.
91.   See Gn 1:1–2:1.
92.   See Gn 5:24.
93.   See Gn 6:5–8:22.
94.   See Gn 12:1.

from whence was the Virgin Mary, who bore Christ, in whom all the nations are blessed.[95] If they are able, let them dare to deny this. This promise was also made to Isaac, the son of Abraham,[96] and to Jacob, the grandson of Abraham.[97] Jacob was also called Israel, and the whole people got their lineage and name from him, so that the God of this people is called the God of Israel. [This is not to say] that he is not also the God of all the nations, whether or not they now know him, but he wished to reveal the power of his promises more clearly among this people. For that people first multiplied in Egypt;[98] then they were freed from slavery there by Moses, with many signs and wonders.[99] They conquered most of the nations and received the land of promise, their kings from the tribe of Judah reigning there. Judah was one of the twelve sons of Israel,[100] Abraham's grandson. From him came the Jews, who did many things with God's help, and who suffered many things when God punished them for their sins, until the promised seed came[101] in whom all the nations would be blessed and [for whom] they willingly broke up the idols of their fathers.

26,40. For what is accomplished by Christians is not just of the Christian era but was predicted long before. The very same Jews who remain enemies of Christ's name, and of whose future treachery these prophetic writings are not silent, possess and read the prophet who says, *O Lord my God and refuge in the day of evil, the nations shall come to you from the ends of the earth and say, Truly our fathers worshiped lying idols, and there is no value in them* (Jer 16:19). Behold, that is now happening. Behold, now the nations are coming to Christ from the ends of the earth, saying such things and breaking their idols. And this is a great thing that God has established beforehand for his Church spread throughout the world. The Jewish people, rightly conquered and dispersed across the earth, carries our prophetic books everywhere, so that no one could suppose they were composed by us. Thus an enemy of our faith has become a witness to our truth. How then can Christ's disciples have taught what they have not learned from Christ, as those ridiculous men in their foolishness claim, in order to destroy the superstition of the gods and idols of the nations? Can they also say that those prophecies that are now read in the books of Christ's enemies were fabricated by Christ's disciples?

26,41. For who other than the God of Israel has overturned them? For divine voices said to this people through Moses, *Hear, O Israel, the Lord our God is one Lord* (Dt 6:4). *You shall not make for yourselves any idol or likeness of anything that is in heaven above or on the earth below* (Ex 20:4; Dt 5:8). Also, so that this people might overturn those things wherever they were able to, they were given this commandment, *You shall not worship their gods, or serve them, or do their*

---

95. See Gal 3:16.
96. See Gn 26:4.
97. See Gn 28:14.
98. See Ex 1:7.
99. See Ex 7:8–11:10.
100. See Gn 29:35.
101. See Gal 3:19.

works, but you shall completely tear them down and utterly destroy their images (Ex 23:24). Who will say that Christ and Christians have no connection to Israel? Israel was the grandson of Abraham, and, as I have mentioned, the following was said first to Abraham, then to his son Isaac, then to his grandson Israel: *In your seed shall all the nations be blessed.* We see this now in Christ. For from [Abraham's line] came that virgin of whom the prophet of the people of Israel and of the God of Israel sang, *Behold, a virgin shall conceive and bear a son, and they shall call his name Emmanuel* (Is 7:14). Emmanuel is interpreted as meaning *God is with us* (Mt 1:23). Therefore the God of Israel has prohibited the worship of other gods, prohibited the making of idols, commanded their overthrow, and predicted through his prophet that the nations from the ends of the earth would say, *Truly, our fathers have worshiped lying idols, in which there is no value* (Jer 16:19). This same God has ordered, promised, and brought about the overthrow of all these superstitions through the name of Christ and the faith of Christians. These gods—that is to say, demons, who fear the name of Christ—have prohibited these miserable people[102] from blaspheming Christ, but they still try in vain to make this doctrine out to be something foreign to him, although Christians use it to argue against idols and to eradicate false religions wherever they can.

27,42. Let them answer now concerning the God of Israel. The books not only of the Christians but also of the Jews[103] testify that he teaches and commands these things. Let them consult their own gods, who prohibit the blaspheming of Christ. If they say anything insulting concerning the God of Israel, let them respond. But whom should they consult? Or where now should they go for advice? Let them read their own books. If they think the God of Israel is Jupiter, as Varro has written (I speak now according to their opinion), why then do they not believe that the idols are to be destroyed by Jupiter? If they think he is Saturn, why do they not worship him? Or why do they not worship him as he has commanded through those prophets through whom he foretold what he has accomplished? Why do they not believe that idols should be overthrown and other gods not worshiped? If he is neither Jupiter nor Saturn (indeed, if he were one of these, he would not speak against the rites of Jupiter and Saturn so much), then who is he? Among the gods, he is the only one not worshiped by them, yet he clearly overthrows the other gods, so that he alone is worshiped; he has humiliated all the proud and exalted[104] who set themselves up against Christ on behalf of their idols, persecuting and killing Christians. Indeed, it is now a question where such people go when they wish to sacrifice, or where they hide their gods to keep them from being found and broken up by Christians. This is done out of fear of the laws and rulers through whom God exercises his power and who are subject to the name of Christ. He promised this long ago, saying through the prophet, *All the kings of the earth shall worship him, all the nations shall serve him* (Ps 72:11).

---

102. I.e., the pagans.
103. I.e., the Old and New Testaments.
104. See Lk 1:51–52.

28,43. Indeed, what was repeatedly said by the prophets is now being fulfilled—that he would abandon his impious people (though not entirely, for many Israelites, such as his apostles, have believed in Christ), and that he would humble all the proud and violent. Thus he alone would be exalted. It would be revealed to people that he alone was high and mighty, until idols are cast away by believers and hidden by unbelievers, when the earth is broken with fear of him and earthly men are subdued by fear [105]—by fearing either the law of [God] himself or that of those believers who rule among the nations and prohibit such sacrilege.

28,44. I say these things briefly and for easier comprehension, as a preface to what the prophet says: *And now you, O house of Jacob, come, let us walk in the light of the Lord. For he has abandoned his people, the house of Israel, because their country is as full as it was at the beginning with their soothsayers, like those of foreigners, and many foreign children are born to them. Their country is full of silver and gold, and there is no counting their treasures. The land is full of horses, and there is no counting their chariots. The land is full of abominations, works of their own hands, and they have worshiped what their own fingers have made. And the ordinary person has bowed down and the strong man has humiliated himself,[106] and I will not forgive them. And now go into the rocks and hide yourselves in the earth from before the fear of the Lord and from the majesty of his power, when he arises to smash the earth. For the eyes of the Lord are high, but man is low. For the haughtiness of men shall be humbled, and the Lord alone shall be exalted on that day. For the day of the Lord of hosts [shall come] upon all who are unjust and proud, and upon all who are high and exalted, and they shall be humbled, upon all the high and exalted cedars of Lebanon, and upon all the trees of the acorn of Bashan, and upon all the mountains and all the high hills, and upon all the ships of the sea and upon all the wondrous beauty of ships. And human audacity shall be humbled and fall, and the Lord alone shall be exalted on that day. And in caves, and in cracks in the rocks, and in caverns of the earth they shall hide all things made by hand from before the fear of the Lord and from the majesty of his power, when he arises to smash the earth. For on that day people shall throw away the abominations of gold and silver, the empty and offensive things that they made to worship, putting them into holes in the solid rock and into cracks in the rocks, from before the fear of the Lord and from the majesty of his power, when he arises to demolish the earth.* (Is 2:5–14.16–17.19–21)

29,45. What do they say of this God of Sabaoth,[107] which means God "of powers" or "of armies," since the powers and armies of angels serve him? What do they say of this God of Israel? For he is the God of that people from whom came

---

105. Punning on *confringitur* ("broken") and *franguntur* ("subdued").

106. "Ordinary person...strong man": *homo...vir.*

107. The title is the same as "Lord of hosts," which Augustine used in the preceding paragraph; here he explains its meaning. It appears frequently in the Old Testament, as in 1 S 1:3; Ps 89:8; Is 48:2.

the seed in which all nations were to be blessed.[108] Why is he alone not worshiped by those who assert that all gods should be worshiped? Why do they not believe in him, since he both disproves and overthrows the other false gods? I have heard one of them say that he had read in some philosopher that one could learn what God the Jews worshiped from what they did in their sacred rites. He said, "He is the ruler of those elements out of which this visible and corporeal world is built,"[109] just as the Holy Scriptures of his prophets clearly show that the people of Israel were commanded to worship the God who made heaven and earth and from whom comes all true wisdom. But there is no need to discuss this further; it is sufficient for me that they presume whatever they please concerning that God, who they cannot deny is God. For, if he is the ruler of the elements of which the world consists,[110] why is he not worshiped instead of Neptune, who is ruler only of the sea? Why not instead of Silvanus, who [is ruler] only of fields and woods? Why not instead of the Sun, who [is ruler] only of the day, or of all heavenly heat? Why not instead of the Moon, who [is ruler] only of the night, or who has special power over moisture? Why not instead of Juno, who is said to have power only over the air? For, clearly, whoever rules the parts must necessarily be under the one who governs all the elements and all this massive universe, but he prohibits the worship of all the others. Why then do they go against the command of the greater one, not only choosing to worship those [lesser ones] but even refusing for their sakes [to worship] him? But they have not discovered anything clear and consistent to say concerning this God of Israel. Nor will they ever discover such until they discover that he is the one true God by whom all things were created.

30,46. I believe that Lucan, one of their great poetic speakers, searched for who the God of the Jews was, using his own reflections as well as books. Since he did not search piously, he did not find him. But since he perceived such great proofs of him, he did not deny he was a god but called him rather the unknown God, whom he did not find. For he says, "...and Judea, dedicated to the worship of an unknown God."[111] And God, the holy and true God of Israel, had not yet done by the name of Christ such things among all the nations as he has done since Lucan's times up to today. Who now is so inflexible that he does not yield? Who is so senseless[112] that he is not inflamed when the Scripture is fulfilled, *There is no one who is hidden from its heat* (Ps 19:6)? Things predicted long ago in the Psalm from which I just cited part of a verse have now been revealed in the clearest light. For Christ's apostles were signified by the word *heavens*, since God directed them in order to announce the Gospel. Now, therefore, *the heavens have proclaimed the glory of God, and the firmament has shown the works of his hands. Day has brought forth speech to day, and night has revealed knowledge to night. Now there*

---

108. See Gn 22:18.
109. Perhaps the philosopher is Numenius, cited in Eusebius, *Preparation for the Gospel* VII,3.
110. See *The City of God* IV,10.
111. Lucan, *Pharsalia* II,592–93.
112. Reading *torpidus*; other editions read *tepidus* ("tepid").

*is no language or dialect in which their voices are not heard. Now their sound
has gone out to all the earth, and their words to the end of the world.* (Ps 19:1–4)
Now he has set his tent, which is his Church, in the sun; that is, [he has made it]
manifest.[113] In order to do this, as it says in the passage quoted, he *came out of his
chamber like a bridegroom* (Ps 19:5); that is, the Word, wedded to human flesh,
came out from the Virgin's womb. Now he has rejoiced like a hero and has run
his course. Now his rising has been made from the end of the heavens, and his
return to the end of the heavens.[114] And therefore it is completely right that the
verse I previously mentioned in part follows, *There is no one who is hidden from
its heat.* And still these people choose to babble about their paltry little objections,
which are like stubble turned to ashes by that fire,[115] rather than like gold purged
of its dross.[116] And now the fraudulent monuments of their false gods have been
overturned, while the true promises of that unknown God have been confirmed.

31,47. Therefore those evil persons who praise Christ but refuse to become
Christians should stop saying that Christ did not teach them to forsake their gods
and break up their idols.[117] For the God of Israel, of whom it was predicted that he
would be called the God of the whole earth,[118] is now called the God of the whole
earth. He predicted this through his prophets, and through Christ he brought it
about at the appropriate time. Indeed, if the God of Israel is now called the God
of the whole earth, then what he commanded must come to pass, for the one who
commands is well known. But he is known through Christ and in Christ, so that
his Church is spread throughout the world; through it the God of Israel is called
the God of the whole earth, as those who wish may read a little earlier in the same
prophet. Indeed, I should cite it myself, for it is not so long as to prevent one from
citing it. For here much is said of the presence, humility, and passion of Christ, and
of the body of which he is the head, that is, his Church,[119] which is called barren,
for it is not so long that it ought to be omitted. For many years the Church had
not yet appeared, although eventually its children, the saints, would be in every
nation, for Christ had not been announced by the evangelists to those who had not
heard the prophets. Further, it says there will be more children for the one who is
deserted than for the one who has a husband,[120] the word *husband* signifying either
the law or the king whom the people of Israel first accepted. For, at the time the
prophet spoke, neither had the gentiles accepted the law nor had a Christian king
yet appeared, although subsequently a more productive and numerous group of
saints has come from the gentiles. Therefore Isaiah speaks thus, starting with the

---

113. See Ps 19:4.
114. See Ps 19:5–6.
115. See Is 47:14.
116. See Prv 17:3.
117. See Ex 34:13; Dt 7:5.
118. See Is 54:5.
119. See Col 1:18.
120. See Is 54:1.

humility of Christ[121] and later turning to address the Church, continuing on to that verse which we have already mentioned, where he says, *The one who brought you out, the God of Israel himself, will be called* [the God] *of the whole earth* (Is 54:5).

Behold, he says, my servant shall be wise and shall be highly exalted and honored. So many shall marvel at you, yet your appearance shall seem dishonorable to everyone, but you shall be honored by them. For many nations shall marvel at him, and kings shall shut their mouths, for those to whom he has not been announced shall see, and those who have not heard shall understand. Lord, who has believed our report? And to whom has the arm of the Lord been revealed? We have proclaimed him as a servant, as a root in dry ground, and he has neither attractiveness nor honor. We have seen him, and he has neither attractiveness nor beauty. But his face is downcast and his shape is unattractive to all people. He is a beaten man, one who knows how to bear infirmities. For this his face is turned away, injured, and not highly esteemed. He bears our infirmities and is in sorrows for us. And we considered him to be sorrowful, beaten, and punished. He was wounded for our sins and laid low for our iniquities. The price of our peace was laid on him, and by his bruises we are healed. Like sheep we have all wandered off, and the Lord gave him up for our sins. And, while he was treated badly, he did not open his mouth. He was led like a sheep to the slaughter and, like a lamb that is silent before its shearer, he did not open his mouth. In humility judgment was passed on him. Who will explain his generation? His life shall be cut off from the land. By the iniquities of my people he is led to death. Therefore I will give up the evil for his burial and the rich for his death. He committed no iniquity and there was no deceit in his mouth. The Lord wishes to cleanse him by beating. If you give your soul for your crimes, you shall see the seed of a very long life. The Lord wishes to remove his soul from sorrows, to show him the light, to make him manifest, and to justify the righteous one who serves many well, and he shall bear their sins. Therefore he shall have many for his inheritance, and he shall divide the spoils of the strong. For this his soul was handed over to death and he was counted among the unjust. He bore the sins of many and was handed over for their iniquities. Rejoice, you barren, you who do not give birth; leap and shout, you who are not in labor, for the children of the one who was abandoned are many more than those of her who has a husband. For the Lord has said, Enlarge the site of your tent and fasten your curtains;[122] *there is no reason to spare. Stretch out your ropes and set your stakes firmly. Again and again expand your area to the right and to the left. For your seed shall inherit the nations and you shall inhabit the cities that were desolate. There is nothing for you to fear, for you shall prevail. And you shall not be ashamed of being despised. For you shall forget your confusion forever. You shall not remember the disgrace of your widowhood, since I am the Lord who made you. The Lord is his name. The one*

---

121. Reading *humilitate*; other editions read *humanitate* ("humanity").
122. Reading *aulaeas* instead of *aulas* ("halls," "courts"). See Letter 105,15; *The City of God* XVIII,29.

who brought you out, the God of Israel himself, shall be called [the God] *of the whole earth.* (Is 52:13–54:5)

31,48. What can be said against this evidence, this expression of things both predicted and fulfilled? If they think that his disciples lied about Christ's divinity, will they also doubt Christ's passion? They are not used to believing in his resurrection, but they readily believe that he suffered all the human things inflicted by men, for they wish to believe that he was only human. So, he was led like a sheep to the slaughter. He was counted among the unjust. He was wounded for our sins. By his bruises we are healed. His face was injured and not highly esteemed, beaten with hands and smeared with spit. His shape was broken on the cross. He was led to death by the iniquities of the people of Israel. He is the one who had neither attractiveness nor beauty when he was struck with blows, when he was crowned with thorns, or when he was mocked as he hung. He is the one who, like a lamb that is silent before its shearer, did not open his mouth when those who insulted him said, *Prophesy to us, O Christ!* (Mt 26:68) But now indeed he is exalted, now he is highly honored. Now indeed many nations marvel at him. Now kings have shut those mouths by which they used to pronounce the cruelest laws against Christians. Those indeed to whom he was not announced now see, and those who have not heard now understand.[123] For those nations to whom the prophets did not speak now see that what the prophets said is true. And those who have not heard Isaiah himself speaking now understand from his writings what he said of him. Even in the very nation of the Jews, who among them believed the prophets' report? To whom has the arm of the Lord been revealed, which is Christ himself who was announced by them? For by their own hands they committed those crimes which had been predicted by the prophets who lived among them. He has indeed now inherited many, and he divides the spoils of the strong, since he has expelled and defeated the devil and the demons and has distributed their possessions for the building of his churches and for other necessities.

32,49. Then what do these perverse praisers of Christ, who are also detractors of Christians, say to these things? Did Christ, by some magical arts, cause those things to be predicted so long ago by the prophets? Or did his disciples fabricate them? Is this why the Church, once barren, is now spread throughout the nations, and rejoices in [having] more children than that Synagogue which had a sort of husband in the law or in its king? Is this why [the Church] enlarges the site of its tent, occupying all nations and languages, extending its ropes beyond the limits of the laws of the Roman Empire, even into Persia and India and other barbarous nations? Is this why both true Christians and even false ones spread his name among so many peoples?[124] Is this why his seed inherits the nations, so that they now inhabit cities that were once empty of the true worship of God and of the true religion? Is this why [the Church] has not feared human threats and furies, even

---

123. See Rom 15:21.
124. See Phil 1:15–18.

when the blood of the martyrs has honorably clothed it like a purple robe? Is this why it has prevailed over its many violent and powerful persecutors? Is this why it has not been ashamed of being despised, when it was a great crime to become or to be a Christian? Is this why it has forever forgotten its confusion, because, where sin abounded, grace abounded all the more.[125] Is this why the disgrace of its widowhood is forgotten, since it was abandoned and derided only for a little while and now flourishes again with outstanding glory? To summarize: the Lord, who made [the Church] and brought it out from the domination of the devil and demons, the very God of Israel, is now called the God of the whole earth. Can it be that Christ's disciples fabricated this when the prophets, whose books are now in the hands of Christ's enemies, predicted this so long before Christ became the Son of Man?

32,50. From this let them understand that this does not remain obscure or doubtful even to the slowest and dullest people. Let those, I say, who perversely praise Christ and curse the Christian religion understand this: against their gods, Christ's disciples have learned and taught what Christ's doctrine contains. For it is clear that the God of Israel commanded that everything these people wish to worship should be hated and destroyed. Because of Christ and Christ's Church, this very God is now called [the God] of the whole earth, just as he promised so long ago. But if in their amazing madness they suppose that Christ worshiped their gods and through them had such power, is it then the case that their gods were also worshiped by the God of Israel, who has fulfilled through Christ his promises that he would be worshiped in all the nations and that the other [gods] would be hated and destroyed?[126] Where are their gods? Where are the ravings of their fanatics and the predictions of their oracles? Where are the signs or omens or divinations or oracles of their demons? Why in their ancient books are there found no warnings or predictions against the Christian faith or against the truth of our prophets, which is now so clearly expressed in every nation? They say, "We have offended our gods and they have deserted us; that is why the Christians prevail against us, and human wellbeing falters, weakened and diminished." But let them read from the books of their soothsayers, where [it is said that] such things would occur because of the Christians. Since they want to believe that Christ worshiped their gods, let them show where at least this God of Israel, who insists on the destruction of others, is disapproved of and hated. But they will never find such a passage unless they fabricate it themselves. If they were to produce such, it would clearly be from themselves, because of the obscurity from which they [supposedly] brought forth such an important thing. For it ought to have been proclaimed in the temples of the gods of all nations before what was predicted had happened, in order to prepare and warn those who now refuse[127] to be Christians.

---

125. See Rom 5:20.
126. See Ex 34:13; Dt 7:5.
127. Reading *nolunt*; other editions read *volunt* ("want").

33,51. Finally, they complain about the waning of human wellbeing during Christian times. But in the books of their own philosophers they will find contempt for those same things that are now being taken away from them, despite their objections and complaints, and therefore Christian times should be given great praise. For what wellbeing is diminished except that which they abused most foully and extravagantly, to the great harm of their creator? Unless these are [the signs of] evil times — that in almost every city the theaters are falling, along with dens of vice and disgraceful public professions, and the markets and strongholds where the demons used to be worshiped are falling as well. Why are they falling except for the fact that they were built for the lustful and sacrilegious use of impotent things? Did not their Cicero, when praising Roscius the actor, say that he was so skillful that he was the only one worthy to step onto a stage, but also that he was such a good man that in his worthiness he alone should not have approached it?[128] What else did he show more clearly than that the stage was so foul that the better a man was, the less he ought to have to do with it? And yet their gods were pleased at such disgraceful things, which he deemed ought to be kept away from good men. We even have an open confession of this same Cicero that he had to appease Flora, the mother of sports, by frequent celebration.[129] These sports usually exhibit such foulness that in comparison to them other things are respectable, even though good men are prohibited from doing them. Who is this mother Flora? What sort of goddess is she who is flattered and appeased by vice that is more frequent and more loosely controlled [than others]? How much more respectable was it for Roscius to go on stage than for Cicero to worship such a goddess? If the gods of the gentiles are offended when the amount of things dedicated to such celebrations is lessened, then this demonstrates what they are like, since they delight in such things. But if they themselves in their anger diminish these, then angering them is more useful than pleasing them. Then let them reject their own philosophers, who condemn such things in profligate people, or else let them tear down their gods, who force their worshipers [to do] such things, if indeed they can find any such [gods] either to tear down or to hide. Let them stop blasphemously blaming Christian times for the decline of their prosperity, which was dissolving into foulness and death; otherwise they only remind us to praise the power of Christ even more fully.

34,52. I could say much more, but the work I have undertaken compels me now to finish this book and return to the original project. For, when the four evangelists seem to some not to be consistent with one another, [this raises] questions about the Gospels that I sought to resolve. I have tried my best to give an explanation of the ideas that they each [express] individually. It occurred to me first to discuss what some often ask, as to why we can produce no writings of Christ himself. For they want to believe that he wrote something, I know not what, that they find

---

128. See Cicero, *On behalf of Roscius* 6,17.
129. See Cicero, *Against Verres* II,5,14,36.

agreeable, and that he had no thoughts against their gods but rather worshiped them with some magic ritual. [They also think] that his disciples not only lied by calling him God, by whom all things were made, when he was only a man of the highest wisdom, but also that they taught about their gods something they had not learned from him. This is why we have attacked them first concerning the God of Israel, who is worshiped by all the nations through the Church of Christians, and who now everywhere overturns their sacrilegious vanities. He predicted this by his prophets long ago, and he has accomplished what he predicted by the name of Christ, in whom he promised all nations would be blessed.[130] From this they ought to understand that Christ could not have known or taught anything about their gods other than what the God of Israel commanded and predicted by his prophets. Through them he promised and sent that same Christ, in whose name, according to the promise made to the fathers, all nations were blessed. This is why the God of Israel is called [the God] of the whole earth. His disciples did not deviate from their teacher's instructions when they prohibited the worship of the gods of the gentiles, so that we would not pray to deaf images or keep company with demons or serve the creature rather than the creator with religious adoration.[131]

35,53. Christ himself is the wisdom of God,[132] by whom all things were created, and no rational mind, either angelic or human, becomes wise except by participation in him with whom we are united by the Holy Spirit, who pours love into our hearts.[133] This Trinity is one God. Therefore, divine providence, mindful of mortals whose temporal life was enthralled by the rising and falling of things, had this wisdom of God take up a man[134] into the unity of his person, so that he could be born in time, live, die, and rise again. Saying, doing, suffering, and bearing things helpful for our salvation, he would be an example to people below of how to return [to God], and an example to the angels above of how to hold on [to God]. For unless at one point in time something that had not existed before came into being in the nature of the rational soul, no one could pass from the lowest and most foolish life to the wisest and most excellent one. For the contemplative, truth enjoys eternal things; for the believer, faith ought to be in things that are created. Thus people are purified through faith in temporal things so that they may receive the truth of eternal things. One of their most renowned men, the philosopher Plato, said in his book called *Timaeus*: "As eternity is related to that which is created, so is truth to faith."[135] Two are above, eternity and truth; two are below, that which is created and faith. So that we may be called back from the lowest to the highest, and so that what is created may receive eternity, we must come through faith to the truth. Because all contraries are made commensurate through some middle

---

130. See Gn 22:18; 26:4; 28:14.
131. See Rom 1:25.
132. See 1 Cor 1:24.
133. See Rom 5:5.
134. "Take up a man": *homine assumpto*. See also below at I,35,54, and p. 58, note 77.
135. *Timaeus* 29c.

term, and because temporal iniquity alienated us from eternal justice, therefore there had to be some temporal justice to go between. This mediation would be temporal in its lowest dimensions but just in its highest. Thus, by connecting with the lowest without breaking away from the highest, it would bring the lowest back to the highest. Therefore Christ was called the mediator between God and man,[136] between the immortal God and mortal humanity, reconciling humanity to God; he remained what he was while becoming what he had not been. Our faith in created things is in him who is the truth of eternal things.

35,54. This great and indescribable promise, this kingdom and priesthood, was revealed by the prophets to the people of ancient times and proclaimed by the Gospel to their descendants. For it was right that at some time what had been promised by one nation would be presented to all nations. He who sent the prophets before his descent also sent his apostles after his ascension. For all his disciples, he is like the head is to the members of his body[137] through the man whom he assumed.[138] Therefore, since they have written what he showed and said to them, it cannot be said that he himself wrote nothing, for his members did what they learned from the head speaking [to them]. For whatever he wished us to read of his deeds and words he commanded them to write down just as if they were his own hands. Anyone who understands this partnership in unity and the members' harmonious collaboration in various capacities under one head will accept what he reads in the accounts of Christ's disciples in the Gospel just as though he had seen the Lord writing it with the very hand that his own body controlled. Let us now rather investigate the kind of passages in which some suppose the evangelists wrote contrary accounts. (They can seem this way only to those who understand too little.) Once these questions have been resolved, it will be clear how the members are in real harmony in the unity of the body not only with the intentions of the head but also by the agreement of their writings.

---

136. See 1 Tim 2:5.
137. See 1 Cor 12:12–31; Eph 5:23.
138. "Through the man whom he assumed": *per hominem quem assumpsit.*

Book Two

1,1. In the first book we completed a lengthy but entirely necessary discussion in which we refuted the foolishness of those who disdain the disciples who wrote Christ's Gospel, because we do not claim to have anything written by Christ himself, whom they do not believe to be God but nevertheless do not hesitate to honor as a person far surpassing others in wisdom. Further, they want it to seem that he left writings that are amenable to their twisted ideas rather than writings that, through study and faith, could correct such twisted ideas. Let us now look at what the four evangelists have written of Christ, in order to see if they agree among themselves. [Let us do] this in such a way that not the least offence will be felt in the Christian faith by those who have more curiosity than understanding, because they have not just glanced at but rather have carefully examined the books of the evangelists, and they believe that they have found there inconsistencies and contradictions which they judge to be part of contentious objections rather than objects of informed consideration.

1,2. The evangelist Matthew begins this way: *The book of the generation of Jesus Christ, son of David, son of Abraham* (Mt 1:1). By his beginning he shows clearly that he is trying to give an account of Christ's generation according to the flesh. For, according to this, Christ is the Son of Man, which he very frequently calls himself,[1] thereby drawing our attention to what he in his glory has mercifully become for us. For that heavenly and eternal generation, according to which he is the only-begotten Son of God, who was before every creature and by whom all things were made,[2] is so ineffable that we must understand the prophet [as speaking] of it when he says, *Who will explain his generation?* (Is 53:8) Matthew therefore follows Christ's human generation, listing his ancestors from Abraham on, continuing them down to Joseph, the husband of Mary, of whom Jesus was born. For it was not appropriate to consider him apart from his marriage to Mary, even though she gave birth to Christ as a virgin and not as the result of sexual intercourse.[3] This example wonderfully shows faithful married people that, even if they mutually consent to remain continent, they can still remain and be called a married couple, for, although there is no bodily association between the sexes, they keep their mental affections. [Mary and Joseph's] example is especially [compelling], since they were able to have a son without that fleshly union that is only to be performed in order to conceive children. Just because Joseph had not begotten him through intercourse was no reason not to call him Christ's father, since one can rightly be the father of [a child] whom he had not begotten with his wife but had adopted from someone else.

1,3. It was also supposed that Christ was Joseph's son in the sense that he was really begotten by him in the flesh, but only those who were ignorant of Mary's

---

1. See, e.g., Mt 8:20; 9:6; 12:8.32; 17:22; 20:18.
2. See Jn 1:3.
3. See Mt 1:18–25.

virginity supposed this. For Luke says, *Then Jesus himself began to be about thirty years old, being, as was supposed, the son of Joseph* (Lk 3:23). But Mary was not his only parent, and Luke did not hesitate at all to name both of them as his parents when he said, *And the boy grew and became strong, filled with wisdom, and the favor of God was on him. And his parents went to Jerusalem every year at the feast of the Passover.* (Lk 2:40–41) But if one were to suppose that *parents* here refers to Mary's relatives together with the mother herself, how would one explain what the same Luke said earlier, *And his father and mother marveled at those things that were said about him* (Lk 2:33)? So he says that Christ was born of Mary the virgin, but not through intercourse with Joseph. How then can he call him his father unless we rightly understand that he was the husband of Mary, without fleshly intercourse but with marital union? And by this he was more intimately the father of Christ, since he was born of his wife, than if he had been adopted from someone else. It is clear from this that he says *as was supposed, the son of Joseph* for the sake of those who say that he was begotten by Joseph in the same way as other people are begotten.

2,4. Therefore, even if one could show that there was no blood tie between Mary and David, one could still consider Christ the son of David[4] by the same reasoning that Joseph is rightly called his father. But, since the apostle Paul clearly states that *Christ was descended from David according to the flesh* (Rom 1:3), we ought not to doubt that Mary had some sort of blood tie with the line of David. Furthermore, Luke is not silent about this woman's being from the priestly family, since he says that her relative Elizabeth was one of the daughters of Aaron;[5] therefore we should most firmly maintain that Christ's flesh descends from both lines, namely, of kings and priests, in whose persons a mystical anointing among the Hebrew people acted as a symbolic figure; this was the *chrisma*, which explained Christ's name so long ago by the pronouncement of this most clear symbolism.[6]

3,5. As for those who are disturbed by the fact that Matthew and Luke list different ancestors [for Christ], Matthew listing them from David down to Joseph, Luke listing them from Joseph up to David, it is easy enough if they consider the fact that Joseph might have had two fathers, one by whom he was begotten, another by whom he might have been adopted. For it was an ancient custom among that people of God that they would by adoption make sons for themselves from those they had not begotten. Setting aside the fact that Pharaoh's daughter adopted Moses, for she was a foreigner,[7] Jacob himself adopted his grandsons, the sons of Joseph, saying in these most clear words, *Now your two sons, who were born to you before I came to you, are mine. Ephraim and Manasseh shall be mine, just as Reuben and Simeon are. As for those of your line born afterwards, they shall be yours.* (Gn 48:5–6) In the same way, there were twelve tribes of Israel, leaving out the

---

4.   See Mt 1:1, 17, 20.
5.   See Lk 1:5.36.
6.   See above at I,13,20; 14,22.
7.   See Ex 2:10.

tribe of Levi, which served in the Temple, because, including that one, there were thirteen, even though there were twelve sons of Jacob. Thus it can be understood why in his Gospel Luke [lists] as the father of Joseph[8] not the man by whom he was begotten but the one by whom he was adopted, listing the ancestors upwards to David. For, since both evangelists, Matthew and Luke, relate the truth, it was necessary that one of them give the lineage of the father who begot Joseph and the other that of him who adopted him. And who should we think would be more likely to give the lineage of the father who adopted him than the [evangelist] who refuses to say that Joseph was begotten by that man whose son [that evangelist] says he is? For it is more appropriate to say that he was the son of the man who adopted him than to say that he was begotten by a man from whose flesh he had not descended. So, when Matthew says, *Abraham begot Isaac, Isaac begot Jacob* (Mt 1:2), and so on in this way, keeping the term *begot* throughout, until finally he says, *Jacob begot Joseph* (Mt 1:16), he shows sufficiently that he is giving the order of the ancestors not up to the father who adopted Joseph but up to the one who begot him.[9]

3,6. But, even though Luke says that Joseph was begotten by Heli,[10] this phrase should not disturb us or make us believe anything other than the fact that the one evangelist mentions the father who begot him and the other the one who adopted him. For it is not absurd to say that one who has adopted a son has begotten him in love, although not in the flesh. Indeed, we have been given the power to become children of God,[11] although he did not beget us from his own nature and substance as he did his only Son, but he did indeed adopt us in love. The Apostle often uses this phrase to distinguish us from the only-begotten Son,[12] who is before all creatures, through whom all things were made,[13] who alone is born of the Father's substance, and who in divine equality is in every way what the Father is. He is said to have been sent to take on the flesh of that race which is ours by our nature; out of love he participated in our mortality, so that by adoption he could make us participants in his divinity. For he says, *When the fullness of time had come, God sent his Son, made from a woman, made under the law, so that he might redeem those who were under the law, so that we might receive the adoption of sons* (Gal 4:4–5). But we are also said to be born of God, for we, who were already human beings, have received the power to be made into his children;[14] we are made such by grace, not by nature, for, if we were children by nature, we could never have been anything else. When John says, *To those who believe in his name he gave the power to become children of God*, he follows it with *who were born not of blood,*

---

8. See Lk 3:23.
9. Augustine makes a slight qualification to his claim that Joseph was adopted in *Revisions* II,16(43). See also *Answer to Faustus, a Manichean* III,3.
10. See Lk 3:23.
11. See Jn 1:12.
12. See Rom 8:14–17.23.
13. See Jn 1:2.
14. See Eph 1:5.

nor of the will of the flesh, nor of the will of man, but of God (Jn 1:12–13). Thus he says that, having received power, they became children of God, which refers to the adoption that Paul mentions, and that they were born of God. And, in order to show more clearly the grace that accomplished this, he continues, *And the Word became flesh and dwelt among us* (Jn 1:14), as if to say, "Why is it incredible that they are made children of God, even though they are flesh, when the only [Son] is made flesh, even though he is the Word?" The two cases differ greatly, however, in that when we are made children of God we are changed for the better, but when the Son of God was made the Son of Man he was not changed into something worse, although he did lower himself. James also says this, *Of his own will he begot us by the word of truth, so that we would be a kind of first fruits of his creatures* (Jas 1:18). So that we would not think that *begot* means that we are made into what [God] himself is, [James] shows us quite clearly that we receive by this adoption a kind of preeminence among his creatures.

3,7. It would not be untrue even if Luke had said that Joseph was begotten by the man who adopted him. For he did beget him, not as a person but as a son, just as God begets us as sons after having made us as human beings. But he begot one, who is not only the Son, which the Father is not, but is also God, which the Father is. Clearly, however, if Luke had used this phrase, it would not at all have been evident which of [the evangelists] had recorded the adoptive father and which had recorded the father who had begotten him from his own flesh. Likewise, if neither of them said *begot*, but the one said that he was the son of one man while the other said that he was the son of another, it would then be unclear who had recorded his biological father and who had recorded his adoptive father. But, in fact, the one says, *Jacob begot Joseph* (Mt 1:16), while the other says, *Joseph, who was the son of Heli* (Lk 3:23). By the difference in phrasing they both elegantly indicate what they each intend. But, as I said, this [idea] would occur easily enough to a religious person who thought it right to seek some [explanation] rather than believe that the evangelist had lied. It would occur easily, I say, to one who inquired as to how one man could have two fathers. This might have occurred to those critics, but they prefer contention to reflection.

4,8. The next matter to be introduced is one that requires a most attentive and careful reader in order for it to be rightly perceived and understood. For it has been keenly observed that Matthew, who undertook to show the royal character of Christ, names forty men besides Christ himself in the series of generations.[15] This number signifies that time during which, in this age and on this earth, we must be ruled by Christ according to that painful discipline of which it is written, *God scourges every son whom he receives* (Heb 12:6), and of which the Apostle says, *Through tribulation we must enter into the kingdom of God* (Acts 14:22). This [discipline] is also signified by that iron rod which one can read about in a Psalm, *You shall rule them with an iron rod* (Ps 2:9), before which it is said, *I have*

---

15. See Mt 1:17.

been set as king by him on Zion, his holy mount (Ps 2:6). For even the good are ruled by an iron rod, as it is said of them, *It is time for judgment to begin with the Lord's household; and if it begins with us, what will be the end for those who do not believe in God's Gospel? And if one who is righteous is barely saved, where will the sinner and impious appear?* (1 Pt 4:17–18) To these the following applies: *You shall smash them like a potter's vessel* (Ps 2:9). For the good are ruled by this discipline, while the evil are destroyed by it. They are mentioned together because the same signs[16] apply to both the evil and the good.

4,9. The following also shows that this number is a sign of that painful time when we shall be under the discipline of Christ and fight the devil. Both Moses and Elijah fasted for forty days,[17] [thereby showing that] both the law and the prophets prescribe a forty-day fast, that is, a humbling of the soul. The Gospel's account of the Lord's fasting also prefigures this. For he was tempted by the devil for forty days,[18] having deigned to take upon himself the flesh of our mortality, just as we are tempted throughout the time of this age. And after the resurrection he wished to stay with the disciples not longer than forty days,[19] engaging humanly with them and sharing with them the food of mortals, even though he would never die again. By these forty days he showed them that, although his presence would be hidden, he would fulfill what he promised when he said, *Behold, I am with you, even until the end of the age* (Mt 28:20). Why this number signifies this temporal and earthly life is suggested most readily by the fact that, although there may be other more secret reasons, the seasons of the year pass in four changes, and the world itself has four regions, which Scripture sometimes records by the names of the winds—east and west, north and south.[20] Furthermore, forty is four times ten, and ten is made by adding together the numbers between one and four.[21]

4,10. Therefore, since Matthew presents Christ as a ruler who came into this world, into this earthly and mortal human life, in order to rule us as we struggle in temptation, he starts with Abraham and lists forty men. For Christ came in the flesh from that very nation of Hebrews whom God set apart from other nations by separating Abraham from his own land and family;[22] this promise was especially made so that the prophecy and prediction of the nation from which he was to come would be more clear. For [Matthew] sets out fourteen generations in three parts, saying that there were fourteen generations from Abraham to David, another fourteen from David to the deportation to Babylon, and another fourteen from then until Christ's birth,[23] but he does not add them together and say that there were forty-two altogether. For, of these ancestors, one is counted twice, that is

---

16.   "Signs": *sacramenta*, as below in the singular.
17.   See Ex 34:28; 1 K 19:8.
18.   See Mt 4:1–11; Mk 1:12–13; Lk 4:1–13.
19.   See Acts 1:3.
20.   See Zc 2:6; 14:4.
21.   See a similar discussion of the numbers four and ten in Philo, *On the Creation* 47.
22.   See Gn 12:1–2.
23.   See Mt 1:17.

Jechoniah,[24] by whom there was a certain turning aside towards foreign nations at the time of the Babylonian deportation. Moreover, when a series is turned from its straightforward order towards something else, it forms a kind of angle in which the member forming the angle is listed twice, once as the end of the preceding series and once as the beginning of the new order. This also prefigured Christ, who in a way passed from the circumcision to the uncircumcision,[25] or from Jerusalem to Babylon, and became the cornerstone to all who believe in him,[26] whether on one side or the other. This was God presenting in figures things that were to come in truth. For this Jechoniah himself, who prefigured this angle, is interpreted as "God's preparation."[27] Therefore, there are not forty-two [generations], which is the result of three times fourteen; because one is counted twice, there are forty-one generations, counting Christ himself, who rules our temporal and earthly life just as he regally presides over this number forty.

4,11. Since Matthew wishes to show [Christ's] descent into participation in mortality with us, he records at the beginning of his Gospel in descending order the generations from Abraham to Joseph, and even up to Christ's own birth.[28] But Luke gives his generations not at the beginning but at Christ's baptism,[29] and not in descending but in ascending order, thus showing him rather as a priest for the expiation of sins, as the voice from heaven declares him[30] and as the testimony of John himself asserts: *Behold him who takes away the sins of the world* (Jn 1:29). And ascending, he passes by Abraham and goes back to God, to whom we are reconciled in purity and expiation.[31] By his merit he has laid the foundation of our adoption, for we become sons of God through adoption[32] by believing in the Son of God. Indeed, it was for us that the Son of God became the Son of Man according to fleshly generation. It has been shown quite clearly that Joseph is not called the son of Heli because he was begotten by him but because he was adopted by him; in the same way Adam was called the son of God because he was made by God, but he was established as his son in paradise by the grace which he afterwards lost through his sin.

4,12. Thus Matthew's genealogy shows how the Lord Christ took on our sins, while Luke's genealogy shows how the Lord Christ took away our sins. This is why the one is in descending order, the other in ascending order. For, when the Apostle says, *God sent his son in the likeness of sinful flesh*, this refers to his taking on of our sins; but when he adds *for sin, in order to condemn sin in the flesh* (Rom 8:3), this [refers] to the removal of sins. Thus Matthew traces his descent

---

24. See Mt 1:11–12.
25. See Eph 2:11.
26. See Eph 2:20.
27. See Jerome, *On Hebrew Names*, 1 Kingdoms, s.v. Jechonia.
28. See Mt 1:2–16; *Answer to Faustus, a Manichean* III,4.
29. See Lk 3:23–38.
30. See Lk 3:22.
31. See Rom 5:10.
32. See Rom 8:15–23.

from David through Solomon, with whose mother [David] sinned,[33] while Luke traces the line up to David through Nathan, the prophet by whom God removed [David's] sin.[34] Moreover, Luke gives a number that most certainly and clearly indicates the removal of sins. For, although he bore in his flesh the iniquities of humanity, there were no related iniquities in Christ; therefore Matthew excludes Christ from the number forty. But on the other hand, by removing all sin from us and purging us, he unites us to the righteousness of himself and his Father, as the Apostle says, *He who joins himself to the Lord is one spirit* (1 Cor 6:17). Therefore Luke's number includes Christ, who begins the list, and God, who ends it, thereby adding up to seventy-seven, which signifies the complete remission and removal of all sins. The Lord himself expressed this idea through the mystery of this number, when he said that a sinner was to be forgiven *not only seven times but seventy-seven times* (Mt 18:22).

4,13. If one inquires carefully, [one can see] how this number relates to the cleansing of all sins. For the ten precepts of the law show that the number ten is the number of righteousness. And sin is going beyond the law,[35] which is analogous to eleven going beyond the number ten: this is why it was commanded that there be eleven goat-hair curtains in the tabernacle.[36] For who can doubt that goat-hair is a reference to sin? And, since all time revolves in cycles of seven days, seven times eleven, or seventy-seven, would aptly show the fullness of all sin. In this number then is the complete remission of sin, as we are atoned for by the flesh of our priest,[37] from whom this number began. We are also reconciled to God, by whom this number is completed through the Holy Spirit, who appeared in the form of a dove at the baptism which is related to this number.[38]

5,14. After listing the generations, Matthew continues in this way: *Christ's birth was thus. When his mother Mary was betrothed to Joseph, before they came together, she was found to be pregnant by the Holy Spirit.* (Mt 1:18) He does not say how this happened, but Luke explains it after his account of John's conception: *In the sixth month the angel Gabriel was sent from the Lord to a city of Galilee named Nazareth, to a virgin betrothed to a man whose name was Joseph, of the house of David, and the virgin's name was Mary. And the angel came to her and said, Hail, full of grace, the Lord is with you, you are blessed among women.*

---

33. See 2 S 11:2–5.
34. See 2 S 12:1–14. In *Revisions* II,16 (43) Augustine makes a clear distinction between Nathan the prophet and Nathan the son of David.
35. "Going beyond the law": *transgressio legis*, or "transgression of the law."
36. See Ex 26:7.
37. See Heb 8:1–13.
38. See Mt 3:16; Mk 1:10; Lk 3:22; Jn 1:32. Since the number seventy-seven is not mentioned at Jesus' baptism, Augustine's reasoning may be as follows: Seventy-seven is mentioned in Mt 18:22 as part of Jesus' teaching on forgiving others, which would bring with it God's forgiveness. Jesus was acknowledged as God's Son at his baptism for the forgiveness of sins by the descent of the Holy Spirit. Therefore this number is related to forgiveness and sonship; forgiveness and sonship are related to baptism; the Holy Spirit came upon Jesus at his baptism; and therefore the Holy Spirit is related to the number seventy-seven.

When she saw this she was troubled at his saying and considered what sort of greeting this might be. And the angel said to her, Fear not, Mary, for you have found favor with God. Behold, you shall conceive in your womb and bear a son and his name shall be Jesus; he shall be great and shall be called the son of the Most High, and the Lord God shall give to him the throne of his father David, and he shall reign in the house of Jacob forever and his kingdom shall have no end. And Mary said to the angel, How will this be, since I do not know a man? And the angel answered, saying to her, The Holy Spirit shall come upon you and the power of the Most High shall overshadow you. Therefore he who is to be born shall be called holy, the Son of God. (Lk 1:26–35) (Other things follow that do not relate to what we are now discussing.) All of this Matthew refers to when he says of Mary, *She was found to be pregnant by the Holy Spirit* (Mt 1:18). There is no contradiction if Luke explains something that Matthew omits, for they both testify that Mary conceived by the Holy Spirit. Nor is there any contradiction when Matthew includes something that Luke omits. For Matthew says the following: *Then her husband Joseph, being a righteous man and unwilling to put her to shame, decided to divorce her privately. And, while he was considering this, behold, an angel of the Lord appeared to him in a dream, saying, Joseph, son of David, do not be afraid to take Mary as your wife, for that which is conceived in her is of the Holy Spirit. She shall bear a son and you shall call his name Jesus, for he shall save his people from their sins. All this happened in order to fulfill what was said by the Lord through his prophet, saying, Behold, a virgin shall conceive and bear a son, and they shall call his name Emmanuel, which is, interpreted, God with us. When Joseph woke up from sleep he did as the angel of the Lord had commanded him and he took his wife, and he did not know her until she had borne her first-born son, and he called his name Jesus. When Jesus was born in Bethlehem of Judea in the days of Herod the king* (Mt 1:19–2:1), and so forth.

5,15. As to the city of Bethlehem, Matthew and Luke agree, but Luke explains how and why they came there,[39] while Matthew omits this. But, as to the journey of the magi from the east, Luke is silent, while Matthew tells us of it immediately after [what was discussed before]: *Behold, magi from the east came to Jerusalem, saying, Where is he who is born king of the Jews? We have seen his star in the east and have come to worship him. And when Herod the king heard this he was troubled* (Mt 2:1–3), and so forth, until where it is written of these magi that, *being warned in a dream not to return to Herod, they departed to their country by a different way* (Mt 2:12). Luke omits this, just as Matthew does not narrate some things that Luke does — that the Lord was laid in a manger,[40] and that an angel announced his birth to the shepherds,[41] and that a great multitude of the host of heaven was with the angel praising God,[42] and that the shepherds came and saw

---

39. See Lk 2:3–5.
40. See Lk 2:7.
41. See Lk 2:8–12.
42. See Lk 2:13–14.

that what the angel had announced to them was true,[43] and that on the day of his circumcision he received his name.[44] Luke also narrates the events that occurred after Mary's days of purification were completed[45] — that they took [Jesus] to Jerusalem and that Simeon and Anna spoke of him in the Temple, when, filled with the Holy Spirit, they recognized him.[46] Matthew is silent concerning all these things.

5,16. Therefore we ought to inquire as to when there occurred the events that Matthew omits but Luke includes and those that Luke omits and Matthew includes. For, after Matthew tells that the magi who had come from the east returned to their own country, he goes on to tell that Joseph was warned by an angel to flee into Egypt with the child, so that he would not be killed by Herod;[47] that Herod could not find [Jesus] but killed the children two years old and under;[48] that upon Herod's death [Joseph] returned from Egypt, and that, when he heard that Archelaus reigned in Judea instead of his father Herod, he went to live with the boy in the region of Galilee in the city of Nazareth.[49] Luke is silent concerning all these things. But it cannot be seen as a disagreement if the one includes what the other omits, and the other records what the one does not. But we must inquire as to when these things that Matthew includes in his story could have happened — their flight into Egypt, their return after Herod's death, and their living in the city of Nazareth, the place that Luke says they returned to after they had completed in the Temple all the things of the Lord's law that pertained to the boy.[50] In this and other similar cases we should be aware of the following, so that it will not affect or disturb our mind again: Each evangelist constructs his narrative so that it appears an orderly account without omissions. He is silent concerning those things that he does not wish to narrate, and he connects the things that he does wish to narrate to what has just been said, so that it appears as an uninterrupted sequence. But, if we carefully consider the order of the narrative at the point where one narrates something that the other omits, we can find the place where the one who omitted something made a leap and connected what he wished to narrate to what came before, as though it followed without interruption. By this we can understand that, when Matthew tells of the dream warning the magi not to go back to Herod and how they returned to their own country a different way, he omits the things that Luke narrates concerning the Lord in the Temple and what was said by Simeon and Anna. On the other hand, Luke omits their flight into Egypt, which Matthew narrates, and thereby [makes it seem] that their return to the city of Nazareth followed immediately.

---

43. See Lk 2:15–20.
44. See Lk 2:21.
45. See Lk 2:22.
46. See Lk 2:25–38.
47. See Mt 2:13–15.
48. See Mt 2:16–18.
49. See Mt 2:19–23.
50. See Lk 2:39.

5,17. But, if someone wished to take all that is said or omitted in these two narratives and make it into one narrative of Christ's nativity and infancy or childhood, it would be in this order:

Now Christ's birth was thus (Mt 2:12). In the days of Herod, king of Judea, there was a priest named Zechariah, of the division of Abijah, and his wife was of the daughters of Aaron, and her name was Elizabeth. They were both righteous before God, walking blamelessly in all the commandments and ordinances of the Lord. And they did not have a child because Elizabeth was barren, and they were both advanced in years. And it happened that, as he was serving as priest before God when his division was on duty, according to the custom of the priesthood, his lot was to burn incense when he entered the Lord's Temple. And the whole multitude of the people was outside praying at the hour of incense. And there appeared to him an angel of the Lord standing at the right side of the altar of incense. And Zechariah was troubled when he saw him, and fear fell upon him. But the angel said to him, Do not be afraid, Zechariah, for your prayer is heard, and your wife Elizabeth shall bear you a son, and you shall call his name John. And you shall have joy and gladness, and many shall rejoice at his birth, for he shall be great before the Lord, and he shall not drink wine or strong drink, and he shall be filled with the Holy Spirit even from his mother's womb. And he shall turn many of the children of Israel to the Lord their God, and he shall go before him in the spirit and power of Elijah, to turn the hearts of fathers to their children, and the unbelieving to the wisdom of the righteous, to make ready for the Lord a perfect people. And Zechariah said to the angel, How shall I know this? For I am an old man, and my wife is advanced in years. And answering, the angel said to him, I am Gabriel, who stand before God, and I was sent to speak to you and to bring this good news to you. And behold, you shall be silent and unable to speak until the day these things happen, because you did not believe my words, which shall be fulfilled in their time. And the people were waiting for Zechariah, and they wondered at his delay in the Temple. And when he came out he could not speak to them, and they perceived that he had seen a vision in the Temple; and he made signs to them and remained mute. And it happened that, when the days of his service were finished, he went to his home. After these days his wife Elizabeth conceived and hid herself for five months, saying, Thus has the Lord done to me in the days when he looked upon me, to take away my reproach among men. In the sixth month the angel Gabriel was sent from God to a city of Galilee named Nazareth, to a virgin betrothed to a man whose name was Joseph, of the house of David, and the virgin's name was Mary. And the angel came in to her and said, Hail, O favored one, the Lord is with you; blessed are you among women. But when she saw him, she was troubled at his saying and considered what sort of greeting this might be. And the angel said to her, Do not be afraid, Mary, for you have found favor with God. Behold, you shall conceive in your womb and bear a son, and you shall call his name Jesus. He shall be great and shall be called the son of the Most High, and the Lord God shall give him the throne of his father

David. And he shall reign in the house of Jacob forever and his kingdom shall have no end. And Mary said to the angel, How will this be, since I do not know man? And the angel answered, saying to her, The Holy Spirit shall come upon you and the power of the Most High shall overshadow you. Therefore he who is to be born shall be called holy, the Son of God. And behold, your relative Eliza-beth in her old age has also conceived a son, and this is the sixth month with her who was called barren. For with God nothing will be impossible. And Mary said, Behold the handmaid of the Lord; let it be done to me according to your word. And the angel departed from her. In those days Mary got up and went with haste into the hill country to a city of Judah and entered into Zechariah's house and greeted Elizabeth. And it happened that, when Elizabeth heard Mary's greeting, the baby leaped in her womb. And Elizabeth was filled with the Holy Spirit, and she cried out with a loud voice, saying, Blessed are you among women, and blessed is the fruit of your womb. How can this be, that the mother of my Lord should come to me? For behold, when the voice of your greeting came to my ears, the baby leaped in my womb for joy. And blessed is she who believed, for there shall be a fulfillment of what was spoken to her by the Lord. And Mary said, My soul magnifies the Lord, and my spirit rejoices in God my savior, for he has regarded the lowliness of his handmaid. For behold, henceforth all generations shall call me blessed, for he who is mighty has done great things for me, and holy is his name. And his mercy is on those who fear him from generation to generation. He has exercised power with his arm, he has scattered the proud in the imagination of their hearts. He has put down the mighty from their throne and exalted the lowly. He has filled the hungry with good things and sent the rich away empty. He has raised up his servant Israel, remembering his mercy, as he said to our fathers, to Abraham and his descendants forever. And Mary stayed with her about three months and returned to her home. (Lk 1:5–56) And she was found to be pregnant by the Holy Spirit. Then her husband Joseph, being a righteous man and unwilling to put her to shame, decided to divorce her privately. And while he was considering this, behold, an angel of the Lord appeared to him in a dream, saying, Joseph, son of David, do not be afraid to take Mary as your wife, for that which is conceived in her is of the Holy Spirit. She shall bear a son and you shall call his name Jesus, for he shall save his people from their sins. All this happened in order to fulfill what was said by the Lord through his prophet, saying, Behold, a virgin shall conceive and bear a son, and they shall call his name Emmanuel, which is, interpreted, God with us. When Joseph woke up from sleep he did as the angel of the Lord had commanded him and he took his wife, and he did not know her. (Mt 1:18–25) Elizabeth's time to give birth had come, and she bore a son. And her neighbors and relatives heard that the Lord had magnified his mercy towards her, and they congratulated her. And it happened that on the eighth day they came to circumcise the child and they would have called him Zechariah after the name of his father. But answering, his mother said, No, he shall be called John. And they said to her, None of your relatives is called by this name. They made signs to his father as to what he wanted to call him. And, asking for a writing tablet, he wrote, saying, His name is John. And they all marveled. Immediately his mouth and tongue were loosed and he spoke, blessing God. And fear came upon all their neighbors, and all these things were spread through all the hill country of Judea. And all who heard them kept them in their hearts, saying, What do you think this child will be? For the hand of the Lord was with him. And his father Zechariah was filled with the Holy Spirit and prophesied, saying, Blessed be the Lord God of Israel, for he has visited and redeemed his people and has raised up a horn of salvation for us in the house of his servant David, as he said by the mouth of his holy everlasting prophets, salvation from our enemies and from the hand of all who hate us, that he would have mercy on our fathers and remember his holy covenant, the oath that he swore to our father Abraham, that he would give us, so that, having been delivered from the hand of our enemies, we might serve him without fear, in holiness and righteousness before him all of our days. And you, child, shall be called the prophet of the Most High, for you shall go before the face of the Lord to prepare his ways, to give knowledge of salvation to his people for the remission of their sins, through the bowels of the mercy of our God, whereby the dawn has come upon us from on high, to give light to those who sit in darkness and in the shadow of death, to guide our feet into the way of peace. And the child grew and became strong in spirit, and he was in the wilderness until the day when he was revealed to Israel. And it happened in those days that a decree went out from Caesar Augustus that the whole world should be enrolled. This was the first enrollment, when Quirinius was governor of Syria. And all went to make their declaration, each in his own city. And Joseph went up from Galilee, from the city of Nazareth, to Judea, to the city of David, which is called Bethlehem, because he was of the house and family of David, to make his declaration with Mary, who was betrothed to be his wife, and who was pregnant. And it happened that while they were there, the time for her to give birth came, and she gave birth to her first-born son and wrapped him in swaddling clothes and laid him in a manger, because there was no room at the inn. And there were shepherds in that area, watching and keeping nighttime guard over their flock. And behold, an angel of the Lord stood by them, and the glory of God shone about them, and they were very afraid. And the angel said to them, Do not be afraid. For behold, I bring you good news of great joy, which shall be to all the people. For to you is born this day in the city of David a savior, who is Christ the Lord. And this shall be a sign to you: you shall find the baby wrapped in swaddling clothes and lying in a manger. And suddenly there was with the angel a multitude of the heavenly host praising God and saying, Glory to God in the highest, and on earth peace to people of good will. And it happened that, as the angels were going away from them into heaven, the shepherds said to one another, Let us go over to Bethlehem and see this thing that has happened, which the Lord has shown us. And they came with haste and found Mary and Joseph, and the baby lying in a manger. And when they had seen it, they remembered what had been said to them about this child. And all who heard of these things also marveled at what was said to them by the shepherds. But Mary kept all these things and pondered them in her heart. And the shepherds returned, glorifying and praising God for all the things they had heard and seen, as it had been told to them. And at the end of eight days, when he was circumcised, his name was called Jesus, as he had been called by the angel before he was conceived in the womb. (Lk 1:57–2:21) *Behold, magi from the east came to Jerusalem, saying, Where is he who is born the king of the Jews? For we have seen his star in the east and have come to worship him. When Herod the king heard this he was troubled, and all Jerusalem with him. And assembling all the chief priests and scribes of the people, he asked them where the Christ was to be born. They said to him, In Bethlehem of Judea. For thus it is written by the prophet, And you, Bethlehem, in the land of Judea, are not the least among the rulers of Judea, for from you shall come a leader who shall rule my people Israel. Then Herod secretly called the magi and diligently inquired of them what time the star had appeared to them. And sending them to Bethlehem, he said, Go and search diligently for the child and, when you have found him, report back to me, so that I may come and worship him too. When they had heard the king they left. And behold, the star that they had seen in the east went before them, until it came and stood over where the child was. When they saw the star, they rejoiced with an exceedingly great joy. And going into the house, they found the child with Mary his mother, and falling down they worshiped him. And opening their treasures, they offered him gifts, gold, frankincense, and myrrh. And being warned in a dream not to return to Herod, they departed for their country by a different way.* (Mt 2:1–12) *And after their departure it was time for her purification according to the law of Moses. They brought him to Jerusalem, to present him to the Lord (as it is written in the law of the Lord, Every male that opens the womb shall be called holy to the Lord), and to offer a sacrifice according to what is said in the law of the Lord, a pair of turtledoves, or two young pigeons. And behold, there was a man in Jerusalem whose name was Simeon, and this man was righteous and devout, hoping for the consolation of Israel, and the Holy Spirit was in him. And it had been revealed to him by the Holy Spirit that he would not see death before he had seen the Lord's Christ. And he came in the spirit into the Temple. And when the parents brought in the child Jesus, to do for him according to the custom of the law, he took him up in his arms and blessed God and said, Lord, now let your servant depart in peace, according to your word. For my eyes have seen your salvation, which you have prepared before the face of all people, a light for revelation to the gentiles, and glory to your people Israel. And his father and mother marveled at what was said about him. And Simeon blessed them and said to Mary his mother, Behold, this one is set for the fall and rise of many in Israel, and for a sign that is spoken against; and a sword shall pierce your own soul too, that the thoughts of many hearts may be revealed. And there was a prophetess, Anna, the daughter of Phanuel, of the tribe of Asher; she was very old, having lived with her husband for seven years from her virgin-*

ity, and as a widow until she was eighty-four. She did not depart from the Temple, worshiping night and day with fasting and prayers. And coming in at that very moment, she testified to God and spoke of him to all who hoped for the redemption of Jerusalem. And, when they had finished everything according to the law of the Lord (Lk 2:22–39), *behold, an angel of the Lord appeared to Joseph in a dream, saying, Rise, and take the child and his mother and flee into Egypt and stay there until I tell you; for Herod will seek the child to destroy him. Rising he took the child and his mother by night and departed to Egypt. And he was there until the death of Herod, in order to fulfill what was said by the Lord through his prophet, Out of Egypt have I called my son. Then Herod, seeing that he had been tricked by the magi, was extremely enraged, and sent to kill all the male children who were in Bethlehem and in all its environs who were two years old and under, according to the time he had determined from the magi. Then was fulfilled what was said by the prophet Jeremiah, A voice was heard in Rama, weeping and loud lamentation, Rachel weeping for her children, and she refused to be consoled, for they were no more. But when Herod died, behold, an angel of the Lord appeared in a dream to Joseph in Egypt, saying, Rise and take the child and his mother and go to the land of Israel, for those who sought the child's life are dead. Rising, he took the child and his mother and came to the land of Israel. But, hearing that Archelaus reigned in Judea in place of his father Herod, he was afraid to go there. And being warned in a dream, he turned aside to the region of Galilee. And he came and lived in a city called Nazareth, in order to fulfill what was said by the prophets, He shall be called a Nazarene.* (Mt 2:13–23) *And the child grew and became strong, filled with wisdom, and the favor of God was on him. And his parents went to Jerusalem every year at the feast of Passover. And, when he was twelve years old, they went up to Jerusalem according to the custom of the feast. And when the days were finished they returned, but the boy Jesus remained in Jerusalem, and his parents did not know it. But supposing him to be in the crowd, they went a day's journey and then looked for him among their relatives and acquaintances. And when they did not find him they returned to Jerusalem to look for him. And it happened that after three days they found him in the Temple, sitting among the teachers, listening to them and questioning them. And all who heard him were amazed at his understanding and answers. And when they saw him they were astonished. And his mother said to him, Son, why have you acted this way towards us? Behold, your father and I have been looking for you sorrowfully. And he said to them, Why have you been looking for me? Did you not know that I must be about my father's business? And they did not understand what he had said to them. And he went down with them and came to Nazareth and was obedient to them. And his mother kept all these things in her heart. And Jesus increased in wisdom, age, and favor with God and men.* (Lk 2:40–52)

6,18. Now at this point begins the narration of John's preaching, which is recorded by all four [evangelists]. For, after the last of his words that I have placed above, where he records the testimony of the prophet, *He shall be called a Naza-*

rene (Mt 2:23), Matthew continues and adds, *In those days came John the Baptist, preaching in the wilderness of Judea* (Mt 3:1), and so forth. And Mark, who says nothing of the Lord's nativity or infancy or childhood, begins his Gospel with this event, that is, John's preaching. For he begins thus: *The beginning of the Gospel of Jesus Christ, the Son of God. As it is written in Isaiah the prophet, Behold, I send my messenger before your face, who shall prepare your way. The voice of one crying in the wilderness: prepare the way of the Lord, make his paths straight. John was in the wilderness, baptizing and preaching a baptism of repentance for the remission of sins* (Mk 1:1–4), and so forth. And after Luke says, *And Jesus increased in wisdom, age, and favor with God and men* (Lk 2:52), he continues by speaking of John's preaching: *In the fifteenth year of the reign of Tiberius Caesar, Pontius Pilate being governor of Judea, and Herod being tetrarch of Galilee, and his brother Philip being tetrarch of the region of Iturea and Trachonitis, and Lysanias being tetrarch of Abilene, Annas and Caiaphas being the high priests, the word of the Lord came upon John, the son of Zechariah, in the wilderness* (Lk 3:1–2), and so forth. The apostle John, most eminent of the four evangelists, after speaking of the Word of God, who is also the Son who was before all the ages of creation, through whom all things were made,[51] also introduces John's preaching and testimony in this context, saying, *There was a man sent from God, whose name was John* (Jn 1:6). Now, it is clear that the four evangelists' narratives of John are not in disagreement with one another, so that it can neither be required nor demanded that we go through everything the way we did with the origins of Christ, who was born of Mary. For in that case [I indicated] how Matthew and Luke agreed, and how we might make one narrative out of the two, showing to the obtuse that, although one might include what the other omits, or one might omit what the other includes, this does not hinder the understanding of the truthfulness of the other's account. By one such example, whether in the way I did it or in another more appropriate way, one can see that what one has observed was done in this case could be done in any similar case.

6,19. Therefore let us now examine the agreement of the four evangelists regarding John the Baptist. Matthew continues thus: *In those days came John the Baptist, preaching in the wilderness of Judea* (Mt 3:1). Mark does not say *in those days* because he tells of no events that went before, regarding which events it would make sense to say *in those days*. But Luke's mentioning of the earthly powers specifies more precisely the time of John's preaching and baptizing. *In the fifteenth year of the reign of Tiberius Caesar, Pontius Pilate being governor of Judea, and Herod being tetrarch of Galilee, and his brother Philip being tetrarch of the region of Ituraea and Trachonitis, and Lysanias being tetrarch of Abilene, Annas and Caiaphas being the high priests, the word of the Lord came upon John, the son of Zechariah, in the wilderness* (Lk 3:1–2). However, when Matthew says *in those days*, we must understand that he does not mean only the period of these

---

51. See Jn 1:1–5.

powers but that he wishes to express a much longer time period when he says *in those days.* For he first narrates the return of Christ from Egypt after the death of Herod,[52] which happened during his infancy or childhood and which is therefore consistent with Luke's account of what happened in the Temple when he was twelve years old.[53] And after he records the recall of the infant or child from Egypt, Matthew continues, *In those days came John the Baptist.* He thereby indicates not only the days of his childhood but all the days from his nativity up until the time when John began preaching and baptizing, at which time Christ was a young man, for he and John were the same age, and it is said that he was about thirty years old when he was baptized by the latter.[54]

7,20. But there are usually some, indeed, who are troubled by the fact that Luke says that Herod was tetrarch of Galilee during the days of John's baptizing, when the Lord was baptized as a young man,[55] whereas Matthew says that the boy Jesus returned from Egypt after Herod's death.[56] Both cannot be true, unless we are to understand that there were two Herods. But who does not know that this is possible? Those who are eager to make false charges against the truth of the Gospels are blindly raving, but their insight is so impoverished that they cannot understand how two men might have had the same name! This is something for which there are plenty of examples everywhere. For this latter Herod is understood to have been the son of the former Herod. [He had other sons] such as Archelaus, who Matthew says succeeded to the rule of Judea after his father's death,[57] and Philip, whom Luke introduces as the brother of Herod the tetrarch and as himself the tetrarch of Ituraea.[58] For it was Herod the king who sought the life of Christ as a child, but the other Herod, his son, was not called a king but a tetrarch, which is a Greek word that indicates one who rules the fourth part of a kingdom.

8,21. Once again, the following may be troubling to some. Matthew says that upon his return Joseph was afraid to go into Judea because Archelaus, the son of Herod, reigned there in his father's place. But why would he go into Galilee, where there was another of his sons, Herod the tetrarch, as Luke declares? But this is only [a problem] if [Joseph] feared for the child's safety at the same time as the events Luke records. But this is clearly not the case, [for Luke says] not that Archelaus was king in Judea but that Pontius Pilate was their governor, who was not the king of the Jews. During his time the sons of Herod the Great, acting under Tiberius Caesar, held not the kingdom but the tetrarchy. These things had not happened when Joseph, fearing Archelaus who was ruling in Judea, went with the child into Galilee, where his city of Nazareth was also located.

---

52. See Mt 2:19–21.
53. See Lk 2:42–50.
54. See Lk 3:23.
55. See Lk 3:1–21.
56. See Mt 2:15.19–21.
57. See Mt 2:22.
58. See Lk 3:1.

9,22. Perhaps it is troubling as well that Matthew says that his parents went with the boy Jesus into Galilee, because they did not want to go into Judea on account of their fear of Archelaus, whereas Luke's account would make it seem rather that they went into Galilee because their city was Nazareth of Galilee. But it must be understood that, when the angel said in a dream to Joseph in Egypt, *Rise, and take the child and his mother and go to the land of Israel* (Mt 2:20), Joseph first understood this to mean that he was commanded to go into Judea, for that was the first interpretation which one could have given to *the land of Israel*. But when he realized that Archelaus, the son of Herod, reigned there, he did not want to expose himself to such danger; then [he saw] that *the land of Israel* could be interpreted to include Galilee, because the people of Israel lived there as well. There is also another way of solving this problem: It might have seemed to Christ's parents that, since they had received such messages from angels concerning the boy, they were supposed to live with him only in Jerusalem, where the Temple of the Lord was. And upon returning from Egypt they might have gone there and lived there, had it not been for their terror of Archelaus's presence. But, since they had not had any divine command to live there, it was not necessary for them to ignore their fear of Archelaus.

10,23. Does anyone ask how it can be that, as Luke reports, during Christ's childhood his parents went every year to Jerusalem,[59] if the fear of Archelaus kept them from going there. It does not seem difficult to me to respond to this, even though none of the evangelists say how long Archelaus reigned there. For it might be that on the feast day, hidden by the huge crowds, they went up to and returned from a place they would have been afraid to live in on other days; they would thus be neither impious for neglecting the festival nor conspicuous for staying there continuously. And, although all [the evangelists] omit mentioning what the length of Archelaus's reign was, this interpretation is still open — that, when Luke says that their custom was to go up to Jerusalem every year, we are to understand this as having happened when Archelaus was no longer feared. But, if some non-gospel history that appears trustworthy should show that Archelaus's reign lasted somewhat longer, then what I have said above should still suffice — namely, that, although the boy's parents feared to live in Jerusalem, their fear of God did not let them neglect the yearly festival, to which they could easily go in secret. For it is not incredible that, by seizing opportune times, either days or hours, people may go places in which they would fear to remain.

11,24. With this another question is answered, too, if it troubles anyone. If Herod the Great was already worried, disturbed by what the magi had told him about the birth of the king of the Jews, then how could [Christ's] mother safely take him up to the Temple when the days of her purification were complete, in order to do for him according to the law of the Lord, as Luke records?[60] But who cannot see that

---

59. See Lk 2:41.
60. See Lk 2:22–40.

this one day might have gone unnoticed by a king who was occupied with many concerns? It does not seem unlikely that by the time Herod, extremely troubled and waiting for the magi's report on the child, realized he had been tricked, the mother's purification was already completed, and the religious rites of the first-born child were already finished in the Temple in Jerusalem, and even their departure into Egypt was accomplished; only then did it occur to him to seek the child's life and to kill so many babies. But if this troubles anyone, I shall not neglect to state the many and important matters that could have drawn away the king's interest, so that for many days his attention was either completely diverted or hindered. Although no one could enumerate the causes that could have brought this about, no one is so ignorant of human affairs as to deny or doubt that there could have been many such important matters. For anyone could imagine that the king might have received announcements, whether true or false, of many other terrible things, so that, rather than fearing some royal child who might after some years prove to be a threat to himself or his sons, he might be agitated by more immediate dangers, his mind drawn from that other worry, and instead occupy himself with other more immediate precautions. But leaving all this aside, I venture to say that, when the magi did not report back to Herod, he could have believed that they were misled by a false vision of a star and, when they did not find the one they thought had been born, that they were too embarrassed to return to him. In this way he dispelled his fears and left off seeking or persecuting the child. But when they had gone with him to Jerusalem after his mother's purification, and those things that Luke reports had been [done] in the Temple,[61] then the prophetic words of Simeon and Anna about him began to be proclaimed by those who heard them, and these recalled the king's mind to its original intention. Then Joseph was warned in a dream to flee into Egypt with the child and his mother,[62] and then, when the things that had been said in the Temple were made public, Herod realized he had been tricked by the magi, and, desiring to bring about Christ's death, he killed many infants, as Matthew records.[63]

12,25. Now Matthew says this about John: *In those days came John the Baptist, preaching in the wilderness of Judea and saying, Repent, for the kingdom of heaven is at hand. For this is he who is spoken of by the prophet Isaiah, saying, The voice of one crying in the wilderness, Prepare the way of the Lord, make his paths straight.* (Mt 3:1–3) Mark and Luke agree that this testimony of Isaiah refers to John.[64] Luke has recorded more words of the same prophet following these in his narrative of John the Baptist.[65] John the evangelist also records that John the Baptist himself applied this same testimony of Isaiah to himself.[66] And Matthew,

---

61. See Lk 2:22–39.
62. See Mt 2:13–16.
63. See Mt 2:16–18.
64. See Mk 1:3; Lk 3:4.
65. Lk 3:5–6 continues the quotation through Is 40:4–5.
66. See Jn 1:23.

too, gives some words of John that the others do not. He says that he was *preaching in the wilderness of Judea and saying, Repent, for the kingdom of heaven is at hand* (Mt 3:1–2). These words of John the others have omitted. But what Matthew puts next — *For this is he who is spoken of by the prophet Isaiah, saying, The voice of one crying in the wilderness, Prepare the way of the Lord, make his paths straight* (Mt 3:3) — is in an ambiguous place. For it is not clear whether Matthew himself is saying this or whether it is a continuation of John's words, so that we are to understand the whole thing as spoken by John, *Repent, for the kingdom of heaven is at hand. For this is he who is spoken of by the prophet Isaiah*, and so forth. And it should not trouble anyone that he does not say, "For I am he who was spoken of by the prophet Isaiah," but says, *For this is he who is spoken of.* This manner of speech is usual for the evangelists Matthew and John to use in reference to themselves. For Matthew says, *He found a man sitting at the tax office* (Mt 9:9), rather than saying, "He found me." And John also says, *This is the disciple who gives testimony of these things and has written these things, and we know that his testimony is true* (Jn 21:24), rather than saying "I am" and so forth, or "my testimony is true." The Lord himself very frequently says *the Son of Man*[67] or *the Son of God*[68] instead of saying "I." And he says, *It was necessary for the Christ to suffer and to rise on the third day* (Lk 24:46), rather than saying, "It was necessary for me to suffer." Therefore it is possible that after saying, *Repent, for the kingdom of heaven is at hand* (Mt 3:2), John the Baptist could have continued and said of himself, *For this is he who is spoken of by the prophet Isaiah*, and so forth. Only after his words does Matthew resume his narrative, *Now, this John had a garment of camel's hair* (Mt 3:4), and so forth. If this is so, then it is not remarkable that when asked he would say of himself, as John the evangelist reports he said, *I am the voice of one crying in the wilderness* (Jn 1:23), since he had already spoken in these terms when warning them to repent. Matthew then goes on to tell us of his clothing and his way of life: *Now, this John had a garment of camel's hair and a leather belt around his waist, and his food was locusts and wild honey* (Mt 3:4). Mark says this in almost the same words,[69] but the other two omit it.

12,26. Matthew continues, then, and says, *Then Jerusalem and all Judea and the whole region around the Jordan went out to him, and they were baptized by him in the Jordan, confessing their sins. But when he saw many of the Pharisees and Sadducees coming for baptism, he said to them, You brood of vipers, who told you to flee the wrath to come? Bear fruit worthy of repentance and do not think to say to yourselves, We have Abraham as our father, for I say to you that God is able from these stones to raise up children to Abraham. For now the axe is laid to the root of the trees; every tree that does not bear good fruit is cut down and thrown into the fire. I indeed baptize you with water for repentance, but he who is coming after me is mightier than I, whose shoes I am not worthy to carry. He*

---

67. See, e.g., Mt 8:20; 9:6; 16:27; 17:9.22; 20:18.28; Mk 8:38; Lk 9:22.58.
68. See, e.g., Jn 5:25.
69. See Mk 1:6.

shall baptize you in the Holy Spirit and with fire, whose winnowing fork is in his hand, and he shall clear his threshing floor and gather his wheat into the granary, but the chaff he shall burn with unquenchable fire. (Mt 3:5–12) Luke also says all this, ascribing almost the same words to John,[70] and where there is any variation in the words, there is no difference in the meaning. For example, Matthew says that John said, *And do not think to say to yourselves, We have Abraham as our father* (Mt 3:9), while Luke says, *And do not begin to say, We have Abraham as our father* (Lk 3:8). Again, the former has, *I indeed baptize you with water for repentance* (Mt 3:11), while the latter adds in the questions of the crowds, as to what they should do, and gives John's response on the good works that are the fruits of repentance,[71] which Matthew omits. And when they were thinking in their hearts about whether he was the Christ, [Luke] has him respond, *I indeed baptize you with water* (Lk 3:16), but he does not say *for repentance.* And in Matthew [John] says, *But he who is coming after me is mightier than I* (Mt 3:11), while [Luke] has him say, *But one mightier than I is coming* (Lk 3:16). Likewise, in Matthew he says, *Whose shoes I am not worthy to carry* (Mt 3:11), but in [Luke], *The strap of whose shoes I am not worthy to unloose* (Lk 3:16), which Mark also says, although he omits other matters. For, after noting his clothing and food, he goes on to say the following: *And he preached, saying, After me is coming one mightier than I, the strap of whose shoes I am not worthy to bend down and unloose. I have baptized you with water, but he shall baptize you with the Holy Spirit.* (Mk 1:7–8) Therefore, as for the shoes, he differs from Luke only by his addition of *bend down*; as for the baptism, [he differs] from both by not saying *and with fire* but only *with the Holy Spirit.* For both Matthew and Luke say the same thing in the same order: *He shall baptize you with the Spirit and with fire*, except that Luke does not add *Holy*,[72] while Matthew says *with the Holy Spirit and with fire.* John the evangelist confirms the other three when he says, *John bears witness to him and cries, saying, This was he of whom I said, He who is coming after me is above me, for he was before me* (Jn 1:15). Thus he shows that this was said at the same time as what [John] said that is recorded by the others. Also, he is repeating and reiterating something that he had already said, when he says, *This was he of whom I said, He who is coming after me.*

12,27. What if one were to ask what the exact words were that John the Baptist said, whether those recorded as spoken by him in Matthew or Luke, or those few included as spoken by him in Mark, who omits the rest? In no way would this be considered a difficulty by anyone who wisely understands that what is necessary in order to know the truth is the meaning and not the exact words used. If there is a difference in the order of words between two of them, that is not really a contradiction. Nor is there a contradiction if the one includes what the other omits. It is clear

---

70. See Lk 3:7–17.
71. See Lk 3:10–15.
72. Luke 3:16, although *Holy* is now accepted as authentic in Luke and not as an interpolation.

that they have set down these things as they remembered them, and as they were moved to be either brief or expansive, while nonetheless expressing one meaning.

12,28. Thus it is quite apparent in what is most related to the present point that the truth of the Gospel is from the word of God, which remains eternal and unchangeable above all that is created. It is spread abroad through the creation of temporal signs and through human language and has the highest level of authority. Therefore one should not suppose that one of [the evangelists] is deceitful if, in their account of something they saw or heard, several people remember it in not exactly the same way or in not exactly the same words but nonetheless describe the same thing; nor if the order of the words is different; nor if some words are in place of others that nonetheless indicate the same thing; nor if something is not said, either because it did not occur to the writer or because it could be inferred from other things that were said; nor if one decides to mention something for the sake of the narrative and, in order to keep the chronological order in place, only touches on part of something rather than explaining it entirely; nor if the person who has the authority to write the narrative should add not something to the subject but rather some words in order to illuminate and explain his meaning; nor if, although he presents the subject well, he tries but does not succeed in remembering and expressing the exact words he heard with complete accuracy. And, if someone says that the evangelists certainly ought to have been given this ability by the power of the Holy Spirit, so that their words would differ in neither kind nor order nor number, then he does not understand that, just as the evangelists' authority is heightened, so too is the credibility strengthened of other people who speak the truth through them. For, if several people narrate the same thing, in no way can one of them be rightly accused of falsehood if he differs from another, because the evangelists give a precedent example in his defense.[73] For, just as it is impossible to consider or say that with the evangelists there is anything false, neither does it appear that there is anything false about a writer who has done his work in the same way as we have shown they have done theirs. And, just as it belongs to the highest morality to guard against falsehood, so too ought we to be ruled by so eminent an authority such that we do not suppose that any narratives which we discover contain variations are therefore false, for there are variations among the evangelists.[74] At the same time we ought to understand that, in matters most closely related to the faithfulness of doctrine, the truth is not to be sought and embraced in mere words but in the things themselves. For with writers who

---

73. Augustine's logic may be summarized in this way: The Gospels are always right, but they do not always agree in language. If this is the case with the Gospels, then it is also possible for ordinary persons to express the same truth while not agreeing language. Whereas a modern person might use the idea of pluralism to argue for the truthfulness of the Gospel, Augustine here uses the gospel truth to defend the possibility of pluralism.

74. Again, Augustine's dense logic may be summarized in this way: It is good that there should be less falsehood in the world. The Gospels are true but contain variations. Therefore other accounts can contain variations but remain true. Hence there is less falsehood in the world than one might initially think.

use different words, but who do not differ in their subjects and ideas, we accept them as established in the same truth.

12,29. Now, what is there in the comparisons I have proposed between the narratives of the evangelists that must be considered contradictory? Is it that one says *whose shoes I am not worthy to carry* (Mt 3:11) while the others say *the strap of whose shoes…to unloose* (Mk 1:7; Lk 3:16; Jn 1:27)? For this seems not to be a matter of words, or of the order of words, or of the mode of speech, but of the subject itself, for the one is about carrying shoes and the others are about unloosing the strap of the shoes. Therefore it may be rightly asked what John said he was unworthy to do — whether to carry the shoes or to unloose the strap of the shoes. For, if he only said one of these things, then the narrative that says what he really said would seem to be the true one; and the other, while not a lie, would nonetheless be a slip of the memory and would be supposed to have said one thing instead of another. But one ought to keep away from the evangelists all charges of falsehood, not only that which comes from lying but also that which comes from forgetfulness. Therefore, if it is relevant to the subject to understand "carrying shoes" to mean one thing, and "unloosing the strap of the shoes" to mean another, then how should one rightly understand it, except that John said both things, either on separate occasions or on the same occasion? For he might have said, "the strap of whose shoes I am not worthy to unloose, and whose shoes I am not worthy to carry," with the result that the one evangelist would have given part of it, and the others the rest, but all would have given truthful accounts. Furthermore, if by mentioning the Lord's shoes John intended to show [the Lord's] greatness and his own lowliness, then, whatever he said, whether it was about unloosing the strap of his shoes or carrying his shoes, the sense is preserved by any writer who mentions the shoes in his own words, thereby expressing the same idea of lowliness and not altering his subject's thought. Therefore, this is a useful method, and one especially worthy to be remembered, that, when we speak of the agreement of the evangelists, there is no falsehood, not even if they say that the subject of a narrative said something which that person did not say, as long as they express the same thought as the one of them who does record the actual words. From this we learn the sound lesson that we ought to seek nothing other than what the person speaking meant.

13,30. Matthew continues, then, and says, *Then Jesus came from Galilee to the Jordan to John, to be baptized by him. But John forbade him, saying, I need to be baptized by you, and you come to me? But answering, Jesus said to him, Let it be so, for thus it is fitting for us to fulfill all righteousness. Then he let him.* (Mt 3:13–15) The others also attest that Jesus came to John.[75] Three record that he was baptized, but they omit one thing which Matthew includes — that John spoke to the Lord and that the Lord answered John.

---

75.   See Mk 1:9; Lk 3:21; Jn 1:32–34.

14,31. Then Matthew continues, *When Jesus was baptized, he immediately went up out of the water. And behold, the heavens were opened to him and he saw the Spirit of God descending like a dove and coming upon him. And behold, a voice from heaven saying, This is my beloved son, with whom I am well pleased.* (Mt 3:16–17) Two of the others, Mark and Luke, tell a similar story.[76] But they express differently the words of the voice that came from heaven even though they keep the sense intact. For, although Matthew says, *This is my beloved son* (Mt 3:17), and the other two say, *You are my beloved son* (Mk 1:11; Lk 3:22), they have the same meaning, as discussed above. For, although the heavenly voice only said one of these things, the evangelist wished to show by this expression, *This is my son*, that it was for the benefit of those listening, to show them that he was the Son of God. Thus he turned *You are my son* into *This is my son*, as though it were being said to them. For it could not be to show Christ something that he already knew but so that those present could hear it, for whose sakes indeed the voice itself was there. But the one says, *with whom I am well pleased* (Mt 3:17), while the other says, *with you I am well pleased* (Mk 1:11), while the third says, *with you it has well pleased me* (Lk 3:22).[77] If you ask which of these reproduce what was said by that voice, any one of them may be accepted, as long as you understand that, although they do not give the exact same phrasing, they give the same sense. This diversity in speech is also useful for this — that, with only one version of the expression, it might be harder to understand it, or it might be interpreted in a way other than the sense of the thing itself. For with the expression, *with whom I am well pleased*, anyone who wanted to understand it to mean that God is pleased with himself in the Son would be warned away from this by the expression, *with you I am well pleased.*[78] On the other hand, if one understands this latter saying to mean that the Father is made pleasing to people by the Son, then one is warned away from this by the expression, *with you it has well pleased me.* From this it is clear enough that whichever evangelist has preserved the actual words of the heavenly voice, the others have varied the words only in order to explain the sense of it more familiarly, so that what is said by all of them might be understood as saying, "In you I have placed my good pleasure," that is to say, "to do what is pleasing to me through you." But again, some of the versions of the Gospel according to Luke say that what was heard in that voice was what was written in the Psalm, *You are my son, today I have begotten you* (Ps 2:7).[79] Although it is said not to be found in the more ancient Greek versions, if it can be confirmed by any trustworthy ones, how else could it be understood than that both were heard from heaven, in whichever word order?

---

76. See Mk 1:10–11; Lk 3:22.
77. There is no difference between Mk 1:11 and Lk 3:22 in the most reliable manuscripts.
78. Augustine's text of Matthew's version reads *In te complacuit mihi* (literally "With you it has well pleased me"), whereas Mark's version reads *In te complacui* (literally "With you I have been well pleased").
79. See *Answer to Faustus, a Manichean* XXIII,2.

15,32. In [the Gospel] according to John, when the dove came down is not told, but the words of John the Baptist reporting what he saw are recorded. Here it must be asked how this can be said: *And I did not know him, but he who sent me to baptize with water said to me, The one on whom you will see the Spirit descend and remain, this is he who baptizes in the Holy Spirit* (Jn 1:33). But if he came to know him only when he saw the dove descending upon him, there is a question as to how he could have said to him when he came to be baptized, *I need rather to be baptized by you* (Mt 3:14), since he said this to him before the dove descended. From this it is clear that, although he already knew him (after all, he leaped in his mother's womb when Mary came to Elizabeth[80]), there was something he did not know, which he learned by the Spirit's descent—that only [Jesus] baptized with the Holy Spirit by his own divine power, so that no one who received baptism from God, even though [John] baptized some, could say that what he handed on was his own nor that the Holy Spirit was given by him.

16,33. Matthew continues and says, *Then Jesus was led by the Spirit into the wilderness to be tempted by the devil. And, when he had fasted forty days and forty nights, he was hungry afterwards. And the tempter came and said to him, If you are the Son of God, speak, so that these stones may be made into bread. But answering he said, It is written, Man does not live on bread alone but by every word that proceeds from the mouth of God* (Mt 4:1–4), and so forth, until where it says, *Then the devil left him, and behold, angels came and ministered to him* (Mt 4:11). Luke tells the whole story similarly but in a different order.[81] This makes it uncertain whether the kingdoms of the earth were shown to him and after that he was taken up to the pinnacle of the Temple, or whether the latter occurred before the former. But this is irrelevant, as long as it is clear that all these things really happened. Although Luke expresses the same ideas in different words, it need not be noted again that there is no loss of truth thereby. For Mark confirms that he was tempted in the wilderness by the devil for forty days and nights, but he does not mention what was said to him or how he replied.[82] But that the angels ministered to him he does not omit, even though Luke does. John, on the other hand, omits this whole passage.

17,34. Matthew continues by saying, *Now, when he heard that John had been handed over, he withdrew into Galilee* (Mt 4:12). Mark says the same,[83] as does Luke,[84] but Luke says nothing in this section about John's being handed over. And the evangelist John says that, before Jesus went into Galilee, Peter and Andrew were with him one day, and that at that time Peter was given the name Peter, having been called Simon before.[85] Likewise the following day, desiring to go into

---

80. See Luke 1:41.
81. See Lk 4:1–13.
82. See Mk 1:12–13.
83. See Mk 1:14.
84. See Lk 4:14.
85. See Jn 1:40–42.

Galilee, he found Philip and told him to follow him.[86] So too he tells the story of Nathanael.[87] On the third day, when he was in Galilee, he performed the miracle at Cana of turning the water into wine.[88] All the other evangelists omit all these things and continue their narratives with Jesus' return to Galilee. It should be understood that some days intervened; John relates those things concerning the disciples that took place at this time. And there is nothing here that contradicts that other passage, where Matthew reports that the Lord said to Peter, *You are Peter, and on this rock I will build my Church* (Mt 16:18). It is not to be understood that this is when he received that name; rather, this [happened] when it was said to him, as John records, *You shall be called Cephas, which means Peter* (Jn 1:42). Thus the Lord could call him by that name later, saying, *You are Peter*, for he does not say [later], *You shall be called Peter* but *You are Peter*, because he had already said to him before, *You shall be called*.

17,35. Then the narrative continues and Matthew says, *And leaving the city of Nazareth he came and dwelt in Capernaum by the sea, on the borders of Zebulun and Naphtali* (Mt 4:13), and so forth, until the end of the sermon that he gave on a mountain.[89] In this section of the narrative he is confirmed by Mark as to the calling of the disciples Peter and Andrew, and a little later, James and John.[90] But, when Matthew continues his narrative with that long sermon that he gave on a mountain, after he cured a multitude and many crowds followed him,[91] Mark instead inserts other things, such as his teaching in the synagogues and the amazement at his teaching.[92] He also says what Matthew says after that long sermon, that *he taught them as one who had authority, and not as the scribes* (Mt 7:29; Mk 1:22). He also tells of the man out of whom the unclean spirit was cast, and then the story of Peter's mother-in-law.[93] Luke too agrees with these things.[94] Matthew, however, gives no account of the demon; he is not silent concerning Peter's mother-in-law, but [he includes the story] later.[95]

17,36. In this passage that we are now considering, after the call of the disciples, who were fishing and whom [Jesus] commanded to follow him, Matthew narrates that he went around Galilee teaching in the synagogues and preaching the Gospel and healing all sicknesses, and, when the crowds had gathered around him, he went up on a mountain and gave that long sermon.[96] This passage leads us to conclude that the things which Mark narrates after the choosing of those disciples must have happened when he was going around Galilee and teaching in

---

86. See Jn 1:43.
87. See Jn 1:45–51.
88. See Jn 2:1–11.
89. See Mt 4:14–7:29.
90. See Mk 1:16–20.
91. See Mt 4:23–25.
92. See Mk 1:21–22.
93. See Mk 1:23–31.
94. See Lk 4:31–39.
95. See Mt 8:14–15.
96. See Mt 4:23–5:1.

their synagogues,[97] as well as the event concerning Peter's mother-in-law. [Matthew] records later what he omits here, although he does not include everything that he omits here in his later narrative.

17,37. But it may be problematic that John says that [the following happened] not in Galilee but near the Jordan: first, that Andrew followed the Lord together with someone else, whose name is not stated; then, that Peter received his name from him; and thirdly, that Philip was called to follow him.[98] But the other three evangelists, especially Matthew and Mark, agree among themselves that they were called while fishing.[99] Although Luke does not mention Andrew by name, one can gather that he was in the boat, based on the account of Matthew and Mark, which briefly summarizes what happened, while Luke gives a clearer account, recording also the miraculous catch of fish as well as the fact that the Lord first spoke to the crowds from that boat.[100] But this would also seem to be a difference — that [Luke] writes, *From now on you shall catch men* (Lk 5:10), as though the Lord said it to Peter alone, while the others record it as though it was said to both brothers.[101] But it may be that this was said first to Peter, when he was marveling at the huge multitude of fish caught, as Luke indicates, and later to both, as the other two record. Therefore what we have said of John should be considered carefully, for it may raise an issue of no small incompatibility, as there is disagreement as to location, time, and the calling itself. For, if it is the case that near the Jordan, before Jesus went into Galilee, two men — Andrew, who immediately brought to Jesus his brother Simon, who then received the name Peter, by which he was subsequently called — followed [Jesus] thanks to the testimony of John the Baptist, how can the other evangelists say that he found them fishing in Galilee and called them to be his disciples? How can this be understood unless, when the Lord was near the Jordan, they did not perceive him to be someone they would inseparably attach themselves to but only learned who he was and, after marveling at him, returned to their usual lives?

17,38. Again, in Cana of Galilee, after he had turned the water into wine, John says that his disciples believed in him. He writes the following: *And on the third day there was a wedding in Cana of Galilee, and Jesus' mother was there. And Jesus was invited to the wedding, along with his disciples.* (Jn 2:1–2) Now, if this was the time when they believed in him, as he says a little later, then they were not his disciples when they were invited to the wedding. But this is a way of speaking and means the same as when we say that the apostle Paul was born in Tarsus of Cilicia,[102] even though he was not an apostle then. So, when we hear that Christ's disciples were invited to the wedding, we ought to understand not that they were

---

97. See Mk 1:16–31.
98. See Jn 1:35–43.
99. See Mt 4:18–22; Mk 1:16–20.
100. See Lk 5:1–11.
101. See Mt 4:19; Mk 1:17.
102. See Acts 22:3.

already his disciples but that they were to become his disciples. For, when this narrative was written down, they were indeed Christ's disciples, and that is why [the evangelist], as the narrator of past times, speaks of them this way.

17,39. And when John says, *After this he went down to Capernaum with his mother and his brothers and his disciples, and they stayed there not many days* (Jn 2:12), it is unclear whether Peter and Andrew and the sons of Zebedee had also already joined him. For Matthew says first that he came and dwelt in Capernaum, and later that he called them from their boats as they were fishing.[103] But [John] says that his disciples came with him to Capernaum. It may be that Matthew goes over here what he had omitted elsewhere. For he does not say, "After this, while walking by the Sea of Galilee, he saw two brothers," but, without any indication of the chronological sequence, he says only, *Walking by the Sea of Galilee, he saw two brothers* (Mt 4:18), and so forth. Therefore it may be that [Matthew] records later not what happened later but something that he had omitted before, so that it may be understood that they came with him to Capernaum, as John says he came with his mother and disciples. Or perhaps these were other disciples, such as Philip, who followed him, and who had been called when he said, *Follow me* (Jn 1:43). For it is not clear from the evangelists' accounts in what order all twelve apostles were called. Not only is the order of their callings not recorded, but not even is the very calling of each one recorded, apart from that of Philip and Peter and Andrew and the sons of Zebedee and Matthew the tax-collector, who was also called Levi.[104] Peter was the first and only one, however, who was singled out to receive a name from him.[105] For he called the sons of Zebedee both together, and not singly, *sons of thunder* (Mk 3:17).

17,40. It should certainly be noted that the Scriptures, both the Gospels and the apostolic writings, use the name "disciples" not only for those twelve but for all who believed in him and were educated by his teaching for the kingdom of heaven. For out of many such [disciples] he called twelve, whom he also named apostles, as Luke records.[106] For a little further on he says, *And he came down with them and stood on a level place with a crowd of his disciples and a great multitude of people.* (Lk 6:17) He surely would not have said *a crowd of disciples* if there were only twelve men. In other passages of Scripture it is also quite apparent that "disciples" refers to anyone who learned from him about eternal life.

17,41. But one may ask how he called the fishermen from their boats by twos, first Peter and Andrew, then going a little further, another two, the sons of Zebedee, as Matthew and Mark say, while Luke says that both their boats were filled with the great catch of fish. He also says that Peter's partners, James and John, the sons of Zebedee, were called upon to help when they could not drag up their full nets, and they marveled at the huge number of fish that had been caught, and

---

103. See Matt 4:13, 19.
104. See Mt 4:18–22; Mk 1:16–20; Lk 5:1–11; Jn 1:35–44.
105. See Jn 1:42.
106. See Lk 6:13.

[Jesus] said to Peter, *Do not be afraid, from now on you shall be catching men* (Lk 5:10). As soon as they drew their boats up to shore, they followed him. From this it should be understood that Luke is showing what happened first—that they were not called by the Lord then but only that it was predicted that Peter would be a catcher of men. Nor was it said that from then on they would not be catching fish, for we read that even after the Lord's resurrection they were fishing.[107] Hence it means that thenceforth he would be catching men; it does not mean that thenceforth he would not be catching fish. From this passage one could assume that they returned to their habit of catching fish. Therefore what Matthew and Mark narrate could have happened later—that he called them by twos and commanded them to follow him, first the pair of Peter and Andrew and then the other two, the sons of Zebedee. For at that time they did not take care to draw up their boats, as though they would return to them, but immediately followed him, as one who had called and commanded them to follow him.

18,42. Further, we must ask how the evangelist John, before John the Baptist is put in prison, says that Jesus went into Galilee. For, after recording that he turned the water into wine in Cana of Galilee and went down to Capernaum with his mother and disciples and remained there not many days,[108] he then says that he went up to Jerusalem for the Passover,[109] and that after this he came into the land of Judea with his disciples and stayed there with them and baptized.[110] He then says that *John also was baptizing in Aenon near Salim, because there was much water there, and they came and were baptized. For John had not yet been put in prison.* (Jn 3:23–24) But Matthew says, *Now, when he heard that John had been handed over, he withdrew into Galilee* (Mt 4:12). Similarly, Mark has, *Now, after John had been handed over, Jesus came into Galilee* (Mk 1:14). Now, Luke says nothing of John's being handed over, but nonetheless, after Christ's baptism and temptation, he, like the other two, says that he went into Galilee. For thus his narrative continues, *And when every temptation was finished, the devil departed from him for a time. And Jesus returned in the power of the Spirit into Galilee, and a report of him went out through all that area.* (Lk 4:13–14) From this it should be understood that these three evangelists do not record anything contrary to the evangelist John but only that they omit the Lord's first arrival into Galilee after his baptism, when he turned the water into wine, for at that time John had not yet been handed over. Into their narratives they insert another arrival of his into Galilee, which occurred after John was handed over. The evangelist John himself also speaks of this return into Galilee: *Now, when Jesus knew that the Pharisees had heard that Jesus was making and baptizing more disciples than John (although Jesus himself did not baptize, but his disciples), he left Judea and departed again into Galilee* (Jn 4:1–3). So we learn that by that time John had

---

107. See Jn 21:3.
108. See Jn 2:1–12.
109. See Jn 2:13.
110. See Jn 3:22.

already been handed over and that the Jews had heard that [Jesus] was making and baptizing more disciples than John had made and baptized.

19,43. Now, as for that long sermon which Matthew says the Lord gave on a mountain, let us see whether or not the other evangelists seem to be in disagreement with it. Mark records none of it, nor even anything similar to it, except some disconnected scattered sentences that the Lord repeated in other places. But he leaves a space in the text of his narrative, where we may understand that this sermon was given, even though it has been omitted. That is where he says, *And he went throughout all of Galilee, preaching in their synagogues and casting out demons* (Mk 1:39). This preaching, which he says took place in all of Galilee, is to be understood as including that sermon which he gave on a mountain and which is recorded by Matthew. For Mark continues, *And a leper came to him, beseeching him, and kneeling said, If you will, you can make me clean* (Mk 1:40), and so forth. He goes on to tell of the leper's cleansing, so that it is to be understood that it is the same cleansing that Matthew records after the Lord came down from his sermon on the mountain. For Matthew says this: *When he came down from the mountain, great crowds followed him. And behold, a leper came and worshiped him, saying, Lord, if you will, you can make me clean* (Mt 8:1–2), and so forth.

19,44. Luke also mentions this leper,[111] not in this order but in the manner in which [the evangelists] were accustomed to record things that they had omitted previously or anticipate things that happened later; they knew these things before, but, as they remembered them later, they were divinely prompted to write them down. Indeed, Luke also gives us his version of the Lord's long sermon, which begins in the same way as Matthew's. For the latter says, *Blessed are the poor in spirit, for theirs is the kingdom of heaven* (Mt 5:3), while the former [says], *Blessed are you poor, for yours is the kingdom of God* (Lk 6:20). Much of what follows from then on in Luke's narrative is similar [to Matthew's]. And the conclusion of the sermon is the same in both, concerning the prudent man who built on rock and the foolish man who built on sand, except that [Luke] speaks of the stream beating against the house, but not the rain and wind as Matthew does.[112] Hence it is easy enough to believe that [Luke] introduces the same sermon of the Lord but omits some phrases that Matthew includes, includes others that [Matthew] does not, and expresses others in such a way that they preserve the fullness of the truth, although not in the same words.

19,45. This could easily be believed, as I have said, unless it should be problematic that Matthew says that the Lord gave this sermon while sitting on a mountain, whereas Luke [says] that the Lord was standing on a level place.[113] This difference makes it seem that the one [refers] to one [sermon] and the other to another. But what would keep Christ from repeating something he had said before, or from doing something he had done before? One need not conclude that these two ser-

---

111. See Lk 5:12–16.
112. See Mt 7:24–27; Lk 6:47–49.
113. See Mt 5:1; Lk 6:17.

mons inserted by Matthew and Luke are not separated by a long period of time, because similar or identical events are narrated before and after both. Therefore it is not absurd to think that these narratives inserted here took place in the same places and times. For Matthew says the following: *And great crowds followed him from Galilee and the Decapolis and Jerusalem and Judea and from beyond the Jordan. Seeing the crowds, he went up on the mountain, and when he sat down his disciples came to him. And opening his mouth, he taught them, saying, Blessed are the poor in spirit, for theirs is the kingdom of heaven* (Mt 4:25–5:3), and so forth. This makes it seem that he wished to avoid the great crowds, so he went up on the mountain to withdraw from the crowds so that he could speak to his disciples alone. This seems to be confirmed by Luke's narrative: *It happened in those days that he went out to a mountain to pray, and all night he was praying to God. And when it was day he called his disciples and chose twelve from them, whom he named apostles: Simon, whom he also named Peter, and Andrew his brother, James and John, Philip and Bartholomew, Matthew and Thomas, James the son of Alphaeus, and Simon, who was called the Zealot, Judas the son of James, and Judas Iscariot, who was the betrayer. And going down with them, he stood on a level place, with a crowd of his disciples and a great multitude of people from all Judea and Jerusalem and the seacoast of Tyre and Sidon, who had come to hear him and to be healed of their diseases. And those who were troubled by unclean spirits were cured. And all the crowd sought to touch him, for power went out from him and healed them all. And he lifted up his eyes to his disciples, and said, Blessed are you poor, for yours is the kingdom of God* (Lk 6:12–20), and so forth. This makes the following seem probable: On the mountain he chose twelve disciples out of many, whom he named apostles, which Matthew omits. Then he gave the sermon, which Matthew includes and Luke omits. Then he came down the mountain and gave another similar [sermon] on a level place, which Matthew omits and Luke does not omit. And both these sermons ended in the same way.

19,46. At the end of that sermon Matthew continues and says the following: *And it happened that, when Jesus had finished these sayings, the crowds were astonished at his teaching* (Mt 7:28). This might make it seem that the crowds of disciples, from whom he chose the twelve, were speaking. And immediately he goes on to say the following: *When he came down from the mountain, great crowds followed him. And behold, a leper came and worshiped him.* (Mt 8:1–2) From this one should understand that this took place after both sermons, not just Matthew's but also the one that Luke inserts. For it is not clear how much time passed after his descent from the mountain. Matthew did not wish to show how much time had intervened but only that, after his descent from the mountain, there were great crowds with the Lord when he cleansed the leper. This is also shown by the fact that Luke says this same leper was cleansed when the Lord was in a city,[114] which Matthew has not bothered to tell us.

---

114. See Lk 5:12.

19,47. The following might also have occurred: Perhaps the Lord was on some higher part of the mountain, only with his disciples, when he chose twelve of them. Then he came down with them from that higher part of the mountain, and not down from the mountain itself, onto a level place—that is, a level place which was on the mountain and which could hold great crowds—and he stood there and the crowds gathered around him.[115] After this he sat down, and his disciples came near him,[116] and he gave one sermon to them and to the other crowds that were present. Matthew and Luke narrate this according to their different narrative styles, but they both speak the truth regarding the [sermon's] subjects and ideas. For we have already noted something that did not need to be noted and should have been immediately evident to anyone—that there is no contradiction if one omits what the other includes, or if one expresses it one way and the other another way, as long as they both express the truth regarding the subjects and ideas.[117] In this way, when Matthew says, *When he came down from the mountain* (Mt 8:1), it may be understood as a level place which could have been on the mountain. Then Matthew tells of the cleansing of the leper, which Mark and Luke [tell] similarly.[118]

20,48. After this Matthew continues and says, *And when he entered Capernaum, a centurion approached him, begging him and saying, Lord, my servant lies at home, paralyzed and terribly tormented* (Mt 8:5–6), and so forth, until the place where it says, *And the servant was healed at that very moment* (Mt 8:13). Luke also records this story of the centurion's servant, although not immediately after the cleansing of the leper, which he had already recorded even though it [happened] later.[119] Luke connects it after the end of that long sermon: *When he had finished all his sayings in the hearing of the people, he entered Capernaum. And a centurion's slave, who was dear to him, was sick to the point of death* (Lk 7:1–2), and so forth, until the place where it says he was healed.[120] Thus it is to be understood that Christ entered Capernaum after he had finished all his sayings in the hearing of the people. This only means that he did not enter there before he had finished these words, but it does not imply anything as to the length of the time interval between the end of the sermon and his entrance into Capernaum. During this interval that leper was cleansed, which Matthew puts in this place, thus recording it later.[121]

---

115. See Lk 6:17.
116. See Mt 5:1.
117. See *Answer to Faustus, a Manichean* XXXIII,7.
118. See Mt 8:2–4; Mk 1:40–45; Lk 5:12–16.
119. See above at II,19,44.
120. See Lk 7:10.
121. Augustine's problem with this passage is twofold. First, Luke puts the cleansing of the leper earlier: Augustine explains this on the basis of the principle enunciated at the beginning of II,19,44, that the evangelists not only postpone until later things that happened earlier but also anticipate things that happened later. Therefore Matthew's chronology is correct, but Luke's is not misleading. Second, Luke makes it seem that the healing of the centurion's servant happened immediately after the sermon on the plain, whereas Matthew makes it seem that the cleansing followed immediately on the sermon and that there was then a passage of time before

20,49. Now let us see whether Matthew and Luke agree with one another concerning the centurion's servant. Matthew says this: *A centurion approached him, begging him and saying, My servant lies at home, paralyzed* (Mt 8:5–6). This seems to be incompatible with what Luke says: *When he heard of Jesus, he sent to him elders of the Jews, begging him to come and heal his slave. And when they came to Jesus, they begged him anxiously, saying, He is worthy for you to do this for him, for he loves our nation and built us our synagogue. And Jesus went with them. And when he was not far from the house, the centurion sent friends to him saying, Lord, do not trouble yourself, for I am not worthy to have you enter under my roof, nor did I consider myself worthy to come to you; but say the word, and my servant will be healed.* (Lk 7:3–7) If this is how it happened, how can it be true, as Matthew says, that *a certain centurion approached him* (Mt 8:5), when he himself did not approach him but sent friends?[122] But, if we examine it carefully, we may understand that Matthew is only using a common way of speaking. For we are in the habit of saying that someone is approaching before he has reached the place that he is said to be approaching; we even speak of "approaching a little" or "approaching more" with respect to something that one wishes to reach. We even frequently say that one has reached the thing which was the reason for the approach, even though the one who reaches may not see the one whom he is reaching, using friends to reach the one whose favor is necessary for him. This is why people who are angling for some position and who use suitable persons to get at others who are powerful but inaccessible are usually called "reachers"[123] in ordinary speech. If, then, one may say that one reaches someone through others, how much more would it be possible [to say] that one approaches someone through others, since [approaching] is less than reaching. For one could do a lot of approaching and still not be able to reach something! It would not at all be unreasonable, then (and, indeed, anyone could understand it), if the centurion approached the Lord through others and that Matthew chooses to express this concisely by saying, *A centurion approached him.*

20,50. We should not carelessly overlook the mystical loftiness of the holy evangelist's language, however, since it resembles what is written in the Psalm, *Approach him and be radiant* (Ps 34:5). For the centurion approached Jesus with such faith that Jesus himself praised it, saying, *I have not found such faith in Israel* (Mt 8:10). The evangelist wisely chooses to say that he—rather than those through whom he sent his words—approached Christ himself. Furthermore, Luke presents the event in such a way that it leads us to understand how someone else who was incapable of falsehood might tell of his approach. In the same way, the woman who suffered from the flow of blood, although she only touched the fringe

---

the entrance into Capernaum. Augustine explains this on the basis of another principle that he invokes several times (at, e.g., II,17,34 and 19,45–46): the fact that events follow one another immediately in the narrative implies nothing about the real time between the two events.

122. See *Answer to Faustus, a Manichean* XXXIII,7.
123. "Reachers": *perventores.*

of his garment, touched him more deeply than did the crowds that pressed upon him.[124] For she touched the Lord more deeply because she believed more deeply, and in the same way the centurion approached the Lord more deeply because he believed more deeply. As for the rest of this section, it would be superfluous to go over the things that are said by one and omitted by the other since, by that rule noted earlier,[125] no contradiction is to be found.

21,51. Matthew continues and says, *And when Jesus came into Peter's house, he saw that his mother-in-law was lying sick and with a fever. And he touched her hand, and the fever left her, and she got up and served them.* (Mt 8:14–15) Matthew does not say when this occurred, whether before or after. For, just because it is placed after an event in the narrative, one need not assume that it occurred after that. Undoubtedly we are to understand that he has mentioned something here that he omitted before. For, before he gives the account of the cleansing of the leper, which seems to be an insertion, Mark narrates what happened after the sermon that was given on the mountain, about which he himself says nothing. Both Luke and Mark place the story of Peter's mother-in-law after the same event,[126] but [Luke] has it before that long sermon that appears to be the same as the one that Matthew says was given on a mountain. But what difference does it make where something is placed, whether it is in order, or whether it is mentioned after it was omitted before, or whether it is anticipated before it happened, as long as it does not contradict anything elsewhere in the same [Gospel] or in the others, whether they are narratives of the same event or of others? For no one has the ability, no matter how great and trustworthy his knowledge of events is, to determine the order in which he will remember them. For whether something comes into a person's mind earlier or later is a matter not of our will but of how it is given to us. It is probable enough that each of the evangelists believed it was his duty to narrate events in the order in which God saw fit to suggest to his recollection the things he was narrating. This would be the case at least with those things where one order or another would in no way diminish the truth and authority of the Gospel.

21,52. The Holy Spirit, who *apportions to each as he wishes* (1 Cor 12:11), undoubtedly governed and ruled the minds of the holy ones by reminding them what to write, so as to place their books at such a height of authority. But he lets one arrange his narrative one way and the other another way; with pious care one may investigate why this is so, and one may even find an answer with divine help. However, that is not the purpose we have set for the present work. We only seek to show that none of the evangelists is inconsistent with either himself or the others, in whatever order he was willing or able to narrate Christ's deeds and words, and whether in reference to the same or different things. Therefore, when the chronological order is not clear, it ought to make no difference to us what narrative order any of them chose; but if it is clear and seems to be inconsistent with

---

124. See Lk 8:42–48; Mt 9:18–26; Mk 5:25–34.
125. See above at II,12,27–28.
126. See Mk 1:21–28; Lk 4:31–37.

its own [narrative] or the others, then it should be an object of our concern — and, indeed, ought to be reflected upon and explained.

22,53. Matthew continues, then, and says, *Now, when it was evening, they brought to him many who had demons, and he cast out the spirits with a word and healed all who were sick. This was to fulfill what was spoken by Isaiah the prophet, saying, He himself took our infirmities and bore our sicknesses.* (Mt 8:16–17) It is quite clear that this was on the same day, because he says, *when it was evening* (Mt 8:16). Similarly, at the end of the healing of Peter's mother-in-law, Mark says, *and she served them* (Mk 1:31), and he then continues thus: *That evening, when the sun went down, they brought to him all who were sick and those who had demons. And the whole city was gathered at the door. And he healed many who were sick with various diseases and cast out many demons, and he did not let them speak, because they knew him. And, rising a long time before dawn, he departed and went out to a lonely place.* (Mk 1:32–35) It appears that Mark has preserved the order here, for, after saying, *when it was evening* (Mk 1:32), he then says, *and, rising a long time before dawn* (Mk 1:35). But, although it is not necessary to suppose that *evening* refers to the evening of that same day or that *dawn* refers to the dawn following that same night, it nonetheless seems that the order of these events preserves the proper chronological order. For although Luke, after telling of Peter's mother-in-law, does not say, *when it was evening*, he does continue by saying something that means the same thing: *Now, when the sun was setting, all those who had any who were sick with various diseases brought them to him; and, laying his hands on every one of them, he healed them. And demons came out of many, crying out and saying, You are the Son of God! But rebuking them, he would not let them speak, because they knew that he was the Christ. And, when it was day, he departed and went to a lonely place.* (Lk 4:40–42) Here we see the same chronological order preserved as we found in Mark. But Matthew does not seem to record the story of Peter's mother-in-law in the order in which it happened but just as it occurred to him after omitting it before. For afterwards he continues his narrative with what happened on that same day at evening, but then, instead of continuing with [the next] morning, he says this: *Now, when Jesus saw great crowds around him, he gave orders to go over to the other side of the lake* (Mt 8:18). This is different from what Mark and Luke say, who go from evening to morning. Therefore, when it says, *Now, when Jesus saw great crowds around him, he gave orders to go over to the other side of the lake*, we ought to understand that [Matthew] has placed here something he recalled — that, on a certain day, when Jesus saw great crowds around himself, he gave orders to go over to the other side of the lake.

23,54. He then adds this, *And a scribe came and said to him, Teacher, I will follow you wherever you go* (Mt 8:19), until where it says, *Let the dead bury their dead* (Mt 8:22). Although this account is given similarly in Luke,[127] it comes after

---

127. See Lk 9:57–62.

many other things and without any real reference to the chronological order, as though he just remembered it. It is also uncertain whether it was omitted earlier or whether it anticipates something that happened after events that now follow it in the narrative. For [Luke] says this: *And it happened that, as they were going along the road, someone said to him, I will follow you wherever you go* (Lk 9:57). And he answers him in just the same way as Matthew reports. But, although Matthew says this happened when [Jesus] gave orders for them to go over to the other side of the lake, while Luke [says it happened] while they were going along the road, there is no contradiction, for they may have been going along the road in order to get to the lake. Matthew and Luke also agree completely as to the man who asked to bury his father first.[128] For the fact that Matthew has the man ask about his father first and then has the Lord say, *Follow me* (Mt 8:22), while Luke has the Lord say, *Follow me* (Lk 9:59), and then has the man [speak], does not change the meaning. Luke also writes of another man who said, *I will follow you, Lord, but first let me say farewell to those who are at home* (Lk 9:61), while Matthew says nothing of him. Luke then continues to another event, and not the one that followed in the temporal order: *And after these things, the Lord appointed seventy-two others* (Lk 10:1). Although it is clear that this happened *after these things*, it is not apparent how long it was before the Lord did this. What Matthew next relates took place in that interval, for Matthew holds to the chronological order as he continues his narrative.

24,55. *And when he got into the boat, his disciples followed him. And behold, there arose a great storm on the sea* (Mt 8:23–24), until where it says, *and he came into his own city* (Mt 9:1). Matthew recounts these two events — regarding the calming of the sea, after Jesus was awakened from his sleep and commanded the winds, and regarding those who had savage demons and who had broken their chains and been led into the wilderness — as though they happened in immediate succession; they are recounted similarly by Mark and Luke.[129] Although they use different words from one another, their sense is not different. For example, Matthew says that [Jesus] said, *Why are you afraid, O you of little faith?* (Mt 8:26) while Mark says, *Why are you afraid? Have you no faith?* (Mk 4:40) By this [Mark] means that perfect [faith] which is like a grain of mustard seed, thereby intending the same as *little faith*. And Luke's [version] is *Where is your faith?* (Lk 8:25) Therefore [Jesus'] whole statement might have been *Why are you afraid? Where is your faith, O you of little faith?* of which each of them has recorded a part. The same sort of thing [happened] with what they said to him when they woke him up. For Matthew [says], *Lord, save us, we are perishing* (Mt 8:25); Mark [says], *Teacher, does it not matter to you that we are perishing?* (Mk 4:38); and Luke [says], *Master, we are perishing* (Lk 8:24). But they all have the same meaning — that they were waking the Lord and that they wished to be saved. Nor is it necessary

---

128. See Mt 8:21; Lk 9:59.
129. See Mk 4:35–41; 5:1–17; Lk 8:22–37.

to inquire which of these was actually said to Christ. For what difference would it make if one of these three was what was said, or even if it was different words which were not recorded by any of the evangelists but which had the same true sense? It is also possible that, when several people were trying at the same time to awaken him, all these things were said, some by one, some by another. Thus also at the calming of the storm they said, according to Matthew, *What sort of man is this, that even the winds and sea obey him?* (Mt 8:27); according to Mark, *Who do you think this is, that the wind and sea obey him?* (Mk 4:41); and according to Luke, *Who do you think this is, that he commands the winds and the sea, and they obey him?* (Lk 8:25) Who could not see that there is one meaning here? For *Who do you think this is?* is equivalent to *What sort of man is this?* And where it does not say *he commands*, it should be understood that one who is obeyed is one who commands.

24,56. As for the fact that Matthew says there were two people who suffered from the legion of demons that he let go into the swine,[130] while Mark and Luke both record only one,[131] it may be supposed that one of them was a kind of distinguished and famous person, who was especially lamented in that area and whose health was of particular concern. Wishing to indicate this, two of the evangelists have decided to record only that one, whose case made the fame of this act spread more widely and remarkably. No doubts should be raised by the evangelists' having different words spoken by the demons, for they may be reduced to the same meaning, or they may be supposed to have all been spoken. Nor is there anything inconsistent in Matthew's having them speak in the plural, while the others have it in the singular, for they also say that when he was asked what he was called, he answered *Legion*, because the demons were many; nor in Mark's [saying] that the herd of swine was around the mountain, while Luke [says] that they were on the mountain, for the herd of swine was so large that part could have been on the mountain and another part around the mountain, for, as Mark says, there were about two thousand swine.

25,57. Then Matthew, still keeping the chronological order, goes on to the following in his narrative: *And getting into a boat, he crossed over and came into his own city. And behold, they brought to him a paralytic, lying on a bed* (Mt 9:1–2), and so forth, until where it says, *And when the crowds saw it, they were afraid, and they glorified God, who had given such power to men* (Mt 9:8). Mark and Luke also tell the story of this paralytic.[132] But, while Matthew says that the Lord said, *Take heart, son, your sins are forgiven you* (Mt 9:2), according to Luke he did not say *son* but *man* (Lk 5:20). But this only makes the Lord's meaning more explicit: the sins of a man were forgiven, because as a man it was not possible for him to say, "I have not sinned," and at the same time this made it known that the one who forgave the man was himself God. Mark has the same words as Matthew, except

---

130. See Mt 8:28–34.
131. See Mk 5:1–17; Lk 8:26–37.
132. See Mk 2:1–12; Lk 5:17–26.

that he does not say, *Take heart.* It is also possible that the whole saying was this: *Take heart, man; your sins are forgiven you, son* or *Take heart, son; your sins are forgiven you, man,* or the order of the words may have been something similar.

25,58. But it may be problematic that Matthew tells the story of the paralytic this way: *And getting into a boat, he crossed over and came into his own city. And behold, they brought to him a paralytic, lying on a bed.* (Mt 9:1–2) For Mark does not say that this happened in his own city, which is called Nazareth, but in Capernaum: *And he entered into Capernaum after some days, and it was heard that he was in the house. And so many were gathered that there was no room for them, not even by the door, and he was speaking the word to them. And they came bringing to him a paralytic carried by four men. And when they could not bring him to him because of the crowd, they uncovered the roof where he was; and when they had made an opening, they let down the cot on which the paralytic lay. And when Jesus saw their faith* (Mk 2:1–5), and so forth. Luke, however, does not record where it happened but tells it this way: *And it happened that on one of those days he was sitting and teaching, and there were Pharisees and teachers of the law sitting by who had come from every village of Galilee and Judea and Jerusalem, and the power of the Lord was there to heal them. And behold, men were carrying on a bed a man who was paralyzed, and they sought to bring him in and lay him before him. But, not finding a way to bring him in, because of the crowd, they went up on the roof and let him down with his bed through the tiles into the midst before Jesus. And when he saw their faith, he said, Man, your sins are forgiven you* (Lk 5:17–20), and so forth. The issue is therefore between Matthew and Mark, for Matthew writes that it happened in the Lord's city, but Mark that it was in Capernaum. This would be more difficult to resolve if Matthew mentioned Nazareth by name. But it is possible to call Galilee Christ's city, since Nazareth was in Galilee, just as the whole empire is made up of so many cities but is called the city of Rome.[133] Similarly, so many nations go to make up that city, of which it is written, *Glorious things are said of you, O city of God* (Ps 87:3). And also God's ancient people, although living in so many cities, were said to be one house, the house of Israel.[134] Who, then, could doubt that Jesus did this in his own city if he did it in the city of Capernaum, which is a city of Galilee, to which he returned when he crossed over from the region of the Gerasenes? Therefore it is correct to say that, when he came into Galilee, he came into his own city, wherever he might have been in Galilee, especially since Capernaum stood out to such a degree in Galilee that it was considered a metropolis. But, even if it was not correct to take Christ's city as [meaning] Galilee, where Nazareth was, nor as Capernaum, which was held up among the cities of Galilee as though it were its capital, we may still say that Matthew omits everything that happened from the time Jesus came into his own city until he came to Capernaum, and he adds the healing of the paralytic

---

133. Augustine's discussion relies on the dual meaning of *civitas*, which may refer to either a city or a state.

134. See Is 5:7; Jer 3:20; Ezk 3:4, 7.

here. This is often done by those who omit intervening material and, without any indication of the omission, add material as though it followed without interruption.

26,59. From this point Matthew continues, then, and says, *And as Jesus passed on from there, he saw a man named Matthew sitting at the tax office, and he said to him, Follow me. And he rose and followed him.* (Mt 9:9) Mark also tells this story in the same order, placing it after the healing of the paralytic: *And he went out by the sea, and all the crowd came to him and he taught them. And as he passed by he saw Levi the son of Alphaeus sitting at the tax office, and he said to him, Follow me. And he rose and followed him.* (Mk 2:13–14) There is nothing inconsistent here, since Matthew and Levi are the same. Luke also adds this story after the healing of the paralytic: *And after these things he went out and saw a tax collector named Levi sitting at the tax office, and he said to him, Follow me. And he left everything and rose and followed him.* (Lk 5:27–28) This shows quite credibly that Matthew is here recording things that he has now remembered after [previously] omitting them. For we ought to believe that Matthew was called before the sermon on the mountain, for Luke reports that on that mountain [Jesus] chose from out of many disciples all those twelve, whom he also named apostles.[135]

27,60. Matthew continues, then, and says, *And it happened that, as he sat at table in the house, behold, many tax collectors and sinners came and sat down with Jesus and his disciples* (Mt 9:10), and so forth, until where it says, *But they put new wine into new wineskins, so that both are preserved* (Mt 9:17). Here Matthew does not say in whose house Jesus was sitting at the table with tax collectors and sinners. Thus it might seem that he has not placed it here according to its sequence but that it happened at another time, and he added it here as it occurred to him. But Mark and Luke give an altogether similar account and show that it was in the house of Levi — in other words, Matthew — that Jesus sat at table and said those things that follow. For Mark says this, preserving the same order: *And it happened that, as he sat at table in his house, many tax collectors and sinners sat with Jesus* (Mk 2:15). When he says *in his house* he must be referring to the one whom he just mentioned, and that is Levi. Similarly, after Luke says, *And he said to him, Follow me. And he left everything, and rose and followed him*, he immediately continues, *And Levi made him a great feast in his own house, and there was a large crowd of tax collectors and others sitting at table with them* (Lk 5:27–29). Thus it is clear in whose house these things happened.

27,61. Now let us look at those words which all three evangelists agree were spoken to the Lord and his responses to them. Matthew says, *And seeing this, the Pharisees said to his disciples, Why does your teacher eat with tax collectors and sinners?* (Mt 9:11) Mark has nearly the same words: *Why does your teacher eat and drink with tax collectors and sinners?* (Mk 2:16) Matthew omits one thing that he includes, the words *and drink*, but what difference does that make, since the same sense is conveyed that they were feasting together? Luke, though, seems to give a somewhat different account: *But the Pharisees and scribes murmured against them and said to his disciples, Why do you eat and drink with tax collectors and sinners?* (Lk 5:30) This is not to be taken as excluding their teacher but means that their objection was against all of them together, his disciples and himself; it was just said to them and not to him, even though it was to be taken as referring to him and them. And Luke himself also says that the Lord responded with *I have come not to call the righteous but sinners to repentance* (Lk 5:32). He would not have responded this way unless their question, *Why do you eat and drink?* had been directed especially against him. Similarly, Matthew and Mark say that the objection made against him was directed to his disciples because, when it was said to them, it was an even greater reproach against the teacher whom they were following and imitating. There is therefore only one sense, and the abiding truth is expressed better through these various words. As for the Lord's reply, in Matthew it is the following: *Those who are well do not need a doctor, but those who are sick. Go and learn what this means: I desire mercy and not sacrifice. For I have come not to call the righteous but sinners.* (Mt 9:12–13) Mark and Luke have the same meaning in almost the same words, except that neither of them adds the testimony of the prophet, *I desire mercy and not sacrifice* (Hos 6:6). After he says, *I have come not to call the righteous but sinners*, Luke adds *to repentance* in order to explain the meaning more fully, so that no one would suppose that Christ loves sinners simply because they are sinners. The comparison with sickness shows this well: when God calls sinners he seeks the same thing as a doctor does with sick persons, their being saved from iniquity as though from sickness, and this comes about through repentance.

27,62. Matthew continues thus: *Then John's disciples came to him, saying, Why do we and the Pharisees fast often?* (Mt 9:14) Mark says something similar: *Now, John's disciples and the Pharisees were fasting, and they came to him and said, Why do the disciples of John and of the Pharisees fast?* (Mk 2:18) The only thing that can be seen as an addition is that here the Pharisees are speaking together with John's disciples, while Matthew says that it was only John's disciples who spoke. But the words that they spoke according to Mark show rather that there were two different groups. It was the dinner guests who came to Jesus, because the disciples of John and the Pharisees were fasting, and they spoke concerning them. So *they came* does not refer to *the disciples of John and the Pharisees were fasting*. But, as they were fasting, others were bothered by this and came to him and said, *Why do the disciples of John and of the Pharisees fast, but yours do not fast?* (Mk 2:18) Luke expresses this more clearly. He is thinking of this when he continues this way, after the Lord responds about his calling sinners by comparing them to those who are sick: *And they said to him, Why do John's disciples fast often and pray, and likewise those of the Pharisees, but yours eat and drink?* (Lk 5:33) As in Mark, he says that one group of people was speaking about others. So how can Matthew say, *Then John's disciples came to him, saying, Why do we and the Pharisees fast?* (Mt 9:14) Perhaps they were all there and were all eager to reproach him in this way as much as possible. The three evangelists express these sentiments in different ways but without deviating from the truth of the matter.

27,63. Matthew and Mark tell similar stories about the children of the bridegroom who do not fast as long as the bridegroom is with them, except that Mark says that they were the children of the marriage and Matthew that they were the children of the bridegroom.[136] But this makes no difference. For *children of the marriage* means to us those of the bridegroom and the bride. Therefore the sense is the same and consistent and not different or incompatible. But Luke does not say, "Can the children of the bridegroom fast?" but instead, *Can you make the children of the bridegroom fast while the bridegroom is with them?* (Lk 5:34) In this way he expresses the same sense while implying something further. For this makes it understood that those who were speaking would make the children of the bridegroom mourn and fast by killing the bridegroom. Also, Matthew first says *mourn* while Mark and Luke [say] *fast*; but later on Matthew says, *Then they will fast* (Mt 9:15) and not "Then they will mourn." But with this expression he shows that, when the Lord spoke of this fasting, it was the kind that is related to the lowliness of tribulation. But [he then moves on to a fasting] that is related to the joy of the mind, upraised in spiritual things and therefore alienated in a certain way from bodily food. The Lord's parables of the new cloth and the new wine show that this kind of fasting is unacceptable to those who are animal and carnal, occupied with the body and on that account trapped in the old senses.[137] The other two [evangelists] tell these parables similarly.[138] For it is clear enough that there is no disagreement if one omits what the other includes, either in phrasing or subject, as long as there is no deviation from the same sense and there is no opposition between them.

28,64. Still keeping to the chronological sequence, Matthew continues, *While he was saying these things to them, behold, a ruler approached and worshiped him, saying, My daughter has just died; but come, lay your hand on her, and she will live* (Mt 9:18), and so forth, until where it says, *and the girl arose, and the fame of this went through all that land* (Mt 9:25–26). The other two, Mark and Luke, also say this, although not in the same order. For they record and insert it at the point where [Jesus] crosses over and returns from the region of the Gerasenes after casting out the demons and letting them go into the swine.[139] Mark connects it after what happened among the Gerasenes: *And when Jesus had crossed again in the boat to the other side, a great crowd gathered around him; and he was by the sea. Then one of the synagogue rulers came, named Jairus, and seeing him fell at his feet* (Mk 5:21–22), and so forth. From this we are to understand that the incident involving the synagogue leader's daughter happened after Jesus had crossed over the lake again in the boat, but it is unclear how long after. But there

---

136. See Mk 2:19; Mt 9:15.
137. See Mt 9:16–17.
138. See Mk 2:21–22; Lk 5:36–39.
139. See Mk 5:21–24.35–43; Lk 8:40–42.49–56.

must have been some interval, or there would not have been time for that feast in his house which Matthew records. Though he tells it in the third person, as is the style of the evangelists, it took place in his own house. And the story of the synagogue leader's daughter follows immediately on that. He has connected it in such a way that the transition itself shows clearly that what is narrated as immediately following is what happened immediately following. For, immediately after Jesus' previous words on the new cloth and new wine, he continues without interruption: *While he was saying these things to them, behold, a ruler approached* (Mt 9:18). If he approached him while he was saying these things, then [Jesus] could not have done or said anything else in between. But in Mark's account it is clear where other things might have intervened, as we have shown. Similarly, when Luke moves from the story of the miracle among the Gerasenes to the story of the synagogue leader's daughter, he does so in a way that does not contradict Matthew, who shows that this happened after the parables of the cloth and wine by saying *while he was saying these things*. For, when he finishes his story of what happened among the Gerasenes, Luke continues in the following way: *And it happened that, when Jesus returned, the crowd welcomed him, for they were all waiting for him. And behold, a man, whose name was Jairus, and who was a ruler of the synagogue, fell at Jesus' feet* (Lk 8:40–41), and so forth. Thus it is to be understood that the crowd welcomed the Lord at that same time, for they were waiting for his return. But when he goes on to say, *And behold, a man, whose name was Jairus* (Lk 8:41), this does not mean that it happened at that same time, for the feast with the tax collectors happened before that, and Matthew has connected these stories in such a way that it is impossible to think that they could have happened in any other order.

28,65. In this narrative, therefore, which we have now begun to consider, all three of these evangelists unquestionably agree as to the woman who suffered from the flow of blood. It makes no difference that one omits what another mentions, or that Mark says, *Who touched my clothes?* (Mk 5:30) while Luke says, *Who touched me?* (Lk 8:45) For the one has used a typical expression, and the other has been more precise, but they both have the same meaning. For it is more common for us to say "You are tearing me" than to say "You are tearing my clothes," but what we wish to be understood is still clear enough.[140]

28,66. But Matthew writes that the ruler of the synagogue did not say to the Lord that his daughter was going to die, or that she was dying, or even that she was on the brink of death, but that she was in fact dead. But the other two [evangelists] say that she was near death but not yet dead; they are clear on this, for they say that people came later who announced her death and who said that the teacher need not bother to come and lay his hands on her to prevent her death, for [they did] not [suppose] that he could raise the dead. So we must consider whether there seems to be a contradiction here. We may understand it thus: Matthew, for the sake of

---

140. "You are tearing me...you are tearing my clothes": *conscindis me...conscindis vestimenta mea.* By Augustine's time the former construction was idiomatically used to refer to abuse ("You are abusing me"), while the latter usage was rare.

brevity, preferred to have them ask the Lord to do what he in fact did, which was that he should raise the dead. For our attention is drawn not to the father's words about his daughter but to what is more important, to what he wants, and therefore he has given such words that they show his real desire. He had left her dying, and he was in such despair that he could not believe that she would be found still alive, so he asked instead that she be brought back to life. So the other two give the actual words spoken by Jairus, but Matthew what he wished and thought. Thus both requests were made to the Lord, that he should either save the dying girl or raise the dead girl. But, since Matthew wished to tell the story briefly, he made the father request what he himself wished and what Christ actually did. Indeed, if one or both of the other two [evangelists] had recorded that the father himself said what those coming from his house said—that Jesus should not be bothered, since the girl had died—then there would be some inconsistency between his thoughts and the words given by Matthew. But it is not written that he agreed with those who reported this and who tried to stop the teacher from coming. And, moreover, when the Lord said to him, *Do not be afraid; only believe, and she will he saved* (Lk 8:50), he was not reprimanding him for disbelief but really confirming him in an even stronger belief. For he had faith like the one who said, *I believe, Lord; help my unbelief* (Mk 9:24).

28,67. Thus, from the evangelists' different but not contradictory ways of speaking, such as we have here, we learn a most useful and necessary lesson. We should look for nothing in a person's words apart from his intent, which it is the purpose of the words to serve. It is not a lie if someone conveys the intent of someone else in words other than what he spoke. Nor should we let those miserable pedants suppose that the truth is somehow tied to the accent marks over letters when, not by words alone but also by every other indication that can be grasped by the mind, it is nothing else than the mind itself that must be sought for.

28,68. But some versions of Matthew have *For the woman is not dead but sleeping* (Mt 9:24), while Mark and Luke testify that she was a girl of twelve.[141] We should understand that Matthew is following the Hebrew way of speaking, for in other places in Scripture we find that not only those who had been with a man but all females, even untouched virgins, are called women. It is written of Eve, *He made it into a woman* (Gn 2:22), and in the Book of Numbers they are commanded to spare from death the women who have not known a man's bed—that is to say, virgins.[142] Paul too speaks like this when he says that Christ was made of a woman.[143] It is better to understand it this way than to believe that a twelve-year-old was married or had been with a man.

29,69. Matthew continues and says, *And passing on from there, two blind men followed him, crying out and saying, Have mercy on us, Son of David* (Mt 9:27), and so forth, until where it says, *But the Pharisees said, He casts out demons by*

---

141. See Mk 5:42; Lk 8:42.
142. See Nm 31:18.
143. See Gal 4:4.

the prince of demons (Mt 9:34). Matthew is the only one who gives this story of the two blind men and the mute demoniac. For these two blind men are not the same as those of whom the others write,[144] although their stories are so similar that, if Matthew had not recorded both,[145] it might be supposed that this story is the same as that told by the other two [evangelists]. So we should carefully bear in mind that [different] events may be similar. This is proved here by the same evangelist's recording both. So, if we ever find some one event in several [of the Gospels] and are unable to resolve some contradiction between them, it should occur to us that this is not the same event but only something similar or something done similarly.

30,70. The order of the following events is not clear. After the two stories of the blind men and the mute demoniac, [Matthew] continues thus: *And Jesus went about all the cities and villages, teaching in their synagogues and preaching the Gospel of the kingdom and healing every disease and every infirmity. And seeing the crowds, he had compassion for them, because they were troubled and cast down, like sheep without a shepherd. Then he said to his disciples, The harvest is great but the workers are few; pray therefore that the Lord of the harvest will send out workers into his harvest. And he called together his twelve disciples and gave them power over unclean spirits* (Mt 9:35–10:1), and so forth, until where it says, *Amen, I say to you, he shall not lose his reward* (Mt 10:42). In this entire passage that we are now considering he gives much advice to his disciples. But, as we said, it is unclear whether Matthew placed these things here in their [temporal] order or whether they are just in the order in which they occurred to him. For Mark seems to have treated this passage more briefly, as he continues, *And he went about among the villages, teaching. And he called together the twelve, and began to send them out by twos, and he gave them power over the unclean spirits* (Mk 6:6–7), and so forth, until where it says, *Shake off the dust from your feet for a testimony against them* (Mk 6:11). But, between this and the story of the raising of the daughter of the synagogue ruler, Mark gives the account of how they marveled at him in his own country, at the source of his wisdom and power, since they knew his family.[146] Matthew records that story after the advice to the disciples and many other things.[147] Therefore it is uncertain whether Matthew records this here after omitting it previously, or whether Mark records it in anticipation [of something that happened later], or which of them keeps to the [chronological] order of events and which to the order of his recollection. Luke also [takes] this passage about the power and advice [given to] the disciples and adds it immediately after the story of the raising of Jairus's daughter and with the same brevity as Mark,[148] but he does not make it clear whether this is the [chronological] order of events. As for the names of the disciples, whom he named earlier when they were chosen on

---

144. See Mk 10:46–52; Lk 18:35–43.
145. See Mt 20:29–34.
146. See Mk 6:1–6.
147. See Mt 13:53–58.
148. See Lk 9:1–6.

the mountain, there is no discrepancy between them except for Judas the son of James, whom Matthew calls Thaddaeus (or, in some versions, Lebbaeus).[149] But who would deny that a man might be called by two or three names?

30,71. It is also often asked how Matthew and Luke can record that the Lord told his disciples not to take a staff,[150] whereas Mark says this: *He commanded them to take nothing on the way except a staff*, and he continues, *no bag, no bread, no money in their belts* (Mk 6:8), in order to show that this narrative is the same as that of the other two, who talk about not taking a staff. This [discrepancy] can be resolved by understanding that the staff which Mark [says] they were not to take must be different than the staff which Matthew and Luke [say] they were to take. The word "temptation" is similarly found to have one meaning when it is said, *God tempts no one* (Jas 1:13), and another when it is said, *The Lord your God tempts you, to know whether you love him* (Dt 13:3). In the former it is seduction, in the latter it is testing. The word "judgment" is similar, as when it is said in one way, *Those who have done good to the resurrection of life, and those who have done evil to the resurrection of judgment* (Jn 5:29), and when it is said in another way, *Judge me, God, and take up my cause, against an unholy nation* (Ps 43:1). In the former "judgment" is damnation, but in the latter it is discernment.

30,72. And there are many words that do not have one meaning but are understood in different ways in different places and are sometimes even given an explanation, as in, *Do not be children in your thinking, but be infants as to evil, so that you may be perfect in thinking* (1 Cor 14:20). Here is a sentence that could have been summarized as "Do not be children, but be children." Similarly: *If anyone among you thinks that he is wise in this age, let him become a fool, so that he may be wise* (1 Cor 3:18). For what is this saying but "One should not be wise, so that he may be wise"? Sometimes these phrases are used in order to exercise the inquirer, as in what is said to the Galatians: *Bear one another's burdens, and so fulfill the law of Christ. For, if anyone thinks he is something when he is nothing, he deceives himself. Let each one test his own work, and then he will have glory in himself and not in another. For each one will bear his own burden.* (Gal 6:2–5)[151] For, unless *burden* can mean different things, one would think without a doubt that the same author has contradicted himself — and in words placed very near each other in a single paragraph. For having just said, *Bear one another's burdens* (Gal 6:2), he goes on to say, *For each one will bear his own burden* (Gal 6:5). But the former refers to the burdens that we share in our infirmity, while the latter are those that we shall give to God in an account of our actions. The former are borne as they are shared with our brothers, and the latter are those carried by each individually. Thus *rod*[152] is meant spiritually when the Apostle says, *Shall I come to you with a*

---

149. See Mt 10:3.
150. See Mt 10:10; Lk 9:3.
151. See *The City of God* XV,6.
152. "Rod": *virga* (the same word used for "staff" above at II,30,71).

rod? (1 Cor 4:21), but corporally when referring to that used on a horse or for some other such purpose. For now we shall omit the other figurative uses of the word.

30,73. Therefore we must accept that the Lord said each of these things to the apostles, both that they should not take a staff and that they should take nothing but a staff. For according to Matthew he said, *Have neither gold nor silver nor money in your belts, no bag for the way, nor two tunics nor shoes nor a staff,* and then he added immediately, *for the worker is worthy of his food* (Mt 10:9–10). He thereby makes it clear enough why they are not to have or to carry these things. It is not that these things are unnecessary for sustaining life. But he sent them to preach the Gospel to those who would believe it in such a way that it would be clear to them that they ought to give these things to [the disciples] just as wages [are due] to soldiers, the fruit of the vine to the planters, and the milk of the flock to the shepherds. Paul says this too: *Who is a soldier at his own expense? Who plants a vineyard and does not eat its fruit? Who tends a flock and does not gather the flock's milk?* (1 Cor 9:7) He says this in reference to the things that are necessary to those who preach the Gospel. A little further on he says this: *If we have sown spiritual things among you, is it too much if we reap carnal things? If others have this power over you, do not we have it even more? But we have not used this power.* (1 Cor 9:11–12) This makes it clear that the Lord did not instruct the evangelists to live only on what was given to them by those to whom they preached the Gospel. (The Apostle himself acted contrary to such a command, for he obtained his living through the works of his own hands so that he would not be a burden to any of them.[153]) But he gave them a power for which they knew they were owed these things. For, when the Lord gives any command, there is a blameworthy disobedience if it is not carried out. But, when a power is given, anyone is free not to use it and thereby to yield his right. Therefore, when the Lord said these things to the disciples, he was doing what the Apostle explained a little further on: *Do you not know that those who work in the Temple eat what is in the Temple and that those who serve at the altar share the things from the altar? In the same way the Lord ordained that those who preach the Gospel should get their living from the Gospel. But I have used none of these things.* (1 Cor 9:13–15) So, when he says that the Lord ordained this but that he has not used it, he shows that it was a power given to him that he might use and not a necessity imposed on him that he had to obey.

30,74. Having ordained what the Apostle says he ordained, that those who preach the Gospel should get their living from the Gospel, the Lord said these things to the apostles so that they would be free from care, not having or carrying the necessities of life, whether great or small. So he said *nor a staff* (Mt 10:10) in order to show that all these things were owed by his faithful to his ministers, although they needed nothing superfluous. And when he added, *for the worker is worthy of his food* (Mt 10:10), he made it clear and intelligible enough how and why he had said all these things. The word *staff* signifies this power, when he said,

---

153. See 1 Thes 2:9.

Take nothing on the way except a staff (Mk 6:8). For he could have summarized it by saying, "Take with you none of the necessities, not even a staff, but only a staff." [Put this way], "not even a staff" would mean "not even the least things"; but in the addition, "but only a staff," "staff" would signify that power given to them by the Lord by which they would not lack the things they were not carrying. Therefore the Lord said both. But, since one evangelist does not record both [phrases], it appears that the one who says that they should take a staff in one sense is contradicting the one who says that they should not take a staff in another sense. But, now that this has been explained, there is no need to suppose this.

30,75. And likewise, when Matthew says they were not to carry shoes on the way, they were warned not to worry that they would lack such things if they did not carry them. And, as for the two tunics, it is to be understood that none of them were to think of taking another apart from the one he was wearing, lest he be afraid, when the power given by [the Lord] guaranteed there would be no such need. Likewise, when Mark says they are to wear open shoes or sandals,[154] he shows that this kind of shoe has some mystical significance, so that the foot is neither covered nor bare to the ground, just as the Gospel is neither hidden nor reliant on earthly things. And here he more clearly forbids not the carrying or having of two tunics but the wearing of them: *Do not put on two tunics* (Mk 6:9). What does he teach them here except that they are to walk not in duplicity but in simplicity?

30,76. Thus there is no doubt of any kind that the Lord said all these things, some in their own sense and some in a figurative sense, but that each evangelist puts some things into his writings and the others other things. In some places two or three or even all four of them say the same thing, but even in these cases they may not have written down everything said or done by him. For, if anyone supposes that in one discourse the Lord could not use language both figuratively and literally, let him examine others of his and he will see how this would be judged as rash and uninformed. For, to give one example that occurs to me now, when he admonishes that the left hand should not know what the right is doing,[155] one would then have to take in a figurative sense both almsgiving itself and whatever else he teaches there.

30,77. But I must give this warning again, which the reader should keep in mind so as not to need such a warning so often: The Lord repeated in different places in his discourses many things that he had already said elsewhere. If the order of the passages is not the same between two evangelists, one might take this as a contradiction, but one should understand it as his saying again something that he had already said, and this observation applies not only to his words but also to his actions. For there is nothing to keep us from believing that the same thing happened more than once. But it is sacrilegious vanity for someone to attack the

---

154. See Mk 6:9.
155. See Mt 6:3.

Gospel because he does not believe in the repetition of some event, which no one can show is an impossibility.

31,78. Matthew continues and says, *And it happened that, when Jesus had finished instructing his twelve disciples, he went on from there to teach and preach in their cities. Now, when John heard in prison about Christ's work, he sent two of his disciples, and he said to him, Are you he who is to come, or shall we wait for another?* (Mt 11:1–3) and so forth, until where it says, *But wisdom is justified by her children* (Mt 11:19). Luke also gives this entire passage on John the Baptist—that he sent to Jesus, the response received by those he sent, and what the Lord said about John after they left. But the order is not the same, and it is unclear which of them gives the order of his recollections and which the [chronological] order of the events themselves.

32,79. Matthew continues and says, *Then he began to reproach the cities in which he had done most of his mighty works, because they did not repent* (Mt 11:20), and so forth, until where it says, *It shall be more tolerable for the land of Sodom on the day of judgment than for you* (Mt 11:24). Luke also records this from the Lord's mouth as part of an extended discourse of his.[156] It appears that he keeps the order in which the Lord said these things, while Matthew has the order in which he remembers them. But when Matthew says, *Then he began to reproach the cities*, even if one supposes that he wished *then* to express the exact moment in time when he said that, rather than some broader time period during which many of these things were done and said, then one could still believe that this was said twice [on different occasions]. For even with respect to one evangelist there are things that the Lord says twice. In Luke one finds the Lord saying in two different places not to take a bag on the way;[157] and it is similar with other things. So why is it remarkable if something that was said twice should have each of its two occurrences reported by two separate [evangelists], each of whom keeps the actual order in which one of them was spoken, although the order seems different between them, because the one reported one occasion on which it was said and the other reported another occasion?

33,80. Matthew continues, *At that time Jesus answered and said, I acknowledge you, Father, Lord of heaven and earth, for you have hidden these things from the wise and prudent* (Mt 11:25), and so forth, until where it says, *For my yoke is easy and my burden is light* (Mt 11:30). Luke also mentions this passage, but only in part. For he does not say, *Come to me, all you who labor* (Mt 11:28), and what follows. But it is plausible that on one occasion these things were said by the Lord, but Luke does not record everything that he said. For Matthew says, *At that time Jesus answered and said*—that is, right after he reproached the cities. But after the reproaching of the cities Luke inserts other material, though not much, and then adds, *At that same hour he rejoiced in the Holy Spirit and said*

---

156. See Lk 7:18–35.
157. See Lk 9:3; 10:4.

(Lk 10:21). But even if Matthew had said *at that same hour* instead of *at that time*, Luke inserted so little in between that it does not seem unreasonable that he said these things at the same time.

34,81. Matthew continues and says, *At that time Jesus went through the grain fields on the sabbath, and his disciples were hungry, and they began to pluck the grain and to eat* (Mt 12:1), and so forth, until where it says, *For the Son of Man is Lord even of the sabbath* (Mt 12:8). Mark and Luke also record this, without any question of inconsistency,[158] although they do not say *at that time*. This makes it more likely that Matthew keeps the chronological order and that they [keep the order] in which they recall it, unless *that time* is understood to be more encompassing, during which many different things happened.

35,82. Matthew continues his account this way, then: *And when he went on from there, he came into their synagogue. And behold, there was a man with a withered hand* (Mt 12:9), and so forth, until where it says, *And it was restored to health like the other* (Mt 12:13). The healing of this man with a withered hand is not omitted by Mark and Luke. Since the [incident] of the grain and the healing are both recorded as having happened on a sabbath, one might suppose that they happened on the same day, but Luke makes it clear that the healing of the withered hand happened on another sabbath. So, when Matthew says, *And when he went on from there, he came into their synagogue*, [it means] that he came in only after he had gone on from there, but it does not state how many days there were between his leaving the field and his going into the synagogue, nor that it followed immediately. This gives room for Luke's story, which says that his hand was healed on another sabbath. But there may be a problem, for Matthew says that they asked the Lord, *Is it lawful to heal on the sabbath?* (Mt 12:10), wishing to find an opportunity to accuse him, to which he proposed the comparison of a sheep: *What man of you, if he has one sheep and it falls into a pit on the sabbath, will not take hold of it and pull it out? Of how much more value is a man than a sheep? Therefore it is lawful to do good on the sabbath.* (Mt 12:11–12) But Mark and Luke say instead that they were asked this by the Lord: *Is it lawful on the sabbath to do good or evil? To save life or to kill?* (Mk 3:4; Lk 6:9) But it may be understood this way: First they asked the Lord, *Is it lawful to heal on the sabbath?* And, since he knew their thoughts, that they were seeking an opportunity to accuse him, he put in their midst the one who was about to be cured and asked them what Mark and Luke record he asked them. And then, when they were silent, he proposed the comparison with a sheep and concluded that it was lawful to do good on the sabbath. And finally, looking around at them with anger, as Mark says, saddened by the blindness of their heart, he said to the man, *Stretch out your hand* (Mk 3:5).

36,83. Matthew continues his narrative thus: *But the Pharisees went out and held a council against him, how they could destroy him. But Jesus, knowing this, withdrew from there. And many followed him, and he healed them all and com-*

---

158. See Mk 2:23–28; Lk 6:1–5.

manded them not to make him known, in order to fulfill what was spoken by the prophet Isaiah, saying (Mt 12:14–17), and so forth, until where it says, *And in his name shall the nations hope* (Mt 12:21). He is the only one to record this, the other two having gone on to other things. Mark in a way seems to have kept to the [chronological] order, for he says that Jesus, knowing that the Jews were badly disposed to him, withdrew to the sea with his disciples, and the crowds flocked to him, and he healed many of them.[159] However, it is unclear when he begins to move on to something other than what followed immediately. It could be when he says that the crowds gathered about him, for that could have happened then or at some other time, or when he says, *And he went up a mountain* (Mk 3:13). Luke also seems to record this when he says, *And it happened that in those days he went out to a mountain to pray* Lk 6:12). For by saying *in those days* he makes it quite clear that it did not follow immediately.

37,84. Matthew continues, then, and says, *Then a person who had a blind and mute demon was brought to him, and he cured him, so that he spoke and saw* (Mt 12:22). Luke records this story not in this order but after many other things, and he says that he is only mute, not blind too.[160] But we need not suppose that he is speaking of another person just because he omits one thing or another, especially since what follows is the same as in Matthew.

38,85. Matthew continues and says, *And all the crowds were amazed and said, Is this not the Son of David? But when the Pharisees heard it they said, It is only by Beelzebul the prince of demons that he casts out demons. But Jesus, knowing their thoughts, said to them, Every kingdom divided against itself is laid waste* (Mt 12:23–25), and so forth, until where it says, *By your words you will be justified, and by your words you will be condemned* (Mt 12:37). Mark does not record this allegation that Jesus casts out demons by Beelzebul right after the story of the mute person. He adds it after some other things that he alone records, either because he recalled it at this point and added it or because, after omitting it previously, he now resumes the sequence. But Luke gives almost the same words as Matthew.[161] When he calls *the Spirit of God* (Mt 12:28) *the finger of God* (Lk 11:20), there is no difference in meaning. Rather, it teaches us how to understand *the finger of God* whenever we read it in the Scriptures. Also, there is no problem with those other things that are omitted by both Mark and Luke, nor with those things that are said differently by them, for their meaning is the same.

39,86. Matthew continues and says, *Then some of the scribes and Pharisees answered him, saying, Teacher, we wish to see a sign from you* (Mt 12:38), and so forth, until where it says, *So shall it be with this evil generation* (Mt 12:45). Luke gives this passage in this place, to be sure, but in a somewhat different order.[162] For, right after the miracle of the mute man, Luke records that they asked the Lord

---

159. See Mk 3:6–12.
160. See Lk 11:14–15.
161. See Lk 11:14–23.
162. See Lk 11:16–32.

for a sign from heaven, but he did not give the Lord's response to this. After the crowds were gathered, though, he tells us his response, and we should understand this as given to those who had previously asked him for a sign from heaven.[163] He adds this only after inserting the story of the woman who said to the Lord, *Blessed is the womb that bore you* (Lk 11:27). And he inserts this story of the woman after he has recorded the Lord's saying about the unclean spirit that went out of a man, which then returned and found the house cleaned.[164] So, after the story of the woman, and after his response to the crowds about their seeking for a sign from heaven, he inserts the comparison with the prophet Jonah, and then he continues the Lord's discourse with his saying about the queen of the south and the Ninevites.[165] So he records what Matthew omits rather than omits what [Matthew] writes in this place. And who cannot see that it is irrelevant to ask about the sequence in which the Lord said these things? From the most high authority of the evangelists we ought to learn that it is not false if someone reports a discourse in a sequence that is not the same as that in which it was spoken, as long as no variation in the sequence affects the subject itself. Luke also shows that this discourse of the Lord was longer, and he records in it things that Matthew had in the sermon on the mountain.[166] So we are to understand that these things were said twice, once then and once at this point. At the end of this discourse Luke goes on to another subject, and it is unclear whether his order keeps to that of the actual events. For he adds, *And while he was speaking, a Pharisee asked him to dine with him* (Lk 11:37). He does not say "while he was saying these things" but *while he was speaking*. If he had said, "while he was saying these things," then this would necessarily have obliged us to understand this as not just the narrated order but as that in which the Lord did these things.

40,87. Matthew, then, continues and says, *While he was still speaking to the crowds, behold, his mother and brothers were standing outside, asking to speak to him* (Mt 12:46), and so forth, until where it says, *For whoever does the will of my Father who is in heaven, he is my brother and sister and mother* (Mt 12:50). Without a doubt, we should understand that this followed immediately upon what was done [previously]. For he begins this narrative with the transition, *While he was still speaking to the crowds.* This *still* shows that he was speaking on the same subject. For it does not say, "While he spoke to the crowds, behold, his mother and brothers" but *While he was still speaking*, by which we must understand, "While he was speaking of those things just mentioned." For Mark also records what the Lord said after he mentioned the blasphemy against the Holy Spirit: *And his mother and brothers came* (Mk 3:31). He omits some things of the Lord's discourse that Matthew gives at greater length than Mark, and Luke at greater length than Matthew. Luke does not keep the sequence of this event, but he anticipates it before

---

163. See Lk 11:29–33.
164. See Lk 11:24–26.
165. See Lk 11:29–32.
166. See Lk 11:33–36; Mt 5:15; 6:22.

it happened, narrating it as he recalls it. Also, he inserts it in such a way that it appears disconnected from what precedes it and what follows it. For, after recording some of the Lord's parables, he inserts the story of his mother and brothers in this way: *Then his mother and his brothers came to him, but they could not reach him because of the crowd* (Lk 8:19); but he does not say exactly when they came to him. Then, when he moves on from this subject, he says, *And it happened that one day he got into a boat with his disciples* (Lk 8:22). By saying, *And it happened that one day,* he shows clearly enough that we need not understand it as the same day that the preceding event occurred, nor the following day. So there is nothing inconsistent between the accounts of Matthew and the other two regarding the incident of the Lord's mother and brothers, neither in the Lord's words nor in the order of the events.

41,88. Matthew continues, *On that day Jesus went out of the house and sat by the seaside. And great crowds gathered around him, so that he got into a boat and sat there, and the whole crowd stood on the shore. And he spoke many things in parables, saying* (Mt 13:1–3), and so forth, until where it says, *Therefore every scribe who has been trained for the kingdom of heaven is like a householder who brings out of his treasure new things and old things* (Mt 13:52). By saying, *On that day Jesus went out of the house and sat by the seaside. And great crowds gathered around him* (Mt 13:1–2), Matthew shows that these things happened immediately after the incident of the Lord's mother and brothers and that his narrative has kept the sequence. For by saying *on that day* he shows quite clearly that this follows immediately on the preceding events, or that not much could have intervened (unless *day* just means "time," as it sometimes does in the Scriptures). The fact that Mark follows the same order makes this even more likely.[167] Luke, however, after giving the account of the Lord's mother and brothers, goes on to something else, but his connection does not seem to be inconsistent with this order. So in all the places where the Lord's discourses are reported the same by Matthew, Mark, and Luke, there is no question of inconsistency. There is even less controversy where Matthew alone reports something.[168] Although the order is somewhat different between them, sometimes keeping to the sequence of events and sometimes to the order in which they were recollected, I see nothing contradictory among them.

42,89. Matthew continues, then: *And it happened that, when Jesus had finished these parables, he went away from there. And coming to his own country, he taught them in their synagogues* (Mt 13:53–54), and so forth, until where it says, *And he did not do many mighty works, because of their unbelief* (Mt 13:58). Thus he goes from the previous discourse composed of parables to this passage, but he does not indicate whether it necessarily followed it immediately. Also, Mark follows the parables not with this passage but with another that is closer to Luke's. This makes

---

167. See Mk 4:1–34.
168. Augustine means that when all three agree there can be no disagreement, because they agree, whereas when only one reports something there can be no disagreement, because there is nothing with which to disagree.

their order seem more credible, when they go on to the story of the boat in which Jesus was asleep and then to the miracle of the expulsion of the demons among the Gerasenes,[169] which two events Matthew had already included as he recalled them.[170] Now we must see whether [Matthew's account of] what the Lord says and what is said to him in his own country is in agreement with that of the other two, Mark and Luke. For, in a very different and dissimilar place in the narrative, John records some words that were spoken either by the Lord or to him[171] and are similar to this passage mentioned by the other three.

42,90. Now, Mark records this passage like Matthew does, except that he says that the Lord was called *the carpenter, the son of Mary* (Mk 6:3) by the people of his town and not, as Matthew says, *the carpenter's son* (Mt 13:55). But this is unremarkable, since he could have been called by both of these names, for they thought he was a carpenter because he was a carpenter's son. Luke gives the same incident more broadly, recording other things connected with this. He inserts this not long after his baptism and temptation, no doubt anticipating something that really happened only after many other intervening events. This brings to our attention something of the greatest importance to the overriding question of the agreement of the evangelists, which we have attempted to answer with God's help. It is not from ignorance that they omit some things, nor is it from ignorance of the actual order of events that they have kept to the order in which they recall things. This can be seen clearly by the fact that Luke, before he gives any account of what the Lord did at Capernaum, anticipates it in the passage that we are now considering, in which the other people of his town marvel at his mighty power and disparage the lowliness of his family. For [Luke] says that he said this to them: *Certainly you will say to me, Physician, heal yourself; what we have heard you did at Capernaum, do here also in your own country* (Lk 4:23). But in Luke's own narrative we have not read of anything that he did in Capernaum. We shall insert the whole passage here, since it is not too long, and it is very easy and most necessary to consider it, [showing] where and how this narrative came to be. After the Lord's baptism and temptation he continues in this way: *And when the devil had finished every temptation, he left him for a time. And Jesus returned in the power of the Spirit into Galilee, and the report of him went out through all the region. And he taught in their synagogues and was praised by everyone. And he came to Nazareth, where he had been brought up. And, as his custom was, he went into the synagogue on the sabbath day, and he stood up to read, and the book of the prophet Isaiah was handed to him. And he opened the book and found the place where it was written, The Spirit of the Lord is upon me, because he has anointed me. He has sent me to preach good news to the poor, to proclaim release to the captives and sight to the blind, to release those who are broken, to proclaim the acceptable year of the Lord and the day of retribution. And, when he had closed*

---

169. See Mk 4:35–5:17; Lk 8:22–37.
170. See Mt 8:23–34.
171. See Jn 6:42.

the book, he gave it back to the assistant and sat down. And the eyes of all in the synagogue were fixed on him. And he began to say to them, Today this scripture has been fulfilled in your hearing. And all gave witness to him and marveled at the gracious words that came out of his mouth, and they said, Is not this Joseph's son? And he said to them, Certainly you will say to me, Physician, heal yourself; what we have heard you did at Capernaum, do here also in your own country (Lk 4:13–23), and so forth, until he finishes this entire passage in his narrative. What could make it clearer that he knows this narrative came later, since he knows and refers to the great deeds done by him in Capernaum but also knows that he has not yet narrated those? This did not occur so long after [Jesus'] baptism that one could suppose that he had forgotten that he had not yet recorded anything that happened in Capernaum; for it is right after the baptism that he gives us this narrative about the Lord.

43,91. Matthew continues, *At that time Herod the tetrarch heard about the fame of Jesus, and he said to his servants, This is John the Baptist; he has risen from the dead and therefore these powers are at work in him* (Mt 14:1–2). Mark records this same passage in the same way but not in the same order.[172] He connects it to the end of the discourse that was partly recorded by him after the Lord sent out the disciples, telling them to take nothing but a staff. But this does not oblige us to understand that these things had to happen right after what preceded. The same goes for Matthew, for he says *at that time* (Mt 14:1), not "on that day" or "hour." But Mark does not say that Herod himself said this, but others: *They said that John the Baptist has risen from the dead* (Mk 6:14). But Matthew has it as Herod himself, for he says, *He said to his servants* (Mt 14:2). Luke also has the same narrative order as Mark, though it does not oblige us to think that he was keeping to the real sequence of events. He records it this way: *But Herod the tetrarch heard of all that was done by him, and he was confused, because it was said by some that John was risen from the dead, by some that Elijah had appeared, and by others that one of the old prophets had risen. And Herod said, John I beheaded, but who is this about whom I hear such things? And he sought to see him.* (Lk 9:7–9) With these words Luke confirms Mark's version, insofar as it was not Herod but others who said that John was risen from the dead. But he also records Herod's confusion and then his statement, *John I beheaded; but who is this about whom I hear such things?* (Lk 9:9) This can be understood [in one of two ways]. Either he was no longer confused but became convinced in his own mind of what others had said, so that he said to his servants, as Matthew reports it, *And he said to his servants, This is John the Baptist; he has risen from the dead and therefore these powers are at work in him* (Mt 14:2). Or he said these words in a way that showed he was confused. For if he had said, "Who is this?" or "Can this perhaps be John the Baptist?" then there would have been no need to indicate how they were said, for they are clearly said with doubt and confusion. But, since these

172. See Mk 6:14–16.

are not the words here, there are two ways they could have been said. Either we can think that he had been convinced by what others had said, so that he believed what he said, or else, as Luke reports, he was still confused. Likewise Mark, who had previously said that it was others who said that John was risen from the dead, in the end has Herod himself say, *John, whom I beheaded, has risen from the dead* (Mk 6:16). These words can also be taken as having been spoken in one of two ways, and they can be understood as being either full of conviction or full of doubt. Also, after Luke records this incident, he passes on to other things. But the other two, Matthew and Mark, narrate at this point how John was killed by Herod.

44,92. Matthew continues, then, and says, *For Herod had seized John and bound him and put him in prison for the sake of Herodias, his brother's wife* (Mt 14:3), and so forth, until the place where it is said, *And his disciples came and took his body and buried it and went and told Jesus* (Mt 14:12). Mark tells this story similarly.[173] Luke, however, does not recall it in this order but places it near the Lord's own baptism.[174] It is to be understood that he anticipates it at that point, putting something that happened much later into that earlier narrative. For he records John's words concerning the Lord, that *the winnowing fork is in his hand, and he shall clear his threshing floor; he shall gather his grain into his barn, but the chaff he shall burn with unquenchable fire* (Lk 3:17). He then immediately goes on to another incident, which John the evangelist shows clearly could not have happened immediately after this. For he records that after Jesus was baptized he went into Galilee, where he turned the water into wine.[175] Then, after staying a few days in Capernaum,[176] he returned to the land of Judea and there he baptized many around the Jordan, and this was before John was put in prison.[177] For what person, with less than perfect knowledge about these writings, would not suppose that it was immediately after those words about the winnowing fork and the cleared floor that Herod became hostile to John and put him in prison? But we have already shown that the order of the narrative here is not the order in which these things happened,[178] and Luke proves this. For, if John was put into prison immediately after those words, how can Luke himself tell the story of Jesus' baptism after he has recorded that John was put into prison? So it is clear that he recalls this incident here and puts it in his narrative before many other things in his narrative that really occurred before this happened to John. But neither do the other two, Matthew and Mark, as shown in their writings, put John's imprisonment in their narratives in the order in which it occurred. For they say that the Lord went into Galilee when John was handed over.[179] And, after many other things that he did in Galilee, they come to Herod's recollection and bewilderment, because John,

---

173. See Mk 6:17–29.
174. See Lk 3:15–20.
175. See Jn 2:1–11.
176. See Jn 2:12.
177. See Jn 3:22–24.
178. See above at II,17,34–18,42.
179. See Mt 4:12; Mk 1:14.

whom he beheaded, had risen from the dead.[180] And in connection with this they tell us of everything related to John's imprisonment and death.

45,93. After saying how John's death was reported to Christ, then, Matthew continues his narrative thus: *When Jesus heard this, he went away from there in a boat to a lonely place apart. And when the crowds heard this, they followed him on foot from the cities. And as he was going he saw a great crowd, and he had compassion and healed their sick.* (Mt 14:13–14) He records this as happening immediately after John's suffering. So what was narrated earlier — the fact that Herod was troubled and said, *John I beheaded* (Lk 9:9) — in fact happened after this. For it should be understood that these things must have happened, and then later they were reported to Herod, who was troubled and confused as to who this could be of whom he heard such things, when he himself had killed John. And Mark, after telling of John's suffering, records that the disciples who had been sent out returned to Jesus and told him all that they had done and taught. And, as he alone recounts, the Lord told them to rest a while in a lonely place, and he then got into a boat with them and left and, when the crowds saw this, they got there ahead of them. And the Lord was compassionate and taught them many things. And when it was late it happened that all who were there ate of the five loaves and two fishes,[181] which is a miracle that all four evangelists record.[182] Luke, who had told the story of John's suffering much earlier, also connects it to the passage that we are now discussing, for he here records Herod's confusion at who the Lord could be[183] and immediately connects it to the same things found in Mark: the apostles returned to him and told him what they had done, and he took them and withdrew to a lonely place, and the crowds followed him, and he spoke to them of the kingdom of God and cured those who needed healing. And then he records that, as the day was drawing to a close, the miracle of the five loaves happened.[184]

45,94. But John differs greatly from the other three evangelists in that he deals more with the Lord's discourses than with his miraculous deeds. For he records that he left Judea and went again into Galilee, which is to be understood as the same [departure] that the other evangelists [speak of] when they say that he went into Galilee when John was handed over. After he records this, John inserts into his narrative many things that he said as he passed through Samaria, when he found the Samaritan woman at the well. And after two days he says he went into Galilee, and then he came into Cana of Galilee, where he had turned the water into wine, and he healed a certain official's son there.[185] But John tells us nothing of the other things he did and said in Galilee according to the other [evangelists]. However, they omit something that he tells us about — that he went up to Jerusa-

---

180. See Mt 14:1–2; Mk 6:14–16.
181. See Mk 6:30–44.
182. See Mt 14:13–21; Lk 9:10–17; Jn 6:1–13.
183. See Lk 9:7–9.
184. See Lk 9:10–17.
185. See Jn 4:1–54.

lem on the feast day and performed there the healing of the man who been ill for thirty-eight years and did not have anyone to put him into the pool where those with various illnesses were healed.[186] He also records how he said many things on that occasion. After this he tells how he went across the Sea of Galilee, which is the Sea of Tiberias, and a great multitude followed him. He then says that he went out to a mountain and sat there with his disciples, and it was nearly the time of the Passover, the feast of the Jews. Then, lifting up his eyes and seeing a great multitude, he fed them with five loaves and two fish,[187] which is also related by the other evangelists. This makes it certain that he omits those things that the others pass through in their narratives on their way to their recording of this miracle. Among them there seems to be a different manner of narration, as those three omit things that [John] includes. This miracle of the five loaves is the meeting point for the three who are following more or less the same course and the one who is more interested in the Lord's discourses. While he is [treating] other matters about which the others are silent, he flies back in some way and rejoins the others in recording the miracle of the five loaves, although it is not long before he flies off again into higher matters.[188]

46,95. Matthew continues, then, and proceeds in order with his narrative to the episode of the five loaves: *When it was evening, his disciples came to him, saying, This is a lonely place, and the time is now past; send the crowds away, so that they can go into the villages and buy food for themselves. But Jesus said to them, They do not have to go; you give them something to eat* (Mt 14:15–16), and so forth, until where it says, *And the number of those who ate was five thousand men, besides women and children* (Mt 14:21). We must examine and discuss this miracle, which all four evangelists record[189] and on which they are thought to disagree. From this one instance we will learn the rules of speech [that apply] to other similar cases that retain the same sense and preserve the same truth, although [expressed] differently. We should begin this examination not with Matthew, although that would be in the order of the evangelists, but rather with John, who tells this story so precisely that he even gives the names of the disciples to whom the Lord spoke about this. He says this: *Then, lifting up his eyes and seeing a great multitude coming towards him, Jesus said to Philip, How are we to buy bread, so that these people may eat? He said this in order to test him, for he knew what he would do. Philip answered him, Two hundred denarii worth of bread would not be enough for each of them to take a little bit. Then one of his disciples, Andrew, Simon Peter's brother, said to him, Here is one boy who has five barley loaves and two fish; but what are those among so many? So Jesus said, Make the people sit down. Now, there was much grass in the place. So the men sat down, in number about five thousand. Jesus took the loaves and, when he had given thanks, he*

---

186. See Jn 5:1–47.
187. See Jn 6:1–13.
188. Augustine is alluding to the fact that John is symbolized by an eagle. See above at I,6,9.
189. See Mk 6:32–44; Lk 9:10–17; Jn 6:1–13.

distributed them to those who were sitting. And the same with the fish, as much as they wanted. And when they were full he said to his disciples, Gather up the leftover fragments, so that they are not lost. So they gathered them up and filled twelve baskets with fragments from the five barley loaves left by those who had eaten. (Jn 6:5–13)

46,96. We need not inquire here about what he says about the kind of loaves, for he does not omit the fact that they were made of barley, which the others do omit. Nor need we inquire about his not saying that there were women and children as well as the five thousand men, as Matthew says.[190] By now it should be clear to everyone and should be taken for granted that, when one includes what the other omits, this is no reason for concern. But we must inquire how it is that the things said by them can all be true, so that one's version does not conflict with another's. For in John's version, when the Lord saw the crowds, he tested Philip by asking him how food could be given to them. But then there is a problem with the truth of the others, who say that first the disciples asked the Lord to send away the crowds, so that they could buy food for themselves in the nearby areas, to which he replied, according to Matthew, *They do not have to go; you give them something to eat* (Mt 14:16). Mark and Luke agree with this, except that they do not say, *They do not have to go.* So it should be understood that after these words the Lord looked at the multitude and said to Philip what John records but the others omit. John then says that Philip replied, while Mark, wishing to show that Philip answered as the spokesperson for the others, says that the response was from the disciples. (Or else they used the plural number for the singular, a most common usage.) And what, then, did Philip say? [According to John], *Two hundred denarii worth of bread would not be enough for each of them to take a little bit* (Jn 6:7), which is also said in Mark, *Shall we go and buy two hundred denarii worth of bread and give it to them to eat?* (Mk 6:37) Mark reports that the Lord said, *How many loaves do you have?* (Mk 6:38) but the others omit this. According to John, Andrew mentioned the five loaves and two fish, while the others say it was the group of disciples, putting it in the plural instead of the singular. And Luke puts the answers of Philip and Andrew together in one sentence. For when he says, *We have no more than five loaves and two fishes*, that is Andrew's response; but when he adds, *unless we are to go and buy food for all this crowd* (Lk 9:13), this would seem to be Philip's response, except that he has left out the two hundred denarii. But perhaps the sense of this can also be understood in Andrew's words, when he said, *Here is one boy who has five barley loaves and two fish*, and then added, *but what are those among so many?* (Jn 6:9) which is the same as saying, "unless we are to go and buy food for all this crowd."

46,97. Although there is great variation in the words, there is agreement as to the subjects and ideas. It is clear enough that this should teach us, for our own good, to seek nothing in people's words other than the speakers' intention, which

---

190. See Mt 14:21.

is what all truthful narrators ought to be attentive to, whether they are speaking of human beings or of angels or of God. For this intention can be expressed in words that are in no way ambiguous with regard to themselves.

46,98. We should certainly not neglect at this point to direct the reader's attention to other matters that may turn out to be of the same kind. For example, Luke says they were commanded to sit down in groups of fifty,[191] while Mark [says] it was in groups of fifty and one hundred.[192] But this is not really a problem, since the one reports the part and the other the whole. For the one who says one hundred has just said what the other has omitted, and this is not a contradiction. Indeed, if the one had only reported fifty and the other only one hundred, this certainly might have seemed to be a contradiction, and it might not have been easy to show that both were said, the one recording only the one and the other the other. But, even in this case, who will not admit that with a more careful examination, [an answer] should have been found? I bring this up because there are often such cases where things that are not contradictory seem so to those who pay too little attention and make a judgment carelessly.

47,99. Matthew continues and says, *And when he had dismissed the crowd he went up on the mountain alone to pray. And when evening came he was there alone. But the boat was in the midst of the sea, tossed by the waves, for the wind was against them. And in the fourth watch of the night he came to them, walking on the sea. And when they saw him walking on the sea they were troubled, saying, It is a ghost* (Mt 14:23–26), and so forth, until where it says, *They came and worshiped him, saying, Truly you are the Son of God* (Mt 14:33). After his account of the miracle of the loaves, Mark also tells of this: *And when it was late, the boat was in the midst of the sea, and he was alone on land. And seeing them struggling at rowing, for the wind was against them* (Mk 6:47–48), and so forth, which is similar, except that he does not mention Peter walking on the water.[193] But we must not be troubled that Mark says of the Lord when he was walking on the water: *And he meant to pass by them* (Mk 6:48). How could they have perceived this except that he was going in the opposite direction and wished to pass them by like strangers to whom he was so unrecognizable that they thought he was a ghost? Who is so stupid as not to notice that this has a mystical significance? But, as they were confused and crying out, he came to their aid, saying, *Have faith, it is I, do not be afraid* (Mk 6:50). So why would he want to pass by those whom he then helped in their terror? It must have been in order to elicit those cries to which he would then respond with help.

47,100. But John spends some time dwelling on these matters. For, after his account of the miracle of the five loaves, he does not fail to mention as well the boat foundering and the Lord walking on the water: *Therefore, when Jesus perceived that they were coming to take him by force and make him king, he left for the*

---

191. See Lk 9:14.
192. See Mk 6:40.
193. See Mt 14:28–31.

mountain alone. And when it was late his disciples went down to the sea, and they got into a boat and went across the sea to Capernaum. And it was now dark, and Jesus had not come to them. And the sea rose because a great wind was blowing (Jn 6:15–18), and so forth. There is nothing in this that appears contrary [to the others], except that Matthew says that, after dismissing the crowds, he went up on the mountain alone to pray, while John says that he was on a mountain when he fed the crowds with the five loaves. But, since John himself says that after this miracle he went off to a mountain, so as not to be taken by the crowds who wished to make him king, it is clear that they must have come down from the mountain to a level place, when those loaves were given to the crowds. So, when he goes up the mountain again there is no contradiction between Matthew and John, except that Matthew says, *He went up* (Mt 14:23), and John says, *He left* (Jn 6:15). But this would only be a contradiction if leaving did not include going up. Nor is there any inconsistency when Matthew says, *He went up on the mountain alone to pray* (Mt 14:23), and John says, *When Jesus perceived that they were coming to take him by force and make him king, he left for the mountain alone* (Jn 6:15), for there is nothing incompatible between praying and leaving. The Lord himself transfigured the body of our humiliation, so that he might make it like the body of his glory.[194] This teaches us that the act of leaving can be the object of profound prayer. Nor is it incompatible that Matthew says that first he commanded the disciples to get into the little boat and go before him across the lake until he dismissed the crowds, and when he had dismissed the crowds he went up on the mountain alone to pray, whereas John reports that first he went off alone to the mountain and then says, *And when it was late his disciples went down to the sea, and they got into a boat* (John 6:16–17), and so forth. But who will not see that in John's summary he says the disciples did something later, which Jesus had already commanded them [to do], before he went off to the mountain? Frequently in speech one comes back to something that had been overlooked before. But if it is not noted that this reference is [to something previous], and if [the mention] is brief and sudden, then those who hear it might suppose that what is mentioned later in fact happened later. So, although he first says that they got into a boat and went across the sea to Capernaum and then says that they were struggling in the sea when the Lord came walking to them on the water, he means that this happened during their crossing to Capernaum.

47,101. But after the miracle of the five loaves Luke goes on to something else and also diverges from this order. For he reports nothing of that boat or of the Lord's passage on the water. Instead he says, *And all ate and were full, and they took up what was left over, twelve baskets of fragments* (Lk 9:17), and he continues, *And it happened that when he was alone praying, the disciples were also with him, and he asked them, saying, Who do the crowds say that I am?* (Lk 9:18) He narrates something here that the other three do not; they instead tell of how the Lord walked on the water and came to the disciples while they were on their journey.

---

194. See Phil 3:21.

But it should not be supposed that he said to the disciples, *Who do the crowds say that I am?* (Lk 9:18) on the mountain that Matthew says he went up on to pray alone. Since Luke says, *As he was praying alone* (Lk 9:18), and Matthew says, *He went up on the mountain alone to pray* (Mt 14:23), it might seem that these two [scenes] are the same, but it is not at all so. For, when he asks this question, he is both alone praying and his disciples are with him. Luke, indeed, says that he was alone but not that the disciples were absent. But, according to Matthew and John, they had left him and gone before him across the sea. But [Luke] adds most explicitly, *The disciples were also with him* (Lk 9:18). So, when he says that he was alone, [he means that] the crowds were gone, for they did not live with him.

48,102. Matthew continues and says, *And when they had crossed over, they came into the land of Genesaret. And when the men of that place recognized him, they sent round to all that region and brought to him all who were sick and asked him if they could touch the edge of his garment. And as many as touched it were healed. Then the scribes and Pharisees came down to him from Jerusalem, saying, Why do your disciples transgress the tradition of the elders? For they do not wash their hands when they eat bread* (Mt 14:34–15:2), and so forth, until where it says, *But to eat with unwashed hands does not defile a man* (Mt 15:20). Mark also reports this, and there is no question of any inconsistency; although there are differences between them in the way things are said, there is no difference in sense. But after the [incident of] the Lord's walking on the sea to come to the boat, John [goes on to what happened] when they got to land; since he is most interested in the Lord's discourses, he reports that he taught them many divine things occasioned by [the miracle of] the bread.[195] After this discourse his narrative is sublimely carried on to other things. But this transition to other things is not incompatible with the [accounts of] the others, although it differs somewhat in order. Nothing would keep us from supposing that the Lord healed some people, as Matthew and Mark report, and that he said those things to the people who followed him across the sea, as John reports. [This is especially likely] since Capernaum, to which John says they were crossing, is near the Lake of Genesaret, the land to which Matthew says they were going.

49,103. Matthew, then, continues his narrative after the Lord's discourse to the Pharisees about unwashed hands. His narrative order preserves the sequence of the following events, as far as we can tell from the transitions: *And Jesus went away from there and withdrew to the region of Tyre and Sidon. And behold, a Canaanite woman came from those areas and cried out, saying to him, Have mercy on me, Lord, Son of David; my daughter is greatly troubled by a demon. But he did not answer her a word* (Mt 15:21–23), and so forth, until where it says, *O woman, great is your faith; be it done to you as you desire. And her daughter was healed that very hour* (Mt 15:28). Mark also records [the story] of this Canaanite woman, giving the same order of events and raising no question of inconsistency apart from

195. See Jn 6:22–71.

saying that the Lord was in a house when the woman came to him pleading for her daughter.[196] It could easily be supposed that, [although] Matthew does not mention the house, he is nonetheless reporting the same event, except that he says that the disciples suggested to the Lord, *Send her away, for she is crying after us* (Mt 15:23). This would seem to indicate that the woman gave voice to these pleas as [she followed] the Lord while he was walking. So how can it have been in a house unless we are to understand that she went into the place where Jesus was, which according to Mark was a house?[197] But when Matthew says, *He did not answer her a word* (Mt 15:23), he hints at what both of them leave unsaid — that, while silent, Jesus left that house. From there on there is no disagreement between them. Mark reports the Lord's response to her, that the children's bread is not to be given to the dogs,[198] while Matthew does not fail to mention some other sayings first. So the disciples must have first begged him concerning her; then he answered them that he was sent only to the lost sheep of the house of Israel; and then she came to him, or rather, followed him; and then she worshiped him, saying, *Help me* (Mt 15:25); and then they said what both evangelists have recorded.

50,104. Matthew continues his narrative thus: *And when Jesus had gone on from there, he came to the shore of the Sea of Galilee. And he went up on a mountain and sat there. And many crowds came to him, bringing with them the mute, blind, lame, maimed, and many others, and they put them at his feet, and he healed them, so that the crowd marveled when they saw the mute speak, the lame walk, the blind see, and they glorified the God of Israel. Then Jesus called his disciples to him and said, I have compassion on the crowd, for they have stayed with me for three days, and have nothing to eat* (Mt 15:29–32), and so forth, until where it says, *Those who ate were four thousand men, besides children and women* (Mt 15:38). This other miracle of the seven loaves and a few fish is also recorded by Mark in almost the same order, except that he inserts [a story], told by none of the others, of a deaf man[199] whose ears the Lord opened by spitting on his fingers and saying, *Ephatha, that is, Be opened* (Mk 7:34).

50,105. It is certainly not unimportant to call attention to this miracle of the seven loaves that the two evangelists, Matthew and Mark, set down. If [only] one of them had recounted this and not recounted that of the five loaves, then one might think that he was contradicting the others. One might then suppose that there was in fact only one [miracle] and that an incomplete and untruthful account was given by one, or by the others, or by all of them, whether it was that one was mistaken and recorded seven instead of five, or that the others [recorded] five instead of seven either from a desire to deceive or from their own forgetfulness. Or one might think

---

196. See Mk 7:24–30.
197. See Mk 7:24.
198. See Mk 7:27.
199. See Mk 7:31–37.

that there was a contradiction between the twelve baskets and the seven hampers,[200] or between the five thousand and the four thousand who were fed. But, since those who narrate the miracle of the seven loaves do not omit that of the five, there is no problem, and anyone can understand that both occurred. We note this so that whenever one finds a similar deed of the Lord [told] by two evangelists in a way that seems so inconsistent that there is no means of reconciling them, one can only understand that it happened twice and that each of them reports one of the incidents. We have already raised this possibility with the seating by hundreds and by fifties, where we also found both [numbers] in one [evangelist], when we might have supposed a contradiction if he had mentioned only one [of the numbers].[201]

51,106. Matthew continues and says, *And, dismissing the crowd, he got into a boat and came to the coast of Magadan* (Mt 15:39), and so forth, until where it says, *An evil and adulterous generation looks for a sign, but no sign shall be given to it except the sign of Jonah* (Mt 16:4). Matthew already said this elsewhere.[202] Hence we must maintain again and again that the Lord frequently said the same thing, Indeed, Mark also keeps to the same order, for after the miracle of the seven loaves he adds the same thing as Matthew, except that Matthew does not say *Dalmanutha*, as in some versions of Mark,[203] but *Magadan*. No one can doubt, however, that it is the same place under a different name. Besides, most versions of Mark have nothing other than *Magadan*. Nor is it a problem that Mark does not mention Jonah in the reply to those who asked for a sign from heaven, as Matthew does,[204] but has the Lord reply, *A sign shall not be given to it* (Mk 8:12). For it can be understood that the kind of sign they sought was one from heaven, and [Mark] just omits mentioning Jonah, which Matthew does record.

52,107. Matthew continues, *And he left them and departed. And when his disciples came across the lake, they had forgotten to bring bread. He said to them, Consider and beware of the leaven of the Pharisees and Sadducees* (Mt 16:4–6), and so forth, until where it says, *Then they understood that he was telling them to beware not of the leaven of bread but of the teaching of the Pharisees and Sadducees* (Mt 16:12). This is also given by Mark, and in the same order.[205]

53,108. Matthew continues, *And Jesus came to the region of Caesarea Philippi, and he asked his disciples saying, Who do people say that I, the Son of Man, am? And they said, Some John the Baptist, others Elijah, and others Jeremiah or one of the prophets* (Mt 16:13–14), and so forth, until it says, *And whatever you loose on earth shall be loosed in heaven* (Mt 16:19). Mark narrates this in nearly the same order, although he first inserts [the story], which he alone records, of the healing of the blind man who said to the Lord, *I see men like walking trees* (Mk

---

200. "Baskets" (Mt 14:20; Mk 6:43 Lk 9:17; Jn 6:13)..."hampers" (Mt 15:37; Mk 8:8): *cophinis... sportis.*
201. See above at II,46,98.
202. See Mt 12:39.
203. See Mk 8:10.
204. See Mt 16:4.
205. See Mk 8:13–21.

8:24). Luke also records this and inserts it after the miracle of the five loaves,[206] but, as we noted above, his recollected order is not inconsistent with their order. But it may be troublesome that Luke says that the Lord asked his disciples about who people said he was while he was alone praying and they were with him,[207] whereas Mark says that he asked them this while they were on the way.[208] But this is troublesome only to someone who has never prayed on the way.

53,109. I recall saying already that it should not be supposed that Peter received that name when he said to him, *You are Peter, and on this rock I will build my Church* (Mt 16:18), for he only received this name at the time that John records it: *You shall be called Cephas, which means Peter* (Jn 1:42).[209] Nor can it be supposed that he received the name Peter at the time when Mark records the names of the twelve apostles, telling how James and John were called sons of thunder,[210] just because he says that he named him Peter, for he says this when he recalls it, not as though it happened at the time.

54,110. Matthew continues and says, *Then he commanded his disciples to tell no one that he was Jesus the Christ. From then on Jesus began to show his disciples that he must go to Jerusalem and suffer many things from the elders and scribes* (Mt 16:20–21), and so forth, until where it says, *You are not thinking of the things that are God's but of those that are men's* (Mt 16:23). Mark and Luke put this in the same order,[211] although Luke omits Peter's opposition to Christ's passion.

55,111. Matthew continues, *Then Jesus told his disciples, If anyone wishes to come after me, let him deny himself and take up his cross and follow me* (Mt 16:24), and so forth, until where it says, *Then he shall repay everyone according to his work* (Mt 16:27). Mark adds this in the same order, although he does not mention the Son of Man coming with his angels to repay everyone according to his work. But he reports what was said by the Lord: *For whoever is ashamed of me and my words in this adulterous and sinful generation, of him the Son of Man shall be ashamed when he comes in his glory with the holy angels* (Mk 8:38). This can be understood as meaning the same as Matthew's statement that he would repay everyone according to his work. Luke adds this in the same order, only varying the words slightly but truthfully giving the same meaning.[212]

56,112. Matthew continues, *Amen, I say to you, there are some standing here who shall not taste death before they see the Son of Man coming in his kingdom. And after six days Jesus took Peter and James and his brother John and led them up a high mountain* (Mt 16:28–17:1), and so forth, until where it says, *Tell no one the vision until the Son of Man rises from the dead* (Mt 17:9). Three disciples—Peter, James, and John—[see] this vision of the Lord on the mountain, and in the same

---

206. See Lk 9:18–20.
207. See Lk 9:18.
208. See Mk 8:27.
209. See above at II,17,34.
210. See Mk 3:16–19.
211. See Mk 8:30–33; Lk 9:21–22.
212. See Lk 9:23–27.

scene the witness of the Father's voice from heaven is related; all of this is given in the same order and with the same exact meaning by three evangelists.[213] But regarding other things readers may see that they use different types of speech, although without any difference in meaning, as we have shown above in other cases.

56,113. But Mark and Matthew say that this happened after six days, while Luke says it was eight days; anyone who is troubled by this should not be treated dismissively but should be instructed by being given reasons. For, when we say "after so many days," sometimes we do not count the day on which we are speaking, or the day on which the event we are predicting or promising is to occur, but the full and complete days that will come in between. This is what Matthew and Mark do. They leave out the day on which Jesus said this and the day on which he showed that memorable vision on the mountain, only considering the days in between, and therefore they say *after six days* (Mt 17:1; Mk 9:2). But [Luke] counts the end days, that is the first and the last, and therefore he says *after eight days* (Lk 9:28), as when one speaks of the part as though it stood for the whole.[214]

56,114. Now, as for what Luke says about Moses and Elijah, *And it happened that when they departed from him, Peter said to Jesus, Master, it is good for us to be here* (Lk 9:33), and so forth, this should not be taken as contradicting what Matthew and Mark say here, as though Peter made this suggestion while Moses and Elijah were still speaking with the Lord. For they do not say that it happened right then, but instead they omit his addition that Peter suggested to the Lord the building of three tents as they were departing.[215] Luke also adds that they were entering the cloud when the voice came from the cloud,[216] which the others do not say, although they do not contradict it either.

57,115. Matthew continues, *And the disciples asked him saying, Why do the scribes say that first Elijah must come? And he replied and said to them, Elijah shall come and restore all things, but I say to you that Elijah has already come, and they did not know him but did to him whatever they wished. So also the Son of Man shall suffer from them. Then the disciples understood that he was speaking to them of John the Baptist.* (Mt 17:10–13) Mark also reports this in the same order, and, although there is some difference in the wording, he in no way departs from the same truthful meaning.[217] But he does not say that the disciples understood that the Lord was referring to John when he said that Elijah had come.

58,116. Matthew continues and says, *And when he came to the crowd, a man approached him, fell on his knees before him, and said, Lord, have mercy on my son, for he is a lunatic and suffers terribly* (Mt 17:14–15), and so forth, until where it says, *But this kind does not come out except by prayer and fasting* (Mt

---

213. See Mt 17:1–9; Mk 9:1–9; Lk 9:27–36.
214. I.e., Luke has counted two partial days as though they were whole days.
215. See Lk 9:33
216. See, Lk 9:34–35.
217. See Mk 9:11–13.

17:20). Mark and Luke also record this in the same order without any question of inconsistency.[218]

59,117. Matthew continues, saying, *While they were in Galilee, Jesus said to them, The Son of Man shall be handed over into the hands of men, and they shall kill him, and on the third day he shall rise. And they were extremely sad.* (Mt 17:22–23) Mark and Luke record this in the same order.[219]

60,118. Matthew continues, *And when they came to Capernaum, those who were collecting the half-drachma tax approached Peter and said to him, Does your teacher pay the half-drachma tax? And he said, Yes* (Mt 17:24–25), and so forth, until where it says, *You will find a piece of money; take that and give it to them for me and you* (Mt 17:27). He alone records this, and after inserting it he again follows the same order as Mark and Luke.

61,119. Matthew then continues in the following way and says, *At that time the disciples came to Jesus, saying, Who do you think is greatest in the kingdom of heaven? And Jesus called a child and stood him in their midst and said, Amen, I say to you, unless you are converted and become as little children, you shall not enter the kingdom of heaven* (Mt 18:1–3), and so forth, until where it says, *So also my heavenly Father shall do to you if each one of you does not forgive your brother from your heart* (Mt 18:35). Mark does not include all of this lengthy discourse of the Lord but only some parts, although these are in the same order, and he also inserts some things that Matthew does not mention.[220] The only interruption in this whole discourse that we have taken into consideration occurs when Peter asks how often a brother should be forgiven.[221] But the Lord spoke in such a way that it is quite clear that Peter's question and the answer to it are part of the same discourse. Luke records none of this in this order, except for the little child who was set before the disciples as someone to be imitated when they were thinking of their own greatness.[222] Although he says other things similar to what is found in this discourse, he recalls them as they were said on other occasions. Similarly, John reports what the Lord said after his resurrection about the forgiveness of sins, that they would be retained if [his disciples] retained anyone's and forgiven if they forgave anyone's.[223] In this discourse Matthew reports that the Lord said something that he already claimed he had said to Peter earlier.[224] This should not trouble us, even though the order of the sayings may appear inconsistent, for Jesus said the same thing often and at different places, which we have frequently observed and which we ought to keep in mind, so that we need not bring it up repeatedly.

62,120. Matthew continues his narrative thus: *And it happened that, when Jesus had finished these sayings, he went away to Galilee and came into the region*

---

218. See Mk 9:14–29; Lk 9:37–43.
219. See Mk 9:30–32; Lk 9:43–45.
220. See Mk 9:33–50.
221. See Mt 18:21.
222. See Lk 9:46–48.
223. See Jn 20:23.
224. See Mt 16:19.

*of Judea beyond the Jordan. And great crowds followed him, and he healed them
there. And Pharisees came up to him, testing him by asking, Is it lawful for a man
to divorce his wife for any cause?* (Mt 19:1–3) and so forth, until where it says,
He who is able to receive this, let him receive it (Mt 19:12). Mark also records
this in the same order. But we must see whether there does not seem to be an
inconsistency here, for Mark says that the Lord asked the Pharisees what Moses
commanded, and they answered that he permitted them a bill of divorce.[225] But
Matthew says that the Lord's words showed from the law how God had joined
male and female[226] and that therefore they should not be separated by a human
being, to which they replied, *Why then did Moses command a bill of divorce to be
given and to send her away?* (Mt 19:7) And he said to them, *For your hardness of
heart Moses allowed you to divorce your wives, but from the beginning it was not
so* (Mt 19:8). Mark does not omit the Lord's response, but he [puts] it after their
answer to his question about the bill of divorce.

62,121. As to the order or the wording, we ought to understand that it makes
no difference to the truth of the matter whether they asked him about the bill
of divorce allowed by Moses, who also wrote that God joined male and female
together,[227] while the Lord was prohibiting divorce and proving his ideas from the
law, or whether they mentioned it in their answer to his question about what Moses
had commanded them. He did not intend to give them a reason for why Moses
had permitted this until after they had mentioned it first. This intentionality of
his is indicated by the question that Mark records. But their intention was that the
authority of Moses, who had commanded them to give a bill of divorce, would
stop him from definitively prohibiting divorce, for they had come to him to say
something that would test him. Their intention is expressed by Matthew, who does
not record that they were questioned but that they asked about Moses's command
so that they could convict the Lord of prohibiting the divorce of spouses. Both
evangelists show the intentions of the speakers, which is what words are supposed
to do; therefore it is of no concern if there are differences in their ways of telling
the story, so long as neither deviates from the truth of the matter.

62,122. It may also be understood in this way: Perhaps, as Mark says, they
first questioned the Lord about divorcing a wife, and then he asked them about
what Moses had commanded. Then they responded that Moses had allowed them
to write a bill of divorce and send her away. Then he answered regarding the
law given by Moses and how God had instituted the joining of male and female,
saying, as Matthew puts it, *Have you not read that he who made them from the
beginning male and female?* (Mt 19:4) and so forth. When they heard this they
repeated what they had answered to his previous question, saying, *Why then did
Moses command a bill of divorce to be given and to send her away?* Then Jesus
showed that the reason was their hardness of heart. Mark had briefly shown this

225. See Mk 10:4.
226. See Mt 19:5.
227. See Gn 1:27.

earlier when [Jesus] answered their response, which Matthew omitted. He judged that wherever he put these words, no damage would be done to the truth, for the statement to which they responded was said twice, and the Lord's response was in these words.

63,123. Matthew continues, *Then little children were brought to him so that he could lay his hands on them and pray. But the disciples rebuked them* (Mt 19:13), and so forth, until where it says, *For many are called, but few are chosen* (Mt 20:16). Mark follows the same order as Matthew here, although Matthew alone inserts the story of the hiring of the workers for the vineyard.[228] Luke first records what he said to those who questioned who would be the greatest among them, and then he adds [the story] of the man they saw casting out demons, although he did not follow [Jesus]; then he diverges from the other two, saying how he set his face to go to Jerusalem,[229] and, after inserting many other things,[230] he rejoins their record with [the story] of the rich man, to whom it was said, *Sell all that you have* (Lk 18:22). This is recorded by all of them in the order that they all have in common.[231] For Luke includes [the story] of the little children right before he mentions the rich man, just as the other two do. As for this rich man, who asks what good he must do in order to obtain eternal life, there may seem to be some discrepancy among them. For according to Matthew [Jesus] said, *Why do you ask me about what is good?* (Mt 19:17) while according to the others he said, *Why do you call me good?* (Mk 10:18; Lk 18:19) *Why do you ask me about the good?* may refer to his question, *What good must I do?* (Mt 19:16) He both called [Jesus] good and asked about the good, but *good teacher* (Mk 10:17; Lk 18:18) is not of itself a question. So the best way to understand this would be that [Jesus] said both *Why do you call me good?* and *Why do you ask me about the good?*

64,124. Matthew continues and says, *And as Jesus was going up to Jerusalem he took the twelve disciples aside and said to them, Behold, we are going up to Jerusalem, and the Son of Man shall be handed over to the chief priests and scribes, and they shall condemn him to death, and they shall hand him over to the gentiles to be mocked, flogged, and crucified, and on the third day he shall rise. Then the mother of the sons of Zebedee came to him with her sons, worshiping him and asking him for something* (Mt 20:17–20), and so forth, until where it says, *Even as the Son of Man came not to be served but to serve and to give his life as a ransom for many* (Mt 20:28). Mark also follows this order, except that

---

228. Cf. Matt 20:1–16.
229. Cf. Luke 9:46–51.
230. This long insertion — Luke 9:52–18:14 — is usually called "The Travel Narrative," since it is (loosely) structured around Jesus' going to Jerusalem, or Luke's "Special Section," since it contains most of the material unique to his Gospel. Its uniqueness allows Augustine to skip over it so easily: once he has established his principle that material unique to one Gospel presents no problem of disagreement with the other Gospels, he can skip over any insertion, no matter how large.
231. I.e., although it occurs much later in Luke, it is in the same order relative to those stories that the three evangelists share.

he has the request come from the sons of Zebedee themselves,[232] while Matthew says it was not from them directly but from their mother, who presented their wish to the Lord. So Mark briefly indicates that the statement is from them rather than from her. But both Matthew and Mark have the Lord reply to them rather than to their mother. Luke, however, after recording in the same order his prediction to the twelve disciples of his passion and resurrection, omits what the others include and rejoins them after this with the report of what happened at Jericho.[233] As for what Matthew and Mark say about the leaders of the gentiles exercising power over their subjects, and that this should not be so with [the disciples] but that the greatest among them should serve the others, Luke says something similar, though not at this point, and his order indicates that this idea was expressed by the Lord on a separate occasion.[234]

65,125. Matthew continues, *And as they left Jericho a great crowd followed. And behold, two blind men sitting by the road heard that Jesus was passing by, and they cried out saying, Lord, have mercy on us, Son of David* (Mt 20:29–30), and so forth, until where it says, *And immediately they could see and they followed him* (Mt 20:34). Mark also records this, though with only one blind man.[235] We can address this question in the same way that we addressed it in the story of the two men who suffered from the legion of demons in the region of the Gerasenes.[236] Only [Matthew] tells of two blind men, but one of them must have been of special standing and fame in that city. This is shown quite clearly by the fact that Mark records the name of both him and his father, which occurs in none of the other healings done by the Lord, except when he mentions the name of the ruler of the synagogue, Jairus, whose daughter Jesus resuscitated,[237] and in that instance it is clear that the ruler of the synagogue was a high-ranking man in that place. So no doubt this Bartimaeus, son of Timaeus, had fallen from some great fortune to a most remarkable and infamous misery, because he was not only blind but even had to sit begging. Therefore Mark chooses to report only that one whose restoration of sight made this miracle as famous as his loss had been remarkable.

65,126. Although Luke has an altogether similar incident, it is nevertheless to be understood as the record of the miracle of another blind man, similar to this miracle.[238] For he says that it happened as he drew near to Jericho, while the others [say that] it was when he was leaving Jericho. Though the name of the city and the similarity of the act encourage one to suppose that there was one event, the fact that the evangelists disagree with one another, in that one says, *As he drew near to Jericho* (Lk 18:35), while the others [say], *As he was leaving Jericho* (Mt 20:29; Mk 10:46), surely persuades one that these are not the same event, unless

---

232. See Mk 10:35.
233. See Lk 18:35–43; Mt 20:29–34; Mk 10:46–52.
234. See Lk 22:24–27; Mt 20:24–28; Mk 10:41–45.
235. See Mk 10:46–52.
236. See above at II, 24,56.
237. See Mk 10:22–43.
238. See Lk 18:35–43.

one is more inclined to believe that the Gospel is false than that Jesus did similar miracles under similar circumstances. All faithful children of the Gospel will easily see which of these is more believable and true; and all antagonists, when they are shown how things are, will either be silent or, if they choose not to be silent, will keep their thoughts to themselves.

66,127. Matthew continues and says, *And when they drew near to Jerusalem and came to Bethpage, to the Mount of Olives, Jesus sent two disciples, saying to them, Go into the village opposite you, and immediately you will find an ass tied, and a colt with her* (Mt 21:1–2), and so forth, until where it says, *Blessed is he who comes in the name of the Lord, hosanna in the highest* (Mt 21:9). Mark reports this in the same order.[239] Luke stays in Jericho longer, recording some things the others omit, such as the story of Zacchaeus, the chief tax-collector, and other things spoken in parables.[240] After this he rejoins the others in reporting on the colt on which Jesus sat.[241] And it is not problematic that Matthew speaks of an ass and a colt, while the others do not mention the ass. For we must remember that rule which we discussed previously in the case of the seating by fifties and by hundreds when the crowds were fed with the five loaves.[242] Once this is remembered, the reader should find no problem here. Even if Matthew had omitted the colt and the others had omitted the ass, one would not need to suppose some great difference because one mentioned an ass and the others the colt of an ass. Hence it is even less of a problem if the one mentions the ass, which the others omit, but also includes the colt, which the others also mention. So, when it is possible to suppose that both things were there, there is no inconsistency if one mentions the one thing and another the other, and there is even less [of a problem] if one [mentions] one and the other both.

66,128. Although John says nothing about the Lord's sending his disciples to bring these animals to him, he nonetheless briefly mentions this colt, along with the same prophetic witness used by Matthew.[243] In this prophetic witness, although there is some difference in wording among the evangelists, there is no difference in their meaning. It could be problematic, however, that Matthew cites this passage as though the prophet mentioned the ass, when this is not the case either in John's version or in the Church's books of the usual translation. But it seems to me that the reason for this is that Matthew is held to have written his Gospel in the Hebrew language. It is clear, furthermore, that the translation known as the Septuagint is not always identical to what is found in the Hebrew by those who know that language and by those who have made translations of those Hebrew books. If one seeks the reason for this difference, or for why the authority of the Septuagint translation differs in so many places from the truth found in the Hebrew books, there is no

---

239. See Mk 11:1–10.
240. See Lk 19:1–27.
241. See Lk 19:28–40.
242. See above at II,46,98.
243. See Jn 12:14–15; Zc 9:9.

more probable explanation than this — that the Spirit [who spoke] through the Septuagint translators was the same Spirit who had earlier spoken those things which they were translating. This is confirmed by that agreement which they are said to have miraculously had with one another.[244] So, although their wording may have varied, they in no way departed from the will of God, from which the words came and to which the words had to be subservient. They wished to show nothing other than that same thing which we now marvel at in the diversity of agreement among the four evangelists, in which it is shown to us that one need not be false if one expresses something in a different way from another, as long as one does not depart from the intention of the One with whom one must be in accord and agreement. Knowing this is advantageous both to morality, for the purpose of guarding against and judging falsehood, and to faith itself, lest we suppose that God would commend the truth to us by giving us not only the thing itself but even the words in which it is expressed, as though they were a kind of deified sound. It is rather the case that the thing which is to be learned is so far above the words by which it is learned that we would not need to ask about them at all if we were able to know the thing itself without them, as God knows it and his angels know it in him.

67,129. Matthew continues and says, *And when he entered Jerusalem, all the city was stirred, saying, Who is this? And the people said, This is the prophet Jesus from Nazareth of Galilee. And Jesus entered the Temple of God and drove out all who sold and bought in the Temple* (Mt 21:10–12), and so forth, until where it says, *But you have made it a den of thieves* (Mt 21:13). All [the evangelists] record this [event] of the crowds of merchants who were cast out of the Temple, but John [does so] in a very different sequence.[245] For, after the testimony of John the Baptist concerning Jesus, he then records his going into Galilee, when he turned the water into wine. And then, after noting his stay in Capernaum for a few days,[246] he says that he went up to Jerusalem at the time of the Jews' Passover and made a whip of small cords to drive the merchants from the Temple. This makes it clear that the Lord did this not once but twice, and John records the first time and the others the last time.

68,130. Matthew continues, *And the blind and lame came to him in the Temple, and he healed them. But when the chief priests and the scribes saw the marvelous things that he was doing, and the children crying out in the Temple saying, Hosanna to the Son of David, they were indignant, and they said to him, Do you hear what these are saying? And Jesus said to them, Yes. Have you never read, Out of the mouth of babes and sucklings you have perfected praise? And leaving them he went out of the city to Bethany and stayed there. In the morning, as he was*

244. Augustine is referring to the legend of the Septuagint's creation, according to which seventy (or seventy-two) translators independently produced Greek translations of the Hebrew Bible in the third century B.C. at the request of the Egyptian king, Ptolemy II. When the translators came together at the end of the project and compared their versions, all were identical in every respect.

245. See Mk 11:15–17; Lk 19:45–46; Jn 2:14–16.

246. See Jn 2:1–12.

returning to the city, he was hungry. And seeing a fig tree on the way, he went up
to it and found nothing on it but leaves only. And he said to it, May no fruit ever
come from you again. And the fig tree withered up at once. And when the disciples
saw it they marveled, saying, How did it wither up at once? But answering, Jesus
said to them, Amen, I say to you, if you have faith and do not doubt, you shall not
only do this to the fig tree but, even if you say to this mountain, Be taken up and
cast into the sea, it shall be done. And whatever you ask for in prayer with faith,
you shall receive. (Mt 21:14–22)

68,131. Mark also mentions this in what follows, but not in the same order.[247] For
what Matthew tells first, that he went into the Temple and cast out those who sold
and bought, Mark does not record [first]. Instead, he says that he looked around at
everything, and when it was evening he went out to Bethany with the twelve. Then,
on another day, when they came from Bethany, he was hungry, and he cursed the
fig tree, as Matthew also reports. Then Mark adds that he came to Jerusalem and
entered the Temple and cast out those who bought and sold, as though it happened
on another day and not on the first. But since Matthew says, *And he left them and*
went out of the city to Bethany (Mt 21:17), and reports that when he returned in the
morning to the city he cursed the fig tree, it is more likely to suppose that he kept
the chronological order of the casting out from the Temple of those who bought
and sold. For when he says, *And he left them and went out*, to whom can this refer
except to those who were indignant when the children cried, *Hosanna to the Son*
of David (Mt 21:9.15)? So Mark omits what happened on the first day, when he
entered the Temple, and records what he recalled at that point—Jesus' finding
nothing but leaves on the fig tree—even though that happened on the second day,
as both of them testify. But the disciples' surprise at the tree's withering, and the
Lord's response to them about faith and about the mountain being cast into the sea,
did not [happen] on the second day, when he said to the tree, *May no one eat fruit*
from you ever again (Mk 11:14), but on the third day. For Mark reports the casting
out of the merchants from the Temple on the second day,[248] which he omits from
the first day. So it is on this second day that Jesus went out of the city at evening.
And the following day when they passed by it in the morning, the disciples saw the
fig tree withered from the roots, and Peter remembered it and said, *Rabbi, behold*
the fig tree that you cursed has withered (Mk 11:21), and then [Jesus] responded
on the power of faith. But Matthew [says that all] this happened on the second
day: [Jesus] said to the tree, *May no fruit ever come from you again* (Mt 21:19),
the withering immediately followed, the disciples marveled when they saw it, and
he responded to them on the power of faith. So it should be understood that Mark
reports as happening on the second day what he omits from the first—the casting
out from the Temple of those who bought and sold. Meanwhile, Matthew reports
what happened on the [second] day—the cursing of the tree as he returned in the

---

247. See Mk 11:11–17.
248. See Mk 11:12.

morning from Bethany to the city. But he omits what Mark records—his entering
the city, leaving it at evening, and the disciples' surprise at the tree's withering
when they passed by it in the morning. He adds to the second day, when the tree
was cursed, things that happened on the third day—the disciples' surprise at the
withering and the Lord's response about the power of faith. He connects them in
such a way that, without Mark's narrative to alert us, we would not have been able
to detect where Matthew has omitted anything. So Matthew says this: *And leaving
them he went out of the city to Bethany and stayed there. In the morning, as he was
returning to the city, he was hungry. And seeing a fig tree on the way, he came up
to it and found nothing on it but leaves only. And he said to it, May no fruit ever
come from you again. And the fig tree withered up at once.* (Mt 21:17–19) Then
he omits some things related to that day and immediately adds the following: *And
when the disciples saw it they marveled, saying, How did it wither up at once?* (Mt
21:20) But it was on another day that they saw this and marveled at it. It should
be understood, though, that it did not wither up when they saw it but as soon as it
was cursed. For they saw it not just withering up but already completely withered
up, and they understood that it had withered up immediately after the Lord's word.

69,132. Matthew continues and says, *And when he came into the Temple, the
chief priests and the elders of the people came up to him as he was teaching, saying, By what authority do you do these things, and who gave you this authority?
Answering, Jesus said to them, I shall also ask you one thing, and if you answer
me I shall tell you by what authority I do these things. Whence was the baptism
of John?* (Mt 21:23–25) and so forth, until where it says, *Neither shall I tell you by
what authority I do these things* (Mt 21:27). The other two, Mark and Luke, tell
all of this in almost the same words.[249] Nor is there any difference in sequence,
except for what was noted previously, that Matthew omits some things from his
account of the second day. Thus, were it not [for Mark's] alerting us, we would
have thought he was referring to the second day, while Mark [shows] it was really
the third. Luke, on the other hand, does not add this as though he were following
the sequence of days, but, after reporting the casting out from the Temple of those
who bought and sold, he omits his going to Bethany, his returning to the city, what
happened to the fig tree, and the response about the power of faith made to the
disciples' surprise. And after omitting this he continues, *And he was teaching daily
in the Temple. And the chief priests and scribes and leaders of the people sought
to destroy him but could not find anything that they could do to him, for all the
people were listening to him attentively. And it happened that one day, as he was
teaching the people in the Temple and preaching the Gospel, the chief priests and
scribes with the elders came up and said to him, Tell us by what authority you
do these things* (Lk 19:47–20:2), and so forth. The other two record these things
also. So there appears to be no difference even in the sequence itself, for when he

---

249. See Mk 11:27–33; Lk 20:1–8.

says, *And it happened that one day* (Lk 20:1), this can be understood as that day to which the others also refer.

70,133. Matthew continues, *Now, what do you think? A man had two sons; and he went to the first and said to him, Go today to work in my vineyard. And answering he said, No, but afterward he repented and went. And he went to the other and said the same. And answering he said, I am going, sir, but he did not go* (Mt 21:28–30), and so forth, until where it says, *And he who falls on this stone shall be broken, but he upon whom it falls, it shall crush him* (Mt 21:44). Mark and Luke do not record this [story] of the two sons who were commanded to go and work in the vineyard. But the next [story] that Matthew tells, of the vineyard that was let out to farmers, who abused the servants sent to them and afterwards killed the beloved son and threw him out of vineyard, is not overlooked by the other two, who give it in the same order.[250] They tell it after the Jews say they are unable to answer the question about John's baptism, to which [Jesus] replies, *Neither do I tell you by what authority I do these things* (Mt 21:27; Mk 11:33).

70,134. There is no question of disagreement here, unless it is because Matthew has the Lord ask the Jews, *When the owner of the vineyard comes, what will he do to those farmers?* (Mt 21:40) and has them respond, *He will destroy those evil men in an evil way and let the vineyard out to other farmers, who will give him the fruits in their seasons* (Mt 21:41). For Mark does not record this as their response but as what was said by the Lord in response to his own question. For [in Mark Jesus] says, *What will the owner of the vineyard do? He will come and destroy the tenants and give the vineyard to others.* (Mk 12:9) But it is easy enough to understand that their words are added here without the addition of "They said" or "They responded," but nonetheless this is to be understood. Or else this response is attributed to the Lord because, when they spoke the truth, he who is himself the truth answered the same as they did.

70,135. But it is more problematic that Luke, like Mark, not only attributes these words to the Lord and so does not say that it was their response but even has them give a contrary response, saying, *Let it not be so!* (Lk 20:16) For this is his version: *What then will the owner of the vineyard do to them? He will come and destroy those tenants and give the vineyard to others. When they heard this, they said, Let it not be so! But he looked at them and said, What then is this that is written: The stone that the builders rejected has become the head of the corner?* (Lk 20:15–17) So how can the same people who say according to Matthew, *He will destroy those evil men in an evil way and let the vineyard out to other farmers, who will give him the fruits in their seasons*, say according to Luke something completely at odds with these words, saying, *Let it not be so?* In fact, what the Lord then says about the stone that was rejected by the builders but became the head of the corner seems to be meant as a witness to discredit those who disagree with the parable. Matthew's report also seems directed against those who disagree:

---

250. See Mt 21:33–46; Mk 12:1–12; Lk 20:9–19.

Have you never read in the Scriptures: The stone that the builders rejected has become the head of the corner? (Mt 21:42) For *Have you never read?* [shows] that their response was in disagreement with this [parable]. Mark also indicates this with these words: *Have you not read this Scripture: The stone that the builders rejected has become the head of the corner?* (Mk 12:10) In Luke's [version] this sentence seems to be in the place where it was said, for it is right after their dissent, *Let it not be so!* And the way that he puts it — *What then is this that is written: The stone that the builders rejected has become the head of the corner?* (Lk 20:17) — is equivalent to the others. For the same meaning is expressed in each of these phrases: *Have you never read? Have you not read? What then is this that is written?*

70,136. It remains then for us to understand that, among the people who were listening then, there were some who responded as Matthew reports: *They said to him, He will destroy those evil men in an evil way and let the vineyard out to other farmers* (Mt 21:41). But there were also some [who said] what Luke does not fail to mention, *Let it not be so!* Those who said *Let it not be so!* were responding to those who made the first reply to the Lord. But this first response has been attributed by Mark and Luke to the Lord, because, as was noted, the truth itself was spoken by them even if they did not know it and even if they were evil. The same [happened] with Caiaphas the high priest, who knew not what he said but still prophesied.[251] It also [happened] with those who did know and who understood and believed, for that multitude was also there, through whom the prophecy was fulfilled[252] when there was a great throng at his arrival and they cried out, *Blessed is he who comes in the name of the Lord!* (Mt 21:9)

70,137. Nor is it a problem that Matthew says that the chief priests and elders of the people came to the Lord and asked him by what authority he did these things and who had given him this authority, and he asked them whether the baptism of John was from heaven or from men. And when they answered that they did not know, he said, *Neither do I tell you by what authority I do these things* (Mt 21:27). And he follows this with the next words spoken: *What do you think? A man had two sons* (Mt 21:28), and so forth. So, according to Matthew this discourse continued without any interruption from things or persons through [the parable] of the vineyard that was let out to farmers. Hence it may be supposed that all these things were said to the chief priests and elders of the people who had asked him about his authority. But if they had asked these things to tempt him as enemies, then it is not possible to suppose that they believed and gave that clear, prophetic witness to the Lord. They must not have been unbelievers but believers in order to give a response like *He will destroy those evil men in an evil way and let the vineyard out to other farmers*. And this should not at all be a problem that would make us suppose that there were no believers in that multitude that heard the Lord's

---

251. See Jn 11:49–51.
252. See Ps 118:26.

parables. For only for the sake of brevity does Matthew omit what Luke does not; this parable was uttered not only to those who had asked him about his authority but to the people, for he says this: *He began to tell the people this parable: A man planted a vineyard* (Lk 20:9), and so forth. It is to be understood that among these people there could have been some who listened to him in the same way as those who said, *Blessed is he who comes in the name of the Lord!* All of these, or some of them, were the ones who responded, *He will destroy those evil men in an evil way and let the vineyard out to other farmers.* Mark and Luke attribute their response to the Lord [for two reasons] — because he himself could very well have said this, since he is the truth,[253] which he often speaks even by means of wicked and ignorant people, moving a person's mind through a certain hidden instinct, not by reason of that person's holiness but by right of his own authority; and also because such people[254] might correctly have already been deemed members of the Lord's body, so that what they said could rightly be attributed to him, whose members they were. For by that time he had baptized more than John[255] and had crowds of disciples, as the evangelists often testify. The apostle Paul reports that after his resurrection he appeared to five hundred brethren,[256] who must have been from this group. Moreover, in the statement according to Matthew — *They said to him, He will destroy those evil men in an evil way* — the *to him* is placed in such a way that it need not be plural,[257] as though the ones responding were the same as those who had deceitfully asked him about his authority. But *They said to him* means "to the Lord himself," the singular pronoun, not the plural, which is unambiguously clear in the Greek versions.

70,138. The evangelist John recounts a discourse of the Lord's that may make this more easily intelligible: *Then Jesus said to those Jews who believed in him, If you continue in my word, you will truly be my disciples, and you will know the truth, and the truth will set you free. And they answered him, We are Abraham's seed and were never in bondage to anyone. Why do you say, You will be set free? Jesus answered them, Amen, amen, I say to you, everyone who commits a sin is a slave to sin. The slave does not stay in the house forever, but the son stays forever. So, if the son sets you free, you will be truly free. I know that you are children of Abraham, but you seek to kill me, because my word has no place in you.* (Jn 8:31–37) He did not say *but you seek to kill me* (Jn 8:37) to those who already believed in him, to whom he had said, *If you continue in my word, you will truly be my disciples* (Jn 8:31). He made this latter statement to those who already believed in him. But there was a multitude present, and among them were

---

253. See Jn 14:6.
254. I.e., the people in the crowd of Jesus' listeners who believed in him.
255. See Jn 4:1.
256. See 1 Cor 15:6.
257. The Latin for *they said to him* reads *aiunt illi. Illi* could be taken as either a nominative plural ("they") or a dative singular ("to him"). In other words the phrase could also be translated simply as "they said." Augustine argues (correctly) that *illi* should be understood as a dative singular.

many of his enemies. Even though the evangelist does not say who it was who responded this way, the way they responded and the type of answer they deserved from him make it clear enough which words should be attributed to which persons. So, just as in this multitude that John [speaks of] there were those who already believed in Jesus and those who sought to kill him, so also in the one that we are now discussing there were those who deceitfully questioned the Lord about the authority by which he did those things, and there were those who not deceitfully but faithfully acclaimed him, *Blessed is he who comes in the name of the Lord!* So there were some there who said, "He will destroy them and give his vineyard to others." And this can rightly be understood as the Lord's own voice either because it is the truth or because of the unity that there is between the members and the head. There were also others who said to this response, *Let it not be so!* because they understood that this parable had been spoken against them.

71,139. Matthew continues, *And when the chief priests and the Pharisees heard his parables, they realized that he was speaking about them. And when they sought to take him they feared the crowds, because they held him to be a prophet. And answering, Jesus again spoke to them in parables, saying, The kingdom of heaven may be compared to a man, a king, who made a wedding feast for his son and sent his servants to call those who were invited to the feast, but they would not come* (Mt 21:45–22:3), and so forth, until where it says, *For many are called, but few are chosen* (Mt 22:14). Only Matthew tells this parable of those invited to the wedding feast. Luke records something similar,[258] but it is not the same, as shown by the sequence alone, although there is some similarity. But Mark and Luke also confirm the things that Matthew adds right after the parable of the vineyard and the killing of the father's son — that the Jews realized that this was said about them and that they began to contrive plots — and they do so in the same order.[259] But after this they go on to something else, adding something that Matthew also puts in the same order after his unique insertion of the parable of the wedding feast.

72,140. Matthew continues, then: *Then the Pharisees went and took counsel how to catch him in his speech. And they sent their disciples to him with the Herodians, saying, Teacher, we know that you are truthful and teach the way of God in truth and do not favor anyone, for you do not regard the person of men. So, tell us what you think: is it lawful to give taxes to Caesar or not?* (Mt 22:15–17), and so forth, until where it says, *And when the crowd heard it, they marveled at his teaching* (Mt 22:33). The Lord [gives] two replies here, one about the coin, in reference to giving tribute to Caesar, and the other about the resurrection, in reference to the woman who married seven brothers in succession. Mark and Luke give similar accounts and do not differ in the order.[260] After all three [evangelists] record the parable about those to whom the vineyard was rented, which was spoken against the Jews and their plotting, these two, Mark and Luke, omit the parable of

258. See Lk 14:16–24.
259. See Mk 12:12; Lk 20:19.
260. See Mk 12:13–27; Lk 20:20–40.

those invited to the wedding feast, which is unique to Matthew. And then these two rejoin the first, telling of the tribute to Caesar and the woman with seven husbands, in the exact same order and without any inconsistency.

73,141. Matthew continues, then, and says, *Now, when the Pharisees heard that he had silenced the Sadducees, they gathered together and one of them, a lawyer, asked him a question to test him: Teacher, which is the greatest commandment in the law? Jesus said to him, You shall love the Lord your God with all your heart and with all your soul and with all your mind. This is the great and first commandment. And the second is similar to it: You shall love your neighbor as yourself. On these two commandments depend all the law and the prophets.* (Mt 22:34–40) Mark also records this in the same order. It is not a problem that Matthew says that the man who questioned the Lord did it to test him, while Mark omits this and concludes by saying that he answered wisely and the Lord said to him, *You are not far from the kingdom of God* (Mk 12:34). For it is possible that, although he approached him in order to test him, the Lord's response nonetheless set him right. Or else we need not assume that the testing was in a bad sense, as from one who wished to deceive an enemy, but rather a precaution, as from one who wished to learn more about some unknown person. For it is rightly written, *He who believes too readily is light-minded and shall be brought low* (Sir 19:4).

73,142. Luke tells something like this, but not in this order and in a totally different place.[261] But it is uncertain whether that refers to this [incident], or whether there was another person to whom the Lord spoke similarly about these two commandments. It seems right that it was another person not only because of the great difference in order but because [in Luke's version] he himself replies to the Lord's question, and it is in his reply that the two commandments are mentioned. And after the Lord told him to do the great thing that he himself had said was in the law — *Do this and you shall live* (Lk 10:28) — the evangelist adds the following: *But he, wishing to justify himself, said, And who is my neighbor?* (Lk 10:29) The Lord then tells the story of the man who was going down from Jerusalem to Jericho and fell among robbers.[262] So, because he is referred to as testing [Jesus] and because he himself responds with the two commandments, he is not commended as a good person after the Lord admonishes him by saying, *Do this and you shall live*, since it is said of him, *But he, wishing to justify himself.* On the other hand, in the incident recorded by both Matthew and Mark in the same order, he is commended so highly that the Lord says to him, *You are not far from the kingdom of God* (Mk 12:34). So it is quite probable that these are to be taken as two separate persons.

74,143. Matthew continues, *Now, while the Pharisees were gathered together, Jesus asked them, What do you think of the Christ? Whose son is he? They said to him, David's. He said to them, How is it, then, that David in the Spirit calls him Lord, saying, The Lord said to my Lord, sit at my right hand, until I make your*

---

261. See Lk 10:25–28.
262. See Lk 10:30–37.

enemies your footstool? If David calls him Lord, how is he his son? And no one was able to answer him a word, and from that day on no one dared ask him any more questions. (Mt 22:41–46) Mark also records this in the same order.[263] After omitting [the story] of the man who asked Jesus about the first commandment in the law, Luke rejoins the same order, too, telling of this question that the Lord asked the Jews about how Christ was the Son of David.[264] It does not make any difference that in Matthew, when Jesus asks them what they think of the Christ and whose son he would be, they respond, *David's* (Mt 22:42), and then he asks them why David called him Lord. But according to the other two, Mark and Luke, we find neither the question nor the answer. We must understand that these two evangelists describe the Lord's thoughts after their response. He spoke to those listeners whom he wished to teach usefully from his authority and to dissuade from the scribes' teaching. [These listeners] knew Christ only as one who was from the seed of David according to the flesh and did not understand that he was God, and the Lord even of David. Therefore these two evangelists report that the Lord spoke of those erroneous [teachers] to those whom he wished to free from their errors. So when he says, "What do you say?" as Matthew tells it, it should be taken as spoken not just to them but to those whom he wished to instruct.

75,144. Matthew continues this way, keeping to the order of the narrative: *Then Jesus spoke to the crowds and to his disciples, saying, The scribes and Pharisees sit on Moses's seat, so observe and do everything they tell you but not what they do. For they say but do not do* (Mt 23:1–3), and so forth, until where it says, *You shall not see me again until you say, Blessed is he who comes in the name of the Lord* (Mt 23:39). Luke reports a similar discourse of the Lord's against the Pharisees and scribes and lawyers, although it [occurs] in the house of a certain Pharisee who had invited him to dinner.[265] When he tells this story he departs from Matthew's order at the point where both of them report what the Lord said of the sign of Jonah's three days and nights, and of the queen of the South, and of the Ninevites, and of the unclean spirit that returned to find the house cleaned.[266] After this discourse Matthew says, *While he was still speaking to the crowds, behold, his mother and brothers stood outside, asking to speak to him* (Mt 12:46). But after this discourse of the Lord's in Luke, he records some things that the Lord said which were omitted by Matthew, and then he departs from the order he had shared with Matthew: *While he was speaking, a certain Pharisee asked him to dine with him, and he went in and sat at table. But the Pharisee was astonished and began to say something, because he did not wash before dinner. And the Lord said to him, Now, you Pharisees clean the outside of the cup and platter.* (Lk 11:37–39) Then he [relates] other sayings against the scribes and Pharisees and lawyers, similar to those in the passage from Matthew that we now have under consideration. When

263. See Mk 12:35–37.
264. See Lk 20:41–44.
265. See Lk 11:37–52.
266. See Lk 11:24–26.29–32; Mt 12:39–45.

Matthew records these things he does not specify that they were said in the house of this Pharisee, but neither does he describe the place in such a way that they could not have been in his house. Yet, since the Lord had already come to Jerusalem from Galilee, and this discourse is in the context of the things [discussed] above [that happened] after his arrival, then we should probably take them as having happened in Jerusalem. But Luke's account is of what the Lord [said] while going to Jerusalem. So it seems to me that these are two similar discourses, and that the one [evangelist] reports the one and the other the other.

75,145. We should certainly consider how it may be said, *You shall not see me again until you say, Blessed is he who comes in the name of the Lord* (Mt 23:39), when according to Matthew they had already said this.[267] And Luke gives this statement as the Lord's response to those who warned him to leave there because Herod wished to kill him. He records the same words as Matthew, but as spoken against Jerusalem itself. For Luke tells it this way: *On that same day some Pharisees came, saying to him, Get out and leave here, for Herod wants to kill you. And he said to them, Go, tell that fox, Behold, I cast out demons and perform cures today and tomorrow, and on the third day I complete my course. Nevertheless I must walk today and tomorrow and the next day, for it cannot be that a prophet should perish outside of Jerusalem. Jerusalem, Jerusalem, which kills the prophets and stones those who are sent to you, how often did I wish to gather your children together, as a bird gathers her nestlings under her wings, but you would not! Behold, your house is abandoned to you. But I say to you, you shall not see me until the time comes when you will say, Blessed is he who comes in the name of the Lord.* (Lk 13:31–35) But this narrative of Luke's does not seem to be inconsistent with the crowds' saying at the Lord's arrival in Jerusalem, *Blessed is he who comes in the name of the Lord.* For, according to Luke's order, he had not come there yet, and this had not been said. But [Luke] does not say that he left there, not to return until the time when that would be said. He continues his journey until he comes to Jerusalem. And when he said, *Behold, I cast out demons and perform cures today and tomorrow, and on the third day I complete my course* (Lk 13:32), this is to be understood as said in a mystical and figurative sense. For he did not suffer on the third day after that, [as shown] when he says right after that, *I must walk today and tomorrow and the next day* (Lk 13:33). So we must also understand this as mystical: *You shall not see me until the time comes when you will say, Blessed is he who comes in the name of the Lord* (Lk 13:35). This refers to his return, when he will be completely revealed. And when he says, *I cast out demons and perform cures today and tomorrow, and on the third day I complete my course,* this refers to his body, which is the Church. For demons are cast out when the gentiles abandon their ancestral superstitions and believe in him, and cures are performed when they live by his commandments, renouncing the devil and this world, all the way to the end, that is, the resurrection. Then there will be that completion of *the*

---

267. See Mt 21:9.

third day, when the Church will be brought to the perfection of angelic fullness by the immortality of the body. Therefore Matthew's order is not to be understood as a digression to something else. Rather, we should understand that either Luke anticipates the events that happened in Jerusalem, inserting them here as he recalls them, before his narrative brings the Lord to Jerusalem, or else, when he was near that city, his reply to those who warned him to beware of Herod was similar to what Matthew says he spoke to the crowds when he was in Jerusalem, when all these things mentioned above had already occurred.

76,146. Matthew continues and says, *And Jesus left the Temple and went away, and his disciples approached him to show him the buildings of the Temple. But he answered, saying to them, Do you see all these? Amen, I say to you, there shall not be one stone left on another that will not be thrown down.* (Mt 24:1–2) Mark also records this in nearly the same order, after he makes a small digression to report the story of the widow who put two coins into the treasury, which only he and Luke record.[268] After the Lord speaks with the Jews about how they think the Christ is David's son, Mark also tells of his warning against the Pharisees and their hypocrisy, a passage that Matthew has given more fully, telling more of the things said then.[269] After this passage, which Mark gives briefly and Matthew gives more fully, Mark goes on, as I said, to the widow who was so poor and yet so generous. Without adding anything else, Mark rejoins Matthew's [order], speaking of the destruction of the Temple.[270] Luke also records the [question] of how the Christ is David's son and then a few of the warnings against the hypocrisy of the Pharisees. Then, like Mark, he goes on to the widow who put two coins in the treasury. And then he goes on to the future destruction of the Temple,[271] as do Matthew and Mark.

77,147. Matthew continues, saying, *As he sat on the Mount of Olives, the disciples came to him privately, saying, Tell us, when will this be, and what will be the sign of your coming and of the end of the age? And answering, Jesus said to them, Watch, so that no one misleads you. For many shall come in my name, saying, I am the Christ, and they shall mislead many* (Mt 24:3–5), and so forth, until where it says, *And they shall go into eternal punishment, but the righteous into eternal life* (Mt 25:46). Now we must consider this long discourse of the Lord's, as it is [reported] in the three evangelists, Matthew, Mark, and Luke. They all include it in nearly the same order.[272] Each of them includes some things that are unique to his version, but none that would make us fear any suspicion of inconsistency. What must be shown, however, is that, where they are speaking similarly, no contradiction can be supposed. For, if such were to be found, one could not say that it was a similar thing said by the Lord at a different time, for the narratives of all three are the same as to subjects and times. Although they do not all keep the same order,

268. See Mk 14:41–44; Lk 21:1–4.
269. See Mk 12:38–40; Mt 23:1–36.
270. See Mt 24:1–2; Mk 13:1–2.
271. See Lk 20:41–21:6.
272. See Mk 13:4–37; Lk 21:7–36.

the same sentiments are expressed by the Lord, and so this should not affect the understanding or expression of the subject itself, so long as their reports of what he said do not contradict one another.

77,148. Matthew says, then, *And this Gospel of the kingdom shall be preached through all the world as a testimony to all nations, and then the end shall come* (Mt 24:14), and this is also reported by Mark in the same order, *The Gospel must first be preached to all nations* (Mk 13:10). Although he does not say, *And then the end shall come*, when he says the word *first* in *The Gospel must first be preached to all nations*, it means the same thing. For, since they had asked him about the end, when he says, *The Gospel must first be preached to all nations, first* means that it will be before the end comes.

77,149. Again, Matthew says, *So, when you see the abomination of desolation spoken of by the prophet Daniel standing in the holy place, let the reader understand* (Mt 24:15), and Mark says it this way, *But when you see the abomination of desolation standing where it should not be, let the reader understand* (Mk 13:14). Although the words are changed, it carries the same meaning. He says *where it should not be* because it should not be in the holy place. Luke says neither *When you see the abomination of desolation standing in the holy place* nor *where it should not be* but instead *But when you see Jerusalem surrounded by an army, then know that its desolation has come near* (Lk 21:20). The abomination of desolation, therefore, will be in the holy place at that time.

77,150. Then Matthew says, *Then let those who are in Judea flee to the mountains; and let him who is on the roof not go down to take anything from his house; and let him who is in the field not turn back to take his tunic* (Mt 24:16–18), and Mark also records this in nearly the same words.[273] Luke says, *Then let those who are in Judea flee to the mountains* (Lk 21:21). This is like what the other two say, but what follows is different: *Let those who are inside*[274] *go out, and let those who are in country not enter it. For these are the days of vengeance, so that everything that has been written may be fulfilled.* (Lk 21:21–22) Now, there seems to be some difference here, for [the first two] say, *Let him who is on the roof not go down to take anything from the house* (Mt 24:7; Mk 13:15), while [Luke] says, *Let those who are inside go out* (Lk 21:21). Perhaps there will be such a huge disturbance in the face of so great and immediate a disaster that those trapped in the siege (who are referred to by the phrase, *who are inside*), will be on the roof, stunned and wishing to see the impending doom or possible escape. But how can he say, *Let them go out*, when he has just said, *But when you see Jerusalem surrounded by an army*? And what follows, *Let those who are in the country not enter it*, seems to be part of one complete warning. And one could see how those who are outside should not enter into it, but how are those who are inside of it to leave when the city is already surrounded by an army? Perhaps this *inside of it* refers to when the

---

273. See Mk 13:14–16.
274. I.e., inside the city.

danger will be so urgent that there will be no time to escape with one's life, so that then the soul should be ready and free, neither occupied with nor weighed down by carnal desires. And the other two indicate this when they say *on the roof* or *up on the roof.* So, when [Luke] says, *Let them go out,* it means that they should not hold on to the desire of this life but should be ready to pass on to another life. This is the same as when the other two say, "Let him not come down to take anything from the house," which means that his affections should not turn towards the flesh, as though it could obtain anything useful. And when [Luke] says, *Let those who are in the country not enter it,* this means that those who have with a good purpose of heart put themselves outside of carnal lust are not to be in it again or desire it. This is the same as when the others say, *Let him who is in the field not return to take his clothes* (Mt 24:18; Mk 13:16), which means being involved with worries that had been stripped away from him.

77,151. What Matthew says, *But pray that your flight may not be in winter or on a sabbath* (Mt 24:20), Mark partly says and partly omits — *Pray that it may not happen in winter* (Mk 13:18). Luke says nothing of this but instead mentions something unique to himself, which it seems to me illuminates the sense that the others have expressed obscurely: *But take heed to yourselves, so that your hearts not be weighed down with hangovers and drunkenness and the cares of this life, lest that day come upon you unexpectedly. Like a snare it shall come upon all those who dwell on the face of the whole earth. But watch at all times, praying that you be found worthy to escape all these things that will happen.* (Lk 21:34–36) This should be understood as the same escape that Matthew records and that should not happen in winter or on a sabbath. *Winter* refers to the cares of this life, which Luke expresses more clearly, while *sabbath* [refers] to hangovers and drunkenness. For sad cares are indeed like winter, and hangovers and drunkenness submerge and bury the heart in carnal pleasure and decadence, which is an evil indicated by the term *sabbath*, for at that time, as is also the case now, the Jews had the most evil habit of indulging in pleasures on that day, while they were ignorant of the spiritual sabbath. But if the words of Matthew and Mark are understood another way, then Luke can also be speaking of something else, and there will be no question of inconsistency to trouble us. We have not now attempted to explain the Gospels but only to defend them from slanderous charges of inaccuracy and deceit. Other things that Matthew and Mark both place in this discourse raise no questions. But what [Matthew has in common] with Luke, Luke does not place in this discourse, although he does agree with his order. Instead, he inserts them as he recalls them, so that they are anticipatory, reporting things earlier that the Lord in fact said later; or else it is to be understood that the Lord said them twice, once at one time, according to Matthew, and once at another, according to [Luke].

78,152. Matthew continues, *And it happened that, when Jesus had finished all these utterances, he said to his disciples, You know that after two days it will be the Passover, and the Son of Man will be handed over to be crucified* (Mt 26:1–2). This is confirmed by the other two, Mark and Luke, who also do not deviate from the same order, but they do not report this as said by the Lord, for they omit any mention of it. Mark himself says, *It was now two days before the Passover and the feast of unleavened bread* (Mk 14:1). And Luke says, *The feast day of unleavened bread drew near, which is called the Passover* (Lk 22:1). *Drew near* can mean the same as *after two days*, but the other two express this more clearly. John reports the nearness of this feast day three separate times — in connection with other things on the previous two occasions, but on this third occasion it is clear that he is speaking of the same events as the other three, that is, when the Lord's passion was already near.

78,153. But to those who investigate this with too little care, the following may seem to be a contradiction. After saying that the Passover was in two days, Matthew and Mark then report that Jesus was in Bethany, where they speak of the precious ointment.[275] But when John tells the story of the ointment he says that Jesus came to Bethany six days before the Passover.[276] How, therefore, can [Matthew and Mark] say that it was two days before the Passover and then tell the same story of the anointing at Bethany as John tells, although he says that it was six days before the Passover? This is a problem only if one does not understand that Matthew and Mark mention the anointing at Bethany as a reminiscence of something that happened earlier, when there were six days before the Passover and not something [that happened] after the statement that it was two days before the Passover. For, after they say that it was two days before the Passover, they do not then go on to the events at Bethany by saying, "After these things, when he was in Bethany." Instead, Matthew says, *Now, when Jesus was in Bethany* (Mt 26:6), and Mark [says], *When he was in Bethany* (Mk 14:3). So it can be understood that they are speaking of a time before what was said two days before the Passover. From John's narrative, then, it can be gathered that six days before the Passover he came to Bethany, where the dinner took place where the precious ointment is mentioned. Then he came to Jerusalem, sitting on an ass. Then those things happened that they record as happening after his arrival in Jerusalem. So, although the evangelists do not note it, we are to understand that from the day he came to Bethany, where he was anointed, to the day when all these things were done and said, four days passed, during which was the day that they specify as being two days before the Passover. Now, when Luke says, *The feast day of unleavened bread drew near* (Lk 22:1), although he does not specify two days, the nearness that he reports ought to be taken as equivalent to these two days. But when John says, *The Passover of the Jews was near* (Jn 11:55), he wishes to express that it was not two days but rather six days before the Passover. So, when he records some things after this statement, he wishes to show how near the Passover was: *Six days before the Passover, Jesus came to Bethany, where Lazarus had died, whom Jesus raised from the dead. There they made him a supper.* (Jn 12:1–2) This

---

275. See Mt 26:6–13; Mk 14:3–9.
276. See Jn 12:1.

is what Matthew and Mark record as a recapitulation after they say that it was two days before the Passover. In their recapitulation they return to that day in Bethany, which was six days before the Passover, and tell the same story as John does of the supper and the ointment. From there he went to Jerusalem and, after those things happened that are narrated, he arrived at the day that was two days before the Passover. Then they digress to recall what had already happened at the anointing in Bethany, and they return from there to the point in their narrative where they had digressed—that is, to the Lord's discourse that was given two days before the Passover. For, if we omit what happened in Bethany, which they tell by way of recapitulation and recollection, we thereby set the order straight, so that what the Lord said reads this way according to Matthew: *You know that after two days is the Passover, and the Son of Man shall be handed over to be crucified. Then the chief priests and the elders of the people gathered in the palace of the high priest, who was called Caiaphas, and took counsel together in order to take Jesus by stealth and kill him. But they said, Not on the feast day, lest there be a tumult among the people.... Then one of the twelve, who was called Judas Iscariot, went to the chief priests* (Mt 26:2–5.14), and so forth.[277] For between where it is said, *Lest there be a tumult among the people* (Mt 26:5), and where it is said, *Then one of the twelve, who was called Judas Iscariot* (Mt 26:14), they have inserted as a recapitulation [the story] of Bethany. And if we omit this we have restored the flow of the narrative in such a way as to show that there is no inconsistency in the sequence. And if we similarly omit from Mark the dinner at Bethany, which he also inserts as a recapitulation, then his narrative will also keep its order, as follows: *It was two days before the Passover and the feast of unleavened bread, and the chief priests and scribes sought how to take him by stealth and kill him. For they said, Not on the feast day, lest there be a tumult among the people.... Then Judas Iscariot, one of the twelve, went to the chief priests in order to hand him over* (Mk 14:1–2.10), and so forth. Again, between where it is said, *Lest there be a tumult among the people* (Mk 14:2), and what we appended to it, *And Judas Iscariot, one of the twelve* (Mk 14:10), the [story] of Bethany is placed as a recapitulation. Luke simply omits what happened at Bethany. This is what we say concerning the six days before the Passover, which John mentions in his story of what happened at Bethany, and the two days before the Passover, which Matthew and Mark mention right before they report the same events in Bethany as John does.

79,154. After this passage that we have now finished considering, Matthew continues his narrative and says, *Then the chief priests and the elders of the people gathered in the palace of the high priest, who was called Caiaphas, and took counsel together in order to take Jesus by stealth and kill him. But they said, Not on the feast day, lest there be a tumult among the people. Now, when Jesus was in Bethany in the house of Simon the leper, a woman came up to him with an*

---

277. Augustine is correct in a way, but the splitting up of the story is usually taken as deliberate Markan artfulness. See J. R. Edwards, "Markan Sandwiches: The Significance of Interpolations in Markan Narratives," in *Novum Testamentum* 31 (1989) 193–216.

alabaster flask of precious ointment and poured it on his head as he sat at table (Mt 26:3–7), and so forth, until where it says, *What she has done shall be told in memory of her* (Mt 26:13). Now, we must consider what happened in Bethany concerning the woman and the precious ointment. Luke reports a similar incident, in which even the name of the man with whom the Lord dined is the same, for he calls him Simon.[278] But just as one person may have two names, so it is even more possible for two people to have one name, and in this there is nothing contrary to either nature or human custom. Therefore it is more believable that the Simon in whose house this happened in Bethany [according to Luke] is different than the leper. And Luke does not say that this happened in Bethany, although he does not report what city or village it happened in; nonetheless, his narrative does not seem to be about the same place. I think there is only one way to understand this. It is not that [the woman in Matthew's version] is different than the woman who was a sinner and came to Jesus' feet and kissed them and washed them with her tears and wiped them with her hair and anointed them with ointment, to whom the Lord applied the parable of the two debtors and said that her many sins were forgiven her because she loved much; rather, it was the same Mary who did this twice. Luke records the first time, when she came with humility and tears and obtained forgiveness for her sins. Although John does not narrate the incident like Luke, he does report it while mentioning the same Mary when he begins to tell the story of the raising of Lazarus, before [Jesus] came to Bethany. His narrative is thus: *Now, a certain man was sick, Lazarus of Bethany, the village of Mary and her sister Martha. It was Mary, who anointed the Lord with ointment and wiped his feet with her hair, whose brother Lazarus was ill.* (Jn 11:1–2) By saying this, John confirms Luke, who said that it was in the house of a certain Simon, a Pharisee, that Mary did this. But what she did again in Bethany is something else, not included in Luke's narrative but told similarly by the [other] three, John, Matthew, and Mark.[279]

79,155. Let us see, then, what the correspondence is among these three, Matthew, Mark, and John. For here there is no doubt that they are telling the same story of what happened in Bethany. All three report that the disciples murmured against the woman because of the costliness of the ointment. Matthew and Mark say the ointment was poured on the Lord's head, but John [says] on his feet. But the rule that we demonstrated in the case of the feeding of the crowds with the five loaves shows that this is not a contradiction. For in that instance one does not fail to report that they sat down by fifties and hundreds, while the other says only fifties, but no contradiction can be found,[280] which could have been the case, however, if one had said only hundreds, and the other only fifties; but even were that so, it ought to have been clear that it was in fact both. This example should remind us, as I counseled before, that, when the evangelists record two different

---

278. See Lk 7:36–50.
279. See Jn 12:1–8; Mt 26:6–13; Mk 14:3–9.
280. See above at II,46,98.

things individually, we should understand both to have happened. So we should accept that the woman poured not only on his head but also on his feet. But perhaps, since Mark reports that she broke the alabaster jar when she poured it on his head, some absurd and slanderous person could deny that there could have been anything left in the broken vessel to pour on his feet. But, while someone who was striving against the truth of the Gospel might argue that it was broken in such a way that there was nothing left in it, someone who was striving for the truth of the Gospel would make a better and more moral argument that it was not broken in such a way that everything was poured out. And if that slanderer is so obstinately blind as to try to break the harmony of the evangelists with this broken alabaster jar, he should rather accept that it was poured on his feet before it was broken. So it remained intact until it was poured on his head, when it was broken and completely emptied. We know that [to go] from the head [down] is an appropriate order, but going from the feet up to the head is also an appropriate order.

79,156. The other things that happen here do not seem to me to raise any question. The other [evangelists] say that the disciples murmured against the wasting of the precious ointment,[281] while John reports that it was Judas, because he was a thief.[282] But I think it is clear that the term *disciples* also indicates Judas, as we showed in regard to Philip at [the miracle] of the five loaves,[283] when the plural was used instead of the singular.[284] Or it may be understood that the other disciples either felt or spoke as [Judas did] or were persuaded by what Judas said, so that Matthew and Mark express in words what everyone was thinking. But Judas said it because he was a thief, while the others [did it] because of their care for the poor. And John chooses to report it as [said] only by that one whose habitual stealing he believed should be shown on this occasion.

80,157. Matthew continues, *Then one of the twelve, who is called Judas Iscariot, went to the chief priests and said to them, What are you willing to give me, and I shall hand him over to you? And they agreed on thirty pieces of silver* (Mt 26:14–15), and so forth, until where it says, *And the disciples did as Jesus had told them, and they prepared the Passover* (Mt 26:19). Nothing in this passage can be thought to be contrary to Mark and Luke, who tell the story similarly.[285] Matthew says, *Go into the city to a certain man, and say to him, The teacher says, my time is at hand; I shall keep the Passover at your house with my disciples* (Mt 26:18). This indicates the same person whom Mark and Luke call *the head of the household* or *the master of the house*, who showed them the upper room where they were to prepare the Passover.[286] So Matthew inserted *a certain man* as his own way of phrasing it, because he wished to show us by a short comment who

---

281. See Mt 26:8–9; Mk 14:4–5. Mark, however, does not actually specify that it was the disciples who murmured.
282. See Jn 12:4–6.
283. See Jn 6:7.
284. See above at II,46,96.
285. See Mk 14:10–16; Lk 22:3–13.
286. See Mk 14:13; Lk 22:10.

this was. For if he had said that the Lord had said, "Go into the city and say to him/it,[287] 'The teacher says, My time is at hand, I shall keep the Passover at your house with my disciples,'" then one might have thought they were to speak to the city itself. So he inserts as his own comment and not as something said by the Lord, whose commands he is narrating, that the Lord told them to go to a certain person. He did this because it seemed to him to be enough to show the meaning of the one giving the commands, without having to state everything. For who does not know that no one says, "Go to someone"? And if it had been "Go to anyone" or "anyone you please," this would be a more natural way of talking, but it would have been unclear to what man they had been sent. Mark and Luke show that he was a particular person, although they omit his name. But the Lord knew to whom he sent them and, so that those he was sending would be able to find that person, he told them something that they should look for—a man carrying a bottle or jar of water. And if they followed him they would come to the house that he intended. So he could not have said, "Go to anyone you please," which is a correct way of speaking but which would not have given the truth of the matter that he was trying to convey here. How much less, then, could he have said, "Go to someone," which is not even a correct way of speaking! So clearly the disciples were not sent by the Lord to anyone they pleased but to *a certain man*, that is, to a particular person. This is something the evangelist could have told us of himself if he had said, "He sent them to a certain person, to say to him, 'I shall keep the Passover at your house.'" Or he could [have said], "He sent them to a certain person, saying, 'Go, say to him, I shall keep the Passover at your house.'" So to the Lord's words, *Go into the city*, he added, *to a certain man* (Mt 26:18), not as though they were spoken by the Lord but to show us that there was in the city a particular person, whose name has been omitted, to whom the Lord's disciples were sent to prepare the Passover. And, after inserting these words of his own, he goes back to the order of the Lord's words, saying, *and say to him, The teacher says* (Mt 26:18). And if you ask to whom [they were to say this], then the correct answer is this: to that man to whom the evangelist indicates that they were sent with the insertion of his own phrase, *to a certain man*. This may be an unusual expression, but it can be understood as correct in this way. Or perhaps, since Matthew is supposed to have written in Hebrew, that language has some rule that would make it a typical idiom, even if the Lord himself uttered the entire phrase; but only those who know [that language] could decide this. Even in Latin one could say something like this: "Go into the city to a certain man, who will be shown to you as the man who meets you carrying a bottle of water." If the command was given this way, one could act upon it without ambiguity. Or even if it was said, "Go into the city to a certain man who lives in this or that place, in such and such a house," then the description of the place and the specification of the house would make it understandable, so one

---

287. The dative pronoun *ei*, which is used here, is ambiguous and can be translated as either "to him" or "to it."

could do it. But when these and other similar indications are left unsaid, and the person says, "Go to a certain man and say to him," it is not possible to obey him. For, although he wishes a particular person to be understood when he says "to a certain man," he has not indicated how he is to be recognized. But, if we take the statement as one made by the evangelist himself, then its necessary brevity will make it obscure but not incorrect. Finally, Mark refers to a bottle and Luke to a jar.[288] One has indicated the kind of vessel, and the other its size, and both have preserved the true sense.

80,158. Matthew continues, *When it was evening he sat with the twelve disciples, and as they were eating he said to them, Amen, I say to you, one of you will hand me over. And they were very sad and began to say to him one after another, Is it I, Lord?* (Mt 26:20–22) and so forth, until where it says, *Then Judas, who betrayed him, answered and said, Is it I, rabbi? He said to him, You have said so* (Mt 26:25). In these things that we have now raised for consideration, the other evangelists, who also record these matters,[289] present nothing questionable.

---

288. "Bottle…jar": *lagenam…amphoram.*
289. See Mk 14:17–21; Lk 22:14–23; Jn 13:21–27.

Book Three

1,1. Now we are at the point in all four Gospels from which they necessarily proceed together to the end without diverging from one another. And if one records something that another omits, it seems to me that we can show more readily that all the evangelists are in agreement if from here on we bring together everything from all of them and arrange it into a single narrative and presentation. It seems to me that what we have been trying to explain will be done more conveniently and easily this way. So we are attempting to make a narrative from all the things recorded through the witness of the evangelists, each of whom recollected out of all these things what he could or what he wished. Moreover, all these things were said by all of them, which shows that there is no disagreement among them in any way.

1,2. Let us begin, then, with Matthew: *As they were eating, Jesus took bread and blessed it and broke it and gave it to his disciples and said, Take and eat, this is my body* (Mt 26:26). Mark and Luke also record this.[1] Although Luke mentions the cup twice, both before and after he gave the bread, this is because when he says it first it is, as usual, in anticipation, and what he inserts in its proper place is not recorded earlier. So, when taken together, the meaning is the same as that in the other Gospels. But John says nothing about the body and blood of the Lord at this point, though he clearly testifies that the Lord said this much more fully at another time.[2] Now he records how the Lord rose from supper and washed the disciples' feet, and he also tells why he acted thus, for the Lord showed in a hidden way through the witness of Scripture that he was to be betrayed by one who ate his bread. Then he comes to the incident that the other three also relate: *When he had said this, Jesus was troubled in spirit and testified and said, Amen, amen, I say to you, one of you will betray me. Then,* John adds, *the disciples looked at one another, uncertain of whom he spoke.* (Jn 13:21–22) *Then they were very sorrowful,* as Matthew and Mark say, *and began to say to him one by one, Is it I?* (Mt 26:22; Mk 14:19) *And he answered, saying,* as Matthew continues, *He who dips his hand in the dish with me is the one who will betray me.* And Matthew continues in this way: *The Son of Man goes as it is written of him. But woe to that man by whom the Son of Man is betrayed! It would have been better for that man if he had not been born.* (Mt 26:23–24) With this Mark is in agreement even as to the order.[3] Then Matthew continues, *Then Judas, who betrayed him, answered and said, Is it I, Rabbi? And he said to him, You have said so.* (Mt 26:25) These words do not indicate whether he was the one. For this may be understood as meaning, "I do not say so." It is possible that Judas said this and the Lord answered without any of the others noticing.

---

1. See Mk 14:17–22; Lk 22:14–23.
2. See Jn 6:32–64.
3. See Mk 14:20–21.

1,3. Matthew then continues, inserting the mystery of the body and blood, as it was given to the disciples by the Lord; Mark and Luke do so likewise.[4] But after he had handed over the cup, he spoke again about his betrayer, as Luke says in the following: *But behold, the hand of him who betrays me is with me on the table. And the Son of Man goes as it has been determined, but woe to that man by whom he is betrayed.* (Lk 22:21–22) Here we should understand that then there follows what John narrates and the others omit, just as John omits some things that they have given. For, after the handing over of the cup and the Lord's words given by Luke, *But behold, the hand of him who betrays me is with me on the table* (Lk 22:21), and so forth, John adds the following: *Now, one of the disciples whom Jesus loved was lying on Jesus' breast, so Simon Peter beckoned to him and said to him, Who is it of whom he speaks? And so, as he lay on Jesus' breast, he said to him, Lord, who is it? Jesus answered, The one to whom I will offer this bread when I have dipped it. And when he had dipped the bread he gave it to Judas, the son of Simon Iscariot. And after the morsel, Satan entered into him.* (Jn 13:23–27)

1,4. This might make it appear that John not only contradicts Luke, who says earlier that Satan entered into the heart of Judas when he agreed with the Jews to betray him for money, but even that he contradicts himself. For John says earlier, before he received the morsel, *During supper, when the devil had already put it into the heart of Judas to betray him* (Jn 13:2). How does he enter into the heart except by putting evil inclinations into the thoughts of evil people? But we ought to understand that Judas was now more fully possessed by the devil. The same sort of thing happened to those good men who received the Holy Spirit after his resurrection when he breathed on them, saying, *Receive the Holy Spirit* (Jn 20:22), for they later received more when he was sent down from above on the day of Pentecost.[5] In the same way Satan then entered into this man after the morsel. And as John then records, *Jesus said to him, What you are going to do, do quickly. Now, no one at the table knew why he said this to him. Some thought that, because Judas had the purse, Jesus had said to him, Buy what we need for the feast, or that he should give something to the poor. So, after receiving the morsel he went out, and it was night. And after he said this, Jesus said, Now the Son of Man is glorified, and God is glorified in him. And God will also glorify him in himself,[6] and will glorify him immediately.* (Jn 13:27–32)

2,5. *Little children, yet a little while I am with you. You will seek me, but, as I said to the Jews, Where I am going you cannot come, and I say this now to you. A new commandment I give to you, that you love one another; as I have loved you, so you also should love one another. By this everyone will know that you are my disciples, if you have love for one another. Simon Peter said to him, Lord, where are you going? Jesus answered, Where I am going you cannot follow me*

---

4.   See Mt 26:26–28; Mk 14:22–24; Lk 22:17–20.
5.   See Acts 2:1.
6.   Some manuscripts add the beginning of the verse, *And if God is glorified in him, God will also*, etc.

now, but you shall follow afterwards. Peter said to him, Why can I not follow you now? I will lay down my life for you. Jesus answered, Will you lay down your life for me? Amen, amen, I say to you, the cock shall not crow till you have denied me three times. (Jn 13:33–38) John, from whose Gospel I have taken this passage, is not the only one to give this prediction to Peter of his own denial, for the other three also record it.[7] They do not all introduce it at the same point in the discourse, however. For Matthew and Mark both put it in the same order and in the same place in their narrative, after the Lord left the house in which they had eaten the Passover, while Luke and John have it before he left there. This might easily be understood either as a recapitulation by two of them or as an anticipation by the other two. But this seems less than likely, as not only the words differ but also the Lord's ideas, which moved Peter to offer his presumptuous statement that he would die with the Lord or for the Lord. This leads us to understand, instead, that he made his presumptuous statement three times, at different points in Christ's discourses, and that the Lord answered three times that, before the cock crowed, he would deny him three times.

2,6. Nor is it incredible that Peter might have been moved to such a presumptuous statement at several distinct times, just as he denied him several times, or that the Lord answered similarly three times, just as after the resurrection Christ asked three times, with no deeds or words intervening, whether he loved him, and that, when Peter gave the same answer three times, he gave the same command three times to feed his sheep.[8] That Peter showed his presumptuousness three times, and that he heard the Lord's warning of his triple denial three times, will be shown to be more believable by the words of the evangelists themselves, who record the Lord's utterances in different words and different contexts. Let us recall that passage from John's Gospel in which he clearly said the following: *Little children, yet a little while I am with you. You will seek me, but, as I said to the Jews, Where I am going you cannot come, and I say this now to you. A new commandment I give to you, that you love one another; as I have loved you, so you also should love one another. By this everyone will know that you are my disciples, if you have love for one another. Simon Peter said to him, Lord, where are you going?* (Jn 13:33–36) Now here it is clear that what moved Peter to say, *Lord, where are you going?* was the Lord's words, for he had heard him say, *Where I am going you cannot come.* Then Jesus answered Peter, *Where I am going, you cannot follow me now, but you shall follow afterwards* (Jn 13:36). And then Peter asked, *Why can I not follow you now? I will lay down my life for you.* (Jn 13:37) The Lord responded to this presumptuous statement by predicting his denial. But Luke records the Lord's words this way: *Simon, behold, Satan asked to have you, so that he could sift you like wheat. But I have prayed for you, that your faith may not fail, and when you have turned around, strengthen your brethren.* (Lk

7.   See Mt 26:33–35; Mk 14:26–31; Lk 22:31–34.
8.   See Jn 21:15–17.

22:31–32) And then he adds Peter's response: *Lord, I am ready to go with you to prison and to death* (Lk 22:33). And he said, *I say to you, Peter, the cock shall not crow today until you deny three times that you know me* (Lk 22:34). Who cannot see that this is a different occasion than the one when Peter was moved to make a presumptuous statement? And Matthew says this: *And when they had sung a hymn, they went out to the Mount of Olives. Then Jesus said to them, You shall all be offended because of me this night, for it is written, I will strike the shepherd, and the sheep of the flock shall be scattered. But after I am raised up, I will go before you to Galilee.* (Mt 26:30–32) Mark says the same.[9] But what similarity is there between these words and their meaning and those in which Peter makes his presumptuous statement either in John or in Luke? And Matthew continues thus: *Peter answered and said to him, Although they are all offended because of you, I will never be offended. And Jesus said to him, Amen, I say to you that this night, before the cock crows, you shall deny me three times. Peter said to him, Even if I must die with you, I will not deny you. And so said all the disciples.* (Mt 26:33–35)

2,7. Mark records this in almost the same words, except that he makes the prediction more specific, giving the Lord's words this way: *Amen, I say to you that today, this very night, before the cock crows twice, you shall deny me three times* (Mk 14:30). Thus they all say that the Lord predicted that Peter would deny him before the cock crowed, but they do not all say how many times the cock would crow; only Mark notes this explicitly. So it seems to some persons that he is not in agreement with the other [evangelists], but this is because they are not careful enough, and especially because their efforts are obscured by the fact that their minds are sunk in animosity against the Gospel. Overall, Peter's denial is a triple denial. For his spirit remained agitated and his purpose remained false until he was reminded of what had been predicted; then he was healed through bitter weeping and sorrow of the heart.[10] But if everything—that is, all three denials—began after the cock crowed once, then three of the accounts would appear to be false. For Matthew says this: *Amen, I say to you that this night, before the cock crows, you shall deny me three times* (Mt 26:34). And Luke says, *I say to you, Peter, the cock shall not crow today until you deny three times that you know me.* And John says, *Amen, amen, I say to you, the cock shall not crow until you have denied me three times* (Jn 13:38). Although the words and their sequence are different, they give the same sense of what the Lord said, namely, that before the cock crowed, Peter was to deny him. But if the whole triple denial happened before the cock began to crow, then Mark obviously attributes to the Lord a superfluous statement: *Amen, I say to you that today, this very night, before the cock crows twice, you shall deny me three times.* But what point is there in saying *before the cock crows twice*? If the whole triple denial was completed before the first cockcrow, then is it not evident that it must also have been completed before the second, third, and

---

9.   See Mk 14:26–28.
10.   See Mt 26:75 par.

any other cockcrows that took place that night? But the three evangelists note that the triple denial began before the first cockcrow, but not when Peter completed it. They note its extent and its beginning—that it was to be repeated three times and begin before the cockcrow. As for Peter's frame of mind before the cockcrow, it is possible to understand it overall. For although the actual words of denial began before the first cockcrow and finished with the whole triple denial before the second cockcrow, Peter's frame of mind and his fear were fully conceived before the first. Nor does it matter how long the intervals of time were between those three announcements if his heart was so completely possessed before the first cockcrow that he was filled with such fear as to be able to deny the Lord when he was asked not just once but twice and even a third time. So, if we look at it more correctly and carefully, it is the same as saying that the man who looks at a woman with lust has already committed adultery in his heart.[11] For Peter's words just expressed that fear that he had so intensely conceived in his mind that he was able to prolong his denial of the Lord to three times; hence the whole triple denial should be assigned to that time when the fear that caused his triple denial took control of him. Even if the actual words of the denial only began to burst forth from him after the first cockcrow, when his heart was assailed by the questions, it would be neither absurd nor untruthful to say that he denied him three times before the cock crowed, since before the cock crowed his mind had already been possessed by a fear that was able to bring him to a third denial. It should trouble us even less if the triple denial and the triple statements of the denier had begun before the cockcrow, even if they were not completed before the first cockcrow. Suppose someone were to say, "Tonight, before the cock crows, you will write me a letter in which you will insult me three times." There would be no reason to call the prediction false if the person began to write before the cock crowed at all and finished after the first cockcrow. Therefore, when Mark has the Lord say, *Before the cock crows twice, you shall deny me three times*, this indicates more clearly the intervals between the sayings. This will be made clear when we come to that section of the gospel narrative, so that the agreement among the evangelists may be shown.

2,8. But if they seek the actual words that the Lord said to Peter, it is impossible to find them and useless to try, for his meaning, which is what he wanted to make known through saying these words, can be completely understood even through the diverse words of the evangelists. Either Peter, moved at different points in the Lord's discourse, made his presumptuous statement at three separate times, and three times the Lord predicted his denial, which is more probable, based on our investigation, or else the records of all the evangelists could be reduced to one version with some other narrative order, so that it could be shown that there was one occasion on which Peter made his presumptuous statement and the Lord made his prediction that he would deny him. But in either case no inconsistency among the evangelists can be shown, for there is none.

---

11.   See Mt 5:28.

3,9. Now, as much as possible, let us follow the very order given by all [of the evangelists]. After this prediction that was made to Peter, according to John, John continues the Lord's discourse: *Let not your heart be troubled. You believe in God; believe also in me. In my Father's house there are many rooms* (Jn 14:1–2), and so forth, narrating the rest of his noble and most sublime discourse until he comes to that place where the Lord says, *O righteous Father, the world has not known you, but I know you, and these know that you have sent me. And I made known to them your name, and I shall make it known, so that the love with which you have loved me will be in them, and I in them.* (Jn 17:25–26) But when *there was a dispute among them as to which of them was to be regarded as the greatest,* as Luke recalls, *he said to them, The kings of the gentiles exercise lordship over them, and those who have authority over them are called benefactors. But not so with you. Rather, let the greatest among you be as the youngest, and the leader as one who serves. For who is greater, the one who sits at table or the one who serves? Is it not the one who sits at table? But I am among you as one who serves. And you are those who have remained with me in my trials. And I assign to you, as my Father assigned to me, a kingdom, so that you may eat and drink at my table in my kingdom and sit on thrones judging the twelve tribes of Israel.* (Lk 22:24–30) Then Luke adds that the Lord said to Simon: *Behold, Satan asked to have you, so that he could sift you like wheat. But I have prayed for you, that your faith may not fail, and when you have turned around, strengthen your brethren. And he said to him, Lord, I am ready to go with you into prison and into death. And he said, I say to you, Peter, the cock shall not crow today until you deny three times that you know me. And he said to them, When I sent you out without a bag, or wallet, or shoes, did you lack anything? They said, Nothing. He said to them, But now, let him who has a bag take it, and likewise a wallet. And let him who does not have a sword sell his clothes and buy one. For I say to you that this scripture must be fulfilled in me, And he was reckoned among the transgressors, for the things concerning me have their fulfillment. And they said, Lord, here are two swords. And he said to them, It is enough.* (Lk 22:31–38) Then, as Matthew and Mark record it: *And when they had sung a hymn, they went out to the Mount of Olives. Then Jesus said to them, You shall all be offended because of me this night. For it is written: I will strike the shepherd, and the sheep of the flock shall be scattered. But after I am raised up, I shall go before you to Galilee. Peter answered and said to him, Though they all are offended because of you, I will never be offended. And Jesus said to him, Amen, I say to you that this night, before the cock crows, you shall deny me three times. Peter said to him, Even if I must die with you, I will not deny you. And so said all the disciples.* (Mt 26:30–35) We have already introduced this in Matthew's version, but Mark also has it in nearly the same number of identical words,[12] except for the difficulty we have already explained concerning the cockcrow.

---

12. See Mk 14:26–31.

4,10. Matthew continues his narrative, then, and says, *Then Jesus came with them to a place called Gethsemane* (Mt 26:36). Mark says the same and so does Luke, although he does not specify the name of the place: *And he came out and went, as was his custom, to the Mount of Olives; and the disciples followed him. And when he came to the place he said to them, Pray that you may not enter into temptation.* (Lk 22:39–40) This is the place which the other two tell us was called Gethsemane. This is to be understood as the garden which John mentions when he says, *When Jesus had spoken these words, he went out with his disciples across the Kidron stream, where there was a garden, which he and his disciples entered* (Jn 18:1). Then, following Matthew's account: *He said to the disciples, Sit here, while I go over there and pray. And taking with him Peter and the two sons of Zebedee, he began to be sorrowful and sad. Then he said to them, My soul is sorrowful even to death; stay here and watch with me. And going a little further, he fell on his face and prayed, saying, My Father, if it be possible, let this cup pass from me; nevertheless, not as I will but as you will. And he came to the disciples and found them sleeping, and he said to Peter, So, could you not watch with me one hour? Watch and pray that you may not enter into temptation. For the spirit indeed is willing, but the flesh is weak. Again, he went away a second time and prayed, saying, My Father, if this cup cannot pass unless I drink from it, your will be done. And he came again and found them sleeping, for their eyes were heavy. And he left them and went away again, and prayed a third time, saying the same thing. Then he came to his disciples and said to them, Sleep now and take your rest. Behold, the hour is at hand, and the Son of Man shall be betrayed into the hands of sinners. Rise, let us go. Behold, the one who will betray me is at hand.* (Mt 26:36–46)

4,11. Mark also gives this in the same way and in the same order, abbreviating some of the phrases and expanding others.[13] However, within Matthew's version these sayings seem to be inconsistent. For, after he returned to his disciples from praying the third time, he said to them, *Sleep now and take your rest. Behold, the hour is at hand, and the Son of Man shall be betrayed into the hands of sinners. Rise, let us go. Behold, the one who will betray me is at hand.* (Mt 26:45–46) How can he say, *Sleep now and take your rest,* and then immediately go on to say, *Behold, the hour is at hand,* and then, *Rise, let us go*? Those who read a disagreement in these words seek to pronounce *Sleep now and take your rest* as if it were said accusingly and not permissively. It could rightly be taken this way if necessary. But Mark records it as follows: first he said, *Sleep now and take your rest,* and then he added, *It is enough,* and finally, *The hour has come. Behold, the Son of Man is betrayed* (Mk 14:41). It can be understood, then, in this way: After he said, *Sleep now and take your rest,* the Lord was silent for a while, so that they did what he had permitted them to do. Then later he said, *Behold, the hour is at hand.* Between these two statements, Mark has him say, *It is enough,* which means, "The

---

13. See Mk 14:32–42.

rest you have had is enough now." But, since the Lord's silence in this interval is not specifically mentioned and the interval is understood as compressed, these words seem to take on a different meaning.

4,12. Luke does not specify how many times he prayed. But he mentions something which the others do not—that while he was praying he was strengthened by an angel, and that as he prayed more earnestly he had bloody sweat, with drops falling down to the ground.[14] So when Luke says, *And when he arose from prayer he came to his disciples* (Lk 22:45), he does not indicate how many times he had prayed. But there is nothing inconsistent between this and the other two. Indeed, John says that he went into the garden with his disciples[15] but does not record what he did there until his betrayer came with the Jews to arrest him.

4,13. So these three narrate the same event, just as one person could do three times with some differences but no real contradiction. For example, Luke is more specific as to how far away he withdrew when he went away to pray, saying that it was *about a stone's throw away* (Lk 22:41). Mark first gives in his own words how the Lord prayed that, *if it were possible, that hour might pass from him* (Mk 14:35), indicating his passion, which he then also signifies with the word *cup*. He then gives the Lord's own words: *Abba, Father, all things are possible to you; remove this cup from me* (Mk 14:36). If we take these words together with those of the other two evangelists, which Mark has given above in his own words, then the whole phrase appears as *Father, if it is possible,* for *all things are possible to you, remove this cup from me.* He said *if it is possible* so that one could not suppose that he minimized the Father's power. For he did not say "if you are able" but *if it is possible,* for whatever he wills is possible. So, to say *if it is possible* is the same as saying "if you will." Mark makes it clear how one should understand *if it is possible* by saying *all things are possible to you.* And when they record that he said, *Nevertheless, not as I will but as you will* (Mt 26:39 par), which means the same as saying, "Nevertheless, not my will but yours be done," it shows quite clearly that Jesus was referring to the Father's will and not to his ability when he said *if it is possible.* Luke shows this even more clearly, for he does not say *if it is possible* but *if you are willing* (Lk 22:42). For even greater clarity we may join Mark's insertion to [Luke's] clearer statement, so that it reads thus: *If you are willing,* for *all things are possible to you, remove this cup from me.*

4,14. As for the fact that Mark records that he said not only *Father* but *Abba, Father,* this is because *abba* is in Hebrew what "father" is in Latin. Perhaps the Lord said this symbolically, wishing to show that he bore this sorrow in that part of him which is his body, the Church, of which he has been made the cornerstone, and which comes to him partly from the Hebrews, to whom he refers when he says *Abba,* and partly from the gentiles, to whom he refers when he says *Father.*[16]

---

14. See Lk 22:43–44, which is not found in the best Greek manuscripts.
15. See Jn 18:1.
16. See Eph 2:11–22.

The apostle Paul does not neglect this mystery[17] when he says, *In whom we cry Abba, Father* (Rom 8:15), and again, *God has sent his Spirit into our hearts, crying, Abba, Father* (Gal 4:6). For it is right that the good teacher and true savior, by suffering together with those who are weaker, should reveal in himself that his martyrs should not despair, even though perhaps at the time of their suffering some sorrow might creep into their hearts because of human weakness. They will vanquish this weakness by preferring the will of God over their own, since he knows what is best for those upon whom he looks. This is not the time to discuss this whole matter fully, for now we are dealing with the agreement of the evangelists, from whose diversity of words we learn to our benefit that the one thing which is necessary in order to hear the truth is not the words but the meaning that the speaker wished to convey. For the word *Father* is the same as the words *Abba, Father*, but, as intimating a mystery, *Abba, Father* is clearer, while *Father* is sufficient to indicate unity. It should be believed, then, that the Lord said *Abba, Father*. But this would not illuminate his meaning, except for the fact that others say only *Father*, thereby showing that these two Churches, one Jewish, the other Greek, are really one. Therefore *Abba, Father* is to be understood in the same way as when the Lord says, *I have other sheep that are not of this fold* (Jn 10:16). This certainly means the gentiles, since he also had sheep among the people of Israel. But he goes on to add, *I must bring them also, so that there may be one fold and one shepherd* (Jn 10:16). So, just as *Abba, Father* includes the Israelites and the gentiles, so too does *Father* alone point to the unity of the flock.

5,15. *While he was still speaking*, as Matthew and Mark say, *behold, Judas, one of the twelve, came, and with him a great crowd with swords and clubs, from the chief priests and elders of the people. The one who betrayed him had given them a sign, saying, The one whom I shall kiss is the man; seize him. And immediately he came up to Jesus and said, Hail, Rabbi, and kissed him.* (Mt 26:47–49)[18] And as Luke tells us, he first said to him, *Judas, do you betray the Son of Man with a kiss?* (Lk 22:48) Then, as Matthew reports, he said, *Friend, why have you come?* (Mt 26:50) Then he said what John records, *Whom do you seek? They answered him, Jesus of Nazareth. Jesus said to them, I am he. And Judas, who betrayed him, stood with them. When he said to them, I am he, they drew back and fell to the ground. Again he asked them, Whom do you seek? And they said, Jesus of Nazareth. Jesus answered, I told you that I am he; so, if you seek me, let these men go. This was to fulfill what had been spoken, Of those whom you gave me, I lost not one.* (Jn 18:4–9)

5,16. Then Luke continues, *And when those who were around him saw what would follow, they said to him, Lord, shall we strike with the sword? And one of them*, as all four [evangelists] tell us, *struck the servant of the high priest, and cut off his ear* (Lk 22:49–50) (Luke and John tell us it was his right ear,[19] and John says

---

17.　"Mystery": *sacramentum*, as immediately below.
18.　See Mk 14:43–45.
19.　See Lk 22:50; Jn 18:10.

it was Peter who struck and that the one who was struck was called Malchus.[20]) Then Luke says, *Jesus answered and said, Let it be for now.* (Lk 22:51) Then we have what Matthew records: *Put your sword back in its place, for all who take the sword shall perish by the sword. Do you think that I cannot ask my Father, and he will at once send me more than twelve legions of angels? But how then should the Scriptures be fulfilled, that it must be so?* (Mt 26:52–54) We may add to these words what John reports he said at that time: *Shall I not drink the cup which the Father has given me?* (Jn 18:11) Then, as Luke says, he touched the ear of the one who had been struck and healed him.[21]

5,17. It should not trouble us as if it were a contradiction when Luke says that, after the disciples asked whether they should strike with the sword, the Lord answered, *Let it be for now*, as though he said this after the blow had been struck and was pleased with what had happened but did not want anything more to be done, whereas the words in Matthew might be understood to mean that the whole incident of Peter's using his sword displeased the Lord. For it is more likely that when they asked him, *Lord, shall we strike with the sword?* (Lk 22:49) and he answered, *Let it be for now*, he meant, "Do not be troubled by what is about to happen. These men will be allowed to go so far, that is, to arrest me and to fulfill what has been written of me." In the time between their question and the Lord's response, however, Peter struck, out of his desire to make a defense and from his greater fervor for the Lord. But, although it is not possible to say two things at once, it is possible to do two things at once. For [Luke] would not have said, *Jesus answered* (Lk 22:51), unless he were responding to their question and not to Peter's deed. Only Matthew records how Jesus judged Peter's deed. But Matthew does not say, "Jesus answered Peter, 'Put your sword back'" but *Then Jesus said to him, Put your sword back* (Mt 26:52), and it seems that the Lord said this after the deed. And when Luke puts it this way, *Jesus answered and said to them, Let it be for now*, this must be taken as his answer to those who questioned him. But as we said, the single blow was struck in the time between the question and the Lord's response; therefore Luke thought it right to narrate it in this order, so he placed it between the question and the answer. There is nothing inconsistent between this and what Matthew says, *For all who take the sword shall perish by the sword* (Mt 26:52), that is, those who may use the sword. But there might appear to be some inconsistency here if the Lord's answer showed approval of this one voluntary use of the sword that produced a non-lethal wound. Overall consistency may be understood, however, in what was said to Peter. As we have remarked before, we may thus put this together with what Luke and Matthew have reported: *Let it be for now, and put your sword back in its place. For all who take the sword shall perish by the sword*, and so forth. I have already explained how *Let it be for now*

---

20.   See Jn 18:10.
21.   See Lk 22:51.

is to be understood. If there is anyone who can explain it better, let him do so, as long as the truth of the evangelists is affirmed.

5,18. After this Matthew continues, recording what he said to the crowds at that moment: *Have you come out as against a robber, with swords and clubs to take me? Daily I sat with you, teaching in the Temple, and you did not seize me.* (Mt 26:55) He then added some other words, which are given by Luke: *But this is your hour, and the power of darkness* (Lk 22:53). And then he said, as Matthew gives it, *But all this has happened so that the Scriptures of the prophets might be fulfilled. Then all the disciples forsook him and fled* (Mt 26:56), as Mark also says.[22] *But a young man followed him, with a linen garment on*, as Mark records, *and they seized him, but he left the linen garment and ran away from them naked* (Mk 14:51–52).

6,19. *Then those who had seized Jesus led him to Caiaphas the high priest, where the scribes and the elders had gathered* (Mt 26:57), as Matthew says. But first he was led to Annas, the father-in-law of Caiaphas, as John tells us.[23] Mark and Luke do not mention the high priest's name at all.[24] Also, as John reports, he was led away bound, and a tribune and a cohort and the servants of the Jews were in that crowd. As Matthew says, *Peter followed him at a distance into the hall of the high priest, and going inside he sat with the servants to see the end* (26:58). At this point in the narrative Mark adds, *And he warmed himself by the fire* (Mk 14:54). Luke records something similar: *Peter followed at a distance; and when they had kindled a fire in the middle of the hall and sat down together, Peter was among them* (Lk 22:54–55). And John says that *Simon Peter followed Jesus, and so did another disciple. And since that other disciple was known to the high priest, he entered the hall of the high priest* (Jn 18:15), as John says. *But Peter stood outside at the door* (Jn 18:16), according to John. *The other disciple, who was known to the high priest, went out and spoke to the woman who kept the door and brought in Peter* (Jn 18:16). This shows how Peter got inside and was in the hall, as the other three also mention.

6,20. *Now, the chief priests and the whole council*, as Matthew says, *sought false testimony against Jesus, so that they could hand him over to death, but they found none, although many false witnesses came forward* (Mt 26:59–60). *For their testimony did not agree* (Mk 14:56), as Mark says when he recalls the same moment. *At last two false witnesses came forward*, as Matthew says, *and said, This man said, I am able to destroy the Temple of God and to build it up in three days* (Mt 26:60–61). Mark too records that there were others who said, *We heard him say, I will destroy this Temple that is made with hands, and in three days I will build another that is not made with hands. And*, as Mark says, *their testimony did not agree.* (Mk 14:58–59). Then Matthew says this: *And standing up, the high priest said to him, Have you no response to make to what they testify against you? But*

---

22. See Mk 14:50.
23. See Jn 18:13.
24. See Mk 14:53–65; Lk 22:54–62.

Jesus was silent. And the high priest said to him, I adjure you by the living God, tell us if you are the Christ, the Son of God. Jesus said to him, You have said so. (Mt 26:62–64) Mark reports this in different words, although he does not mention that the high priest adjured him. But he shows how it is the same whether Jesus said *You have said so* or *I am* (Mk 14:62), for Mark says the following: *And Jesus said, I am. And you shall see the Son of Man seated at the right hand of power, and coming with the clouds of heaven.* (Mk 14:62) Matthew also says this, although he does not say that Jesus answered, *I am.* Matthew records the following: *Then the high priest tore his clothes and said, He has spoken blasphemy. Why do we still need witnesses? Behold, you have now heard his blasphemy. What do you think? And they answered and said, He deserves death.* (Mt 26:65–66) Mark says the same.[25] And Matthew continues, *Then they spat in his face and beat him, and others slapped him in the face with the palms of their hands, saying, Prophesy to us, Christ! Who is it that struck you?* (Mt 26:67–68) Mark says this too, although he also reports that they covered his face.[26] Luke testifies to these things as well.[27]

6,21. It should be understood that the Lord endured these things until morning in the high priest's house, to which he was first led and where Peter also was tested. But, as for Peter's testing, which took place as the Lord was being subjected to these indignities, [the evangelists] do not all give their account in the same order. For Matthew and Mark record them first and then the testing of Peter,[28] whereas Luke presents first the testing of Peter and then the indignities enacted against the Lord.[29] John begins with Peter's testing, then goes on to some of the indignities enacted against the Lord, then mentions that he was sent to Caiaphas the high priest, then resumes the story that he had begun of Peter's testing in the house where he had first been led, and then resumes the sequence, showing how the Lord was led to Caiaphas.[30]

6,22. Matthew, then, continues thus: *Now Peter was sitting outside in the hall. And a maid came up to him and said, You also were with Jesus the Galilean. But he denied it before them all, saying, I do not know what you mean. And when he went out to the porch, another maid saw him and said to those who were there, This man was with Jesus of Nazareth. And again he denied it with an oath: I do not know the man. And after a little while those who stood by came up and said to Peter, Certainly you also are one of them, for your speech makes you known. Then he began to curse and swear that he did not know the man. And immediately the cock crowed.* (Mt 26:69–74) Such is Matthew's version. But it is to be understood that after he went out, when he had denied him once, the cock crowed the first time; although Matthew does not mention this, Mark does.[31]

25. See Mk 14:63–64.
26. See Mk 14:65.
27. See Lk 22:63–65.
28. See Mt 26:69–75; Mk 14:66–72.
29. See Lk 22:56–62.
30. See Jn 18:15–27.
31. See Mk 14:66–72.

6,23. It was not when he was outside the door, however, that he denied the Lord again but when he returned to the fireplace, although it was not necessary to record when he returned there. Mark, then, continues his story thus: *And he went out the door of the hall, and the cock crowed. And a maid saw him again and began to say to those who stood by, This man is one of them. And he denied it again.* (Mk 14:68–70) This is not the same maid, though, but another one, as Matthew tells us. Indeed, it should be understood that at the second denial he was accused by two people—the maid, mentioned by Matthew and Mark, and another person, mentioned by Luke. For Luke tells the story this way: *Peter followed at a distance, and when they had kindled a fire in the middle of the hall and sat down together, Peter was among them. But a maid saw him sitting in the light, and she looked at him intently and said, This man also was with him. But he denied it, saying, Woman, I do not know him. And after a little while another person saw him and said, You also are one of them.* (Lk 22:54–58) When Luke says, *And after a little while*, this indicates the time during which Peter went outside and the first cock crowed. And then he came back, which is why John says he was standing by the fireplace when he denied him again. John not only does not mention the cock crowing for the first time at Peter's first denial (which the others do, except Mark), but he also does not report that he was sitting by the fire when the maid recognized him; this is all that he says: *The maid who kept the door said to Peter, Are not you also one of this man's disciples? He said, I am not.* (Jn 18:17) Then he goes on to those things that happened with Jesus in that house, recording those that seemed right to him to include: *Now the servants and attendants were standing by the coals warming themselves, because it was cold. Peter also was with them, standing and warming himself.* (Jn 18:17–18) Therefore it should be understood that at this point Peter had gone out and come back again. For at first he had been sitting by the fire, and then, after returning, he began to stand there.

6,24. But perhaps someone will say that Peter had not gone out but had only gotten up in order to go out. This might be said by someone who thought that the second questioning and denial happened outside the door. Let us see, then, how John continues: *The high priest then asked Jesus about his disciples and his teaching. Jesus answered him, I have spoken openly to the world. I have always taught in the synagogue and in the Temple, where all the Jews come together. I have said nothing in secret. Why do you ask me? Ask those who heard me what I said to them. Behold, they know what I said. When he had said this, one of the attendants standing by slapped Jesus, saying, Is that how you answer the high priest? Jesus answered him, If I have spoken wrongly, bear witness to the wrong; but if I have spoken well, why do you hit me? And Annas sent him bound to Caiaphas the high priest.* (Jn 18:19–24) This clearly shows that Annas was high priest, for he had not yet been sent to Caiaphas when he was asked, *Is that how you answer the high priest?* (Jn 18:22) And at the beginning of his Gospel Luke records that these two,

Annas and Caiaphas, were high priests.[32] After this, John returns to the story he had begun of Peter's denial—that is, back to the house where the things he is narrating happened. It was from there that Jesus was sent to Caiaphas, to whom he was being led at the beginning of this scene, as Matthew reports.[33] John records these things as a recapitulation of Peter's story, rejoining it in order to complete the narrative of the triple denial: *Now Peter was standing and warming himself. They said to him, Are not you also one of his disciples? He denied it and said, I am not.* (Jn 18:25) We find here, then, that Peter's second denial occurred while he was standing by the fireplace, not by the door. But this could not have been the case unless he had returned after having gone outside. So it is not that he went out and the other maid saw him outside but that she saw him as he was going out, as he was getting up to go out. She noticed him then and said to those who were around the fire inside the hall, *This man was with Jesus of Nazareth* (Mt 26:71). Upon hearing this, the one who had gone out came back in and swore to those who were incensed against him that he did not know the man. Mark also says of this maid, *And she began to say to those who were standing around, This man is one of them* (Mk 14:69). Although she was not speaking to him but to those who had remained when he went out, he nonetheless heard her and returned to stand by the fire again and responded to their words with a negative. It is at this point that John says, *They said, Are not you also one of his disciples?* (Jn 18:25) We understand that this was said when he had returned and was standing there, which accords with the fact that Peter had to deal not only with that other maid mentioned by Matthew and Mark at the second denial but also with that other person whom Luke mentions. This is why John says, *They said to him* (Jn 18:25). It may be that, after he went out, the maid said to those who were with her in the hall, *This man is one of them* (Mk 14:69), and that Peter heard this and came back in order to clear himself in some way by a denial. Or, as seems more probable, perhaps he did not hear what was said about him as he went out, and that afterwards he returned, and the maid and that other person mentioned by Luke said to him, *Are not you also one of his disciples?* and he said, *I am not.* And when the other person mentioned by Luke insisted more tenaciously, saying, *You also are one of them*, Peter said, *Man, I am not* (Lk 22:58). But when we bring together all the testimony of the evangelists on this subject, it becomes clear that Peter's second denial happened inside the hall by the fire and not at the door. Matthew and Mark, who record that he went out, have for the sake of brevity not mentioned his return.

6,25. Now let us consider how much agreement there is in the third denial, which we have only examined in Matthew's version. Mark continues, then, and says, *And after a little while those who were standing by said to Peter, Certainly you are one of them, for you are a Galilean. But he began to curse and swear, I do not know this man of whom you speak. And immediately the cock crowed a*

---

32. See Lk 3:2.
33. See Mt 26:57.

second time. (Mk 14:70–72) Luke continues his narrative this way: *And after about an hour another one insisted, saying, Certainly this man also was with him, for he is a Galilean. And Peter said, Man, I do not know what you are saying. And immediately, while he was still speaking, the cock crowed.* (Lk 22:59–60) John continues his account of Peter's third denial thus: *One of the high priest's servants, a relative of the man whose ear Peter had cut off, said, Did I not see you in the garden with him? Peter again denied it, and immediately the cock crowed.* (Jn 18:26–27) The amount of time Matthew and Mark mean by *after a little while* is specified by Luke, who says, *and after about an hour.* John, however, does not mention this interval. Matthew and Mark do not use the singular but the plural number when talking about those who set upon Peter, while Luke speaks of only one, and John specifies this as a relative of the man whose ear Peter cut off. But it is easy to understand that Matthew and Mark use the plural in place of the singular, which is a common way of talking, or else that one of those who knew and had seen Peter was foremost in the attack and that the others followed his confidence in pressing upon Peter. So two of the evangelists speak of the group together in the plural number, while the other two prefer to single out the one who was the leader of the group. But Matthew claims that this was said to Peter himself: *Certainly you also are one of them, for your speech makes you known* (Mt 26:73). Likewise, John claims that this was said to Peter: *Did I not see you in the garden with him?* (Jn 18:26) But Mark presents them as talking among themselves about Peter, *Surely he is one of them, for he is a Galilean* (Mk 14:70; Lk 22:59),[34] just as Luke says that this was said about Peter but not to him—*Another one insisted, saying, Certainly this man also was with him, for he is a Galilean* (Lk 22:59). We may either understand that those who speak of Peter as the one addressed are holding to the sense, for talking about him right in front of him is more or less the same as talking to him. Or perhaps both these happened, and some record the one way, others the other way. Finally, we understand that the second cockcrow happened after the third denial, as Mark indicates.

6,26. Matthew, then, continues thus and says, *And Peter remembered the word of Jesus that he had said to him, Before the cock crows, you shall deny me three times. And he went out and wept bitterly.* (Mt 26:75) Mark puts it this way: *Peter remembered the word that Jesus had said to him, Before the cock crows twice, you shall deny me three times. And he began to weep.* (Mk 14:72) Luke says this: *And the Lord turned and looked at Peter. And Peter remembered the Lord's word, how he had said, Before the cock crows, you shall deny me three times. And Peter went out and wept bitterly.* (Lk 22:61–62) John does not mention that Peter remembered and wept. Luke's statement, that *the Lord turned and looked at Peter* (Lk 22:61), needs more careful consideration as to how it is to be taken. For, although both inner and outer halls might be called the same thing,

---

34. This conflation of Mk 14:70 and Lk 22:59 is noteworthy in that Augustine quotes the former correctly (in the second person) at the beginning of III,6,25 above.

Peter was in an outer hall with the servants, who were warming themselves along with him at the fire. And it is not plausible that the Lord would have been heard by the Jews in such a place, so this cannot refer to a bodily look. For, when Matthew said, *Then they spat in his face and beat him, and others slapped him in the face with the palms of their hands, saying, Prophesy to us, Christ! Who is it that struck you?* he went on to say, *Now, Peter was sitting outside in the hall* (Mt 26:69), which he would not have said unless those things that were being done to the Lord were going on inside. And it can be gathered from Mark's narrative that these things happened not only inside but in the upper parts of the house. For after Mark narrates these things, he continues and says, *And as Peter was below in the hall* (Mk 14:66). Matthew says, *Now, Peter was sitting outside in the hall*, in order to show that the other things happened inside, just as Mark says, *And as Peter was below in the hall*, in order to show that these other things happened not only inside but in the upper parts of the building. How, then, could the Lord have looked at Peter in a bodily way? For this reason it seems to me that it must have been a look from God himself that brought before his mind how many times he had denied him and how the Lord had predicted it, and thus the Lord's merciful look moved him to repentance and salutary weeping. We speak this way every day when we say, "Lord, look upon me" or "The Lord looked upon him," when the divine mercy has delivered someone from some danger or hardship, and that is how it is said, *Look upon me and hear me* (Ps 13:3) and *Turn, O Lord, and deliver my soul* (Ps 6:4). I think that this should be taken the same way: *The Lord turned and looked at Peter. And Peter remembered the Lord's word.* (Lk 22:61) Moreover, although [the evangelists] use *Jesus* more frequently in the narratives than *Lord*, here Luke puts *Lord*: *The Lord turned and looked at Peter. And Peter remembered the Lord's word.* Matthew and Mark, who do not mention this look, do not say that he remembered *the Lord's word* but *the word of Jesus* (Mt 26:75).[35] Therefore we understand this look from Jesus not as one made by a human eye but by the eye of God.

7,27. Matthew continues, then, and says, *When morning came, all the chief priests and elders of the people took counsel against Jesus to put him to death. And when they had bound him, they led him away and delivered him to Pontius Pilate, the governor.* (Mt 27:1–2) Mark says the same: *As soon as it was morning, the chief priests held a meeting with the elders and scribes and the whole council, and they bound Jesus and led him away and delivered him to Pilate* (Mk 15:1). And Luke, after finishing his account of Peter's denial, summarizes what was done to Jesus towards morning, as seems to be the case: *Now, the men who were holding Jesus mocked him and beat him; and when they had blindfolded him they struck his face and asked him, saying, Prophesy to us! Who is it that struck you? And they said many other blasphemous things against him. And when it was day, the elders of the people and the chief priests and the scribes came together and led*

---

35. See Mk 14:72.

him to their council, saying, If you are the Christ, tell us. But he said to them, If I tell you, you will not believe me; and if I also ask you, you will not answer me or let me go. But from now on the Son of Man shall be seated at the right hand of the power of God. And they all said, Are you the Son of God, then? And he said, You say that I am. And they said, What further testimony do we need? We ourselves have heard it from his own mouth. And the whole multitude of them arose and brought him before Pilate. (Lk 22:63–23:1) Luke narrates all this, and it should be understood that Matthew and Mark narrate similar things—that the Lord was asked whether he was the Son of God and that he said, *I say to you that hereafter you shall see the Son of Man sitting at the right hand of the Power and coming in the clouds of heaven* (Mt 26:64).[36] These things seem to have happened at daybreak, for Luke says, *And when it was day* (Lk 22:66). So his narrative is similar, although he also records something that the others omit. We understand that the false witnesses spoke against the Lord at night; this is briefly recorded by Matthew and Mark and omitted by Luke, although he narrates what happened at daybreak. Matthew and Mark give continuous narratives of what happened to the Lord up until morning, but then they resume the story of Peter's denial; when this is over they return to the events of the morning, so that they produce a complete account of what happened to the Lord. But they do not record what happened at daybreak. John also, after telling what happened to the Lord as much as seemed right to him and recording the whole story of Peter's denial, says, *Then they led* Jesus *to Caiaphas in the praetorium. It was early.* (Jn 18:28) From this we are to understand either that there was some compelling reason for Caiaphas to be at the praetorium so that he was not present when the other chief priests interrogated the Lord, or else that the praetorium was in his house. In the latter case they must from the beginning have been leading Jesus to Caiaphas, whom he now finally met at the end. But since they brought Jesus to him as one who was already guilty of a crime, and since it already seemed to Caiaphas that Jesus ought to die, there was no delay in handing him over to Pilate for death. This is why at this point Matthew narrates what happened between Pilate and the Lord.

7,28. But first he makes a digression to record the end of Judas the traitor, which he alone narrates, and he says, *Then Judas, who had betrayed him, seeing that he was condemned, repented and brought back the thirty silver pieces to the chief priests and elders, saying, I have sinned by betraying innocent blood. They said, What is that to us? You see to it. And he threw the silver pieces into the Temple and left and went and hanged himself. But the chief priests took the silver pieces and said, It is not lawful to put them in the treasury, since they are blood money. And they took counsel and bought with them the potter's field in which to bury strangers. Therefore that field has been called Akeldama, that is, Field of Blood, to this day.*[37] *Then was fulfilled what was spoken by the prophet Jeremiah, saying,*

36. See Mk 14:62.
37. Augustine is conflating here Mt 27:8 and Acts 1:19.

*And they took the thirty silver pieces, the price of the one on whom a price had
been set, on whom some of the children of Israel had put a price, and they gave
them for the potter's field, as the Lord directed me.* (Mt 27:3–10)

7,29. But if it troubles someone that this testimony is not found in the writings of the prophet Jeremiah, [38] so that it damages his trust in the evangelist, let
him note first that not all the copies of the Gospels have it that this was said by
Jeremiah but only by a prophet. So we can say that those copies are more accurate
that do not include the name of Jeremiah, for this was said by a prophet, but that
prophet was Zechariah. Hence it seems that those copies that include the name of
Jeremiah are inaccurate, for they ought to have had the name of Zechariah or no
name at all; one such copy does this, saying that it was by a prophet, which could be
understood to be Zechariah. But this defense may be used by anyone who pleases.
It is not satisfactory to me, because most copies include the name of Jeremiah,
and those who study the Gospels most carefully in Greek declare that it is found
in the more ancient Greek copies. Moreover, there would have been no reason to
add this name and thereby make the copy misleading. But there would have been
a reason to remove it from so many copies; bold ignorance would have led to this
when faced with the problem of why this testimony is not found in Jeremiah.

7,30. But how is this to be understood, except that it must have been brought
about by the secret plan of God's providence that ruled over the evangelists' minds?
It might have been that Jeremiah instead of Zechariah occurred to Matthew's
mind as he wrote his Gospel. But if this had happened, he would undoubtedly
have corrected it, since others would have noticed it as they read his work while
he was still alive in the flesh. But he must have thought as he was writing, under
the guidance of the Holy Spirit, that the name of the one prophet would not have
occurred to him instead of the other unless the Lord wanted it to be written this
way. But why did the Lord want it this way? One certainly ought to consider this
first and most useful reason, that it shows the miracle of how all the holy prophets spoke with one voice, remaining in agreement with one another—a miracle
much greater than if all the things said by all the prophets had been said by the
mouth of one single man. Therefore one ought to accept without question whatever
the Holy Spirit says through them, and to accept what is said by one as said by
all and what is said by any as said by each. If the utterances of Jeremiah are as
much Zechariah's as Jeremiah's, then, and if the utterances of Zechariah are as
much Jeremiah's as Zechariah's, why would Matthew correct it when he looked
back over what he had written and found that the one name had occurred to him
instead of the other? Would he not rather follow the authority of the Holy Spirit,
by whom he felt his mind to be ruled more than we do, and therefore leave his
writing unchanged, as the Lord had directed him by his influence? This was done
to show us that there is such agreement among the words of the prophets that

---

38. The quotation from "Jeremiah" is notoriously problematic, as it corresponds to no one passage
in Jeremiah or anywhere else. It seems to be a combination of references to Jer 18:1–6; 19:1–12;
32:6–44; Zc 11:12–13.

it is not ridiculous but most appropriate if we cite Jeremiah for something that Zechariah said. Consider the following present-day example. Suppose someone wished to show us someone else's words, but he said the name of someone other than the person who said them. But this other person was the closest friend and confidant of the person who had said the words. As soon as the person says the one name instead of the other, he realizes his mistake and corrects it but says, "I did speak truthfully, however." How would we interpret this, except that there is such agreement between the speaker whom he wished to name and the person whose name actually occurred to him that one can credit either with the words? This ought to be so much the more understood and approved of in the case of the holy prophets that we should accept the books of all of them as though they were one single book. One ought to believe that in this book there are no discrepancies as to the subject matter—as indeed none would be found—and that in it there is a greater consistency of truthfulness than if all these things had been said by one man, even if he were the most learned. Therefore, although there are those among the unbelieving or ignorant who seek to make this into some kind of argument to show the discord among the holy evangelists, the faithful and learned ought rather to claim that this shows the unity of the holy prophets.

7,31. There is another reason why the authority of the Holy Spirit did not just allow the name of Jeremiah to be put here instead of Zechariah but actually commanded it, although it seems to me that I should explore this more fully at another time and not prolong this discussion further, since necessity demands an end to this work. In Jeremiah we find that he bought a field from his brother's son and gave him money for it,[39] but the price—thirty silver pieces—is not mentioned there, as it is in Zechariah, whereas the purchase of the field is not mentioned in Zechariah. It is clear that the evangelist interprets the prophecy of the thirty silver pieces as fulfilled by the Lord, for this was his price. But perhaps Matthew wishes to show by a mysterious symbol that what Jeremiah said about the purchase of a field also related to Jesus, so he did not give the name of Zechariah, who mentioned the thirty silver pieces, but Jeremiah, who mentioned the purchase of a field. So, on reading the Gospel and finding there the name of Jeremiah, and then reading Jeremiah and not finding any testimony about thirty silver pieces there but finding instead mention of the purchase of a field, the reader would be encouraged to compare the two and thus unlock the real meaning of the prophecy and how it relates to what was fulfilled in the Lord. For that is what Matthew adds to his testimony when he says, *Upon whom the sons of Israel put a price, and they gave them for the potter's field, as the Lord directed me* (Mt 27:9–10). This is in neither Zechariah nor Jeremiah. So we must accept it as a beautiful and mysterious addition made by the evangelist himself; it had been given to him by revelation from the Lord that a prophecy of this kind related to the price that had been put upon the Lord. In Jeremiah he is commanded to put the record of the purchase of the

---

39. See Jer 32:6–44.

field into a pottery vessel. In the Gospel the price of the Lord was used to buy the potter's field for the burial of strangers, showing that there is permanent rest for those who are strangers in this age and are buried with Christ through baptism.[40] This purchase of a field also signifies what the Lord said to Jeremiah, that in the land there would a remnant freed from their captivity.[41] I thought it right to lay this out in order to show how one should carefully and precisely find the unity of the prophetic witnesses and then compare it with the gospel narrative. This is what Matthew inserts regarding the traitor Judas.

8,32. Then he continues and says, *Jesus stood before the governor, who questioned him, saying, Are you the king of the Jews? Jesus said to him, You say so. But when he was accused by the chief priests and the elders, he gave no answer. Then Pilate said to him, Do you not hear how many things they testify against you. But he did not answer him with a single word, so that he wondered greatly. Now, on the feast day he was accustomed to release to the people one prisoner, whomever they wished. And they had then a notorious prisoner called Barabbas. So, when they had gathered, Pilate said to them, Whom do you want me to release to you, Barabbas or Jesus, who is called Christ? For he knew that they had handed him over out of envy. But while he was sitting on the judgment seat his wife sent word to him, saying, Have nothing to do with that just man, for I have suffered many things today in a dream because of him. The chief priests and the elders, however, persuaded the people to ask for Barabbas and destroy Jesus. But the governor answered and said to them, Which of the two do you want me to release to you? And they said, Barabbas! Pilate said to them, Then what shall I do with Jesus, who is called Christ? They all said, Let him be crucified! He said to them, Why, what evil has he done? They cried out the more, saying, Let him be crucified! So, when Pilate saw that he was not gaining anything but that instead a riot was beginning, he took water and washed his hands before the people saying, I am innocent of this just man's blood; you see to it. And all the people answered and said, His blood be on us and on our children. Then he released Barabbas to them. And having scourged Jesus he handed him over to be crucified.* (Mt 27:11–26) These are the things that Matthew reports were done by Pilate in regard to the Lord.

8,33. Mark agrees with this in both wording and content.[42] But Pilate's words, when he answered the people's request to release one prisoner according to the custom of the feast day, he gives as follows: *But Pilate answered them and said, Do you want me to release to you the king of the Jews?* (Mk 15:9) Matthew, however, puts it this way: *So, when they had gathered, Pilate said to them, Whom do you want me to release to you, Barabbas or Jesus, who is called Christ?* (Mt 27:17) No difficulty is raised by the fact that Matthew does not mention that they asked for one to be released. But it may be asked what words Pilate said, whether those

---

40.   See Rom 6:4; Col 2:12.
41.   See Jer 40:11–12.
42.   See Mk 15:2–15.

given by Matthew or those given by Mark, for there seems to be some difference between *Whom do you want me to release to you, Barabbas or Jesus, who is called Christ?* and *Do you want me to release to you the king of the Jews?* (Mk 15:9) But, since they called their kings "anointed ones,"[43] one could say one or the other, so it is clear that he asked them if they wanted him to release to them the king of the Jews, that is, the Christ. It makes no difference in the meaning that Mark does not mention Barabbas, for he wishes to speak only of what relates to the Lord. He makes it quite clear in their reply whom they wished to have released: *But the chief priests stirred up the crowd, that he should release Barabbas instead. And Pilate answered and said again to them, Then what do you want me to do with the king of the Jews?* (Mk 15:11–12) This makes it quite clear that, by saying *the king of the Jews*, Mark meant to indicate the same thing as Matthew did by saying *Christ*, since kings were not called "anointed ones" except by the Jews, for in that same place Matthew says, *Pilate said to them, Then what shall I do with Jesus, who is called Christ?* (Mt 27:22) Mark, then, continues, *And they cried out again, Crucify him!* (Mk 15:13) which [Matthew] puts this way: *They all said, Let him be crucified!* (Mt 27:22). And Mark continues, *Pilate said to them, Why, what evil has he done? And they cried out the more, Crucify him!* (Mk 15:14) Matthew does not say this, but, because he says, *When Pilate saw that he was not gaining anything, however, but that instead a riot was beginning* (Mt 27:24), he also says that he washed his hands before the people in order to show that he was innocent of this just man's blood, which Mark and the others do not mention. Matthew also shows quite clearly how the governor dealt with the people in an attempt to have Jesus released. Mark indicates this briefly when he reports that Pilate said, *Why, what evil has he done?* And then he concludes his account of what happened between Pilate and the Lord in this way: *So Pilate, wishing to satisfy the crowd, released Barabbas to them; and having scourged Jesus, he handed him over to be crucified* (Mk 15:15). This is what Mark narrates happened with the governor.

8,34. Luke narrates what happened with Pilate this way: *And they began to accuse him, saying, We found this man perverting our nation and forbidding us to give tribute to Caesar and saying that he is Christ, a king* (Lk 23:2). The other two evangelists do not report this, although they do say that they were accusing him.[44] Thus [Luke] is the one who reveals what the false charges were that were brought against him. He omits, however, what Pilate said to him— *Have you no answer to make? See how many charges they bring against you* (Mk 15:4)—although he continues and says what they also say: *And Pilate asked him, Are you the king of the Jews? And he answered and said, You say so.* (Lk 23:3) Matthew and Mark also record this before they mention that Jesus was rebuked for not answering his accusers.[45] It makes no difference to the truth in what order Luke gives these things, nor does it make any difference if one omits what another records. Consider in that

---

43. "Anointed ones": *christos*, i.e., "christs."
44. See Mt 27:12; Mk 14:56–59.
45. See Mt 27:11; Mk 15:2.

regard what [Luke] says next: *Then Pilate said to the chief priests and the crowds,
I find no crime in this man. But they grew more vehement, saying, He stirs up the
people, teaching throughout Judea, from Galilee even to here. When Pilate heard
of Galilee, he asked if the man were a Galilean. And when he learned that he was
under Herod's jurisdiction, he sent him to Herod, who was himself in Jerusalem
at that time. When Herod saw Jesus he was very glad, for he had desired to see
him for a long time because he had heard much about him, and he hoped to see
some sign done by him. So he questioned him at length, but he did not answer.
The chief priests and scribes stood by, roundly accusing him. And Herod with his
soldiers insulted him, mocked him, and, dressing him in rich clothes, sent him back
to Pilate. And Herod and Pilate became friends that day, for previously they had
been each other's enemies.* (Lk 23:4–12) Only Luke records all these things—that
Pilate sent the Lord to Herod, and what happened there—even though some of the
things that he says here are similar to things that can be found elsewhere with the
other [evangelists]. But the others at this point wish only to report what happened
with Pilate up until the time when the Lord was handed over for crucifixion. Before
resuming his account of what happened with the governor, Luke digresses to tell
what happened with Herod, and he continues thus: *But Pilate called together the
chief priests and the rulers and the people and said to them, You brought this man
to me as one who was perverting the people. And behold, having examined him
before you, I have found no cause in this man for the things of which you accuse
him.* (Lk 23:13–14) Here we notice that Luke does not mention that Pilate asked
the Lord how he would answer his accusers. Then Luke continues, *Neither did
Herod, for I sent you back to him,*[46] *and behold, nothing worthy of death has been
done by him. Therefore I shall chastise him and release him. For he was obliged
to release one man to them at the festival. But the whole crowd cried out together,
saying, Away with this man, and release to us Barabbas! who had been put in
prison for making an insurrection in the city and for murder. Pilate spoke to them
again, wanting to release Jesus. But they shouted back, saying, Crucify, crucify
him! A third time he said to them, Why, what evil has he done? I find no reason
to put him to death, so I shall chastise him and release him. But they insisted,
demanding with loud voices that he be crucified, and their voices prevailed.* (Lk
23:15–23) Matthew confirms that Pilate tried several times to change their mind,
since he desired to release Jesus, although he puts this in very few words when he
says, *When Pilate saw that he was not gaining anything, however, but that instead
a riot was beginning* (Mt 27:24). [Matthew] would not have said this unless [Pilate]
had made several efforts, although he does not mention how many times he tried
to save Jesus from their fury. And Luke concludes his account of what happened
with the governor this way: *So Pilate passed sentence to do as they asked. He*

---

46. This is Augustine's reading, as well as that of the Vulgate. The Greek original makes much
    more sense: *He sent him back to us.*

released to them the man who had been put in prison for murder and insurrection, whom they had requested, but he handed Jesus over to their will. (Lk 23:24–25)

8,35. Now let us consider the same events as presented by John, that is, what was done by Pilate: *They themselves did not enter the praetorium, so that they would not be defiled but might eat the Passover. So Pilate went out to them and said, What accusation do you bring against this man? They answered and said to him, If this man were not a criminal, we would not have handed him over to you.* (Jn 18:28–30) It must be seen whether this is inconsistent with Luke's version, which says that specific charges were brought against him and says what those were: *And they began to accuse him, saying, We found this man perverting our nation and forbidding us to give tribute to Caesar and saying that he is Christ, a king.* But according to John's record it seems that the Jews were unwilling to state any charges. For when Pilate asked them, *What accusation do you bring against this man?* (Jn 18:29) their only reply was, *If this man were not a criminal, we would not have handed him over to you* (Jn 18:30). They said this as though [Pilate] was to follow their authority, stop his inquiry, and believe Jesus guilty based solely on the fact that they thought it right to hand him over to him. Therefore we ought to understand that all these things were said, both what is reported by [John] and what is reported by Luke. For there were many statements and answers made, and out of these the writers chose what seemed right for their narratives, putting into them what they thought sufficient. John himself says that there were charges, as we shall see in their proper place. So he continues, *Pilate said to them, then, Take him yourselves and judge him according to your own law. Then the Jews said to him, It is not lawful for us to put anyone to death. This was to fulfill what Jesus had said to show how he would die. Then Pilate entered the praetorium again and called Jesus and said to him, Are you the king of the Jews? Jesus answered, Do you say this yourself, or did others tell it to you about me?* (Jn 18:31–34) This would not seem to agree with what was said by the others— *Jesus answered, You say so* (Mt 27:11; Mk 15:2; Lk 23:3)—unless it can be shown in what follows that both were said. And John shows that what he now says is something that was omitted by the other evangelists rather than something that the Lord did not say. Note, then, how he continues: *Pilate answered, Am I a Jew? Your own nation and the high priests have handed you over to me. What have you done? Jesus answered, My kingdom is not of this world; if my kingdom were of this world, my servants would fight that I might not be handed over to the Jews. But now my kingdom is not of this world. Then Pilate said to him, Are you a king, then? Jesus answered, You say that I am a king.* (Jn 18:35–37) See how he rejoins at this point the account given by the other evangelists. Then he continues with what the Lord goes on to say that the others omit: *For this I was born, and for this I have come into the world, to bear witness to the truth. Everyone who is of the truth hears my voice. Pilate said to him, What is truth? And when he had said this he went out again to the Jews and said to them, I find no fault in this man. But you have a custom that I release one man to you at Passover. Do you wish me to release to you the king of the Jews?*

Then they all cried out again, saying, Not this man but Barabbas! Now Barabbas was a robber. Then Pilate took Jesus and scourged him. And the soldiers plaited a crown of thorns, put it on his head, and put a purple robe on him. And they came to him and said, Hail, King of the Jews, and struck him with their hands. Pilate went out again and said to them, Behold, I am bringing him out to you, so that you may know that I find no fault in him. Then Jesus came out, wearing the crown of thorns and the purple robe. And Pilate said to them, Behold the man. When the chief priests and the servants saw him, they cried out, saying, Crucify! Crucify! Pilate said to them, Take him yourselves and crucify him, for I find no fault in him. The Jews answered him, We have a law, and by that law he ought to die, for he made himself the Son of God. (Jn 18:37–19:7) This could be consistent with what Luke records was the Jews' accusation, *We found this man perverting our nation* (Lk 23:2), for they could then have added, *for he made himself the Son of God* (Jn 19:7). John continues, then, and says, *When Pilate heard them say this, he was the more afraid. And he entered the praetorium again and said to Jesus, Where are you from? But Jesus gave no answer to him. So Pilate said to him, You will not speak to me? Do you not know that I have the power to crucify you and the power to release you? Jesus answered, You would have no power over me unless it had been given to you from above; therefore the one who handed me over to you has the greater sin. From then on Pilate sought to release him. But the Jews cried out, saying, If you release this man, you are not Caesar's friend; everyone who makes himself a king is speaking against Caesar.* (Jn 19:8–12) It is possible that this coincides with what Luke says was the Jews' accusation. For after they say, *We found him perverting our nation*, he adds, *and forbidding us to give tribute to Caesar and saying that he is Christ, a king* (Lk 23:2). This could also solve the problem that arises when one supposes that the Jews made no specific charge against the Lord in John's version, when they responded and said to [Pilate], *If this man were not a criminal, we would not have handed him over to you* (Jn 18:30). John continues, then, and says, *When Pilate heard these things, then, he brought Jesus outside and sat on the judgment seat in the place called The Pavement, or in Hebrew, Gabbatha. Now it was the day of the preparation of the Passover, at about the sixth hour. And he said to the Jews, Behold your king. But they cried out, Take him and crucify him! Pilate said to them, Shall I crucify your king? The chief priests answered, We have no king but Caesar. Then he handed him over to them to be crucified.* (Jn 19:13–16) This is what John says concerning the things done by Pilate.

9,36. We have now come to where we may examine the Lord's passion itself, according to the witness of the four evangelists, which Matthew begins this way: *Then the governor's soldiers took Jesus into the praetorium and gathered before him the whole troop. And they stripped him and put a scarlet robe on him. And plaiting a crown of thorns, they put it on his head and put a reed in his right hand. And they knelt before him and mocked him, saying, Hail, King of the Jews.* (Mt 27:27–29) At the same point in the narrative, Mark puts it thus: *And the soldiers*

led him to the hall of the praetorium, and they called together the whole troop.
And they clothed him in purple and, having plaited a crown of thorns, they put
it on him. And they began to salute him, Hail, King of the Jews. And they struck
his head with a reed and spat upon him, and kneeling they worshiped him. (Mk
15:16–19) So it is clear that where Matthew says, *They put a scarlet robe on him*
(Mt 27:28), Mark says, *They clothed him in purple* (Mk 15:17). Perhaps the mock-
ers used a scarlet robe instead of a royal purple one; or perhaps it was a reddish-
purple very similar to scarlet; or perhaps Mark mentioned the purple that was in
the robe, even though it was scarlet. Luke says nothing of this. But before he says
that Pilate handed him over to be crucified, John mentions this and says, *Then*
Pilate took Jesus and scourged him. And the soldiers plaited a crown of thorns,
put it on his head, and put a purple robe on him. And they came to him and said,
Hail, King of the Jews, and struck him with their hands. (Jn 19:1–3) So it is evident
that Matthew and Mark have reported this in summary form and that it did not
actually happen when Pilate handed him over to be crucified, for John says quite
clearly that these things happened when he was with Pilate. So the others, having omitted it previously, include it here. What Matthew says subsequently also
pertains to this: *And they spat upon him and took the reed and struck him on the*
head. And after that they mocked him and stripped him of the robe and put his
own clothes on him and led him away to crucify him. (Mt 27:30–31) From this we
are to understand that they stripped him of the robe and put his own clothes on
him when all of this was over, just before he was led away. Mark puts it this way:
And after they had mocked him they stripped him of the purple and put his own
clothes on him (Mk 15:20).

10,37. Matthew continues, then: *As they went out, they found a man of Cyrene*
named Simon; they compelled this man to carry his cross (Mt 27:32). Mark also
says, *And they led him out to crucify him. And they compelled a passerby, Simon of*
Cyrene, who was coming in from the country, the father of Alexander and Rufus,
to carry his cross. (Mk 15:20–21) Luke says this: *And as they led him away, they*
seized one Simon of Cyrene, who was coming in from the country, and laid the
cross on him to carry behind Jesus (Lk 23:26). John, however, narrates it thus: *So*
they took Jesus and led him out. And carrying his own cross, he went to the place
called The Place of a Skull, or in Hebrew, Golgotha, where they crucified him.
(Jn 19:16–18) From this it is to be understood that Jesus was carrying his cross
himself when he was going to the place mentioned. But on the way Simon, whom
the other three mention, was seized, and the cross was given to him to carry the
rest of the way. So we find that both things happened—at the beginning as John
says, and then as the other three say.

11,38. Matthew continues, *And they came to a place called Golgotha, that is,*
The Place of a Skull (Mt 27:33). (As to the place, they are most obvious in their
agreement.) Then Matthew adds this: *And they gave him wine to drink, mixed*
with gall; and when he tasted it, he would not drink it (Mt 27:34). Mark puts it
this way: *And they gave him wine mixed with myrrh to drink, and he did not take*

it (Mk 15:23). This is to be understood as the same as Matthew's statement that it was mixed with gall. For Matthew mentions gall because of its bitterness, and wine mixed with myrrh is most bitter; or perhaps the wine was mixed with both gall and myrrh. And when Mark says that he did not take it, it is to be understood that he did not take it and drink it, although he did taste it, as Matthew testifies. So, when Matthew says, *He would not drink it*, it is the same as when Mark says, *He did not take it*, but he is silent as to whether he tasted it.

12,39. Matthew continues, *And after they crucified him they divided his clothes by casting lots. And sitting down, they watched him.* (Mt 27:35–36) Mark puts it this way: *And crucifying him, they divided his clothes by casting lots for what each one would take* (Mk 15:24). Luke says it this way: *They cast lots to divide his clothes. And the people stood by, watching.* (Lk 23:34–35) So this incident is given briefly by these three. John, though, describes what happened in more detail: *When the soldiers had crucified him they took his clothes and made four parts, one part for each soldier, and the same with his tunic. But the tunic was seamless, woven from the top throughout. So they said to one another, Let us not tear it but cast lots for it, to see whose it will be. This was to fulfill what was said in the Scriptures, They parted my clothes among them, and for my garment they cast lots.* (Jn 19:23–24)

13,40. Matthew continues, *And over his head they put his charge in writing, This is Jesus, the King of the Jews* (Mt 27:37). But before Mark says that, he notes, *It was the third hour, and they crucified him* (Mk 15:25). He adds this right after he describes the dividing of the clothes. We must examine this very carefully in order to avoid a great error. For some think that the Lord was crucified at the third hour and that then, from the sixth to the ninth hour, there was darkness. Understood this way, there must have been three hours between when he was crucified and when darkness fell. This could be the right way to understand this, except for the fact that John says it was about the sixth hour when Pilate sat *on the judgment seat in the place called The Pavement, or in Hebrew, Gabbatha* (Jn 19:13). He continues, *Now it was the day of the preparation of the Passover, at about the sixth hour. And he said to the Jews, Behold your king. But they cried out, Take him, take him, crucify him! Pilate said to them, Shall I crucify your king? The chief priests answered, We have no king but Caesar. Then he handed him over to them to be crucified.* (Jn 19:14–16) If it was about the sixth hour when Pilate was sitting on the judgment seat and handed Jesus over to the Jews to be crucified, how could he have been crucified at the third hour, as some have thought who do not understand Mark's words?

13,41. First let us consider at what hour he could have been crucified, and then we shall see why Mark says he was crucified at the third hour. As stated above, it was about the sixth hour when Pilate was sitting on the judgment seat and handed him over to be crucified. It was not exactly the sixth hour but about the sixth hour; that is, the fifth hour had passed and the sixth had begun. But they could not say "five and a quarter" or "five and a third" or "five and a half" or anything like that.

For the Scriptures customarily speak of whole numbers rather than parts, especially when it comes to time. For example, they say that after eight days [Jesus] went up on a mountain,[47] but Matthew and Mark say it was after six days, because they only count the days in between.[48] John's statement is most judicious: he does not say "sixth" but *about the sixth* (Jn 19:14). But even if he had not said this but had said that it was the sixth hour, we could still understand this as an example of that scriptural style which, as I have said, speaks of whole numbers and not parts. So sometime after the end of the fifth hour and the beginning of the sixth those things happened which are narrated concerning our Lord's crucifixion. And he hung there until the end of the sixth hour, when darkness fell, as attested by three evangelists, Matthew, Mark, and Luke.[49]

13,42. Now we must inquire why Mark, after reporting that, as they were *crucifying him, they divided his clothes by casting lots for what each one would take* (Mk 15:24), goes on to add that *it was the third hour, and they crucified him* (Mk 15:25). He had already said that *crucifying him, they divided his clothes*, and it is confirmed by the others that when he was crucified they divided his clothes. But if Mark's purpose was to note the time, then he could have just said, *It was the third hour.* So why would he add *and they crucified him*? He must have wanted this repetition to indicate something that could be found by investigation, for this Scripture was read at a time when the whole Church knew at what hour the Lord was hung upon a tree and could either correct an error or refute a falsehood. But, since Mark knew that the Lord had been hung by the soldiers and not by the Jews, as John clearly indicates,[50] his hidden purpose here was to show that those who cried out for his crucifixion were the ones who really crucified him, more than those who only obeyed their leader according to their duty. So it is to be understood that it was the third hour when the Jews cried out that the Lord should be crucified, and this shows most truly that they crucified him at the time when they cried out. It is especially important to note this, because they were unwilling to do it themselves and therefore handed him over to Pilate. This is shown quite clearly by John, for when Pilate said to them, *What accusation do you bring against this man? They answered and said to him, If this man were not a criminal, we would not have handed him over to you. Then Pilate said to them, Take him yourselves and judge him according to your own law. Then the Jews said to him, It is not lawful for us to put anyone to death.* (Jn 18:29–31) So Mark shows that they did at the third hour what they were most unwilling to appear to be doing; he judged most truly that the Lord was murdered more by the Jews' tongue than by the soldiers' hand.[51]

---

47. See Lk 9:28.
48. See Mt 17:1; Mk 9:1. The discrepancy is discussed above at II,56,113.
49. See Mt 27:45; Mk 15:33; Lk 23:44.
50. See Jn 19:23.
51. Augustine's anti-Semitism is particularly egregious here, although it is not unique in early Christian literature. For a useful brief discussion of Augustine's treatment of the Jews see Allan D. Fitzgerald, ed., *Augustine through the Ages: An Encyclopedia* (Grand Rapids: Eerdmans, 1999) 470–474.

13,43. But if someone should say that it was not the third hour when the Jews first cried out in this way, then he shows that he is a most insane enemy of the Gospel, unless he can perhaps resolve this question otherwise. But he cannot demonstrate that it was not the third hour, so we should rather believe an honest evangelist than the contentious suspicions of men. But were someone to ask how it could be proved that it was the third hour, I would make this response: I believe the evangelists. If you believe them too, then show me how the Lord could have been crucified at both the sixth hour and the third. For we must admit that John's narrative puts it at the sixth hour, while Mark reports it was at the third. So if we believe both of them, show me another way in which both could have happened and I shall gladly accept your explanation. For what I value is not my own idea but the truth of the Gospel. Would that others would discover more solutions to this problem! But until they do, please use mine. And if no other solution is found, this one alone will suffice. If there can be another, however, then when it is demonstrated we shall choose between them. But do not ever suppose that any one of all four evangelists has lied or has fallen into error from such a holy and high authority.

13,44. But perhaps someone will try to prove from this that it was not the third hour when the Jews cried out in this way because, after Mark says, *And Pilate answered and said again to them, Then what do you want me to do with the king of the Jews? And they cried out again, Crucify him!* (Mk 15:12–13), there are then no other events in Mark's narrative, but it continues immediately with Pilate's handing the Lord over to be crucified, which John reports happened at about the sixth hour. But I say that it must be understood that Mark omitted many things that happened during the time when Pilate was seeking a way to save [Jesus] from the Jews and striving with all his might against their mad will by every means possible.[52] For Matthew says, Pilate said to them, *Then what shall I do with Jesus, who is called Christ? They all said, Let him be crucified!* (Mt 27:22) We say that at that time it was the third hour. But when Matthew then continues and says, *Pilate saw that he was not gaining anything, however, but that instead a riot was beginning* (Mt 27:24), we understand that two hours passed, during which time Pilate tried to save the Lord and the Jews were demonstrating against his efforts. Therefore, by this time the sixth hour had begun, and during the sixth hour those things occurred that are described as having happened between Pilate's handing over of the Lord and the onset of darkness. Matthew had previously recorded the following: *But while he was sitting on the judgment seat, his wife sent word to him, saying, Have nothing to do with that just man, for I have suffered many things today in a dream because of him* (Mt 27:19). Although Pilate really sat on the judgment seat later, Matthew recorded the incident with Pilate's wife earlier in his narrative in order to show why Pilate so intently wished, up to the very end, not to hand Jesus over to the Jews.

---

52. Augustine's readiness to blame the Jews for Jesus' death is combined with an exculpatory attitude toward Pilate, which is also not unique in early Christian literature.

13,45. Luke, then, reports that Pilate said, *I shall therefore chastise him and release him* (Lk 23:16), and then that the whole crowd cried out, *Take this man away, and release to us Barabbas!* (Lk 23:18) But perhaps they had not yet said, *Crucify him!* (Lk 23:21) Luke continues, *Pilate spoke to them again, wishing to release Jesus. But they cried out, saying, Crucify him!* (Lk 23:20–21) This is understood to have been at the third hour. Luke continues, then, and says, *A third time he said to them, Why, what evil has he done? I find no reason to put him to death, so I shall chastise him and release him. But they insisted, demanding with loud voices that he be crucified, and their voices prevailed.* (Lk 23:22–23) This is sufficient indication that there was a great tumult. It is also quite evident, as far as our investigation into the truth is concerned, how much time passed before he said to them a third time, *Why, what evil has he done?* (Lk 23:22) And when he goes on to say, *They insisted with loud voices, and their voices prevailed* (Lk 23:23), who cannot understand that they did this because they saw that Pilate was unwilling to hand the Lord over to them? And, since he was so unwilling to do this, he did not give up in just a moment, but more than two hours passed as he hesitated.

13,46. Examine John likewise and you will see how great was Pilate's hesitation and refusal to perform such a shameful deed. For John records these events in more detail, although even he does not tell us everything that happened in those two hours and in part of the sixth. For after Pilate scourged Jesus and allowed the soldiers to put the robe on him as a mockery and allowed him to be mistreated and insulted in many other ways (which, I believe, he did to mitigate their fury, so that they would not continue in their savage lust for his death), John continues, *Pilate went out again and said to them, Behold, I am bringing him out to you, so that you may know that I find no fault in him. Then Jesus came out wearing the crown of thorns and the purple robe. And Pilate said to them, Behold the man.* (Jn 19:4–5) He said this so that they would be placated by seeing his ignominious appearance. But he continues and says, *When the chief priests and the servants saw him, they cried out, saying, Crucify! Crucify!* (Jn 19:6) We say that this was at the third hour. Note what follows: *Pilate said to them, Take him yourselves and crucify him, for I find no fault in him. The Jews answered him, We have a law, and by that law he ought to die, for he made himself the Son of God. When Pilate heard them say this, he was the more afraid. And he entered the praetorium again and said to Jesus, Where are you from? But Jesus gave no answer to him. So Pilate said to him, You will not speak to me? Do you not know that I have the power to crucify you and the power to release you? Jesus answered, You would have no power over me unless it had been given to you from above; therefore the one who handed me over to you has the greater sin. From then on, Pilate sought to release him.* (Jn 19:6–12) The fact that Pilate sought to release him is significant, for we may suppose that this attempt took some time, and the evangelist has omitted many things said by Pilate as well as the objections made by the Jews, until the Jews finally overwhelmed him and made him capitulate. For [John] continues thus: *But the Jews cried out, saying, If you release this man, you are not*

Caesar's friend; everyone who makes himself a king is speaking against Caesar. When Pilate heard these things, he brought Jesus outside and sat on the judgment seat in the place called The Pavement, or in Hebrew, Gabbatha. Now it was the day of the preparation of the Passover, at about the sixth hour. (Jn 19:12–14) So when the Jews first cried out *Crucify!* it was the third hour. But two hours then passed, while Pilate hesitated and the Jews raised a tumult, before he sat on the judgment seat. Then the fifth hour passed and the sixth hour began. *He said to the Jews,* then, *Behold your king. But they cried out, Take him and crucify him!* (Jn 19:14–15) But still Pilate, who was not troubled by fear of their slandering him, did not give in easily. For now his wife sent word to him while he was sitting on the judgment seat; only Matthew reports this, but he puts it earlier in his narrative,[53] placing it where he thought it more appropriate. Then Pilate, attempting to stop the process from going forward, said to them, *Shall I crucify your king? The chief priests answered, We have no king but Caesar. Then he handed him over to them to be crucified.* (Jn 19:15–16) By the time that Jesus went there and was crucified with the two robbers, and the division of his clothes was decided by lot, as was the possession of his tunic, and he was insulted in various ways (for while these things were happening insults were also hurled at him), the sixth hour was over, and the darkness came, as Matthew, Mark, and Luke report.[54]

13,47. And so, let us cast off impious obstinacy and believe that the Lord Jesus Christ was crucified at the third hour by the Jews' mouths and at the sixth hour by the soldiers' hands. For while the Jews were threatening to riot and Pilate was irresolute, two hours passed from when they had first said *Crucify!* Even Mark, a master of brevity, wanted briefly to show Pilate's desire and effort in favor of the Lord's life. First he notes, *They cried out again, Crucify him!* (Mk 15:13), showing thereby that they had cried out before, when they asked him to release Barabbas. Then he adds, *Then Pilate was saying to them, Why, what evil has he done?* (Mk 15:14) In this way he condenses things that took place over a long period of time. However, keeping in mind that we are trying to understand what Mark intended, it is significant that he did not say "Pilate said to them" but *Pilate was saying to them, Why, what evil has he done?* For if he had said "said," then we might have thought he said it only once, but by saying *he was saying* he indicates quite clearly to the intelligent that he said it several times in different ways up until the beginning of the sixth hour.[55] Let us consider, then, how brief Mark's version is in comparison to Matthew's, how brief Matthew's is in comparison to Luke's, and how brief Luke's is in comparison to John's, although each records something unique to himself. And even John's version is brief in comparison to how many things happened and

---

53. See Mt 27:19.
54. See Mt 27:45; Mk 15:33; Lk 23:44.
55. "Said...was saying": *dixit...dicebat*. The difference is between the perfect tense, which usually indicates completed action, and the imperfect tense, which usually indicates ongoing action in the past.

how long it took them to happen. Let us stop this madness and believe that more than two hours could have elapsed.

13,48. But if this is how it happened, then someone might object that Mark could have said it was the third hour when it was the third hour, when the voice of the Jews called out for the Lord's crucifixion, or that he could have said it was the Jews themselves who then crucified him. Such an objection comes from boundless pride and seeks to impose laws on the narrators of truth. One might as well say that, if one were to narrate these events himself, then however he narrated them, they would have to be narrated in the same way and in the same order by anyone else who narrated them. Let him instead reckon that the evangelist Mark's understanding was superior to his own, and that Mark decided to put this statement where divine inspiration directed him. For their recollections were governed by the hand of the one who governs the waters however it pleases him, as it is written.[56] For human memory drifts through a variety of thoughts, and no one can control what kind of thought comes into his mind, nor when it does so. These holy and truthful men committed their scattered recollections regarding the order of their narratives to God's hidden power, to which nothing is scattered. Therefore no one who is far from and wandering away from the eyes of God ought to say that something should be put in a different place, for he is completely ignorant of why God wished to put it in the place where it is. The Apostle says, *If our Gospel is hidden, it is hidden to those who are perishing* (2 Cor 4:3) and *We are a fragrance of life to life to some, but to others a fragrance of death to death* (2 Cor 2:16), adding immediately, *And who is sufficient for these things?* (2 Cor 2:16)—that is, "Who is sufficient to understand how this can be done justly?" For the Lord himself says, *For I have come so that those who do not see may see, and those who do see may become blind* (Jn 9:39). For it is out of the depths of the riches of God's wisdom and knowledge[57] that from one lump one vessel is made for honor, another for base use,[58] and that to flesh and blood it is said, *O man, who are you to answer back to God?* (Rom 9:20) So, in this matter who knows the mind of God, or who has been his adviser?[59] But God governed the hearts of the evangelists in their recollections and raised them to such a height of authority in the Church so that those things that may seem contradictory in them may blind many, deservedly handing them over to the lusts of their hearts and to their base mind,[60] and so that many may be exercised in perfecting a devout understanding in accord with the hidden justice of the Omnipotent. For a prophet speaks to the Lord this way: *Your thoughts are very deep. An imprudent man will not know and a foolish man will not understand these things.* (Ps 92:5–6)

---

56. See Pss 29:3; 33:7; 77:16.
57. See Rom 11:33.
58. See Rom 9:21.
59. See Rom 11:34.
60. See Rom 1:24–28.

13,49. But I ask and warn all who have read what we have explicated with the Lord's help to bear the following in mind, so that it need not be repeated. This discussion, which I have judged it right to introduce at this point, applies in all similar difficult questions. All who wish to rid themselves of the hardness of impiety and to examine the question can easily see that the place where Mark mentions the third hour is most opportune. At the very point where Mark records what the soldiers did as their duty, one is reminded that the Jews crucified the Lord at the third hour, even though they wished to transfer the blame for the crime to the Romans, either the leaders or the soldiers. For he says, *And crucifying him, they divided his clothes among them by casting lots for what each one would take* (Mk 15:24). Who was doing this except the soldiers, as John confirms?[61] Therefore, so that no one would turn the idea of so great a crime away from the Jews and blame only the soldiers, [Mark] says, *It was the third hour, and they crucified him* (Mk 15:25), so that the reader may see who really crucified him. A careful investigator would find that this was done by those who cried out for his crucifixion at the third hour, while noting that what the soldiers did happened at the sixth hour.

13,50. Although John records that *it was the preparation of the Passover, about the sixth hour* (Jn 19:14), there are those who understand that the preparation happened at the third hour of the day, when Pilate sat on the judgment seat. Thus the end of the third hour would seem to be when he was crucified, and he hung on the tree for another three hours before he gave up his spirit.[62] Under this theory, the darkness fell when he died, that is, at the sixth hour of the day, and lasted until the ninth. For they say that the preparation of the Jewish Passover happened on the day before the sabbath, for the days of unleavened bread begin with that sabbath. But the true Passover, which was brought about by the Lord's passion, is not the Jewish Passover but the Christian. This began to be prepared—that is, to have its preparation—from the ninth hour of the night, when the Lord was being prepared to be killed by the Jews, for the term that they use, *parasceve*, means "preparation." From the ninth hour of the night up to his crucifixion, then, there passed what John calls the sixth hour of the preparation and what Mark calls the third hour of the day. So Mark does not mention the hour when the Jews cried out, *Crucify! Crucify!* as a summary but gives the third hour as the time when the Lord was fastened to the tree. Any believer would accept this solution to the question if only we could find something that would fit with everything else and would connect the ninth hour with the beginning of the preparation of our Passover, that is, the preparation of Christ's death. For, if we say that it began when the Lord was arrested by the Jews, then this was only at the beginning of the night. Perhaps it was when he was led to the house of Caiaphas's father-in-law, where the chief priests also heard him, but we gather that at this time the cock had not yet crowed, for Peter's denial occurred when it was heard. Perhaps it was when he was handed over to Pilate, but Scripture

---

61. See Jn 19:23.
62. See Mt 27:50 par.

clearly says that then it was morning. So the only remaining explanation is that the preparation of the Passover, that is, the preparation of the Lord's death, began when the chief priests, having first heard him, answered and said, *He deserves death* (Mt 26:66), which is found in both Matthew and Mark.[63] (Therefore we are to understand the report of Peter's denial as a recapitulation of something that happened earlier.) And it is not at all unlikely to suppose, as I said, that the time when they pronounced him guilty of death was in fact the ninth hour of the night. Between that time and the time when Pilate sat on the judgment seat, the sixth hour passed—not the sixth hour of the day but the sixth hour of the preparation of the sacrifice of the Lord, which is the true Passover. So the Lord was hung on the tree at the end of that sixth hour of preparation, which was the end of the third hour of the day. We may choose, therefore, either to understand it this way or to suppose that Mark mentioned the third hour because he wished especially to focus on the condemnation of the Jews for their part in the Lord's crucifixion. For they are understood to have cried out for his crucifixion so much that we may consider that they themselves crucified him, rather than those who with their own hands hung him from the tree. This is similar to how the centurion approached the Lord more closely than the friends whom he sent.[64] But without a doubt we now have an answer to the question of the time of the Lord's passion, which can greatly stir up the shamelessness of the contentious and disturb the ignorance of the weak.

14,51. Matthew continues and says, *Then two robbers were crucified with him, one on the right and one on the left* (Mt 27:38). Mark and Luke give it similarly.[65] No difficulty is caused by the fact that John says nothing about the robbers, for he says, *And two others with him, one on either side, and Jesus between them* (Jn 19:18). There would only have been a contradiction if, when the others call them robbers, [John] had called them innocent.

15,52. Matthew continues and says, *And those who passed by reviled him, shaking their heads and saying, You who would destroy the Temple and rebuild it in three days, save yourself. If you are the Son of God, come down from the cross.* (Mt 27:39–40) Mark says the same, almost word for word.[66] Then Matthew continues and says, *The chief priests, along with the scribes and elders, did the same, mocking him and saying, He saved others; he cannot save himself. If he is the king of Israel, let him come down now from the cross and we shall believe him. He trusted in God, let him deliver him now if he wishes. For he said, I am the Son of God.* (Mt 27:41–43) Mark and Luke agree with the sense of this, although they use different words, and the one omits what the other records.[67] Neither is silent concerning the fact that the chief priests insulted the crucified Lord. Mark, on the other hand, is silent concerning the elders, whereas Luke mentions chiefs but does

---

63. See Mk 14:64.
64. See above at II,20,48–50.
65. See Mk 15:27; Lk 23:33.
66. See Mk 15:29–30.
67. See Mk 15:29–32; Lk 23:35–37.

not specify priests,[68] thereby indicating by this general label all the leaders, which we can understand as including both scribes and elders.

16,53. Matthew continues and says, *And the robbers who were crucified with him also insulted him* (Mt 27:44). Mark does not differ from this, saying the same thing in different words.[69] But Luke might be thought to be inconsistent in this regard unless we keep in mind a certain style of speech that is quite common. For Luke says, *One of the robbers who were hanging reviled him, saying, If you are the Christ, save yourself and us* (Lk 23:39). He continues and adds the following: *But the other rebuked him, answering and saying, Do you not fear God, since you are under the same condemnation? And we indeed justly, for we are receiving the due reward for our deeds, but this man has done no wrong. And he said to Jesus, Lord, remember me when you come into your kingdom. And Jesus said to him, Amen, I say to you, today you shall be with me in paradise.* (Lk 27:40–43) How, then, can we explain that Matthew says, *The robbers who were crucified with him insulted him*, and that Mark says, *And those who were crucified with him reviled him* (Mk 15:32), while Luke's testimony is that one of them reviled him but that the other one rebuked the first and believed in the Lord? We must understand that Matthew and Mark, touching on the subject briefly here, use the plural for the singular. Similarly, we find the plural in the Epistle to the Hebrews, *They stopped the mouths of lions* (Heb 11:33), when this can only be understood as referring to Daniel alone.[70] It is also said in the plural, *They were sawn in two* (Heb 11:37), when this death has been reported only of Isaiah.[71] When it says in a Psalm, *The kings of the earth set themselves, and the rulers came together* (Ps 2:2), this must be the plural for the singular, for, when the passage is explained in the Acts of the Apostles, those who apply the testimony of the Psalm understand *kings* to refer to Herod and *rulers* to Pilate.[72] And since the pagans often slander the Gospels, let them consider how it can be that their own authors write of more than one Phaedra, Medea, and Clytemnestra, when there was only one of each.[73] And is it not common to say, "Country people are offensive to me," even though only one is offensive? There would be an inconsistency, then, in the fact that Luke mentioned only one if [the other evangelists] had specified that both robbers reviled the Lord, for then it would not be possible to understand the plural number as referring to just one of them. But, since they say *the robbers* or *those who were crucified with him* and

---

68. See Lk 23:35. "Chiefs": *principes*, or "rulers."
69. See Mk 15:32.
70. See Dan 6:16–22.
71. Augustine is referring to a tradition that made its first appearance in the apocryphal *Martyrdom and Ascension of Isaiah* 5 and was accepted by several early Christian writers.
72. See Acts 4:26–27.
73. Augustine here claims that the evangelists are no more inconsistent or misleading than the Greek tragedians Aeschylus, Sophocles, and Euripides, who have quite different versions of the stories involving these characters (e.g., all three wrote plays recounting how Orestes and Electra killed their mother, Clytemnestra), although these stories are deemed accurate, or even authoritative.

do not add "both," this could mean that both of them did it or that just one of them did it, the plural number being used according to a common method of speech.

17,54. Matthew continues and says, *From the sixth hour until the ninth hour there was darkness over all the land* (Mt 27:45). Two of the others confirm this, although Luke adds that the darkness was brought about because the sun was obscured.[74] Matthew continues, *And about the ninth hour Jesus cried out with a loud voice, saying, Eli, Eli, lama sabachthani? that is, My God, my God, why have you forsaken me? But some of those who stood by, when they heard it, said, This man is calling for Elijah.* (Mt 27:46–47) Mark is almost identical in wording, and in meaning he agrees not almost but completely. Matthew continues, *And one of them immediately ran and took a sponge, filled it with vinegar and put it on a reed and gave it to him to drink* (Mt 27:48). Mark says it thus: *One ran and filled a sponge with vinegar, put it on a reed, and gave it to him to drink, saying, Wait, let us see whether Elijah will come to take him down* (Mk 15:36). But Matthew reports that the words concerning Elijah were not said by the one who offered the sponge with vinegar but by others, for he says, *But others said, Wait, let us see whether Elijah will come to save him* (Mt 27:49). Therefore we understand that this was said by both the one man and the others. Before he reports the robbers' insults, however, Luke mentions the vinegar in this way: *The soldiers also mocked him, coming up to him and offering him vinegar, saying, If you are the king of the Jews, save yourself!* (Lk 23:36–37) Luke wished this to include both what the soldiers did and what they said. Therefore it ought not to present any difficulty if he does not say that it was one of them who offered the vinegar. It is a way of speaking, which we have already discussed, of giving the plural number for the singular.[75] John also mentions the vinegar: *After this, Jesus, knowing that all was now fulfilled, so that the Scripture might be fulfilled, said, I thirst. Now, there was a vessel full of vinegar there, so they filled a sponge with vinegar and put it on hyssop and put it to his mouth.* (Jn 19:28–29) Although John reports that he said, *I thirst* (Jn 19:28), and that there was a vessel full of vinegar there, which the others omit, there is nothing remarkable in this.

18,55. Matthew continues, *Jesus cried again with a loud voice and yielded up his spirit* (Mt 27:50). Mark says similarly, *Jesus cried with a loud voice and died* (Mk 15:37). Luke tells what he said in a loud voice, for he says, *And crying with a loud voice, Jesus said, Father, into your hands I commit my spirit. And having said this he died.* (Lk 23:46) John, who does not mention the first cry of *Eli, Eli* (Mt 27:46; Mk 15:34), as reported by Matthew and Mark, also does not mention the cry of *Father, into your hands I commit my spirit* (Lk 23:46), which only Luke includes, while the other two refer to it as *a loud voice*. Luke also reports that this was said with a loud voice, so that we may understand that it is the same as the loud voice reported by Matthew and Mark. But John reports something that none of

---

74. See Lk 23:45.
75. See above at III,16,53.

the other three do, which is that he said, *It is finished* (Jn 19:30). He said this after he took the vinegar, and we understand that this was said before the loud cry, for these are John's words: *When Jesus had received the vinegar, he said, It is finished, and he bowed his head and gave up his spirit* (Jn 19:30). So in the time between when he said, *It is finished*, and the time when it says that *he bowed his head and handed over his spirit* (Jn 19:30), he uttered that cry in a loud voice which John omits but the other three record. So the order would appear to be as follows: first he said, *It is finished*, when the things prophesied of him were fulfilled in him; then he committed and handed over his spirit, like one who had been expecting this and died when he wished it. But, whichever sequence one deems most likely for these sayings, one should take the greatest care not to suppose that any one of the evangelists is inconsistent with any other, whether one omits what another mentions or one mentions what another omits.

19,56. Matthew continues, *And behold, the curtain of the Temple was torn in two, from top to bottom* (Mt 27:51). Mark says it thus: *And the curtain of the Temple was torn in two, from top to bottom* (Mk 15:38). Luke says it similarly: *And the curtain of the Temple was torn in the middle* (Lk 23:45). He does not give it in the same order, however, for, wishing to add miracle upon miracle, he says, *The sun was darkened* (Lk 23:45), and then he deems it right to add immediately, *And the curtain of the Temple was torn in the middle.* So he places this earlier in the narrative, for it really happened when the Lord died. He then goes on to summarize the things that took place at the drinking of the vinegar, the cry in a loud voice, and the death itself, all of which we understand happened before the tearing of the curtain and after the onset of darkness. For Matthew says, *Jesus cried again with a loud voice and yielded up his spirit*, and then he immediately adds, *And behold, the curtain of the Temple was torn.* He thereby shows quite clearly that it was torn after Jesus yielded up the spirit. If he had not added *And behold* but had just said, *The curtain of the Temple was torn*, then it would have been unclear whether he and Mark had recorded this as a summary and Luke had kept to the real order, or Luke had given a summary of what they had placed in the real order.

20,57. Matthew continues, *And the earth shook, and the rocks split, and tombs were opened, and many bodies of the saints who had been asleep arose, and coming out of the tombs after his resurrection they went into the holy city and appeared to many* (Mt 27:51–53). Though he alone narrates these things, there is no reason to fear that they appear inconsistent with anything said by the others. He continues, *When the centurion and those who were with him watching Jesus saw the earthquake and those things that happened, they were greatly afraid, saying, Truly this was the Son of God* (Mt 27:54). Mark puts it this way: *And when the centurion who stood facing him saw that he cried out and breathed his last, he said, Truly this man was the Son of God* (Mk 15:39). Luke says it thus: *Now, when the centurion saw what had happened, he glorified God, saying, Truly this was a righteous man* (Lk 23:47). There is no inconsistency here. Matthew says that the amazement of the centurion and those with him was at the sight of the earthquake, while Luke says the amazement was at his cry at the moment of death, showing that he had power over when he would die. But since Matthew says that they saw not only the earthquake but also the things that happened, he shows that it is accurate for Luke to say at this point that the centurion marveled at the Lord's death, for this was one of the miraculous things that happened then. Even if Matthew had not put it this way, one could have supposed that many miraculous things happened then and that the centurion and those with him marveled at all of them; therefore the narrators were free to choose to record any one of these as the object of their amazement. Nor is there any inconsistency if one says it was one event and another says it was another at which they marveled, for all these things amazed them. And anyone who remembers the many similar cases already mentioned and discussed will not be bothered by the fact that one reports that the centurion said, *Truly this was the Son of God*, and another that he said, *Truly this man was the Son of God*. For both these sets of words carry the same meaning. There is no contradiction if one omits the word *man* while the other includes it. It might appear more discrepant that Luke does not report that the centurion said *This was the Son of God* but rather *This was a righteous man*. Either we ought to understand that the centurion said both and that the one statement is given by two of the evangelists and the other by the third, or else that Luke wished to show what the centurion meant by saying that Jesus was the Son of God. Perhaps the centurion did not understand that he was the Only Begotten, equal to the Father, but he called him the Son of God because he believed him to be a righteous man, as many other righteous men are called sons of God. When Luke says, *When the centurion saw what had happened*, he includes in this way all those marvelous things that happened at that time, recording all the miraculous members and parts as if they were one marvelous event. And, as for the fact that Matthew mentions those who were with the centurion while the others do not, this is explained by the frequently-noted rule that there is no contradiction if one mentions what another omits.[76] And while Matthew says, *They were greatly afraid* (Mt 27:54), Luke does not say that he feared but that he glorified God. But who would not understand that he glorified God by his fear of him?

21,58. Matthew continues, *But there were many women there, far off, who had followed Jesus from Galilee, ministering to him. Among them were Mary Magdalene, and Mary the mother of James and Joseph, and the mother of the sons of Zebedee.* (Mt 27:55–56). Mark says this: *There were also women watching from afar, among whom were Mary Magdalene, and Mary the mother of James the younger and of Joseph, and Salome, who, when he was in Galilee, followed him and ministered to him, and many other women who came up with him to Jerusalem* (Mk 15:40–41). I see nothing here that could be supposed to be inconsistent. For what difference can it make to the truth that some women are named in both and some in just one? Luke, for his part, continues his narrative this way: *And all*

---

76. See, e.g., above at II,12,27–28.

the crowds of those who had assembled for that sight, when they saw what had happened, beat their breasts and returned home. And all his acquaintances and the women who had followed him from Galilee stood far off, seeing these things. (Lk 23:48–49) Clearly he is consistent with the other two as to the presence of the women, although he mentions none of them by name. As for the crowds who were there, saw what happened and beat their breasts and returned home, this is also consistent with Matthew, who specifies *the centurion and those who were with him* (Mt 27:54). Thus Luke is unique only in his mention of Jesus' acquaintances, who stood far off. For John also records the presence of the women before the Lord yielded up his spirit: *But standing by the cross of Jesus were his mother, and his mother's sister, Mary the wife of Cleophas, and Mary Magdalene. When Jesus saw his mother and the disciple whom he loved standing there, he said to his mother, Woman, behold your son. Then he said to the disciple, Behold your mother. And from that hour the disciple took her into his own house.* (Jn 19:25–27) Except for the fact that Matthew and Mark name Mary Magdalene as one who was near the cross, we might have been able to say that there were some women far away, and some right by the cross, for none of the others mentions the Lord's mother except John. But this is how we are to understand that Mary Magdalene was standing far off with the other women, as Matthew and Mark say, and also right by the cross, as John says: they were at such a distance that one could say that they were near, since they were right there in his sight, but also that they were far off in comparison to the crowds standing there with the centurion and the soldiers. Hence we ought to suppose that those women who were there with the Lord's mother, after he commended her to the disciple, began to move away to escape the press of the crowd, and they saw the rest of what happened from a distance. So the other evangelists, who mention these women after the Lord's death, report that they were then standing far off.

22,59. Matthew continues, *When it was evening, there came a certain rich man from Arimathea, named Joseph, who also was a disciple of Jesus. He went to Pilate and asked for Jesus' body. Then Pilate ordered the body to be given to him.* (Mt 27:57–58) Mark says the following: *And when it was evening, since it was the day of preparation, that is, the day before the sabbath, Joseph of Arimathea, a respected member of the council, who also looked for the kingdom of God, came and went boldly to Pilate and asked for Jesus' body. And Pilate wondered if he were already dead, and calling the centurion, he asked him if he were already dead. And when he heard the centurion's answer, he gave the body to Joseph.* (Mk 15:42–45) Luke says the following: *And behold, there was a man named Joseph, a councilman, who was a good and righteous man (he had not consented to their purpose and actions). He was from Arimathea, a Jewish city, and he was looking for the kingdom of God. He went to Pilate and asked for Jesus' body.* (Lk 23:50–52) But John tells of the breaking of the legs of those crucified with the Lord, and the piercing of the Lord's side, all of which he alone relates,[77] and then he goes on to mention Joseph in terms that agree with the others: *And after this, Joseph of Arimathea, who was a disciple of Jesus, but a secret one for fear of the Jews, asked Pilate if he might take away the body, and Pilate allowed it. So he came and took Jesus' body.* (Jn 19:38) Here there is nothing in any one of them that could seem inconsistent with any other. But one might ask whether John is inconsistent with himself, for he says along with the others that Joseph asked for Jesus' body, but he alone says that he was a disciple of the Lord in secret for fear of the Jews. For it is a legitimate question how someone who was a disciple in secret out of fear would dare to ask for his body, which none of his declared followers dared to do. We are to understand that he did this out of confidence in his status, which enabled him to approach Pilate with great familiarity. In the end, the duty of performing the burial made him worry less about the Jews, even though previously he had been used to hearing the Lord while avoiding their hostility.

23,60. Matthew continues, *And Joseph took the body and wrapped it in a clean linen shroud and laid it in his own new tomb, which he had hewn out of a rock. And he rolled a great stone to the entrance of the tomb, and he left.* (Mt 27:59–60) Mark says this: *And Joseph bought a linen shroud and, taking him down, wrapped him in the linen shroud and laid him in a tomb, which had been hewn out of the rock. And he rolled a stone to the entrance of the tomb.* (Mk 15:46) Luke says this: *And he took it down and wrapped it in a linen shroud and laid it in a tomb hewn out of the rock, in which no one had ever before been laid* (Lk 23:53). With these three no question of disagreement can be raised. But John reports that Nicodemus as well as Joseph performed the Lord's burial; in what follows he begins in this way with Nicodemus: *Nicodemus also came, who had at first come to Jesus by night, bringing a mixture of myrrh and aloes, weighing about a hundred pounds* (Jn 19:39). Then he returns to Joseph and says, *They took Jesus' body and bound it in linen cloths with spices, as is the burial custom of the Jews. Now, in the place where he was crucified there was a garden, and in the garden a new tomb where no one had ever been laid. Then, because of the Jewish day of preparation, since the tomb was nearby, they laid Jesus there.* (Jn 19:40–42) There is nothing here to put off those who have a correct understanding, since [the evangelists] who do not mention Nicodemus do not say that the Lord was buried by Joseph alone, even though they make mention only of him. Moreover, although they say that he was wrapped in linen by Joseph, this would not keep us from supposing that Nicodemus brought other cloths and added them, which is why John speaks the truth when he says that he was wrapped not in one cloth but in cloths. Furthermore, since there was a handkerchief around the head, and other strips bound around all the rest of the body, and all of these were made of linen, then there really was one linen shroud, and yet one could say with complete truthfulness that they bound it in linen cloths, for one can say "linen cloths" of anything made of linen.

---

77. See Jn 19:30–37.

24,61. Matthew continues, *Mary Magdalene and the other Mary were there, sitting opposite the sepulcher* (Mt 27:61). Marks puts it this way: *Mary Magdalene and Mary the mother of Joseph saw where he was laid* (Mk 15:47). There is clearly no discrepancy between them.

24,62. Matthew continues, *Now, the next day after the day of preparation, the chief priests and Pharisees came together before Pilate, saying, Sir, we remember how that deceiver said while he was still alive, After three days I will rise again. Therefore order that the sepulcher be made secure until the third day, so that his disciples cannot come and steal him and say to the people, He has risen from the dead, so that the last fraud will be worse than the first. Pilate said to them, You have a guard. Go, and make it as secure as you know how. So they went and secured the sepulcher, sealing the stone and setting guards.* (Mt 27:62–66). Matthew alone narrates this, but there is nothing in the others that would seem to contradict it.

24,63. Matthew then continues and says, *Now, on the evening of the sabbath,*[78] *at dawn of the first day of the week, Mary Magdalene and the other Mary came to see the sepulcher. And behold, there was a great earthquake, for an angel of the Lord descended from heaven and came and rolled back the stone and sat upon it. His appearance was like lightning and his clothes white as snow. For fear of him the guards trembled and became like dead men. And the angel answered and said to the women, Do not be afraid, for I know that you seek Jesus, who was crucified. He is not here, for he has risen, as he said. Come and see the place where the Lord was laid. And go quickly and tell his disciples that he has risen. And behold, he is going before you to Galilee; there you will see him. Behold, I have told you.* (Mt 28:1–7) Mark agrees with this.[79] But it might be a problem that, according to Matthew, the rock was already rolled away from the tomb and the angel was sitting on it, whereas Mark says that the women went into the tomb and saw a young man sitting there on the right, covered in a white robe, and they were amazed. But perhaps we are to suppose that Matthew has not mentioned the angel that they saw when they entered the tomb, and Mark has not mentioned the one that they saw outside sitting on the rock. So they saw two angels and heard what both of them said about Jesus. First they listened to the one that they saw outside sitting on the rock, then they heard the one that they saw sitting on the right when they entered the tomb. The one sitting outside encouraged them to enter by saying, *Come and see the place where the Lord was laid* (Mt 28:6). When they came, as was said, and entered, they saw the angel that Matthew does not mention and that Mark says was sitting on the right, from whom they heard things similar to what the first had told them. Or perhaps we ought to accept the explanation that when they entered the tomb area they came to a part that was walled in, which it is reasonable to suppose was contiguous with the rock wall in which the sepulcher was hewn. In this area they saw the angel sitting to the right, who Matthew says

---

78. The Greek original does not mention evening, so it does not raise the problem that Augustine's Latin version does, which he deals with at length below at III,24,65.

79. See Mk 16:1–8.

was sitting on the stone, which he had rolled away from the entrance of the tomb during the earthquake, in the area of the sepulcher that was hewn in the rock.

24,64. It can also be asked how Mark can say, *And they went out and fled from the tomb, for trembling and fear had seized them; and they said nothing to anyone, for they were afraid* (Mk 18:8), whereas Matthew says, *And they quickly departed from the tomb with fear and great joy and ran to tell his disciples* (Mk 28:8). Perhaps we are to suppose that they dared to say nothing to the angels themselves—that is, they could not respond to what they had heard from them—or indeed to the guards whom they saw lying there. For the joy mentioned by Matthew is not inconsistent with the fear described by Mark. So we ought to suppose that both these feelings were in their souls, even though Matthew does not at first mention the fear. But when he says, *And they quickly departed from the tomb with fear and great joy*, no question can remain on this point.

24,65. But a question arises that is not to be disparaged, which concerns the time at which the women came to the tomb. For inasmuch as Matthew says, *Now, on the evening of the sabbath, at dawn of the first day of the week, Mary Magdalene and the other Mary came to see the sepulcher* (Mt 28:1), how is it that Mark says, *And very early in the morning of the first day of the week they came to the tomb at sunrise* (Mk 16:2)? Mark's statement is not inconsistent with the other two, Luke and John, for Luke says *early dawn* (Lk 24:1) and John says *morning, while it was still dark* (Jn 20:1). These mean the same as Mark's *very early...at sunrise*. They all refer to the time when the sky was brightening in the east, which only happens when the sun is about to rise. This brightening is usually called dawn. Nor is there any inconsistency between this and the one who says *while it was still dark*, for when the day is breaking the remaining darkness recedes as the light advances. For one need not take *very early in the morning* to mean that the sun itself was already seen over the lands; rather, it is an expression we often use when we wish to show someone that something is to be done at a certain time. If we were to say just "morning," someone might suppose that we meant that the sun was visible over the earth; to avoid this we would add to it and say "early morning," so that they would know we meant daybreak. Likewise, it is common that after several cockcrows, when people begin to think that the day is starting, they say, "It is morning." But if after saying this they notice that the sun is rising, that is, when they see that the sun is coming near these parts and reddening or brightening the sky, then they add to "It is morning" and say "It is early morning." Neither explanation makes any difference so long as we understand that when Mark says *morning* it means the same as what Luke calls *dawn*; furthermore, that *very early in the morning* means the same as *early dawn* and the same as when John says *morning, while it was still dark*; and finally, that *sunrise* means that the sun's rising was just beginning to illuminate the sky. But how can Matthew be in agreement with these three, since he does not say *dawn* or *morning* but *on the evening of the sabbath, at dawn of the first day of the week*? This should be carefully investigated. When Matthew refers to the first part of the night, which he calls *evening*, he wishes to indicate that night at the end of which the women came to the tomb. It should be supposed that he calls attention to this night, because at that time in the evening it was lawful for them to bring the spices, since the sabbath was then over. Therefore, since it was the sabbath that prevented them from doing it, Matthew indicates the time of night at which it became lawful for them to do it, at whatever time of night they actually chose to do this. So he says *evening of the sabbath* to mean the night of the sabbath, that is, the night that followed the day of the sabbath. His words indicate this quite clearly, since he says, *Now, on the evening of the sabbath, at dawn of the first day of the week*. Hence we cannot understand *evening* to mean the first part of the night, that is, only the beginning of the night. For the dawn of the first day of the week does not come at the beginning of the night but during the night itself, which the light is beginning to bring to an end, since the end of the first part of the night is the beginning of the second part, but light is the end of the whole night. So one could not say that during the evening it was dawning on the first day of the week, unless one were to understand the word "evening" to mean the night itself, which ends with the light. It is a common way of speaking in Divine Scripture to use the part to refer to the whole. Therefore "evening" means the whole night, which ends at dawn. Those women came to the tomb at dawn; this is the same as saying that they came at night, which is referred to here as *evening*. The whole night is designated by that word, as I said. Therefore, whatever time of night they came, they came during that night. Therefore, if they came at the very end of that night, they still came unquestionably on that night. And it could not have been *on the evening... at dawn of the first day of the week* unless one understands that this refers to the whole night. Therefore those who came in the night came in the evening, and they came in the night even if they came at the very end of that night.

24,66. The three days between the Lord's death and his resurrection cannot be rightly understood except by the way of speaking that takes the part for the whole. Indeed, he himself said, *For as Jonah was three days and three nights in the whale's belly, so shall the Son of Man be three days and three nights in the heart of the earth* (Mt 12:40). However we calculate the time, whether from when he yielded up his spirit or from when he was buried, it will not come out right unless we count each of the following as a whole day—the sabbath (with its night), the day of preparation, and the first day of the week (which we call the Lord's Day). It is of no use to us that there are some who are troubled by these difficulties and are ignorant of the important role that this way of speaking of the part as the whole has in resolving questions in the Holy Scriptures. They wish to count as a night those three hours from the sixth to the ninth when the sun was hidden, and to count as a day those other three hours when the sun reappeared on earth, that is, from the ninth hour until sunset. There then follows the night of the sabbath and, counting it with its day, there would then be two nights and two days.[80] Then there

---

80. Augustine's discussion, confusing enough as it is, is rendered more complex by the custom of reckoning days (as in Jewish law) from sunset to sunset; although many usually think of the sabbath as Saturday, in fact it extends from sundown on Friday to sundown on Saturday.

comes the night after the sabbath, the night of the first day of the week, which ends with the dawning of the Lord's Day; it was at this time that the Lord rose. By this calculation there were two nights, two days, and one more night (we would have to take this last one as a complete night and not show that this dawn was the very end of it). Therefore, not even by taking these six hours—three of darkness and three of light—and counting them this way could one come up with the three days and three nights. So we must calculate the time based on that way of speaking of the part as the whole that is so common in the Scriptures. Consequently we must take the day of preparation, on which the Lord was crucified and buried, as a complete day and night, even though its night was already over. Likewise, we must take the sabbath as a complete whole and not just a part. Finally, the third day must be counted from its first part; that is, its night must count as the whole day, including its daylight portion. Thus there were three days, in the same way as there were eight days after which the Lord went up onto a mountain. In that case Matthew and Mark only count the intervening complete days and therefore say *after six days* (Mt 17:1; Mk 9:2), whereas Luke says *after eight days* (Lk 9:28).[81]

24,67. Now let us examine the others as to whether they agree with Matthew. For Luke says most clearly that the women who came to the tomb saw two angels. We have understood that these two angels are reported separately by the first two evangelists. Matthew speaks of the one who was outside the tomb sitting on the rock, while Mark speaks of the one who was inside the tomb sitting on the right. But Luke puts it this way: *It was the day of preparation, and the sabbath was beginning. The women who had come with him from Galilee followed, and they saw the tomb and how his body was laid. And they returned and prepared spices and ointments. And on the sabbath they rested according to the commandment. But on the first day of the week, at early dawn, they came to the tomb carrying the spices they had prepared. And they found the stone rolled away from the tomb, and when they went in they did not find the body of the Lord Jesus. And it happened that, as their minds were perplexed about this, behold, two men stood by them in shining apparel. And as they were afraid and were bowing their faces to the ground, they said to them, Why do you seek the living among the dead? He is not here but has risen. Remember how he spoke to you while he was still in Galilee, saying, The Son of Man must be delivered into the hands of sinful men, and be crucified, and on the third day rise. And they remembered his words. And returning from the tomb, they announced all this to the eleven and to all the rest.* (Lk 23:54–24:9) Although they spoke to the women similarly, how can these two [angels] have been seen separately, one sitting outside on the rock, according to Matthew, and the other sitting inside on the right, according to Mark, if Luke says they both stood beside the women? Perhaps we can understand that both Matthew and Mark describe the women as having seen one angel, as we discussed above. We may take it that when the women came into the area of the tomb they entered

---

81.   See above at II,56,113.

a place with a wall around it, thereby entering the space in front of the stone sepulcher. And it was there that they saw the angel sitting on the rock that had been rolled away from the tomb, as Matthew reports, which meant he was sitting on the right, as Mark says. Then going inside, the women looked at the place where the body of the Lord had lain, and they saw two other angels standing there, as reported by Luke. These angels said similar things to them, encouraging their souls and lifting up their faith.

24,68. But let us also examine what John says, to see whether and in what way it agrees with [Matthew, Mark and Luke]. John says this, then: *Now, on the first day of the week, Mary Magdalene came to the tomb in the morning, while it was still dark, and saw that the stone was taken away from the tomb. So she ran and came to Simon Peter and to the other disciple, whom Jesus loved, and said to them, They have taken the Lord out of the tomb, and we do not know where they have put him. So Peter and that other disciple went out and came to the tomb. The two ran together, and that other disciple ran faster than Peter and came to the tomb first. And when he stooped down, he saw the linen cloths, but he did not go in. Then Simon Peter came, following him, and went into the tomb; and he saw the linen cloths lying, and the handkerchief that had been on his head, not lying with the linen cloths but rolled up in a place by itself. Then the disciple who had reached the tomb first also entered, and he saw and believed. For he did not yet know the Scripture, that he had to rise from the dead. Then the disciples went back again to their homes, but Mary stood weeping outside the tomb. As she was weeping, then, she stooped down and looked into the tomb and saw two angels in white, sitting where the body of Jesus had been placed, one at the head and one at the feet. They said to her, Woman, why are you weeping? She said to them, Because they have taken away my Lord, and I do not know where they have put him. When she said this, she turned around and saw Jesus standing but did not know that it was Jesus. Jesus said to her, Woman, why are you weeping? Whom are you seeking? Thinking that he was the gardener, she said to him, Sir, if you have carried him away, tell me where you have put him, and I shall take him away. Jesus said to her, Mary. She turned and said to him, Rabboni, which means teacher. Jesus said to her, Do not touch me, for I have not yet ascended to my Father, but go to my brothers and tell them that I am ascending to my Father and your Father, to my God and your God. Mary Magdalene came and told the disciples, I have seen the Lord, and he told me these things.* (Jn 20:1–18) John's narrative agrees with the others as to the day and time when they came to the tomb. As to the two angels who were seen, he agrees with Luke. But regarding whether the angels were standing or sitting, and other matters which the authors do not mention, it remains for us to show how there are no discrepancies among them and in which order these things happened. Unless we consider this carefully, there may appear to be inconsistencies among them.

24,69. Therefore, with the Lord's help, let us take all these things that happened at the time of the Lord's resurrection, according to the testimonies of all the evangelists, and arrange them into one narrative, as they could have occurred. At dawn of the first day of the week, as they all agree, they came to the tomb. By then the things recorded by Matthew alone had occurred—the earthquake, the rolling away of the stone, and the guards' fear, which in some way prostrated them like dead men.[82] Then, as John says, Mary Magdalene came, whose love was unquestionably more fervent than that of the other women who had ministered to the Lord;[83] therefore it is not unwarranted of John to mention her alone and to omit the others who came with her, who are mentioned by the other evangelists. So she came and saw the stone taken away from the tomb; she did not make any more careful investigation, for she had no doubt that Jesus' body was gone, so she ran, as John reports, and told this to Peter and to John himself, who is the disciple whom Jesus loved. And they began to run to the tomb; John arrived first, and he stooped down and saw the linen cloths lying there, but he did not enter. Peter followed next, and he did enter the tomb, and *he saw the linen cloths lying, and the handkerchief that had been on his head, not lying with the other cloths but rolled up in a place by itself* (Jn 20:6–7). Then John entered and saw the same things, and he believed what Mary had told him, that the Lord had been taken from the tomb. *For they did not yet know the Scripture, that he had to rise from the dead. Then the disciples went back again to their homes, but Mary stood outside the tomb weeping.* (Jn 20:9–11) She was outside the place where the sepulcher was hewn but inside the area that they had entered. There was a garden there, as John reports.[84] Then they saw the angel sitting on the rock on the right side, as described by both Matthew and Mark.[85] Then he said to them, *Do not be afraid, for I know that you seek Jesus, who was crucified. He is not here, for he has risen, as he said. Come and see the place where the Lord was laid. And go quickly and tell his disciples that he has risen. And behold, he is going before you to Galilee. There you will see him. Behold, I have told you.* (Mt 28:5–7) Mark describes this similarly.[86] At these words, Mary, still weeping, *stooped down and looked into the tomb and saw two angels in white,* as John says, *sitting where the body of Jesus had been placed, one at the head and one at the feet. They said to her, Woman, why are you weeping? She said to them, Because they have taken away my Lord, and I do not know where they have put him.* (Jn 20:12–13) We must suppose that the angels got up at this point, so that they were also seen standing, as Luke reports,[87] and, according to Luke, they said to the frightened women as they were bowing their faces to the ground, *Why do you seek the living among the dead? He is not here but has risen. Remember how he spoke to you while he was still in Galilee, saying, The Son of Man must be delivered into the hands of sinful men, and be crucified, and on the*

82. See Mt 28:2–4.
83. See Lk 7:36–50.
84. See Jn 19:41.
85. See Mt 28:2; Mk 16:5.
86. See Mk 16:6–7.
87. See Lk 24:4.

third day rise. And they remembered his words. (Lk 24:5–8) After this, John tells us that Mary *turned around and saw Jesus standing but did not know that it was Jesus. Jesus said to her, Woman, why are you weeping? Whom are you seeking? Thinking that he was the gardener, she said to him, Sir, if you have carried him away, tell me where you have put him, and I shall take him away. Jesus said to her, Mary. She turned and said to him, Rabboni, which means teacher. Jesus said to her, Do not touch me, for I have not yet ascended to my Father, but go to my brothers and tell them that I am ascending to my Father and your Father, to my God and your God.* (Jn 20:14–17) Then she left the tomb, that is, the place where there was a garden in front of the hewn rock. With her were the other women, who Mark tells us were seized with fear and trembling; these were the ones who said nothing to anyone.[88] Now we return to Matthew's account: *Behold, Jesus met them and said, Hail! They came up to him and took hold of his feet and worshiped him.* (Mt 28:9) From this we gather that the angels spoke to them twice when they came to the tomb. The Lord spoke twice as well, once when Mary thought he was the gardener and once now when he met them on the way, repeating himself in order to strengthen them and lift them out of their fear: *Then he said to them, Do not be afraid, but go, tell my brothers to go into Galilee, and there they will see me* (Mt 28:10). Then Mary Magdalene came and told the disciples that she had seen the Lord and that he had said these things to her[89]—and not just to her but also to others, as Luke reports; they announced these things to the eleven disciples and to all the others,[90] *but these words seemed crazy to them, and they did not believe them* (Lk 24:11). This is confirmed by Mark. For, after reporting that they left the tomb with fear and trembling and said nothing to anyone,[91] he adds that the Lord rose early on the first day of the week and *appeared first to Mary Magdalene, from whom he had cast out seven demons,* and that *she went and told those who had been with him as they mourned and wept,* and that *when they heard that he was alive and had been seen by her, they did not believe it* (Mk 16:9–11). Matthew also inserts that, as the women who had seen and heard all these things were going away, some of the guards, who had been lying like dead men, came to the city and told the chief priests everything that had happened, or at least everything that they themselves had been able to witness. Then they gathered with the elders and took counsel, and they gave a large sum of money to the soldiers to say that his disciples had come and stolen him while they were asleep; they also promised to protect them from the governor, who had supplied those guards. And they took the money and did as they were taught, and this story is widespread among the Jews until this day.[92]

---

88. See Mk 16:8.
89. See Jn 20:18.
90. See Lk 24:10.
91. See Mk 16:8.
92. See Mt 28:11–15.

25,70. Now we must consider how the Lord appeared to the disciples after his resurrection, so as to show not only the agreement of the four evangelists in this matter but also how they are in harmony with the apostle Paul, who speaks of this as follows in his First Epistle to the Corinthians: *For I delivered to you in the first place what I also received, that Christ died for our sins in accordance with the Scriptures, and that he was buried, and that he rose on the third day in accordance with the Scriptures, and that he appeared to Cephas, afterwards to the twelve. Then he appeared to more than five hundred brethren at one time, most of whom remain today, though some have fallen asleep. Afterwards he appeared to James, then to all the apostles. Last of all, as to one born out of time, he appeared also to me.* (1 Cor 15:3–8) None of the evangelists give this order, so we must consider whether their order is not in opposition to this. [Paul] does not include everything, and neither do they, but what must be examined is whether, among all the things that they report, they show any inconsistency among themselves. Luke is the only one of the four evangelists who does not mention that the women saw the Lord but only the angels.[93] Matthew says that he met them as they returned from the tomb.[94] Mark says that he was first seen by Mary Magdalene;[95] John says this too.[96] Mark does not say how he appeared, although this is explained by John. Luke, however, not only fails to mention that he appeared to the women, as I said, but he also tells of the two men, one of whom was Cleophas, who spoke with him before they recognized him. He thereby makes it seem that the women had only told of the appearance to them of the angels, who had said that he was alive, for this is what he narrates: *Behold, that day two of them were going to a village named Emmaus, which was sixty stadia from Jerusalem, and they were talking to one another about all these things that had occurred. And it happened that, as they were speaking and discussing together, Jesus himself drew near and went with them. But their eyes were kept from recognizing him. And he said to them, What are these things that you are saying to one another as you are walking along and are sad? Then the one named Cleophas answered and said to him, Are you the only visitor in Jerusalem who does not know what has happened there in these days? He said to them, What things? And they said, Concerning Jesus of Nazareth, who was a prophet mighty in deed and word before God and all the people, and how the chief priests and our rulers handed him over to be condemned to death, and crucified him. But we had hoped that he was the one who would redeem Israel. And now, besides all this, it is the third day since this happened. And some women among us amazed us. Before it was light they went to the tomb and did not find his body. They came back, saying that they had seen a vision of angels, who had said that he was alive. And some among us went to the tomb and found it just as*

---

93. Augustine is presumably referring to Lk 24:4–7, but in fact this passage does not say that the angels saw the Lord.
94. See Mt 28:8–10.
95. See Mk 16:9.
96. See Jn 20:14–17.

the women had said, but him they did not see. (Lk 24:13–24) According to Luke, this is what they said. They spoke as they were able to recall what the women had said, or what the disciples had said after they had run to the tomb upon hearing that his body was gone from there. Luke himself also says that in fact only Peter ran to the tomb and, bending down, saw the linen cloths lying by themselves, and he went home, wondering at what had happened.[97] He mentions this about Peter before he gives the account of the two whom [Jesus] found on the way and after he gives the account of the women who had seen the angels and heard from them that Jesus had risen, as though it were at this point that Peter ran to the tomb. But, rather, it should be supposed that Luke puts it here as a recapitulation. For Peter and John ran to the tomb at the same time, and when they ran there they only knew what the women, especially Mary Magdalene, had told them—that the body was gone. Mary announced this when she saw the stone rolled away from the tomb. It was later that they saw the angels and then the Lord himself, who appeared to the women twice, once at the tomb and again when he met them as they were returning from the tomb. And this happened before he was seen on the way by the two, one of whom was Cleophas. When Cleophas was speaking with the Lord, before he recognized him, he did not say that Peter had gone to the tomb but that *some among us went to the tomb and found it just as the women had said* (Lk 24:24). This also is to be understood as a recapitulation, since it refers to when the women came and told Peter and John that the Lord's body was gone. So when Luke says that Peter ran to the tomb and that Cleophas said that some of them went to the tomb, this is to be understood as confirming John's account, which said that two ran to the tomb. Luke mentions only Peter at first, because Mary told him first. It may be troubling that Luke does not say that Peter entered but only that he bent down and saw the linen cloths by themselves and then left in wonderment, whereas John says that it was he himself, since he was the disciple whom Jesus loved, who saw this, for he did not enter the tomb, but, arriving there first, stooped down and saw the linen cloths laid there, although he says that he entered later. So we must suppose that Peter first bent down and saw, as Luke reports but John does not mention; then he entered before John did. Hence, as we can see, all these speak accurately and without any inconsistency.

25,71. We must bring together, then, the Lord's appearances to the male disciples, leaving out what he said to the women, and show the order of events as they were able to take place, in accordance not only with the testimony of the four evangelists but also with that of Paul. Of all the men, then, we may suppose that he appeared to Peter first; at least this seems to be the case from the records of all four evangelists and the apostle Paul. But who would be bold enough either to affirm or deny that he might have appeared before Peter to someone who is not mentioned by any of the witnesses? For Paul does not say, "He appeared first to Cephas" but *He appeared to Cephas, afterwards to the twelve. Then he appeared to more than*

---

97. See Lk 24:12.

five hundred brethren at one time. (1 Cor 15:5–6) Thus it is not clear who these twelve were, or who these five hundred were. It is possible that these were twelve unknown people out of the crowd of disciples. If [Paul] meant those whom [Jesus] named apostles, then he would have said eleven and not twelve, as indeed some versions have. But I think that this is an emendation inserted by some who were troubled by this text, for they supposed that this referred to the twelve apostles, who were only eleven after the demise of Judas. So it may be that those versions that read *eleven* are more correct, or that the apostle Paul wished to indicate some other twelve disciples, or that he wanted to retain that sacred number even after they were only eleven, because the fact that there were twelve apostles had such a mystical importance that they had to elect just one person, Matthias, to take Judas's place,[98] in order to preserve this sacred number.[99] But whichever of these is the case, there is nothing that appears inconsistent with the truth or inconsistent among these most truthful writers. It seems probable that, after appearing to Peter, he then appeared to those two, of whom one was Cleophas, and about whom Luke gives a complete account and Mark only a brief note: *After this*, he says, *he appeared in another form to two of them as they were walking and going to a village* (Mk 16:12). For it is not ridiculous to suppose that a settlement could also be called a village.[100] Indeed, Bethlehem itself is now called a village, even though formerly it was called a city,[101] and despite the fact that its honor has grown as the name of the Lord born there has been spread throughout the churches of all nations. In the Greek we find *farm* rather than *village*.[102] But "farm" refers not only to settlements but also to towns and colonies beyond the city, which is the head and mother, as it were, of the rest, which is why it is called a metropolis.[103]

25,72. As for the fact that Mark says that the Lord appeared to them in another form, Luke expresses the same thing when he says that their eyes were kept from recognizing him, for something happened to their eyes, and they were allowed to remain this way until the breaking of the bread, for the sake of an undoubted mystery.[104] So he really did appear to them in a different form, and they did not recognize him until the breaking of the bread, as Luke's version shows. So, just as their minds could not comprehend that Christ had to die and rise again, something similar happened to their eyes. It was not that the truth misled them but that they themselves were incapable of perceiving the truth and therefore thought of it as

98. See Acts 1:26.
99. "This sacred number": *sacramentum eiusdem numeri*, i.e., "the sacrament of this same number."
100. "Settlement...village": *castellum...villam*. Augustine comments on this because Luke refers to Emmaus, the destination of the two disciples, as a *castellum* (Lk 24:13), whereas Mark calls it a *villa* (Mk 16:12).
101. See Lk 2:4.
102. Augustine is referring now once again to Lk 24:13, where the Greek has *kome*, which in fact also translates as "village."
103. The word "metropolis" derives from two Greek words meaning "mother" and "city."
104. "For the sake of an undoubted mystery": *certi mysterii causa*. From what follows it is clear that Augustine is referring to the breaking of the bread at Emmaus as a foreshadowing of the mystery, or the sacrament, of the eucharist.

something else. So one cannot think that one knows Christ unless one is part of his body, the Church, the unity of which the Apostle indicates in the sacrament of the bread: *One bread, we who are many are one body* (1 Cor 10:17). When he handed them the bread he had blessed, their eyes were opened and they recognized him. They were opened to knowledge of him by the removal of that obstacle that had kept them from recognizing him, for clearly they were not walking with their eyes closed, but there was something in them that kept them from recognizing what they saw, which often happens because of dullness or a certain kind of disposition. It is not that the Lord could not transform his flesh in such a way that his form really would be different from the one they were used to seeing. Indeed, even before his passion he was transfigured on the mountain, so that his face shone like the sun.[105] He could change any body into any other kind of body that he wished to, just as he changed real water into real wine.[106] It is just that he did not do so when he appeared in a different form to those two people. To them he did not appear to be what he was because their eyes were kept from recognizing him. It would not be inappropriate for us to suppose that this obstacle to their sight came from Satan, so that they would not recognize Jesus. But Christ allowed this, nonetheless, until the sacrament of the bread, showing that participation in the unity of his body removes the enemy's obstacle, so that Christ can be recognized.

25,73. We should believe that these are the same persons that Mark describes, for he says that they went and told the others, just as Luke says that they got up at that same hour and returned to Jerusalem and found the eleven gathered together and those who were with them, who said that the Lord had truly risen and appeared to Simon, and then goes on to have them tell what had happened on the way, and how they knew him in the breaking of bread.[107] By that time, therefore, Jesus' resurrection had been made known by those women and by Simon Peter, to whom he had already appeared. So, when these two people came to the ones in Jerusalem, they found them talking about this. It may have been fear that kept them from mentioning on the way that they had heard of his resurrection, when they said that only angels had been seen by the women. Since they did not know to whom they were speaking, it would have been reasonable for them to be worried about discussing Christ's resurrection in an incautious way, lest they fall into the hands of the Jews. Mark says, *They told the others, but they did not believe them* (Mk 16:13), while Luke says that they were already talking about the Lord's resurrection and his appearance to Simon.[108] Should we not then suppose that there were some there who refused to believe them? And to whom can it not be clear that Mark omits some things that Luke explains more fully in his narrative, such as the conversation they had with Jesus before they recognized him, and how they recognized him in the breaking of bread? For, after he says that Jesus appeared

---

105. See Mt 17:2.
106. See Jn 2:1–11.
107. See Lk 24:33–35.
108. See Lk 24:34.

to them in a different form as they were going into a village, he continues thus: *And they went and told the others, but they did not believe them* (Mk 16:13). But how could they speak of someone whom they did not recognize, or how could they recognize someone who appeared to them in a different form? Mark, to be sure, leaves out how they came to recognize him so that they could tell the others. We ought to keep this in mind so that we may become accustomed to noticing the evangelists' habit of omitting the things that they do not record and connecting the things that they do record; there is no greater source of error than not taking this practice into consideration, which leads some to suppose there are inconsistencies among [the evangelists].

25,74. Luke continues, then, and says, *As they were talking about these things, Jesus stood in their midst and said to them, Peace to you; it is I; do not be afraid.*[109] *But they were startled and frightened and thought that they were seeing a spirit. And he said to them, Why are you troubled, and why do thoughts arise in your hearts? Look at my hands and feet, that it is I. Touch and see, for a spirit does not have flesh and bones as you see I have. And when he had said this, he showed them his hands and feet.* (Lk 24:36–40) We are to suppose that John is referring to the same manifestation of the Lord when he says the following: *Then, when it was late on the first day of the week, the doors being shut where the disciples were for fear of the Jews, Jesus came and stood in their midst and said to them, Peace to you. And when he had said this, he showed them his hands and side.* (Jn 20:19–20) And with these words from John we may connect some things that Luke mentions but which John omits, for Luke continues thus: *And while they did not believe for joy, and were in wonderment, he said, Do you have anything here to eat? And they gave him a piece of broiled fish and a honeycomb.*[110] *And when he had eaten before them, he took what was left and gave it to them.* (Lk 24:41–43)[111] One should connect these words to some that are omitted by Luke but given by John: *The disciples were glad, then, when they saw the Lord. He said to them again, Peace to you. As the Father has sent me, so also I send you. When he had said this, he breathed on them and said to them, Receive the Holy Spirit. If you forgive the sins of any, then they are forgiven, and if you retain the sins of any, then they are retained.* (Jn 20:20–23) On the other hand, one should add to this something that John omits but Luke records: *And he said to them, These are my words which I spoke to you while I was still with you, that everything written about me in the law of Moses and the prophets and the Psalms must be fulfilled. Then he opened their minds to understand the Scriptures, and he said to them, Thus it is written, that the Christ must suffer and rise from the dead on the third*

---

109. This first sentence of the gospel citation exists in at least two other versions, which omit parts of Augustine's version.
110. Although the Latin version of Lk 24:42 that Augustine knew included the words *and a honeycomb*, they are not found in the best Greek manuscripts.
111. The last sentence, Lk 24:43, is shorter in most Greek manuscripts: *And he took it and ate before them.*

day and that repentance and forgiveness of sins should be preached in his name in all nations, beginning from Jerusalem. You are witnesses of these things. And I am sending the promise of my Father upon you. But stay here until you are clothed with power from on high. (Lk 24:44–49) See how Luke records the promise of the Holy Spirit, which we do not find that the Lord makes elsewhere, except in John's Gospel.[112] This merits more than just a passing notice, so that we may bear in mind how the evangelists confirm one another, even regarding things that they do not themselves record but that they nonetheless know have been recorded. After this, Luke omits everything else that happened, recording nothing other than Jesus' ascent into heaven.[113] And he connects this in such a way that it seems as though it happened immediately after [Jesus] said these words, together with the other things that occurred on the first day of the week, that is, the day on which the Lord rose, but Luke himself says in the Acts of the Apostles that this took place on the fortieth day after his resurrection.[114] Finally, John says that the apostle Thomas was not with them at this time,[115] while Luke says that the two persons, one of whom was Cleophas, returned to Jerusalem and found the eleven gathered together and those who were with them.[116] There is no doubt that we should suppose that Thomas left there before the Lord appeared to them while they were discussing these things.

25,75. John then reports another manifestation of the Lord to the disciples eight days later. Thomas was present this time, though he had not seen him the first time. John continues, *And eight days later his disciples were again inside, and Thomas was with them. Jesus came in, although the doors were shut, and stood in their midst and said, Peace to you. Then he said to Thomas, Put your finger here, and look at my hands, and put out your hand and put it in my side. And do not be disbelieving but believing. Thomas answered and said to him, My Lord and my God! Jesus said to him, Because you have seen, you have believed; blessed are those who have not seen and have believed.* (Jn 20:26–29) This second appearance of the Lord to the disciples—that is, the one that John records as second—might have seemed to be the same as the one that Mark refers to in his usual brief style, except that it is problematic that he says, *Lastly*[117] *he appeared to the eleven as they sat at table* (Mk 16:14). The problem is not that John does not mention their sitting at table, for he might have omitted that, but rather that [Mark] says *lastly* as though he did not appear to them after that, whereas John reports a third manifestation by the sea of Tiberias. Moreover, Mark says that he reproached *their unbelief and hardness of heart, because they had not believed those who saw him after he had risen* (Mk 16:14). This refers to the two who were on their way to the village and saw him after he had risen, and to Peter, who first saw him, as our investigation of

---

112. See Jn 14:26; 15:26.
113. See Lk 24:50–51.
114. See Acts 1:3.
115. See Jn 20:24.
116. See Lk 24:33.
117. "Lastly": *novissime.* This is not a problem in the original, where the Greek word means only "afterwards."

Luke showed,[118] and possibly to Mary Magdalene and the other women who went with her when he appeared to them at the tomb, and again when he met them on their way back.[119] For Mark constructs his narrative so that there is first a brief report of the two who saw him as they were on their way to the village; then they tell this to the others, who do not believe them; and then, *Lastly he appeared to the eleven as they sat at table, and he reproached their unbelief and hardness of heart, because they had not believed those who saw him after he had risen* (Mk 16:14). How are we to take *lastly*—as if they did not see him after this? For the last time that the apostles saw the Lord on the earth was when he ascended into heaven, which happened forty days after his resurrection.[120] But why would he reproach them then for not believing those who had seen him after he had risen, when by then they themselves had often seen him after his resurrection? Indeed, they themselves had seen him on the very day of his resurrection, that is, on the first day of the week, around nighttime, as Luke and John report it.[121] Therefore we must suppose that all these things happened on the day of his resurrection, that is, the first day of the week. On that day Mary and the other women with her saw him at dawn. Peter also saw him then. Also, those two, one of whom was Cleophas, saw him, as Mark seems to record as well.[122] Then around nighttime he appeared to the eleven, except Thomas, and those who were with them, and it was to this group that those people had told what they had seen. Mark wishes to record all this in his usual brief style. So when he says *lastly* it is because this was the last thing to happen on that day. Night was beginning to fall as the two returned from the settlement, where they had recognized him in the breaking of bread, to Jerusalem, where Luke says they found the eleven and those who were with them discussing the Lord's resurrection and his appearance to Peter. These two told them what had happened on the way and how they had recognized him in the breaking of bread.[123] But there must have been some there who did not believe, which shows the truth of Mark's statement that *they did not believe them* (Mk 16:13). They were sitting at table then, as Mark says,[124] and discussing these things, as Luke says,[125] when the Lord stood among them and said to them, *Peace to you* (Lk 24:36; Jn 20:19.26), as Luke and John report. Also, the doors were closed when he entered, as John alone records.[126] And among those things that the Lord said to the disciples, as Luke and John report, there was also this reproach, regarding which Mark says that they did not believe those who had seen him after he had risen.

---

118. See Lk 24:13–35.
119. See Mt 28:1–10 par.
120. See Acts 1:3.9.
121. See Lk 24:1; Jn 20:1.
122. See Mk 16:12.
123. See Lk 24:33–35.
124. See Mk 16:14.
125. See Lk 24:36.
126. See Jn 20:19.26.

25,76. But perhaps it is troubling, again, that Mark says that he appeared to the eleven as they sat at table,[127] whereas Luke and John report that it was the beginning of the night of the Lord's Day.[128] John clearly says that the apostle Thomas was not with them then;[129] we believe that he went out before the Lord entered but after those two returned from the settlement and were speaking with the eleven, as we find in Luke. Indeed, in Luke's narrative there is a point at which one may suppose that, as they were speaking, Thomas left and then the Lord entered.[130] But since Mark says, *Lastly he appeared to the eleven as they sat at table*, this obliges us to admit that Thomas was still with them. But perhaps, despite the absence of one, he still chose to call them *the eleven* because the company of apostles was called by this number before Matthias was elected to take Judas's place. Or, if there is a difficulty in accepting this, we may suppose that, after he had made so many manifestations of his presence to the disciples during the forty days, he also appeared to the eleven one last time as they sat at table on the fortieth day itself. And at that time, as he was about to ascend into heaven, he wished on that day especially to reproach them for not believing those who had seen him after he had risen, until they themselves had seen him. He did this because after his ascension they would be preaching the Gospel to the gentiles, who would have to believe what they did not see. Right after this reproach, in fact, Mark says, *And he said to them, Go into the whole world and preach the Gospel to every creature. He who believes and is baptized shall be saved, but he who does not believe shall be condemned.* (Mk 16:15–16) So, if they were to preach that one who does not believe will be condemned, and what one does not believe is that which one cannot see, should he not have reproached them? For before they themselves saw the Lord they did not believe those to whom he had appeared.

25,77. There is a further reason for us to believe that this was the last time that the Lord manifested himself bodily on earth to the apostles, for Mark continues thus: *And these signs shall follow those who believe: in my name they shall cast out demons; they shall speak in new tongues; they shall pick up snakes, and if they drink anything deadly it shall not hurt them; they shall lay their hands on the sick, and they shall recover* (Mk 16:17–18). Then he adds, *And the Lord, after he had spoken to them, was taken up into heaven and took his seat at the right hand of God. Then they went forth and preached everywhere, the Lord working with them and confirming the message with the signs that followed it.* (Mk 16:19–20) When he says, *And the Lord, after he had spoken to them, was taken up into heaven* (Mk 16:19), this would seem to show quite clearly that this was the last time he spoke to them on earth, although it does not seem to exclude any other meaning, for he does not say "after he had said these things to them" but rather *after he had spoken to them*. So, if necessary, it would be possible to suppose that

127. See Mk 16:14.
128. See Lk 24:29.36; Jn 20:19.
129. See Jn 20:24.
130. It is hard to ascertain what Augustine had in mind and when this point occurs.

this was neither the last time that he spoke to them nor the last day that he was present with them on earth. Perhaps all the things he spoke to them on all those days are implied in the one phrase, *After he had spoken to them, he was taken up into heaven*, but our previous discussion has persuaded us rather that this was the last day.[131] So we need not suppose that this happened previously, when they were only ten, because of Thomas's absence. After these words, then, that Mark records, and after those said by the disciples and by the Lord that are recorded in the Acts of the Apostles,[132] we believe that the Lord was taken up into heaven on the fortieth day after the day of his resurrection.

25,78. But John, although he admits that he has omitted many of the things that Jesus did,[133] nonetheless wishes to record a third appearance to the disciples after his resurrection. This happened at the Sea of Tiberias to seven disciples—Peter, Thomas, Nathanael, the sons of Zebedee, and two others who are not named.[134] While they were fishing, and at his command, they cast the net on the right side and drew out many fish, one hundred and fifty-three. At this time he also asked Peter three times whether he loved him, and he told him to feed his sheep. He also predicted what Peter would suffer, and he said of John himself, *I wish him to remain until I come* (Jn 21:23). With this John ends his Gospel.

25,79. Now we must inquire what his first appearance to the disciples in Galilee was, because the one that John places third happened in Galilee by the Sea of Tiberias. This is obvious if one recalls the miracle of the five loaves, which John begins to recount by saying, *After this Jesus went across the Sea of Galilee, of Tiberias* (Jn 6:1). And where else but Galilee could one suppose that he ought to have appeared first to his disciples after his resurrection? One should recall the angel's words, given by Matthew, spoken to the women as they came to the tomb: *Do not be afraid, for I know that you seek Jesus who was crucified. He is not here, for he has risen, as he said. Come, see the place where the Lord was laid. And go quickly and tell his disciples that he has risen. And behold, he is going before you to Galilee; there you will see him. Behold, I have told you.* (Mt 28:5–7) Mark's version is similar, whether it is the same angel or a different one: *Do not be amazed. You seek Jesus of Nazareth, who was crucified. He is risen, he is not here. Behold the place where they laid him. But go, tell his disciples and Peter that he is going before you to Galilee. There you will see him, as he told you.* (Mk 16:6–7) These words seem to indicate that Jesus was not going to show himself to his disciples after his resurrection, except in Galilee. But Mark himself does not report this appearance, even though he says that he appeared first to Mary Magdalene early in the morning of the first day of the week. She then told the disciples who had been with him, as they mourned and wept, but they did not believe her. After this he appeared to two people as they were going to a village, and they told what had

---

131. See above at III,25,76.
132. See Acts 1:1–8.
133. See Jn 21:24–25.
134. See Jn 21:1–23.

happened to the others; Luke and John both confirm that this happened in Jerusalem on the very day of his resurrection, at the beginning of the night. Then Mark comes to that appearance which he calls the last, made to the eleven as they sat at table; after this he says he was taken up into heaven, which we know happened on the Mount of Olives, not far from Jerusalem.[135] So Mark never records the carrying out of what he testifies was predicted by the angel. Matthew mentions no earlier or later appearance, and he says that the disciples saw the Lord in no place other than Galilee, as the angel had predicted. Matthew first describes how the angel spoke to the women; then he says that, as they were going, the guards were bribed to lie; and then he goes on to describe the appearance in Galilee, as though it followed immediately on the preceding. Indeed, when the angel said, *He has risen. And behold, he is going before you to Galilee; there you will see him* (Mt 28:7), it made it seem as though this would follow immediately. *Then*, he says, *the eleven disciples went to Galilee, to the mountain where Jesus had directed them. And when they saw him they worshiped him, but some doubted. And Jesus came and spoke to them, saying, All power in heaven and on earth has been given to me. Go therefore and teach all the nations, baptizing them in the name of the Father and of the Son and of the Holy Spirit, teaching them to observe all that I have commanded you. And behold, I am with you all days until the end of the age.* (Mt 28:16–20) With that Matthew concludes his Gospel.

25,80. From this we might have thought that the Lord's first appearance to the disciples after his resurrection was nowhere else than in Galilee, but we are obliged by reflection on the others' narratives to investigate this more carefully. Likewise, if Mark had failed to mention the angel's prediction, one might have supposed that Matthew told of the disciples going to the mountain in Galilee and worshiping the Lord in order to make it seem that the angel's command and prediction, which Matthew had narrated, had indeed been fulfilled. But Luke and John make it sufficiently clear that on the very day of his resurrection the Lord was seen in Jerusalem by his disciples,[136] which is so far from Galilee that it would have been impossible for him to be seen on the same day by the same people in both places. And Mark, who gives a similar prediction by the angel, does not report an appearance in Galilee by the Lord to the disciples after his resurrection. These facts strongly urge us to investigate what is meant when it is said, *Behold, he is going before you to Galilee; there you will see him* (Mt 28:7; Mk 16:7). If Matthew had never said that the eleven disciples went away to the mountain in Galilee that Jesus had directed them to and saw him and worshiped him there, we might have supposed that this prediction was not literally fulfilled but was a prediction with a completely figurative meaning. This would be similar to what we found in Luke, *Behold, I cast out demons and perform cures today and tomorrow, and on the third day I complete my course* (Lk 13:32), which was clearly not fulfilled literal-

---

135. See Mk 16:9–19.
136. See Lk 24:33–36; Jn 20:19.

ly.[137] If the angel had said, *He is going before you into Galilee,* and then continued by saying, "there you will see him first" or "only there will you see him" or "you will see him nowhere else but there," then without a doubt Matthew would be incompatible with the others. But he only says, *Behold, he is going before you to Galilee; there you will see him.* He does not say when this will be, or whether it will be the first appearance before he is seen by them elsewhere, or whether it will be after they have seen him in places other than Galilee. Furthermore, although Matthew says that the disciples went to a mountain in Galilee, he does not say on what day this happened, nor does he order his narrative to make us suppose that this was necessarily the first appearance. So he is not opposed to the narratives of the others, and we may understand and accept their accounts as well at this point. Nonetheless, although the Lord did not indicate where he would first appear, he did indicate that he had to appear later in Galilee. He indicated this both through the angel's words, *Behold, he is going before you to Galilee; there you will see him,* and his own, *Go, tell my brothers to go to Galilee; there they will see me* (Mt 28:10). This would make any believer eager to find out how to understand this mysterious saying.

25,81. First we must consider when he might have appeared bodily in Galilee, for Matthew says, *Then the eleven disciples went away to Galilee, to the mountain where the Lord had directed them. And when they saw him they worshiped him, but some doubted.* (Mt 28:16–17) Clearly this was not on the day of his resurrection, for Luke and John most clearly agree that on that day he was seen in Jerusalem at the beginning of the night.[138] Mark is not so clear about this. So when did they see the Lord in Galilee? It cannot have been the appearance described by John at the Sea of Tiberias, for there were only seven there, and they were found fishing.[139] We are seeking when the appearance described by Matthew occurred, when the eleven went to the mountain to which Jesus had gone before them, as the angel predicted. For he seems to say this in order to show that they found him there, because he had gone before them as planned. This did not happen on the day of his resurrection, nor in the eight days following, after which John says that the Lord appeared to the disciples, and Thomas saw him for the first time, for he had not seen him on the day of his resurrection.[140] How could the eleven have seen him on the mountain in Galilee during those eight days if Thomas, who was one of the eleven, only saw him for the first time after those eight days, unless these eleven were not those eleven called apostles but some other eleven disciples from out of the large number of his disciples? For those eleven were the only ones called apostles, but they were not the only disciples. It could be, then, that some of the apostles were there, although not all, and that other disciples were with them, so that they totaled eleven. And Thomas, who only saw the Lord for the first time after eight days,

---

137. See above at II,75,145.
138. See Lk 24:33–36; Jn 20:19.
139. See Jn 21:1–14.
140. See Jn 20:19–29.

was not there. When Mark mentions these eleven, he does not just say "eleven" but that *he appeared to the eleven* (Mk 16:14). Luke also says, *They returned to Jerusalem and found the eleven gathered together and those who were with them* (Lk 24:33). This shows that *the eleven* means the apostles. For when he adds *and those who were with them*, he shows quite clearly that these others were with some people who were called *the eleven* as a signal of their status, and so they may be understood to be those who were called apostles. Thus it may be that, out of the number of apostles and other disciples, there was a total of eleven disciples who saw Jesus on the mountain in Galilee sometime during those eight days.

25,82. But another problem arises here. When John reports the Lord's appearance to the seven who were fishing on the Sea of Tiberias, rather than to the eleven on the mountain, he says, *This was now the third time that Jesus revealed himself to the disciples after he rose from the dead* (Jn 21:14). But if we accept that the Lord appeared to the eleven disciples during those eight days before Thomas saw him, then this appearance by the Sea of Tiberias is not the third but the fourth. And we ought to be careful lest anyone think that, by saying that this was the third, John meant there were only three appearances. Rather, this should be understood to refer to the number of days and not to the number of appearances, and John himself testifies that these days are not successive but separated by intervals. For it is clear in the Gospel that on the day of his resurrection he revealed himself three times, not counting the appearance to the women—first to Peter;[141] then to those two, one of whom was Cleophas; and a third time to the many who were conversing as night fell. John counts all these together as one,[142] for they happened on one day. The second was when Thomas saw him, for this was on another day. Then the third appearance was by the Sea of Tiberias, not because it was his third appearance but because it was the third day of his appearances. This obliges us to suppose that it was after all these things that the eleven disciples then saw him on a mountain in Galilee, as Matthew reports. He went there before them, as planned, so that what had been predicted by the angel and by himself would be fulfilled to the very letter.

25,83. We find, then, that the four evangelists report ten appearances of the Lord to different people after his resurrection—first, to the women at the tomb;[143] second, again to them as they returned from the tomb;[144] third, to Peter;[145] fourth, to the two who were going to the settlement;[146] fifth, to the many in Jerusalem, when Thomas was absent;[147] sixth, when Thomas saw him;[148] seventh, by the Sea

---

141. A first appearance to Peter is in fact not mentioned explicitly in the Gospels, although Augustine may think that Lk 24:34 (*The Lord has risen indeed and has appeared to Simon*) is such a mention.

142. It is hard to know what Augustine means by this, since the only appearance of these three that John might be alluding to occurs at 20:19.

143. See Jn 20:14–18; Mk 16:9–11.

144. See Mt 28:9–10; Lk 24:9–11.

145. See Lk 24:34 and note 141 above.

146. See Lk 24:15–33.

147. See Jn 20:19–24; Lk 24:36–43.

148. See Jn 20:26–29.

of Tiberias;[149] eighth, on the mountain in Galilee, as Matthew describes it;[150] ninth, when Mark says, *Lastly, as they sat at table* (Mk 16:14), for they would dine no more with him on earth; tenth, on that same day, not on the earth but raised on a cloud as he ascended into heaven, as Mark and Luke report. Mark gives this last appearance immediately after he appeared to them as they sat at table: *And after the Lord had spoken to them, he was taken up into heaven* (Mk 16:19). Luke omits all that might have happened between him and his disciples during the forty days. The day of his resurrection, when he appeared to many, Luke joins directly to the last day, when he ascended into heaven: *Then he led them out as far as Bethany, and lifting up his hands he blessed them. And it happened that, as he blessed them, he parted from them and was carried up into heaven.* (Lk 24:50–51) So they saw him not only on earth but also as he was carried into heaven. This, then, is how many times the Books of the Gospels report that he was seen by people before ascending into heaven—namely, nine times on earth and once in the air as he was ascending.

25,84. But not everything has been written down, as John attests,[151] for he had many encounters with people during the forty days before he ascended into heaven,[152] although he did not appear to them continuously throughout the forty days. For John says that after the day of his resurrection there were eight other days, after which he appeared to them again,[153] but the third time was by the Sea of Tiberias,[154] and it may have happened on the next day, as there is nothing to refute this. And then he appeared to them as he wished, according to his previous direction and prediction, going before them to the mountain in Galilee. Throughout these forty days he appeared whenever, to whomever, and however he wished. Peter says as much when he was proclaiming [Jesus] to Cornelius and those who were with him: *To us who ate and drank with him*, he says, *after he rose from the dead, over the course of forty days* (Acts 10:41). They did not eat and drink with him, however, every day of the forty days. That would contradict John, who mentions the eight days during which he was not seen and then goes on to his third appearance by the Sea of Tiberias. But even if they saw him and lived with him every day after that, there would be no inconsistency. And perhaps the phrase, *over the course of forty days*, which is four times ten, mysteriously refers either to the whole world or to the whole earthly age; then the first ten days of that period, during which those eight days fall, can not unreasonably be counted as a part of the whole, a common way of speaking in the Scriptures.[155]

---

149. See Jn 21:1–24.
150. See Mt 28:16–17.
151. See Jn 21:25.
152. See Acts 1:3.
153. See Jn 20:26.
154. See Jn 21:14.
155. Augustine's rather complicated point seems to be that Jesus could be said to have appeared on every day of the forty days, even though he did not appear on eight of them, because if he

25,85. Now let us examine what the apostle Paul says, to see whether it raises any question: *He rose on the third day,* he says, *according to the Scriptures, and appeared to Cephas* (1 Cor 15:4–5). He does not say that he appeared first to Cephas, because this would contradict what is written in the Gospel, that he appeared first to the women. *Afterwards to the twelve* (1 Cor 15:5), he says. Whoever they were and at whatever hour this happened, it must nonetheless have been on the very day of the resurrection. Paul continues, *Then he appeared to more than five hundred brethren at one time* (1 Cor 15:6). It makes no difference whether this refers to the time when Jesus came to the eleven, who were gathered together behind closed doors out of fear of the Jews after Thomas had left, or to some other time after the eight days. *Afterwards,* he says, *he appeared to James* (1 Cor 15:7). We need not suppose that this was the first time that he appeared to James; instead, it may have been a special appearance to him by himself. *Then to all the apostles* (1 Cor 15:7), which does not mean that this was the first time he appeared to them but that from then until the day of his ascension he had more familiar encounters with them. *Last of all,* he says, *as to one born out of time, he appeared also to me* (1 Cor 15:8). But that was from heaven, a long time after his ascension.

25,86. Now let us examine the question that we put aside. We must find the significance of the mysterious saying, given in Matthew and Mark, that [Jesus] uttered as a command when he rose, *I shall go before you to Galilee; there you will see me.*[156] Even if this took place, it did not take place until a long time later. But it is stated as though one would expect this appearance to be either the only one or the first one, although this is not an absolutely necessary interpretation of it. It is undoubtedly significant, nonetheless, that this is not said as part of the evangelists' narrative comments but that it comes from the angel (under the Lord's command) and then from the Lord himself; it is in the evangelists' narratives but, because it is said by the angel and by the Lord, it must be taken prophetically. *Galilee* may mean either "transmigration" or "revelation."[157] If we take the first meaning, "transmigration," then there is no other way to understand *He is going before you to Galilee; there you will see him* (Mt 28:7; Mk 16:7) than as the grace of Christ that was about to transmigrate from the people of Israel to the gentiles. They would never have believed the apostles' preaching of the Gospel if the Lord himself had not prepared a way for it in human hearts, and that is the meaning of *He is going before you to Galilee.* And they would be joyful and amazed at the destruction and removal of the obstacles that would open a door for them in the Lord through the enlightenment of the faithful, which is the meaning of *There you will see him*—that is, "There you will find his members, there you will recognize

---

appeared during part of the forty, then he could be said to have appeared on any of the forty, since Scripture often uses the part in place of the whole.

156. This is a conflation of Jesus' prediction of his resurrection (Mt 26:32; Mk 14:28), the words of the angel (Mt 28:7; Mk 16:7) and Jesus' words at his resurrection (Mt 28:10).

157. For its meaning as "transmigration" see Jerome, *Interpretation of Hebrew Names,* Luke, s.v. Galilaea.

his living body in those who receive you." If we take *Galilee* in its second sense, as "revelation," then it must mean that he will no longer be in the form of a servant but in that form which is equal to the Father.[158] He promised this to those who loved him, as he said in John, *And I shall love him and manifest myself to him* (Jn 14:21). He was not to appear as they had seen him before, nor as they had seen and touched him after his rising, still with his scars, but he would appear as that ineffable light which enlightens every person who comes into this world, whereby he shines in the darkness and the darkness does not grasp him.[159] In this way he goes before us, coming to us without leaving that place and going before us without leaving us behind. This will be a revelation like the true Galilee, when we shall be like him; there we shall see him as he is.[160] If we embrace his commandments, we shall experience that more blessed transmigration from this age to that eternity, to be seated apart at his right hand. Then those at his left hand will go to eternal burning, but the righteous to eternal life.[161] From there they will transmigrate thither and see him, as the wicked do not see him. The wicked man shall be taken away *so that he may not see the brightness of the Lord* (Is 26:10), and wicked persons will not see the light. *But this is eternal life,* it says, *that they may know you, the only true God, and Jesus Christ whom you have sent* (Jn 17:3), as he is known in that eternity to which he leads his servants by way of the form of a servant, so that in freedom they may contemplate the form of the Lord.

---

158. See Phil 2:6–7.
159. See Jn 1:5–9.
160. See 1 Jn 3:2.
161. See Mt 25:46.

Book Four

1,1. Now we have examined Matthew's continuous narrative, comparing it with the other three [evangelists] through to the end, and have found that none of them contains anything inconsistent with either his own narrative or those of the others. Let us now examine Mark in a similar way. We shall set aside the things that he has in common with Matthew, for we have already investigated them, and it seems we are done with them. Now we shall inspect and compare the other parts and show that there is no inconsistency among them, up to the Lord's supper. For we have already treated everything from that point to the end in all four Gospels, showing how they agree.

1,2. Mark commences, then, in this way: *The beginning of the Gospel of Jesus Christ, the Son of God. As it is written in Isaiah the prophet* (Mk 1:1–2), and so forth, until where it says, *And they went into Capernaum, and immediately on the sabbath he entered the synagogue and taught them* (Mk 1:21). Everything in this context has already been examined above in Matthew. What Mark says, that he entered the synagogue in Capernaum and taught them on the sabbath, is also said by Luke,[1] but it raises no problems.

2,3. Mark continues and says, *And they were astonished at his teaching, for he taught them as one with authority and not as the scribes. And there was in their synagogue a man with an unclean spirit, and he cried out, saying, What have you to do with us, Jesus of Nazareth? Have you come to destroy us?* (Mk 1:22–24), and so forth, until the place where it says, *And he was preaching in their synagogues throughout all Galilee, and casting out demons* (Mk 1:39). Although there are some things here unique to Mark and Luke, we have nonetheless discussed everything in this section when we treated Matthew's continuous narrative, for these things occurred in the same sequence in such a way that I did not think they ought to be overlooked. But Luke says that the unclean spirit came out of the man without harming him,[2] whereas Mark says, *And the unclean spirit, mangling him and crying out in a loud voice, came out of him* (Mk 1:26). This may seem to be a contradiction, for how can he speak of *mangling him,* or, as some codices have, *pressing upon him,* when Luke says that it did him no harm? But Luke himself says, *And when the demon had thrown him down in the midst, it came out of him and did him no harm* (Lk 4:35). So it should be understood that when Mark says that it pressed upon him, this is the same as when Luke says, *when it had thrown him down in the midst.* And when he adds, *it did him no harm,* it means that the tossing about and shaking of his limbs did not injure him, which often happens when demons leave someone, even to the point of breaking the limbs as the shaking is subsiding.

---

1. See Lk 4:31.
2. See Lk 4:35.

3,4. Mark continues, *And a leper came to him, beseeching him, and kneeling said, If you will, you can make me clean* (Mk 1:40), and so forth, until where it says, *You are the Son of God. And he strictly charged them not to make him known* (Mk 3:11–12). Luke says something similar to the last part of this passage,[3] though without any question of inconsistency. Mark continues, *And he went up on the mountain and called to himself those whom he wished, and they came to him. And he appointed twelve to be with him and to be sent out to preach. And he gave to them the power to cure illnesses[4] and cast out demons. Simon, whom he renamed Peter* (Mk 3:13–16), and so forth, until where it says, *And he went away and began to proclaim in the Decapolis how much Jesus had done for him, and everyone marveled* (Mk 5:20). I know that I have already spoken of the names of the disciples when following Matthew's order,[5] but I repeat the caution again here—namely, that no one should suppose that Simon received the name Peter now for the first time or that there is any disagreement here with John, who reports that *You shall be called Cephas, which means Peter* (Jn 1:42) was said to him a long time before. For John records the exact words of the Lord by which he renamed him, whereas Mark is summarizing in this passage when he mentions *Simon, whom he renamed Peter* (Mk 3:16). Since he wants to give a list of the twelve apostles' names, he has to mention Peter, but he wishes to note briefly that he had not always been called that but that the Lord had given the name to him. It was not given to him at that time but at the time when John places the Lord's exact words. The rest is not inconsistent in any way, and it has already been treated before.

4,5. Mark continues, *And when Jesus had crossed over again in the boat to the other side, a great crowd gathered near him, and he was by the sea* (Mk 5:21), and so forth, until where it says, *And the apostles returned to Jesus and told him everything they had done and taught* (Mk 6:30). This last part is also given by Luke without any disagreement,[6] and the rest has already been discussed. Mark continues, *And he said to them, Come away by yourselves to a deserted place and rest a little* (Mk 6:31), and so forth, until where it says, *But the more he charged them, the more they proclaimed it. And they were the more astonished, saying, He has done all things well; he even makes the deaf hear and the mute speak* (Mk 7:36–37). Here there seems to be no inconsistency between Luke and Mark, and we already considered all of these things when we were comparing Matthew with the others. But there should be this caution: one should not suppose that this last statement from Mark's Gospel is inconsistent with all the passages in the Gospels that show that in most of his other deeds and words he knew what was going on within people; in other words, they could not hide their thoughts and desires from him. John says this most clearly: *But Jesus did not trust himself to them, because he knew everyone and he did not need anyone to bear testimony concerning a*

---

3.   See Lk 4:41.
4.   *To cure illnesses* is not in the Greek original.
5.   See above at II,17,34–41; 53,108–109.
6.   See Lk 9:10.

man, for he himself knew what was in man (Jn 2:24–25). But it is not remarkable
that he could see people's present desires, for he predicted to Peter what he would
wish in the future, which he did not at that time, when he was presumptuously
saying that he would die for him or with him.[7] Since this is so, it seems that such
great knowledge and foreknowledge is contradicted when Mark says, *He charged
them to tell no one; but the more he charged them, the more they proclaimed it*
(Mk 7:36). For if he had knowledge of people's present and future desires, then
he would have known that the more he charged them not to proclaim it, the more
they would proclaim it, so why would he charge them not to? Perhaps he wished
to show to the idle how much more zealously and fervently they ought to preach,
if he commands them to, since the ones whom he prohibits from preaching cannot keep silent.

5,6. Mark continues, *In those days, when once again a great crowd was
there and they had nothing to eat* (Mk 8:1), and so forth, until where it says, *John
answered, saying to him, Teacher, we saw someone who does not follow us, casting out demons in your name, and we forbade him. But Jesus said, Do not forbid
him, for there is no one who does a mighty deed in my name who can then speak
evil of me, for he who is not against you is for you* (Mk 9:38–39). Luke narrates
this similarly,[8] although he does not say, *For there is no one who does a mighty
deed in my name who can then speak evil of me* (Mk 9:39). So there is no question
of inconsistency between these. But we must see whether this can be supposed to
contradict another of the Lord's statements: *He who is not with me is against me,
and he who does not gather with me scatters* (Mt 12:30; Lk 11:23). How was this
man not against him because he was not with him, when John says that he did not
follow them, and that whoever was not with him was against him? Or if he was
against him, how does he say to the disciples, *Do not forbid him. For he who is
not against you is for you* (Mk 9:39)? Anyone will note the important difference,
inasmuch as here he says to the disciples, *He who is not against you is for you*
(Mk 9:39), whereas in the other passage he said of himself, *He who is not with me
is against me* (Mt 12:30; Lk 11:23). Is it possible in some way not to be with him
but to be associated with his disciples, who are his very limbs? But then how can
these sayings be true—*He who receives you receives me* (Mt 10:40), and *What
you have done to one of the least of mine you have done to me* (Mt 25:40)? Or is
it possible for someone not to be against him, although he is against his disciples?
What then will we do with *He who rejects you rejects me* (Lk 10:16), and *What you
have not done to one of the least of mine you have not done to me*, and *Saul, Saul,
why do you persecute me?* (Acts 9:4) when Saul was persecuting his disciples? But
certainly this is what he wished this to mean: so far as someone is not with him,
to that extent he is against him; and so far as someone is not against him, to that
extent he is with him. Take for example this man who was doing mighty works in

---

7.   See Mt 26:33–35 par.
8.   See Lk 9:49–50.

Christ's name but was not in the community of Christ's disciples. Inasmuch as he was performing mighty works in his name, to that extent he was with them and was not against them. But inasmuch as he was not a member of their community, to that extent he was not with them and was against them. But because they had forbidden him to do that whereby he was with them, for that reason the Lord said to them, *Do not forbid him* (Mk 9:39). For they ought to have forbidden his being outside their community, so that they could bring him into the unity of the Church, and not the very thing on which he was one with them, namely, raising up the name of their teacher and Lord in the expulsion of demons. The Catholic Church follows this practice, not condemning those sacraments among the heretics that are held in common, for in these they are with us and not against us.[9] But it condemns and forbids division and separation or any opinion opposed to peace and truth, for in this they are against us, because in this they are not with us; they do not gather, and therefore they scatter.

6,7. Mark continues and says, *For whoever gives you a cup of water to drink in my name, because you are Christ's, amen I say to you, shall not lose his reward. And whoever causes one of these little ones who believe in me to stumble, it would be better for him if a millstone were hung around his neck and he were cast into the sea. And if your hand causes you to stumble, cut it off; it is better for you to enter life maimed than with two hands to go to hell, to the unquenchable fire, where their worm does not die and the fire is not quenched* (Mk 9:41–43),[10] and so forth, until where it says, *Have salt in yourselves, and have peace among yourselves* (Mk 9:50). Mark presents the Lord as saying this right after he made them stop prohibiting the man from casting out demons in his name, because he did not follow him with the disciples. In this section he also records some things that are not in any of the other evangelists, and some that are also in Matthew, and some that are also in Matthew and Luke. But these things are in the other Gospels in different contexts and in another order, and not at the point where he is told of the man who cast out demons in his name although he did not follow him with Christ's disciples. Therefore it seems to me that, as Mark faithfully reports, in this passage and also in other passages, insofar as they were related to his meaning here, the Lord said that he forbade them from stopping someone from performing mighty deeds in his name, even if that person did not follow him with his disciples. For he connects the two passages as follows: *For he who is not against you is for you. For whoever gives you a cup of water to drink in my name, because you are Christ's, amen I say to you, shall not lose his reward.* (Mk 9:40–41) This shows that even this man, whom John mentions, thereby beginning [Jesus'] discourse, had not separated himself from the community of the disciples as though he were a heretic who was condemning it. People often do something similar, not dar-

---

9. Augustine almost certainly is referring here to the Donatists who, although separated from the Catholic Church, were recognized as sharing valid sacraments with it.

10. The final phrase (*where their worm...quenched*) is counted as Mk 9:44 but is not found in the best Greek manuscripts.

ing to take Christ's sacraments but nonetheless favoring the Christian name, so that they even accept and are favorable towards Christians, just because they are Christians and not for any other reason.[11] It is of such people that he says that they will not lose their reward. Yet they ought not to think themselves safe and secure, even though they are not washed in Christ's baptism or incorporated into his unity, because of their benevolence towards Christians. Rather, the point is that they are being guided by God's mercy, so that they may achieve these things and leave this world safely. Even before they join the ranks of Christians, these people really are more profitable servants than those who, although they are called Christians and are initiated in the Christian sacraments,[12] recommend to others the kinds of things that, if they are persuaded to follow them, will drag them both into eternal punishment. These are those whom he refers to as members of the body, such as the hand or eye, that lead astray, and which he commands to be cut off from the body, that is, from the unity of the community, so that without them it may enter into life rather than with them go into Gehenna. They are also separated from those from whom they separate themselves by the fact that when they seek to persuade those others to do evil things—that is, to cause them to stumble—they are resisted. And indeed, if any good people who know them detect their real perversity, then they are completely cut off from any community and even from participation in the divine sacraments. But if only some people know them, while the majority is ignorant of their perversity, then they must be tolerated as chaff is tolerated on the threshing floor before the winnowing.[13] One must not agree with them in the fellowship of iniquity or leave the community of the good on account of them. This is what is done by those have salt in themselves and have peace among themselves.

7,8. Mark continues, *And he arose from there and came to the territory of Judea beyond the Jordan. And again crowds came to him and, as was his custom, he again taught them* (Mk 10:1), and so forth, until where it says, *For they all gave to them out of their abundance, but she out of her poverty gave everything she had, her whole living* (Mk 12:44). Every part of this section was examined previously to see if there was any disagreement when we were comparing Matthew in sequence with the others. This story of the poor widow, who put two mites into the treasury, is told only by two evangelists, Mark and Luke,[14] but with no doubts as to their agreement. From here to the Lord's supper, from which point we considered everything in all the Gospels together,[15] Mark says nothing that would oblige us to compare or inquire as to whether there seems to be any disagreement.

8,9. Now, then, let us deal with Luke's Gospel in order, setting aside those parts that he has in common with Matthew and Mark, for all of these have already

---

11. See the case of Victorinus in *Confessions* VIII,2,3–5, which made a significant impression on Augustine.
12. "Initiated in the Christian sacraments": *christianis sacramentis imbuti*. The original meaning of *imbuti* is "to have been moistened," and hence the word suggests baptism.
13. See Mt 13:24–30.
14. See Mk 12:41–44; Lk 21:1–4.
15. See above at III passim.

been treated. Luke begins this way, then: *Inasmuch as many have attempted to set in order a narrative of the things which have been fulfilled among us, just as they were delivered to us by those who from the beginning saw and were ministers, it seemed good to me also, having carefully followed everything from the very beginning, to write carefully an orderly account for you, most excellent Theophilus, so that you may know the truth of those words that you have been told.* (Lk 1:1–4) This beginning not only applies to the narrative of the Gospel, but it alerts us to the fact that Luke also wrote the book which is called the Acts of the Apostles. It is not just the presence of the name of Theophilus there that leads to this conclusion, for there could have been someone else named Theophilus, and, even if it were the same one, someone else could have written something to him, just as the Gospel was written to him from Luke. Rather, it is because it begins this way: *I composed the first book, O Theophilus, about everything that Jesus began to do and teach, until the day when, through the Holy Spirit, he chose the apostles and gave them the command to preach the Gospel* (Acts 1:1–2).[16] From this we are to understand that he wrote one of those four books of the Gospel that are held in the highest authority by the Church. But, just because he says that he composed his book about everything that Jesus began to do and teach until that day when he commanded the apostles, one should not suppose that he wrote in his Gospel everything that Jesus did and said while he was with the apostles on earth. This would contradict John's statement that Jesus did many other things, and that, if they were all written down, the whole world could not contain that many books.[17] There are in fact not a few things that the other evangelists narrate, upon which Luke himself has not touched. He put together his report about everything, then, by selecting from all of them to make his report, judging what was fitting and appropriate to fulfill his devoted responsibility. And when he refers to the many who attempted *to set in order a narrative of the things which have been fulfilled among us* (Lk 1:1), he seems to mean those who were not able to finish the task that they had taken upon themselves. Hence he says that it seemed good to him *to write carefully an orderly account, inasmuch as many have attempted* (Lk 1:3.1). But we should suppose that this refers to those who have no authority in the Church, because they were in no way capable of finishing what they attempted. He does not take his narrative only up to the Lord's resurrection and assumption, though, so that, thanks to his labor, he has an honored place among the four authors of the gospel writings, but he continues with what was done by the apostles, writing down those things that he believed were necessary to build up the faith of his readers or hearers. He wrote it in such a way that only the book with his account is considered worthy of credibility in the Church with respect to the acts of the apostles. All the others who wrote of the apostles' deeds and words have been rejected because they are

---

16. Augustine departs from both the Vulgate and the Greek original by omitting *when he was taken up* and inserting *to preach the Gospel*.
17. See Jn 21:25.

not faithful accounts, as they should have been.[18] Indeed, Mark and Luke wrote at a time when it would have been possible for both the Church of Christ and the apostles themselves, who were still living in the flesh, to judge the accuracy of their writings.

9,10. Luke, then, begins to narrate his Gospel in this way: *In the days of Herod, king of Judea, there was a priest named Zechariah, of the division of Abijah, and his wife was of the daughters of Aaron, and her name was Elizabeth* (Lk 1:5), and so forth, until the passage where it says, *And when he had ceased speaking, he said to Simon, Go out into the deep and let down your nets for a catch* (Lk 5:4). There is nothing in this section to raise any question of inconsistency. John, indeed, seems to say something similar, but what happened at the Sea of Tiberias after the Lord's resurrection is really quite different. It is not just that the time is totally different, but the events themselves are quite distinct. For [in John] the nets were cast from the right side, and one hundred fifty-three fish were caught, and they were large ones. It even seemed relevant to the evangelist to say that, although they were so big, the nets were not ripped.[19] He must have had in mind the event that Luke records, in which the nets were torn by the huge number of fish.[20] For everything else Luke does not report the same things as John does except what concerns the Lord's passion and resurrection. The whole section from the Lord's supper to the end has been treated by us, with a comparison of all the testimonies revealing no inconsistency.[21]

10,11. John is the last, and there remains nothing with which to compare him. For although each [evangelist] individually reports things that the others do not, it is difficult to raise a question of inconsistency from this. It is clearly the case that these three—namely, Matthew, Mark, and Luke—are mostly concerned with the humanity of our Lord Jesus Christ, according to which he is both king and priest. Mark seems to be shown as the figure of a human being in that mystery of the four animals.[22] He also seems to have been Matthew's companion, for he has more in common with him than with the others; this would suit the kingly character, already commented on in the first book,[23] which is not accustomed to go unaccompanied. Or it is more likely to understand that he goes together with both [Matthew and Luke], for, although Mark agrees with Matthew in more places, nonetheless in other places he agrees more with Luke. This shows that Mark relates to both the lion and the ox, that is, to the royal character emphasized by Matthew and to the priestly character emphasized by Luke. Christ is human in both these ways, and Mark's symbol pertains to both. But John takes up some points for special empha-

---

18. The reference here is undoubtedly to the numerous apocryphal Acts (like those of John, Peter and Paul) that were circulating in Christian antiquity.
19. See Jn 21:1–11.
20. See Lk 5:6.
21. See above at III passim.
22. See Rv 4:6–7. A comparison is made between the evangelists and the four animals above at I,6,9.
23. See above at I,3,6.

sis—Christ's divinity, his equality with the Father, according to which he is the Word and God with God,[24] and the fact that the Word was made flesh in order to dwell among us,[25] according to which he and the Father are one.[26] Like an eagle [John] dwells on things that Christ spoke of more loftily, and only rarely does he in some way descend to earth. For example, though he clearly shows that he knows Christ's mother,[27] John nonetheless, unlike Matthew and Luke, says nothing of his nativity. Nor, unlike the other three, does he record his baptism; instead, he only gives John's testimony in a lofty and elevated way,[28] and then he departs from the others and goes on to the wedding in Cana of Galilee.[29] Although the evangelist himself records that his mother was there, nonetheless he says, *Woman, what have I to do with you?* (Jn 2:4) It is not that he was putting off the one who gave him flesh but rather that he was indicating his divinity then in a very special way, as he was about to turn water into wine—the divinity which had created that woman and which was not created in her.

10,12. After those few days spent in Capernaum he returned to the Temple, where John records that he spoke of the temple of his body: *Destroy this temple and in three days I will raise it up* (Jn 2:19). This shows most definitely not only that God was in the temple in the form of the Word made flesh but also that he himself raised that flesh by no other means than by reason of the fact that he is one with the Father, not doing anything separately from him. In other passages in Scripture, and perhaps in all of them, it says that God raised him; nor does it say anywhere that, when God raised Christ, Christ raised himself, because he is one God with the Father, just as in this passage, where it says, *Destroy this temple and in three days I will raise it up.*

10,13. How great and how divine are the words spoken to Nicodemus after that![30] From there [the evangelist] returns again to John's testimony, noting that the bridegroom's friend cannot help but rejoice at the bridegroom's voice.[31] This warns us that the human soul has no light in and of itself and that it cannot be blessed unless it participates in the unchangeable wisdom. Then he goes on to the Samaritan woman, mentioning the water that will never allow a person to thirst again if he drinks from it.[32] Then he returns to Cana of Galilee, where [Jesus] had made water into wine. [33] There he reports what [Jesus] said to the official whose son was sick: *Unless you see signs and wonders you will not believe* (Jn 4:48). By saying this he wished to lift the believer's mind far above all changeable things, for

---

24. See Jn 1:1.
25. See Jn 1:14.
26. See Jn 10:30.
27. See Jn 2:1–11; 19:26–27.
28. See Jn 1:15–34.
29. See Jn 2:1–11.
30. See Jn 3:1–21.
31. See Jn 3:22–36.
32. See Jn 4:1–42.
33. See Jn 4:43–54.

he did not wish the faithful to seek after the miracles themselves, which, although they are signs of divinity, nonetheless occur in mutable bodies.

10,14. Then [John] returns to Jerusalem, where a man who was sick for thirty-eight years is healed.[34] What things are said on this occasion! And how many things are said! Here it is said, *The Jews sought to kill him not only because he broke the sabbath but also because he called God his Father, making himself equal with God* (Jn 5:18), which clearly shows that he did not call God his Father in the way that holy people often do but that he meant he was equal to him. Indeed, right before that he had said to those who were slandering him on account of the sabbath, *My Father is working until now, and I am working* (Jn 5:17). Then they were enraged not because he said that God was his Father but because he wanted it to be understood that he was equal with God when he said, *My Father is working until now, and I am working*—indicating, as a consequence, that as the Father works, so too does the Son work, because the Father does not work without the Son. This was right before he said to those who were angry with him, *For whatever he does, the Son does this likewise* (Jn 5:19).

10,15. Then John descends to where the other three are walking with the Lord on the earth, recording the feeding of the five thousand with the five loaves,[35] although only he reports that, when they wanted to make him king, he fled by himself to a mountain.[36] It seems to me that here [John] wishes to remind the rational soul that [Jesus] rules our minds and reason, in which respect he is so far above us that he has no natural connection with human beings but is alone because he is the Only-Begotten of the Father. Because it is so sublime, this mystery escapes those carnal people who creep about in lower regions. Hence he flees to a mountain, away from those who long for his kingdom with an earthly mind; as he says elsewhere, *My kingdom is not of this world* (Jn 18:36). This also is reported only by John, who soars as it were in the upper air over the earth, rejoicing in the light of the sun of righteousness.[37] Then, passing on from this mountain after the miracle of the five loaves, he stays with the other three a little longer, until the crossing of the sea, when [Jesus] walked on the water.[38] But then he rises again to the Lord's words, so great, so extensive, so lofty and elevated for such a long time, spoken on the occasion of the loaves, when he said to the crowds, *Amen, amen, I say to you, you seek me not because you saw signs but because you ate and were filled with the loaves. Do not work for the food that perishes but for that which endures to eternal life.* (Jn 6:26–27) After this he says other such things most excellently and for a very long time. Then some, who did not walk with him from then on, fell away from the loftiness of this discourse.[39] But some really clung to him, who

---

34. See Jn 5:1–47.
35. See Jn 6:1–15; Mt 14:13–21; Mk 6:32–44; Lk 9:10–17.
36. See Jn 6:15.
37. See Mal 4:2.
38. See Jn 6:16–21.
39. See Jn 6:66.

were able to understand that *it is the spirit that gives life, but the flesh is of no use* (Jn 6:63), because the spirit is of use even by way of the flesh, and only the spirit is of use, whereas the flesh without the spirit is of no use.

10,16. Then his brothers—that is, those related to his flesh—suggested that he go up to the feast day so that he might make himself known to the multitude, to which he responded with great sublimity: *My time has not yet come, but your time is always ready. The world cannot hate you, but it hates me, because I give testimony of it, that its works are evil.* (Jn 7:6–7) *Your time is always ready* must mean "You long for that day of which the prophet says, *But I have not labored, following you, O Lord, and you know that I have not desired the day of men*" (Jer 17:16). The right kind of desire is to fly to the light of the Word and to long for that day which Abraham longed to see, and *he saw it and was glad* (Jn 8:56). And when he went up to the Temple on the feast day, John reports what he said, and it was so amazing, so divine, so lofty! He said that they would be unable to come to where he was.[40] He said that they knew him and knew where he was from, and that he who had sent him was true, whom they did not know.[41] This is the same as saying, "You both know and do not know where I am from." What could he have meant to be understood by this except that they could know him according to the flesh, both his ancestry and country, but be ignorant as to his divinity? By speaking of the gift of the Holy Spirit[42] he also showed them who he was, since it was his office to give that highest gift.

10,17. Again, how great are the things which [John] reports that [Jesus] said after he returned from the Mount of Olives! Here he forgave the adulteress, whom his tempters had presented to him as one worthy of stoning.[43] Here he wrote with his finger on the ground, as if to show that people such as these accusers would be written on the earth and not in heaven;[44] he had similarly admonished the disciples when he told them to rejoice that their names were written in heaven.[45] Or perhaps he was showing that it was by humbling himself, which he indicated by lowering his head, that he made signs on the earth,[46] or that it was time for his law to be written on earth, which would yield fruit, and no longer on sterile stone, as before.[47] After this he said that he was the light of the world and that whoever followed him would not walk in darkness but have the light of life.[48] He also said

---

40. See Jn 7:34.
41. See Jn 7:28.
42. See Jn 7:37–39.
43. See Jn 8:1–11.
44. See Jn 8:6.8
45. See Lk 10:20.
46. Augustine is engaging in wordplay here: Jesus was making signs on the earth by writing in the dirt to show what he meant, but he also performed miracles while on earth, and these are often referred to by John as signs—i.e., indications of who he was and what he intended. He was only able to perform these signs because he had lowered his head—i.e., because he had humbled himself to enter into the human condition on earth.
47. See 2 Cor 3:3.
48. See Jn 8:12.

that he was the beginning, who had spoken to them.[49] By applying this name to himself he distinguished himself from the light which he made, and he showed that he was the light by which all things were made. So, when he said that he was the light of the world, this should not be understood in the same way as when he told his disciples, *You are the light of the world* (Mt 5:14). They are only compared to a lamp that is not put under a bushel but on a stand,[50] as John the Baptist is: *He was*, it says, *a burning and shining lamp* (Jn 5:35). [Jesus] himself, however, is the beginning, of whom it is said, *From his fullness we have all received* (Jn 1:16). Here he says that he, the Son, is the truth that makes free, without which no one will be free.[51]

10,18. Then, after [Jesus] has brought sight to the man who was blind from birth,[52] John lingers over the long discourse given on that occasion, which is about the sheep and the shepherd and the door, and about [Jesus'] power to lay down his life and take it up again;[53] all this showed the highest power of his divinity. Then [John] reports how, at the feast of the Dedication in Jerusalem, the Jews said to him, *How long will you keep our minds in suspense? If you are the Christ, tell us plainly.* (Jn 10:24) Then he tells of those sublime words that [Jesus] spoke on the occasion of a discourse, when he said, *I and the Father are one* (Jn 10:30). Then he tells of [Jesus'] raising of Lazarus,[54] when he said, *I am the resurrection and the life. Whoever believes in me, even though he has died, yet shall live. And all who live and believe in me shall never die.* (Jn 10:25–26) What do we recognize in these words except the loftiness of his divinity, by sharing in which we shall live forever? Then John rejoins Matthew and Mark in Bethany, where the incident of the costly ointment occurred that Mary poured out on [Jesus'] feet and head.[55] From then on to the Lord's passion and resurrection John proceeds with the other three evangelists, at least insofar as they speak of the same situations.

10,19. But, regarding the Lord's discourses from this point on, John does not cease to raise up the more sublime and lengthy things said by him. When, by way of Philip and Andrew, the gentiles say that they want to see him, he gives a lofty discourse, which none of the other evangelists includes.[56] There he again reports the striking things that he said about the light which enlightens and makes people children of light. Although none of the evangelists fails to mention the supper, how many and how great are the words that only John records, which the others omit! There is not only the example of humility that he gives by washing his disciples' feet[57] but, after the betrayer has been indicated with a morsel and has gone out,[58]

---

49. See Jn 8:25.
50. See Mt 5:15.
51. See Jn 8:36.
52. See Jn 9:1–41.
53. See Jn 10:1–21.
54. See Jn 11:1–44.
55. See Jn 12:1–8; Mt 26:6–13; Mk 14:3–9.
56. See Jn 12:20–50.
57. See Jn 13:1–20.
58. See Jn 13:21–30.

there is also his wonderfully amazing and most lengthy discourse given to the eleven who remained with him.[59] John dwells on this discourse, in which [Jesus] says, *He who has seen me has seen the Father* (Jn 14:9). Here he also says many things about the Holy Spirit, the Paraclete, whom he was to send to them,[60] and about his own glory that he had with the Father before the world was.[61] He also speaks about making us one in himself, as he and the Father are one;[62] this does not mean that he and the Father and we should be one, but that we should be one as they are one. And he says many other marvelously lofty things, but if we were to examine these things as they deserve, even if we were capable of doing so, it would not relate to what we are attempting to do in the present work. Although this would perhaps be a worthy work of interpretation at another time, it certainly is not what is required here, for we wish to show those who are lovers of the Word of God and students of the holy truth that John is a proclaimer and preacher of Christ, who is true and truthful. It is the same with the other three who wrote the Gospels, and also with the other apostles. Even if they themselves did not attempt to write narratives, they nonetheless fulfilled the official duty of preaching about him. But John is carried up higher in Christ from the very beginning of his book, and only rarely is he on the same level as the others, which is the case first by the Jordan, concerning the testimony of John the Baptist;[63] then on the other side of the Sea of Tiberias, when [Jesus] fed the crowds with the five loaves and then walked on the water;[64] and thirdly in Bethany, when the costly ointment was poured over him by the devotion of a woman's faith.[65] Thus he goes on, up to the time of the passion, where his narrative necessarily runs parallel to theirs. Yet at the Lord's supper, which none of them fail to mention, John gives a much fuller version, drawn from the storehouse of the Lord's breast, on which he used to recline.[66] In John [Jesus] strikes Pilate with loftier words, saying that his kingdom is not of this earth, and that he was born to be a king, and that he came into this world in order to give witness to the truth.[67] It is also in John that he comes to Mary after the resurrection and with mystical depth says, *Do not touch me, for I have not yet ascended to the Father* (Jn 20:17). It is also in John that he gives the Holy Spirit to the disciples by breathing on them,[68] lest it be thought that the Spirit, who is consubstantial and coeternal with the Trinity, is only the Father's and not also the Son's Spirit.[69]

---

59. See Jn 14:1–17:26.
60. See Jn 14:16–17.26; 15:26; 16:7.13–14.
61. See Jn 17:5.
62. See Jn 17:11.
63. See Jn 1:19–34.
64. See Jn 6:1–21.
65. See Jn 12:1–8.
66. See Jn 13:23.
67. See Jn 18:36–37.
68. See Jn 20:22.
69. Augustine comes close here to expressing the doctrine that the Spirit proceeds equally from both the Father and the Son, which is known as the *Filioque* ("and from the Son") and which appears in fully elaborated form in *The Trinity* XV,17,29.

10,20. Finally, after committing his sheep to Peter, who loves him and who confesses this love three times, [Jesus] then says that he wishes John to remain until he comes.[70] It seems to me that here he teaches a lofty mystery. John's evangelical commission carries him up into the clearest light of the Word, where one can see the equality and immutability of the Trinity and especially how greatly there differs from others the man by whose assumption the Word became flesh,[71] which cannot be distinguished or clearly known until the Lord himself comes. Thus it will remain, therefore, until he comes. Now it will remain in the faith of believers, but then it will be contemplated face to face,[72] when he, our life, will appear, and we shall appear with him in glory.[73] But, if someone supposes that in this mortal life he can reach this in such a way that he could cast off and scatter every cloud of corporeal and carnal phantasms, thereby obtaining the serenest light of immutable truth, to which one would cling constantly and unchangeably, having thoroughly severed the mind from the habits of this life, he understands neither what he is seeking nor who it is who is doing the seeking. Let him believe, rather, that lofty authority which has no falsehood, which says that, as long as we are in the body, we are away from the Lord and walk by faith and not by sight.[74] So one must with perseverance hold onto and guard faith, hope, and charity, striving towards the sight, the promise of which we have received from the Holy Spirit, who will teach us all truth,[75] when God, who raised Jesus Christ from the dead, vivifies our mortal bodies by his Spirit living in us.[76] But before the body, which is mortal because of sin, is vivified, it is undoubtedly corruptible and weighs down the soul.[77] And if someone is helped to go beyond this cloud that covers the whole earth,[78] which is the carnal darkness that covers all earthly life, it is only a quick movement, and he returns to his weakness, for the desire remains to be excited again, and the purity is not sufficient to make one withstand it. The more one can do this, the greater one is; and the less one can do this, the less one is. But if someone's mind has thus far had no experience of any such thing, yet Christ lives in it through faith, then that person ought to strive to minimize and eliminate these worldly lusts by the practice of moral virtue, walking as it were in the company of those three evangelists[79] with Christ the mediator. With the joy of great hope let him faithfully hold onto him who is always the Son of God and for

---

70. See Jn 21:15–23.
71. "The man by whose assumption the Word became flesh": *homo cuius susceptione Verbum caro factum est*. This is an instance of *homo assumptus / susceptus* Christology, which was popular in the early Church and in Augustine's earlier writings. See p. 58, note 77.
72. See 1 Cor 13:12.
73. See Col 3:4.
74. See 2 Cor 5:6–7.
75. See Jn 16:13.
76. See Rom 8:10–11.
77. See Wis 9:15.
78. See Sir 24:3. Augustine takes the cloud in a negative sense, whereas in Sir 24:3 (assuming that he is alluding to that verse) it is identified with divine wisdom.
79. I.e., Matthew, Mark and Luke.

our sake became the Son of Man, so that his eternal power and divinity might be joined with our weakness and mortality, using what is ours to make a way for us in him and to him. Let him who is ruled by Christ the king not sin; if he happens to sin, let him be atoned for by Christ the priest.[80] Thus, having been nourished by the practice of a good manner of life, and having been carried away from the earth by a double love[81] as though by two strong wings, he will be enlightened by Christ the Word himself, the Word that was in the beginning, and the Word that was with God, and the Word that was God.[82] Although this will be in a mirror dimly,[83] it will nonetheless be greatly superior to any bodily imitation. So in the first three [Gospels] the gifts of active [virtue] shine forth, while in the Gospel of John it is those of contemplative virtue, which are able to recognize these higher things.[84] But even the Gospel of John, because it is partial, will [only] remain until that which is perfect comes.[85] The word of wisdom is given through the Spirit to one person, and through the same Spirit the word of knowledge is given to another.[86] One person draws sustenance from the Lord's Day,[87] another drinks purer nourishment from the Lord's breast,[88] another is even taken up to the third heaven and hears unutterable words,[89] but all of these, as long as they are in the body, are away from the Lord,[90] and for all who are faithful to a good hope and who are written in the book of life[91] there is reserved what is said: *And I shall love him and manifest myself to him* (Jn 14:21). Nonetheless, even during this absence [from the Lord], whoever is making progress in the understanding and knowledge of these things should be all the more on guard against the diabolical vices of pride and envy. One should keep in mind that this very Gospel of John, which raises one more fully to the contemplation of the truth, also commands more fully the sweetness of love. And because that commandment—*The greater you are, the more you should humble yourself in all things* (Sir 3:18)—is most true and most beneficial, the evangelist who commends Christ more sublimely than the others has him wash his disciples' feet.[92]

---

80. See 1 Jn 2:1–2.
81. Augustine is most likely referring to the love of God and neighbor. See Mt 22:37–40 par.
82. See Jn 1:1.
83. See 1 Cor 13:12.
84. Augustine frequently discusses the relation between the active and contemplative lives, and the superiority of the latter, as at I,5,8 above.
85. See 1 Cor 13:9–10.
86. See 1 Cor 12:8.
87. I.e., from the eucharist, celebrated on Sunday. See Rom 14:6.
88. See Jn 13:23.
89. See 2 Cor 12:2–4.
90. See 2 Cor 5:6.
91. See Rv 21:27.
92. See Jn 13:5–11.

INDEX

*The first numeral in the Index is the Book number. The numbers following
the colons are the Chapter numbers, then the Section numbers in parentheses. (Additional numbers, preceded by the letter n, indicate footnotes.)*

QUESTIONS ON THE GOSPELS

(Quaestiones evangeliorum)

Introduction

Questions on the Gospels and *Seventeen Questions on Matthew* both belong to the literary genre of *quaestiones et responsiones*, or "questions and answers." That genre was used in classical Greek literature under the title of *zetemata kai luseis* and also in Jewish and Christian works on questions of biblical interpretation as well as on other subjects.[1] The *quaestiones* format is found in many of Augustine's works, some of whose titles — such as *Eighty-three Questions, Miscellany of Questions in Response to Simplician, Questions on the Heptateuch,* and *Eight Questions of Dulcitius* — make it clear that they are in this category. Others have been added to the list by various scholars, although their titles may not immediately indicate that they belong to the *quaestiones* genre.[2] But not all of Augustine's works in this genre deal with exegetical questions about Scripture as the present two works, *Questions on the Gospels* and *Seventeen Questions on Matthew*, clearly do.

Questions on the Gospels is divided into two books, one on questions about various passages from Matthew's Gospel and the other on questions about passages from Luke's Gospel. In the prologue Augustine explains that these questions arose when the Gospels were being read with a disciple and that they do not present an orderly commentary but contain only responses to the questions that were posed at the time. He also says that in their published form the questions do not entirely follow the sequence of the gospel narratives and that some questions were inserted later where there was room in the manuscript. To simplify the problem of finding the discussion of a specific topic, Augustine numbered the questions and put a numerical list of them at the beginning of each book.

It is difficult to determine precisely the date of the composition of *Questions on the Gospels*. It is listed in *Revisions* II,12, where it appears as the sixth work after the *Confessions* and the fourth work after the *Answer to Felix, A Manichean* — two writings that can be securely dated to 397–398 and December 404 respectively. The location of the work in the *Revisions*, however, may indicate either the starting point of its composition or the date of its publication. After consideration of various clues, Barbara Fenati concludes that the date proposed by the Maurist editors in the seventeenth century for its composition, namely, around 400, is the most probable.[3]

In her introduction to the critical edition of the text, Almut Mutzenbecher lists both Greek and Latin authors among Augustine's sources. Among the Greeks she points to Origen and Gregory of Nyssa — to Origen, for example, for the interpretation of the parable of the Good Samaritan and to Gregory of Nyssa for that

---

1. See the introduction to the Italian translation of *Quaestiones evangeliorum* by Barbara Fenati in *Nuova Biblioteca Agostiniana* (NBA) X/2,289. On the use of this genre in early Christian literature see Annelie Volgers and Claudio Zumagni, eds., *Erotapokriseis: Early Christian Question-and-Answer Literature* (Leuven: Peeters, 2004).
2. On Augustine's works in the question-and-answer genre see my "Augustine and the Quaestiones et Responsiones Literature," in *Eratapokriseis* 127–144.
3. See NBA 10/2, 290–291.

of the parable of the wedding feast. Among the Latin, or Western, authors whom Mutzenbecher singles out are Irenaeus, Tertullian, Cyprian, Optatus of Milevis, and Ambrose.[4]

Some of the questions receive brief and straightforward answers in literal interpretations of the text, such as the explanation of how Joseph's father could have had two different names[5] or how Jonah was in the belly of the whale and Jesus in the tomb for three days and three nights.[6] But the vast majority of the questions have figurative or allegorical responses that go well beyond what the modern reader is likely to expect. Many of the gospel passages about which the questions arise are themselves figurative, and Augustine's answer provides a more figurative meaning in his interpretation. For example, Christ said about someone who scandalized a little child that it would be better for him that a millstone be hung around his neck and that he be thrown into the sea.[7] Here Augustine explains that his punishment means that it is fitting that the one who gives such scandal be bound by the love of temporal things and brought down in chains to the depth of perdition.[8] Similarly, Augustine explains figuratively Christ's figurative words to his disciples about telling the mountain to pick itself up and cast itself into the sea as what a servant of God ought to say to pride in order to drive it off from himself. But he also suggests an alternative interpretation, that is, that it could be understood in a figurative sense about Christ, who is the mountain, taken from the Jews and cast among the sea of the gentiles.[9] Such multiple interpretations are frequently offered and show that Augustine held that a passage could have many true interpretations.[10]

To understand Augustine's extensive use of figurative or allegorical interpretation of the biblical text, it is helpful to recall that he had personally found a literal reading of the Scriptures a deadly process until he discovered in listening to Ambrose's preaching in Milan that spiritual people in the Catholic Church did not always understand the Scriptures according to their literal sense.[11] He tells us that he had been especially troubled by the anthropomorphic language of the Bible, which seemed to say that God had the shape and body parts of a human being.[12] The Manicheans, to whom Augustine belonged as a hearer for at least eleven years, used to mock Catholics for believing that "man was made to the image and likeness of God. For they note the shape of our body and mistakenly ask whether

---

4. See CCSL (*Corpus Christianorum Series Latina*) 44/B,xxvii-xxix.
5. See II,5.
6. See I,7.
7. See Mt 18:6.
8. See I,24.
9. See I,29.
10. On the notion that a single passage of Scripture could have several legitimate interpretations see *Confessions* XII,30,41–42.
11. See ibid. V,14,24.
12. See ibid. VI,3,4.

God has a nose, teeth, beard, other inferior members, and the other things that we need. But it is ridiculous and even wicked to believe that such things are in God."[13]

While listening to Ambrose preach, Augustine came to realize that spiritual persons in the Church, like Ambrose himself, did not interpret the Scriptures in a literal sense, and he gradually came to see, especially once he was introduced to the books of the Platonists, that God was not to be thought of in bodily terms. As he tells us in the *Confessions*, his inability to understand what a spiritual substance was had been the greatest and almost the sole cause of his errors.[14] Hence, his ability to understand anthropomorphic language about God in a spiritual sense came as a great liberation from the Manichaean and Stoic corporealism that was the common philosophical patrimony of the Roman world, except where Neoplatonic spiritualism had been introduced, as was the case in the Milanese church.[15]

Such spiritual interpretation did not, however, resolve all Augustine's problems with the Scriptures, for there are many scriptural texts that raise difficulties when they are interpreted according to the letter, such as some that touch on the seemingly immoral conduct of the Old Testament patriarchs and, in the New Testament, the parable about the unjust steward.[16] For the latter seems to praise the steward for cheating his master and consequently to encourage the Lord's disciples to do the same. In *On Genesis: A Refutation of the Manicheans*, Augustine held a rather sober position, which Jean Pépin has called the absurdity criterion for figurative interpretation of a biblical text, namely, that "the principal indication that a biblical text had been written with an allegorical intent and ought to be understood as such is the absurdity of the text as long as one sticks to the literal sense."[17] But Augustine clearly went beyond this criterion in *Teaching Christianity*, where he wrote, "You should know that whatever in the word of God cannot in the proper sense be referred to the goodness of morals or the truth of the faith is figurative."[18] Henri-Irénée Marrou called this Augustine's fundamental law of spiritual interpretation,[19] and it clearly maximizes the amount of Scripture that requires a figurative interpretation. In his *Answer to Faustus, a Manichaean* Augustine went so far as to say that Christ speaks to him in all of Scripture.[20] For example, in the parable of the Good Samaritan,[21] Augustine explains that the man who went down from Jerusalem to Jericho is Adam and the whole human race in him, that Jerusalem is beatitude, Jericho mortality, the robbers the devil and his angels, the priest and Levite the priesthood and ministry of the Old Testament,

---

13. See *On Genesis: A Refutation of the Manicheans* I,17,27.
14. See *Confessions* V,10,19.
15. See Roland Teske, "Spirituals and Spiritual Interpretation in Augustine," in *Augustinian Studies* 15 (1984) 65–81.
16. See Lk 16:1–13.
17. Jean Pépin, "A propos de l'histoire de l'exégèse allégorique: l'absurdité signe de l'allégorie," in *Texte und Untersuchungen* 63 (1955) 397.
18. *Teaching Christianity* III,10,14.
19. Henri-Irénée Marrou, *Saint Augustin et la fin de la culture antique* (Paris: Boccard, 1938) 478.
20. See *Answer to Faustus, a Manichaean* 12, 27.
21. See Lk 10:30–37.

the Samaritan Christ, his animal Christ's flesh, the inn the Church, and so on.[22] Such exegesis is an example of Augustine's ability to find Christ in a text that, in and of itself, has a true and moral literal sense.

In *The Literal Meaning of Genesis* Augustine states his two goals in undertaking the exposition of Genesis. The first is "to show that what some superficial or unbelieving readers might think impossible or contrary to the authority of Holy Scripture…was neither impossible nor contrary to it," which comes close to the absurdity criterion of figurative interpretation. But his second goal is to show that "what appears possible and has no semblance of contradictoriness, but could seem to certain people to be either superfluous or even lacking sense, was not something produced in the natural or ordinary course of events. Thus we might believe that it has a mystical meaning, since nothing can be found there that is lacking sense."[23] Marrou has suggested two reasons for holding this maximizing criterion for figurative interpretation. The first is that Augustine took seriously the words from 2 Tm 3:16 that *all divinely inspired Scripture is useful.* On the basis of these words, Marrou argued, "We have then to seek a hidden meaning for all those passages whose usefulness is not apparent in the literal sense."[24] His second reason for Augustine's having adopted the maximizing criterion for figurative interpretation is that Augustine's training in rhetoric taught him to study a text verse by verse and word by word rather than sentence by sentence.[25] As Joseph Lienhard says, "The ancients' first unit of understanding was not the pericope, or the sentence, but the single word. The word as the starting point for understanding was an assumption of ancient education in poetics and rhetoric."[26] Finally, Augustine's adherence to the maximizing interpretation is tied to his conviction that Scripture contains only a few truths to be believed and a few moral precepts to be followed. After stating his fundamental law, he points out that "good moral conduct has to do with loving God and the neighbor, and the truth of the faith has to do with knowing God and the neighbor."[27] Thus, given his view that the essence of Scripture is contained in the creed and in the commandments to love God and neighbor, most of the Bible would be superfluous and without sense unless it contained hidden meanings and figures to be grasped by those who would understand the word of God figuratively.

To return, then, to *Questions on the Gospels*, most of the answers to the questions in the first book are quite short, but those in the second book are often much longer. Among other things, Augustine takes delight in numerical symbolism. For instance, in the Lucan genealogy there are seventy-seven persons mentioned.[28]

---

22. See II,19.
23. *The Literal Meaning of Genesis* IX,12,22.
24. Marrou 479.
25. See ibid. 480.
26. Joseph Lienhard, "'The Glue Itself is Charity': Ps 62:9 in Augustine's Thought," in J. Lienhard, E. Muller, and R. Teske, eds., *Collectanea Augustiniana: Presbyter Factus Sum* (New York: Peter Lang, 1993) 375–384, here 381.
27. *Teaching Christianity* III,10,14.
28. See Lk 3:23–38.

Augustine notes that Christ told Peter that one should forgive a brother's sins seventy-seven times, and by this number he taught that we should forgive all sins, since he through whom all sins were forgiven came in the seventy-seventh generation.[29] Augustine insists that Christ would not have come in that seventy-seventh generation had there not been "something hidden in that number which pertains to signifying all sins."[30] He explains that one may see this in the numbers eleven and seven, which when multiplied by each other make seventy-seven. Eleven represents the transgression of the perfect number ten, which signifies beatitude, symbolized by the denarius, or ten pennies, that the workers in the vineyard were paid. Ten, moreover, is the sum of the union of the seven-part human creature, that is, heart, soul, and mind plus the four dimensions of the body, with the triune God. Hence "it is evident," Augustine says, "that the transgression of the number ten"—that is, going beyond it—"signifies the sin of pride."[31] And of course, according to the Book of Sirach, pride is the beginning of all sin.[32] Similarly, on the mission of the seventy-two disciples,[33] Augustine explains that, as the sun circles the earth in twenty-four hours, and as the world is enlightened by the sun, so the seventy-two disciples were sent to enlighten the world with the Gospel of the Trinity. For three times twenty-four makes seventy-two. And they were sent in twos because of the twofold commandment of love or because love can exist only between two or more.[34]

Augustine spends considerable time on the parables. He gives the one on the Good Samaritan a christological interpretation that he clearly derived from Origen and Ambrose, in which, as already mentioned, the man who went down from Jerusalem to Jericho represents the whole human race, and Christ is the good Samaritan who cares for him after he is left half-dead by robbers.[35] The parable of the Prodigal Son receives the lengthiest interpretation, in which Augustine explains that we need to view its content from the very beginning of creation. From that perspective the elder son, for example, represents the part of the human race that remained faithful to the worship of the true God, while the younger son represents the nations that went off to worship idols. In using his natural gifts wrongly the younger son departed for a distant region and thus abandoned his father. His hunger is his longing for the word of God, even as he forgets his father in the distant region. Augustine goes on to spell out the significance of the other elements of the parable in great detail.[36]

Given Augustine's principles for spiritual or figurative interpretation, in accord with which nothing is said in Scripture without meaning, his answers to the various

29.   See II,6,1.
30.   II,6,2.
31.   Ibid.
32.   See Sir 10:13, in Augustine's Latin version, but not in the best Greek and Hebrew manuscripts.
33.   See Lk 10:1.
34.   See II,14.
35.   See Roland Teske, "St. Augustine on the Good Samaritan," in Frederick Van Fleteren and Joseph Schaubelt, eds., *Augustine the Exegete* (New York: Peter Lang, 2001) 347–367.
36.   See II,33,1–7.

questions are clear enough without further explanation. It should not be surprising that he who warned that we would have to give an account for every idle word we speak[37] would not himself have included any idle words among the words of God.

*   *   *

The Latin text translated here is that found in the critical edition by Almut Mutzenbecher in CCSL 44/B, with some attention to the text and translation found in NBA 10/2. Aside from two nineteenth-century French translations in two separate editions, each entitled *Oeuvres complètes de Saint Augustin* (Bar-le-Duc 1864–1873; Paris 1869–1878), and the Italian translation in NBA 10/2, there do not seem to be any translations into modern languages.

---

37. See Mt 12:36.

Revisions II,12 (39)

These are some explanations of certain passages from the Gospel according to Matthew and likewise others from the Gospel according to Luke. The former were published in one book, the latter in another. The title of this work is *Questions on the Gospels*. But my prologue indicates well enough why only those passages from the above-mentioned Gospels were explained that are contained in my books, and it indicates which ones they are by adding and numbering the same questions so that anyone may find what he wants to read by following the numbers.

In the first book, then, where it says that the Lord foretold his passion to two disciples apart from the rest,[1] the faultiness of the codex misled us. For *to twelve*, not "to two," was written in the Gospel. In the second book, in wanting to explain how Joseph, whose wife was the virgin Mary, could have two fathers, I said that what is suggested, namely, that a brother took the wife of a deceased brother in order to raise up offspring for him according to the law,[2] is weak, because the law commanded that the one who would be born take the name of the deceased brother,[3] and that is not true. For the law commanded that the name of the deceased brother be used so that he would be called his son, not so that he would take his name.

The work begins as follows: *This work was not written as if.*

---

1. See I,27.
2. See Dt 25:5.
3. See II,5.

Prologue

This work was not written as if we had undertaken to explain the Gospel in order, but in accord with the choice and time of the person who consulted us, with whom it was being read, if something seemed unclear to him. For this reason many things, and perhaps some that are more obscure, have been passed over, because the person who was asking about what he did not yet know already knew them, and he did not want to be slowed down on those matters that he had already grasped; thus, by his diligence in listening and in handling the questions, he might commit the matter to memory solidly and firmly. Some things are also found to be explained here not in the same order in which they are narrated in the Gospel, because some things that were deferred out of haste were considered later when we were given time and were written in an empty place that followed in the order of things already explained. After I discovered this, so that anyone who wanted to read something in this work that troubled him in the Gospel and moved him to ask would not be put off by the bother of the disrupted order (since I know that those things that were dictated piecemeal were gathered together and combined into one work), I arranged things so that he might easily find what he needed by the titles written before them in numerical order.

Titles of the Questions of the First Book

1. That he says, *No one knows the Son except the Father.*

2. That the Lord's disciples began to pluck the ears and eat.

3. On the smoldering wick.

4. On the blind and mute man.

5. That he says, *And if I cast out demons by Beelzebul.*

6. That he says, *Brood of vipers.*

7. That he says, *As Jonah was in the belly of the whale three days and three nights.*

8. That he says, *When the unclean spirit has gone out of the man.*

9. On the hundredfold, sixtyfold, and thirtyfold fruit.

10. That he says, *Gather the weeds first.*

11. On the mustard seed that becomes larger than all the plants.

12. On the yeast that the woman took and hid in three measures of wheat.

13. On the treasure hidden in a field.

14. That the Jews said, *From where does he have this wisdom and these powers?*

15. That he walked on the sea toward the disciples.

16. What this means: *Whatever gift comes from me will be counted toward your good.*

17. That he says, *Every planting that my Father has not planted shall be uprooted.*

18. On the son of the centurion and the daughter of the Canaanite woman.

19. What the mute and the blind and the deaf and the lame signify who were presented to the Lord to be cured.

20. That he says, *When evening comes you say, It will be clear, for the sky is red.*

21. That he says, *Elijah shall certainly come and restore all things.*

22. On the man who often fell into the fire and at times into the water.

23. That he says, *Therefore the sons are free*, when tribute is asked for.

24. That he says, *But whoever scandalizes one of these little ones.*

25. That the man who owed ten thousand talents was brought to him.

26. On the rich man who does not enter the kingdom of God.

27. That he indicates to two disciples apart from the rest that he is going to suffer.

28. That, when he left Jericho, he restored sight to two blind men.

29. That he said to the disciples, *You shall say to this mountain, Rise up and throw yourself into the sea.*

30. That he said, *And whoever stumbles over this stone shall be broken.*

31. On the man who was a king who held a wedding feast for his son.

32. On the seven brothers who had one wife.

33. What does it mean that he said, *The whole law depends on these two commandments*?

34. That he said, *For which is greater, the gold or the Temple that makes the gold holy?*

35. That he said, *Straining out a gnat but swallowing a camel.*

36. That he said, *How often have I wanted to gather your children as a hen.*

37. That he said, *Pray that your flight may not be in winter or on the sabbath.*

38. That he said, *As lightning goes forth from the east and reaches all the way to the west.*

39. That he said, *But learn a lesson from the fig tree.*

40. That he said about Judas, *It was better for him not to be born.*

41. That he was sold for thirty pieces of silver.

42. That he said, *Where the body is, there the eagles will be gathered.*

43. That he said, *I shall not drink henceforth of this fruit of the vine.*

44. That they spat in his face and struck him with blows.

45. On Peter's threefold denial.

46. That he followed the Lord at a distance as he entered upon his passion.

47. That the Lord prayed three times before he was handed over.

First Book

1

When he said, *No one knows the Son except the Father,* he did not say, "and him to whom the Father wished to reveal him," as was the case when he said, *No one knows the Father except the Son,* and he added, *and him to whom the Son wished to reveal him* (Mt 11:27). This is not to be understood in the sense that the Son could be known by no one except by the Father alone but that the Father could be known not only by the Son but also by those to whom the Son revealed him. For it was said, rather, so that we would understand that both the Father and the Son are revealed through the Son, because he is himself the light for our mind, so that you would understand what he added afterward, *and him to whom the Son wished to reveal* not only the Father but also the Son. For what he said was added to the whole. For the Father makes himself known by his Word, but the Word not only makes known what is made known by the Word but also makes himself known.

2

That the disciples of the Lord *began to pluck ears and eat* (Mt 12:1)), which they could not do without shucking them,[1] means *put to death your members that are on the earth* (Col 3:5), that is, because no one enters into the body of Christ unless he has been stripped of carnal clothing. Hence there is *Lay aside the old man* (Col 3:9), and hence there is also *By the circumcision not made by hand in the stripping off of the flesh* (Col 2:11).

3

Regarding the smoldering wick[2] one should note that, when it ceases to give light, it makes a stink.

4

Then there was brought to him a blind and mute man who had a demon (Mt 12:22), that is, one who does not believe and is subject to the devil, who does not understand and does not confess the faith of which it was said, *By the mouth confession is made unto salvation* (Rom 10:10), or who does not give praise to God.

5

That he said, *And if I cast out demons by Beelzebul, therefore,* even according to your own view, *the kingdom of God has arrived among you* (Mt 12:27–28), for

---

1. See Lk 6:1.
2. See Mt 12:20.

the kingdom of the devil cannot stand, which you say is divided against itself.[3] What he now calls the *kingdom of God* means that by which the wicked are condemned and separated by their sins from the faithful who are now doing penance. He calls him *the strong man* (Mt 12:29) because he held them in such a way that people could not tear themselves away from him by their own strength but by the grace of God. He calls all nonbelievers his possessions.[4] *Unless he has first bound up the strong man* (Mt 12:29). *He has bound up* means that he took from him the power of preventing the will of the faithful from following Christ and attaining the kingdom of God.

6

He calls them *brood of vipers* (Mt 12:34) because he also calls them children of the devil.[5] For one becomes his child to the extent that he imitates him in sinning.

7

As Jonah was in the belly of the whale three days and three nights, so the Son of Man shall be in the heart of the earth three days and three nights (Mt 12:40). Take part of the Friday on which he was buried along with the previous night for a night and day, that is, for a whole day, the sabbath night and day, and the night of the Lord's Day with the dawn of the same day, and in that way, by taking a part for the whole, you have three days and three nights. For, when a woman is said to be pregnant for ten months, there are nine full months, but the beginning of the tenth is taken as though it were a whole. And one evangelist says that the Lord revealed himself on the mountain after six days,[6] while another says after eight days,[7] counting as whole and complete days the last part of the first day on which the Lord promised this and the first part of the last day on which what he promised was fulfilled. In that way you can understand that the one who said *after six days* was mentioning only the ones in between, which were truly whole and complete. For in Genesis a day begins with light and ends with darkness[8] in order to signify the fall of man. But now a day begins from darkness and ends at light, as it was said, *Light shines forth from the darkness* (2 Cor 4:6), because a person set free from sins has come to the light of righteousness.

8

When the unclean spirit has gone out of the man (Mt 12:43), and so forth. This signifies that some are going to believe in such a way that they cannot endure

---

3.   See Mt 26:26.
4.   See Mt 12:29.
5.   See Jn 8:44.
6.   See Mt 17:1; Mk 9:2.
7.   See Lk 9:28.
8.   See Gn 1:5.

the labors of continence and are going to return to the world. The words, *He takes with him seven others* (Mt 12:45), are to be understood in the sense that, when someone falls away from righteousness, he will also pretend to be virtuous. For, when the lust of the flesh has been driven off from its usual actions by penance and *does not find* delights *in which to rest* (Mt 12:43), it returns with greater desire and again occupies the mind of the man, if he becomes negligent after it has been driven out, so that the word of God may not be brought in as the inhabitant of a house that has been cleansed[9] by sound doctrine. And the man will have not only those seven vices that are contrary to the seven spiritual virtues[10] but will also through hypocrisy pretend that he has the virtues themselves, and for this reason, *having taken seven others worse than itself* (Mt 12:45), that is, those seven by pretense, that concupiscence *returns so that the last state of the man is worse than the first* (Mt 12:45).

9

As to his words, *One a hundredfold, another sixtyfold, still another thirtyfold* (Mt 13:8), the hundredfold belongs to the martyrs on account of their holiness of life and their contempt for death, the sixtyfold belongs to the virgins on account of their interior leisure, because they do not have to fight against the sinful habits of the flesh — for leisure is usually granted to men of sixty after military service or after public service — and the thirtyfold belongs to married people, because this is the age of those engaged in the battle. For they have a fiercer conflict not to be overcome by their passions.

10[11]

Every impurity in the wheat is called weeds. The weeds are said to be separated first, because nonbelievers will be separated from believers by a prior tribulation. It is understood that this will be done by the good angels, because the good ones can carry out the duties of justice with a good intention, like a king or like a judge, but the evil ones cannot fulfill the duties of mercy.

11

On account of[12] the fervor of faith or because it is said to drive out poisons, a mustard seed becomes larger than all the plants,[13] that is, than other teachings.

---

9. See Mt 12:44.
10. It is not clear whether Augustine has seven particular vices in mind, but he seems to be referring to seven particular virtues — perhaps the three theological virtues (faith, hope and charity) and the four cardinal virtues (prudence, justice, fortitude and temperance).
11. This question deals with Mt 13:24–30.36–43.
12. Reading *ob* in PL instead of *ad* in CCSL.
13. See Mt 13:31–32.

These teachings are, however, the opinions of the sects, that is, what has pleased the individual sects.[14]

12

A woman took the yeast and hid it in three measures of wheat (Mt 13:33). He calls wisdom *a woman* and love *the yeast*, because it warms and raises up. But *in three measures of wheat* signifies either these three in a human being, *from the whole heart, and from the whole soul, and from the whole mind* (Mt 12:30), or these three degrees of fruitfulness, *a hundredfold, sixtyfold, thirtyfold* (Mt 13:8), or these three kinds of men, *Noah, Daniel, and Job* (Ez 14:14).[15]

13

He called the two covenants of the law *a treasure hidden in a field* (Mt 13:44), and when someone finds it through his intellect, he realizes that great things are hidden in it, and *he goes and sells all he has and buys that field* (Mt 13:44), that is, by contempt for temporal things he buys leisure for himself so that he may be rich in the knowledge of God.

14

The Jews said, *From where does he have this wisdom and these powers?* (Mt 13:54) — *wisdom* in what he said and *powers* in what he did. And for this reason too, when the Apostle said, *Christ the power of God and the wisdom of God* (1 Cor 1:24), by *power* he referred to signs done for the sake of the Jews, but by *wisdom* to teaching for the sake of the Greeks, that is, the gentiles.

15[16]

When the disciples said that it was a ghost, this signifies the same thing as the words, *Do you think that he will find faith on earth?* (Lk 18:8), for some who give in to the devil will have doubts about the coming of Christ. But that Peter pleads for help from the Lord lest he drown signifies that the Church is going to be purified by certain tribulations even after the last persecution. And Paul too signifies this when he says, *He will be saved, but as through fire* (1 Cor 3:15). What follows, namely, that in adoration all in the boat said, *Truly you are the Son of God* (Mt 14:33), signifies that his glory will then be evident to those who now walk through faith when they see through vision.[17]

---

14. "Opinions...has pleased": *placita...placuit.*
15. A similar but more extended comparison is made below at II,44,2.
16. This question deals with Mt 14:26–33.
17. See 2 Cor 5:7.

16

Whatever gift comes from me will be counted toward your good (Mt 15:5), that is, a gift that you offer because of me will now pertain to you. By these words children signify that it is no longer the task of parents to offer sacrifices for them, because they have come to the age at which they can now offer them for themselves. The Pharisees, therefore, denied that those who had attained the age when they could say this to their parents were guilty if they did not offer honor to their parents.[18]

17

Every planting that my heavenly Father has not planted shall be uprooted (Mt 15:13), that is, carnal desire, for those whose thoughts were in accord with it were offended when the signs of things or even their own traditions were treated dismissively, but they did not care about the commandments of life that cleanse the soul from desire.[19]

18

That he cures the son of the centurion and the daughter of the Canaanite woman without coming to their homes[20] signifies that the gentiles to whom he does not come will be saved by his word. By the fact that the children are healed when their parents ask,[21] the person of the Church is to be understood, because she is in herself both mother and children. For she is called mother for all those people together who make up the Church, but the same people as individuals are called her children.

19

The crowds presented to the Lord mute persons, who do not praise God or confess the faith, blind persons, who do not understand, although they obey those who command, deaf persons, who do not obey, although they understand, and lame persons, who do not carry out the commandments.[22]

20

The Lord said, *When evening comes you say, It will be clear, for the sky is red* (Mt 16:2), that is, by the blood of Christ's passion the forgiveness of sins is given in his first coming. *And in the morning you say, It will be stormy today, for the sky is red with gloom* (Mt 16:3), that is, because in his second coming he will come with fire preceding him. *Do you know, then, how to judge the face of*

---

18. See Mt 15:5.
19. See Mt 15:1–9.
20. See Mt 8:5–13; 15:22–28.
21. See Mt 8:5–6; 15:22.
22. See Mt 15:30.

the sky, but you cannot judge the signs of the times? (Mt 16:4) He said *the signs of the times* with reference to his coming or his passion, to which a red sky in the evening is similar. And he likewise said *the sky is red with gloom* with reference to the tribulation before his future coming, to which a red morning is similar.

21

The Lord said, *Elijah shall certainly come and restore all things* (Mt 17:11), that is, those whom the persecution of the Antichrist has thrown into disruption, or, alternatively, he himself will restore by dying the things that he ought.

22

When he said, *He often falls into the fire and at times into water* (Mt 17:14), *fire* stands for anger, because it seeks to move upward, and *water* for the pleasures of the flesh. Likewise, when the disciples say, *Why were we not able to cast him out?* (Mt 17:18), this happened lest they be lifted up in pride by working miracles. Instead they were admonished through the lowliness of faith, as though through a mustard seed, in order to cure their earthly pride, which is signified by the term *mountain*,[23] so that it would pass away.

23[24]

When he said, *Therefore the children are free* (Mt 17:25), one should understand that in every kingdom the children are free, that is, not subject to taxes. Therefore the children of that kingdom, under which are all earthly kingdoms, ought to be that much freer.

24

What the Lord says, *But whoever scandalizes one of these little ones* (Mt 18:6), either by not obeying or by disobeying, refers to humble people, such as the Lord wants his disciples to be. *It is better for him that a huge millstone be hung on his neck and that he be cast into the depth of the sea* (Mt 18:6), much the same as the Apostle said when speaking of Alexander the coppersmith.[25] In other words, it is fitting for him that the desire for temporal things, to which the foolish and blind are bound, drag him down to destruction, enchained by their weight.

---

23. See Mt 17:20.
24. This question deals with Mt 17:24–27.
25. See 2 Tm 4:14.

25²⁶

That *a man who owed ten thousand talents was brought before his master, and he ordered that he be sold along with his wife and children and all that he had and that he be repaid* (Mt 18:24–25) should be understood as meaning that he was in debt with regard to the ten commandments of the law, and that he had to pay the penalty for his greed and actions as it were by means of his wife and children, which is his price; the price of a person who has been sold is understood to be the punishment of a condemned person. That he said, *He refused to pardon his fellow servant but went off and cast him into prison* (Mt 18:29–30), and so forth, should be understood as meaning that the master held against him his desire to punish his fellow servant. But by his fellow servants who reported his actions to the master one can understand the Church, which looses him and binds him.²⁷

26

The Lord says that a rich man does not enter the kingdom of God,²⁸ and his disciples say, *Who can be saved?* (Mt 19:25) Since there are few rich people compared to the very many who are poor, it should be understood that all those who desire such things are considered to be numbered among them.

27

The Lord tells two of his disciples apart from the rest that he is going to suffer.²⁹ He did this to strengthen their testimony for the future, because he said, *On the lips of two or three witnesses every word will stand firm* (Mt 18:16). For, in order that what he said might not be made public and yet not lack the strength of human testimony, he could not say this to fewer than two. Or he said it to reveal the mystery of love,³⁰ for it cannot exist between fewer than two.³¹ He was going to suffer out of love, however, not because of what he owed on account of his own sin but in order to absolve our sins.

28³²

The Lord departs from Jericho, on his way to leaving the earth by his resurrection. Large crowds follow him, and peoples and nations believe in him. But the two blind men sitting alongside the road signify certain individuals from both

---

26. This question deals with Mt 18:24–31.
27. See Mt 18:18.
28. See Mt 19:23.
29. See Mt 20:17. See also *Revisions* II,12(39), where Augustine claims that a faulty codex led him to say "two" rather than "twelve" disciples.
30. "Mystery of love": *sacramentum caritatis.*
31. See also below at II,14.
32. This question deals with Mt 20:29–34.

peoples[33] who through faith are now clinging to the temporal dispensation of salvation, in accord with which Christ is the way,[34] and desiring to be given sight, that is, to understand something about the eternity of the Word, which they desire to obtain as Jesus passes, that is, through the merit of the faith by which they believe that the Son of God has both been born as man and has suffered for us. For Jesus passes, as it were, through this temporal dispensation, since such actions take place in time. But they had to shout enough to overcome the noise of the crowd that held them back, that is, they had to apply their minds with perseverance to praying and knocking until they overcame by their very strong insistence the habit of carnal desires that, like a crowd, shouts against the thoughts of someone trying to see the light of the eternal truth, or until they overcame the multitude of carnal human beings that impedes spiritual pursuits. Therefore, when Jesus — who says, *To the one who asks it shall be given, and one who seeks shall find, and to the one who knocks it shall be opened* (Mt 7:7) — hears those who come to him, that is, who come with ardent desire for what they desire, he stands still, touches them, and grants them sight. For the eternity of the Word that, *remaining in itself, renews all things* (Wis 7:27), does not pass as that temporal dispensation does. Hence, because faith in the incarnation that takes place in time prepares us to understand eternal realities, they were admonished by Jesus' passing so that their eyes might be opened, and their eyes were opened by his standing still. For temporal things pass, while eternal things stand still.

29

When the Lord said to his disciples, *You shall say to this mountain, Rise up and throw yourself into the sea* (Mt 21:21), he was speaking of the pride that worldly people have. A servant of God ought to say this to himself in order to drive that pride away from himself, because it is not fitting for him. Alternatively, through the faith of [the disciples], because the Gospel was preached by them, the Lord himself, who is called a mountain,[35] was taken away from the Jews in order that he might be cast far off into the gentiles as though into the sea.

30

When the Lord says, *And whoever stumbles over this stone will be broken, but it will crush him upon whom it falls* (Mt 21:44), in saying that they are stumbling over him he is speaking about the people who now despise or insult him. For this reason they are not yet completely perishing, but they are still being broken so that they may not walk correctly. But he will come to those upon whom he falls from above in judgment with the punishment of perdition. For this reason he said that

---

33. I.e., Jews and gentiles.
34. See Jn 14:6.
35. See Is 2:2; Dn 2:35.45.

it would crush them, so that the wicked would be *like dust that the wind blows from the face of the earth* (Ps 1:4).

31

When the Lord said, *The kingdom of heaven is like a man who was a king who held a wedding feast for his son* (Mt 22:1–2), he called the incarnate Word a wedding because the Church was united to God in the man that he assumed.[36] When he said, *My bulls and fatlings have been slaughtered* (Mt 22:4), he called the princes of the people *bulls*, but *fatlings* all those who were fed. When the Lord said, *Go out to the roadways and invite to the wedding feast whomever you find* (Mt 22:9), the roads are understood as the teachings of the gentiles, because from all of them they came to the wedding feast, that is, they believed in Christ.

32

When the Sadducees said to the Lord, *There were among us seven brothers, and one having taken a wife passed away, and the second, and the others as well* (Mt 22:25–26), they are understood to be wicked persons who were unable to bear the fruit of righteousness on the earth through all the seven ages of the world in which this earth has existed.[37] For afterward even the earth itself will pass away, through which all those seven husbands fruitlessly passed.

33

When the Lord said, *On these two commandments the whole law and the prophets depend* (Mt 22:40), he said *depend* as indicating something that is ordered to an end.

34

When the Lord said, *For which is greater, the gold or the Temple that makes it holy?* (Mt 23:17), and when he likewise said, *For which is greater, the gift or the altar that makes the gift holy?* (Mt 23:19), the Temple and the altar should be understood as Christ himself, and the gold and the gift as the praises and the sacrifices of prayers that we offer in him through him. For he is not made holy through them, but they are through him.

---

36. "The man that he assumed": *homine suscepto*. This is an instance of the *homo assumptus* (or *susceptus*) terminology that Augustine used in some of his earlier writings to refer to Christ's incarnation. See p. 58, note 77. See also below at I,36, 42 and 43.
37. Augustine usually speaks of six ages, from Adam to the Christian era, with a seventh (and eighth) age yet to come, as most notably in *The City of God* XXII,30. See below at I,41.

35

When the Lord said, *Straining out the gnat* (Mt 23:24), it refers to his having said that [the Pharisees] pay the tithe on any little things,[38] and *swallowing a camel* (Mt 23:24) refers to his having said, *You pass over the more important matters of the law, mercy and justice and faith* (Mt 23:24). Hence the meaning is: you observe the littlest things, but you scorn the biggest ones. For from this perversity there also comes upon them what these things can be referred to by allegory. Thus they released Barabbas[39] because he did not violate the sabbath,[40] which they observed in a carnal sense with great diligence, but they killed the Lord, who taught a spiritual observance of the sabbath *through mercy and justice and faith*, which they very greatly scorned. For the term *gnat* not unreasonably symbolizes a seditious murderer, because this creature arouses disquiet by its buzzing and is delighted by blood, and, on account of the greatness that lowers itself to take on burdens, the term *camel* appropriately suggests the Lord.[41]

36

The Lord said to Jerusalem, *How often have I wanted to gather your children as a hen gathers her chicks, and you refused!* (Mt 23:37) This kind of animal has such a great affection for its offspring that, moved by their weakness, it too becomes weak and shelters her offspring with her wings and fights against a hawk, which is something that you will scarcely find in other animals. In that way our mother, the wisdom of God,[42] having in a sense become weak through the assumption of flesh, protects our weakness, which is why the Apostle says, *That of God which is weak is stronger than human beings* (1 Cor 1:25), and she resists the devil so that he does not carry us off. And, in that act of defense, what that mother tries to do against a hawk with love, this one succeeds in doing against the devil with power.

37

When the Lord said, *Pray that your flight may not be in winter or on the sabbath* (Mt 26:20), it means that you should not be held back by any hindrance, because one is hindered from a journey by winter, rains, cold, or the sabbath, when one is not permitted to set out. Alternatively, it means that that day should not find anyone in sorrow or joy over temporal things.

---

38. See Mt 23:23.
39. See Mt 26:20.
40. The Gospels say nothing about Barrabas's observance of the sabbath.
41. See also below at II,47.
42. See 1 Cor 1:24.

38

When the Lord said, *For as lightning goes forth from the east and reaches all the way to the west, so shall be the coming of the Son of Man* (Mt 24:27), he wanted to signify by the terms *east* and *west* the whole world through which the Gospel was going to spread, beginning in Jerusalem,[43] in accord with the sense in which he said, *Hereafter you shall see the Son of Man coming in the clouds* (Mt 26:64). For he now fittingly called the Church *lightning*, which usually flashes forth from the clouds. Therefore, once the authority of the Church has been established as clear and evident throughout the world, she then warns her disciples and all the faithful and those who wish to believe in him not to believe schismatics and heretics. For every schism and every heresy either has its place in the world, occupying some part of it, or takes advantage of people's curiosity by its hidden and dark assemblies. To this there pertains what he says, *If someone says to you, See, Christ is here or there* (Mt 24:23), which signifies parts of lands or provinces, or, *in the interior of the house or in the desert* (Mt 24:26), which signifies the hidden and dark assemblies of heretics. When he says that his coming will reach from the east to the west, it is directed against those who are mentioned through small parts of lands and say that Christ is with them. When he says *as lightning*, it is directed against those who assemble in secret, as *in the interior of houses*, and against the few, as *in the desert*. The term *lightning* pertains to the evidence and light of the Church and also indicates the night and clouds of this world, for then the brightness of lightning is seen.

39

When the Lord says, *But learn a lesson from the fig tree* (Mt 24:32), understand the fig tree as the human race on account of the itching of the flesh.[44] *For when its branch is supple* (Mt 24:32) means when the children of men advance through faith in Christ to spiritual fruitfulness, and the honor of their adoption as children of God shines forth.

40

When the Lord said about Judas, *It was better for him not to be born* (Mt 26:24), did he mean being born into this life, so that he was speaking in the ordinary sense? For something cannot be good for one who does not exist. And if anyone claims that there is a life before this one,[45] it is clear that not to be born is better not only for Judas but for everyone. Or does he mean that it is better not to be born to the devil for sin? Or does he even mean that it was better that he not be born to Christ through his calling, so that he would not be an apostate?

---

43. See Lk 24:47.
44. Augustine may be referring either to the fact that Adam and Eve covered their nakedness with fig leaves (Gn 3:7) or to the slight scratchiness of fig leaves, which could cause itching.
45. Augustine is probably referring to a view attributed to Origen in Jerome, Letter 124,5.

41

That the Lord was sold for thirty pieces of silver signified by means of Judas the wicked Jews who, in pursuing carnal and temporal things that pertain to the five senses of the body, refused to possess Christ. And that they did this in the sixth age of the world signified that they received that sum of six times five as the price of the Lord who was sold. With regard to that time the prophet mocks such people when he says, *Sons of men, how long will you be heavy of heart? Why do you follow after vanity and seek a lie?* (Ps 4:3), in the sense that, if there had been an excuse for pursuing vanity in five ages, at least in the sixth age they ought to have grasped the truth that the Lord Jesus preached and made known, just as on the sixth day man was made to the image of God.[46] And because they rejected this, they have the image of the prince of the world impressed on them six times five times,[47] and they do not have Christ through whom *the light of your countenance, Lord* (Ps 4:7) was impressed upon us. And because the words of the Lord are silver,[48] but they understood even the law itself in a carnal manner, they held onto the image of worldly rule as though impressed on silver, while they lost the Lord.

42

When the Lord says, *Where the body is, there the eagles will be gathered* (Mt 24:28), he means into heaven, where he raised up along with himself the body in the man he assumed, which is also called a cadaver, because he was speaking as one about to die. *There the eagles will be gathered* is said of the spiritual people who, in imitating his suffering and humility, are as if filled from his body. For he assumed a body on account of his humility and suffering for us.

43

When the Lord says to his disciples before the time of his passion, *I shall not drink henceforth of this fruit of the vine until that day when I shall drink it anew with you in the kingdom of my Father* (Mt 26:29), he wants the former to be understood as old when he calls the latter new. Because from the offspring of Adam, then, who is called *the old man* (Rom 6:6), he assumed the body that he would hand over to death in his passion, for which reason he also commends his blood through the sacrament of the wine, what else ought we to understand the new wine to be but the immortality of bodies brought to a newness of life? And when he says, *I shall drink with you*, he also promises them the resurrection of the body for the sake of being clothed with immortality. For *with you* must be understood to be said not as referring to the same time but as referring to the same renewal.

---

46. See Gn 1:26.
47. I.e., thirty times, corresponding to the thirty pieces of silver.
48. See Ps 11:7.

For the Apostle too says that we have risen with Christ,[49] so that the hope for what lies in the future may bring present joy. But when he says of this fruit of the vine that it is new, he is signifying that the same bodies will rise in accord with the heavenly renewal that are now going to die in terms of their earthly oldness. But if you understand as the Jews themselves *the vine* from whose oldness he drinks this chalice of his passion, this signifies that this nation would come to the body of Christ through newness of life when, after the multitude of the gentiles has entered, all of Israel will be saved.[50]

44

What was said, *They spat in his face* (Mt 26:67), signified those who spit back the presence of his grace. Likewise, they strike *him* as *by blows* (Mt 26:67) signifies those who prefer their honors to him. They put *their palms to his face* (Mt 26:67) signifies those who, blinded by unbelief, claim that he has not come, as if undoing and repelling his presence.

45

Because Peter was not yet firm in faith, he denied him three times.[51] This triple denial seems to designate the evil error of the heretics, for the error of the heretics about Christ is reduced to three kinds, for they are mistaken either about his divinity or about his humanity or about both.

46

That Peter follows the Lord from afar as he goes toward his passion[52] signifies that the Church was certainly going to follow, that is, imitate the passion of the Lord, but in a far different way, for the Church suffers for itself, but he suffers for the Church.

47

As the temptation of desire is threefold, so the temptation of fear is also threefold. The fear of death is opposed to the desire that is in curiosity, for, as in the latter there is the desire to know things, so in the former there is the fear of losing such knowledge. The fear of shame and insults is opposed to the desire for honor and praise. The fear of pain is opposed to the desire for pleasure. It is, therefore, not absurd to understand that, on account of the threefold temptation of his passion, the Lord prayed three times that the chalice would pass, but in such a way, rather, that the will of the Father would be fulfilled.[53]

---

49. See Col 2:12.
50. See Rom 11:26.
51. See Mt 26:69–74.
52. See Mt 26:58.
53. See Mt 26:39.42.44.

Titles of the Questions of the Second Book

1. That Zechariah heard from the angel, *Your prayer has been answered.*

2. That he teaches the crowds from a boat.

3. That he says to the leper who was cleansed, *Go, show yourself to the priest.*

4. On the paralytic who was lowered to him through the roof.

5. How Joseph could have had two fathers.

6. On the seventy-seven generations.

7. On the man who had a withered right hand.

8. That he says, *They will pour into your lap a good measure heaped up, shaken down, and overflowing.*

9. That he says, *Can a blind person lead a blind person?*

10. On the man who dug deep and laid a foundation on rock.

11. On the children sitting in the marketplace and shouting to one another.

12. That he says, *No one lights a lamp and covers it with a bucket or puts it under a bed.*

13. On the man in whom there was a legion of demons.

14. On the seventy-two disciples.

15. That he says, *If the light that is in you is darkness, how great is the darkness itself!*

16. That he says, *Now, you Pharisees clean what is outside the cup and the bowl.*

17. On the finger of God.

18. On the fast of the bridegroom's guests.

19. On the man who went down from Jerusalem to Jericho and fell among thieves.

20. That Martha received him into her home, where Mary sat at his feet.

21. On the man who in the middle of the night asks for three loaves of bread from his friend.

22. On the bread and the fish and the egg.

23. That he says, *You have carried the key of knowledge.*

24. That he says, *The soul is more valuable than food.*

25. That he says, *Let your loins be girt and your lamps burning.*

26. On the measure of wheat that the faithful steward gives to the family.

27. That he says, *When you see a cloud rising from the west.*

28. What he says about the stature of the body to which they could not add anything.

29. That he says, *Do not be raised high up.*

30. On those invited to the banquet.

31. On the expenses for building the tower and on the king who had twenty thousand men.

32. On the salt that lost its savor and the lost sheep.

33. On the two sons, the younger of whom set out for a faraway region.

34. That he says, *Make friends for yourselves with the mammon of iniquity.*

35. That he says, *If you were not trustworthy in regard to someone else's property.*

36. That he says, *No one can serve two masters.*

37. That he says, *The kingdom of heaven suffers violence.*

38. On the rich man at whose door Lazarus lay with his sores.

39. That the disciples said, *Increase our faith.*

40. On the ten lepers.

41. On the man who is on the roof and his belongings in the house.

42. On the man in the field who should not return.

43. On Lot's wife.

44. On the two in a bed and the two at the millstone and the two in the field.

45. On the unjust judge whom the widow was entreating.

46. On the nobleman who went off to a faraway region to receive a kingdom for himself.

47. On the camel passing through the eye of a needle.

48. On the blind man whose sight was restored when he approached Jericho.

49. On the life of the saints after they rose from the dead.

50. That he says, *Pray that you do not enter into temptation.*

51. What is written about the Lord: *He pretended to go further.*

Second Book

1

When Zechariah is praying for the people he hears from an angel, *Your prayer has been answered. Behold, your wife Elizabeth shall conceive and bear a son, and you shall call his name John.* (Lk 1:13) What you should first notice here is that it is not likely that an old man who had an elderly wife could have set aside the prayers for the people and prayed to have children, especially since no one prays to receive what he has given up hope that he will receive. But he had already so utterly given up hope that he was going to have children that he did not believe the promise of the angel. After all, he was offering prayers for the sins or for the salvation or redemption of the people, and the people were waiting for him while he offered them. Therefore what is said to him, *Your prayer has been answered,* should be understood as spoken for the sake of the people. For that people's salvation and redemption and the remission of their sins was going to come about through Christ, which is why it is announced to Zechariah that a son was going to be born, because he was destined to be Christ's precursor. But because he does not believe the angel, the same angel said to him, *And behold, you shall be unable to speak until these things are fulfilled in their time* (Lk 1:20). We should understand that this signified that, until John, prophecy would be as though silent with respect to any intelligible words, because it was not understood until it was fulfilled in the Lord.

2[1]

That the Lord teaches the crowds from a boat signified the present time, when the Lord teaches the nations from the authority of the Church. That the Lord climbs into the boat that belonged to Peter and asks him to pull back a little from the shore signifies either that one should speak to the crowds with moderation, so that one does not preach earthly things to them and so that one does not move off from earthly things into the deeper aspects of the mysteries[2] in such a way that the people do not understand them at all; or that one should first preach to the peoples in the nearby regions, just as what he says to Peter, *Head out into the deep, and lower your nets for the catch* (Lk 5:4), likewise pertains to the more remote peoples who were preached to at a later time, as Isaiah says, *Raise up the standard among the peoples for those that are near and for those that are far off* (Is 62:10; 57:19). Thus, that the nets were also breaking from the abundance of fish and that the boats were so full that they were sinking signifies that there will be a great number of carnal people in the Church. And it will continue to be great despite the disruption of the peace that occurs when heresies and schisms leave it,

---

1. This question deals with Lk 5:3–11.
2. "Deeper aspects of the mysteries": *profundiora sacramentorum.*

and it will suffer so great a loss of faith and of good morals that such a Church will seem to say to Christ, *Depart from me, because I am a sinful man* (Lk 5:8), as if, filled with crowds of carnal people and almost submerged by their moral behavior, it may somehow drive off from itself the rule of spiritual persons, in whom the person of Christ stands out most of all. For these people do not say this to the good servants of God with the voice of their tongue in order to drive them away from them, but they urge them by the voice of their moral behavior and actions to draw back from them so that they are not governed by them. And, insofar as they offer them honor with greater fervor, they still admonish them by their deeds to withdraw from them. Thus, as Peter falling at the Lord's feet signified their offering them honor, he signified their morals by his words, *Depart from me, Lord, because I am a sinful man.* That the Lord did not do this, however, for he did not withdraw from them but brought them to the shore by the boats that had withdrawn from the land, signifies that good and spiritual men, troubled by the sins of the crowds where they live, need not have the will to abandon the service of the Church in order to live, as it were, more securely and peacefully. The fact, therefore, that *when the boats were brought back to land*, Peter and James and John *left everything and followed him* (Lk 5:9) can signify the end of time, when those who have clung to Christ will completely withdraw from the sea of this world.

3

When the Lord says to the leper who was cleansed, *Go, show yourself to the priest and offer the gift for your cleansing, as Moses commanded, in testimony to them* (Lk 5:14), he seems to approve of the sacrifice that was commanded by Moses,[3] although the Church has not accepted it. He can be understood to have ordered this because the sacrifice, the holy of holies,[4] which is his body, had not yet begun, for he had not yet offered his holocaust in his passion. When that sacrifice was established among the believing people, the Temple was overthrown in which those sacrifices were customarily offered. This happened in accordance with the prophecy of Daniel.[5] For it was not appropriate to abolish the sacrifices that signified it before the sacrifice that they signified was established through the testimony of the apostles who preached it and the faith of the people who believed them.

4[6]

In the paralytic one can see a soul crippled in its members, that is, in good works, seeking Christ, that is, the will of the Word of God. But he is prevented by the crowds, unless he opens the roof, that is, the veil over the Scriptures,[7] and in

---

3. See Lv 14:10.
4. See Lv 6:25.
5. See Dn 9:27.
6. This question deals with Lk 5:18–25.
7. See 2 Cor 3:12–18.

that way comes through them to the knowledge of Christ, that is, comes down to his lowliness by the piety of faith. Those by whom he is lowered can signify good teachers in the Church. That he was lowered with his bed signifies that Christ must be known by a person while he is still living in this flesh. And by the fact that, after being healed, he is then ordered to carry his bed and go to his home, one may understand that there remains for the members of the soul, which are convalescing through good hope by the forgiveness of sins, this task, namely, that the weakness of the soul should no longer rest in carnal delights, as in a bed, but should hold in check carnal loves and aim at repose in the depths of its heart.

5

1. The question is not unreasonably raised about how Joseph could have two fathers. For Matthew says that he was begotten of someone called Jacob,[8] whereas Luke says that he is the son of someone called Heli.[9] And in this passage it cannot be said that, as clearly is often the case not only among the gentiles but also among the Jews, one man has two names, since someone who thinks this is easily refuted by the remaining series of the generations. For what is he going to say about grandfathers, great-grandfathers, great-great-grandfathers, and other ancestors, whose names each of the two evangelists has woven into his account? What, finally, is he going to say about their number, since Luke lists forty-three generations from the Lord to David,[10] while Matthew lists twenty-eight or twenty-seven from David to the Lord,[11] for one is counted twice for a mysterious purpose[12] both up to the exile and likewise from the exile.

2. One must ask, then, how Joseph could have two fathers. And at the moment three reasons occur to me, one of which motivated the evangelist. For either one was Joseph's natural father and the other adopted him. Or, according to the custom of the Jews, when one died without children his brother took his wife and credited the son he begot to his brother;[13] thus, since Joseph was begotten by the one brother for the other, he would fittingly be said to have two fathers. Or one evangelist named as his father the man by whom he was begotten, but the other listed his maternal grandfather or one of his ancestors, for, on account of the bond of consanguinity, Joseph would not unreasonably be considered as his son, so that he did not report the same order of generations from there back to David. Among these reasons the one that we put in the second place seems weak, because, when a Jew produced a child from his wife for his deceased brother or relative, the one born usually took the name of the deceased.[14] Therefore either adoption solves this

---

8. See Mt 1:16.
9. See Lk 3:23.
10. See Lk 3:23–31.
11. See Mt 1:6–16.
12. "For a mysterious purpose"; *certi enim sacramenti gratia.*
13. See Dt 25:5–6.
14. See *Revisions* II,12,3.

question, or the origin of his ancestors, or some other reason that does not occur to us at present. Hence the madness of those who more readily fall into accusing one of the evangelists of a lie than look for reasons why the individual evangelist mentioned diverse names of the fathers is very great, since it is rashly said that there are only two reasons why it could correctly have happened, when it is nonetheless sufficient to find merely one to resolve the question.

6

1. It can be asked why seventy-seven persons are found in the genealogy that Luke followed.[15] After all, the Lord also mentioned this number when Peter asked him about forgiving a brother's sins, for the Lord says that he should be forgiven not only seven times but seventy-seven times.[16] Hence, one correctly believes that by mentioning this number he commanded that all sins be forgiven, since he through whom all sins were forgiven deigned to come as a man to human beings in the seventy-seventh generation, according to the testimony of the previously mentioned evangelist. But, although his series of generations is different than Matthew presents,[17] he most suitably enumerated the generations through seventy-seven persons back from the baptism of the Lord. For this movement back, when one ascends into the past through those generations, has the appearance of a kind of ascent to God, to whom we are reconciled after the forgiveness of sins. And indeed the forgiveness of all sins, which is signified by that number, is certainly produced through baptism.[18] For sins were not forgiven for the Lord himself in the Lord's baptism, but in it the forgiveness of all sins, which was bestowed upon human beings by his mercy and power, was consecrated and signified by the Lord's baptism and by that number of generations.

2. Nor did the Lord come by chance and without reason to abolish all sins in that seventy-seventh generation, for there is something hidden in that number that pertains to the signification of all sins. This needs to be considered in reference to the numbers eleven and seven which, when multiplied by each other, come to that number, for eleven times seven or seven times eleven comes to seventy-seven. But eleven signifies a transgression of the number ten.[19] And if the perfection of beatitude is signified by the number ten, that is why all those who were hired for the vineyard were paid a denarius worth ten pennies,[20] which is produced when the number seven, represented by the creature, is united with the Trinity of the creator. It is evident that the transgression of the number ten signifies sin through

---

15. See Lk 3:23–38.
16. See Mt 18:22.
17. See Mt 1:1–17.
18. See Acts 2:38.
19. I.e., in the sense that it goes beyond the number ten, but also in the sense that it represents a transgression of the perfection that ten symbolizes.
20. See Lk 20:2–10. The Roman denarius was worth a bit more, but it has been translated so as to preserve the correspondence with the number ten.

the pride of one who wants to have something more and loses integrity and perfection. But this is repeated seven times in order to signify the transgression produced by a person's action.[21] For the incorporeal part of a human being is signified by the number three; hence it is that we are commanded to love God from our whole heart, and from our whole soul, and from our whole mind.[22] But the body is signified by the number four, for the nature of the body is found to be quadripartite in many ways.[23] A human being consisting of the union of these, therefore, is not unreasonably signified by the number seven. But action is not expressed in numbers when we say "one, two, three, four," and so forth, but rather when we say "once, twice, three times, four times," and so forth. Hence, as I said, not seven and eleven but seven times eleven signifies transgression, which is produced by the action of a person who sins, that is, who goes beyond the stability of his perfection by the desire for having something more.[24] Thus long afterwards the prophet said to the soul, "You hoped that if you departed from me you would have something more."[25] From that beginning of pride all sins sprout up,[26] and, when they are forgiven, we are admonished to forgive seventy-seven times, so that we may understand that no sin is excluded that is not forgiven for one who does penance and asks for pardon through the Church, whose person Peter represents.

7

When the Lord said to the Jews concerning the man who had a withered right hand, *I shall ask you whether it is permitted to do good or evil on the sabbath, to save a soul or to destroy it* (Lk 6:9), the question arises as to why, once he healed the body, he asked in this way, *to save a soul or to destroy it.* One could say either that he worked those miracles on account of the faith in which the salvation of the soul consists, or that the very healing of the right hand signified the salvation of the soul that, when it ceased from good works, seemed in some sense to have a withered right hand, or he used *soul* instead of "human being," as we are accustomed to say, "So many souls were there."

8

When the Lord says, *Give, and it will be given to you. They will pour into your lap a good measure, heaped up, shaken down, and overflowing* (Lk 6:38), one can understand from those words what he says in another passage, *So that they may receive you into eternal dwelling places* (Lk 16:9). Thus the commandment given to the people in the words, *Give, and it will be given to you*, seems to

---

21. See Gn 2:15–3:24. It is clear from the mention a few lines later of the prophet who spoke "long afterwards" that Augustine is referring here to the sin of Adam.
22. See Dt 6:5; Mt 2:7.
23. The possession of four limbs is the most obvious way that the body is quadripartite.
24. See Gn 3:1–7.
25. The source of this "prophetic" quotation, which Augustine also cites in Sermon 51,34, is unknown.
26. See Sir 10:14–15.

be in accord with the Apostle's statement, *Let him who has been instructed in the word share in all good things with the one who instructs him* (Gal 6:6). For he would not say, *They will pour into your lap*, were it not because they will deserve to receive a heavenly reward through the merits of those to whom they give even a cup of cold water in the name of a disciple.[27]

9

When the Lord says, *Can a blind person lead a blind person? Will not both fall into a ditch?* (Lk 6:39), perhaps he added this so that they would not expect to receive from the Levites that measure of which he said, *They will pour* it *into your lap* (Lk 6:38), because they were giving tithes[28] to those he called blind, since they did not accept the Gospel. Thus the people would now begin instead to expect that reward from the Lord's disciples. And, wanting to show that they were imitators of him, he also added, *A disciple is not above his teacher* (Lk 6:40).

10

When the Lord says, *Everyone who comes to me and hears my words and keeps them, I shall show you whom he is like. He is like a man who, in building a house, dug deep and laid the foundation upon rock* (Lk 6:47–48), he said that he dug by Christian humility and removed everything earthly so that he would not worship God on account of anything of that sort. But he digs deep until he reaches rock, insofar as he follows Christ freely and worships him gratuitously, not only not on account of superfluous things, but not even on account of those that seem necessary for this life and that can be taken and possessed by any righteous person without sin, although they are still temporal and earthly.

11[29]

On the children sitting in the marketplace and shouting to one another he replies in reverse order to the questions set before him. For his words, *We lamented and you did not weep*, pertain to John, whose abstinence from food and drink signified the sadness of penance. But his words, *We sang to you with pipes and you did not dance* (Lk 7:32), pertain to the Lord himself, who in using food and drink with others symbolized the joy of the kingdom. But they wanted neither to be humble with John nor to rejoice with Christ, since they said that John had a demon and that Christ was a glutton and drunkard, a friend of publicans and sinners. But what he adds, *And wisdom is declared righteous by all her children* (Lk 7:35), shows that the children of wisdom understand that righteousness does not consist in either abstaining or eating but in peace of soul in enduring want, in temperance in not

---

27. See Mt 10:42.
28. See Nm 18:26.
29. This question deals with Lk 7:32–35.

being corrupted by abundance, and in taking or not taking those things not whose use but whose desire is reprehensible. For it makes no difference at all what foods you take to support the needs of the body, provided that in the sorts of foods you are in harmony with those among whom you have to live.[30] Nor does how much you take make much difference, since we see that some people's bellies are quickly satisfied but that those who are satisfied by that small amount crave it passionately, unbearably, and utterly shamefully, while others, indeed, are satisfied by a little more but suffer a lack with endurance and look calmly upon feasts set before them to partake of and do not even touch them if at that time there is need or necessity. Therefore it does not make much difference what or how much food one takes in accord with what is suitable for human beings and for one's own person or the needs of one's health, but it makes a considerable difference with what ease or calmness of soul one goes without them when one should or even must go without them. In that way what the Apostle says is fulfilled in the mind of a Christian: *I know how to have less, and I know how to have an abundance. For I have experienced all things and all conditions, both being satisfied and being hungry, both having an abundance and suffering need. I can do all things in him who strengthens me.* (Phil 4:12–13) And this: *If we eat we shall not have an abundance, nor shall we be in need if we do not eat* (1 Cor 8:8). And this: *The kingdom of God is not food and drink but righteousness and peace and joy.* And, because people usually rejoice much over feasts for the body, he added *in the Holy Spirit.* (Rom 14:17) Therefore *wisdom is declared righteous by all her children* (Lk 7:35),who understand that the times ought to be suitable for using temporal things, but the ease in going without such things and a love of enjoying eternal ones ought not to vary with the times but should be maintained perpetually.

12

The Lord says, *But no one lights a lamp and covers it with a bucket or puts it under a bed but on a candlestick, in order that those entering may see the light* (Lk 8:16). Someone who hides the word of God out of the fear of temporal difficulties certainly prefers the flesh to the revelation of the truth and covers it out of fear of preaching the word. Therefore he referred to the person who does this as a bucket and a bed, under which, he says, one who does this places the light.

13[31]

When, in the territory of the Gerasenes, the Lord cured the man in whom there was a legion of demons, the gentiles, who were serving many demons, are signified. That he was without clothes signifies that he was without faith. That he did not live in a house signifies that he was not at peace in his conscience. That he

---

30. See 1 Cor 8:7–13.
31. This question deals with Lk 8:26–39.

stayed among the tombs signifies that he found delight in dead works, that is, in sins. That he was bound in iron fetters and chains signifies the heavy and harsh laws of the gentiles, by which sins are held in check also in their republic. That, after he broke these bonds, he was driven into the desert by a demon signifies that, after he broke these laws, he was also led to those crimes by a passion that even went beyond common moral acceptance. That the demons were permitted to enter the swine that were feeding in the mountains signifies the unclean and proud persons over whom the demons ruled through the worship of idols. That they were hurled down into the lake signifies that, once the Church has shone forth with light and the people of the gentiles has been set free from the domination of demons, those who refused to believe in Christ perform their sacrilegious rites in hiding, submerged in their blind and deep curiosity. That the swine herders fled and reported these events signifies that, although some of the leaders of the nonbelievers flee from the Christian law, they still proclaim its power among the nations by their awe and admiration. That the Gerasenes come forth to see what happened and find the man clothed and sitting with a sound mind at the feet of Jesus, recognize what happened, and ask Jesus to depart from them, since they were stricken with great fear, signifies that the multitude is delighted with their old life and, while honoring the Christian law, is unwilling to endure its burdens, since they say that they cannot fulfill it, and yet they admire the faithful people who have been healed of their former sinful way of life. That the man now wants to be with Christ and is told, *Return to your home and recount the great things that God has done to you* (Lk 8:39), can be correctly understood from the words of the Apostle, when he says, *To die and be with Christ is by far better, but to remain in the flesh is necessary on your account* (Phil 1:23). In that way each person should understand that, after the forgiveness of sins, he must return to a good conscience and serve the Gospel for the sake of the salvation of others, so that afterwards he may rest with Christ. For, in his desire to be with Christ with excessive haste, he must not neglect the ministry of preaching suited to the redemption of his brethren.

14[32]

On the seventy-two disciples.[33] Just as the whole earth goes through its phases in twenty-four hours and is illuminated by the sun, so the ministry of giving light to the world through the Gospel of the Trinity is conveyed by the seventy-two disciples, for we put twenty-four into seventy-two three times.[34] But that he sends them in twos is the mystery of love[35] either because there are two commandments of love[36] or because no love can exist between fewer than two people.

32. This question deals with Lk 10:12.
33. The title is added as in PL.
34. The reading in PL is followed rather than that in the critical edition.
35. "Mystery of love": *sacramentum…caritatis.*
36. See Mt 22:37–40.

15

If the light that is in you is darkness, how great is the darkness itself! (Lk 11:35) He called *light* the good intention of the mind by which we act, but he calls *darkness* the works themselves either because others do not know the intention with which we do them or because even we ourselves do not know their result, that is, how they go forth and benefit those for whom we do them with a good intention. For they are often harmed by using our good works wrongly, although we do them out of mercy and with a benevolent intention.

16

Now, you Pharisees clean what is outside the cup and the bowl (Lk 11:39). What he says here and hereafter against the Pharisees and teachers of the law is what he said previously, *He set his face toward Jerusalem* (Lk 9:51), in order to tell them openly their vices and sins.

17

The Holy Spirit is called *the finger of God* (Lk 11:20) on account of the division of the gifts that are given by him, which are proper either to human beings or to angels. For in none of our members is division more apparent than in our fingers.

18[37]

Fasting is done either in tribulation or in joy — in tribulation to propitiate God for sins, but in joy when we find less delight in things of flesh to the extent that nourishment from spiritual things is greater. When the Lord was asked why his disciples did not fast, then, he replied concerning both fasts. For his statement that the guests of the bridegroom will fast when the bridegroom has been taken from them pertains to the fact that people usually fast in tribulation, for they will then be left desolate and will be in sorrow and grief until they receive consoling joys from the Holy Spirit. And once they have received that gift they will most appropriately practice the other kind of fasting that is done in joy, after they have been renewed for the spiritual life. He says that before they receive it they are like old garments on which a new patch is not fittingly sown, that is, some piece of teaching that pertains to regulating the new life, since, if that is done, the teaching itself is in a sense torn, and the piece of it that holds for fasting from foods is not handed on in an appropriate manner, since it teaches a general fasting not merely from a desire for foods but from all the joys of temporal pleasure. And he says that a patch of it, that is, the part that pertains to foods, ought not to be imparted to persons who are still attached to their old way of life, since a tear is seen to be produced from it and it does not fit with the old fabric. He also says that they are

---

37. This question deals with Lk 5:33–39.

like old wineskins, which he says are more easily burst by new wine, that is, by spiritual commandments, than they hold it. But they were new wineskins when, after the ascension of the Lord, they were renewed by the desire for his consolation through prayer and hope, for then they received the Holy Spirit, and, filled by him, were said to be full of wine when they spoke with the languages of all those who were present from different nations.[38] For the new wine had now come to the new wineskins.

19[39]

A certain man was going down from Jerusalem to Jericho (Lk 10:30). He is understood to be Adam himself, representing the human race. *Jerusalem* is that city of peace[40] from whose blessedness he fell. *Jericho* is translated as "moon"[41] and signifies our mortality, because it begins, increases, grows old, and sets.[42] The robbers are the devil and his angels, *who stripped him* of immortality, *and having beat with blows*, by persuading him to sinfulness, *left him half alive* (Lk 10:30), because the man was alive in the part by which he could understand and know God, and he was dead in the part in which he was wasting away and weighed down by sins. And for this reason he is said to be half alive. But the priest and the Levite who saw him and passed him by signify the priesthood and ministry of the Old Testament, which could not be of benefit toward salvation. *Samaritan* is translated as "guardian,"[43] and for this reason the Lord himself is signified by this name. The binding of the wounds is the holding of sins in check. The oil is the consolation of good hope because of the forgiveness given for the reconciliation of peace. The wine is an exhortation to work with a fervent spirit. His beast of burden is the flesh in which he deigned to come to us. To be placed on the beast of burden is to believe in Christ's incarnation. The stable is the Church where travelers are refreshed from the journey as they return to the eternal fatherland. The following day is after the resurrection of the Lord. The two denarii are the two commandments of love[44] that the apostles received though the Holy Spirit in order to bring the Gospel to others, or they are the promise of the present and future life, for in accord with those two promises it was said, *He shall receive seven times as much in this world, and in the world to come he shall attain eternal life* (Mt 19:29). The innkeeper, then, is the Apostle. The extra expense is either the counsel he gave — *But about virgins I do not have a commandment of the Lord, but I give a counsel* (1 Cor 7:25) — or the fact he even worked with his own hands,[45] so that

---

38. See Acts 1:1–13.
39. This question deals with Lk 10:30–37.
40. See Jerome, *Interpretation of Hebrew Names*, Isaiah, s.v. *Jerusalem* ("vision of peace").
41. See ibid., Numbers, s.v. *Jerio*.
42. See also below at II,48,1.
43. See Jerome, *Interpretation of Hebrew Names*, Luke, s.v. *Samaritae*.
44. See Mt 22:37–40.
45. See 1 Cor 4:12.

he would not be a burden to anyone in the newness of the Gospel,[46] although he was permitted to earn his food from the Gospel.[47]

20[48]

That *Martha received him into her home* (Lk 10:38) signifies the Church that exists now, which welcomes the Lord into her heart. *Her sister, Mary, who sat at the Lord's feet and listened to his word* (Lk 10:39) signifies the same Church, but in the age to come, when she ceases from work and service to the needy and enjoys wisdom alone. Martha, therefore, is occupied with much service, because the Church is now burdened with such works. Her question about why her sister does not help, however, provides an occasion for the Lord's statement, in which he shows that this Church is now worried and bothered about many things, although only that one thing is necessary, which it attains through the merits of this service. But he says that Mary chose the better part, which will not be taken away from her, and it is understood to be the best, because through this present part one tends to that which is to come, and it will not be taken away. But that service, although good, will be taken away when the need that it serves has passed.

21[49]

The story of the friend to whom the man comes in the middle of the night so that he might lend him three loaves is actually a simile in accord with which someone who is encompassed by tribulation asks God to give him an understanding of the Trinity whereby he may alleviate the burdens of the present life. But the comparison is from the lesser to the greater. For, if the human friend gets up from his bed and gives him the loaves, motivated not by friendship but by annoyance, how much more does God give, who gives what is asked for with the greatest abundance and without any annoyance, but who wants to be asked so that those who ask may acquire the capacity to receive his gifts. The three loaves signify that the Trinity is one in substance. The friend, who the man asking for the loaves says came from a journey and whom he has nothing to offer, is understood to be a person's appetite, which ought always to obey reason. The man was enslaved to temporal habits, which he calls a journey on account of the fact that all things pass through time. When a person has turned toward God, that appetite is also called back from such habits. But, if joy over the spiritual teaching by which the Trinity of the creator is preached does not console him interiorly, a person whom the bitterness of mortality weighs down experiences great difficulties when he is commanded to abstain from the external things in which he finds delight and he does not interiorly have refreshment from the joy of salutary teaching. The middle

---

46. See 2 Thes 3:8–9.
47. See 1 Cor 9:14.
48. This question deals with Lk 10:38–42.
49. This question deals with Lk 11:5–8.

of the night, in which he is compelled to persist strongly in asking to receive three loaves, is the difficulty itself. But that it is said to him from within that the door is already closed, and that the man's children are with him in bed, signifies a time of hunger for the word, when understanding is closed and the children of the father of the family, who have preached the wisdom of the Gospel and disbursed it like bread throughout the world, are already in their hidden repose with the Lord. And yet it comes about through prayer that anyone who desires understanding receives it from God himself, even when there is no one to preach wisdom.

22[50]

With respect to the bread, the fish, and the egg, with which the stone, the serpent, and the scorpion are contrasted, the bread is understood as charity, on account of the greater desire for it and because it is so necessary that without it other things are nothing, just as a table without bread is deficient. Its contrary is hardness of heart, which he compared to a stone. But the fish is understood as the belief in invisible realities, either on account of the water of baptism or because it is caught in places that are unseen, for faith that is not broken, even when battered by the waves of this world, is correctly compared to a fish. He contrasts it with a serpent, on account of the venom of falsity that it sowed in wickedly persuading even the first man.[51] In the egg hope is understood, for an egg is not yet a full-grown chick, but one is hoped for by fostering it. He contrasts it with a scorpion, from whose poisonous sting one must draw back in fear, just as the contrary of hope is to look back, since hope for the things to come also stretches out to those that lie ahead.[52]

23

The Lord says to the scribes and teachers of the Jews, *You have carried the key of knowledge. You yourselves have not entered, and you have prevented those who were entering* (Lk 11:52), because neither did they themselves want to understand Christ's humility in God's Scripture nor did they want others to understand it.

24

The Lord says to his disciples, *The soul is more valuable than food, and the body more valuable than clothes* (Lk 12:33), and surely, if he has given you what is more valuable, how much the more will he give what is less!

---

50. This question deals with Lk 11:11–12.
51. See Gn 3:1–6.
52. See Phil 3:13; 1 Cor 13:13.

25

The Lord says, *Let your loins be girt*, for the sake of holding in check the love of worldly things, *and your lamps burning* (Lk 12:35), so that you may do this for the true end and with the right intention.

26

When the Lord said to Peter, *Who do you think is the faithful and wise steward whom the Lord will set over his household to give them a measure of wheat at the proper time?* (Lk 12:42), he speaks of a measure in reference to the degree of capacity of certain listeners.

27

When the Lord said, *When you see a cloud rising from the west* (Lk 12:54), he is signifying his flesh rising from death, for from it the rain of evangelical preaching has been poured out on all lands. *The south wind blowing* (Lk 12:55) before the heat of summer signifies the lighter tribulations before the judgment.

28

The Lord said, *For if you cannot do that which is least* (Lk 12:26), when he was speaking about increasing the stature of the body; the *least* means this, namely, for God to produce bodies.

29

1. When he was telling his disciples that they should not be worried about foods, he said, *And do not be raised high up* (Lk 12:29).[53] For a person seeks these things first in order to fulfill his needs, but, when he has these in abundance, he also begins to be proud over such things. This is like a wounded person who boasts that he has many bandages in his home, when it would be better for him not to have wounds and not to need even a single bandage.

2. He fittingly compared a man with dropsy to an animal that fell into a well,[54] for he was suffering from excessive fluid, just as he compared that woman, who he said was afflicted for eighteen years and whom he freed from that affliction, to a beast of burden that is set free so that it may be led to water.[55] But we correctly compare a person with dropsy to an avaricious rich man. For, just as the more a man with dropsy abounds in excessive fluid, the more he thirsts, so the more a rich man abounds in riches that he does not use well, the more he desires such

---

53. The English for this verse is usually rendered along the lines of *nor be of anxious mind*, as in the RSV. But both the Latin text that Augustine used and the original Greek allow for this meaning.
54. See Lk 14:2.5.
55. See Lk 13:11–16.

things. But we correctly compare that woman who was so bent over by illness that she could not stand up straight to a soul so weakened and oppressed by earthly concerns that it cannot think of divine things.

30[56]

That he brings in those whom he has invited to the banquet from the city refers to those who believed from the people of the Jews, who were weak from sins and who had no pride as though in the false righteousness that kept their leaders from grace. But the others whom he ordered to be brought in from the hedges and paths, since there was still room, signify the gentiles, on account of the diverse paths of their sects and the thorns of their sins.

31[57]

The expenses for building a tower signify the strength needed for becoming a disciple of Christ, and the ten thousand who were going to fight with the king who had twenty thousand signify the simplicity of a Christian who is going to fight with the duplicity of the devil, that is, with his deceits and lies.[58] He placed this in the context of the love of one who renounces everything that he has, for he concludes in this way: *So each one of you who does not renounce all the things that he has cannot be my disciple* (Lk 14:33). And among all those things must be included even temporal life itself, which one should possess for a time in such a way that someone who threatened to take it away would not keep you from eternal life. But, just as in regard to the unfinished tower [Christ] counseled delay by invoking the criticisms of those who were saying, *This man began to build but could not complete it* (Lk 14:30), so, in the case of the king with whom [the other king] was going to fight, he laid responsibility on peace itself when he said, *When he was still far off, he sent a delegation and asked for terms of peace* (Lk 14:32), which also signified that people who do not renounce all that they possess do not endure the threats of the devil's imminent temptations and make peace with him by consenting to him to commit sins. To build a tower and to fight against that king is of course to be a disciple of Christ, but to have the money to build the tower and to have ten thousand strong men against the twenty thousand of the king is to renounce everything that one possesses.

32

He referred to an apostate as the salt that has lost its savor[59] and to all sinners who are reconciled to God through penance as the lost sheep, and he carries

---

56. This question deals with Lk 14:16–24.
57. This question deals with Lk 14:28–33.
58. Simplicity verses duplicity because the first digit of ten thousand is one, which symbolizes simplicity, while the first digit of twenty thousand is two, which symbolizes duplicity.
59. See Lk 14:34.

the lost sheep on his shoulders[60] because he raised up such sinners by humbling himself. But for this reason he said that the ninety-nine that he left in the desert signify the proud, like those who cherish solitude in their soul and wish to be seen to stand alone, to whose perfection one thing is lacking. For when a person is torn from true oneness, he is torn by pride. Desiring to be in his own power, he does not follow the One that is God. Hence he signified by both the ninety-nine sheep and the nine drachmas those who, relying on themselves, preferred themselves to sinners returning to salvation. For one is lacking to nine to be ten, and to ninety-nine to be one hundred, and so forth through other numbers, when you reflect on it. Similarly, one is lacking to nine hundred and ninety-nine to be one thousand, and one is lacking to nine thousand nine hundred and ninety-nine to be ten thousand. Therefore there can be different numbers great and small that are lacking one in order to be perfect.[61] But the One itself, which abides in itself without any variation, produces perfection when it is added, and [Christ] ascribes this to all who have been reconciled through penance, which is obtained by humility.

33[62]

1. The man with two sons is understood to be God, who has two peoples, like two families of the human race, one of whom abode in the worship of the one God, the other of whom abandoned him even so far as to worship idols. Our consideration, however, should begin from the origin of the creation of mortals. The elder son, then, pertains to the worship of the one God. [Christ] says that the younger set out for a faraway region. He asked his father to give him the part of the inheritance that would come to him, like a soul delighting in its own powers, that is, in the possession of life, understanding, memory, and excellence in quick wit; all of these are divine gifts. Taking these under his control through free choice, because the father divided his wealth between his sons, the younger son set out for a faraway region by wrongly using these natural goods, since he abandoned his father out of a desire to enjoy a creature after leaving the creator himself.[63] He said that, after not many days, it happened that he gathered up everything and went away from home into a faraway region because, not long after the creation of the human race, the soul chose to take with itself through free choice a certain power as it were of nature and to abandon him by whom it was created, overconfident in its resources, which the soul exhausts more quickly to the extent that it abandons him by whom they were given. And for this reason he calls this life prodigal, which loves to spend and spread itself out in external display while becoming interiorly empty, when anyone pursues those things that flow forth from it[64] and abandons

---

60. See Lk 15:3–7.
61. On the number one as having the possibility to bring an incomplete number to completion see also below at II,40,4.
62. This question deals with Lk 15:11–32.
63. See Rom 1:25.
64. I.e., this prodigal life.

him who is interior to him. The faraway region, then, is forgetfulness of God, and the hunger in that region is the need for the word of truth. The citizen of that region is a prince of the air who belongs to the army of the devil, his farm is the extent of his power, the swine are the unclean spirits under him, and the husks with which he was feeding the swine are worldly teachings that resound with empty vanity, and from them the praises of the idols and myths pertaining to the gods of the gentiles are uttered in various languages and in songs that delight the demons. Hence, when he desired to be filled with them, he wanted to find in such things something solid and correct that pertained to the happy life and could not find any. For this is what he said: *And no one gave him any* (Lk 15:16).

2. *But returning into himself*—that is, withdrawing his attention now in the interiority of his conscience from those external and empty things that are enticing and seductive—*he said, How many hired men of my father have abundant bread!* (Lk 15:16) How could he, in whom there was as great a forgetfulness of God as there was among all the idolaters, be aware of this if this recollection were not already the sign of one who had come to his senses when the Gospel was preached? For he was now able to notice that many preach the truth, among whom there are some who are not led by the love of the truth but by the desire for obtaining worldly advantages. Of these the Apostle said that there are some who *announce the good news without sincerity* (Phil 1:17), thinking *that gain is piety* (1 Tm 6:5). They do not preach something else like the heretics but the same thing as the apostle Paul does, although not with the same intention as the apostle Paul. Hence they are rightly called hirelings who, in the same house, to be sure, offer the same bread of the word yet are not called to an eternal heritage but hired for a temporal reward. Of such persons it has been said, *Amen, I say to you, They have received their reward* (Mt 6:2). And so he says, *I am perishing here of hunger* (Lk 15:17).Then he says, *I shall rise up*, because he was lying flat, *and I shall go*, because he was far away, *to the house of my father* (Lk 15:18), because he was under the prince of swine.[65] The remaining words are those of someone considering repentance in the confession of sin but not yet those of someone repenting, for he does not yet say them to his father, but he promises that he will say them when he arrives. You should understand, therefore, that this coming to the father should now to be taken as being a member of the Church through faith, where it is now possible to make a legitimate and fruitful confession of sins.[66] Why, then, does he say that he will say to his father, *Father, I have sinned against heaven and before you, and I am no longer worthy to be called your son. Treat me as one of your hired men* (Lk 15:18–19) Does *I have sinned against heaven* mean the same as *before you*? In that case he was referring to the very loftiness of the Father as *heaven*, which is why it also says in the Psalm, *His going forth is from the height of heaven* (Ps 18:7), since he wants this understood of the Father himself. Or, on the other hand,

---

65. See Mt 8:28–34 par.

66. Augustine is perhaps referring to the practice of penance, or *exomolgesis*, which in the early Church could be exercised only once in a lifetime.

does *I have sinned against heaven* mean before all the holy souls in whom is God's seat, while *before you* means in the interior chamber of one's conscience?

3. *And rising up, he went to his father. But when he was still far off,* before he understood God, but when he was nonetheless piously seeking him, *his father saw him* (Lk 15:20), for he is rightly said not to see the impious and proud, as though not holding them before his eyes, since usually only those who are loved are said to be held before one's eyes. *And he was moved by compassion, and he ran and fell upon his neck* (Lk 15:20), for the Father did not abandon his only-begotten Son, in whom he ran and came down even to our distant wandering, because *God was in Christ reconciling the world to himself* (2 Cor 5:19), and the Lord himself says, *Remaining in me, the Father himself does his works* (Jn 14:10). But what does falling upon his neck mean but to bend down and lower his arm for an embrace? *And to whom was the arm of the Lord revealed?* (Is 53:1)—which is certainly our Lord Jesus Christ. *And he kissed him* (Lk 15:20). That he merits a kiss of love from his father, after he has returned from long journeying, means that he is consoled by the word of God's grace with the hope of the forgiveness of sins, and, as a member of the Church, he now begins to confess his sins. He does not say everything that he had promised that he was going to say but only *I am not worthy to be called your son* (Lk 15:21), for he wants that to be done through grace, of which he admits that he is unworthy by his merits. He does not add what he has said in considering repentance, *Treat me as one of your hired men* (Lk 15:19), for, when he did not have bread, he wanted at least to be a hired man, and after his father's most generous kiss he now disdains this. The best robe is the dignity that Adam lost; the servants who bring it forth are those who preach reconciliation; the ring on his hand is the pledge of the Holy Spirit[67] on account of the bestowal of grace, which is rightly signified by the finger; the sandals on his feet are the preparation for preaching the good news without touching earthly things; the fattened calf is the Lord himself, but stuffed with opprobrium in terms of the flesh. What does the command to bring it forth mean but to preach him and, by proclaiming him, to make him enter into the belly of the hungry son worn out by starvation? For he also orders that they slay it, that is, that they announce his death, for he is slain for a person when he believes that he was killed. *And let us feast* (Lk 15:23), he says. That refers to the joy that impels him to say next, *Because this son of mine was dead and has come back to life; he was lost and has been found* (Lk 15:24). And this banquet and festival is now celebrated in the Church, which is spread out and diffused throughout the world. For that calf is both offered to the Father in the Lord's body and blood and feeds the whole house.

4. Meanwhile, although the elder son, the people of Israel according to the flesh, did not set out for a faraway region, he is nonetheless not in the house; he is, instead, in the field, that is, he is working upon earthly things in the hereditary riches of the law and the prophets and in certain Israelite concerns. For many of

67. See 2 Cor 5:5.

that sort have been found and are often found among them. Coming from the field, he begins to draw near to the house, that is, having rejected the labor of servile work, he has given thought to the freedom of the Church from the same Scriptures. He hears the music and dancing, that is, those filled with the Spirit preaching the Gospel with harmonious voice,[68] to whom it is said, *I beg you, brothers, in the name of our Lord Jesus Christ, that you all say the same thing* (1 Cor 1:10), and he sees[69] the one heart and one soul[70] of those living for the praise of God. He calls one of the servants and asks what those sounds are, that is, he picks up one of the prophets to read and, searching in him, in a sense asks why these feasts are celebrated in the Church, where he does not see that he himself is. The prophet, a servant of the Father, answers him and says, *"Your brother has come, and your father has slain the fattened calf, because he has got him back safe* (Lk 15:27), for your brother was in the remotest parts of the earth. There is great rejoicing over this on the part of those singing *a new song unto the Lord* (Ps 95:5), because his praise comes from the remotest parts of the earth.[71] And for the sake of him who was absent a man was slain who was exposed to blows and who knew how to bear weakness,[72] because those have seen who were not told of him, and those have understood who did not hear."[73] But [the elder son] is now indignant as well and still does not want to enter.

5. When the fullness of the gentiles has entered, therefore, his father will go out at the right time so that all of Israel may also be saved. Its blindness was partly caused as though in the case of him who was absent in the field, until the fullness of the younger son, who was living far away in the idolatry of the gentiles, returned and entered to eat the calf.[74] For the calling of the Jews to the salvation of the Gospel will eventually be manifest. He calls the disclosure of their calling the father's going out to plead with the elder son. Then, what the same elder son answered raises two questions, namely, how that people is understood never to have transgressed a commandment of God and what he means by the goat that he never received, so that he might have a feast with his friends. But it is easy to think that it was said about a commandment that was not violated, and not about every commandment but about the one that is most necessary, by which [that people] was commanded to worship no other God than the one creator of all things.[75] Nor is this son understood to represent the person of all the Israelites but only of those who never turned away from the one God to idols. For, although this son who was working in the field desired earthly things, he still desired these good things from

---

68. See Acts 2:4.
69. The editor of the CCSL text notes a missing word here, which we have conjectured as "sees" (*videt*).
70. See Acts 4:32.
71. See Is 42:10.
72. See Is 53:3.
73. See Is 52:15.
74. See Rom 11:25.
75. See Ex 20:3.

the one God, even though a human being has them in common with the animals. Hence, the words in the Psalm, *I have become like cattle before you, and I am with you always* (Ps 73:22), are appropriately understood to apply to the Synagogue, which is translated as Asaph.[76] And this is also shown by the testimony of the father when he says, *You are always with me* (Lk 15:31), for he did not accuse him of lying, but he approves his perseverance and invites him to the enjoyment of greater and more joyous exultation.

6. What then is the goat that he never received for feasting? To be sure, a sinner is often signified by the term "goat."[77] But heaven forbid that I should understand the Antichrist, for this does not seem to me to be the way to grasp the sense of the word. It is, after all, quite absurd that the one to whom the father said, *You are always with me*, would have wanted from his father that he would believe in the Antichrist. It is not at all correct to understand this son among those Jews who are going to believe in the Antichrist. But if the goat was the Antichrist, how was he who did not believe in him going to feast on him? Or, if to feast over the slaying of the goat is to rejoice over the destruction of the Antichrist, how does the son whom the father welcomes say that the father never gave him this, since all the sons of God are going to rejoice over the condemnation of that adversary? Without prejudice to a more careful investigation, then, I would say on this very obscure point that it is indisputable that he is complaining that the Lord himself is being denied him for eating, as long as he thinks that he is a sinner. For he is a goat for that people who did not merit to enjoy his feasts, that is, when they think that he violates the sabbath[78] and transgresses the law.[79] Thus, when he says, *You never gave me a goat so that I might feast with my friends* (Lk 15:29), it is equivalent to saying, "You never gave me for feasting him who I thought was a goat, not granting me this for the very reason that I thought that he was a goat." But when he says *with my friends*, it is understood as representing either the leaders along with the people or the people of Jerusalem along with the other peoples of Judah. The prostitutes, however, with whom the younger son was accused of wasting his livelihood, are rightly understood as the superstitions which, after a person has abandoned the one legitimate marriage with the Word of God,[80] fornicate with a crowd of demons in the foulest lust.

7. Finally, what does it mean that, when the father said, *You are always with me* (which has already been discussed), he added, *and all things of mine are yours* (Lk 15:31)? On this question you must first watch out that you do not understand *all things of mine are yours* in such a way that they would not also be his brother's

---

76. See Jerome, *Interpretation of Hebrew Names*, Psalms, s.v. *Asaph*. Jerome translates Asaph as *congregans* ("congregating"), which is roughly the meaning of the word "synagogue." The title of Ps 73 reads *A Psalm of Asaph*—hence, as Augustine understands it, "A Psalm of the Synagogue."

77. See, e.g., Mt 25:32–33.
78. See, e.g., Mt 12:1–13.
79. See, e.g., Mt 5:17.
80. See Eph 5:21–33; Rv 21:2.9.

or in such a way that you would be troubled, as though this were an earthly inheritance, as to how all things could belong to the elder brother if the younger also has a part of them. For sons who are perfect and purified and immortal possess all things in such a way that each of those things belongs to all of them and all of them belong to each of them, for, while covetousness possesses nothing without difficulty, charity possesses nothing with difficulty. But how do they have all things? Are we to suppose that God has made subject to such a son, someone asks, the angels and lofty virtues and powers[81] and all the heavenly ministers of God? If you understand possession in the sense that the one who has a possession is its lord, they certainly do not have all things, for those of whom it is said, *They will be equal to the angels of God* (Mt 22:30), will not be lords of the angels but rather their companions. But if possession is understood in the way that we correctly say that souls possess the truth, I do not see why we cannot truly and in the proper sense understand *all things* in the sense of all things, for we do not say that in the sense that souls are the lords of the truth, which we do say that they possess. Or, if we are kept from this sense by the term "possession," let it too be removed. For the father does not say, "I shall give all things into your possession" or "You possess" or "will possess all things of mine" but *All things of mine are yours*. And yet they are not his as they are God's. For what is counted as our property can be our family's food or furniture or something of the sort. And surely, since he could correctly call his father his own, I do not see what of his he could not correctly call his own, although in different ways. For when we obtain that blessedness, the higher beings will be ours to see,[82] the equal ones will be ours to live with, and the lower ones will be ours to rule over.[83] Let the elder brother rejoice with the greatest security, because the younger brother *was dead and has come back to life, had perished and has been found* (Lk 15:32).

34[84]

1. In the story of the steward whom his lord[85] threw out of his stewardship and praised because he looked out for his future, we should not take everything for our imitation. For we should not commit some fraud against our own lord so that we might give alms from that fraud, nor is it right to understand those by whom we want to be welcomed into eternal dwelling places as those in debt to our God and Lord, since this passage is speaking about the righteous and holy who will bring into eternal dwelling places those who have given a share of their temporal goods

---

81. See 1 Pt 3:22.
82. Following the reading in PL, *ad videndum* ("to see"), rather than that in CCSL, *ad vivendum* ("to live").
83. "The higher beings" (*superiora*) are presumably the persons of the Trinity, "the equal ones" (*aequalia*) are of course the angels, but who "the lower ones" (*inferiora*) are is unclear; perhaps the demons are meant.
84. This question deals with Lk 16:1–9.
85. "Lord": *dominus*, usually translated in this case as "master," although translating it in that way here would destroy the parallelism between an earthly lord and master and the divine Lord.

for their needs. The Lord also says about them that, if anyone gives only a cup of cold water to one of them, he will not lose his reward.[86] But these likenesses are drawn from their contraries so that we might understand that, if he who committed a fraud could be praised by his lord, how much more would those please the Lord God who did those deeds in accord with his commandment. In the same way he also compared the unjust judge, with whom the widow pleaded, to God our judge, to whom the unjust judge should in no way be compared.[87]

2. But the fact that he had the one who owed one hundred flasks of oil write fifty and the one who owed one hundred bushels of wheat write eighty means nothing else, I believe, than that anyone who does for the Church of Christ those things that the Jews similarly do for the Levites should be more righteous than the scribes and Pharisees.[88] Thus, since they used to give ten percent,[89] he should give fifty percent, just as Zacchaeus did, not from his profits but from his very possessions,[90] or by giving twenty percent he should at least surpass the offerings of the Jews. But the Lord called this money that we possess for a time *the mammon of iniquity* (Lk 16:9), because *mammon* is translated as "riches," and these are riches only for the iniquitous, who put in them their hope and their whole happiness. But when the righteous possess them, this is, of course, property, but they have only heavenly and spiritual riches, by which they make up for their spiritual deficiencies by removing the misery of neediness and are enriched with an abundance of happiness.

35

When he says, *If you were not trustworthy in regard to someone else's property* (Lk 16:12), he calls earthly resources *someone else's* because no one takes them with him when he dies.[91] This is what David says: *Do not be afraid when a man has become rich and when the glory of his house has increased, because when he dies he will not take all these things, nor will his glory go down with him* (Ps 48:17–18).

36

When he says, *Either he will hate the one and love the other, or he will cling to the one and hold the other in contempt* (Lk 16:13), these words are to be distinguished with care, for they were not said casually or as though rashly. For when asked whether he loves the devil, no one answers that he loves him but rather that he hates him. On the other hand, almost everyone claims to love God. Therefore *he will hate the one and love the other*, as one ought to do, that is, he will hate the

---

86. See Mt 10:42.
87. See Lk 18:2–8.
88. See Mt 5:20.
89. See Nm 18:21.
90. See Lk 19:8.
91. See 1 Tm 6:7.

devil and love God. But he added, *or he will cling to the one and hold the other in contempt*, that is, he will cling to the devil when he pursues temporal things as his possessions, but he will hold God in contempt. He does not say that he will hate but that he will hold in contempt, like those who are in the habit of putting their desires ahead of his threats and who console themselves on the basis of his goodness that they will escape punishment. To these persons Solomon says, *Do not add sin upon sin and say, God's mercy is great* (Sir 5:6–7).

37[92]

The kingdom of heaven suffers violence, and the violent are carrying it off (Mt 11:12).[93] This was said so that anyone would hold in contempt not only those things but also the tongues of those who deride a person who holds such things in contempt. For by acting somehow with this kind of violence one enters the kingdom of heaven like a violent robber. For the evangelist added this after he had said that Jesus was mocked by the Pharisees when he was speaking about scorning earthly riches.[94]

38[95]

1. *There was a certain rich man, and he was clothed in purple and linen, and he feasted splendidly every day* (Lk 16:19). This and what follows can be taken allegorically. Thus, in the rich man there may be understood the proud among the Jews who do not know the righteousness of God and want to establish their own.[96] The purple and linen are the dignity of the kingdom. [Christ] says, *And the kingdom of heaven shall be taken away from you and shall be given to the people that practices righteousness* (Mt 21:43). The splendid feasting is their bragging about the law in which they boasted, misusing it more for the display of their pridefulness than using it for the necessity of salvation. The beggar by the name of Lazarus, which is interpreted as "one who has been helped,"[97] signifies someone in need, like a gentile or a publican, who is helped more to the extent that he counts less on the abundance of his resources. Such were those two who prayed in the Temple, the one a publican, the other a Pharisee.[98] The rich man, therefore, as though he were [already] satiated with righteousness and were not to be counted among those blessed ones who [still] hunger and thirst for righteousness,[99] says, *I give you thanks that I am not like this tax collector* (Lk 18:11), whereas the poor man who desires to be helped says, *Be merciful to me, a sinner* (Lk 18:13). As he

---

92. This question continues the thought of the preceding one.
93. See also Lk 16:16.
94. See Lk 16:14.
95. This question deals with Lk 16:19–31.
96. See Rom 10:3.
97. See Jerome, *Interpretation of Hebrew Names*, Luke, s.v. *adjutus*.
98. See Lk 18:10.
99. See Mt 5:6.

lies at the door he nonetheless desires to be filled from the crumbs that fall from the rich man's table, for he was not admitted to the feasts of the one who was not using them well and did not give to someone in need, like the scribe who holds the keys of the kingdom of the heaven and who neither enters himself nor allows others to enter.[100] The crumbs falling from the rich man's table are certain words of the law that in their boastfulness they in a sense cast upon the earth when they spoke proudly to the people. The sores are the confessions of sins, like bad humors bursting forth from the interior of the body. The dogs that lick them are very wicked human beings, lovers of sin, who with their tongues out do not cease from praising aloud the evil works that the other detests, groaning and confessing within himself. The bosom of Abraham is the repose of the blessed poor to whom the kingdom of heaven belongs,[101] where they are welcomed after this life. The burial indicates the depth of the punishments in the underworld that will devour the proud and merciless after this life. In this narrative the Lord says that they will see from a distance and observe the repose of the blessed, where of course they cannot go.

2. That [the rich man] wanted his tongue to be cooled, although he was certainly burning up entirely in the flames, signifies what is said in Scripture, *Death and life are in the hands of the tongue* (Prv 18:21), and that *by the tongue confession is made unto salvation* (Rom 10:10), which that man in his pride did not do. The tip of the finger signifies even the least work of mercy, by which help is given through the Holy Spirit. When it is said to him, *You received good things in your life* (Lk 16:25), this touches upon the fact that he loved the happiness of the world and loved no other life than that in which he, as a proud man, was puffed up. But he says that Lazarus received evils because he understood that this life's mortality, labors, sorrows, and bitterness are the punishment of sin, about which Scripture says, *We too were by nature children of wrath, just like the others* (Eph 2:3). About this Scripture also says that not even an infant whose life on this earth is one day is clean from sin,[102] because we all die in Adam,[103] who became mortal by his transgression.[104]

3. When he says that, even if they should want to do so, the righteous cannot cross over to those places where the unrighteous are being tormented, what else does this mean but that through the immutability of the divine sentence the righteous can offer no help of mercy after this life, even if they should want to offer it, to those who have been imprisoned, so that they may not get out of there until they have paid the last cent?[105] And in this way people are admonished to help those whom they can in this life, lest afterwards, even if they have been received into heaven, they cannot help those whom they love. For what Scripture says,

---

100. See Lk 11:52.
101. See Mt 5:3.
102. See Jb 14:4–5.
103. See 1 Cor 15:22.
104. See Gn 3:6–19.
105. See Mt 5:26.

That they may also receive you into eternal dwellings (Lk 16:9), was not written about the proud and merciless, such as this rich man is shown to have been, so that they might merit to be received by the saints into such eternal dwellings, but instead about those who made friends for themselves by their most faithful works of mercy. Yet even the righteous receive them not as if they were doing them a favor by their own power but rather by the promise and permission of him who admonished them to make friends for themselves and who, by his goodness as the redeemer, deigned to be fed, clothed, hospitably received, and visited himself in any one of his least brethren.[106] But it is no small question whether that reception takes place immediately after this life or at the end of the world in the resurrection of the dead and the final retribution of judgment. Whenever it takes place, though, there is certainly no scripture passage that promises it to such people as that rich man was known to have been.

4. The five brothers whom he says that he has in the house of his father signify the Jews. There are said to be five because they were held under the law of Moses, who wrote five books.[107] He asks that Lazarus be sent to his brothers, for he perceives that he himself is certainly unworthy to bear witness to the truth, and, since he did not obtain a little cooling for his tongue, much less does he believe that he could be released from the underworld to preach the truth. When Abraham says that, if they want to believe, *they have Moses and the prophets* (Lk 16:29), he did not place them above the Gospel; rather, because, as the Apostle says, the Gospel has testimony from the law and the prophets,[108] he indicates that by believing them they could come to the Gospel, just as in another place the Lord himself says, *If you believed Moses, you would also believe me, for he wrote concerning me* (Jn 5:46). Finally, apropos of this is what he also says later, *If they do not hear Moses and the prophets, neither will they believe if someone rises from the dead* (Lk 16:31), because Moses and the prophets foretold him who rose from the dead. And, since they do not believe even them about the very fact that he was going to rise from the dead, they certainly do not want to believe Christ. Much less, then, can they believe anyone who has risen from the dead when they do not want to believe him whose resurrection Moses and the prophets predicted, whom they refuse to believe.

5. This story can be understood in another way, so that we take Lazarus, lying at the door of that rich man, to signify the Lord, because he lowered himself by the humility of the incarnation to the very proud ears of the Jews, as one desiring to be filled with the crumbs that fell from the rich man's table, asking of them even the least works of righteousness that they have not, through pride, usurped for their table, that is, for their own power, and they do these works of mercy and humility, although very little ones and without the discipline and perseverance of a good life, at least occasionally or by chance, as crumbs are wont to fall from

---

106. See Mt 25:35–40.
107. Moses was universally believed to have written the Books of Genesis, Exodus, Leviticus, Numbers and Deuteronomy. See also below at II,46,3.
108. See Rom 3:21.

a table. The sores are the sufferings of the Lord from the infirmity of the flesh that he deigned to assume for our sake. The dogs that licked them, then, are the gentiles whom the Jews said were sinful and unclean people, and yet now, throughout the whole world, they lick the sufferings of the Lord in the sacraments of his body and blood with the most devout tenderness. The bosom of Abraham is now understood as the Father's hidden chamber, where the Lord was taken when he rose after his passion,[109] and I believe the saying that he was carried there by the angels, because the angels announced to the onlooking disciples this reception by which he went off to the Father's hidden chamber. For in saying, *Why are you standing here, looking up to heaven?* (Acts 1:11), what else did they say but that the eyes of human beings can in no way penetrate to that hidden chamber where the Lord went, when in the sight of the apostles he was borne to heaven? Now the rest can be understood in accord with the previous explanation, because the Father's hidden chamber can be quite well understood as the place where the souls of the righteous will live with God before the resurrection. For God is more truly everywhere insofar as he is contained by no place, as it was also said to the thief, *This day you shall be with me in paradise* (Lk 23:43), from where the Son of God never departed, although through the flesh that he assumed he suffered greatly from human beings in the city of the Jews.

39

1. When the disciples said, *Lord, increase our faith* (Lk 17:5), it can certainly be understood that they were asking that this faith, whereby one believes those things that are not seen, might be increased for them. Yet faith in realities is also being spoken of, when there is belief not in words but in present realities themselves. And that will be the case when the very wisdom of God, by which all things were made,[110] will present itself to the saints to be contemplated through vision. Perhaps the apostle Paul is speaking of that faith in realities and of the showing of that light when he says, *For the righteousness of God is revealed in him from faith to faith* (Rom 1:17), for in another passage he says, *But gazing upon the glory of the Lord with face unveiled, we are being transformed into the same image from glory to glory, as by the Spirit of the Lord* (2 Cor 3:18). In the latter instance, when he says *from glory to glory*, he means from the glory of the Gospel, whereby believers are now enlightened, to the glory of the immutable and manifest truth itself, which those once transformed will then enjoy. In the same way, in the former instance, when he says *from faith to faith*, he means from faith in words, whereby we now believe what we do not yet see, to that faith in realities by which we shall obtain for eternity what we now believe. In accord with this view John also said in the

---

109. See Mk 16:19.
110. See Ps 104:24.

Epistle to the Parthians,[111] *Beloved, we are now children of God, and what we shall be has not yet appeared. We know that when he appears, we shall be like him, because we shall see him as he is.* (1 Jn 3:2) For how are we now children of God unless he has given the power to become children of God to us who believe in his name,[112] so that we may see *in an enigma* (1 Cor 13:12)? But how shall we be like him then if not because, as he says, *we shall see him as he is*? And this was also said: *But then face to face* (1 Cor 13:12).

2. But, since many do not understand that faith in this most present truth, our Lord can seem not to have responded to his disciples' request. For, when they said, *Lord, increase our faith* (Lk 17:5), he said to them, *If you had faith like a mustard seed, you would say to this mulberry tree, be uprooted and planted in the sea, and it would obey you* (Lk 17:6). Then there follows, *Who of you, having a servant plowing or keeping sheep, says to him when he has returned from the field, Go, take your rest right away, and does not say to him, Prepare supper for me; gird yourself, and wait on me, while I eat and drink, and after that you will eat and drink? Is he grateful to that servant because he did what he was told? I do not think so. In the same way, when you have done all that you were commanded, say, We are useless servants. We have done what we ought to have done.* (Lk 17:7–10) It is difficult to see why this pertains to what was said—*Lord, increase our faith*—unless we understand that the words signified that they are being transferred *from faith to faith*, that is, from this faith by which we serve God here to that faith in which we enjoy God. For faith is increased when belief is given first to the words of those who preach it and then to the realities that are seen. But that contemplation includes the supreme peace which is given in the eternal kingdom of God, and that supreme peace is the reward of just labors which are carried out in the ministry of the Church. And for this reason, although the servant is plowing or keeping sheep in the field—that is, although in the life of this world he is either carrying on earthly business or serving foolish people who are like animals—it is necessary that after those labors he come home, that is, be united with the Church, and also labor there, serving the Lord while he eats and drinks. For when [Christ] was hungry he looked for fruit on the tree,[113] and when he was thirsty he asked for water from the Samaritan woman.[114] Let him eat and drink the confession and faith of the gentiles, then, while his servants minister to him, that is, preach the Gospel.

3. To this there also pertains what he initially answered about the mustard seed, namely, that they must first have the faith necessary for the present life, which seems very small as long as it remains in clay vessels[115] but expands and

---

111. For reasons unknown Augustine occasionally refers to the First Epistle of John as the Epistle to the Parthians.
112. See Jn 1:12.
113. See Mt 21:18–19.
114. See Jn 4:7
115. See 2 Cor 4:7.

germinates with great vigor.[116] For, although our Lord Jesus Christ wants to be fed by the ministry of his servants, that is, he wants to transfer believers into his body as slain and eaten, he also feeds them here by the word of faith and the sacrament of his passion.[117] For he *did not come to be served but to serve* (Mt 20:28). Let those servants, therefore, speak to this mulberry tree through the mustard seed, that is, to the Gospel of the Lord's cross through the bleeding fruit hanging on the tree, like wounds, which is going to give nourishment to the peoples. Let them say to it, then, that it be uprooted from the unbelief of the Jews and transferred and planted into the sea of the gentiles. For by that service in the house they will minister to the Lord who hungers and thirsts.[118]

4. Let them then at last seek to enjoy the incorruptible food of divine wisdom when they say, "*We are useless servants. We have done what we ought to have done.* (Lk 17:10) No work remains for us. We have finished the race; we have completed the struggle; there remains for us the crown of justice."[119] Concerning that ineffable enjoyment of the truth everything can be said, and can be said all the more to the extent that it cannot be said worthily. For it is the light of those who have been enlightened and the repose of those who have struggled and the fatherland of those returning and the food of the needy and the crown of the victorious; and, whatever temporal passing goods the error of unbelievers seeks in parts of creation, the piety of the faithful will find as truer, all at once, and abiding for eternity in the creator.

40[120]

1. When the Lord says concerning the ten lepers whom he cleansed, *Go, show yourselves to the priests* (Lk 17:14), many questions can be asked that rightly trouble those who ask them, and not merely about their number, that is, what it means that there were ten and only one of them offered thanks. For these questions are readily asked without interfering at all or only a little with the aim of the reader, even if they are not pursued. But the question is, rather, why he sent them to the priests so that they would be cleansed as they were on their way. For none of those to whom he gave such bodily benefits is found to have been sent to the priests except lepers, for he had also cleansed from leprosy that man to whom he said, *Go, show yourself to the priests, and offer the sacrifice for yourself as testimony to them as Moses commanded* (Lk 5:14). Then, what sort of spiritual cleansing can be understood in the case of those whom he blamed for being ungrateful? For it is easy to see that in terms of the body a person can be free from leprosy and still lack goodness of

---

116. See Mt 13:31–32.
117. "The word of faith" and "the sacrament of his passion," taken in tandem, suggest the basic structure of the eucharistic liturgy.
118. See Mt 25:35.40.
119. See 2 Tm 4:7–8.
120. This question deals with Lk 17:12–19.

soul, but in terms of the meaning of this miracle it is disturbing to someone who reflects on how an ungrateful person could be said to be clean.

2. The question that must be asked, then, is what this leprosy means. For those who did not have it are said not to be healthy but clean. It is in fact a problem that has to do with external appearance rather than with the health or integrity of the senses and members. Hence lepers can not unreasonably be understood to be those who have no knowledge of the true faith and who profess various erroneous teachings, for they do not even hide their ignorance but bring it forth into the light as the height of knowledge and reveal it with their boastful speech. But there is no false teaching that does not have some truths mingled with it. Truth and falsehood, therefore, mixed randomly in someone's argument or account, as though manifesting itself in the appearance of one body, signify leprosy as it changes and mars human bodies by familiar true and false characteristics. But these must be so avoided by the Church that, if possible, they stand far off and plead with Christ with a loud cry, as these ten *stood at a distance and raised their voice, saying, Jesus, teacher, have mercy on us* (Lk 17:12–13). For I think that the fact that they call him *teacher*, a title by which I do not know that anyone called the Lord for bodily healing, clearly signifies that leprosy is false teaching that the good teacher removes.

3. Assuredly, hardly any of the faithful doubt that the priesthood of the Jews was a symbol of the royal priesthood to come, which exists in the Church and by which are consecrated all who belong to the body of Christ, the highest and true prince of priests. For now all are anointed, which was then the case only with kings and priests. And what Peter said when he wrote to the Christian people, *a royal priesthood* (1 Pt 2:9), has made it clear that both designations belong to the people who had that anointing. And so the Lord heals and corrects by himself the other defects of health and of the members, as it were, of the soul and the senses interiorly in the conscience and intellect. But the teaching on initiation through the sacraments and on catechizing through the spoken word and reading are properly attributed to the Church, where a certain true and pure color is understood, because it is readily accessible and externally visible, for these things are done not in hidden thoughts but in visible actions. Therefore, when he heard the Lord's voice, *Why are you persecuting me?* and *I am Jesus whom you are persecuting* (Act 9:4–5), Paul himself was sent to Ananias in order that, by the priesthood that was established in the Church, he might receive the sacrament of the teaching of the faith[121] and its true color might be proved.[122] This is not because the Lord cannot do all things by himself—for who else does these things in the Church?—but in order that the society of the faithful gathered together might have as it were a single true appearance by approving one another and sharing the teaching of the true faith in everything that is said by words or signified by the sacraments. Pertinent to this is what the same Apostle says, *Then, after fourteen years I went up to Jerusalem with*

---

121. "The sacrament of the teaching of the faith": *sacramentum doctrinae fidei.*
122. See Acts 9:10–18.

Barnabas, taking Titus along with me. But I went up in accord with a revelation, and I explained to them the Gospel that I preach among the gentiles, but I did this privately with the leaders, lest I be running or have run in vain. (Gal 2:1–2) And a little later he says, *When they recognized the grace that was given to me, James, Peter, and John, who seemed to be the pillars, gave me and Barnabas their right hands in fellowship* (Gal 2:9). For the meeting revealed a single form of teaching without any variance, which he also warns the Corinthians about in a salutary fashion when he says, *But I beg you, brothers, in the name of our Lord Jesus Christ, that you all say the same thing* (1 Cor 1:10). Also, when Cornelius was told by an angel that his alms were received and his prayers were heard, he is still ordered to send men to Peter for the sake of the unity of the teaching and the sacraments,[123] as if it were said to him and his family, *Go, show yourselves to the priests.* For when they went, they were cleansed. For Peter had already come to them, but, since they had not received the sacrament of baptism, they had not spiritually come to the priests, and yet their cleansing was shown by the outpouring of the Spirit and by wonderful gift of tongues.[124]

4. Since this is so, it is now easy to see that it is possible that whoever in the community of the Church grasps the whole and true teaching, and says everything in accord with the rule of the Catholic faith,[125] distinguishes the creature from the creator,[126] and by that is shown to be without various errors, like leprosy, may still be ungrateful to his God and Lord who has cleansed him, because, lifted up with pride, he is not brought to his knees in the pious humility of giving thanks and becomes like those of whom the Apostle says, *Although they knew God, they did not glorify him or give him thanks* (Rom 1:21). For, when he says that they knew God, he shows that they had been cleansed from leprosy, and yet he immediately blames them for being ungrateful. Hence such people will remain in the number nine as imperfect. For, if one is added to nine, a certain image of unity is realized, and so complete is it that that number goes no further without returning to one, and this rule is maintained through infinity. The nine need one, therefore, in order to be bound together by the form of unity and become ten, whereas one does not need them in order to keep its unity. Consequently, just as those nine who did not give thanks met with disapproval and were excluded from sharing in unity, so that one who did give thanks was approved and praised because he signified the oneness of the Church. And, because they were Jews, they are shown to have missed through pride the kingdom of heaven, where unity is most perfectly guarded. But the one, who was a Samaritan, which is translated as "guardian,"[127] attributed what he received to him from whom he received it, and as if singing the verse from the

---

123. See Acts 10:1–5.
124. See Acts 10:44–48.
125. "The rule of the Catholic faith": *catholicae fidei regulam,* i.e, an informal statement of belief, similar to the more formal creed.
126. See Rom 1:25.
127. See above at p. 388, note 43.

Psalm, *I shall guard my strength for you* (Ps 59:9), he was subject to the king in gratitude and preserved the unity of the kingdom by his humble devotion.

41

What does it mean when the Lord says, *He who is on the roof and his belongings are in the house should not come down to get them* (Lk 17:31)? He is *on the roof* who, standing above things of the flesh, lives spiritually as if in the open air. *His belongings in the house* are the senses of the flesh which many have used to investigate the truth that is grasped by the intellect and have erred greatly. Therefore, these belongings of this spiritual man lie idle in the house, because he has risen above the body by the mind through the keenness of his intelligence, as if he were on a roof, and he enjoys the clarity of wisdom like a completely cloudless sky. He should beware, then, lest on the day of tribulation he be delighted by the life of the flesh, which is fed through the senses of the body, and again come down to get belongings of this kind.

42

What does it mean when it is said, *Likewise, the one who is in the field should not go back* (Lk 17:31)? Let one who works in the Church and, like Paul and Apollo, plants and waters,[128] not look back to the worldly hope that he renounced.

43

What did Lot's wife signify?[129] Those who in tribulation look back and turn away from God's promise. And for this reason she became a pillar of salt;[130] thus, by warning people not to do this, she seasons their heart lest they be without savor.

44[131]

1. Who are the two men in a bed on that night and the two women together at the mill and the two in the field, from all of which pairs one is taken and one is left behind? Three sorts of people seem to be signified here. The first of them has chosen leisure and repose, busy neither in worldly occupations nor in ecclesiastical ones. Their repose is signified by the term *bed*. The second of them is situated among peoples and governed by teachers, doing the things that pertain to this world. They are signified by the term *women*, because it is best for them that they are, as I said, ruled by those with knowledge, and he said that they were grinding at the mill because of the constant round of temporal occupations. Yet he says that

---

128. See 1 Cor 3:6.
129. See Lk 17:32.
130. See Gn 19:26.
131. This question deals with Lk 17:34–36. Lk 17:36 (*Two men will be in the field; one will be taken and the other left*) does not appear in all manuscripts.

they are grinding together insofar as, from their possessions and occupations, they contribute to the needs of the Church. The third of them works in the ministry of the Church as though in God's field, and the Apostle speaks of this work of cultivating the field.[132] In these three pairs, again, there are two kinds of people in each, and they are distinguished in accord with the strength of their abilities. For, although all of them appear to indicate members of the Church, nonetheless, when the trial of tribulation comes, some will remain and some will fall away from those who are at leisure and from those who are involved in the occupations of the world and from those who serve God in the ministry of the Church. Those who remain are taken; those who fall away are left. Therefore *one will be taken and the other left behind* (Lk 17:35)—not as if this is said of two people but of two kinds of loves in the three different kinds of professions. When he said *that night* (Lk 17:34), then, he meant "in that tribulation."

2. To the three kinds that are taken I think that there also pertain those three names of the holy men who the prophet Ezekiel declares were the only ones to be set free—Noah, Daniel, and Job.[133] For Noah seems to pertain to those who rule the Church, as in the waters he governed the ark that prefigured the Church.[134] But because Daniel chose the celibate life[135]—that is, he scorned an earthly marriage so that, as the Apostle says, he might live without preoccupations with his thoughts focused upon God[136]—he symbolizes the kind who are at leisure but are still very strong in the face of temptation, so that they can be taken. But because Job had a wife and children and ample supplies of temporal possessions,[137] he pertains to the kind that was assigned to those grinding at the mill, since they are very strong in the face of temptation, as he was, for otherwise they could not be taken. And I do not think that there are other kinds of people of which the Church is composed than these three, which have two differences, being taken and being left behind, although in individuals there can be found many diverse pursuits and choices that nevertheless work together for harmony and unity.

45[138]

1. Why is it that, in order to teach us to pray always and not to give up, the Lord chose to present the parable about the unjust judge? Although he neither feared God nor respected human beings, yet he gave in to the widow's persistent petitions that he avenge her, so that she would not cause him such bother. For this is what he says: *So that she does not come and wear me out* (Lk 18:5). The Lord presents some parables in terms of similarity, as in the case of the servant whom he forgave

---

132. See 1 Cor 3:9.
133. See Ez 14:14.
134. See Gn 6:11–8:22.
135. Daniel's celibacy is not explicitly stated in Scripture.
136. See 1 Cor 7:32–34.
137. See Jb 1:1–5; 2:9; 42:10–17.
138. This question deals with Lk 18:1–8.

what he was found to owe when the accounting was made, while he refused to grant his fellow servant even a delay;[139] and in that of the moneylender, who, having pardoned two debtors, received more love from the one to whom he had pardoned more;[140] and in that of the man who had two sons, the elder remaining nearby and working in the field, but the younger living luxuriously far away;[141] and in that of countless others of this sort. For the understanding of what they are used to teach or to investigate is derived from these things insofar as they are similar. Or he makes a point by way of dissimilarity, such as this: *If God so clothes the grass of the field that exists today and is tomorrow cast into the furnace, how much more will he clothe you, people of little faith!* (Mt 6:30) To this kind there also pertains what he says concerning the servant who the master declared was removed from his stewardship.[142] He surely cheated his master, for, by falsifying the records of those indebted to his master, he freed them insofar as it was to his advantage. And the Lord in no way encourages us to commit fraud against him, but if he says that he was praised by his master insofar as he looked out for himself for the future, with how much greater alacrity ought those to look out for themselves for eternal life who are ordered to make friends with the mammon of iniquity by working righteously, as was explained in its place![143] To this kind there also pertains the man who, though asleep, is awakened to supply three loaves of bread to his friend not out of friendship but in order to be free of the nuisance.[144] For, if he gave them to be free of the nuisance, how much more does God, who loves his people and urges us to ask, give good things to those who ask him![145] Therefore, that first kind of parable above can be completed by these words: "As the one is, so is the other." But the latter kind can be completed by these words: "If that is so, then how much more is this, or if that is not so, how much less is this!" But in some places these are expressed obscurely and in others clearly.

2. Therefore, the unjust judge is presented here not from the perspective of similarity but from that of dissimilarity, so that the Lord might show how much more certain they ought to be who perseveringly ask God, the fountain of justice and mercy — or if anything more excellent can be said or heard, since before the most unjust judge perseverance was able to effect his granting the desire of her who was beseeching him. But that widow can have similarity to the Church, because she seems all alone until the Lord comes, who even now secretly takes care of her. But if it troubles someone that God's chosen ones pray that he avenge them, which is also said in John's Apocalypse regarding the martyrs,[146] since we are very

---

139. See Mt 18:23–35.
140. See Lk 7:41–43.
141. See Lk 15:11–32.
142. See Lk 16:1–9.
143. See above at II,34.
144. See Lk 11:5–8.
145. See Mt 7:7–11.
146. See Rv 6:10.

clearly admonished to pray for our enemies and those who persecute us,[147] it should be understood that avenging the righteous means that all the evil perish. But they perish in two ways—either by conversion to righteousness or by the loss through punishment of the power by which they are now able to do something against the good, as long as this is to the benefit of the good or for a time. Therefore, even if all human beings were converted to God, among whom there are also the enemies for whom we are commanded to pray, nonetheless the devil, who is at work in the children of disobedience,[148] would remain to be condemned at the end of the world. And when the righteous desire that end, even though they pray for their enemies, they are still not inappropriately said to desire that God avenge them.

46[149]

1. *A certain nobleman went off to a faraway region to receive a kingdom for himself and to return* (Lk 19:12). He is understood to be our Lord Jesus Christ. The faraway region is the Church of the gentiles, reaching to the ends of the earth. Yet he says that he will return, for he went off in order that the fullness of the gentiles might enter; he will return in order that all of Israel may be saved.[150] By the ten pounds he signifies the law, on account of the Decalogue,[151] and by the ten servants he signifies those to whom grace was preached while they were living under the law. Hence it should be understood that they were given the ten pounds to use after they realized that, once the veil had been removed,[152] that very law pertained to the Gospel. His citizens, who sent a delegation after him saying that they did not want him to reign over them, are the Jews, who even after his resurrection sent persecutors against the apostles and rejected the preaching of the Gospel. But he returned, after having received the kingdom, because he who appeared to them as lowly when he said, *My kingdom is not of this world* (Jn 18:36), is going to return in the most manifest and sublime glory.[153]

2. That the servants who gave an account of what they received are praised for having made a profit signifies that those who have made good use of what they had received to increase the Lord's riches through those who believe in him gave a good account. Those who refused to do this are signified by the one who kept his pound wrapped in a cloth, for they are people who fool themselves by this perversity and say, "It is enough that each person give an account of himself. What need is there to preach or minister to others, so that one has to give an account of them as well, since they too, to whom the law was not given and fell asleep in death without having heard the Gospel, are without excuse before the Lord? For through the creature

---

147. See Mt 5:44.
148. See Eph 2:2.
149. This question deals with Lk 19:12–27.
150. See Rom 11:25–26.
151. I.e., the Ten Commandments.
152. See 2 Cor 3:16.
153. See Mt 16:27.

they were able to know the creator, whose invisible realities, understood from the things that were made, are seen from the creation of the world.[154] For this is like reaping where one has not sown,[155] that is, holding even those guilty of impiety to whom the word of the law or of the Gospel was not presented." But, as if trying to avoid the peril of judgment, these people absent themselves from the ministry of the word out of a lazy weariness, which is like hiding what they received in a cloth. We understand the bank where the money should have been put as the profession of religion itself, which is set forth publicly as a necessary means for salvation.

3. But that one of them who made good use of the money acquired ten and another five signifies that those who understood the law through grace were gathered into God's flock, either because it is contained in the Decalogue or because he through whom it was given wrote five books.[156] To this there also pertains the ten and five cities over which he appointed them. For the increase of understanding of the truth that emanates from each commandment or from each book is reduced to one, and it forms, as it were, one city of living and eternal reasons. For the city is not a gathering of just any living beings but of rational ones, bound together in a society of one law. But that it was taken away from the one who refused to use what he was given and given to the one who had ten signifies that one who, while having the gift of God does not have it, in other words does not use it well, can lose it, and also that it is increased in the one who has it when he has it, that is, uses it well. His enemies, whom he orders be slain before him, then, signify the impiety of the Jews who did not want him to rule over them.

47

What does it means that he says, *It is easier for a camel to pass through the eye of a needle than for a rich man to enter the kingdom of God* (Lk 18:25)? Here he calls a rich man one who covets temporal possessions and is proud of such things. The poor in spirit, to whom the kingdom of heaven belongs,[157] are the opposite of these rich people. It is obvious from this that all the covetous, even if they lack the resources of this world, are included among the sort of rich people who were rebuked, since afterwards those who were listening to him said, *And who can be saved*? (Lk 18:26), for the number of poor people is incomparably greater. Thus we understand that there are counted in that number those who, although they do not have such resources, are still caught up in the desire to have them. The sense, however, is that Christ more readily suffers for the lovers of this world than the lovers of this world can be converted to Christ. He wanted himself to be understood by the term *camel*, because he lowered himself and carried burdens. For of whom are these words of Scripture more clearly understood than of him: *The greater*

---

154. See Rom 1:20.
155. See Mt 25:26.
156. See p. 402, note 107 above.
157. See Mt 5:3.

you are, lower yourself in all things (Sir 3:18)? By the needle he signifies being pierced, and being pierced signifies the sufferings received in his passion. The sufferings of his passion, then, he calls *the eye of a needle.* But the words, *What is impossible for men is possible for God* (Lk 18:27), are not to be understood in the sense that the covetous and the proud, who are signified by that rich man, are going to enter into the kingdom of heaven, but that it is possible for God that they be converted by his word, as we see has already happened and is happening daily, from the desire for temporal things to the love of eternal ones and from a pernicious pride to a most salutary humility.

48[158]

1. We could understand of those approaching Jericho that, although they had already left there, they were still near that city. It is of course not usually put that way, but this could nonetheless seem to have been said, because Matthew says that sight was restored for the two blind men who were sitting by the road when they were leaving Jericho.[159] There would certainly be no question regarding the number if one of the evangelists had said nothing of the one while mentioning the other, for Mark mentions one when he says that his sight was restored when they were leaving Jericho, and he mentions his name and his father so that we would understand that he was someone well-known while the other was unknown;[160] thus the well-known man alone was also fittingly mentioned. But, since what follows in the Gospel of Luke very clearly shows that what he narrates was done as they were still coming to Jericho, nothing else remains to be understood but that [Christ] performed this miracle twice — once on the one man when he was still coming to that city and again on the two when he was leaving there. Thus Luke recounted the one and Mark the other, and this is not without some mystery.[161] For, if we interpret *Jericho* as "moon," and for this reason as mortality,[162] as the Lord was approaching death he commanded that the light of the Gospel be preached to the Jews alone,[163] who were signified by that one blind man whom Luke mentioned, but that it be preached to both the Jews and the gentiles when he rose from the dead and ascended.[164] For those two blind men mentioned by Matthew seem to signify the two peoples.

2. Understand the temple in the Gospel to be Christ as man or with his body, which is the Church united to him.[165] Insofar as he is the head of the Church, he said, *Destroy this temple and in three days I will raise it up* (Jn 2:19). But insofar

---

158. This question deals with Lk 18:35–43.
159. See Mt 20:29–34.
160. See Mk 10:46–52.
161. "Mystery": *sacramento.*
162. See above at II,19 and p. 388, note 41.
163. See, e.g., Mt 10:5–6.
164. See Mt 28:16–20.
165. See Col 1:18.

as he is understood to be the temple with the Church joined to him, he is seen to have said, *Take these out of here. It is written, My house will be called a house of prayer, but you have made it a house of business* (Jn 2:16) or *a den of thieves* (Mt 21:13). For he signified that in the Church there would be those who would rather do their own business or have a refuge there to hide their crimes than to imitate the love of Christ and be corrected after having received forgiveness through the confession of their sins.

49

He said, *For thereafter they are not going to die* (Lk 20:36), because marriages exist for the sake of children, children for the sake of succeeding generations, and succeeding generations for the sake of death. Therefore, where death will not exist, marriages will not either.[166] For, as our speaking is now carried out and completed by syllables that pass away and are succeeded by others, so human beings themselves, who have speech, carry out and complete the order of this world that is composed of the beauty of temporal realities. But, since the Word of God that we shall enjoy in that life is complete without the passing and succession of syllables but possesses simultaneously everything that it possesses by abiding forever, so those who partake of it, for whom it alone will be their life, will neither pass away by dying nor succeed others by being born.

50

When the Lord said to his disciples, *Pray that you do not enter into temptation. And he was removed from them as far as a stone's throw* (Lk 22:40–41), it was as though this was an admonition that they should direct a stone at him, that is, that they should direct at him the content of the law, which was written on stone.[167] For that stone can only reach as far as him, inasmuch as *Christ is the end of the law unto justice for every believer* (Rom 10:4).

51

1. What is written about the Lord, *He pretended to go further* (Lk 24:28), does not count as a lie. For not everything that we pretend is a lie, but when we pretend that which signifies nothing, then there is a lie. When our pretense has some signification, however, it is not a lie but a figure of speech. Otherwise all those things that were said figuratively by wise and holy men and by the Lord himself will be considered lies, because the truth for such statements is not found in terms of their usual understanding. For in the case of the man who had two sons, the younger of whom, having received a part of his inheritance, set out for a

---

166. See Lk 20:35.
167. See Ex 31:18; 34:4.

faraway region, and the other things that are woven into that narrative[168] — these things are spoken of as if there really was some man who either experienced or did this in the case of his two sons. These things were, therefore, made up to signify something so much greater and so incomparably different that the true God might be understood through the fictitious man. But just as things are said so also things are done without mendacity in order to signify something. For example, there is also what the same Lord did in seeking fruit from a fig tree at the season when there was as yet no fruit,[169] for there is no doubt that his seeking the fruit was not genuine, inasmuch as anyone would know, if not by its barrenness, then at least by the season, that the tree had no fruit. A pretense, therefore, that conveys some truth is a figure, and one that does not is a lie.

2. What does it signify, then, that the Lord *pretended to go further* when he was accompanying his disciples and explaining the Scriptures to them who did not know whether it was he? What do we suppose but that he intimated that people could come to recognize him by offering hospitality? In that way, although he departed far from men above all the heavens, he is still with those who show these services to his servants. Thus, when they would begin to say, *Lord, when did we see you a stranger and welcome you?* (Mt 25:38), that is, as one who had departed far from them, he would answer, *When you did this to the least of mine, you did it to me* (Mt 25:40). Whoever has been instructed in the word, therefore, shares with the one who instructs him all the good things that he has — as the Apostle says, *Let him who has been instructed in the word share in all good things with the one who instructs him* (Gal 6:6) — and holds onto Christ so that he does not depart far away from him. And in another passage, after he said, *Share with the saints in their needs*, he immediately added, *practicing hospitality* (Rom 12:13). And they were instructed in the word[170] when he explained the Scriptures to them, and, because they practiced hospitality, they recognized in the breaking of the bread him whom they did not recognize in the explanation of the Scriptures.[171] *For it is not the hearers of the law who are just before God, but those who carry out the law will be justified* (Rom 2:13).

3.[172] The fact that the Lord was stripped of his own clothes in the passion and wrapped in a scarlet garment[173] signifies the heretics who say that he did not have a real body but a fictitious one.[174]

---

168. See Lk 15:11–32.
169. See Mk 11:13.
170. "Instructed in the word": *catechizati erant verbo*. This phrase could also be correctly translated as "instructed by the Word."
171. See Lk 24:27–35.
172. This last paragraph is omitted in CCSL.
173. See Mt 27:28.
174. Augustine is referring to Docetists and Gnostics, who maintained this opinion.

INDEX

SEVENTEEN QUESTIONS ON MATTHEW

(Quaestiones XVII in Matthaeum)

Introduction

The treatise that follows is a small collection of questions on the Gospel of Matthew, along with their responses. In the manuscript tradition and in the first printed editions the *Seventeen Questions on Matthew* always follows the *Questions on the Gospels* either under the same title or without a title of its own. The title itself, *Seventeen Questions on Matthew*, first appears in the Maurist edition of 1680, which kept the longstanding division of the eleventh question into two parts. *Patrologia Latina* (PL) 35 reproduced the Maurist text, while the recent critical edition by Almut Mutzenbecher in *Corpus Christianorum Series Latina* (CCSL) 44/B reunited the two questions, entitled the work *Sixteen Questions on Matthew*, and treated it as an appendix to the *Questions on the Gospels*. The Italian translation in *Nuova Biblioteca Agostiniana* (NBA) 10/2, while acknowledging the unity of questions 11 and 12, has preserved the traditional title, which the present translation also does, while reuniting the two questions.

The *Seventeen Questions on Matthew* has often but not always been attributed to Augustine. Significantly, it is not mentioned by him in his *Revisions*, nor is it listed in the *Indiculus*, the extensive catalogue of Augustine's writings put together by Possidius, his protégé. In addition, the work's date of composition is unclear. For a good summary of the arguments for and against Augustinian authorship of the questions, and for a discussion of their date of composition, see Barbara Fenati's introduction to the work in NBA 10/2, 421–426 and Mutzenbecher's introduction to the critical edition in CCSL 44/B, xxiii–xxxii. One can hardly do better than follow Mutzenbecher's conclusion: "After all we can only suppose that the sixteen questions originated on the same or on a similar occasion as Augustine described in the prologue to the *Questions on the Gospels*."[1] But Mutzenbecher argues that it is doubtful that the work is the result of the same reading of Matthew as the first book of the *Questions on the Gospel*, since Mt 13:25–30 is dealt with in both works and is the only such passage that appears in each. Inasmuch as the work is not mentioned in the *Revisions*, the Maurist editors supposed that it was written after 427, when the *Revisions* were published. In her introduction, however, Fenati poses a problem, summarily discussed below in reference to Question 11, with a late dating based on Augustine's interpretation of the field in which the wheat and the weeds are sown.[2]

Most of the questions are treated quite briefly. Question 11 (11–12 in PL) elicits the longest response. In it Augustine explains in detail whether the weeds sown among the wheat are to be understood as heretics or schismatics or Catholics living a bad life, and he draws careful distinctions among the three. In the preface to *Heresies*, which was composed in 428–429 in response to letters from Quodvultdeus, a deacon of Carthage, Augustine had written: "What it is that makes

---

1. See CCSL 44/B,xxv.
2. See Mt 13:38, discussed by Fenati in NBA 10/2,422.

one a heretic, in my opinion, cannot at all, or can only with difficulty, be grasped by a definition in accord with the rules."[3] Hence the present work may reflect an earlier confidence about drawing such distinctions, or *Heresies* may be speaking of "definition" in a more technical sense. In any case the dating of the present work seems an open question.

Paragraphs two to five in the final question are omitted in the critical edition, although they are preserved in the NBA text and translation and are translated here. These paragraphs do not belong to the work, and they are not in the *quaestiones* format.[4] They are in fact the beginning of a pseudo-Augustinian work entitled *Eight Questions on the Old Testament.*[5]

*   *   *

The Latin text translated here is that found in the critical edition by Mutzen-becher, although I have followed the text in NBA in preserving the PL numbering of the questions, while noting the numbering in CCSL. I have also included the concluding paragraphs in the last question that are omitted from the text in CCSL and clearly do not belong to the work. They are, however, included in the NBA text and translation.

Aside from the Italian translation in NBA and two nineteenth-century French translations in the editions mentioned previously,[6] I have found no other translation into a modern language.

---

3. See *Heresies*, preface 7; my translation in *Arianism and Other Heresies* (Hyde Park: New City Press, 1995) 190.
4. See above at p. 351.
5. See Gustav Morin, "Un traité inédit attribué à saint Augustin, le De VIII quaestionibus ex vet. test. du catalogue de Lorsch," in *Revue Bénédictine* 28 (1911) 8ff.
6. See above at p. 356.

1

The words *infants two years old and younger were killed* (Mt 2:16) signify that the humble who have twofold charity,[7] like children of two years, can die for Christ.

2

What I am saying to you in darkness, that is, when you are still in carnal fear, because there is fear in the darkness, *say in the light* (Mt 10:27), that is, in the confidence of the truth, once you have received the Holy Spirit. *And what you hear in your ear, proclaim on the rooftops* (Mt 10:27), that is, what you hear in secret, proclaim once you have trodden underfoot your bodily dwelling place.

3

Do not suppose that I have come to bring peace to the earth. I have come not to bring peace but the sword. For I have come to set a man against his father (Mt 10:34–35), that is, because one renounces the devil who was his father.[8] *And a daughter against her mother* (Mt 10:35), that is, the people of God against the worldly city, namely, the pernicious society of the human race, which Scripture signifies sometimes by Babylon, sometimes by Egypt, sometimes by Sodom,[9] and sometimes by various other names. *A daughter-in-law against her mother-in-law* (Mt 10:35), that is, the Church against the Synagogue, which in terms of the flesh begot Christ,[10] the bridegroom of the Church.[11] But they are divided by the sword of the Spirit, which is the Word of God.[12] *And the enemies of a man will be the members of his household* (Mt 10:36), with whom he was formerly bound by his manner of life.

4

But coming down from the mountain (Mt 8:1), after he gave the commandments to his disciples and to the multitude, *he immediately stretches out his hand and heals a leper* (Mt 8:3), signifies that those who are doubtful about fulfilling the commandments are cleansed from hesitation of this sort by his help.

5

What *the Lord said to the scribe who wanted to follow him, Foxes have lairs and birds of the air nests, but the Son of Man has nowhere to lay his head* (Mt 8:19–20), indicates that, moved by the miracles of the Lord, the scribe wanted to

---

7.   See Mt 22:27–40.
8.   See Jn 8:44.
9.   See Rv 11:8.
10. See Rom 9:5.
11. See Eph 5:21–33.
12. See Eph 6:17.

follow him out of vain boasting, which the birds signify, but he pretended to have the obedience of a disciple, and that pretense is signified by the mention of foxes.[13] But by the laying down of his head he signified his own humility, for which that pretentious and proud man had no room.

6

Let the dead bury their dead (Mt 8:22). Here he calls *dead* those who do not believe, and he calls *their dead* those who have nonetheless left the body without faith.

7

Shake the dust from your feet (Mt 10:13) either as testimony to the earthly labor that they had fruitlessly undertaken for them, or in order to show to what point they seek nothing earthly from them so that they do not allow even the dust from their earth to cling to them.

8

Be, therefore, prudent like serpents (Mt 10:16) in order to avoid evil by guarding one's head, which is Christ.[14] For a serpent presents its whole body for the sake of its head to one who is pursuing it. Alternatively, by forcing itself through narrow places it is renewed by having stripped off its old skin, which those to whom it was said, *Enter through the narrow gate* (Mt 7:13), imitate when they are stripped of the old human being.[15] For if he warned them to avoid evil to the point that they resisted the evil with violence, he would not have said, *I am sending you like sheep in the midst of wolves* (Mt 10:16). But he wanted them to be *simple like doves* (Mt 10:16), for this kind of bird kills absolutely no living being, not merely big ones against which it does not have the power but even the littlest ones on which the smallest sparrows feed. But all non-rational animals have a certain single society among themselves, just as rational animals, that is, human beings, have not only with one another but also with the angels. Let them learn, then, from the example of the doves to harm no one at all who, by partaking in reason, belongs to their society.

9

I confess to you, Father, Lord of heaven and earth (Mt 11:25). One should note that "confession" is used here for praise of God. For the Lord does not confess sins,

---

13. On the fox as a symbol of pretence and deceit see *Physiologus* 18.
14. See 1 Cor 11:3.
15. See Col 3:9. For these and other traits commonly attributed to serpents, as well as for some of the same scriptural references that Augustine uses, see *Physiologus* 13.

since he has none,[16] especially since another evangelist mentions that he said this while he was exulting,[17] and yet the words themselves that he says leave no doubt that they are said in praise of God. Therefore, Scripture generally calls confession whatever is spoken openly as it is seen. For he says, *If anyone confesses me before men, I shall also confess him before my Father* (Mt 10:32), or, as it is said elsewhere, *Before the angels of God* (Lk 12:8). One who confesses Christ certainly does not confess sins. But if some think that it is called confession because the mention of the name of Christ was regarded as a crime in the time of persecution, does Christ also in that way confess before his Father or before the angels the person who confesses him? It is also stated in this way in Ecclesiasticus, *And you shall say these things in confession, for all the works of the Lord are very good* (Sir 39:20–21), and by this passage the praises of the Lord are heaped up. These things are said on account of the ignorance of brethren who, when they hear this word when a lector reads it, immediately strike their breasts, not paying attention to the context in which it is said, as if there could only be a confession of sins.[18]

10

It should be noted that, because the Jews thought that the disciples acted illicitly when they plucked ears on the sabbath, they were given one example of royal power concerning David and another of priestly power concerning those who violate the sabbath through the temple ministry.[19] Far less, then, does the charge of plucking ears on the sabbath pertain to him who is true king and true priest and, for this reason, *Lord of the sabbath* (Mt 12:8).

11

1. *When the men went to sleep, his enemy came and sowed weeds in the midst of the wheat and went off* (Mt 13:25). When those placed in charge of the Church acted rather negligently, or when the apostles accepted the sleep of death, the devil came and sowed after them those whom the Lord interpreted as evil sons.[20] But one is right to ask whether they are heretics or Catholics living bad lives, for heretics can also be called evil sons, because they were procreated from the same seed of the Gospel and by the name of Christ and were converted to false teachings by evil opinions. But, because he says that they were sown *in the midst of the wheat*, it seems as if he was signifying those who belong to one communion. Nonetheless, because the Lord interpreted the field not as the Church but as this world,[21] heretics are correctly understood, because they are mingled with the good people

16. See 1 Pt 2:29.
17. See Lk 10:21.
18. A telling observation on rote behavior during the liturgy in fifth-century Hippo.
19. See Mt 12:1–5.
20. See Mt 13:38.
21. See Mt 13:38.

in this world not by being associated with one Church or one faith but by being associated with the Christian name alone. Thus bad people in the same faith are counted as chaff rather than as weeds,[22] because chaff has the same foundation and root in common with wheat. It is clearly not absurd to understand that there are bad Catholics in that net in which both good and bad fish are caught.[23] For the sea that signifies this world is one thing, but the net is another, which, it seems, represents the communion of one faith and one Church. The difference between heretics and bad Catholics is that heretics believe what is false, whereas bad Catholics believe what is true but do not live as they believe.

2. But it is often asked as well how schismatics differ from heretics, and one finds that it is not diversity in faith that makes schismatics but a breaking of communion within a single society. Still, one can wonder whether they should be counted among the weeds. They seem instead to be like spoiled ears of grain, as Scripture says, *A bad son is spoiled by the wind* (Prv 10:5 Vulg), or like chaff broken or cut from the corn and removed from the grain. For the higher, that is, the prouder, they are, the more fragile and insubstantial they are. Yet it does not follow that every heretic or schismatic is bodily separated from the Church. For, if one believes what is false about God or about some part of the teaching that pertains to the upbuilding of the faith[24] in such a way that he is not restrained by the hesitation characteristic of a questioner but firmly dissents with the erroneous opinion of a believer who has no knowledge whatsoever, he is a heretic and spiritually outside [the Church] while seeming to be corporeally within it. The Church has many of that sort, since they do not defend their false opinions in such a way as to make the majority take note, although, if they do so, they are expelled. Likewise, all those who hate good people by looking for occasions to exclude them or degrade them, or are in that way ready to defend their crimes if they are brought against them or disclosed, so that they even consider stirring up the separations of their gatherings or disturbances of the Church, are already schismatic and cut off from unity in their heart, although they are joined to the sacrament of the Church[25] by their bodily life, since their deeds have not been discovered or their behavior has not been observed.

3. Hence they are rightly considered to be merely bad Catholics who live outrageously and sinfully, contrary to how they believe one should live, despite the fact that they believe the truths that pertain to the teaching of the faith. And, if perhaps they do not know something or think that it should be asked about, they discuss it without any prejudice to the truth and with no loss to piety, and they love and honor good people or those whom they consider good to the extent that they can. For even if such people are disclosed or accused, rebuked for the sake of the Church's discipline and their own salvation, or suspended from communion, in

---

22. See Mt 2:12.
23. See Mt 13:47–48.
24. See Eph 4:29.
25. "The sacrament of the Church": *sacramento ecclesiae*.

no way do they think that they need to withdraw from the Catholic communion as they try to make satisfaction in whatever way permissible. And at times they are changed into grain through penance, after being rebuked or removed or terrified by the word of God, without anyone accusing or rebuking them by name. At times, however, even under the name of penitents they live as they are accustomed or not much better, although some live even worse, yet in no way do they abandon Catholic unity. And if death overtakes them while they are living in that way, they are considered chaff up to the end. Even they themselves believe this. For if they believe and unshakably hold otherwise, they should already be counted among heretics, since they believe that God will grant forgiveness to everyone, even to those who persevere in great iniquity up to the end of life, only because they held onto the unity of the Church not out of sincere love—for they would live differently—but rather out of fear of punishment. These people, therefore, do not believe or firmly hold this, even if they are perhaps still seeking it, but the hope of having more time deceives them, since they think that they will live longer and at some time change their bad morals for the better. Against them it is said, *Do not delay to turn to the Lord, and do not put it off from day to day, for his wrath will come suddenly, and he will destroy you in the time of vengeance* (Sir 5:8–9). For they turn to him who begin to live rightly, for this is to return to God. But those who persevere in following their passions in some way have their back to God, although, while remaining in unity, they often try to see him by turning their neck. Therefore these too, as the prophet says, *are flesh and a spirit that walks and does not return* (Ps 77:39). But still, as was said, on account of the same faith and the unity of the Church they are not counted among the weeds, because the weeds were uprooted, nor are they counted among the chaff of the ears that dares to place itself even above the grain by its harsh dissension and fragile elation, but, although placed under the grain, they are still among the chaff that will be separated by the final winnowing.[26]

4. But good Catholics are those who possess both faith in its fullness and good morals. They seek what pertains to the teaching of the faith, however, in such a way that, if they have some question, there is no perilous conflict either for the questioner or for the one with whom the question is raised or for those who hear their discussion. If, on the other hand, they have something that needs to be taught, they teach it so that they convey familiar and settled matters in the most secure, confident, and gentle way they can, but they convey unfamiliar matters, although they see them with the clearest understanding of the truth, like a seeker rather than like a teacher and legislator, on account of the frailty of the student. For, if some truth has such great depth that it exceeds the abilities of the one who is learning, he should stop in order to allow the learner to grow and not impose it and drive off the child. That is why the Lord says, *When the Son of Man comes, will he find faith on the earth?* (Lk 18:8) At times, however, one must hide the truth, but with

---

26. See Mt 3:12.

encouraging hope, so that a lack of hope may not cool their interest but so that desire may increase their capacity. That is why the Lord says, *I have many things to say to you, but you cannot bear them yet* (Jn 16:12). But what pertains to morals is stated well and briefly: One must struggle with the love of temporal goods so that it does not win out. Either it ought to be tamed and held under control so that, even when it tries to rise up, it is easily shoved back down, or it ought to be eliminated such that it is not aroused at all in any way. The result of this is that, on account of the truth, some face death bravely, others calmly, and still others gladly. And these are the three kinds of fruit of the fertile land—thirtyfold and sixtyfold and a hundredfold.[27] A person must be part of one of these kinds at the time of his death if he plans to leave this life in the right way.

(12)

5. But the weeds are to be tolerated until the harvest. For although the devil sowed them later by spreading evil errors and false opinions—that is, he spread about heresies after the name of Christ was preached—he himself was concealed and became completely hidden. For this is what was meant by *and he went off* (Mt 13:25), but the chaff also remains hidden until the winnowing.[28] And the weight of the grain is more effectively proved only by disturbing the chaff, and, since the grain cannot hold the chaff down with the defense of the truth, it gives it up with the preservation of unity. And yet in this parable, as the Lord concluded in his explanation, he is understood to have signified by the term *weeds* not just some but *all scandals and those who work iniquity* (Mt 13:41).

6. *But when the grain grew and bore fruit, then the weeds also appeared* (Mt 13:26). For when the spiritual person begins to be one who judges all things,[29] then he begins to see errors. *But the servants said to him, Do you want us to go and gather them?* (Mt 13:28) Are they the servants whom he later calls harvesters? Or, since in the explanation of the parable he said that the harvesters are the angels,[30] and since no one would dare to say that the angels did not know who had sown the weeds and that the angels first saw them when the grain bore fruit, does it not make more sense to understand that believers were signified in this passage by the term *servants*, whom he also called *good seed* (Mt 13:24)? It is not surprising if they are called *good seed* and *servants* of the father of the family in the same way that he also says of himself that he is the gate and that he is the shepherd.[31] For one thing often has many and different similarities from the different things it signifies. And this is especially the case since, when he was speaking to the servants, he did not say, "At the time of the harvest I shall say to you, Gather the weeds first"; rather, he says, *I shall say to the harvesters* (Mt 13:30). From this it

---

27. See Mt 13:8.23.
28. See Mt 3:12.
29. See 1 Cor 2:15.
30. See Mt 12:39.
31. See Jn 10:17.

is clear that the ministries of gathering the weeds to burn belong to others and that no son of the Church ought to think that this office pertains to him.

7. Therefore, when anyone has begun to be spiritual, he recognizes the errors of heretics and competently judges and discerns when whatever he may hear or read departs from the rule of the truth.[32] But until he has become perfect in the same spiritual matters and in a sense matures into the fruit that wheat produces, it can trouble him why so many errors of the heretics have emerged under the Christian name. This is why the servants say, *Did you not sow good seed in your field? Where then did the weeds come from?* (Mt 13:27) Then, after one realizes that the devil devised this deception, since he sees that he can do nothing against the authority of so great a name[33] and thus conceals heresies under that same name, the desire can arise in him to remove such people from human affairs if he has some temporal power. But he consults the justice of God whether he ought to do so, whether he commands or permits him to do this and wants this responsibility to belong to human beings. Hence it is that the servants say, *Do you want us to go and gather them?* (Mt 13:28) And Truth himself replies to them that a man was not put in this life in such a way that he could be certain how anyone whose error he sees at present is going to turn out later, or how his error might also contribute to the development of those who are good, and that for this reason they are not to be removed from this life. Otherwise, when he tries to kill the evil he may kill the good, who they will perhaps become, or he may hinder the good to whom they may be useful, albeit unwillingly. But their removal becomes appropriate when in the end there no longer remains time to reform one's life or to make progress toward the truth on the occasion of and by comparison with some other error. But this will not be done then by human beings but by angels. For this reason the father of the family replies, *No, lest in gathering the weeds you also uproot the wheat at the same time. But at the time of the harvest I shall say to the harvesters* (Mt 13:29–30), and so on. And in this way he renders them most patient and calm.

8. But when he says, *Tie up the bundles to burn* (Mt 13:30), one can question why he did not tell them to make one bundle or one pile of the weeds, unless perhaps, on account of the variety of heretics in disagreement not only with the wheat but also with one another, he was signifying by the term *bundles* the particular assemblies of each heresy, in which they are separately bound by their own communion. In this way they would begin to be bound for burning when, separated from the Catholic communion, they would have started to have something like their own churches. Thus their burning would occur at the end of the world, but the binding of the bundles would occur now. Yet if that were the case, many would not break away from their error by coming to their senses and returning to the Catholic Church. Hence, the tying of the bundles also takes place at the end, so

---

32. "Rule of truth": *regular veritatis*. This is equivalent to the rule of (the Catholic) faith mentioned in *Questions on the Gospels* II,40,4.
33. I.e., the name of Christ.

that the stubbornness of each error may be punished in accord with the manner of its perversity.

9. *Lest in gathering the weeds you also uproot the wheat at the same time* (Mt 13:29). This can be the case because, when they are still weak, good people sometimes need to be mingled with the bad either in order to be tried by them or in order that, from comparison with them, they may be strongly exhorted to strive for what is better. If they were removed, the grandeur of charity would fade, as if torn away — that is, uprooted, for, as the Apostle says, *So that, rooted in and founded on charity, you may be able to grasp* (Eph 3:17–18). Or perhaps the wheat would be uprooted at the same time as the weeds are removed because many are weeds first and become wheat afterwards, and, unless they are patiently tolerated when they are bad, they do not attain to a praiseworthy betterment; hence, if they are torn out, the wheat that they would have become if they were spared would also be uprooted.

12 (13)

The kingdom of heaven is like a merchant searching for fine pearls. But when he found one precious pearl he went off, sold all that he had, and bought it. (Mt 13:45–46) The question is why he moves from the plural number to the singular so that, although the man is seeking fine pearls, he finds one precious pearl that he buys after selling all that he has. Either, then, he is seeking good men with whom he might usefully live and, instead of *all*, he finds *one* without sin,[34] *the mediator of God and men, the man Christ Jesus* (1 Tm 2:5). Or he is seeking commandments by the observance of which he might live uprightly with human beings, and he finds the love of neighbor. The Apostle says that *all* are contained in that *one*, such that *you shall not kill, you shall not commit adultery, you shall not steal, you shall not give false testimony, and if there is some other commandment* (Rom 13:8–9) are individual pearls that are summed up in these words, *You shall love your neighbor as yourself* (Mt 19:19). Or the man is seeking good intelligible words and finds that *one* in which *all* are contained: the Word in the beginning, and the Word with God, and God the Word,[35] bright with the splendor of the truth and solid with the strength of eternity and in every respect equal to itself with the beauty of divinity, who is to be understood as God once the shell of the flesh has been pierced. For that man had come to the pearl that had once lain hidden under the wrappings of mortality, like the shell of an oyster, in the depth of this world and amid the rocky hardness of the Jews. He who had already come upon that very pearl, then, says, *And if we once knew Christ according to the flesh, we do not now know him* (2 Cor 5:16). There is nothing else at all that is worthy of being understood by the name *pearl* apart from him to whom one comes when all the coverings of the flesh have been removed by which he is concealed either by human words or by likenesses

---

34. See 2 Cor 5:21.
35. See Jn 1:1.

that surround him, so that he is seen by sure reason as pure, solid, and never out of harmony with himself. That one intelligible word, nonetheless, through whom all things were made and which is the Word of God,[36] contains all those true and solid and perfect intelligible words.

But whichever of the three explanations it is, or if something else could be thought up that might be signified by the reference to that unique and precious pearl, we ourselves are its price—we who are not free to possess it unless for the sake of our deliverance we hold in contempt everything that we possess in time. For when we have sold all our possessions we receive no greater recompense for them than ourselves, because when we were bound to such things we were not our own, so that we in turn might exchange ourselves for that pearl, not indeed because of our great value but because we cannot give more.

13 (14)

1. *And they closed their eyes lest at any time they see with their eyes* (Mt 13:15), that is, they themselves were the reason that God closed their eyes. For another evangelist says, *He closed their eyes* (Jn 12:40). But was it so that they would never see, or was it so that in that way they might not see for a time, displeased with themselves and sorrowing over themselves because of their blindness, and humbled and moved by this to confess their sins and piously seek God? For this is what Mark says: *Lest they be converted and their sins be forgiven* (Mk 4:12). There they are understood to have merited not to understand by reason of their sins, and yet this was mercifully done to them so that they would acknowledge their sins and, having been converted, merit pardon. But what John says in this respect—*Hence they were not able to believe, because Isaiah again said, He blinded their eyes and hardened their heart so that they would not see with their eyes and understand with their heart and be converted and I might save them* (Jn 12:39–40)—may seem to be opposed to this view and absolutely oblige one not to accept what is said here, *lest at any time they see with their eyes*—not, indeed, that they might not see for a time but rather that they might not see at all, inasmuch as it plainly says, *so that they would not see with their eyes* (Jn 12:40). And the words, *Hence they were not able to believe* (Jn 12:39), show quite well that their blindness was not produced so that, moved by it and sorrowing that they did not understand, they might at some time be converted through penance. For they could not do this unless they first believed, so that by believing they might be converted, that by conversion they might be healed, and that by healing they might understand; they were blinded, instead, so that they might not believe, for he says very plainly, *Hence they were not able to believe.*

2. If that is so, who would not rise up in defense of the Jews to declare that they were blameless in their unbelief? For they were not able to believe because he blinded their eyes. But, since we ought rather to understand that God is blame-

---

36. See Jn 1:3.

less, we are obliged to say that they merited to be blinded in that way by certain other sins, but because of that blindness they could not believe. For these are the words of John: *Hence they were not able to believe, because Isaiah again said, He blinded their eyes* (Jn 12:39–40). It is fruitless, then, for us to try to understand that they were blinded in order that they might be converted, for they could not be converted because they did not believe, and they could not believe because they were blinded. Or perhaps it is not absurd for us to say that certain Jews might have been healed but that they were still endangered by such a great swelling of pride that it was better for them not to believe at first; and that they were blinded so that they would not understand the Lord when he spoke in parables; and that because they did not understand them they did not believe in him; and that, not believing with the others who were without hope, they crucified him; and that after his resurrection they were converted so that, having been more humbled by guilt over the Lord's death, they would love him more ardently and rejoice that they were forgiven so great a crime. For their pride was so great that it had to be cast down by such humiliation. Someone might suppose that this was not appropriately stated if he did not read quite clearly in the Acts of the Apostles[37] that this was how it turned out. Therefore, John's words, *Hence, they were not able to believe... because he blinded their eyes... so that they would not see* (Jn 12:39–40), are not incompatible with the view by which we understand that they were blinded so that they would be converted.[38] That is, the thoughts of the Lord were hidden by the obscurity of his language so that after his resurrection they would come to their senses by a more salutary penance. For, blinded by the obscurity of his language, they did not understand the Lord's words, and in not understanding them they did not believe in him, and in not believing they crucified him, and in that way after the resurrection, filled with terror by the miracles that were done in his name, they were pierced by a greater guilt over their crime and laid low through repentance, and then, having received forgiveness, they were converted to obedience with a most ardent love.

3. As for those whom that blindness, which was produced through the language of the parables, did not benefit, the prophet says in another passage that the Apostle also mentioned when he was dealing with the obscurity of languages, *In other languages and in other tongues I will speak to this people, and in that way they shall not hear me, says the Lord* (1 Cor 14:21; Is 28:11). For *and in that way they shall not hear me* would not have been said unless this was done so that they would hear, that is, so that it would lead to humble confession, diligent searching, obedient conversion, and fervent love. But this is also the manner of bodily medicine, for very many medications often first cause pain in order to heal, and if drops have to be put into one's eyes, they cannot be of benefit unless they first cloud and disturb the sense of sight.

---

37. See Acts 2:36–41.
38. See Mk 4:12.

4. Do not let what the same prophet says disturb you, *Unless you believe, you will not understand* (Is 7:9), as if it were contrary to what John says, *Hence, they were not able to believe...because he blinded their eyes*, that is, because those parables were spoken in such a way that they could not understand them. For someone says, "If they had to believe in order to understand, how were they unable to believe, because they did not understand, that is, because *he blinded their eyes* (Jn 12:40)?" But Isaiah's words, *Unless you believe, you will not understand*, were said about that understanding of ineffable things in which one will abide forever. But when what is believed is said, one can only believe if he understands what is said. Therefore, what is said must be understood in order that those things that could be said may be believed, but those that could be said must be believed in order that those that cannot be said may be understood.

14 (15)

And without parables he did not speak to them (Mt 13:34), not because he said nothing in its proper sense but because he rarely spoke without signifying something by way of a parable, although he also said some things in it in their proper sense, such that his entire speech is often found to be in the form of parables, whereas no discourse is found to be spoken entirely in a proper sense. What I call a discourse occurs when, prompted by some matter or other, he begins to speak, until he brings to an end whatever pertains to that matter and moves on to another. At times, in fact, one evangelist has brought together what another indicates was said at different times. For each of them has arranged the narrative that he began not entirely according to the order of events but according to the extent of his recollection.

15 (16)

Have you understood all these things? They say to him, Yes. He says to them, And for this reason every scribe learned in the kingdom of God is like the head of a family who brings forth from his treasure new and old things. (Mt 13:51–52) Did he want to explain by these concluding words what he said was a treasure hidden in a field,[39] because the Holy Scriptures are being implied, which are included under the name of two testaments, new and old, just as in another evangelist the Lord seems to explain the two-edged sword by that conclusion?[40] Or, because he said these things in parables and, when he asked them whether they understood, they answered that they understood, did he perhaps want to show—by that last metaphor of the head of a family who brings forth new and old things from his treasure—that he should be regarded as a learned man in the Church who understood even the old Scriptures as presented in parables, taking the rules from the new ones, because the Lord stated those new things through parables? For Christ

---

39. See Mt 13:44.
40. See Rv 1:16. The "other evangelist" is John, the putative author of the Book of Revelation.

himself is the end of all things[41] in the sense that the old Scriptures are fulfilled in him. Hence, if he in whom all things are fulfilled and made manifest still speaks through parables until his passion tears the veil in half,[42] so that nothing is hidden that is not revealed,[43] we should with much better reason know that those things that were written about him so long ago to announce such a great salvation were cloaked in parables, and, when the Jews took them literally, they refused to be learned in the kingdom of God and to cross over to Christ in order that the veil might be removed that was placed over their heart.[44]

16 (17)

1. *Are not his brothers James and Joseph and Simon and Jude, and are not all his sisters among us? Where then has his man got all these things from? And they were scandalized by him.* (Mt 13:55–57) To such an extent is it beyond dispute that, among the Jews, relatives are called brothers that not only those of the same generation, like the sons of brothers and sisters who are customarily also called brothers among us, but even an uncle and a sister's son, as Jacob and Laban were to each other, are also found to have been referred to as brothers.[45] It is not surprising, then, that any male relatives on his mother's side were called the Lord's brothers, since those from Joseph's kin could also be called his brothers by those who thought that he was the Lord's father.

2.[46] A person does not violate general justice unless, driven by desire, he commits a transgression either against a norm of human society, such as by theft, robbery, adultery, incest, and that sort of thing; or against nature, such as by insult, slaughter, murder, sodomy or bestiality; or against due measure in what is permitted, such as by beating a slave or a son more than is necessary, eating or drinking more than is necessary, or having intercourse with one's wife more than is necessary, and similar things.

3. The Holy Spirit is correctly understood to have given to human beings the first gift of languages[47] — which were instituted by the agreement and decision of human beings and are learned from the habit of hearing them externally through the senses of the body — in order to show them how easily he could make them wise through the wisdom of God, which is internal.

4. Again, the will of the eternal Word is forever stable, because it simultaneously possesses all things, but our will does not stay the same, because it does not simultaneously possess all things, and for this reason we will now this and

---

41.   See Rom 10:4.
42.   See Mt 27:51.
43.   See Mt 10:26.
44.   See 2 Cor 3:15–16.
45.   See Gn 29:10–15. Augustine's ordering of the names is misleading: Laban was the uncle and Jacob was the son of Laban's sister Rebekah.
46.   What follows from here to the end is omitted in the critical edition and does not belong to it. See p. 430 for the explanation.
47.   See Acts 2:4.

now that. Likewise, all the things that were made were in that Word, and the very assumption of a man[48] was foreknown by him, just as, if a painter knows the place where he has to paint, he wants to paint an entire house and thinks of and also has the whole project in his art, preparation, and will, although he carries out each step at its proper time. In that way every creature, and the very man who was going to bear the person of the same Wisdom mysteriously and by an ineffable assumption, was always in that divine Wisdom as in the eternal art of God, although it produces each thing in its proper time, while it stretches from end to end mightily, arranges all things pleasantly,[49] and, while remaining in itself, renews all things.[50]

5. Again, how would one want to will to die if he has come to want to die, when he now has the correct faith and sees where he must arrive, so that he has now come to the point that he would willingly leave this life? For to see where one must arrive is not the same as loving it and desiring to be there now, which have to be brought about in a person's soul in order that he may willingly die. Without reason, therefore, do some people who have sound faith say that they do not want to die so that they may make progress, since their progress has already reached the point that they want to die. If they want to be truthful, then, they should not say, "I do not want to die so that I may make progress" but "I do not want to die because I have made too little progress." And so, for believers not to want to die is not a design for making progress but an indication that they have made too little progress. Therefore, let them will what they do not want in order to be perfect, and they are perfect.

---

48. "The very assumption of a man": *ipsa susceptio hominis.* This is an allusion to so-called *homo assumptus* (or *susceptus*) christology, which also appears later in the paragraph in the reference to "the very man who was going to bear the person...." See p. 58, note 77.

49. See Wis 8:1.

50. See Wis 7:27.

INDEX

(Prepared by Kathleen Strattan)

The first numbers in the Index are the Question numbers. The numbers following the colons are the Paragraph numbers.

WORKS OF ST. AUGUSTINE:
A TRANSLATION FOR THE 21ST CENTURY

New City Press, in conjunction with the Augustinian Heritage Institute, will provide the complete works of Saint Augustine for the first time in the English language. New translations, introductions and notes are written by renowned Augustinian scholars. Foreseen are 48 volumes. See the list below for books already published. Future publication plans available upon request. Standing Order customers receive a 10% discount on each volume in the Works of Saint Augustine series.

Part I — Books

Autobiographical Works

The Confessions (I/1)
  cloth, 978-1-56548-468-9, $59.00
  paper, 978-1-56548-445-0, $24.95
  pocket, 978-1-56548-154-1, $9.95

Revisions (I/2)
  cloth, 978-1-56548-360-6, $39.95

Philosophical-Dogmatic Works

The Trinity (I/5)
  cloth, 978-0-911782-89-9, $64.00
  paper, 978-1-56548-446-7, $29.95

The City of God 1-10 (I/6)
  cloth, 978-1-56548-454-2, $49.00
  paper, 978-1-56548-455-9, $29.95

The City of God 11-22 (I/7)
  cloth, 978-1-56548-479-5, $59.00
  paper, 978-1-56548-481-8, $39.95

On Christian Belief (I/8)
  cloth, 978-1-56548-233-3, $44.00
  paper, 978-1-56548-234-0, $29.95

Pastoral Works

Marriage and Virginity (I/9)
  cloth, 978-1-56548-104-6, $39.00
  paper, 978-1-56548-222-7, $19.95

Exegetical Works

Teaching Christianity (I/11)
    cloth, 978-1-56548-048-3, $29.95
    paper, 978-1-56548-049-0, $24.95

Responses to Miscellaneous Questions (I/12)
    cloth, 978-1-56548-277-7, $44.00

On Genesis (I/13)
    cloth, 978-1-56548-175-6, $44.00
    paper, 978-1-56548-201-2, $29.95

New Testament I and II (I/15 and I/16)
    cloth, 978-1-56548-529-7, $49.00
    paper, 978-1-56548-531-0, $29.95

Polemical Works

Arianism and Other Heresies (I/18)
    cloth, 978-1-56548-038-4, $49.00

Manichean Debate (I/19)
    cloth, 978-1-56548-247-0, $44.00

Answer to Faustus, a Manichean (I/20)
    cloth, 978-1-56548-264-7, $49.00

Answer to the Pelagians (I/23)
    cloth, 978-1-56548-092-6, $59.00

Answer to the Pelagians (I/24)
    cloth, 978-1-56548-107-7, $44.00

Answer To The Pelagians (I/25)
    cloth, 978-1-56548-129-9, $89.00

Answer to the Pelagians (I/26)
    cloth, 978-1-56548-136-7, $49.00

Part II — Letters

Letters 1-99 (II/1)
    cloth, 978-1-56548-163-3, $44.00

Letters 100-155 (II/2)
    cloth, 978-1-56548-186-2, $44.00

Letters 156-210 (II/3)
    cloth, 978-1-56548-200-5, $44.00

Letters 211-270 (II/4)
    cloth, 978-1-56548-209-8, $44.00

Part III — Homilies

Sermons 1-19 (III/1)
    cloth, 978-0-911782-75-2, $44.00

Sermons 20-50 (III/2)
    cloth, 978-0-911782-78-3, $44.00

Sermons 51-94 (III/3)
cloth, 978-0-911782-85-1, $44.00

Sermons 94A-150 (III/4)
cloth, 978-1-56548-000-1, $44.00

Sermons 151-183 (III/5)
cloth, 978-1-56548-007-0, $59.00

Sermons 184-229 (III/6)
cloth, 978-1-56548-050-6, $59.00

Sermons 230-272 (III/7)
cloth, 978-1-56548-059-9, $59.00

Sermons 273-305A (III/8)
cloth, 978-1-56548-060-5, $59.00

Sermons 306-340A (III/9)
cloth, 978-1-56548-068-1, $44.00

Sermons 341-400 (III/10)
cloth, 978-1-56548-028-5, $59.00

Sermons Newly Discovered Since 1990 (III/11)
cloth, 978-1-56548-103-9, $64.00

Homilies on the Gospel of John 1-40 (III/12)
cloth, 978-1-56548-319-4, $59.00
paper, 978-1-56548-318-7, $39.95

Homilies on the First Letter of John (III/14)
cloth, 978-1-56548-288-3, $27.00
paper, 978-1-56548-289-0, $19.95

Expositions of the Psalms 1-32 (III/15)
cloth, 978-1-56548-126-8, $49.00
paper, 978-1-56548-140-4, $27.95

Expositions of the Psalms 33-50 (III/16)
cloth, 978-1-56548-147-3, $59.00
paper, 978-1-56548-146-6, $39.95

Expositions of the Psalms 51-72 (III/17)
cloth, 978-1-56548-156-5, $44.00
paper, 978-1-56548-155-8, $27.95

Expositions of the Psalms 73-98 (III/18)
cloth, 978-1-56548-167-1, $44.00
paper, 978-1-56548-166-4, $27.95

Expositions of the Psalms 99-120 (III/19)
cloth, 978-1-56548-197-8, $49.00
paper, 978-1-56548-196-1, $29.95

Expositions of the Psalms 121-150 (III/20)
cloth, 978-1-56548-211-1, $49.00
paper, 978-1-56548-210-4, $29.95

Essential Texts Created for Classroom Use

Augustine Catechism: Enchiridion on Faith Hope and Love
 paper, 978-1-56548-298-2, $14.95

Essential Sermons
 paper, 978-1-56548-276-0, $29.95

Instructing Beginners in Faith
 paper, 978-1-56548-239-5, $13.95

Monastic Rules
 paper, 978-1-56548-130-5, $13.95

Prayers from The Confessions
 paper, 978-1-56548-188-6, $13.95

Selected Writings on Grace and Pelagianism
 paper, 978-1-56548-372-9, $39.95

Soliloquies: Augustine's Inner Dialogue
 paper, 978-1-56548-142-8, $11.95

Trilogy on Faith and Happiness
 paper, 978-1-56548-359-0, $13.95

Ebooks Available

 *City of God, Books I-X, Essential Sermons, Homilies on the First Letter
 of John, Revisions, The Confessions, Trilogy on Faith and Happiness, The
 Trinity, The Augustine Catechism: The Enchiridion on Faith, Hope and
 Love.*

Custom Syllabus

Universities that wish to create a resource that matches their specific needs using
selections from any of the above titles should contact New City Press.

NEW CITY PRESS
of the Focolare
Hyde Park, New York

About New City Press of the Focolare

New City Press is one of more than 20 publishing houses sponsored by the Focolare, a movement founded by Chiara Lubich to help bring about the realization of Jesus' prayer: "That all may be one" (John 17:21). In view of that goal, New City Press publishes books and resources that enrich the lives of people and help all to strive toward the unity of the entire human family. We are a member of the Association of Catholic Publishers.

Further Reading

15 Days of Prayer with St. Augustine, Jaime Garcia, 978-1-56548-489-4, $12.95

Roots of Christian Mysticism, Olivier Clement, 978-1-56548-485-6, $29.95

From Big Bang to Big Mystery, Brendan Purcell, 978-1-56548-433-7, $34.95

A Critical Study of the Rule of Benedict, Adalbert de Vogüé, 978-1-56548-494-8, $39.95

Periodicals
Living City Magazine,
www.livingcitymagazine.com

Scan to join our mailing list for discounts and promotions or go to www.newcitypress.com and click on "join our email list."